T0333974

Regulating and Combating Money Laundering and Terrorist Financing

This book analytically reviews the impact of the global anti-money laundering and counter-terrorist financing (AML/CFT) framework on the compliance trajectory of a number of jurisdictions to this framework.

The work begins by examining the international financial sector reform and its evolution to inculcate the global framework for AML/CFT regulations. It challenges the resulting uniform AML/CFT due to its paradoxical impact on the compliance trajectory of African countries and emerging economies (ACs/EEs). This is done through an examination of the pre-conditions for effective regulation and compliance drivers for ACs/EEs that reveals the behavioural impact of the AML/CFT standards on the bloc of countries. Through the application of agency theory, it explores the relationship between ACs/EEs on the one hand and the international financial institutions that formulate, disseminate and facilitate compliance with the global framework for AML/CFT standards on the other. The remaining chapters review empirically the compliance pressures and resulting compliance trajectory of ACs/EEs with the AML/CFT standards. The final part of the book provides a detailed explanation of the compliance challenges of ACs/EEs and the legitimacy concerns that facilitate this.

This book offers a new direction on the impact of global AML/CFT standards on ACs/EEs and contributes to the understanding of the conditions under which the global standards are likely to facilitate proactive compliance within these blocs of countries. As such it will be a valuable resource for academics, researchers and policy-makers working in this area.

Nkechikwu Valerie Azinge-Egbiri is a Senior Lecturer in Corporate and Financial Law in the Department of Law, University of Lincoln, UK.

The Law of Financial Crime

Series Editor: Nicholas Ryder

For more information about this series, please visit: www.routledge.com/The
-Law-of-Financial-Crime/book-series/FINCRIME.

Regulating and Combating Money Laundering and Terrorist Financing

The Law in Emerging Economies

Nkechikwu Valerie Azinge-Egbiri

Routledge
Taylor & Francis Group

LONDON AND NEW YORK

First published 2021
by Routledge
2 Park Square, Milton Park, Abingdon, Oxon OX14 4RN

and by Routledge
52 Vanderbilt Avenue, New York, NY 10017

Routledge is an imprint of the Taylor & Francis Group, an informa business

British Library Cataloguing-in-Publication Data
A catalogue record for this book is available from the British Library

Library of Congress Cataloging-in-Publication Data
A catalog record has been requested for this book

Names: Azinge, Nkechikwu Valerie (Azinge-Egbiri), author.
Title: Regulating and combating money laundering and terrorist
  financing :
the law in emerging economies / Nkechikwu Valerie Azinge.

Description: Milton Park, Abingdon, Oxon ; New York, NY :
  Routledge, 2021.
| Series: The law of financial crime | Includes bibliographical
references and index.

Identifiers: LCCN 2020042529 (print) | LCCN 2020042530
(ebook) | ISBN
  9780367861421 (hardback) | ISBN 9781003017158 (ebook)

Subjects: LCSH: Money laundering–Law and legislation. | Money
  laundering–Prevention. | Terrorism–Finance–Law and legislation. |
  Terrorism–Finance–Prevention.

Classification: LCC K1089 .A995 2021 (print) | LCC K1089 (ebook)
| DDC
345/.0268–dc23

LC record available at https://lccn.loc.gov/2020042529

LC ebook record available at https://lccn.loc.gov/2020042530

ISBN: 978-0-367-86142-1 (hbk)
ISBN: 978-1-003-01715-8 (ebk)

Typeset in Galliard
by Deanta Global Publishing Services, Chennai, India

Contents

Acknowledgement

I am thankful to the many people that have assisted me during the write up of this book. Firstly, I would like to thank Professor Dalvinder Singh, my colleagues and friends who reviewed my draft chapters. The usual caveat applies for all errors and omissions. I am also grateful to staff of the institutions interviewed, for deeper insights into the workings of financial crime across countries. My penultimate acknowledgement goes to my husband, parents, siblings, cousins and friends for encouraging me to embrace this journey and blessing me with their unconditional love and support. Finally, this book is dedicated to countries with crippling economic growth and development due to financial crime.

Abbreviations

AC/EE	African Countries and Emerging Economies.
AfDB	African Development Bank.
AGOA	Africa Growth and Opportunity Act.
AML	Anti-Money Laundering.
AML/CFT	Anti-Money Laundering and Counter Terrorist Financing.
APRM	African Peer Review Mechanism.
AU	African Union.
BCBS	Basel Committee on Banking Supervision.
BCCI	Bank of Credit and Commerce International.
BVN	Bank Verification Number.
BoE	Bank of England.
BRICS	Brazil, Russia, India, China, South Africa.
BWI	Bretton Woods Institutions.
CAS	Country Assistance Strategies.
CBA	Compliance-Based Approach.
CCB	China Construction Bank Corporation.
CBR	Correspondent Banking Relationship.
CDD	Customer Due Diligence.
CFATF	Caribbean Financial Action Task Force.
CFLAMLR	Chinese Financial Institutions Anti-Money Laundering Regulation.
CRR	Country Review Reports.
DBA	Deterrence-Based Approach.
DNFBPs	Designated Non-Financial Businesses and Professions.
EAC	East Africa Community.
EAG	Eurasia Group.
EFCC	Economic and Financial Crimes Commission.
ESAMMG	Eastern and Southern Africa Anti-Money Laundering Group.
EP	Extended Principals.
EU	European Union.
FATF	Financial Action Task Force.
FCA	Financial Conduct Authority.
FIs	Financial Institutions.

FIC	Financial Intelligence Centre.
FIG	Financial Integrity Group.
FIU	Financial Intelligence Units.
FSA	Financial Sector Assessment.
FSAP	Financial Sector Assessment Programme.
FSB	Financial Stability Board.
FSF	Financial Stability Forum.
FSSAs	Financial System Stability Assessments.
FSRB	FATF-Style Regional Bodies.
GAFISUD	Financial Action Task Force of South America against Money Laundering.
GDP	Gross Domestic Product.
GFC	Global Financial Crisis.
GIABA	Inter-Governmental Group against Money Laundering in West Africa.
GWP	Global World Product.
G7	Group of Seven.
HDI	Human Development Index.
HLM	High Level Meetings.
HRMJ	High Risk and Other Monitored Jurisdictions.
HP	High Priority.
IAIS	International Association of Insurance Supervisors.
ICBC	Industrial and Commercial Bank of China.
ICPC	Independent Corrupt Practices Commission.
ICRC	International Cooperation Review Group.
IBRD	International Bank for Reconstruction and Development.
IFIs	International Financial Institutions.
IFR	International Financial Regulation.
IIs	International Institutions
INCSR	International Narcotics Control Strategy Report.
IADI	International Association of Deposit Insurers.
IMF	International Monetary Fund.
INCB	International Narcotics Control Board.
IOSCO	International Organisation for Securities and Exchange Commission.
KYC	Know Your Customer.
LCC	Less Compliant Countries.
LOLR	Lender of Last Resort.
LP	Low Priority.
MENAFATF	Middle East and North Africa Region FATF.
MER	Mutual Evaluation Reports.
ML	Money Laundering.
ML/C	Money Laundering and Corruption.
MP	Mid Priority.
NATO	North Atlantic Treaty Organisation.

NC	Non-Compliant.
NCCTs	Non-Cooperative Countries and Territories.
NDIC	Nigerian Deposit Insurance Corporation.
NDLEA	Nigerian Drug Law Enforcement Agency.
NEPAD	New Partnership for Africa's Development.
NFIU	Nigerian Financial Intelligence Unit.
NIFA	New International Financial Architecture.
OAU	Organisation of African Unity.
OFP	Offshore Centre Programme.
OECD	Organisation for Economic Cooperation and Development.
PC	Partially Compliant.
PCC	Pearson Correlation Coefficient
PDG	Policy Development Group.
PP	Proximate Principal.
PPP	Purchasing Power-Parity.
RBA	Risk-Based Approach.
ROSCs	Reports on Observance of Standards and Codes.
RMQ	Ratio of Quasi Money.
SA	South Africa.
SIM	Subscriber Identity Module.
STR	Suspicious Transaction Reports.
TA	Technical Assistance.
TBML	Trade-Based Money Laundering.
TF	Terrorism Financing.
TGNs	Trans-governmental Networks.
TIFA	Trade and Investment Framework Agency.
TOCU	Bank of Sierra Leone and Transnational Organised Crime Unit.
TRIEN	FATF Training and Research Institute.
UBA	Uncertainty-Based Approach.
UN	United Nations.
UNCTC	United Nations Counter-Terrorism Committee.
UNDP, RBA	United Nations Development Programme, The Regional Bureau Africa.
UNECA	United Nations Economic Commission for Africa.
UNODC	United Nations Office on Drugs and Crime.
UNSC	United Nations Security Council.
U.S.	United States.
WW1	First World War.
WW2	Second World War.

1 Compliance with the Global Anti-Money Laundering and Counter-Terrorist Financing (AML/CFT) Regulation

Parameters and Paradoxes of Regulation in African Countries and Emerging Economies (AC/EEs)

Introduction

Whilst African Countries (ACs) struggle with compliance with the AML/CFT regulations enunciated by the Financial Action Task Force (FATF), emerging economies (EEs) record better compliance levels. This is irrespective of the similar socio-economic and political challenges facing these countries. The difficulties faced by ACs in achieving meaningful AML/CFT compliance levels is unsettling, coming at a time when ACs are striving towards global financial integration demonstrably evidenced by their persistent economic growth.[1]

Surprisingly, the drive for improved AML/CFT compliance by ACs usually fosters a regulatory paradox. For instance, the FATF's standard on customer due diligence (CDD) compels financial institutions to 'identify the customer and verify that customer's identity using reliable, independent source documents, data or information'.[2] On its face value, this requirement appears logically framed, but in ACs a large percentage of the population are excluded from mainstream consumer banking due to lack of acceptable identification documentation largely driven by illiteracy, unemployment and poverty.[3] Hence, the strict enforcement

---

1 AfDB, 'Africa's Economic Performance Improves in 2017' (*AfDB*, 12 October 2017) <https ://www.afdb.org/en/news-and-events/africas-economic-performance-improves-in-2017 -17424/ > accessed 10 January 2018.
2 FATF, 'FATF Recommendations' (*FATF*, 2012) <http://www.fatf-gafi.org/media/fatf/ documents/recommendations/pdfs/FATF%20Recommendations%202012.pdf> accessed 10 January 2018.
3 The regulatory circular mandates that no formal identification is necessary for accounts with amounts below 200,000 naira (in Nigeria). In practice, this is hardly the case. See CBN, 'Circular to All Banks and Other Financial Institutions: Implementation of Three-tiered Know Your Customer Requirements' (*Central Bank of Nigeria*, 18 January 2013) <https://ww w.cbn.gov.ng/out/2013/ccd/3%20tiered%20kyc%20requirements.pdf> accessed 30 July 2017; FATF, 'FATF Guidance: Anti-Money Laundering and Terrorist Financing Measures and Financial Inclusion – With a Supplement on Customer Due Diligence' (*FATF Guidance*, November 2017) <https://www.fatf-gafi.org/media/fatf/content/images/Updated-2017- FATF-2013-Guidance.pdf> accessed 10 March 2018.

of CDD would only heighten financial exclusion,[4] which is antithetical to the FATF's financial integrity objective.

More broadly, the FATF recommendations are expected to trigger regulatory law reforms even in jurisdictions where the legal structures are deemed inefficient. FATF recommendation 4 states that 'Countries should adopt measures similar to those set forth in the Vienna and Palermo Convention, and the Terrorist Financing Convention, including legislative measures'.[5] However, anecdotal evidence and statistical findings reveal that developing (especially African) countries struggle with harnessing these standards.[6] This is attributable to weak legal structures under-pinned by socio-economic and political limitations peculiar to these states.

The complexities involved in ACs' attainment of compliance is further heightened by the FATF's perception that the global financial system is only as strong as its weakest link and hence all countries should be equally subject to the FATF's requirement.[7] Scholars have supported this assertion, arguing that it is paramount for all countries to inculcate the FATF's global standard for com-bating illicit crimes[8] particularly as the borderless nature of money laundering (ML)[9] and terrorist financing (TF)[10] reinforces the need for an internationally coordinated response.[11] Furthermore, scholars argue that the various methods by which illicit crimes are carried out remain shrouded in secrecy, therefore uncur-tailed liberalisation of ACs/EEs'[12] market economies can give rise to adverse socio-economic effects,[13] as these crimes pose a threat to the stability of the

---

4   Ibid.
5   *FATF* (n 2) recommendation 4.
6   Concepcion Verdugo Yepes, 'Compliance with The AML/CFT International Standard: Lessons from A Cross-Country Analysis' (2011) International Monetary Fund Working Paper WP/11/177, 9 <https://papers.ssrn.com/sol3/papers.cfm?abstract_id=1899578> accessed 19 April 2015.
7   Paul Allan Schott, 'Reference Guide to Anti-Money Laundering and Combating the Financ-ing of Terrorism: Second Edition and Supplement on Special Recommendation IX' (*World Bank*, 2016) <https://openknowledge.worldbank.org/bitstream/handle/10986/6977/3 50520Referenc1Money01OFFICIAL0USE1.pdf?sequence=1&isAllowed=y> accessed 10 December 2017.
8   Ibid.
9   FATF, 'What is Money Laundering?' <http://www.fatf-gafi.org/faq/moneylaundering/> accessed 10 February 2015.; Nicholas Ryder, *Financial Crime in the 21st Century, Law and Policy* (Edward Publishing Limited 2011) 10.; Eleni Tsingou, 'Global Financial Governance and the Developing Anti-Money Laundering Regime: What Lessons for International Politi-cal Economy' (2005) Centre for the Study of Globalization and Regionalization (CSGR) Working Paper No 161/05 <http://wrap.warwick.ac.uk/1959/1/WRAP_Tsingou_wp16 105.pdf> accessed 11 February 2015.
10 Ilias Bantekas, 'The International Law of Terrorist Financing' [2003] 97 AJIL 315, 315.
11 Michael Barnett and Martha Finnemore, *Rules for the World: International Organizations in Global Politics* (CUP 2004) 9.
12 *Tsingou* (n 9).
13 Paul Ashin, 'Dirty Money, Real Pain' [2012] 49 (2) Finance and Development 38, 38.; Raul Hernández-Coss, Chinyere Egwuagu, Jennifer Isern and David Porteus, 'AML/CFT Regu-lation: Implications for Financial Service Providers that Serve Low-income People' (2005)

financial system.[14] However, requiring that all countries meet the same AML/CFT standard douses regulatory effectiveness and creates a paradox. Moreover, this approach is blindsided to the threat posed to the sovereignty of countries.[15]

A background to the coordinated response to illicit crimes provides a synopsis to the quagmire faced by ACs, and indeed EEs, in attaining desirable compliance levels. The AML/CFT regulation was inculcated in the financial sector reform which involved various global, continental and regional financial institutions.[16] Most prominent of the institutions are the FATF, the International Monetary Fund (IMF) and the World Bank. The latter two are collectively known as the international financial institutions (IFIs). These institutions recognised the dire consequences that money laundering/terrorist financing (ML/TF) can have on the integrity of the international financial market and its likely contribution to financial crises.[17] Hence, the institutional reactions were directed at setting, disseminating and continually assessing AML/CFT standards. The FATF, strengthened by the IFIs, was established to advance standards and ensure compliance with AML/CFT regulation. The standards set by the FATF impose restraints on the supervisory approach of regulatory bodies with the goal of determining how they regulate financial institutions (FIs).[18]

However, an examination of the structure and processes involved in regulating and disseminating the AML/CFT standards has exposed the institutions to criticisms of legitimacy deficiency. This is particularly because ACs/EEs were sidelined from contributing to the standards which they are now subjected to. As can be imagined, these standards, mainly created by the Group of Seven (G7) countries are unreflective of the ACs/EEs' peculiarities. This can further be illuminated by an inquiry into the behavioural impact of the FATF's provisions and the significant relationship between international regulatory standards and state behaviour. To correct this perceived anomaly, the FATF introduced the risk-based approach (RBA) in 2012 to harness the peculiarities of individual countries

The International Bank for Reconstruction and Development/The World Bank, 14 <http://documents.worldbank.org/curated/en/497161468140979952/pdf/361690AML0CFT0regulation01PUBLIC1.pdf> accessed June 12 2012.; See the website of the United Nations Office on Drugs and Crime (UNODC) <www.odccp.org> accessed 10 January 2015.

14 Saby Ghoshray, 'Compliance Convergence in FATF Rulemaking: The Conflict Between Agency Capture and Soft Law' [2014–2015] 59 N.Y.L. Sch. L. Rev. 521, 533.

15 Herbert Morais, 'The Quest for International Standards: Global Governance vs. Sovereignty' [2001] 50 U. Kan. L. Rev. 779, 779.

16 Kevin Davis, 'Regulatory Reform Post the Global Financial Crisis: An Overview 2' [2011] Report for Melbourne APEC Financial Centre, Australasian APEC Study. Centre at RMIT University <http://www.apec.org.au/docs/11_CON_GFC/Regulatory%20Reform%20Post%20GFC-%20Overview%20Paper.pdf> accessed 10 July 2015.

17 FATF, 'Global Money Laundering & Terrorist Financing Threat Assessment' (FATF, July 2010), <https://www.imolin.org/pdf/imolin/Global_Threat_assessment.pdf> accessed 20 July 2015.

18 Ibid.

and ease the assimilation of the AML/CFT standards.[19] The effectiveness is, however, debatable.

Against this backdrop, central to this book is the argument that there is an unfavourable agency relationship between ACs/EEs and the international community. The IFIs/FATF, as collective principals, mandate compliance by ACs/EEs to the FATF's standards and sanction non-compliance. This facilitates a situation where ACs/EEs face a heightened degree of exclusion from the global economy. The sanctions do not consider the unique challenges of these countries in meeting the demands of compliance with AML/CFT standards. This argument exposes a design flaw in AML/CFT standards and processes for benchmarking compliance, irrespective of the adoption of the RBA to compliance.[20] Hence, the current standards and processes have to be re-evaluated to adequately take account of the peculiarities of ACs/EEs[21] with the aim of facilitating actual and proactive compliance.

Examining the varying legal structures underpinned by dire socio-economic and political circumstances reveals that uniform standards, even where supported by the RBA, are antithetical to proactive compliance. Thus, uniform standards may be setting too high a bar for ACs/EEs, which may continually fail to meet the expected compliance standards. This underscores a regulatory paradox, where regulations achieve effects contrary to their intention, which undermines compliance prospects and hinders financial integration of ACs/EEs due to sanctions.

1. Consequently, this **book advances the following questions**: Has the evolution of IFIs/FATF facilitated an agency slack between these international institutions and ACs/EEs with resulting legitimacy crises?
2. Do the compliance drivers and level of compliance attained in ACs/EEs indicate a misalignment of incentives between these countries and IFIs/FATF?
3. What factors exacerbate information asymmetry between IFIs/FATF and ACs/EEs? Can the agency slack that arises from countries acting in their self-interest to hinder information sharing with other countries be resolved?
4. Does the risk-based approach sufficiently take into consideration the peculiarities of countries and facilitate increased legitimacy of the FATF?

Scope of Book

This book focuses on the interrelationship between IFIs/FATF and ACs/EEs, and how this relationship affects the compliance of these countries to the FATF standards. This encompasses an examination of the evolution and legal status of the key actors in the global regulation of AML/CFT: the IMF and the World

---

19 *FATF* (n 2) recommendation 1.
20 Abdullahi Usman Bello and Jackie Harvey, 'From a Risk-based Approach to an Uncertainty Based Approach to Anti-Money Laundering' [2017] 30 (1) Security Journal.
21 Emerging economies refers to Brazil, Russia, India, China and South Africa.

Bank, the FATF and its regional affiliates. Such examination unveils unfavourable agency and legitimacy concerns, thereby challenging the perspective that AML/CFT measures can be implemented uniformly across ACs/EEs.[22] Central to this would be the recognition of socio-economic and political differences within ACs/EEs[23]coupled with the capacity deficit in these blocs of countries that hinder their ability to harness the AML/CFT regime. Consequently, it assesses the pre-conditions for effective AML/CFT regulation and the factors that engineer compliance within these blocs of countries. It concludes that the unsuitability of the current global AML/CFT regime which has not been remedied by the adoption of the RBA necessitates amendments to ensure proactive compliance.

It is imperative to make clear that however scarce, literature exists on the global AML/CFT governance, especially as regards the transplantation of international policies.[24] Eminent scholars such as Rainer Hulsee,[25] Chris Brummer[26] and Jason Sharman[27] have discussed extensively on the suitability of the FATF standards to countries around the world. More particularly, Norman Mugarura has examined the adaptability of the FATF standards across various jurisdictions, especially developing countries and argued that the framework should be designed with 'flexibility' to ensure its adaptability.[28] Inspired by these literatures, this book goes deeper in examining whether the evolution of the IFIs/FATF creates an agency slack and evident legitimacy crises that facilitate strategic communication between ACs/EEs and IFIs/FATF to project actual or proactive compliance. It also questions the suitability of the 'flexibility' introduced through the risk-based approach and whether it serves its purpose. Crucially, it examines the compliance drivers that propel or repel compliance with the FATF standards and how these are influenced by the uneven development of the 'law and confidence' in ACs/EEs underpinned by socio-economic and political factors. Arguments are buttressed with empirical findings from secondary data, which illustrate the compliance variances across countries, indicating that internal dynamics affect compliance.

---

22 Ibid. African Countries – mainly restricted to Nigeria, examples are applicable to other African countries.

23 For instance – unsophisticated legal system, lack or absence of skilled financial institution staff, ineffective regulatory bodies, prevalence of corruption and financial crimes, unemployment and conflict.

24 Norman Mugarura, *The Global Anti-Money Laundering Regulatory Landscape in Less Developed Countries* (First Published 2012, Routledge 2016); Jae-Myong Koh, *Suppressing Terrorist Financing and Money Laundering: The Evolution and Implementation of International Standards* (Springer, 2006).

25 Rainer Hulsee, 'Even Clubs Can't Do without Legitimacy: Why the Anti-Money Laundering Blacklist was Suspended' [2008] 2 Regulation & Governance 459–479.

26 Chris Brummer, *Soft Law and the Global Financial System: Rule Making in the 21st Century* (CUP, 2012).

27 Jason Sharman, 'Power and Discourse in Policy Diffusion: Anti-Money Laundering in Developed States [2008] 52 (3) International Studies Quarterly 635–656.

28 Norman Mugarura (n 24).

Consequently, the critical contribution to knowledge are findings that the level of integration of ACs/EEs to the global economy and their perceived compliance levels to the FATF standards are crucial in determining:

a. Their delegation powers to the IFIs/FATF.
b. Their communication strategy with these institutions.

These in turn can propel or limit their compliance levels as well as inhibit the effectiveness of the FATF regime over these states.

This study seeks to fill the literature gap on the current global AML/CFT framework and its suitability across jurisdictions. Therefore, it explores the interplay between national and global factors and how they play out in the implementation of the global AML/CFT framework across jurisdictions. In doing so, it evaluates the role, composition, competencies and legitimacy of IFIs/FATF and the mechanisms they employ to cause behavioural changes. Conversely, the pressure on ACs/EEs to comply may occasion creative implementation and compliance. This discourse unveils the conflicting interests of the IFIs/FATF and ACs/EEs, which also results in conflicts of interest for implementing authorities. Indeed, this hinders proactive compliance with FATF standards when they do not necessarily promote national interests. The resulting divergent implementation and compliance outcomes have consequences for ACs/EEs.

Thus, this study reveals that the increasing number of countries becoming associate members of the FATF is indicative of the importance attached to the institution, not of their willingness to actually implement or comply with its standards. By examining the dynamics of implementation and compliance, this study aims to contribute to understanding conditions that are likely to make the current recommendations effective. It also seeks to contribute to the wider debate about potential reform of the FATF standards and processes.

Whilst this study is focused on the compliance of countries to AML/CFT standards, it is limited in scope to the technical compliance of countries with myopic focus on the 'effectiveness' of countries. Furthermore, it is not a study of illicit financial crimes in ACs/EEs, rather the regulatory responses to ML/TF through the FATF strategies. Through the lens of the agency theory, the focus is on the transplantation to national legislation and implementation of the FATF regulations and recommendations and how ACs/EEs have responded to them.

Why IMF/World Bank and the FATF?

The IMF and the World Bank, which are IFIs, are considered alongside the FATF for two key reasons. Firstly, these are the paramount institutions that govern AML/CFT regulations globally. These institutions, even with diverse legal status, work in concert in re-formulating, assessing and facilitating compliance with the FATF standards. Hence, scrutinising their evolution, legal status, legitimacy and role in AML/CFT regulation is a crucial starting point for examining how AML/CFT regulation operates at a global level, the interrelationship between IFIs/

FATF and countries, and how this relationship facilitates or hinders compliance. It is imperative to state that there is limited focus on pre-existing United Nations (UN) Conventions on ML/TF given that the FATF has inculcated the UN Convention Against Illicit Traffic in Narcotic Drugs and Psychotropic Substances of 1988 (Vienna Convention), and the UN Convention against Transnational Organised Crime (Palermo Convention) into its recommendations.[29]

Secondly, through the agency theory application, the degree of proximity of these institutions to countries in setting and implementing standards can be examined. Through the prism of the agency theory, the FATF is the proximate principal to countries, whilst the IFIs, as observers on the FATF, have an extended principal position. Their positions are however not static within the agency theory. Interestingly, the dynamics of their non-static position unearth legitimacy concerns which are core to this book.

Why African Countries and Emerging Economies?

Limited literature discusses the bias that ACs/EEs encounter in complying with AML/CFT regulations due to their limited integration to the global economy. Hence, it is interesting to see how these blocs of countries, which had no participation in the AML/CFT policy formulation, have come to align with the global standards. This book shows how such alignments are problematic due to the deficient legal framework of ACs, underpinned by socio-economic and political difficulties. This is enriched by assessing the compliance drivers to AML/CFT standards within EEs who face similar issues but are better equipped to deal with them.

The similarities and differences inherent in this bloc of countries allow for some generalisations in considering their likely behavioural responses to the FATF recommendations. Similarities within and across each bloc include factors such as entrenched cash-based economies, capacity deficiencies and corruption ingrained in legal, institutional and political structures. However, EEs usually have more robust capacity, stronger financial institutions and a greater degree of integration with the international financial economy. Additionally, they have greater macroeconomic and political stability than ACs, which is crucial in explaining the variation in countries' compliance behaviour.

Clarification of Key Terms

Implementation and compliance are used interchangeably; however, they are significantly different. Implementation technically refers to the transplantation of standards into domestic law, coupled with the measures geared at putting international recommendations into practice at the domestic level. Compliance, however, transcends implementation; it refers to an actor's behavioural conformity

---

29 *FATF* (n 2).

to specific recommendations.[30] For example, when the state introduces national laws and regulations on AML/CFT, compliance entails ensuring that the standards are obeyed and not observed in breach. This indicates that implementation is a pre-condition for compliance. Understanding the concept of compliance drivers is critical in constructing the design of recommendations to ensure proactive compliance. These concepts are crucial themes within this book and are key to understanding the conflict of interest between IFIs and states.

Effectiveness cannot be divorced from these concepts. There are varying perspectives on the concept of 'effectiveness' within international law. It may relate to whether an international law attains its objectives[31] or the extent of behavioural improvements within targeted countries. The FATF sees effectiveness assessment as the former, given its definition of the term as 'the extent to which the defined outcomes are achieved'.[32] This book however views effectiveness as the degree to which the recommendations are met through desired changes in state behaviour.[33]

Additionally, the terms 'standards', 'recommendations' and 'rules' are used interchangeably in reference to the FATF recommendations. Whilst the FATF recommendations are referred to as soft law standards, the hardening of these standards during the transplantation process acknowledges their transformation to hard law; thus the reference to rules.

Furthermore, the term 'developing countries' is used interchangeably with African countries. Likewise, 'illicit crimes, activities or transactions' refer to ML/TF and its predicate offences.

Contents Overview

This book is divided into eight chapters. The second chapter of this book examines the evolution of AML/CFT standards, the institutions central to the AML/CFT administration and the influence of these on state compliance. In contextualising the global regulatory progression, this chapter links ML/TF regulation and the financial sector reform. Such a link unearths the hegemonic imposition of a global agenda on AC/EEs, countries not privy to the formation of the AML/CFT standards but bound to comply. This chapter highlights how

---

30 Roger Fisher, 'Improving Compliance with International Law' (1981); Benedict Kingsbury, 'The Concept of Compliance as a Function of Competing Conceptions of International Law' [1998] 10 Mich. J. Int'l 345.

31 Edith Weiss and Harold Jacobson, 'Compliance with the International Environmental Accords' [1995] 119 Global Governance 119, 123.

32 FATF, 'Methodology for Assessing Technical Compliance with the FATF Recommendations and the Effectiveness of AML/CFT Systems' (*FATF*, 2012) <http://www.fatf-gafi.org/media/fatf/documents/methodology/FATF%20Methodology%2022%20Feb%202013.pdf> accessed 14 July 2015.

33 Oran Young & Marc Levy (with the assistance of Gail Osherenko), 'The Effectiveness of International Environmental Regimes', *in* Oran R. Young, *The Effectiveness of International Environmental Regimes: Casual Connections and Behavioral Mechanisms* (MIT Press, Cambridge, MA, 1999).

disproportionately affected ACs/EEs are by the global AML/CFT standards. The third chapter examines the pre-conditions for effective AML/CFT regulation and illustrates how the absence of these factors affects the compliance trajectory of ACs/EEs. In particular, this chapter highlights factors that propel compliance which illuminates the agency slack that exists in standards delegation. Chapter Four further examines the interrelationship between the institutions central to AML/CFT regulation, the International Monetary Fund, the World Bank and the FATF. It employs the agency theory to unveil the power dynamics between these institutions, the countries that created and lead them, and ACs/EEs. It highlights the importance of information sharing between critical institutions and ACs/EEs in combating ML/TF, the factors that are critical to these and the incentives for symmetrical information sharing. This chapter further examines the agency relationship between highly integrated countries and lowly integrated countries. The fifth chapter investigates the compliance drivers and levels in ACs, whose AML/CFT compliance often fall short of that demanded by the international community. The sixth chapter deals with EEs, whose changing position in the global economy provides an interesting set of conclusions on their compliance drivers and its impact on their compliance levels. The penultimate chapter addresses the claim that the risk-based approach to AML/CFT has cured the legitimacy concerns. The final chapter of this book presents the major findings of this analysis and provides suggestions for further research.

Research Methods

This multidisciplinary research (law of institutions and law and economics perspectives) questions the suitability of uniform standards and benchmarking. It adopts a mixture of quantitative and qualitative analyses to draw its conclusions. Empirical data is utilised in evaluating the current compliance level of countries to the FATF recommendations. This involves re-coding secondary data derived from the FATF's assigned compliance levels (from non-compliant to compliant ranked 0–4) to countries on each of the 40 recommendations. The data is gathered from an examination of 43 mutual evaluation reports and further follow-up reports.

Furthermore, to understand the research questions posed by this book, a qualitative study is undertaken, which engages semi-structured interviews as the prime data collection medium. This entailed interviewing high-level staff of the IMF, FATF-styled regional bodies, Development Banks, the Central Bank of Nigeria and the Nigerian Financial Intelligence Unit. In recognition of the potential for bias, interviews are conducted in strict adherence to acknowledged ethical guidelines. For anonymity, interviewees are referenced as *EENA*.

Research Methodology

The applicable theory is enhanced by interview responses from IFIs/ FATF-style regional bodies (FSRB) staff. These staff better understand the relationship IFIs/

FATF share with countries and also can illuminate on the challenges that hinder compliance by ACs – knowledge garnered through practice. Hence, the interviews are tremendously crucial to this book.

Additionally, it utilises an empirical research approach as an extension of the theoretical framework. It provides the opportunity to evaluate the interaction between institutions and countries, and how institutions rein in compliance by countries. It engages in an expository methodological approach in examining the internal and external drivers of compliance across ACs/EEs, which are categorised as legal and non-legal factors. Moreover, it provides understanding of the interaction between developed and developing countries, illustrating interest-driven compliance, which is sometimes circumvented by capacity deficiency.

This book recommends a regulatory framework that recognises the peculiarities of ACs/EEs, whilst also advocating for regional and state involvement in a manner that does not disrupt international finance. If properly re-evaluated, this book would serve as a catalyst for improved compliance, whilst fortifying the integrity of the international financial architecture.

Further Reading

1. Abdullahi Usman Bello and Jackie Harvey, 'From a Risk-based Approach to an Uncertainty Based Approach to Anti-Money Laundering' [2017] 30 (1) Security Journal.
2. AfDB, 'Africa's Economic Performance Improves in 2017' (AfDB, 12 October 2017) <https://www.afdb.org/en/news-and-events/africas-economic-performance-improves-in-2017-17424/> accessed 10 January 2018.
3. Barnett Michael and Martha Finnemore, *Rules for the World: International Organizations in Global Politics* (Cambridge University Press, 2004).
4. Central Bank of Nigeria, 'Circular to All Banks and Other Financial Institutions: Implementation of Three-tiered Know Your Customer Requirements' (Central Bank of Nigeria, 18 January 2013) <https://www.cbn.gov.ng/out/2013/ccd/3%20tiered%20kyc%20requirements.pdf> accessed 30 July 2017.
5. Concepcion Verdugo Yepes, 'Compliance with The AML/CFT International Standard: Lessons from A Cross-Country Analysis' (2011) International Monetary Fund Working Paper WP/11/177, 9 <https://papers.ssrn.com/sol3/papers.cfm?abstract_id=1899578> accessed 19 April 2015.
6. Chris Brummer, *Soft Law and the Global Financial System: Rule Making in the 21st Century* (Cambridge University Press, 2012).
7. Edith Weiss and Harold Jacobson, 'Compliance with the International Environmental Accords' [1995] 119 *Global Governance* 119, 123.
8. Eleni Tsingou, 'Global Financial Governance and the Developing Anti-Money Laundering Regime: What Lessons for International Political Economy' (2005) *Centre for the Study of Globalization and Regionalization (CSGR)* Working Paper No 161/05 <http://wrap.warwick.ac.uk/1959/1/WRAP_Tsingou_wp16105.pdf> accessed 11 February 2015.
9. FATF, 'FATF Guidance: Anti-Money Laundering and Terrorist Financing Measures and Financial Inclusion – With a Supplement on Customer Due Diligence' (FATF Guidance, November 2017) <https://www.fatf-gafi.org

/media/fatf/content/images/Updated-2017-FATF-2013-Guidance.pdf> accessed 10 March 2018.

10. FATF, 'Global Money Laundering & Terrorist Financing Threat Assessment' (FATF, July 2010), <https://www.imolin.org/pdf/imolin/Global_Threat_assessment.pdf> accessed 20 July 2015.

11. FATF, 'Methodology for Assessing Technical Compliance with the FATF Recommendations and the Effectiveness of AML/CFT Systems' (*FATF*, 2012) <http://www.fatf-gafi.org/media/fatf/documents/methodology/FATF%20Methodology%2022%20Feb%202013.pdf> accessed 14 July 2015.

12. FATF, 'What is Money Laundering?' <http://www.fatf-gafi.org/faq/moneylaundering/> accessed 10 February 2015.

13. Herbert Morais, 'The Quest for International Standards: Global Governance vs. Sovereignty' [2001] 50 *U. Kan. Law Review* 779, 779.

14. Ilias Bantekas, 'The International Law of Terrorist Financing' [2003] 97 *AJIL* 315, 315.

15. Jae-Myong Koh, *Suppressing Terrorist Financing and Money Laundering: The Evolution and Implementation of International Standards* (Springer, 2006).

16. Jason Sharman, 'Power and Discourse in Policy Diffusion: Anti-Money Laundering in Developed States' [2008] 52 (3) *International Studies Quarterly* 635–656.

17. Kevin Davis, 'Regulatory Reform Post the Global Financial Crisis: An Overview 2'[2011] *Report for Melbourne APEC Financial Centre, Australasian APEC Study. Centre at RMIT University* <http://www.apec.org.au/docs/11_CON_GFC/Regulatory%20Reform%20Post%20GFC-%20Overview%20Paper.pdf> accessed 10 July 2015.

18. Nicholas Ryder, *Financial Crime in the 21st Century, Law and Policy* (Edward Publishing Limited, 2011).

19. Norman Mugarura, *The Global Anti-Money Laundering Regulatory Landscape in Less Developed Countries* (First Published 2012, Routledge, 2016).

20. Oran Young and Marc Levy (with the assistance of Gail Osherenko), 'The Effectiveness of International Environmental Regimes' in Oran R. Young (ed.) *The Effectiveness of International Environmental Regimes: Casual Connections and Behavioral Mechanisms* (MIT Press, Cambridge, MA, 1999).

21. Paul Allan Schott, 'Reference Guide to Anti-Money Laundering and Combating the Financing of Terrorism: Second Edition and Supplement on Special Recommendation IX' (World Bank, 2016) <https://openknowledge.worldbank.org/bitstream/handle/10986/6977/350520Referenc1Money01OFFICIAL0USE1.pdf?sequence=1&isAllowed=y> accessed 10 December 2017.

22. Paul Ashin, 'Dirty Money, Real Pain' [2012] 49 (2) *Finance and Development* 38, 38.

23. Rainer Hulsee, 'Even Clubs Can't Do Without Legitimacy: Why the Anti-Money Laundering Blacklist was Suspended' [2008] 2 *Regulation & Governance* 459–479.

24. Raul Hernández-Coss, Chinyere Egwuagu, Jennifer Isern and David Porteus, 'AML/CFT Regulation: Implications for Financial Service Providers that Serve Low-Income People' (2005) *The International Bank for Reconstruction and Development/ The World Bank*, 14 <http://documents.worldbank.org/curated/en/497161468140979952/pdf/361690AML0CFT0regulation01PUBLIC1.pdf> accessed 12 June 2012.

25. Roger Fisher, 'Improving Compliance with International Law (1981); Benedict Kingsbury, The Concept of Compliance as a Function of Competing Conceptions of International Law' [1998] 10 *Michigan Journal of International Law* 345.

26. Saby Ghoshray, 'Compliance Convergence in FATF Rulemaking: The Conflict Between Agency Capture and Soft Law' [2014–2015] 59 *N.Y.L. S. Law Review* 521, 533.

2 The International Financial Sector Reform and International Legal Framework for Anti-Money Laundering and Counter-Terrorist Financing (AML/CFT) Regulation

Introduction

Financial liberalisation and the accompanying illicit crimes prompted international harmonisation of a patchwork of domestic regulations on AML/CFT regulation. This process of global regulation, driven by international financial institutions (IFIs) and the Financial Action Task Force (FATF), was in response to the growing complexity of illicit crimes which increasingly occurred on a cross-border level. The relationship between the evolution of the IFIs/FATF and the suitability of the AML/CFT regulations has been questioned, particularly regarding the ability of the regulations to elicit compliance by countries. This has been examined in relation to developed countries such as the United Kingdom[1] and the United States[2] and also the continental blocs, such as Europe.[3] Parochial emphasis on African countries and emerging economies (ACs/EEs) has however occasioned arguments that the global design of IFIs/FATF allows for suitable regulation of, and compliance with, AML/CFT standards globally.[4] Yet, this is not the case; rather, the hegemonic subjection of these countries and consequent agency slack are indicative of a regulatory paradox.

This chapter seeks to understand the mechanics of this. It does this by examining the rationale for international financial regulation, the historical underpinnings and legal structures of the IFIs/FATF and how these affect the suitability of the global standards.

The first section of this chapter focuses on the nature and rationale for international financial regulations as instruments for curbing cross-border externalities.

---

1 Nicholas Ryder, *Money Laundering – An Endless Cycle? A Comparative Analysis of Anti-Money Laundering Policies in the United States of America, the United Kingdom, Australia and Canada* (First Published 2012, Routledge 2012) 8–39, 73.

2 James Gathii, 'The Financial Action Task Force and Global Administrative Law' [2010] 197 J. Prof. Law 1, 2–11; Saby Ghoshray 'Compliance Convergence in FATF Rulemaking: The Conflict Between Agency Capture and Soft Law' [2014–2015] 59 N.Y.L. Sch. L. Rev. 521, 533.

3 Ines Sofia De Oliveria, 'The Anti-Money Laundering Struggle: Actors, Interest and the EU' (4th ECPR Graduate Conference, 2012).

4 Norman Mugarura, *The Global Anti-Money Laundering Regulatory Landscape in Less Developed Countries* (2nd edn, Routledge, 2016) 145.

The second and third sections examine the evolution of international financial regulation (IFR) with an emphasis on the historical and legal status of the IFIs/ FATF, coupled with justifications and reactive steps taken to tackle illicit crimes. The sections highlight that the backing of the FATF by IFIs has hardened the trajectory of the AML/CFT standards and led to a move towards mandatory compliance. The fourth section engages the agency theory to understand how the evolution of IFIs/FATF facilitates compliance with AML/CFT regulations within countries. It argues that the existing 'reverse and continuing international delegation' has created a global hegemony that hinders the suitability of the standards, thus limiting compliance. The fifth section deconstructs the concept of legitimacy and its compliance potential. This section also examines how agency issues flow from legitimacy crises. The sixth section draws the strands together and concludes.

The Nature of International Financial Regulation

As a sub-set of public and, arguably, private international law, IFR is focused on facilitating cross-border financial relations to bolster trade whilst maintaining financial integrity and stability.[5] Such regulation, which is designed to avoid or minimise the probabilities of systemic risk across borders[6] is derived from sources such as soft law standards and treaty agreements.

Treaties are presumed to serve as the primary source of international financial standards given their ability to compel enforcement. This is not the case. Rather, soft law standards which are non-binding agreements have surfaced as the primary means through which international financial standards are set. However, the role of treaty bodies, such as the International Monetary Fund (IMF)/World Bank in regulating international finance cannot be relegated to history. Although they are not standards-setting institutions, the treaties of the IMF/World Bank contain regulations and policies that affect financial institutions (FIs). For instance, the IMF's Articles of Agreement state that it shall oversee members' compliance with their general obligations.[7] This underscores the monitoring and enforcement powers of the IMF to ensure member states comply with their obligations and other relevant soft-law standards. The IMF's backing hardens the trajectory of soft laws, giving them binding authority. This bolsters the argument by scholars that soft law and hard law interact on a continuum and are not necessarily opposites.[8]

---

5 Shapovalov Mikhail Alexeevitch, 'History, Current State and Prospects of Development of International Financial Law' [2015] 43 Revista de Derecho 350.

6 John William Anderson, Jr., 'Regulatory and Supervisory Independence: Is there a Case for Independent Monetary Authorities in Brazil?' [2004] 10 L & Bus Rev. AM. 253; Rolf H. Weber and Douglas Arner, 'Towards a New Design for International Financial Regulation' [2007] 29 (2) Penn.LJ Int'l Econ. Law. 510.

7 See Article IV Section 1 (ii) IMF, Articles of Agreement, 1944.

8 Kenneth Abbott and Duncan Snidal, 'Why States Act through Formal International Organizations' [1998] 42 (1) Journal of Conflict Resolution 3; Kern Alexander, 'The Role of Soft Law

This book focuses on IFR, a crucial aspect of international law which can pre-empt and possibly forestall a financial crisis when armed with the requisite tools.

Rationale for International Financial Regulation

A pro-cyclical relationship exists between the internationalisation of finance and regulation, one which becomes more prominent after a financial crisis.[9] Thus, increasing integration occasions cross-border capital flows which heighten the case for international regulation and national adaptation of international standards to forestall a financial crisis.[10] This position is advanced by the proponents of financial regulatory convergence.[11] Kern Alexander et al. argue that 'as financial markets become integrated…states must form IFIs to manage systemic risk and other types of financial risk in the global market'.[12] Brown adds that 'because today's financial markets are global, we need proper national supervision, and a fundamental reform – global financial regulation'.[13] These views capture the potential damage imminent from international deregulation, whilst projecting the need for international regulation.

An unregulated integrated financial system creates various risks. For instance, it can trigger a 'dominant neighbour' case, where, according to Jordan et al., a country's economy can be significantly affected by the proximity of an economically buoyant neighbour.[14] Such situations prompt the affected neighbour to align its standards with international regulations to level the playing field and attract liquid foreign investment.[15] Barring such an alignment, information asymmetry and negative externalities, which are the principal drivers of market failure, are bound to arise. Information asymmetry thrives in the absence of regulation,

---

in the Legalization of International Banking Supervision: A Conceptual Approach' (2000), ESRC Centre for Business Research, University of Cambridge 168 <https://www.cbr.cam. ac.uk/fileadmin/user_upload/centre-for-business-research/downloads/working-papers/ wp168.pdf> accessed 10 July 2015.

9 Carmen Reinhart and Kenneth Rogoff, 'Regulation Should Be International' (*Financial Times*, 18 November 2008) <https://www.ft.com/content/983724fc-b589-11dd-ab71-0000779fd18c > accessed 28 August 2017.

10 Cally Jordan and Giovanni Majnoni, 'Financial Regulatory Harmonization and the Globalization of Finance' [2002] World Bank Policy Research Working Paper 2919 <https://op enknowledge.worldbank.org/bitstream/handle/10986/19224/multi0page.pdf?sequence =1&isAllowed=y > accessed 11 June 2015.

11 Kern Alexander, Rahul Dhumale and John Eatwell, *Global Governance of Financial Systems: The International Regulation of Systemic Risk* (OUP, 2006) 35.

12 Ibid.

13 HM Treasury, 'Speech by the Chancellor of the Exchequer, Gordon Brown MP at the Council for Foreign Relations in New York' (HM Treasury, 16 September 1999) <http:// webarchive.nationalarchives.gov.uk/20100407173039/http://www.hm-treasury.gov.uk/s peech_chex_160999.htm> accessed 10 June 2015.

14 *Jordan and Majnoni* (n 10).

15 Ibid.; Thomas Oatley, 'The Dilemmas of International Financial Regulation' [2000] 23 (4) Regulation 36; Gianni De-Nicolo, Giovanni Favara and Lev Ratnovski, 'Externalities and Macro Prudential Policy' [2012] SDN12/5 IMF Staff Discussion Note.

when countries decide not to disclose damning financial information that could be dissuasive to an investor. Additionally, the interconnectedness of cross-border systemic financial institutions precipitates risk of contagion in the event of a bank failure. This can propel negative externalities resulting in systemic risk.[16] Gianni De Nicolo et al. agree that high interconnectedness intensifies large shocks as they can reach more counterparts.[17] Hence, the argument that regulation should mandate some level of transparency across countries with the sole aim of ensuring or restoring financial stability.[18]

The risk associated with international regulation has propelled some scholars' arguments that market forces alone should regulate the global financial market. These scholars believe that excessive regulation can damage financial markets' functioning and reduce economic utility.[19] Additionally, there is the perception that the cost of regulation may be too high for small countries, thereby leading to an uneven application of regulations.[20] This is undoubtedly a critical problem in the development of robust standards in a world with numerous jurisdictions. For this reason, Oatley believes that national regulation and international agreements can handle risk and insurance issues; and international regulations are simply a political response to avoid a race to the bottom for less regulated states caused by international competition.[21] He exemplifies this with the Basel Accord I which mandated an 8% minimum capital requirement for internationally active banks and additional capital for loans considered riskier.[22] He finds that banks in affected countries engaged in regulatory arbitrage to maintain an appearance of compliance to these standards. He states that irrespective of the advantages it brings, international regulation could cause greater harm to financial systems and less safe banking systems.[23]

Though strong, Oatley's argument does not consider that the failure of a financial system within an integrated global structure can create negative externalities. Furthermore, it can lead to the movement of capital towards less regulated systems, thus potentially causing financial instability. Moreover, the general

---

16 Rick Gorvett, 'Systemic Risk as a Negative Externality' [2009] Risk Management: Part Two – Systemic Risk, Financial Reform and Moving Forward from the Financial Crisis, Society of Actuaries (SOA) 33; Pawel Smaga, 'The Concept of Systemic Risk' [2014] SRC Special Paper No 5, 13.

17 *De Nicolo, Favara and Ratnovski* (n 15) 1, 10.

18 Frederic Mishkin and National Bureau of Economic Research, 'Financial Stability and Globalization: Getting it Right' (Bank of Spain Conference – Central Banks in the 21st Century, 2006).

19 George Selgin, 'Proposal – Let Market Forces Play a Greater Role' (*Global Economic Symposium*, 2014) <http://www.global-economic-symposium.org/knowledgebase/the-new-global-financial-architecture/proposals/let-market-forces-play-a-great-role> accessed 10 September 2017; Masahiro Kawai and Micheal Pomerleono, 'Who Should Regulate Systemic Stability Risk? The Relevance for Asia' *in* Masahiro Kawal, Eswar Prasad (eds.), *Financial Market Regulation and Reforms in Emerging Markets* (Brookings Institution Press, 2011).

20 *Oatley* (n 15) 36, 37.

21 Ibid.

22 Basel Accord 1988.

23 *Oatley* (n 15) 36, 37.

welfare considerations as regard systemic risks suggest that market forces may be inadequate to ensure regulatory harmonisation.

However, Oatley's argument cannot be fully discarded, particularly his recognition of the inequalities that occasion the application of international standards. From a functionalist perspective, the role of IFR is to ensure financial liberalisation, stability and integrity, and goals with some attendant shortcomings.[24] This is evidenced by the uniform regulatory standards and benchmarking mechanisms applicable to all countries, irrespective of their legal developmental stages. Such arrangements give credence to the argument that international standards are prejudicial, as they establish a hierarchy of values, some of which are superfluous.[25] Although the standards aim at efficiency, integrity and stability, the need for an equitable or legitimate regime suitable for all countries is disregarded.[26] This is reflected in uniform standards, which are difficult to transplant and result in information asymmetry between countries and standard setters, particularly with ACs/EEs. Shortcomings in compliance levels, particularly in ACs, reveal this.

Undoubtedly, the international standards are a projection of the inequalities in the distribution of power within the regulatory sphere, spearheaded by developed countries pushing their domestic policy objectives, laws and commercial preferences through as international standards.[27] Consequently, these standards have failed to take sufficient account of the interests and preferences of ACs/EEs and can potentially stifle the regulatory structures and policies of ACs, whilst producing marginal gains for ACs/EEs.[28] These shortcomings add to the view that international regulatory standards may be unsuitable.[29]

Evolution of International Financial Regulation and Institutions

Prior to the First World War (WW1), global finance was sparsely regulated, both internationally and nationally.[30] During the inter-war period, market activities

---

24 This perspective focuses on the operational functions of the international financial regime.
25 Naomi Haynes and Jason Hickel, 'Hierarchy, Value and the Value of Hierarchy' [2016] 60 Social Analysis 1; Myres S. McDougal, 'Jurisprudence for a Free Society' [1966] 2583 Faculty Scholarship Series 1, 6.
26 Norman Mugarura, *The Global Anti-Money Laundering Regulatory Landscape in Less Developed Countries* (2nd edn, Routledge, 2016) 145.
27 The FATF recommendations were derived from a combination of national strategies from Switzerland, the United Kingdom and the United States, coupled with recommendations from the Basel Committee from 1998. See Mark Pieth and Gemma Aiolfi, 'The Private Sector Becomes Active: The Wolfsberg Process' [2003] 10 (4) Journal of Financial Crime 359, 359–360; Chris Brummer, *Soft Law and the Global Financial System: Rule Making in the 21st Century* (CUP, 2015) 183.
28 Norman Mugarura, *The Global Anti-Money Laundering Regulatory Landscape in Less Developed Countries* (2nd edn, Routledge, 2016) 145.
29 *Brummer* (n 27) 184; Jason Sharman, 'The Global Anti- Money Laundering Regime and Developing Countries: Damned if They Do, Damned if They Don't' [2006] Paper Presented at the ISAA Conference 1, 13.
30 Gerald Epstein, 'Should Financial Flows Be Regulated? Yes' *in* Jomo Kwame SundaraM (eds.) *Reforming the International Financial System for Development* (CUP 2011) 194.;

collapsed, and economies crashed. Countries raised barriers by curtailing financial freedom and risking potential currency devaluation.[31] Undoubtedly, this was self-defeating, leading to a decline in world trade and destruction of international monetary cooperation. After the Second World War (WW2), when trade regulation started emerging, there was still no structure for the regulation of international finance.[32] It was paradoxical that only trade was regulated given that finance flows more easily across borders than goods and services. Nevertheless, given the gradual breakdown of the gold standard (instituted pre-WW1 for monetary stability), finance was now based on closed domestic systems with limited capital flows and a fixed exchange rate due to the disintegration of the world economy.[33]

IFIs, particularly the IMF, were created on the heel of WW2 to facilitate cross-border monetary transactions and ensure currency stability. The IFIs' founders generally excluded a regime for capital movements from the IFIs' structures as this was considered antithetical to trade and investment capital.[34] Keynes and White believed that, although progressive, cross-border transactions could have destabilising consequences within states.[35] Following their concerns, the IMF's Article IV recognised the right of members to impose capital controls, as long as this did not restrict payments for transactions on the current account.[36] This design, which ensured adequate national macroeconomic management, was based on a concept of embedded liberalism. It was rooted in Keynesian ideology and White's perspective that not only favoured nationalistic capital controls but perceived unregulated capital mobility as an example of market failure.[37]

Lance Taylor, 'Global Macroeconomic Management' *in* Peepak Nayyar (eds.) *Governing Globalization: Issues and Institutions* (OUP 2002) 51, 52.

31 Richard Overy, *The Inter-War Crisis* (Routledge, 2016) 1, 62; Richard S. Grossman, 'Banking Crisis' (2006) Wesleyan Economic Working Papers 001 <http://repec.wesleyan.edu /pdf/rgrossman/2016001_grossman.pdf> accessed 13 July 2015; Michele Fratianni and Federico Giri, 'The Tale of Two Great Crises' [2017] 81 Journal of Economic Dynamics and Control 1, 25.

32 Yilmaz Akyuz, 'Towards Reform of the International Financial Architecture: Which Way Forward' *in* Yilmaz Akyuz (eds.), *Reforming the Global Financial Architecture: Issues and Proposals* (Zed Books 2002) 1.

33 *Weber and Arner* (n 6) 510.

34 *Akyuz* (n 32); Ross Buckley, *International Financial System: Policy and Regulation* (Kluwer Law International, 2009) 1, 105.

35 James Boughton, 'The IMF and the Force of History: Ten Events and Ten Ideas that have Shaped the Institution' [2004] IMF Working Paper 04/75 <https://goo.gl/Vhc6pr> accessed 9 November 2015; Benjamin Cohen, 'Monetary Governance and Capital Mobility in Historical Perspective' *in* Rainer Grote and Thilo Maruahn (eds.) *The Regulation of International Financial Markets: Perspectives for Reform* (CUP 2006) 48–50.

36 Ibid.; See Article IV, IMF Articles of Agreement, 1944.

37 Jonathan Kirsher, 'Keynes, Capital Mobility and the Crisis of Embedded Liberalism' [1999] 6 (3) Review of International Political Economy 313; Ikuo Gonoi and Hiroaki Ataka, 'Conceptual Relevance of "Embedded Liberalism" and its Critical Social Consequences' [2006] Artigo aspresentado no ISA-South Annual Conference: PAIS Graduate Working Papers 3

Such failure was based on the inability of countries to pursue tailored economic policies or maintain fixed exchange rates.[38] Capital controls were thus perceived to be necessary for the smooth functioning of an open international economy. Indeed, this ideology resulted in a surge of economic prosperity in the 1950s and 1960s.[39]

However, the increasing risk occasioned by the internationalisation of finance in the late 1970s[40] and the ensuing financial and socio-economic crisis raised questions about the continued application of the embedded-liberalism ideology. The resulting neo-liberalist ideology mandated the replacement of the fixed exchange rates with a flexible exchange rate to restore stability.[41] This ideology also led to the creation of informal committees, including the Basel Committee on Banking Supervision (BCBS) and the International Organisation of Securities Commissions (IOSCO) to formulate unified approaches to curtail crises, especially as regards emerging economies.[42] Agreements resulting from the findings of the neo-liberalists were to be implemented via domestic and regulatory systems. Although the BCBS and IOSCO recorded successes, repeated financial crises such as the developing countries' debt crisis of the 1980s, the global stock market collapse of 1987 and the periodic collapses of financial intermediaries illustrated their limitations in dealing with trends that fundamentally altered the financial landscape.[43]

For instance, the Asian financial crisis was the sharpest to hit the developing world since the 1982 debt crisis.[44] The dynamics of this crisis prompted academic controversy as to its immediate cause.[45] There was consensus that the absence of sound regulatory oversight was significant, especially in the advent of liberalisation

---

(6) <https://warwick.ac.uk/fac/soc/pais/currentstudents/phd/resources/crips/working _papers/2006/working_paper_3_gonoi_and_ataka.pdf> accessed 19 November 2016.

38 Ibid.

39 David Harvey, *A Brief History of Neoliberalism* (OUP, 2005) 178.

40 Richard O'Brien, *Global Financial Integration: The End of Geography* [1992] Royal Institute of International Affairs.

41 Katja Freistein and Philip Liste, 'Introduction: Fragmented Territoriality' [2016] 19 (2) Journal of International Relations and Development 193.

42 *Weber and Arner* (n 6) 391, 403; *Jordan and Majnoni* (n 10).

43 Ibid. 391, 403. For the trends listed: technological innovation, liberalisation of capital, disintermediation of financial markets, reduction in centralized decision makers' role, Bretton Woods Institutions' breakdown.

44 Steven Radelet and Jeffrey Sachs, 'The Onset of the East Asian Financial Crisis' (1998) NBER Working Paper Series, Working Paper 6680, National Bureau of Economic Research 2 <http://www.nber.org/chapters/c8691.pdf> accessed 7 June 2016; Ivan Savic, 'Explaining Compliance with International Commitments to Combat Financial Crisis: The IMF and the G7' (47th Annual ISA Convention, 2006).

45 Goldstein Morris, *The Asian Financial Crisis: Causes, Cures and Systemic Implications* (Institute for International Economics, Washington DC, 1998); Biag Taimur and Ilan Glodfajn, 'Financial Market Contagion in the Asian Crisis' (1998) IMF Working Paper 26/2 <https://link.springer.com/article/10.2307/3867666> accessed 19 April 2016.

in developing countries.[46] Avgouleas notes that attention was focused on policies aimed at abolishing capital restrictions and opening up the market, without regard to the domestic competence or expertise of its regulatory institutions.[47] He also observes that international governance structures were inadequate to sustain the pressure from these policies. Combined with the financial panic that arose from weaknesses in the economies, these precipitated the Asian financial crisis,[48] which demonstrated that the financial sector of domestic economies is uniquely able to inflict damage on the broader economy.[49]

The Asian crisis triggered financial sector reforms aimed at promoting financial stability across borders and providing early warning signals.[50] Measures were installed to identify potential vulnerabilities in national financial systems to forestall any potential localised financial crisis[51] and ensure effective resolution.[52] This myopic reform, which occasioned a New International Financial Architecture (NIFA), encompassed the enhanced involvement of transnational governance institutions wielding soft law instruments as standards setters with supervision from the IMF/World Bank.[53] Concurrently, the IMF sought to amend its Articles of Agreement, to make the promotion of capital account liberalisation its specific purpose.[54] This would give it jurisdiction over capital movements and the power to mandate unrestricted capital flows as a condition for membership.[55] From a Keynesian perspective, this would be unsuitable in curbing future crisis.

Additionally, although the NIFA structure broadened representation of EEs and reinforcement of the roles of standard-setting bodies, its legitimacy was however limited by two factors: the marginalisation of developing countries in the

---

46 *Brummer* (n 27) 13; Gregory Noble and John Ravenhill, 'Cause and Consequences of the Asian Financial Crises', in Gregory Noble and John Ravenhill, (eds.), *The Asian Financial Crisis and the Architecture of the Global Finance*, ed., (CUP 2000) 1.

47 Emilios Avgouleas, 'Governance of Global Financial Markets': *The Law, the Economics, the Politics*' (CUP 2012) 185.

48 Giancarlo Corsetti, Paolo Pesenti and Nouriel Roubini, 'What Caused the Asian Financial Crisis? Part 1: A Macroeconomic Overview' (1998) NBER Working Paper No.6833 <http://www.nber.org/papers/w6833.pdf> accessed 24 May 2016.

49 *Brummer* (n 27) 69; GAO Report, 'International Finance: Actions Taken to Reform Financial Sectors in Asian Emerging Markets' (*GAO/GGD -99 – 57*, Sept 1999) <https://www.gao.gov/assets/230/228224.pdf> accessed 24 May 2016.

50 Cally Jordan, 'The Dangerous Illusion of International Financial Standards and the Legacy of the Financial Stability Forum' [2010] 12 The San Diego Int'l LJ 333, 336.

51 *Brummer* (n 27) 68.

52 Barry Eichengreen, *Towards a New International Financial Architecture: A Practical Post-Asia Agenda* (Peterson Institute Press: All Books, 1999); *Weber and Arner* (n 6) 391, 403.

53 *Brummer* (n 27) 68; the IMF (transparency and liquidity) and the World Bank (technical assistance); Lawrence Baxter, 'Understanding the Global in Global Finance and Regulation' *in* Ross Buckley, Doug Arner, & Emilios Avgouleas (eds.) Reconceptualizing Global Finance and its Regulation (CUP 2015) 1, 2.

54 IMF Survey, 'IMF Wins Mandate to Cover Capital Accounts, Debt Initiative Put in Motion' [1997] 26.9 IMF 131.

55 Pierre Goad, 'Acceptance of Capital Controls is Spreading' [1998] Asian Wall Street Journal.

standard-setting process[56] and the inability of the Financial Stability Board (FSB) to effectively exercise its mandate in generating standards, not even voluntary ones.[57]

Although well intentioned, the eruption of global financial crisis (GFC) on a larger scale a decade later[58] revealed the ineffectiveness of the NIFA to restore confidence in the financial system. Avgouleas attributed the GFC not to the inadequate effectiveness of regulatory initiatives, but rather to the absence of compulsory monitoring mechanisms and a binding framework for managing cross-border crisis[59] under the NIFA.[60] Disputing this, Brummer argued that the NIFA was itself riddled with ambiguities, buttressing his argument with the abstruse mandate, technique and implementation style of the Financial Stability Forum (FSF).[61] These criticisms were predicated on the soft law approach adopted by the FSF, which lacked the transparency and contestation of the legislative process.[62] These arguments reveal that though the NIFA was not fundamentally the cause of the GFC, it was inefficient in meeting the realities of global finance and its attendant risks.

Towards Effective Regulation of International Finance and AML/CFT

The factors considered as precipitants to previous financial crises were listed by the FSB and the Financial Sector Assessment Programme (FSAP).[63] However broad, the compendium of standards compiled by the FSB enumerates 12 economic and financial standards that are internationally acknowledged as crucial for a functional financial system.[64] The FSB emphasised that these standards deserved priority implementation.[65] Amongst the standards identified for rating a financial system were the recommendations of the FATF on AML/CFT.[66] The IMF/

---

56 Robert Delonis, 'International Financial Standards and Codes: Mandatory Regulation without Representation' [2004] 36 NYU J. INT'L L.& POL.563, 631–633.
57 *Alexander, Dhumale and Eatwell* (n 11).
58 Emilios Avgouleas, *Governance of Global Financial Markets: The Law, the Economics, the Politics* (First Published 2012, CUP 2012) 185.
59 Ibid.
60 Ibid. (n 54)
61 *Brummer* (n 27); See also John Eatwell, 'The Challenges Facing International Financial Regulation' [2001] Western Economic Association p 14; Stavros Gadinis, 'The Finacial Stability Board: The New Politics of International Financial Regulation' [2013] 48 (2) Texas International Law Journal 165.
62 *Jordan* (n 50) 1, 17.
63 FSB, 'Table of Key Standards for Sound Financial Systems' <http://www.financialstabilityb oard.org/what-we-do/about-the-compendium-of-standards/key_standards/table-of-key -standards-for-sound-financial-systems/> accessed 13 March 2015.
64 See OECD, *OECD Reviews of Risk Management Policies: Future Global Shocks, Improving Risk Governance* (OECD Publishing, 2011) 1, 110.
65 *FSB* (n 63).
66 Ibid.

World Bank endorsed these with an agreement to monitor the compliance levels of countries.[67]

The addition of AML/CFT to the 12 FSB standards generated a debate[68] that their inclusion was undemocratic, but rather based on the lobbying, networking strength and support for the governing body of the standard-setting organisation.[69] Furthermore, it is argued that banks are not harmed by being used as a conduit for illicit funds; rather illicit funds can be profitable to economies, banks and depositors and thus do not warrant international regulation.[70] The international community has nevertheless continued to include the regulation of money laundering and terrorist financing (ML/TF) in its agenda.

Justification for the Inclusion of AML/CFT Regulation in Financial Sector Reform

To justify the inclusion of the AML/CFT regulation in the international financial sector regime, it is crucial to parallel their aims.

Financial sector reforms were aimed at enhancing combined regulatory supervision to prevent or mitigate a financial crisis, also one of the main aims for regulating ML/TF. This is because these illicit activities can harm financial stability and integrity, a triggering factor for a financial crisis. This argument is not far-fetched. Tsingou postulates that ML/TF is the price for financial liberalisation.[71] Echoing this assertion, Schroeder argues that illegal proceeds are easily converted into seemingly legitimate funds due to increased trade liberalisation and the expansion of the global financial system.[72] Increased and unanticipated cross-border transfer of illicit funds can however have a destabilising macroeconomic effect.[73] Such transfers can lead to inexplicable changes in the demand for money, resulting in an unhealthy volatility of international capital flows and exchange

---

67 David William, 'Development and Global Governance: The World Bank, Financial Sector Reform and the Will to Govern' [2008] 45 (2) International Politics 1, 220–221.

68 Douglas Arner, 'Organizations of International Co-operation in Standard Setting and Regulation' *in* Garard Caprio (eds.) *Handbook of Safeguarding Global Financial Stability: Political, Social, Cultural and Economic Theories and Models* (Elsevier 2013) 484–485.

69 Ibid.

70 Antoinette Verhage, 'Between the Hammer and the Anvil? Money Laundering-Complex and its Interactions with the Compliance Industry' [2009] 52 (1) Crime Law Soc. Change 1, 9–32.

71 Eleni Tsiongou, 'Global Finance Governance and the Developing Anti-Money Laundering Regime: What Lessons for International Political Economy?' [2010] 47 (6) International Politics 617, 627.

72 William Schroeder, 'A Global Threat and the International Community's Response' [2001] 70 FBI Law Enforcement Bulletin 1.

73 Bartlett Brent, 'The Negative Effects of Money Laundering on Economic Development' [2002] 5967 Asian Development Bank Regional Technical Assistance Project; The World Bank, 'Combating Money Laundering and the Financing of Terrorism – A Comprehensive Training Guide' (2009) 1, 19.

rates.[74] This reveals an interesting link between market abuse and financial instability – triggering factors for a crisis.

The occasional association of financial crisis with 'run on banks'[75] can be likened to the effect of ML/TF on banks and the financial sector as a whole. Morais adds that these illicit crimes erode the integrity of FIs, weakening or destroying their positions as repositories of trust and confidence.[76] He states that in the long run, there is the real risk that if left unchecked, criminal interests could assume greater control of FIs.[77] Thus, illicit activities can undermine the soundness of FIs and occasion material damage and loss of confidence or reputation as a result of fraud.[78]

Additionally, illicit transfers through FIs can harm a country's economic growth and development. This can be viewed from two perspectives. On the one hand, ML/TF channel resources to less industrious activities, thus facilitating domestic corruption and crime.[79] In a bid to legalise funds, launderers may channel their monies into sterile investments such as luxury goods or front companies.[80] This diversion of funds can undermine legitimate businesses and harm a country's economic progression. On the other hand, unconstrained illicit transfers, especially in countries with weak regulatory capacity can weaken the financial sector's role in a country's economic progression. The Asian and subsequent international crises illustrated that financial institutions that allow themselves to be abused by ML will bring serious detrimental effect to the economies of their countries.

Thus, it is also clear that ML/TF depresses the revenue of states, particularly where tax evasion is involved.[81] Consequently, various countries, particu-

---

74 *Schroeder* (n 72) 1, 19; Antoinette Verhage, *The Anti Money Laundering Complex and the Compliance of Industry* (Taylor and Francis 2011) 37; Pierre – Laurent Chatain, 'The World Bank's Role in the Fight Against Money Laundering and Terrorist Financing' [2004] 6 Int'l LFD Int'l 1, 192.

75 Garton Gary, 'Some Reflections on the Recent Financial Crisis ' (2012) National Bureau of Economic Research Working Paper Series 18397, 3 <http://risk.econ.queensu.ca/wp-cont ent/uploads/2013/10/Gorton-Some-reflections-on-the-recent-Crisis-2012.pdf> accessed 10 July 2015.

76 *Herbert v. Morais*, 'The War Against Money Laundering, Terrorism and the Financing of Terrorism' [2002] Lawasia J 1,6.

77 *Verhage* (n 70).

78 *Verhage* (n 74); The World Bank, 'Combating Money Laundering and the Financing of Terrorism – A Comprehensive Training Guide' (2009) 1, 19.

79 *Brent* (n 73); Joshua Chesoli, 'Exploring the Concept, Significance and Adverse Impact of Money Laundering'; Paul Allan Schott, *Reference Guide to Anti-Money Laundering and Combatting the Financing of Terrorism* (World Bank Publication 2006) II–1, II–6.

80 Paul Allan Schott, *Reference Guide to Anti-Money Laundering and Combating the Financing of Terrorism* (World Bank Publication 2006) II–1, II–6; Loretta Napoleon, *Terrorism and the Economy: How the War on Terror is Bankrupting the Economy* (SSP 2014) 1, 73.

81 Peter Alldridge, *Money Laundering Law: Forfeiture, Confiscation, Civil Recovery, Criminal Laundering and Taxation of the Proceeds of Crime* (Hart Publishing 2003) II–6; Max Everest – Phillips 'The Political Economy of Controlling Tax Evasion and Illicit Flows' *in* Peter

larly developed economies, have successfully argued for the inclusion of proceeds of illicit crimes in the national gross domestic profit.[82] The European statistical guideline states that illegal transactions backed by consent should be included in measurements of economic size.[83] The argument runs that the exclusion of these activities from national accounts gives rise to discrepancies as the income earned from illegal means are often invested in legal assets.[84] Critics have questioned the methodology utilised in generating the data and argued that this inclusion is likely to provide an unrealistic representation of economic development.[85] This has attendant consequences, such as investor distrust in a perceived 'inauthentic estimate of GDP', a catalyst for reduced investment. Regardless, the European Union restated its position on mandatory illicit transactions accounting in the 2010 version of the European Systems of Accounts.[86]

According to the European Union, illicit transactions have become bothersome and reporting them as part of GDP may heighten the capital flight of funds to jurisdictions that abide by this requirement.[87] This may damage the reputation of countries, particularly developing states whose funds are laundered. It may also deter foreign investments[88] and discourage foreign banks from continuing correspondent relationships with FIs in countries that report illicit transactions as part of GDP.[89]

The 'victimless' nature of ML/TF has been contested. Adopting Mill's argument, Groot postulates that where there are valid contracts on predicate offences, such as drug transactions, such agreements cannot be assumed to harm anyone.[90]

Reuter (eds.) *Draining Development? Controlling Flows of Illicit Funds from Developing Countries* (The World Bank, 2012) 1, 69.

82 Richard Summerfield, 'GDP to include illegal activity' (*Financier Worldwide*, 2014) <https://www.financierworldwide.com/gdp-to-include-illegal-activity/#.WZM5Ha2ZPUo> accessed 10 August 2017.

83 Sarah O'Connor, 'Drugs and Prostitutions Add £10bn to UK Economy' (*Financial Times*, May 29 2014) <https://www.ft.com/content/65704ba0-e730-11e3-88be-00144feabdc0> accessed 10 August 2017.

84 OECD, 'OECD Handbook' (*OECD*) <https://www.oecd.org/std/na/NOE-Handbook-%20Chapter9.pdf> accessed 10 August 2015.

85 *Richard Summerfield* (n 82).

86 Eurostat European Commission, 'European System of Accounts: ESA 2010' (EU, 2013) <http://ec.europa.eu/eurostat/cache/metadata/Annexes/nasa_10_f_esms_an1.pdf> accessed 20 August 2017.

87 James Boyce and Leonce Ndikumana, 'Capital Flight from Sub Saharan African Countries: Updated Estimates, 1970–2010' [2012] Political Economy Research Institute Research Report 1, 6; Raymond Baker, 'The Scale of the Global Financial Structure Facilitating Money Laundering' *in* Brigitte Unger and Daan Van Der Inde (eds.) *Research Handbook on Money Laundering* (Edward Elgar Publishing Limited 2013) 194, 195.

88 *Chatain* (n 74)

89 FATF 'FATF Recommendations' (*FATF*, 2013) <http://www.fatf-gafi.org/media/fatf/documents/recommendations/pdfs/fatf_recommendations.pdf> accessed 20 April 2015.

90 Loek Groot, 'Money Laundering, Drugs and Prostitution as Victimless Crimes' *in* Brigitte Unger, Daan Van Der Inde (eds.) *Research Handbook on Money Laundering* (Edward Elgar Publishing Limited 2013) 59.

He argues, in line with Posner's cost–benefit analysis that criminalising money laundering would not be beneficial to society.[91] Consequently, he contends that, in the absence of a direct victim, ML should not be regulated. Ferwerda asserts that these illicit crimes have social, economic and political effects.[92] These catalyse inflation, insolvency and bankruptcy, as well as increased housing and living costs, which have spillover effects. These implications defeat the 'victimless nature' argument, conferring undue advantage on launderers to the detriment of society.[93] Moreover, by the very act of aiding terrorism, TF causes security challenges, leading to loss of lives and livelihood, and creates an atmosphere of fear.[94]

Increasingly disturbing was the evidence by experts that ML/TF is more detrimental to emerging and developing economies, which have less sophisticated FIs.[95] Identifying that a 'break' in the chain of AML/CFT regime, especially in developing countries, can expose other countries to the detrimental effects of ML/TF, the international community prompted the inclusion of AML/CFT regimes in financial sector reforms. This was based on the recognition that strengthening AML/CFT regimes could significantly improve prospects for sustainable growth, development and social cohesion.

Interestingly, the regulation of ML, once predicated on the need to combat drug crimes,[96] has gone beyond considerations of financial stability.[97] This became evident post 9/11 attacks, spurring the innovation of the FATF's nine additional recommendations on TF.[98] These mandated adherence to the International Convention for the Suppression of the Financing of Terrorism[99] and imposed more stringent recommendations and attendant punitive measures on TF regulation.[100] This move prompted scholars to question why discussions on an international CFT regime occurred only in response to the attack in the United States and was not triggered by earlier terror activities in Africa, the Middle East and

---

91 Ibid.
92 Ferweda Joras, 'The Multidisciplinary Economics of Money Laundering' [2012] Tjalling C. Koopmans Institute Discussion Paper Series 1, 30–31; *Chatain* (n 74).
93 Van de Werdt and P. Speenkenbrink, 'Witwassen, een koud kunstje' Jaarboek Compliance (2008) 201, 201–216; *Chatain* (n 74).
94 David Altheide, 'Terrorism and the Politics of Fear' [2006] 6.4 Cultural Studies Critical Methodologies 415, 415–439; Harmon Christopher, *Terrorism Today* (Routledge 2013) 66.
95 Their financial sectors are lower, less diverse and more susceptible to manipulation than those of developed countries, see *Chatain* (n 74).
96 *The United Nations Convention against Illicit Traffic in Narcotic Drugs and Psychotropic Substances (The Vienna Convention) in 1988.*
97 Arnone Marco and Pier Pardoan, 'Anti-Money Laundering by International Institutions: A Preliminary Assessment' [2008] 26.3 European Journal of Law and Economics 1, 9.
98 FATF, 'FATF Recommendations on Terrorist Financing' (*FATF*, 2013) <http://www.fatf -gafi.org/media/fatf/documents/recommendations/pdfs/fatf_recommendations.pdf> accessed 17 May 2015.
99 Ibid.
100 Ibid. (n 94).

Europe.[101] On close scrutiny, it is clear that, unlike other terrorist attacks, the 9/11 attacks unearthed a pervasive network of underground banking and other financial channels used to finance terrorism.[102] Facing these dramatic new threats, AML/CFT was perceived as a way of ensuring global security.[103] Thus, the international community was able to mandate countries to agree on a consensus for reasons that went beyond financial stability.

These arguments reinforce the reasons why the international community has, although belatedly, recognised as crucial, the regulation of ML/TF.[104]

IFIs and soft law bodies are at the forefront of putting these agenda forward. This book restricts its scope to the IMF/World Bank and the FATF.

THE IMF AND THE WORLD BANK: FINANCIAL SECTOR ASSESSMENT PROGRAMME

Although 45 countries attended the Bretton Woods meeting in 1944 and agreed to establish a framework for international economic cooperation, only 29 countries signed the IMF Articles of Agreement by the following year.[105] These select countries formed the initial members of the IMF. The World Bank, which was formed alongside the IMF, was described as an 'afterthought', given initial resistance by the United Kingdom (UK) government. Support from the United States government however saw to its creation. This is not unsurprising as all accounts show that while each of the IMF and the World Bank articles was signed by several countries, their establishment was negotiated between representatives of the UK and the United States.[106] Whilst WW2 provided the impe-

---

101   *Morais* (n 76) 1, 14. No international CFT regime was discussed even with multiple terrorist activities across African countries (Kenya and Tanzania), Middle Eastern countries (Saudi Arabia and Yemen) and Europe (Scotland in 1988).

102   Ibid. 1. Is there any terror attack without some measure of funding? The United States might only have been uncovered due to technological advances and time.

103   It is questionable whether the 'world' was facing dramatic changes, or the United States was foisting its fears on the world.

104   The World Bank only recognized AML's detrimental effect on the formal financial sector in 1995. See David Scott, 'Money Laundering and International Efforts to Fight it' (Public Policy for the Private Sector, May 1995) <http://siteresources.worldbank.org/EXTFINANCIALSECTOR/Resources/282884-1303327122200/048scott.pdf> accessed 15 March 2015.; Michel Camdessus, 'Money Laundering: The Importance of International Countermeasures', address to the plenary meeting of the FATF (*IMF*, 10 February 1998) <https://www.imf.org/external/np/speeches/1998/021098.htm> accessed 10 January 2015. Anti-terrorism and corruption became critical subjects of consideration at the 1997 Denver Summit – Emilio Avgouleas, *Governance of Global Financial Markets: The Law, the Economics, the Politics* (CUP 2012) 189.

105   IMF, 'Cooperation and Reconstruction (1944–71)' (*IMF*) <https://www.imf.org/external/about/histcoop.htm> accessed 10 September 2017.

106   Kenneth Hover, *Economics as Ideology* (Rowman & Littlefield Publishers, Inc., 2003) 127; Elizabeth Borgwardt, *A New Deal for the World: America's Vision for Human Rights* (The Belknap Press of HUP, Cambridge, Massachusetts. London, 2005) 125–128.

tus to expedite the creation of these institutions, the closed negotiation process was arguably critical for expediency. However, this may have been achieved in a manner detrimental to excluded countries, particularly developing countries – a theme that will run through this book.

The IMF and the World Bank are treaty bodies with detailed articles which impose legally binding obligations on their member states.[107] Their precise rules backed by obligations and enforcement capabilities warrant their classification as 'hard-law' bodies.[108] Accession to their treaties deprives countries of adopting a flexible approach towards the interpretation of their articles, breach of which can result in the imposition of sanctions such as the withdrawal of membership or access to resources. Whilst this may constrain the behaviour or sovereignty of states, it has the advantage of reducing transaction costs and strengthening the credibility of their commitments, particularly at a macroeconomic level.

Whilst the IMF has responsibility for facilitating macroeconomic stability, the World Bank is responsible for reconstruction and development.[109] However, their mandates have evolved to meet global changes. The IMF has become involved in financial stability, an area that was strictly the domain of Central Banks.[110] Minton-Beddoes states that this expansion reflects its yearning for a pioneering role post the deterioration of Bretton Woods Institution.[111] Notwithstanding its underlying motivation, the IMF was critical in lending to countries to assuage financial crises.[112] For this reason, this chapter aligns with the argument by Arner and Taylor that the IMF's involvement is largely because that it has come to regard these issues as ancillary to its mandate.[113] This is buttressed with the Asian crisis experience, which illustrated how large contingent liabilities on government budgets result from poorly regulated banking systems; financial stability was therefore crucial for fiscal discipline and by extension, the balance of payments mandate.

---

107 Articles of Agreement of the IMF (*IMF* 2016) <https://www.imf.org/external/pubs/ ft/aa/pdf/aa.pdf> accessed 25 July 2017; Article 1 of the Articles of Agreement of the IBRD (*IBRD*, 1989) <http://siteresources.worldbank.org/EXTABOUTUS/Resources/ ibrd-articlesofagreement.pdf> accessed 15 April 2015.

108 Kenneth Abbott and Duncan Snidal, 'Hard and Soft Law in International Governance' [2000] 54 (3) International Organization 421, 426.

109 Article 1 of the Articles of Agreement IMF (*IMF,* 2016) <https://www.imf.org/external /pubs/ft/aa/pdf/aa.pdf> accessed 25 July 2017; Article 1 of the Articles of Agreement of the IBRD (*IBRD*, 1989) <http://siteresources.worldbank.org/EXTABOUTUS/Reso urces/ibrd-articlesofagreement.pdf> accessed 15 April 2015.

110 Douglas Arner and Michael Taylor, 'The Global Financial Crisis and the Financial Stability Board: Hardening the Soft Law of International Financial Regulation?' [2009] 32 UNSWLJ 32 488, 505.

111 Zanny Minton-Beddoes, 'Why the IMF Needs Reform' [1995] Foreign Affairs p. 123, 124; Morris Goldstein, Graciela Kaminsky, Carmen Reinhart, *Assessing Financial Vulnerability: An Early Warning System for Emerging Markets* (PIP 2000).

112 The Asian Crisis and the Global Financial Crisis.

113 *Arner and Taylor* (n 110) 488, 504. Contrast with *Jordan* (n 50).

The IMF seeks to ensure that countries comply with key regulatory areas through its core functions of surveillance, financial assistance and technical assistance.[114] These key functions allow the IMF to assess members' economic and monetary policies against its purpose to determine the probability of the risk they pose as against the stability of the international financial systems. These tools equip the IMF with some level of intrusion, giving it power to mandate that countries make changes to monetary and economic policies to assuage existing risk.

Two agencies make up the World Bank: The International Bank for Reconstruction and Development (IBRD) and the International Development Association.[115] The World Bank's primary aim is to act as a financial intermediary, a development institute and a development agency for countries. Interestingly, financial sector reform has been on the World Bank agenda for a considerable length of time. This is evidenced by the Bank's financial and technical support for structural reforms[116] and improvements in country capacity building to oversee the financial systems through trainings and legislative changes. The World Bank's mandate has further evolved to cover banking supervision, creating a legal environment for the financial system, accounting and auditing practices and information provision. This resulted from the Asian financial crisis and is justified based on a substantial spillover threat from badly governed financial systems.

The cornerstone of the IFI's approach is the FSAP; an investigative tool launched jointly by the IMF and the World Bank post the financial crisis.[117] Described as the primary architecture for supporting the monitoring of international financial standards at global level, the FSAP was established to harness the respective strengths of IFIs in identifying financial sector vulnerabilities and developmental needs.[118] Additionally, FSAPs determine countries' compliance levels with international standards of financial regulation and supervision. The overarching aim remains to ensure diminished likelihood of a crisis, thus fostering financial stability.[119]

Seabrooke and Tsiongou strongly argue that the FSAP was introduced for two interrelated reasons; to ensure the control of policy location for financial sector reform and to rescue the IFIs from their battered reputations following their shortcomings during the 1997 financial crisis.[120] They stated that it was

114 Articles of Agreement of the IMF, 'Articles IV and V' (International Monetary Fund, 2016) <http://www.imf.org/external/pubs/ft/aa/> accessed 19 May 2015.
115 See IBRD Articles of Agreement 1989 and IDA Articles of Agreement 1960.
116 *William* (n 67) 212, 216.
117 Haizhou Huang and S. Kal Wajid, 'Financial Stability in the World of Global Finance' [2002] 39.1 Finance and Development, a Quarterly Magazine of the IMF 1, 3.
118 Paul Kupiec, 'The IMF-World Bank Financial Sector Assessment Program: A View from the Inside' *in* Douglas Evanoff and George Kaufman (eds.), *Systematic Financial Crisis, Resolving Large Bank Insolvencies* (World Scientific Publishing Co. Pte. Ltd. 2005) 69.
119 Ibid.; *Huang and Wajid* (n 117) 1, 3.
120 Leonard Seabrooke and Eleni Tsiongou, 'Revolving Doors and Linked Ecologies in the World Economy: Policy Locations and the Practice of International Financial Reform'

an attention-gaining strategy employed by the IFIs during this period.[121] There was however evidence that the FSAP presented the fora where issues concerning international financial systems could be effectively discussed, especially the evolving problems of AML/CFT. Moreover, the IFIs possessed the technical expertise and ability to monitor compliance in these areas.[122] The advantages of these structures made a case for its establishment.

However, the IFIs remained reluctant to intervene due to reservations held by developing countries over additional conditionalities and fears regarding the IFIs expertise in AML/CFT.[123] The IFIs were however prompted to intervene by the Group of Seven (G7) in 2000. This intervention is the foremost cooperative approach of stakeholders to take a more significant role in countering ML/TF.[124] No doubt this was significantly facilitated by the 9/11 terrorist attack on the United States[125] which quelled the reservations of developing countries on the role of the IFIs in addressing AML/CFT issues. During this period, the AML/CFT policies served as shock therapy.[126]

The IFIs have endorsed a list of 12 areas of concern under which AML/CFT is incorporated[127] in the form of the 40 recommendations of the FATF.[128] These indicate an accommodation of AML/CFT into the mandate of both institutions. The IFIs also commenced assessments of countries against the FATF's methodologies to ensure compliance with the FATF's standards. This marked the contracting out of assessments of compliance with the FATF recommendations to the IMF and the World Bank.[129] Compliance and implementation records are documented in the 'Reports on Observance of Standards and Codes' (ROSCs),[130] which constitutes the basis for the publication of the Financial System Stability Assessments (FSSAs) in the IMF and the Financial Sector Assessment (FSA) in the World Bank. AML/CFT issues related to financial supervision and regulation by the IMF are covered under its Article IV consultation.[131] Thus, broadening the scope of financial sector monitoring. Interestingly, the IFIs now integrate FSAP

(2009) 260/09 CSGR Working Paper, 14 <https://warwick.ac.uk/fac/soc/pais/research/researchcentres/csgr/papers/workingpapers/2009/26009.pdf> accessed 10 July 2015.

121 Ibid.
122 *Arnone and Pardoan* (n 97) 361, 361–386.
123 *Seabrooke and Tsiongou, (n 120)*.
124 David Williams, 'Governance, Security and "Development": The Case of Money Laundering' [2008] Working Paper on Transnational Politics 1, 11.
125 *Arnone and Pardoan* (n 97).
126 Naomi Klein, *The Shock Doctrine: The Rise of Disaster Capitalism* (Macmillan, 2007).
127 IMF, the World Bank, 'International Standards: Strengthening Surveillance, Domestic Institutions and International Markets' (IMF, World Bank, 2003) < https://www.imf.org/external/np/pdr/sac/2003/030503.pdf> accessed 17 July 2015.
128 *FATF* (n 89)
129 *Chatain* (n 74).
130 Laurence Ravillon, Helene Tourard and Eric Loquin, 'Informal Sources of International Business Law' [2011] Int'l Bus. LJ 1, 2.
131 *Morais* (n 76), 23.

reports into Country Assistance Strategies (CAS) for borrower countries;[132] making it a regular part of their work. The infusion of AML/CFT regulation into the activities of these institutions illustrates the extent to which it is considered vital in protecting the financial system and safeguarding lives.

The engagement of the IFIs in ensuring compliance to AML/CFT regulations is further enhanced by their observer status within the FATF. However, this indicates a paradox as notwithstanding the repulsion to the centralisation of standard formulation and coercive authority through governments, the FATF utilises the IMF/World Bank framework, given their membership base. Their participation however raises questions about the involvement of governments.[133] The FATF addressed this paradox, which permits the exclusion of governments for their agents[134] whilst seemingly maintaining the uniformity of standards with a measure of flexibility.

THE FINANCIAL ACTION TASK FORCE

The legal status of the FATF differs from that of treaty bodies. Established by the G7 to respond to the threat of ML/TF, the FATF is a 'soft-law'[135] international standard-setting body for AML/CFT regulation. It is so described due to the nature of its standards and its operational base. The FATF's standards are perceived to lack compulsion and precision.[136] They are considered as minimum standards on AML/CFT which countries are encouraged but not bound to implement. Unlike the treaty options which require lengthy ratification processes, this model allows for flexibility of the standard-making process, permitting the swift response of soft law bodies to issues such as ML/TF that pose real-time threats.[137]

Additionally, the FATF standards are not formulated or disseminated at state level, but rather, through a regulatory alliance between countries represented by Ministers of Finance and/or Central Bank Governors. This subnational participation, exercised independently of national governments, gives the FATF its transgovernmental regulatory character.[138]

Furthermore, the operational base of networks is still relatively light in comparison to the IFIs.[139] For instance, the FATF relies on the Organisation for

---

132 *Williams* (n 124).

133 Anne-Marie Slaughter, *A New World Order* (PUP 2004) 54.

134 The FATF interacts with government representatives such as ministers who cannot bind their governments, except where the minister has express executive authority to.

135 *Slaughter* (n 133) 54.

136 *Abbott and Snidal* (n 108).

137 *Slaughter* (n 133) 19; Kal Raustiala, 'The Architecture of International Cooperation: Transgovernmental Networks and the Future of International law' [2002] 43 (1) Virginia Journal of International law 1, 26.

138 Kenneth Blazejewski, 'The FATF and its Institutional Partners: Improving the Effectiveness and Accountability of Transgovernmental Networks' [2008] 22 Temple Int'l & Comp. L.J 1, 8.

139 Ayelet Berman and Ramses Wessel, 'The International Legal Status of Informal International Law-Making Bodies: Consequences for Accountability' *in* J. Pauwelyn, R.A. Wessel

Economic Cooperation and Development (OECD) for secretarial service. It has few employees, a limited budget, a website and operates through consultations.

The context of the legal status of the FATF allows for in-depth understanding of the body. The FATF began operations in 1989, with the role of issuing AML/CFT recommendations addressed to countries.[140] Tsiongou recognises that the regime, which is backed by interpretative guidance and periodic updates, is developing on two fronts: prevention and enforcement.[141] Prevention is focused on regulation, supervision, reporting, consumer due diligence and sanctions. The FATF recommendations' preventive role also includes risk assessment and financing terrorism laws. Enforcement is however designed to be more punitive, centred on investigation, confiscation, prosecution and punishment. Tsiongou identifies the development of the regime across international and regional levels; whilst standards are formulated at international level, regional-styled bodies undertake monitoring, enforcement and implementation.[142] Actual adoption, a precondition for effective compliance is at the national level.[143] Continental bodies like the African Union have also been influential in necessitating the implementation and compliance of ACs to FATF recommendations.

The FATF has necessitated the development of an intrinsic commercial position towards AML/CFT from financial and non-financial institutions. As a self-protective reflex, these institutions have engaged in compliance to protect against regulatory and reputational risks. Nevertheless, in certain instances, they fall short, signalling a low level of compliance by their host country.[144] In the absence of legally binding authority and direct supervisory enforcement ability to bind countries to its recommendations,[145] the FATF employs soft law techniques to ensure compliance. It places failing countries on a High Risk and Other Monitored Jurisdictions (HRMJ) document,[146] which comes with attendant con-

---

and J. Wouters (eds.), *Informal International Lawmaking: Mapping the Action and Testing Concepts of Accountability and Effectiveness* (OUP, 2012).

140 FATF, 'History of the FATF' (FATF, 2017) <http://www.fatf-gafi.org/pages/aboutus/historyofthefatf/> accessed 21 May 2017.

141 Eleni Tsiongou, 'Global Governance and Transnational Financial Crime: Opportunities and Tensions in the Global Anti-Money Laundering Regime' (2005) 161/05 CSGR Working Paper, 5 <https://warwick.ac.uk/fac/soc/pais/research/researchcentres/csgr/papers/workingpapers/2005/wp16105.pdf> accessed 19 June 2015.

142 Implementation monitoring is through self-assessments conducted by countries and subsequently through external evaluation assessments involving onsite visits to governments and concerned institutions.

143 *Tsiongou* (n 141).

144 FATF, High-Risk and Non-Cooperative Jurisdictions (*FATF*) <http://www.fatf-gafi.org/topics/high-riskandnon-cooperativejurisdictions/> accessed 1 December 2014.

145 Navin Beekarry, 'The International Anti-Money Laundering and Combating the Financing of Terrorism Regulatory Strategy: A Critical Analysis of Compliance Determinants in International Law' [2010] 31 NW.J. INT'L L & BUS, 137, 155–166; *Gathii* (n 2) 198.

146 Previously the NCCT list, see FATF, 'Topic: High-Risk and Other Monitored Jurisdictions' (*FATF*, 2018) <http://www.fatf-gafi.org/publications/high-riskandnon-cooperativejurisdictions/?hf=10&b=0&s=desc(fatf_releasedate)> accessed 17 January 2018. There are two listed public documents: the 'countries or jurisdictions with such serious

sequences, including financial isolation.[147] This sanction gains its vitality from the FATF's linkages with the IMF/World Bank, the United Nations Security Council and other related international institutions,[148] which have given it force of compliance.[149] On this basis, various scholars have argued that the FATF's relationship with established supranational bodies has 'hardened' the trajectory of its soft laws, allowing it to exert sufficient authority as a legitimate supervisory body capable of setting international standards.[150]

Critics have however questioned the FATF's global effectiveness in the absence of hard-law making ability.[151] The soft law nature has been critiqued as ineffective because various countries on the previous HRMJ document formerly known as the Non-Cooperative Countries or Territories (NCCT) list have remained unperturbed by the constant 'naming and shaming'.[152] However, given the scope of the FATF's regulation, hard law treaty-based solutions might be unsuitable as it would involve harmonisation of the rulebooks of national regulators.[153] The majority of domestic financial regulation takes place not through legislation but rules promulgated and enforced by regulatory agencies.[154] Arner and Taylor argue that such synchronisation is highly impracticable as typified by the European Union's (EU) failed experiment on regulatory harmonisation. The EU eventually shifted focus to minimum standards, leaving substantial discretion to national authorities on the implementation of standards.[155] This indicates the impracticality of having a hard law regulatory framework. States would be unwilling to agree to a single regulatory system or structure, a process further hindered by the differences in legal systems. Notwithstanding its perceived enforcement shortcomings, the FATF's sanctions are arguably effective, especially as the IMF/World Bank give it some measure of validity. Moreover, given the increasing significance of trans-governmental networks (TGNs), the FATF's soft law approach cannot be underestimated.[156]

---

strategic deficiencies that the FATF calls on members and non-members to apply counter measures' or the 'call on members to apply enhanced due diligence measures proportionate to the risk arising from the deficiencies associated with the country'.

147 *Brummer* (n 27) 155.

148 *Tsiongou* (n 141).

149 *Gathii* (n 2) 198.

150 *Ghoshray* (n 2) 521, 530; Dieter Kerwer and Rainer Hulsee, 'How International Organizations Rule the World: The Case of the Financial Action Task Force on Money Laundering' [2011] 2 J Int'l Org. Stud. 50, 53.

151 Global Witness, 'How FATF Can Measure and Promote an Effective Anti-Money Laundering System' (*Global Witness*) <https://www.globalwitness.org/sites/default/files/libra ry/How%20FATF%20can%20measure%20and%20promote%20an%20effective%20anti-money%20laundering%20system.pdf> accessed 1 June 2015.

152 For Instance, Iran, North Korea, Algeria.

153 Hard law is characterized by legally enforceable commitments, which take shape within international legal parlance as customary laws, self-executing treaties and binding international agreements.

154 *Arner and Taylor* (n 110) 488, 504.

155 Ibid. 488, 505.

156 *O'Brien* (n 40).

The next part of this chapter questions whether the global design of AML/CFT regulation propagated by IFIs/the FATF is suitable by allowing for effective interactions between the FATF/the IFIs and states without a form of hegemonic subjection of a set of countries. This book will answer this question through the lens of the agency theory in light of the concept of legitimacy.

The Agency Theory: Defining International Delegation

The powers wielded by the IFIs/the FATF is best described as 'delegated authority'. The concept of international delegation is derived from the 'agency theory' which is built on the idea of a relationship that involves the contractual engagement of, and subsequent delegation of authority from a principal to an agent.[157] This conditional delegation requires that the agent acts within the confines of the authority bestowed on it and always in the interest of the principal when making decisions.[158] The agent is granted some measure of autonomy and discretion to carry out its responsibilities effectively.[159] This process entails the assumption that at some point, the agent's interest and risk perspective would diverge from that of the principal. This might occasion agency slack, which comes with a cost to the principal.[160] It is the resulting dilemma that the agency theory seeks to resolve whilst avoiding a revocation of delegated authority.

Applying this theory to international delegation, the central idea is that states transfer rulemaking and adjudication authority belonging to their governments to international institutions (IIs) such as the IFIs by signing treaties concerning these institutions. This means that the ability of the FATF and the IFIs to prescribe standards is determined by delegation of authority by a state or its representative.

However straightforward the concept of international delegation seems, its true nature has been subject to scholarly debate. Guzman and Landsidle contend that international delegation is largely mythical in rulemaking and adjudication, as states usually refrain from handing over significant authority to international institutions.[161] Belanger agrees that there is no true international delegation of

---

157 Don Delves and Brian Patrick, 'Agency Theory Summary' [2008]; Josh Bendickson, Jeff Muldoon, Eric W. Liguori and Phillip E. Davis, 'Agency Theory: Background and Epistemology' [2016] 22 (4) JMH 437, 441; *Hawkins, Lake, Nielson and Tierney* (157).

158 William Meckling and Michael Jensen, 'Theory of the Firm: Managerial Behaviour, Agency Costs and Ownership Structure' [1976] 3 (4) JFE 305, 313; Michael C. Jensen, *A Theory of the Firm: Governance, Residual Claims and Organisational Forms*, (1st edn, HUP, 2003); *Hawkins, Lake, Nielson and Tierney* (157).

159 Discretion is sometimes intentionally designed by the principal into its contract with the agent; autonomy is an unavoidable by-product of imperfect control over agents.

160 Kiewiet D. Roderick and Mathew D. McCubbins, *The Logic of Delegation: Congressional Parties and the Appropriations Process* (UCP, 1991). Agency slack encompasses agency slippage and shrinkage. Whilst the former refers to policy shift away from the principal's outcome to the agent's own preference, the latter refers to a maximization of the agent's effort to act on the principal's behalf.

161 Andrew Guzman and Jennifer Landsilde, 'The Myth of International Delegation' [2008] 96 Cal. L. Rev. 1693, 1695.

authority in rulemaking, and any such delegation is limited to the interpretation of rules.[162] Their argument challenges the definition of international delegation as the assignment of responsibilities from states to international institutions.[163] In opposing this, Belanger argues that the state usually retains the responsibility of drafting its own rules, as such, there is no separate agent involved in international delegation.[164] The argument runs that states do not surrender significant degrees of autonomy or sovereignty when engaging in rulemaking.[165] Backing this assertion, Oliveria contends that although member states delegate power to IIs, these member states retain control through established mechanisms and provide guides to the IIs.[166] Whilst these arguments have merits, they fail to consider the true role of specialised staff of IIs in the delegation process.[167] Considering this, Swaine contends that international delegation simply describes the arrangements that 'vest continuing law-making authority' in international institutions.[168]

The concept of international delegation is distinct in its own right. For instance, the authority assigned to IIs is revocable and conditional, and can be withdrawn by a state should it choose to.[169]

There has however been a noticeable change in this arrangement. Previously, the validity of international delegation was dependent on its binding nature,[170] which was perceived to be a pre-requisite for good governance in the public interest.[171] However, in recognition of the emergence of 'disaggregated states' (a term which signifies power wielded by separate components of a state without, theoretically speaking, legal authority to bind the state),[172] Bradley et al. contend that states also delegate to soft law institutions such as standard-setting bodies.[173] This

---

162 Belanger Louis, 'Governing the North American Free-Trade Area: International Rule-Making and Delegation in NAFTA, the SPP and Beyond' (International Political Science Association, 21st World Congress, July 2009).

163 Darren Hawkins, David Lake, Daniel Neilson and Michael Tierney, 'States, International Organizations, and Principal-Agent Theory', in Darren Hawkins, David Lake, Daniel Neilson and Michael Tierney (eds.), *Delegation and Agency in International Organizations* (CUP, 2006).

164 *Louis* (n 162).

165 Ibid.

166 *Oliveria* (n 3).

167 Rainer Hulsse and Dieter Kerwer, 'Global Standards in Action: Insights from AML Regulation' [2007]14 (5) Organisation 629, 630.

168 Edward Swaine, 'The Constitutionality of International Delegation' [2004] 104 Colum. L. Rev. 1492, 1494; Curtis A. Bradley and Judith G. Kelley, 'The Concept of International Delegation' [2008] 71 (1) Law and Contemp. Probs.

169 *Hawkins, Lake, Nielson and Tierney* (157).

170 Scott Cooper, Darren Hawkins, Wade Jacoby and Daniel Nielson, 'Yielding Sovereignty to International Institutions: Bringing Systems Structure Bank in' [2008] 10 (3) International Studies Review 501, 524.

171 Zurn Michael and Christian Joerges (eds.) *Law and Governance in Post-national Europe: Compliance Beyond the Nation-State* (CUP, 2005).

172 Such as the ministers or regulatory bodies as opposed to the elected state officials, see *Slaughter* (n 133) 12.

173 *Bradley and Kelley* (n 168).

position shows that binding authorities do not reflect the realities of global regulations, as international delegation is not invalidated if a state grants non-binding powers to an institution such as the FATF to issue standards or resolutions.

In international delegation, the difference between binding and non-binding arrangements can be appreciated by examining the historical underpinnings of the institutions concerned. For instance, IFIs were established by a group of states at the end of WW2, a phase which ushered in a period of decolonisation[174] and marked the political/economic autonomy of Asian and African countries.[175] This transition from imperialism to a regime founded on the principle of sovereignty propelled increasing nationalism, which occasioned lack of cooperation and served as a catalyst for political conflict amongst states.[176] Hence, IFIs were justified by the need to overcome political conflicts through cooperation and integration of technical tasks.[177] With 189 member states each, a measure of cooperation was achieved and collectively, these states (principals), through authority delegated to the IMF/World Bank's boards (agents), made binding decisions on monetary policies and development, respectively.[178]

This grant of state power to IFIs is however not without its problems, primarily because it conflicts with state sovereignty.[179] Daugirdas argues that international delegation is 'constitutionally suspect' as it is far removed from the people in nation-states[180] and reduces democratic control.[181] This is particularly accurate given the chain of delegation within the states which ousts the input of certain communities/electorates in the delegation process coupled with the contested legitimacy and democratic processes in IFIs. This crisis denotes that states may have different objectives from IFIs, generating a principal-agent problem.[182] Moreover, IIs may be subject to capture by interest groups such as multinational

---

174 Lawrence James, *Rise and Fall of the British Empire* (Time Warner Books, UK, 1999) 426; Gary Thorn, *End of Empires: European Decolonisation, 1919–80* (London: Hodder & Stoughton Educational, 2000) 50.

175 Ibid.

176 Jon Pevehouse and Inken Von Borzyskowski, 'International Organisations in World Politics' *in* Jacob Katz Cogan, Ian Hurd and Ian Johnstone (eds.) *The Oxford Handbook of International Organisations* (OUP, 2006).

177 Ernst B. Haas, *Beyond the Nation-State: Functionalism and International Organisation* (Stanford, CA: SUP, 1964); Robert O. Keohane, *After Hegemony: Power and Discord in International Politics* (Princeton, NJ: PUP, 1984) 6.

178 Daniel Neilson and Michael Tierney, 'Delegation to International Organisations: Agency Theory and World Bank Environmental Reform' [2003] 57 (02) Int.Org 244. These authors note that a delegation relationship can have one or more principals who come together for respect of sovereignty and distaste for domination by a supposed super ruler.

179 Oona Hathaway, 'International Delegation and State Sovereignty' [2008] 883. Faculty Scholarship Series 115, 120.

180 Kristina Daugirdas, 'International Delegation and Administrative Law' [2007] 66 Md. L. Rev. 707, 710.

181 Ibid.

182 Syed Azhar Hussain Shah, Akher Hussain Shah and Sajawal Khan, 'Governance of Money Laundering: An Application of the Principal-Agent Model' [2006] 45 (4) The Pakistan Development Review 1117, 1124.

institutions or global non-governmental organisations, who can influence rule-making to serve their interests. IFIs are also critiqued on their inflexibility and lethargic response to critical issues, attributable to the difficult process of treaty amendment.

Irrespective of these problems, international delegation to IFIs remains largely beneficial and allows for specialisation, and cross-country collaboration towards a unified response to these issues. Moreover, it often makes for cheaper policymaking and expertise.

Conversely, non-binding, soft law bodies such as TGNs emerged in the early 1950s[183] and evolved to meet critical issues such as oil price crisis, security issues, ML/TF – crimes in which wrongdoers present a networked front.[184] Unlike treaty bodies, these TGNs do not operate through formalised stovepipe hierarchies.[185] Instead, they are usually flexible, responsive and collaborative. They engineer regulatory alliance between countries, a unique power-allocation approach that has earned them the tag of disaggregated state.[186]

However, like IFIs, TGNs are usually created by a collection of countries or networks and so suffer from similar legitimacy concerns. For instance, the FATF was created by the G7 countries, a networked body with persuasive but decisive powers. These countries (principals) delegated authority to the FATF (agent) to create standards on AML/CFT.[187] Yet, due to the non-binding nature of these standards, there were concerns that it imposed no real obligations, thus occasioning a weakening of the standards adopted globally. This concern was allayed by collaborations with treaty bodies, from which TGNs gain their enforcement validity, illustrating how non-binding rules can become consequential irrespective of their voluntary nature.

International delegation to binding or non-binding institutions has also been criticised because it escalates agency costs and slippage.[188] Such situations, where an agent (FATF/IFIs) starts to act beyond the powers granted and towards its preference cause concern. Hence, countries usually engage monitoring tools such as the use of representative boards on the IFIs and membership status at the FATF. Countries have also threatened to withdraw their funding from these institutions as a means of limiting agency slippage.[189] These methods have been critiqued as unsuitable given their limited capability in resolving information asymmetry and consequential escalation of agency costs that exist in international delegation. This is comparative to the minimal agency costs that accrue in domestic delegation from arms of government to regulatory institutions, attributable

---

183 Anne-Marie Slaughter, 'The Accountability of Government Networks' [2001] 8 (2) Indiana Journal of Global Legal Studies 347, 350.
184 *Slaughter* (n 133) 54.
185 Ibid.
186 Ibid. 12.
187 *Oliveria* (n 3).
188 Agency slack encompasses agency slippage and shrinkage. See (n 160).
189 *Nielson and Tierney* (n 178).

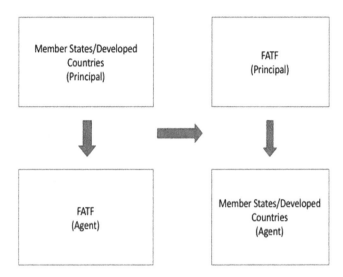

Figure 2.1 Pictorial Representation of the 'Reverse International Delegation'.

more to the proximity of monitoring mechanisms than to agents determined to ensure transparency.[190] Given the absence of proximity, and the fact that IIs are not representative of one country, countries are restricted from employing certain domestic oversight over IIs,[191] thereby according some level of respect for states' sovereignty.

This bottom-up delegation from states to IFIs/TGNs is one half of the delegation process which classes core members of these institutions (G7 and OECD countries) as principals to the FATF. This is attributable to the role of these countries in the establishment of the FATF and the formulation of its standards. This delegation process does not however inculcate how these countries are bound by the standards and processes promulgated by IFIs/TGNs, requiring transplantation and implementation.[192] This reverse position, which allows the IFIs/FATF to evaluate compliance levels of its core members and possibly issue sanctions, is referred to in this book as 'reverse international delegation' (Figure 2.1).

For belated and associate members, there is no initial delegation, as the initial delegation only comes from core FATF member countries. EEs had no input in

190 Daniel Abebe, 'Rethinking the Costs of International Delegations' (2012) University of Chicago Public Law & Legal Theory Working Paper 391 <https://chicagounbound .uchicago.edu/cgi/viewcontent.cgi?referer=https://www.google.co.uk/&httpsredir=1 &article=1260&context=public_law_and_legal_theory> accessed 7 July 2015.

191 Ibid.

192 Anthea Roberts, 'Traditional and Modern Approaches to Customary International Law: A Re-Conciliation' [2001] 95 AM.J.INT'L L 757.

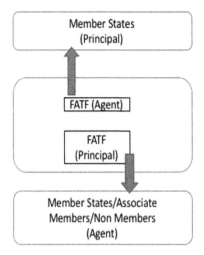

Figure 2.2 Pictorial Representation of the 'Reverse and Continuing International Delegation'.

the FATF establishment process and have only had some measure of involvement in the FATF's standards re-formulation process, which demonstrates their role as 'rule takers' because of their belated membership. ACs suffer a worse off fate with minimal input in standards re-formulation, which restricts them from contributing to the FATF standards and adding their peculiarities, yet ACs are still subject to the FATF rules. The position of ACs/EEs indicates a 'continuing delegation' relationship with the FATF, as their 'rule-taking' position has only experienced a minimal shift, whilst the position of developed countries reversed. These models are discussed within the context of AML/CFT regulation (Figure 2.2).

Reverse and Continuing International Delegation in AML/CFT Regulation

That the G7 delegated authority to the FATF to procure global standards and rules for combating ML/TF reveals a complex agency relationship. Scholarly opinions are divided on the precise nature of the relationship between the FATF and its member states. As we would see, the divergence of views reveals that the FATF's relationship with states is not static but depends on the membership position of states.[193] This refutes the rationalist position projected by Oliveria that the FATF can always be classed as an agent of sovereign states,[194] a myopic perspective

---

193 Membership can also move – so there are two angles to the non-static nature. However, since 1992, the FATF has closed its membership ranks.
194 *Oliveria* (n 3).

which advances the stance of developed member countries represented by the European Commission within the FATF.[195] Shah et al. project a more holistic but knotty viewpoint which emphasises developing countries' position as agents to developed countries through international institutions or networked bodies.[196] They assert that in its interactions with developing countries, the FATF assumes principal responsibilities, often delegating tasks to these countries to ensure they imbibe the AML/CFT standards promulgated by developed countries in their national legislations, whilst benchmarking them to ensure implementation.[197] Accordingly, when there is a conflict between FATF standards and national legislations (for instance, on financial secrecy), the backing and enforcement powers of the IFIs ensure that the standard-rules will take precedence.[198] Within this context, the FATF is subservient to developed countries and acts according to their requests. This illustrates the duality of the FATF role in the delegation arrangements which are dependent on the developmental stage of countries – a criterion for FATF membership.[199]

This model, which considers legitimacy issues, is not devoid of agency problems. Whilst certain agent-states, particularly ACs/EE, are driven to preserve laws for reasons of financial secrecy, exclusion or other self-serving objectives, the principal is besotted with the goal of financial integrity and stability, which are antithetical to the limited objectives of these states. To resolve this problem, the principal often relies on oversight and incentive-laden mechanisms to curb the use of agent-states as instruments for facilitating ML/TF. These tools have been critiqued as unsuitable because they are incapable of resolving information asymmetry or conflict of interests. The effectivity of these mechanisms in resolving agency problems will be examined in the context of the agency relationship between principal and agents.

The Agency Relationship between IFIs/FATF and Agent-States

In the agency relationship between the IFIs/the FATF (collective principals) and agent-states, the FATF formulates and delegates AML/CFT standards and, together with the other principals, assesses the agent's compliance levels to resolve pending conflict of interests. The reports derived from these assessments determine whether to issue sanctions, heighten supervision or engage in capacity training. Assessments are utilised to ensure that the agent's objectives remain aligned with that of the principal. This observatory tool coupled with training and incentives, such as deeper financial integration and withholding of sanctions,

---

195 *Abebe* (n 190).
196 *Shah, Shah, Khan* (n 182) 1117, 1118.
197 Ibid.
198 This raises the question of supremacy of international law to national law. See Hans Kelsen, *General Theory of Law and State* (HUP, 1945) 121.
199 FATF, 'FATF Membership Policy' <http://www.fatf-gafi.org/about/membersandobservers/fatfmembershippolicy.html> accessed 20 April 2017.

are employed by the principals to reduce information asymmetry in interactions with agents. The idea is that symmetrical information exchange would indicate improved interface on confidential information between actors. This is the optimal position which would aid the collective principals in tailor-fitting country assistance programmes, or in reformulating standards whilst encouraging agent-states to share private findings on their socio-economic and political information. This mutual exchange of information, derived from the observatory and incentive mechanisms, is encouraged. Principals own some private information and expertise gained from in-house research, cross-country interactions and credit agencies, which would help in analysing information derived from countries.

Whilst seemingly ideal, the effectivity of these mechanisms in achieving symmetrical information and resultant compliance is uncertain. Allan and Fisher assert that tools employed by the principal may have limited ability to discern the actions of agents or outcomes resulting from such actions.[200] This indicates that information derived from agent-governments are imperfectly observable, meaning that the agent's efforts or true actions cannot be fully ascertained,[201] thus hindering the principal's contractual ability to rein in the agent. Furthermore, Deleanu's empirical findings signal that where there is conflict of interests and an opportunity to misinform the international community about AML combating efforts, agents are likely to manipulate indicators during assessments.[202] Benabou et al. affirm that manipulation is possible because detection is imperfect.[203] Rational economists reject this argument, contending that agents are rational and would restrain from cheating with official statistics or information, as the market would detect such slip.[204] Evidence has however shown that the market does not always detect this slip.[205] Rather, there is confirmation that when governments anticipate correction strategies by the principal which threaten flows to capital and access to market, they may decide to communicate with the principals strategically[206] by either omitting or manipulating statistics to project compliance.[207]

It is however pertinent to state that not all agency slack is attributable to information asymmetry. Even when the principal monitors the agent effectively, peculiarities within a country may hinder compliance. In the absence of full knowledge of these peculiarities, incentives for compliance based on actions would at best be imperfect.

200 Drazen Allan and Stanley Fisher, 'Conditionality and Selectivity in Lending by International Financial Institutions' [1997] Washington: IMF 002.
201 Loana Deleanu, 'Do Countries Consistently Engage in Misinforming the International Community about their Efforts to Combat Money Laundering? Evidence Using Benford's Law' [2017] 21(1) Plos One 2, 19.
202 Ibid.
203 Benabou Roland and Laroque Gug, 'Using Privileged Information to Manipulate Markets: Insiders, Gurus and Credibility' [1992] 107 (3) QJE 921, 941.
204 Manne Henry, *Insider Trading and the Stock Market* (First Edition, Free Press, 1996).
205 *Deleanu* (n 201).
206 Vincent Crawford and Joel Sobel, 'Strategic Informational Transmission' [1982] Econometrica: Journal of the Econometric Society, 1431, 1451.
207 *Manne Henry* (n 204).

Against this backdrop, the argument runs that a reduction in information asymmetry may also occasion robust standards design and implementation. This can enhance legitimacy within the structural framework of principals. For instance, the FATF sets recommendations for recipient states, a step that does not hinder its interaction with 'all' states in the re-formulation process of the recommendations or the evaluation and technical assistance provision.

Unravelling the Agency Quandary

An examination of the reverse and continuing agency model reveals complexities inherent in the formation and membership structure of the proximate principal (FATF) which has resulted in an augmented legitimacy crisis. This crisis is inherent in the overlap in the FATF's position as both principal and agent to developed countries. As earlier discussed, the FATF is the agent of the developed countries, given their role in the formation and continued membership of the FATF. On the other hand, the FATF's principal relationship with these countries is predicated on the fact that its rules are binding on its member states. ACs are not involved in the FATF formation process and do not hold core membership positions. They are however subject to the FATF's rules.

As we will see, the disparity in the FATF relationship within its members and between 'non-members', the resulting FATF standards derived mainly from 'original member states', coupled with the gravitation of decision-making authority from the national to the international level occasions questions on accountability, transparency and legitimacy. Furthermore, questions abound on the suitability of the standards for the ACs/EEs, particularly due to the uniqueness of their terrain, such as their cash-based economy. A solution-driven approach adopted with the aim of ensuring improved compliance and clarifying the nature of the legitimacy crisis is necessary.

Deconstructing the Concept of Legitimacy in International Law and Governance

The phrase 'legitimacy crisis' may presuppose the existence of a legal difficulty, given the conjecture by positivists that 'legitimacy' is the presence of valid and acceptable law, in the absence of which a legal crisis subsists.[208] This perspective aligns with the origin of the word in law. The Merriam-Webster Online Dictionary defines legitimacy as 'the quality or state of being legitimate', whilst 'Legitimate' refers to 'accordant with law or with established legal forms and requirements'.[209] It is also described as 'conforming to recognised principles or accepted rules and standards'.[210] Whilst the former definition constricts the usage

208 C. Schmitt, *Law and Legitimacy* Transl. J. Seitzer (Durham: DUP, 2004).
209 Merriam Webster, 'Legitimate' (*Merriam-Webster*, 1828) <https://www.merriam-webster .com/dictionary/legitimate> accessed 21 May 2017.
210 Ibid.

of the word to legal matters, the latter indicates its applicability in other contexts when it is backed with 'justification of authority'.[211] This indicates that once 'illegal' standards are justifiable or accepted, they are cloaked with the garment of legitimacy. For instance, slave trade was justified for economic purposes and codified constitutionally, giving it a cloak of legitimacy.[212] Those who argued that slave trade was repugnant to the British Constitution and Christian values were considered as acting 'illegitimately'. Hence, whilst treaty organisations and nation-states mirrored the law-based definition of legitimate, the justification-based definition illustrates the varied application of the word.

Treaty bodies such as the IFIs contend with a legitimacy crisis on the grounds of lack of democracy and an asymmetrical decision-making process, which affects their perceived normative legitimacy. 'Normative legitimacy' in this sense means the 'right to rule' when attempting to secure compliance with standards.[213] This right, however contestable, is justified by the legal root of the IFIs in state accession or consent to treaty making.[214] This state-consent positivist approach, which asserts that the IFIs derive legitimacy from the consent of states, is focused on the source of power as a means of justifying legitimacy.[215] Conversely, decentred regulatory regimes, such as the BCBS, the IOSCO and the FATF do not have the state as the locus of authority.[216] They have no clear legal structures such as legislative bodies, courts, national authorities or ombudsman which can ensure their accountability. Additionally, they do not have clear jurisdictional boundaries or an identifiable set of potential democratic participants in their processes,[217] which raises questions about their legitimacy. Black however postulates that using law

---

211 Daniel Bodansky, 'The Legitimacy of International Governance: A Coming Challenge for International Environmental Law?' [1999] 93 (3) American Journal of International Law 596, 601.

212 Clackson Thomas, 'An Essay on the Slavery and Commerce of the Human Species: Particularly the Africans' [1969]; Earl Griggs, *Thomas Clarkson, the Friend of Slaves* (London: G. Allen & Unwin, 1936).

213 Allen Buchanan and Robert Keohane, 'The Legitimacy of Global Governance Institutions' *in* Jovan Babic and Petar Bojanic (eds.) *World Governance: Do We Need It, Is It Possible, What Could It All Mean?* (Cambridge Scholars Publishing, 2010) 214.

214 Jan Klabbers, Anne Peters and Geir Ulfstein, *The Constitutionalization of International Law* (OUP, 2009); Lukas Meyer and Pranay Sanklecha, 'Introduction to Legitimacy, Justice and Public International Law' (CUP, 2009); *Bodansky* (n 211); Rudiger Wolfrum, 'Legitimacy of International Law from a Legal Perspective: Some Introductory Considerations' *in* Rudiger Wolfrum (eds.), *Legitimacy in International Law* (Springer, Berlin, Heidelberg, 2008) cf. with Nienke Grossman, 'The Normative Legitimacy of International Courts' [2013] 86 Temp.L.Rev 61, 76 argues that state consent and procedural fairness are insufficient to ground the legitimacy of institutions. Mathias Kumm, 'The Legitimacy of International Law: A Constitutionalist Framework of Analysis' [2004] 15 (5) The European Journal of International Law 907, 914.

215 *Schmitt* (n 208) 1, 15.

216 Julia Black, 'Constructing and Contesting Legitimacy and Accountability in Polycentric Regulatory Regimes' [2008] 2 (2) Regulation and Governance 137, 142.

217 Ibid.

or legal validity to assess the legitimacy of these institutions would be futile.[218] Such transnational organisations have informed the extended definition of legitimacy in international law to encapsulate 'the perception of actors on the acceptability of an institution'.[219]

Such fluid construction of 'legitimacy' postulates that a soft-law regulatory body perceived as holding the normative right to govern by those on whose behalf it administers is 'legitimate'.[220] Thomas describes this ascription to an objective perspective on legitimacy by actors as 'legitimisation', a process by which actors come to believe in the normative legitimacy of an object.[221] This extended perception grants decentralised bodies another basis for legitimacy which is rooted in the reasons for acceptance. Black categorises these reasons as 'pragmatically based', 'morally based' and 'cognitively based'.[222] Pragmatically based legitimacy suggests the belief held by persons that the institution will pursue their interest directly or indirectly. Morally based legitimacy implies the perception of the institution and its procedures as morally appropriate. Cognitively based legitimacy refers to the perception of the institution as necessary or inevitable based on its knowledge and expertise. These different approaches to legitimacy reveal the fluidity of the concept. Whereas some actors may view legitimacy on a set of values and beliefs, others may base their reasons on different factors.[223] Notwithstanding the factors that may inform legitimacy, any institution or body recognised as legitimate provides a reservoir of loyalty from which leaders or institutions can draw to govern effectively.[224]

The Importance of Legitimacy

Ensuring compliance with regulatory standards informs the need for deeming legitimacy vital. Black states that legitimacy is fundamental in motivating

---

218 Ibid. 137, 145.
219 Chris A. Thomas, 'The Concept of Legitimacy and International Law' (2013) LSE Law, Society and Economy Working Papers 12/2013, 14 <http://eprints.lse.ac.uk/51746 /1/__libfile_repository_Content_Law%2C%20society%20and%20economics%20working %20papers_2013_WPS2013-12_Thomas.pdf> accessed 10 November 2017; *Black* (n 216) 137, 150.
220 John Jost and Brenda Major, *The Psychology of Legitimacy* (CUP 2001); Ian Hurd, Legitimacy and the United Nations (2011) Princeton University Working Paper <https://po seidon01.ssrn.com/delivery.php?ID=667085003073003079126114095021119107 001083027043001020067123115118106114027073093105058102060012110200 911506409608810307109410406000503501501507610702910012710009503401 900309911900610811411170890050730060200200680840691041011250191130 9106901311009 0088&EXT=pdf> accessed 8 May 2015.
221 *Thomas* (n 219).
222 *Black* (n 216) 137, 144; cf. with Thomas who categorises these reasons as 'legal, moral or social' bases for legitimacy in *Thomas* (n 219).
223 *Black* (n 216) 137, 145.
224 Tom R. Tyler, *Why People Obey the Law* (PUP, 2006).

behavioural responses.[225] Arguably, when members consider their institutions legitimate, they are more likely to ensure actual or proactive compliance to established standards, as opposed to formal or constructive compliance.[226] What then does the term 'compliance' connote?

Despite various definitions ascribed to compliance, its meaning in a regulatory context is widely accepted. Hoe describes compliance with international laws in terms of compulsion, defining it as the conformation of state behaviour to international law.[227] Shelton sees compliance as the adherence of countries to international norms or accords and the implementation of measures instituted.[228] Both Hoe and Shelton agree that implementation is a precondition for compliance and that effectiveness is divorced from compliance.[229] Given the above definitions, this chapter accepts the meaning of compliance as state or private institution behaviour, stimulated by international norms and laws – inclusive of national motivations.

Compliance may be actual, constructive or proactive. Actual compliance in this case denotes effective adherence to the spirit of the global regulatory standards, which is usually done voluntarily.[230] Tyler asserts that voluntary observance to the law is preferred by legal authorities, given its cost-effective nature.[231] This varies from formal or constructive compliance which requires higher enforcement cost, is usually achieved through a coercive manner and is harder for law authorities to effectively monitor. These snags can however be avoided when compliance is voluntary and participatory, which is proactive, as opposed to coerced.[232] This illustrates that the presence of coercion negates effectiveness of 'legitimate' standards. Irrespective of the nature of compliance, what is evident is the role of legitimacy in ensuring responses from institutions and persons.

Additionally, the concern of 'legitimacy' can project the need for inward re-evaluation that results in the re-engineering of an institution and its standards to become objectively legitimate. According to Shaffer, such re-engineering must be able to stand the test of input, throughput and output legitimacy.[233] Input legitimacy is concerned with the membership and participation of countries in

225 *Black* (n 216) 137, 148.
226 Rainer Hulsee, 'Even Clubs Can't Do Without Legitimacy: Why the Anti-Money Laundering Blacklist Was Suspended' [2008] 2 Regulation and Governance 459, 466.
227 Daniel Hoe, 'Compliance and the International Soft Law: Why Do Countries Implement the Basel Accord' [2002] Journal of International Economic Law (OUP).
228 Dinah Shelton, *Commitment and Compliance: The Role of Non-Binding Norms in the International Legal System* (OUP, 2003).
229 Ibid.; H.K. Jacobson and Brown Weiss, 'Compliance with the International Environmental Accords' 1995] 119 Global Governance 119, 123.
230 *Hulsee* (n 226) 459, 460.
231 *Tyler* (n 224).
232 Cf with Rainer Hulsee who argues that coercion may be a more cost-effective and simpler option for institutions to disseminate an unpopular regime. See *Hulsee* (n 226) 459, 460.
233 Gregory Shaffer, *Transnational Legal Ordering and State Change* (Cambridge Studies in Law and Society, 2014) 50; cf. with Bodnasky who asserts that legitimacy can be viewed in

decision-making processes within institutions.[234] Throughput legitimacy focuses on the quality of procedural fairness and deliberations in the absence of coercion, whilst output legitimacy deals with the effectiveness of the response of an institution to a problem.[235] Any restructuring to inculcate these forms of legitimacy must ensure that all actors (states) have a voice in the process of standard formulation, its procedures are fair, devoid of coercion and its overall output is effective towards meeting set goals.[236] This perspective on legitimacy was not reflected within the FATF's original processes and an overhaul is required to gain compliance and acceptability within developing countries.[237] Emphasising the need for the club-like bodies to gain acceptability, Weber's argument that perceived institutional legitimacy translates to effectiveness aligns with Shaffer's tests for legitimacy.[238] This further buttresses the fact that a legitimate TGN would foster dialogue and reciprocal exchange of information where persuasion would be wielded as opposed to coercion.[239] Against this backdrop, it can be argued that the need for re-engineering foretells the presence of 'illegitimacy' in the FATF institutional processes and standards.[240]

As the terminology suggests, input legitimacy simply means the ability of all actors to have a voice in the FATF's processes.[241] 'Voice' here denotes a right to uniform votes and participation through equivalent membership rights. More significantly, it symbolises involvement in the formation process of institutions and standards. Having a voice is considered crucial in generating a sense of collective ownership in the fight against ML/TF within countries, whilst achieving geographical balance.[242] Hulsee argues that this sense of ownership can propel proactive compliance, which is futuristic and effective in curbing illicit crimes in dynamic environments.[243] Differentiating actual from proactive compliance, Hulsee argues that whilst the former is focused on implementing enshrined TGN

---

terms of representativeness, procedures and effectiveness. Contrast to Bodansky (legitimacy in terms of sources, procedures and outcomes). *Bodansky* (n 211).

234 *Shaffer* (n 233) 50.
235 Ibid. 51.
236 Ibid. (n 237) 50.
237 At the time of original blacklisting, prior to 2006 (herein referred to as Black1) and also prior to the establishment of the FSRB and partnership with the IFIs in 2001.
238 Max Weber, *Economy and Society* (Guenther Roth and Clau Wittich eds., 1968).
239 *Brummer* (n 27).
240 There was an absence of 'voice-able' members in the standards formulation, lack of representativeness and procedural unfairness in its processes. These signalled accountability and transparency issues thus had the capability of hindering effectives.
241 Chris Brummer, 'How International Financial Law Works (and How It Doesn't)' [2011] 99 Georgetown Law Journal 257, 307; Marie Wilke, 'Emerging Informal Network Structures in Global Governance: Inside the Anti-Money Laundering Regime' [2008] 77 Nordic Journal of International Law 509, 520.
242 See the FATF-GAFI, 'Financial Action Task Force Annual Report 2005–2006' (*FATF*, 23 June 2006) <http://www.fatf-gafi.org/media/fatf/documents/reports/2005%202006%20ENG.pdf> accessed 30th May 2017.
243 *Hulsee* (n 226) 460, 467.

rules into law, the latter is focused on ensuring that even when there is a lapse in the international rules or the risk envisaged by the international rules has transformed at the implementation stage, the country goes further to deal with emergent risk.[244] In the latter example, countries comply out of self-interest and not coercion or dictation. For instance, the FATF rules last revised in 2012 did not cover emerging issues like cryptocurrencies which, as is envisaged, pose huge ML/TF challenge. However, the EEs have all reacted to this by issuing an outright ban. This may not be the most innovative approach, as signalled by the IMF's step towards understanding the risks posed by these currencies to ML/TF and how it operates.[245] However, it signals that a sense of 'ownership' may have facilitated such a futuristic move.

Given the initial presence of the G7 and certain OECD countries in the formation process, it is trite to say that any re-engineering towards input legitimacy would be 'too-late' to guarantee any involvement in the formation of institutions or standards. Consequently, this resulted in a membership asymmetry led by the global hegemon, the US (which constituted the rule makers) on one end, and the ACs/EEs who represented the rule takers on the other.[246] To correct this emerging defect, the FATF continually reformed and expanded its membership. Subsequently, membership of the FATF grew from G7 and OECD countries to the current 35 countries and two gulf regions, although growth was restricted to 'strategically important countries'.[247] Later members of the FATF appear to have been forced to incorporate the regime, whilst non-members are sidelined from the decision-making processes.[248] Coerced members and non-members who are usually rendered reticent in decision-making processes suffer the consequences of their non-participation during the transplantation process. One plausible outcome is the inability to foster voluntary actual or proactive compliance with national legislations derived from global standards, due to lack of legitimacy at

---

244 Ibid.; Christian Reus-Smit, 'International Crises of Legitimacy' [2007] 44 International Politics 157, 170.

245 Dong He et al., 'IMF Staff Discussion Note: Virtual Currencies and Beyond: Initial Considerations' (IMF Staff Team, 2016) <https://www.imf.org/external/pubs/ft/sdn/2016/sdn1603.pdf> accessed 21 May 2017.

246 Mark Suchman, 'Managing Legitimacy: Strategic and Institutional Approaches' [1995] 20 (3) Academy of Management Review 571, 588; Eric Helleiner, 'State Power and the Regulation of Illicit Activity in Global Finance' *in* R.H. Friman and P. Andreas (eds.) *The Illicit Global Economy and State Power* (Rowman & Littlefield, Lanham, 1999).

247 *FATF* (n 199).

248 Zakhele Hlophe, 'Regulating Money Laundering in Developing Countries: A Critical Analysis of South Africa's Incorporation and Implementation of the Global FATF Standards' [2013] Doctoral Thesis, Kings College London; Jason Sharman, 'Power and Discourse in Policy Diffusion: Anti-Money Laundering and Developing Countries' [2008] 52 International Studies Quarterly 635, 644; Rainer Hulsee, 'Creating Demand for Global Governance: The Making of a Global Money Laundering Problem' [2007] 21 (2) Global Society 155, 167; *Hulsee* (n 226) 459, 462; Daniel Drezner, 'Globalisation, Coercion and Competition: The Different Pathways to Policy Convergence' [2005] 12 (5) Journal of European Public Policy 1, 18.

the international level. This is especially so when countries do not consider the standards to be in their best interest or suitable to their terrain.

Black suggests that the variance in 'interests' is usually prominent when there is a long chain of delegation.[249] For instance, the FATF usually delegates to the executive arm of government, such as ministers, which further delegates to related regulatory bodies, such as the Financial Intelligence Units (FIUs), the Central Banks, Securities and Exchange Commissions etc. This chain of delegation habitually bypasses the elected state representatives. For this reason, delegates to the FATF are often accosted from entering compromising agreements with the institution, which has an uneven effect on particular communities that bear the costs of compliance. This can be typified with the international investment arbitration process which has formed a global governance niche monopolised by an exclusive number of countries that ousts Africa and other developing countries. Furthermore, professionals from ousted countries are deprived the opportunity to contribute to the development processes governed by past judges from developed countries and influenced by multinationals.[250] This has negative implications for socio-economic development, as countries that are far removed from the processes are forced to imbibe the rulings made.[251] Hence, acceding to coercion by the existing hegemony can be considered illegitimate, requiring normative legitimisation.[252]

Throughput legitimacy which is based on the quality of procedural fairness and deliberations devoid of coercion is crucial because it proves some level of normative legitimacy. To achieve this, the FATF entered into a partnership with the IFIs – through sharing of methodologies for evaluation. Cooperation between these institutions opens the FATF's standards and methodologies to increased scrutiny by the boards of the IFIs which represent about 189 countries and are thus considered legitimate. The input of the IFIs' boards was presumed to give non-members of the FATF increased input in the FATF standards whilst enhancing the quality of the input process. This argument is however blindsided to the asymmetries within the IFIs. Although emerging economies have high quotas, ACs have far lesser quotas resulting in a smaller voice in the decision-making process. Thus, it can be argued that some level of 'double-illegitimacy' exists, particularly towards ACs. The FATF tried to cure this illegitimacy through its FATF-Style Regional Bodies (FSRBs)[253] in the belief that an endorsement of the institution's standards would translate to an increased partnership between

---

249 *Black* (n 216) 137, 142.
250 Amazu Asouzu, *International Commercial Arbitration and African States: Practice, Participation and Institutional Development* (CUP, 2001) 452.
251 Ibid.
252 Whilst acknowledging that an equally advantageous global regulatory process is almost unachievable due to varying norms and values.
253 The Caribbean Financial Action Task Force (CFATF) established in 1990, the Middle East and North Africa (MENAFATF), Eurasia (EAG), South America (GAFISUD) and West Africa (GIABA).

the FSRB and the FATF. It was hoped that elevation from observer status to membership would ensure increased sense of ownership and local acceptability amongst FSRBs countries, which would in turn secure improved compliance at the regional level.[254] However, this continually fell short of expectations as the non-member/associate member countries were only given 'second-class membership'. This permitted only a slight increase in the input of these countries in the plenary deliberations, indicating that the issue on non-suitability of standards persisted. Hence, it can be argued that the FSRB were nothing more than vehicles for imposing and preserving the FATF regime.

Other limits to procedural fairness can also be attributed to a resource factor. Countries with more resources focused on AML/CFT could afford to send more delegates, and thus have increased input in the FATF's deliberation processes on standards and mutual evaluation reports.

Additionally, to build procedural fairness devoid of coercion, the FATF blacklisting sanctions, which was targeted at non-member countries, was considered illegitimate, as it alienated certain countries from deliberation processes.[255] This hindered actual or even proactive compliance, as alienated countries refrained from investing their resources or energy to combating ML/TF. The FATF blacklisting sanctions were expunged as a breach of the sovereignty norm due to the effect of financial isolation and the double standards that arose therefrom, which were only applicable to non-member states.[256] Furthermore, it was argued that it contravened the AML/CFT regime of voluntary participation and non-binding rules.[257] Sharman refutes this contention, arguing that the elimination of the blacklisting process was based on the accomplishment of the objective which it sought.[258] Contesting this, Hulsee argued that the evaluation process to warrant sanctions for non-compliance by the FATF was still ongo-

254 FATF, Financial Action Task Force: Annual Report (2005–2006) 23 June 2006.

255 *Reus-Smit* (n 244) 157, 172.

256 Jason Sharman, 'International Organization and Implementation by Blacklisting' (Paper presented at ISA Annual Convention, Chicago, February 28–March 3 2007).; Reuter Truman, *Chasing Dirty Money: Progress on Anti-Money Laundering* (Institute for International Economics, Washington, DC, 2004) 165–170; Levi M., 'Money Laundering and its Regulation' [2002] 582 Annals of the American Academy of Political Social Science 181, 182; V. Mitsilegas, 'Countering the Chameleon Threat of Dirty Money: Hard and Soft Law in the Emergence of a Global Regime against Money Laundering and Terrorist Finance' *in* A. Edwards and P. Gill (eds.) *Transnational Organised Crime: Perspectives on Global Security* (Routledge, London, 2004); Kathrin Daepp, Le Regulation Selective De de la Finance Internationale: L' Initiative Sur Les Pays Ou Territoires Non Cooperatifs du GAFI' Universite De Lausanne. Travaux De Dcience Politique (2006) Political Science Working Paper Series <https://www.unil.ch/iephi/files/live/sites/iephi/files/publications/TSP/28DaeppTSP.pdf> accessed 6 May 2015.

257 T. Doyle, 'Cleaning Up Anti-Money Laundering Strategies: Current FATF Tactics Needlessly Violate International Law' [2002] 24 (2) Houston Journal of International Law 279, 298.

258 Jason Sharman, *Havens in a Storm: The Struggle for Global Tax Regulation* (CUP, Ithaca, NY, 2006). Sharman argues that the removal of this process came head on with its rebuttal

ing when the blacklisting process was truncated.[259] Hulsee thus maintained that the illegitimacy of the process fostered a re-evaluation. Nevertheless, the re-engineering did not last long as it has been replaced with a two-tier list compiled by the International Cooperation Review Group (ICRG).[260] As earlier discussed, a closer examination of these lists – the 'call on members to apply counter-measures' list and the 'call for enhanced due diligence risk proportionate to the risk arising from defaulting countries' reveals that similar deficiencies exist. This two-tier list can easily be categorised as a 'black-2' and 'grey' list. The effect of the earlier blacklist that was expunged in the form of financial isolation is still present in the 'black-2' list and more subtly present in the 'grey list'. Thus, there is a need to refine this to ensure procedural fairness and deliberations devoid of any form of coercion.

Flowing from input and throughput legitimacy is output legitimacy. This is concerned with the effective response of institutions to a problem. Whilst it is arguable that the FATF would be perceived to have output legitimacy when input legitimacy is accounted for, this is not necessarily the case, particularly when output is determined by expertise. Hulsee and Kerwer argue that the FATF standards are derived from expertise rather than membership politics.[261] Acceding to this, Vibert asserts that the IFIs and the TGNs belong to the knowledge world where their decision-making skills are dependent on epistemic authority.[262] This indicates that they draw on the natural and social sciences procedure to identify complications and frame policy responses.[263] Thus, Winer asserts that the product of the FATF's plenary sessions reflected in its standards are considered 'neutral... and fair'.[264] This illustrates the projection of the FATF as legitimate on the basis of the expertise wielded by its secretariat and staff in its processes. This position is blindsided to the politics of the agenda within the institution and its effect on the FATF's design and compliance. The politics is evident in the composition of experts from the private and public sectors, who are mainly representatives of developed countries. This configuration does not encompass or represent the views of developing countries, and is thus capable of stifling the compliance of these countries to the FATF standards. Thus, any restructuring should de-politicise the FATF and ensure a truly 'expertise' process that includes the views of developing countries.

---

by the IFIs with whom the FATF sought partnership due to resource constraints, as it was considered to be against the nature of the fund's seemingly voluntary agenda.

259 Hulsee argues that this illustrates the power of stronger organisations over soft law bodies. However, he argued that the G7 and OECD could have given the FATF similar power as the IFIs and it is not for this reason that blacklisting was recoiled. *Hulsee* (n 226) 460, 467.

260 *FATF* (n 144).

261 *Kerwer and Hulsee* (n 150).

262 Frank Vibert, 'Reforming International Rule-Making' [2012] 3 (3) Global Policy 391, 391.

263 Ibid.

264 Winer Jonathan and Trifin Roule, 'Fighting Terrorist Finance' [2002] 44 Survival 84.

Conclusion

This chapter examines the evolution of AML/CFT standards, the institutions central to AML/CFT administration and the influence of these factors on state compliance. This chapter starts by establishing a link between the regulation of ML/TF and the financial sector reform, thus reinforcing the decision to incorporate this theme into global regulation. The AML/CFT standards had a contentious beginning but emerged as a crucial theme during financial sector reforms. This is attributable to the challenges posed to financial integrity by financial liberalisation, especially as regards cross-border financial relations.

Whilst the FATF was initially responsible for the setting and dissemination of standards, the IFIs evolution through various cross-border crises occasioned their perception of illicit crimes as auxiliary to their mandate. The IFIs are now involved in ensuring compliance with AML/CFT standards through participation in assessment processes. Consequently, as observers on the FATF, the IFIs hardened the FATF's soft law trajectory– a means of mandating global participation and compliance. This collaborative support between the IFIs and the FATF was aimed at facilitating compliance with AML/CFT standards.

However well intentioned, the evolution of the IFIs and the FATF, although at different historical points, only inculcated a select group of developed countries. Consequently, standards recommended, and processes, were at best suited to combating ML/TF within these countries. Given the lack of transparency, accountability and legitimacy, the AC/EE have suffered a compliance deficit. This predicament is understood through the lens of the agency theory which unearths a legitimacy crisis, showing that the AC/EE are disproportionately involved and inexplicably affected by the regulations – an indication of hegemonic subjection.

Further Reading

1. Andrew Guzman and Jennifer Landsilde, 'The Myth of International Delegation' [2008] 96 *California Law Review*.
2. Allen Buchanan and Robert O. Keohane, 'The Legitimacy of Global Governance Institutions' *in* Jovan Babic and Petar Bojanic (eds.) *World Governance: Do We Need It, Is It Possible, What Could It All Mean?* (Cambridge Scholars Publishing, 2010).
3. Amazu Asouzu, *International Commercial Arbitration and African States: Practice, Participation and Institutional Development* (Cambridge University Press, 2001).
4. Anne-Marie Slaughter, *A New World Order* (Princeton University Press, 2004).
5. Anne-Marie Slaughter, 'The Accountability of Government Networks' [2001] 8 (2) *Indiana Journal of Global Legal Studies*.
6. Anthea Roberts, 'Traditional and Modern Approaches to Customary International Law: A Re-Conciliation' [2001] 95 *American Journal of International Law*.
7. Antoinette Verhage, 'Between the Hammer and the Anvil? Money Laundering-Complex and its Interactions with the Compliance Industry' [2009] 52 (1) *Crime Law Social Change* 70.

8. Antoinette Verhage, *The Anti Money Laundering Complex and the Compliance of Industry* (Taylor and Francis 2011). 74.

9. Arnone Marco and Pier Pardoan, 'Anti-Money Laundering by International Institutions: A Preliminary Assessment' [2008] 26(3) *European Journal of Law and Economics*.

10. Article 1 of the Articles of Agreement of the IBRD (IBRD, 1989) <http://siteresources.worldbank.org/EXTABOUTUS/Resources/ibrd-articlesofagreement.pdf> accessed 15 April 2015.

11. Ayelet Berman and Ramses Wessel, 'The International Legal Status of Informal International Law-Making Bodies: Consequences for Accountability' *in* J. Pauwelyn, R.A. Wessel and J. Wouters (eds.) *Informal International Lawmaking: Mapping the Action and Testing Concepts of Accountability and Effectiveness* (Oxford University Press, Oxford, 2012).

12. Barry J. Eichengreen, *Towards a New International Financial Architecture: A Practical Post-Asia Agenda* (Peterson Institute Press: All Books, 1999).

13. Bartlett Brent, 'The Negative Effects of Money Laundering on Economic Development' [2002] 5967 *Asian Development Bank Regional Technical Assistance Project; The World Bank, Combating Money Laundering and the Financing of Terrorism – A Comprehensive Training Guide* (2009).

14. Belanger Louis, 'Governing the North American Free-Trade Area: International Rule-Making and Delegation in NAFTA, the SPP and Beyond' (International Political Science Association, 21st World Congress, July 2009).

15. Benabou Roland and Laroque Gug, 'Using Privileged Information to Manipulate Markets: Insiders, Gurus and Credibility' [1992] 107 (3) *QJE*.

16. Benjamin Cohen, 'Monetary Governance and Capital Mobility in Historical Perspective' *in* Rainer Grote and Thilo Maruahn (eds.) *The Regulation of International Financial Markets: Perspectives for Reform* (Cambridge University Press, Cambridge, 2006).

17. Biag Taimur and Ilan Glodfajn, 'Financial Market Contagion in the Asian Crisis' (1998) IMF Working Paper 26/2 <https://link.springer.com/article/10.2307/3867666> accessed 19 April 2016.

18. C. Schmitt, *Law and Legitimacy*, Transl. J. Seitzer (DUP, Durham, 2004).

19. Cally Jordan, 'The Dangerous Illusion of International Financial Standards and the Legacy of the Financial Stability Forum' [2010] 12 The San Diego International Law Journal.

20. Cally Jordan and Giovanni Majnoni, 'Financial Regulatory Harmonization and the Globalization of Finance' [2002] World Bank Policy Research Working Paper 2919 <https://openknowledge.worldbank.org/bitstream/handle/10986/19224/multi0page.pdf?sequence=1&isAllowed=y> accessed 11 June 2015.

21. Carmen Reinhart and Kenneth Rogoff, 'Regulation Should Be International' (*Financial Times*, 18 November 2008) <https://www.ft.com/content/983724fc-b589-11dd-ab71-0000779fd18c> accessed 28 August 2017.

22. Chris Brummer, 'How International Financial Law Works (and How It Doesn't)' [2011] 99 Georgetown Law Journal.

23. Chris Brummer, *Soft Law and the Global Financial System: Rule Making in the 21st Century* (First Published 2012, Cambridge University Press, 2012). 27.

24. Chris Thomas, 'The Concept of Legitimacy and International Law' (2013) *LSE Law, Society and Economy Working Papers 12/2013*, 14 <http://eprints.lse.ac.uk/51746/1/__libfile_repository_Content_Law%2C%20society%2

0and%20economics%20working%20papers_2013_WPS2013-12_Thomas.pdf>
accessed 10 November 2017.

25. Christian Reus-Smit, 'International Crises of Legitimacy' [2007] 44 *International Politics.*

26. Clackson Thomas, 'An Essay on the Slavery and Commerce of the Human Species: Particularly the Africans' [1969] *Honoured with First Prize in the University of Cambridge for the Year 1975 Mnemosyne Publications.*

27. Vincent Crawford and Joel Sobel, 'Strategic Informational Transmission' [1982] *Econometrica: Journal of the Econometric Society.*

28. Curtis Bradley and Judith Kelley, 'The Concept of International Delegation' [2008] 71 (1) *Law and Contemporary Problems.*

29. Kathrin Daepp, 'Le Regulation Selective De de la Finance Internationale: L' Initiative Sur Les Pays Ou Territoires Non Cooperatifs du GAFI' Universite De Lausanne. Travaux De Dcience Politique' (2006) *Political Science Working Paper Series* <https://www.unil.ch/iephi/files/live/sites/iephi/files/publi cations/TSP/28DaeppTSP.pdf> accessed 6 May 2015.

30. Daniel Abebe, 'Rethinking the Costs of International Delegations' (2013) *University of Chicago Law School Public Law and Legal Theory Working Papers*, No. 391, 16 <https://chicagounbound.uchicago.edu/cgi/viewcontent.cgi ?referer=https://www.google.co.uk/&httpsredir=1&article=1260&context =public_law:and_legal_theory> accessed 9 July 2015.

31. Daniel Hoe, 'Compliance and the International Soft Law: Why Do Countries Implement the Basel Accord' [2002] Journal of International Economic Law (OUP).

32. Daniel Bodansky, 'The Legitimacy of International Governance: A Coming Challenge for International Environmental Law?' [1999] 93 (3) American Journal of International Law.

33. Daniel Drezner, 'Globalisation, Coercion and Competition: The Different Pathways to Policy Convergence' [2005] 12 (5) Journal of European Public Policy.

34. Daniel Nielson and Michael Tierney, 'Delegation to International Organizations: Agency Theory and World Bank Environmental Reform' [2003] 57 (2) International Organizations.

35. Darren Hawkins, David Lake, Daniel Nielson and Michael Tierney, 'Delegation Under Anarchy: States, International Organisations and Principal-Agent Theory' *in* Darren Hawkins, David Lake, Daniel Nielson and Michael Tierney (eds.) *Delegation and Agency in International Organisations* (Cambridge University Press, Cambridge, 2006).

36. David Altheide, 'Terrorism and the Politics of Fear' [2006] 6 (4) *Cultural Studies Critical Methodologies* 415, 415–439; Harmon Christopher, *Terrorism Today* (Routledge, 2013).

37. David Harvey, *A Brief History of Neoliberalism* (Oxford University Press, 2005).

38. David Scott, 'Money Laundering and International Efforts to Fight it' (Public Policy for the Private Sector, May 1995) <http://siteresources.worldbank .org/EXTFINANCIALSECTOR/Resources/282884-1303327122200/ 048scott.pdf> accessed 15 March 2015.

39. David Williams, 'Governance, Security and "Development": The Case of Money Laundering' [2008] Working Paper on Transnational Politics.

40. David William, "'Development" and Global Governance: The World Bank, Financial Sector Reform and the "Will to Govern"' [2008] 45 International Politics.

41. Dieter Kerwer and Rainer Hulsee, 'How International Organisations Rule the World: The Case of the Financial Action Task Force on Money Laundering' [2011] 2 Journal of International Organizations Studies.

42. Dinah Shelton, *Commitment and Compliance: The Role of Non-Binding Norms in the International Legal System* (Oxford University Press, 2003).

43. Drazen Allan and Stanley Fisher, 'Conditionality and Selectivity in Lending by International Financial Institutions' [1997] *Washington: International Monetary Fund* 002.

44. Dong He et al., 'IMF Staff Discussion Note: Virtual Currencies and Beyond: Initial Considerations' (IMF Staff Team, 2016) <https://www.imf.org/exter nal/pubs/ft/sdn/2016/sdn1603.pdf> accessed 21 May 2017.

45. Don Delves and Brian Patrick, 'Agency Theory Summary' [2008].

46. Douglas Arner, 'Organizations of International Co-Operation in Standard Setting and Regulation' *in* Garard Caprio (ed.) *Handbook of Safeguarding Global Financial Stability: Political, Social, Cultural and Economic Theories and Models* (Elsevier, 2013).

47. Douglas Arner and Michael Taylor, 'The Global Financial Crisis and the Financial Stability Board: Hardening the Soft Law of International Financial Regulation?' [2009] 32 *UNSWLJ*.

48. T. Doyle, 'Cleaning Up Anti-Money Laundering Strategies: Current FATF Tactics Needlessly Violate International Law' [2002] 24 (2) Houston Journal of International Law.

49. Earl Leslie Griggs, *Thomas Clarkson, the Friend of Slaves* (G. Allen & Unwin, London, 1936).

50. Edward Swaine, 'The Constitutionality of International Delegation' [2004] 104 Columbia Law Review.

51. Eleni Tsiongou, 'Global Finance Governance and the Developing Anti-Money Laundering Regime: What Lessons for International Political Economy?' [2010] 47 (6) *International Politics*.

52. Elizabeth Borgwardt, *A New Deal for the World: America's Vision for Human Rights* (The Belknap Press of HUP, London, 2005).

53. Emilios Avgouleas, *Governance of Global Financial Markets: The Law, the Economics, the Politics* (First Published 2012, Cambridge University Press, 2012).

54. Eric Helleiner, 'State Power and the Regulation of Illicit Activity in Global Finance' *in* R.H. Friman and P. Andreas (eds.) *The Illicit Global Economy and State Power* (Rowman & Littlefield, Lanham, 1999).

55. Ernst Haas, *Beyond the Nation-State: Functionalism and International Organisation* (Stanford University Press, Stanford, CA, 1964).

56. Eurostat European Commission, 'European System of Accounts: ESA 2010' (European Union, 2013) <http://ec.europa.eu/eurostat/cache/metadata/A nnexes/nasa_10_f_esms_an1.pdf> accessed 20 August 2017.

57. FATF, 'FATF Recommendations' (*FATF*, 2013) <http://www.fatf-gafi.org/ media/fatf/documents/recommendations/pdfs/fatf_recommendations.pdf> accessed 12 May 2015.

58. FATF, 'FATF Recommendations on Terrorist Financing' (*FATF*, 2013) <http://www.fatf-gafi.org/media/fatf/documents/recommendations/pdfs/fatf_recommendations.pdf> accessed 17 May 2015.

59. FATF, 'FATF Membership Policy' (*FATF*, 2017) <http://www.fatf-gafi.org/about/membersandobservers/fatfmembershippolicy.html> accessed 21 May 2017.

60. FATF, *Financial Action Task Force: Annual Report (2005 – 2006)* (23 June 2006).

61. FATF, 'High-Risk and Non-Cooperative Jurisdictions' (*FATF*) <http://www.fatf-gafi.org/topics/high-riskandnon-cooperativejurisdictions/> accessed 1 December 2014.

62. FATF, 'History of the FATF' (*FATF*, 2017) <http://www.fatf-gafi.org/pages/aboutus/historyofthefatf/> accessed 21 May 2017.

63. FATF, 'Topic: High-Risk and Other Monitored Jurisdictions' (*FATF*, 2018) <http://www.fatf-gafi.org/publications/high-riskandnon-cooperativejurisdictions/?hf=10&b=0&s=desc(fatf_releasedate)> accessed 17 January 2018.

64. FATF-GAFI, 'Financial Action Task Force Annual Report 2005–2006' (*FATF*, 23 June 2006) <http://www.fatf-gafi.org/media/fatf/documents/reports/2005%202006%20ENG.pdf> accessed 30 May 2017.

65. Ferweda Joras, 'The Multidisciplinary Economics of Money Laundering' [2012] *Tjalling C. Koopmans Institute Discussion Paper Series*.

66. Frederic Mishkin and National Bureau of Economic Research, 'Financial Stability and Globalization: Getting it Right' (Bank of Spain Conference – Central Banks in the 21st Century, 2006).

67. Frank Vibert, 'Reforming International Rule-Making' [2012] 3 (3) Global Policy.

68. FSB, 'Table of Key Standards for Sound Financial Systems' <http://www.financialstabilityboard.org/what-we-do/about-the-compendium-of-standards/key_standards/table-of-key-standards-for-sound-financial-systems/> accessed 13 March 2015.

69. GAO Report, 'International Finance: Actions Taken to Reform Financial Sectors in Asian Emerging Markets' (GAO/GGD –99–57, September 1999) <https://www.gao.gov/assets/230/228224.pdf> accessed 24 May 2016.

70. Garton Gary, 'Some Reflections on the Recent Financial Crisis' (2012) *National Bureau of Economic Research Working Paper Series 18397*, 3 <http://risk.econ.queensu.ca/wp-content/uploads/2013/10/Gorton-Some-reflections-on-the-recent-Crisis-2012.pdf> accessed 10 July 2015.

71. George Selgin, 'Proposal – Let Market Forces Play a Greater Role' (*Global Economic Symposium*, 2014) <http://www.global-economic-symposium.org/knowledgebase/the-new-global-financial-architecture/proposals/let-market-forces-play-a-great-role> accessed 10 September 2017.

72. Gerald Epstein, 'Should Financial Flows Be Regulated? Yes' *in* Jomo Kwame and M. Sundara (eds.) *Reforming the International Financial System for Development* (Cambridge University Press, Cambridge, 2011).

73. Giancarlo Corsetti, Paolo Pesenti and Nouriel Roubini, 'What Caused the Asian Financial Crisis? Part 1: A Macroeconomic Overview' (1998) NBER Working Paper No.6833 <http://www.nber.org/papers/w6833.pdf> accessed 24 May 2016.

74. Gianni De Nicolo, Giovanni Favara and Lev Ratnovski, 'Externalities and Macro Prudential Policy' [2012] *SDN12/5 IMF Staff Discussion Note.*

75. Global Witness, 'How FATF Can Measure and Promote an Effective Anti-Money Laundering System' (*Global Witness*) <https://www.globalwitness .org/sites/default/files/library/How%20FATF%20can%20measure%20and %20promote%20an%20effective%20anti-money%20laundering%20system.pdf> accessed 1 June 2015.

76. Goldstein Morris, *The Asian Financial Crisis: Causes, Cures and Systemic Implications* (Institute for International Economics, Washington DC, 1998).

77. Gregory Shaffer, *Transnational Legal Ordering and State Change* (Cambridge Studies in Law and Society, 2014).

78. Gregory Noble and John Ravenhill, 'Cause and Consequences of the Asian Financial Crises' *in* Gregory W. Noble and John Ravenhill, (eds.), *The Asian Financial Crisis and the Architecture of the Global Finance* (Cambridge University Press, Cambridge, 2000).

79. Groot Loek, 'Money Laundering, Drugs and Prostitution as Victimless Crimes' *in* Brigitte Unger and Daan Van Der Inde (eds.) *Research Handbook on Money Laundering* (Edward Elgar Publishing Limited, 2013).

80. Haizhou Huang and S. Wajid, 'Financial Stability in the World of Global Finance' [2002] 39 (1) *Finance and Development, a Quarterly Magazine of the IMF.*

81. Hans Kelsen, *General Theory of Law and State* (Harvard University Press, 1945).

82. Herbert Morais, 'The War Against Money Laundering, Terrorism and the Financing of Terrorism' [2002] *Lawasia Journal.*

83. HM Treasury, 'Speech by the Chancellor of the Exchequer, Gordon Brown MP at the Council for Foreign Relations in New York' (*HM Treasury*, 16 September 1999) <http://webarchive.nationalarchives.gov.uk/20100407173039/http:// www.hm-treasury.gov.uk/speech_chex_160999.htm> accessed 10 June 2015.

84. Max Weber, *Economy and Society* (Guenther Roth & Clau Wittich, 1968).

85. Ikuo Gonoi and Hiroaki Ataka, 'Conceptual Relevance of "Embedded Liberalism" and its Critical Social Consequences' [2006] *Artigo aspresentado no ISA-South Annual Conference: PAIS Graduate Working Papers*, 3 (6) <https ://warwick.ac.uk/fac/soc/pais/currentstudents/phd/resources/crips/ working_papers/2006/working_paper_3_gonoi_and_ataka.pdf> accessed 19 November 2016.

86. IMF, 'Cooperation and Reconstruction (1944–71)' (*IMF*) <https://www.imf .org/external/about/histcoop.htm> accessed 10 September 2017.

87. IMF, the World Bank, 'International Standards: Strengthening Surveillance, Domestic Institutions and International Markets' (IMF, World Bank, 2003) <https://www.imf.org/external/np/pdr/sac/2003/030503.pdf> accessed 17 July 2015.

88. IMF Survey, 'IMF Wins Mandate to Cover Capital Accounts, Debt Initiative Put in Motion' [1997] 26 (9) IMF.

89. Ines Sofia De Oliveria, 'The Anti-Money Laundering Struggle: Actors, Interest and the EU' (4th ECPR Graduate Conference, 2012).

90. Ivan Savic, 'Explaining Compliance with International Commitments to Combat Financial Crisis: The IMF and the G7' (47th Annual ISA Convention, 2006).

91. H.K. Jacobson and E. Brown Weiss, 'Compliance with the International Environmental Accords' [1995] 119 *Global Governance.*

92. Jan Klabbers, Anne Peters and Geir Ulfstein, *The Constitutionalization of International Law* (Oxford University Press, 2009).

93. James Boughton, 'The IMF and the Force of History: Ten Events and Ten Ideas That Have Shaped the Institution' [2004] IMF Working Paper 04/75 <https://goo.gl/Vhc6pr> accessed 9 November 2015.

94. James Boyce and Leonce Ndikumana, 'Capital Flight from Sub Saharan African Countries: Updated Estimates, 1970–2010' [2012] *Political Economy Research Institute Research Report.*

95. James Gathii, 'The Financial Action Task Force and Global Administrative Law' [2010] Journal of Professional Law.

96. Jason Sharman, *Havens in a Storm: The Struggle for Global Tax Regulation* (Cambridge University Press, Ithaca, NY, 2006).

97. Jason Sharman, 'International Organization and Implementation by Blacklisting' (Paper presented at ISA Annual Convention, Chicago, 28 February–3 March 2007).

98. Jason Sharman, 'The Global Anti- Money Laundering Regime and Developing Countries: Damned if They Do, Damned if They Don't' [2006] Paper Presented at the International Studies Association Annual Conference.

99. Jason Sharman, 'Power and Discourse in Policy Diffusion: Anti-Money Laundering and Developing Countries' [2008] 52 *International Studies Quarterly.*

100. John Eatwell, 'The Challenges Facing International Financial Regulation' [2001] *Western Economic Association.*

101. John Jost and Brenda Major, *The Psychology of Legitimacy* (Cambridge University Press, 2001); Ian Hurd, 'Legitimacy and the United Nations' (2011) Princeton University Working Paper <https://poseidon01.ssrn.c om/delivery.php?ID=667085003073003079126114095021119107001083027043001020067123115118106114027073093105058102060121102009115064096088103071094104060005035015015076107029100127100095034019003099119006108114117089005073006020020068084069104101125019113091069013110090088&EXT=pdf> accessed 8 May 2015.

102. John William Anderson, Jr., 'Regulatory and Supervisory Independence: Is There a Case for Independent Monetary Authorities in Brazil?' [2004] 10 Law and Business Review America.

103. Jon Pevehouse and Inken Von Borzyskowski, 'International Organisations in World Politics' *in* Jacob Katz Cogan, Ian Hurd and Ian Johnstone (eds.) *The Oxford Handbook of International Organisations* (Oxford University Press, Oxford, 2006).

104. Jose Alvarez, 'The Return of the State' [2011] 20 Minnesota Journal of International Law.

105. Joshua Chesoli, 'Exploring the Concept, Significance and Adverse Impact of Money Laundering'; Paul Allan Schott, *Reference Guide to Anti-Money Laundering and Combatting the Financing of Terrorism* (World Bank Publication, 2006).

106. Josh Bendickson, Jeff Muldoon, Eric Liguori and Phillip Davis, 'Agency Theory: Background and Epistemology' [2016] 22 (4) JMH.

107. Julia Black, 'Constructing and Contesting Legitimacy and Accountability in Polycentric Regulatory Regimes' [2008] 2 (2) Regulation and Governance.
108. Kal Raustiala, 'The Architecture of International Cooperation: Transgovernmental Networks and the Future of International law' [2002] 43 (1) *Virginia Journal of International Law.*
109. Katja Freistein and Philip Liste, 'Introduction: Fragmented Territoriality' [2016] 19 (2) Journal of International Relations and Development.
110. Kenneth Abbott and Duncan Snidal, 'Hard and Soft Law in International Governance' [2000] 54 (3) International Organizations.
111. Kenneth Abbott and Duncan Snidal, 'Why States Act Through Formal International Organizations' [1998] 42 (1) Journal of Conflict Resolution.
112. Kenneth Blazejewski, 'The FATF and its Institutional Partners: Improving the Effectiveness and Accountability of Transgovernmental Networks' [2008] 22 Temple International and Comparative Law Journal.
113. Kenneth Hover, *Economics as Ideology* (Rowman & Littlefield Publishers, Inc., 2003).
114. Kern Alexander, 'The Role of Soft Law in the Legalization of International Banking Supervision: A Conceptual Approach' (2000) *ESRC Centre for Business Research, University of Cambridge 168* <https://www.cbr.cam.ac.uk/fileadmin/user_upload/centre-for-business-research/downloads/working-papers/wp168.pdf> accessed 10 July 2015.
115. Kern Alexander, Rahul Dhumale and John Eatwell, *Global Governance of Financial Systems: The International Regulation of Systemic Risk* (Oxford University Press, 2006) 11.
116. Roderick Kiewiet and Mathew McCubbins, *The Logic of Delegation: Congressional Parties and the Appropriations Process* (Cambridge University Press, 1991).
117. Kristina Daugirdas, 'International Delegation and Administrative Law' [2007] 66 *Maryland Law Review.*
118. Lance Taylor, 'Global Macroeconomic Management' *in* Peepak Nayyar (ed.) *Governing Globalization: Issues and Institutions* (Oxford University Press, Oxford, 2002).
119. Laurence Ravillon, Helene Tourard and Eric Loquin, 'Informal Sources of International Business Law' [2011] *International Business Law Journal.*
120. Lawrence Baxter, 'Understanding the Global in Global Finance and Regulation' *in* Ross Buckley, Doug Arner and Emilios Avgouleas (eds.) *Reconceptualizing Global Finance and its Regulation* (Cambridge University Press, Cambridge, 2015).
121. Lawrence James, *Rise and Fall of the British Empire* (Time Warner Books, 1999) 426; Gary Thorn, *End of Empires: European Decolonisation, 1919–80* (Hodder & Stoughton Educational, London, 2000).
122. M. Levi, 'Money Laundering and its Regulation' [2002] 582 *Annals of the American Academy of Political Social Science.*
123. Leonard Seabrooke and Eleni Tsiongou, 'Revolving Doors and Linked Ecologies in the World Economy: Policy Locations and the Practice of International Financial Reform' (2009) 260/09 CSGR Working Paper, 14 <https://warwick.ac.uk/fac/soc/pais/research/researchcentres/csgr/papers/workingpapers/2009/26009.pdf> accessed 10 July 2015.

124. Loana Deleanu, 'Do Countries Consistently Engage in Misinforming the International Community about Their Efforts to Combat Money Laundering? Evidence Using Benford's Law' [2017] 21 (1) Plos One.
125. Loretta Napoleon, *Terrorism and the Economy: How the War on Terror is Bankrupting the Economy* (SSP, 2014).
126. Lukas Meyer and Pranay Sanklecha, *Introduction to Legitimacy, Justice and Public International Law* (Cambridge University Press, 2009).
127. Henry Manne, *Insider Trading and the Stock Market* (1st edn, Free Press, 1996).
128. Marco Arnone and Pier Pardoan, 'Anti-Money Laundering by International Institutions: A Preliminary Assessment' [2008] 26 European Journal of Law and Economics.
129. Marie Wilke, 'Emerging Informal Network Structures in Global Governance: Inside the Anti-Money Laundering Regime' [2008] 77 Nordic Journal of International Law.
130. Mark Pieth and Gemma Aiolfi, 'The Private Sector Becomes Active: The Wolfsberg Process' [2003] 10 (4) Journal of Financial Crime.
131. Mark Suchman, 'Managing Legitimacy: Strategic and Institutional Approaches' [1995] 20 (3) *Academy of Management Review*.
132. Masahiro Kawai and Micheal Pomerleono, 'Who Should Regulate Systemic Stability Risk? The Relevance for Asia' *in* Masahiro Kawal and Eswar Prasad (eds.) *Financial Market Regulation and Reforms in Emerging Markets* (Brookings Institution Press, 2011).
133. Mathias Kumm, 'The Legitimacy of International Law: A Constitutionalist Framework of Analysis' [2004] 15 (5) The European Journal of International Law.
134. Max Everest–Phillips 'The Political Economy of Controlling Tax Evasion and Illicit Flows' *in* Peter Reuter (ed.) *Draining Development? Controlling Flows of Illicit Funds from Developing Countries* (The World Bank, 2012).
135. Wiliam   Meckling and Michael C. Jensen, 'Theory of the Firm: Managerial Behaviour, Agency Costs and Ownership Structure' [1976] 3 (4) JFE.
136. Michael Jensen, *A Theory of the Firm: Governance, Residual Claims and Organisational Forms* (1st edn, Harvard University Press, 2003).
137. Michele Fratianni and Federico Giri, 'The Tale of Two Great Crises' [2017] 81 Journal of Economic Dynamics and Control.
138. Michel Camdessus, 'Money Laundering: The Importance of International Countermeasures', Address to the Plenary Meeting of the FATF (*IMF*, 10 February 1998) <https://www.imf.org/external/np/speeches/1998/0210 98.htm> accessed 10 January 2015.
139. Morris Goldstein, Graciela Laura Kaminsky and Carmen M. Reinhart, *Assessing Financial Vulnerability: An Early Warning System for Emerging Markets* (PIP, 2000).
140. Myres McDougal, 'Jurisprudence for a Free Society' [1966] 2583 *Faculty Scholarship Series*.
141. Naomi Haynes and Jason Hickel, 'Hierarchy, Value and the Value of Hierarchy' [2016] 60 *Social Analysis*.
142. Naomi Klein, *The Shock Doctrine: The Rise of Disaster Capitalism* (Macmillan, 2007).

143. Navin Beekarry, 'The International Anti-Money Laundering and Combating the Financing of Terrorism Regulatory Strategy: A Critical Analysis of Compliance Determinants in International Law' [2010] 31 Northwestern Journal of International Law and Business.

144. Nicholas Ryder, *Money Laundering – An Endless Cycle? A Comparative Analysis of Anti-Money Laundering Policies in the United States of America, the United Kingdom, Australia and Canada* (First Published 2012, Routledge, 2012).

145. Nienke Grossman, 'The Normative Legitimacy of International Courts' [2013] 86 Temple Law Review.

146. Norman Mugarura, *The Global Anti-Money Laundering Regulatory Landscape in Less Developed Countries* (2nd edn, Routledge, 2016).

147. OECD, 'OECD Handbook' (*OECD*) <https://www.oecd.org/std/na/NOE -Handbook-%20Chapter9.pdf> accessed 10 August 2015.

148. OECD, *OECD Reviews of Risk Management Policies: Future Global Shocks, Improving Risk Governance* (OECD Publishing, 2011).

149. Oona Hathaway, *International Delegation and State Sovereignty* [2008] 883 *Faculty Scholarship Series.*

150. Paul Allan Schott, *Reference Guide to Anti-Money Laundering and Combating the Financing of Terrorism* (World Bank Publication, 2006).

151. Paul Kupiec, 'The IMF-World Bank Financial Sector Assessment Program: A View from the Inside' *in* Douglas D. Evanoff and George G. Kaufman (eds.) *Systematic Financial Crisis, Resolving Large Bank Insolvencies* (World Scientific Publishing Co. Pte. Ltd., 2005).

152. Pawel Smaga, 'The Concept of Systemic Risk' [2014] *SRC Special Paper No.*

153. Pierre Goad, 'Acceptance of Capital Controls is Spreading' [1998] Asian Wall Street Journal.

154. Pierre–Laurent Chatain, 'The World Bank's Role in the Fight Against Money Laundering and Terrorist Financing' [2004] 74 *International Law FORUM du droit International.*

155. Rainer Hulsee, 'Even Clubs Can't Do Without Legitimacy: Why the Anti-Money Laundering Blacklist Was Suspended' [2008] 2 *Regulation and Governance.*

156. Rainer Hulsee, 'Creating Demand for Global Governance: The Making of a Global Money Laundering Problem' [2007] 21 (2) Global Society.

157. Rainer Hulsse and Dieter Kerwer, 'Global Standards in Action: Insights from AML Regulation' [2007]14 (5) Organisation.

158. Raymond Baker, 'The Scale of the Global Financial Structure Facilitating Money Laundering' *in* Brigitte Unger and Daan Van Der Inde (eds.) *Research Handbook on Money Laundering* (Edward Elgar Publishing Limited, 2013).

159. P. Reuter and E.M. Truman, *Chasing Dirty Money: Progress on Anti-Money Laundering* (Institute for International Economics, Washington, DC, 2004).

160. Richard O'Brien, 'Global Financial Integration: The End of Geography' [1992] *Royal Institute of International Affairs.*

161. Richard Overy, *The Inter-War Crisis* (Routledge, 2016). 1, 62; Richard S. Grossman, 'Banking Crisis' (2006) Wesleyan Economic Working Papers 001 <http://repec.wesleyan.edu/pdf/rgrossman/2016001_grossman.pdf> accessed 13 July 2015.

162. Richard Summerfield, 'GDP to Include Illegal Activity' (*Financier Worldwide*, 2014) <https://www.financierworldwide.com/gdp-to-include-illegal-activit y/#.WZM5Ha2ZPUo> accessed 10 August 2017.
163. Rick Gorvett, 'Systemic Risk as a Negative Externality' [2009] *Risk Management: Part – Two Systemic Risk, Financial Reform and Moving Forward from the Financial Crisis, Society of Actuaries (SOA).*
164. Robert Delonis, 'International Financial Standards and Codes: Mandatory Regulation Without Representation' [2004] 36 New York University Journal of International Law and Politics.
165. Robert O. Keohane, *After Hegemony: Power and Discord in International Politics* (Princeton, NJ: Princeton University Press, 1984).
166. Ross Buckley, *International Financial System: Policy and Regulation* (Kluwer Law International, 2009).
167. Rudiger Wolfrum, 'Legitimacy of International Law from a Legal Perspective: Some Introductory Considerations' *in* Rudiger Wolfrum (eds.), *Legitimacy in International Law* (Springer, Berlin, 2008).
168. Saby Ghoshray, 'Compliance Convergence in FATF Rulemaking: The Conflict Between Agency Capture and Soft Law' [2014–2015] 59 *New York Law School Law Review.*
169. Sarah O'Connor, 'Drugs and Prostitutions Add £10bn to UK Economy' (*Financial Times*, May 29 2014) <https://www.ft.com/content/65704ba0 -e730-11e3-88be-00144feabdc0> accessed 10 August 2017.
170. Scott Cooper, Darren Hawkins, Wade Jacoby and Daniel Nielson, 'Yielding Sovereignty to International Institutions: Bringing Systems Structure Bank in' [2008] 10 (3) International Studies Review.
171. Shapovalov Alexeevitch, 'History, Current State and Prospects of Development of International Financial Law' [2015] 43 *Revista de Derecho.*
172. Stavros Gadinis, 'The Financial Stability Board: The New Politics of International Financial Regulation' [2013] 48 (2) Texas International Law Journal.
173. Steven Radelet and Jeffrey Sachs, 'The Onset of the East Asian Financial Crisis' (1998) *NBER Working Paper Series, Working Paper 6680, National Bureau of Economic Research 2* <http://www.nber.org/chapters/c8691.pdf> accessed 7 June 2016.
174. Syed Azhar Hussain Shah, Akher Hussain Shah and Sajawal Khan, 'Governance of Money Laundering: An Application of the Principal-Agent Model' [2006] 45 (4) The Pakistan Development Review.
175. Thomas Oatley, 'The Dilemmas of International Financial Regulation' [2000] 23 (4) Regulation.
176. Tom R. Tyler, *Why People Obey the Law* (Princeton University Press, 2006).
177. E. Van de Werdt and P. Speenkenbrink, 'Witwassen, een koud kunstje' (2008) *Jaarboek Compliance.*
178. H. Weber Rolf and Douglas W. Arner, 'Towards a New Design for International Financial Regulation' [2007] 29 (2) *Pennsylvania Journal of International Economic Law.*
179. William R. Schroeder, 'A Global Threat and the International Community's Response' [2001] 70 *FBI Law Enforcement Bulletin.*
180. Winer Jonathan and Trifin Roule, 'Fighting Terrorist Finance' [2002] 44 *Survival.*

181. Yilmaz Akyuz, 'Towards Reform of the International Financial Architecture: Which Way Forward' *in* Yilmaz Akyuz (eds.), *Reforming the Global Financial Architecture: Issues and Proposals* (Zed Books, 2002).
182. Zanny Minton-Beddoes, 'Why the IMF Needs Reform' [1995] *Foreign Affairs*.
183. Zakhele Hlophe, 'Regulating Money Laundering in Developing Countries: A Critical Analysis of South Africa's Incorporation and Implementation of the Global FATF Standards' [2013] Doctoral Thesis, Kings College London.

3 Preconditions for Effective Regulations of Anti-Money Laundering and Counter-Terrorist Financing (AML/CFT) and Compliance Drivers in African Countries and Emerging Economies (AC/EEs)

Introduction

The preconditions for effective AML/CFT regulation aimed at forestalling illicit transfers and the role of law in its development have been the subject of a distinguished body of research.[1] This literature, although limited, has propelled debates on whether law is crucial to the in-country development of robust AML/CFT structures; and if it is, the design it ought to take to combat illicit crimes. Whilst the development of the 'law matters' thesis in AML/CFT regulation is still unresolved, there is recognition that law has to be situated with 'confidence' for countries to effectively combat illicit crimes.

The presence of 'law and confidence' across ACs/EEs does not necessarily result in similar domestic circumstances to effectively combat illicit crimes. Unlike EEs, a majority of ACs have continued to deviate from the expected outcomes in terms of compliance. This can be attributed to a range of factors such as reputational concerns, capacity and resource disparities. Such challenges feed into the compliance drivers in different jurisdictions. An examination of the preconditions for effective regulation and possible compliance drivers illustrate divergent effects on ACs/EEs, further indicating the possible unsuitability of the current regime in effectively combating money laundering/terrorist financing (ML/TF) in ACs.

The first section examines the possibility of law as a precondition for effective regulation. Whilst acknowledging counterarguments, it posits that law does serve as a bedrock for financial regulation. Additionally, it contends that the design of law is imperative given that with weak drafting, laws can and will be gamed. Furthermore, it argues the robustness of law is largely dependent on other factors

---

1 BCBS, 'Consultative Document: Core Principles for Effective Banking Supervision' (*BCBS*, 20 March 2012) <http://www.bis.org/publ/bcbs213.pdf> accessed 1 February 2016; IOSCO, 'Methodology for Assessing Implementation of the IOSCO Objectives and Principles of Securities Regulation' (OICU-IOSCO February 2008); IMF, 'Canada: FSAP: IOSCO Objectives and Principles of Securities Regulation – Detailed Assessment of Implementation 2014' (IMF Country Report No. 14/73).

which are internal to a country. The second section encapsulates these factors as 'confidence' and discusses this as a precondition for effective regulation. Confidence is examined within the framework of financial stability and governmental, political and institutional systems within a country. These factors are required for the well-functioning of law, attainable through the design of the law. The third section discusses the variances in confidence and the resulting effect of legal transplantation across ACs/EEs. The fourth section discusses the perspective on compliance with global standards. It builds on previous sections given that the preconditions for effective regulations feed into the compliance drivers. The fifth section advances the claim that compliance is a function of legal and non-legal factors. The sixth section focuses on how countries are benchmarked against their compliance to international standards. It argues that the process of benchmarking reveals agency problems and further raises legitimacy concerns. The eighth section concludes by drawing the strands together.

Preconditions for Effective Regulations of AML/CFT in African Countries and Emerging Economies

Drawing from categorisation by international financial institutions (IFIs) and trans-governmental networks (TGNs),[2] this chapter contends that there are two interrelated preconditions for effective regulation of AML/CFT – law and confidence. It argues that these factors are critical in ensuring robust regulation and compliance to the AML/CFT standards.

Law as a Precondition for Effective Regulation

Creating a regulated framework within which banks can thrive and advance economic growth in the absence of financial crime is challenging. Indeed, it is surprising that the banking sector still exists despite the numerous crises that eroded the confidence of depositors and the economy as a whole. The viability of banks as the suitable savings or investment option has been threatened with 'run on the bank' in jurisdictions like the United Kingdom.[3] Such an atmosphere indicates the need for tougher regulations. Consequently, reactive laws have resulted from the need to address the vulnerabilities in the banking system. This indicates an assumption that safe banking activities can only function in a tightly

---

2 BCBS 'Sound Management of Risks Related to Money Laundering and Financing of Terrorism' (*BCBS*, June 2017) <http://www.bis.org/bcbs/publ/d405.pdf> accessed August 2017; IAIS, 'Guidance Paper on Anti-Money Laundering and Combating the Financing of Terrorism' (2004); The Joint Forum, 'Initiatives by the BCBS, IAIS and IOSCO to Combat Money Laundering and the Financing of Terrorism' (June 2003) <http://www.bis.org/publ/joint05.pdf> accessed 1 May 2016.
3 Hyun Shin, 'Reflections on Northern Rock: The Bank Run that Heralded the Global Financial Crisis' [2009] 23 (1) Journal of Economic Perspectives 101, 101.

regulated space.[4] This is highlighted by contract law which governs the relationship between banks, their investors and depositors, and mandates adherence to conduct of business regulations. Furthermore, there is increased legislation on such issues as money laundering, cybercrime and tax evasion[5] in ACs/EEs. Statutory supremacy mandates that these legislations are adhered to,[6] and that a breach will result in attendant consequences.

The assumption that rigid regulation catalyses bank safety informed the Financial Action Task Force's (FATF's) mandate on AML/CFT regulation which is designed to 'promote effective implementation of *legal, regulatory and operational measures* for combatting money laundering, terrorist financing and the financing of proliferation, and other related threats to the integrity of the financial system'.[7]

The emphasis on the implementation of legal measures is an indication of the assumption that in the absence of enforcement actions, ML/TF will persist. More importantly, it signifies that robust legislation is required to guide implementation of legal measures. Additionally, it indicates that in the absence of tough laws, countries' capacity to combat illicit crimes and their predicate offences will be severely restricted.[8] Reverberating this perception, the IMF states that:

> 'Money launderers and terrorist financiers exploit loopholes and differences among national AML/CFT systems and move their funds to or through jurisdictions with *weak or ineffective legal* and institutional frameworks' (emphasis added).[9]

An examination of this International Monetary Fund's (IMF's) statement suggests that weak or ineffective laws are unsuitable for curbing laundering because criminals are specialists in understudying the jurisdictional laws of different

4 Gerard Caprio, Jr, 'Financial Regulation After the Crisis: How Did We Get Here and How Do We Get Out?' [2013] Federal Reserve of San Francisco Proceedings 1, 19; Stijin Classens, Daniela Klingebiel and Luc Laeven, 'Resolving Systemic Financial Crisis: Policies and Institutions' (2004) 3377 The World Bank, 13 <http://documents.worldbank.org/curated/en/306631468780599186/126526322_20041117165058/additional/wps3377.pdf> accessed 18 November 2015.

5 Indian Income Tax Act 1961 and subsequently the Finance Act 2015; Article 201 People of China Criminal Law Amendment 2015.

6 Albert Dicey, *Introduction to the Study of the Law of the Constitution* (8th Edition, Liberty Classics 1982) 3–4.

7 FATF, 'The FATF Recommendations' (*FATF*, 2013) <http://www.fatf-gafi.org/media/fatf/documents/recommendations/pdfs/fatf_recommendations.pdf> accessed 12 May 2015.

8 FATF, 'FATF Recommendation 3 and 4' (*FATF*, 2013) <http://www.fatf-gafi.org/media/fatf/documents/recommendations/pdfs/fatf_recommendations.pdf> accessed 12 May 2015.

9 IMF, Anti-Money Laundering/Combating the Financing of Terrorism Topics – The Fund's Involvement In AML/CFT (*IMF*) <https://www.imf.org/external/np/leg/amlcft/eng/aml1.htm> accessed 20 June 2016.

countries – a crucial determinant factor for where to invest in.[10] Interestingly, launderers also look at other business indicators such as openness and transparency of institutions to determine the strength of laws.[11] For instance, sequel to the collapse of the Central Government of Comoros, each island started exerting fiscal sovereignty.[12] Of the three existing islands, Anjouan created a business-friendly and stress-free regulatory environment which permitted the licensing of banks within 48 hours and acceded to the operation of shell banks with limited information on beneficial owners.[13] This indicated its commitment to promote financial secrecy.[14] Furthermore, Anjouan restrained from cooperating with foreign governments except regarding serious criminal cases which excluded tax-related matters.[15] A few months after the creation of this island as an offshore location, launderers from Russia started opening shell banks and companies through which they transferred money.[16] In 2008, it was reported that 300 offshore banks operated in Anjouan, many of which were shell banks.[17]

It is crucial to note that developed countries are not exempt from this difficulty. England's weak regulations on real estate investments have encouraged launderers and corrupt foreign politicians to invest in this sector.[18]

These examples demonstrate a pattern in the operation of launderers when dealing with jurisdictions with weak domestic legislations. Premised on these assumptions, the FATF makes soft law recommendations for countries that respond by promulgating legislation on AML/CFT.[19]

10 EENA1, Consulting Counsel, Financial Integrity Unit, IMF, Interview with EENA1, 'Telephone Call' (2017).

11 Ibid.

12 Tax Justice Network-Africa, *Why Africa Should Stand Up for Tax Justice* (Pambazuka Press, 2011) 36.

13 Hilton McCann, *Offshore Finance* (CUP, 2009) 450.

14 *Tax Justice Network-Africa* (n 12) 33.

15 *McCann* (n 13).

16 Scott Senccal, Murat Akuyev and Yulia Somomakhina, 'Offshores Restricted From Participation in Privatisation and Acquisition of Russian Strategic Companies' (*Cleary Gottlieb*, Alert Memorandum, 10 July 2017) <https://www.clearygottlieb.com/~/media/cgsh/files/2017/publications/alert-memos/offshores-restricted-from-participation-in-privatizations-and-acquisitions-of-russian-7-10-17.pdf> accessed 21 August 2017.

17 *Tax Justice Network-Africa* (n 12) 37.

18 Robert Booth, 'MPs Decry "Failed" Effort to Stop UK Property Money Laundering' (*The Guardian*, 15 July 2016) <https://www.theguardian.com/money/2016/jul/15/mps-decry-inadequate-efforts-stop-money-laundering-uk-property> accessed 10 August 2017; Damien Gayle, 'Foreign Criminals Use London Housing Market to Launder Billions of Pounds' (*The Guardian*, 25 July 2015) <https://www.theguardian.com/uk-news/2015/jul/25/london-housing-market-launder-offshore-tax-havens> accessed 10 August 2017.

19 Saby Ghoshray, 'Compliance Convergence in FATF Rulemaking: The Conflict Between Agency Capture and Soft Law' [2014–2015] 59 N.Y.L. SCH.L.REV. 521, 537.

This legislative process is followed by a monitoring and evaluation exercise by the FATF and or the IFIs to determine the extent of compliance.[20] Where the exercise indicates that countries have failed to enact laws based on the FATF recommendations, or were faulted in their implementation, such countries are characterised as 'weak' or 'non-compliant'. This measurement of compliance is indicative of the failure to align legislative frameworks with the Vienna and Palermo Conventions. Consequentially, pressure is mounted on countries to elicit compliance in the formulation and construction of their laws.[21] The primary reactionary motives of countries are usually to avoid placement on the 'black-2' and 'grey list' and the penalties associated therewith.[22] This is a key reason behind the adaptation of laws perceived as a mechanism for improved compliance and financial stability.[23] While it is plausible that a system of laws guiding businesses including corporate laws, AML/CFT laws, bankruptcy laws, contract, consumer protection and property laws may serve as a precondition for effective regulation, the extent to which they can has been debated.

Law as the Bedrock for Financial Regulation

Some scholars have argued that robust laws would lead to effective supervision, efficient risk management and good corporate governance practices within banks.[24] The assumption is that this would serve as a catalyst for improving confidence in the banking system, thus possibly limiting the extent of any potential financial instability.[25] Singh highlights the importance of the law in ensuring financial stability, stating that it is crucial in preserving confidence in institutions and holding government agencies accountable.[26]

---

20 FATF, 'Methodology: For Assessing Technical Compliance with the FATF Recommendations and the Effectiveness of AML/CFT System' (*FATF*, 2013) <http://www.fatf-gafi.org/media/fatf/documents/methodology/FATF%20Methodology%2022%20Feb%202013.pdf> accessed 10 August 2017.
21 This is usually done through sanctions.
22 Previously referred to as the Non-Cooperative Countries and Territories (NCCT). Leonardo Borlini, 'The Financial Action Task Force: An Introduction' (U4 Brief, January 2015) <https://assets.publishing.service.gov.uk/media/57a0898ee5274a27b2000137/U4Brief-2015-02WEB.pdf> accessed 18 March 2016.
23 Hemeiri Shahar and Lee Jones, 'Regulatory Regionalism and Anti-Money Laundering Governance in Asia' [2015] 69 (2) Australian Journal of International Affairs 144, 145; Jackie Johnson, 'Blacklisting: Initial Reactions, Responses and Repercussion' [2001] 4 (2) Journal of Money Laundering Control 211, 213.
24 Klaus Hopt, 'Corporate Governance of Banks after the Financial Crisis' *in* E. Wymeersch, K.J. Hopt and G. Ferrarini (eds.), *Financial Regulation and Supervision, A Post-Crisis Analysis* (Oxford University Press 2012) 3; Klaus Hopt, 'Better Governance of Financial Institutions' (2013) European Corporate Governance Institute Working Paper 207/2013, 23 <http://personal.lse.ac.uk/schustee/hopt%20governance.pdf> accessed 6 May 2016.
25 Klaus Hopt, 'Better Governance of Financial Institutions' (2013) European Corporate Governance Institute Working Paper 207/2013, 23 <http://personal.lse.ac.uk/schustee/hopt%20governance.pdf> accessed 6 May 2016.
26 Dalvinder Singh and John Raymond La Brosse, 'Developing a Framework for Effective Financial Crisis Management' [2012] 2 OECD Journal: Financial Market Trends 1,7.

Acknowledging law's diverse application, Medish contends that laws form the basis for microeconomic change; therefore, laws of economics do not get a proper chance to work without the rule of law.[27] His argument underscores that accountability, transparency and legitimacy of regulatory actions are dependent on the functional rule of law. This indicates subjection of all institutions, entities and the state itself to legislation,[28] which provides for judicial independence and consistent enforcement. These assertions feed into the five criteria for effective regulation enumerated by Baldwin et al., the top criterion listed as a robust legislative mandate.[29] They argue that regulatory action deserves support when authorised by parliament, the recognised bedrock of democratic authority.[30] As a supervisory law, banking law is a specialised area of administrative law. It elucidates how agencies operate and circumstances where the rights of citizens can be contained by the state.[31]

However, there is the recognition that the strength of laws are predicated on the system in which they operate.[32] Chinn and Ito argue that financial openness can only be beneficial when appropriate legal systems and institutions are in place.[33] This study reveals that equity market development can be spurred by financial openness if a threshold of legal development has been attained.[34] Cooter, Schafer and Ulen argue that the differences across legal institutions reflect the development level in countries.[35] An application of these studies to global regulation of AML/CFT provides some explanation for the disparities in the assimilation of the FATF recommendations by ACs/EEs. Through a historical perspective, the following sub-sections will illustrate that, in comparison with

---

27 Mark Medish, 'Lesson from Economies in Transition During Global Financial Crisis', in Joseph R. Sisignano, Wiliam C. Hunter, George Kaufman, *Global Financial Crises: Lessons from Recent Events* (Bank for International Settlement Federal Reserve Bank of Chicago, 2000) 61.

28 *Dicey* (n 6) 191.

29 Robert Baldwin, Martin Cave and Martin Lodge, *Understanding Regulation: Theory, Strategy and Practice* (First published 2012, 2nd edn, OUP 2014) 27.

30 *Dicey* (n 6).

31 Wouter Bossu and Dawn Chew, "But We Are Different!" 12 Common Weaknesses in Banking Laws, and What to Do About Them (2015) IMF Working Paper WP/15/2000 <https://poseidon01.ssrn.com/delivery.php?ID=576121020003020082097102019092078064 000043077033024024075002002042074000025083108029104081102046010030 00400211709811611608802409207207102507109307100709510807708901003 0086006021071&EXT=pdf> accessed 19 May 2016.

32 Rahmat Mohamad, 'Access to International Justice: The Role of the International Criminal Court in Aiding National Prosecutions of International Crimes' [2012] 1 (2) AALCO Journal of International Law 1.8.

33 Chinn Menzie and Ito Hiro, 'What Matters for Financial Development? Capital Controls, Institutions and Interactions' [2006] 81 (1) Journal of Development Economics 163, 165.

34 Ibid. 163, 187.

35 R. Cooter and H.B. Schafer, *Solomon's Knot: How Law Can End the Poverty of Nations* (First published 2012, Princeton University Press 2012) 173; T. Ulen, 'The Uneasy Case for Competition Law and Regulation as Decisive Factors in Development: Some Lessons for China' *in* M. Faure and Z. Xang (eds.), *Competition Policy and Regulation. Recent Developments in China, the US and Europe* (Edward Elgar 2011) 13–44.

ACs, EEs have more robust legislative responses due to stronger legislative capacity; however, they do not necessarily have a stronger rule of law. Nevertheless, legislative capacity amplifies their ability to adopt tougher laws to combat illicit crimes. Additionally, the economic position of EEs makes it imperative to address reputational concerns before they manifest, an issue which is easier to address in countries with sturdier legal structures.

LEGISLATIVE CHANGES IN AFRICAN COUNTRIES RESULTING FROM
AML/CFT LAWS

The importance of law as a bedrock of financial regulation can be exemplified with the significant changes recorded within countries resulting from AML/CFT legislations, particularly in ACs, as can be seen through the continent's legislative and technical evolution post the colonial era.[36]

It is imperative to state that during the colonial period, the crime of 'money laundering' was nonexistent although certain predicate offences like bribery, corruption, extortion and other offences had been acknowledged to exist. Attesting to this, Rodney stated that 'colonialism was not merely a system of exploitation, but one whose essential purpose was to repatriate the profits to the so-called motherland'.[37] Rodney speaks of an era dominated by slave trade and a gradual move to a period characterised by the exploitation of labour and forced labour where 'Africans in their country were forced to grow cash crops by gun and whip'.[38] The gradual change evidences the tactical means employed by colonial masters to circumvent the 1833 Abolition of Slave Trade Act, which allowed the laundering of ill-gotten wealth to capitalist economies. Interestingly, during this dictatorial period, such 'illicit' transfers, exorbitant taxation and exclusive rights of exploitation granted to British and European firms over mineral and natural resources were legalised.[39]

The prevalent exploitation that riddled the colonial era set the tone for the decolonisation struggle, given that the structures instituted by the colonial masters hindered the fight for independence in ACs. Colonial masters struggled to give up power, arguing instead that their colonies were politically corrupt and unable to handle independence. For instance, colonial masters contended that Nigeria was ridden with 'corruption and bribery'[40] and hence required 'ceaseless vigilance of the British Staff to maintain a high standard of integrity and…prevent

---

36 Focus will be on Nigeria, a prism through which other African countries can be viewed.

37 Walter Rodney, *How Europe Underdeveloped Africa* (Bogle L'Ouverture Publications Ltd, London 1988).

38 Ibid.

39 Austine Ejovi, Mgbonyebi Charles and Akpokighe Okiemute Raymond, 'Corruption in Nigeria: A Historical Perspective' [2013] 3 (16) Research Humanities and Social Sciences Journal 1, 19.

40 Robert Tignor, 'Political Corruption in Nigeria before Independence' [1993] 31 (2) Journal of Modern African Studies 175, 178.

the oppression of peasantry'.[41] Tignor, however, argued that the colonial masters had expected their collaborators to behave this way.[42] Hence, as the struggle for independence grew, colonial masters continually produced reports which indicted leaders of the movement as corrupt and unjustly enriched to the detriment of their people.[43] Nevertheless, ACs began to gain their independence in the 1950s.

During the decolonisation period, the ruling class amassed ill-gotten wealth. They were made ministers or chairmen of parastatals, with power to issue licences, award contracts or scholarships, subject only to veto powers of colonial authority.[44] They exploited these positions to gain 'kickbacks' which are illegal pre-payments of a percentage of the contract awarded to the official in power.[45] This was predominant in Nigeria after it gained independence in 1960, a period marred by widespread corruption. To combat these illicit crimes, the disregard for rule of law and lack of accountability, military takeover commenced in 1966 and dominated for about 32 years.[46] Over six successful military coups occurred aimed at curbing corruption.[47] The regimes of Murtala Mohammed in 1975 and Mohammadu Buhari in 1983 made considerable progress.[48] Murtala Mohammed was killed six months into his regime, whilst Mohammadu Buhari was deposed by another military coup in 1985.[49] Sadly, the deplorable situation remained mainstream, most prominently during the Sani Abacha regime, which looted about £5 billion from Nigeria's coffers and stashed in jurisdictions including the United Kingdom and Switzerland.[50]

Whilst Nigerian governments continually addressed corruption, there was limited focus on money laundering until Nigeria's accession to the 1988 Vienna Convention. This culminated in Nigeria's first significant piece of legislation (by decree) – the Drug Law Enforcement Agency (NDLEA) Act, imbuing the

---

41 Lord Lugard, *The Dual Mandate in Tropical Africa* (6th edn, Routledge 1922) 198; Colonial Office, Report of the Commission of Enquiry into the Disorders of the Eastern Province of Nigeria, November, 1949 (London, 1950) 12 and 30.

42 *Tignor* (n 40).

43 Ibid. 175, 201.

44 B.J. Dudley, *Instability and Political Order: Politics and Crisis in Nigeria* (Ibadan, Ibadan University Press, 1973).

45 Ajayi Isaac, 'Military Regimes and Nation Building in Nigeria, 1966–1999' [2013] 5 (7) African Journal of History and Culture 138, 141.

46 Ibid. 138, 140. It should be noted that a period of civilian rule existed between 1979 and December 1983 under President Shehu Shagari.

47 Ibid.

48 Ogbewere Ijewereme, 'Anatomy of Corruption in the Nigeria Public Sector: Theoretical Perspectives and some Empirical Explanations' [2015] Sage Open 1, 7.

49 Ibid. 1, 4.

50 The Associated Press, 'Late Nigerian Dictator Looted Nearly $500 Million, Swiss Say' (*New York Times*, 19 August 2004) <http://www.nytimes.com/2004/08/19/world/late-nigerian-dictator-looted-nearly-500-million-swiss-say.html> accessed 29 September 2017; Michael Ogbedi, 'Political Leadership and Corruption in Nigeria Since 1960: A Socio-Economic Analysis' [2012] 1 (2) Journal of Nigeria Studies 1, 9.

NDLEA with enforcement powers against drug crime. Mirroring the Vienna Convention, the NDLEA decree focused on tackling money laundering through a fight on drugs alone. At that time, Nigeria had developed large-scale drug trafficking and was classed as second only to China in the trafficking of drugs to the United States.[51] The environment was facilitated by drug lords who operated from a relatively safe home-base given the absence of laws. The NDLEA cracked down on drug lords at the point of cultivation, processing, sale and trafficking.[52] However, the NDLEA decree did not cover other crimes in Nigeria, such as corruption, bribery, etc. This led to the enactment of the Money Laundering Decree (MLD) 1995.[53]

A perusal of the MLD reveals the recognition that the use of financial institutions as a conduit to launder funds could potentially trigger financial instability.[54] In addressing these concerns, the decree pioneered the commencement of Customer Due Diligence (CDD) by financial institutions and individuals with regards to cash payment above a threshold, a process which kickstarts once a customer seeks to open an account.[55] The decree mandated banks to comply with these requirements given the force of law and the regimented structure put in place to combat money laundering. Financial institutions were also mandated to disclose overseas transfers and ensure that all details are precise.[56] It also required casinos and gambling houses to adhere to its CDD and record-keeping requirements.[57] More importantly, this decree required a sustained relationship between financial institutions and the NDLEA, to continually combat drug trafficking.[58]

These decrees, which changed the landscape of AML regulation in Nigeria, had their limitations. For instance, the MLD which required CDD by financial institutions failed as it provided discretionary powers to financial institutions on whether to report suspicious transactions. Additionally, penalties were only targeted at staff of the financial institution and not the institutions themselves, a shortcoming that hindered compliance. Furthermore, the decree was unclear regarding its definition of money laundering. More so, Nigeria was still largely a cash-based economy where less than 37% of adults had access to financial services.[59] Hence, like drugs, money was usually laundered physically – mainly through

---

51 Chibuike Uche, 'The Adoption of a Money Laundering Regime in Nigeria' [1988] 1 (3) JMLC 220, 220.
52 National Drug Law Enforcement Agency Act 1989.
53 Adegboyega Ige, 'A Review of the Legislative and Institutional Frameworks for Combating Money Laundering in Nigeria' [2011] 1 NIALS; Nlerum Okogbule, 'Combating Money Laundering in Nigeria: An Appraisal of the Money Laundering Act 2004' [2007] 28 (2) Statute Law Review 156, 157.
54 Money Laundering Decree 1995.
55 Ibid. S 1 (a) (b), S 10 (2).
56 Ibid.
57 Ibid.
58 Ibid S 4 (1) (a); S 4(1) (b).
59 Financial Inclusion Insights, 'Nigeria: Wave 3 Report, FII Tracker Survey Conducted August–September 2015' (*FinInclusion.org*, 2015) <http://finclusion.org/uploads/file/

airports or seaports, an area unaddressed by the MLD. These deficiencies proved the limitations of legislative capacity in terms of comprehension of the scale of the problems and how best to tackle it. It showed that Nigeria was ill prepared to tackle money laundering or its predicate offences. The decree focused mainly on criminalisation and enforcement (breeding a 'don't-be-caught' mentality), not necessarily on prevention. These shortcomings led to the FATF blacklisting of Nigeria in 2001.

To get delisted, Nigeria enacted the Money Laundering (Amendment) Act 2002. This Act expanded the scope of predicate offences to other illegal acts. It also extended AML obligations to other non-financial institutions and required enhanced due diligence. The FATF however still faulted the Act, leading to the enactment of the Money Laundering (Prohibition) Act 2004 which repealed the 2002 Act. The 2004 Act was modelled to ensure the delisting of Nigeria from the FATF's blacklist. Hence, it limited the amount of cash that private individuals and corporate entities could hold for making payments of five hundred thousand naira (N500,000) and one million naira (N1,000,000), respectively.[60] It also provided that transfers above the stipulated amount be done through a financial institution. Additionally, it limited international transfers to ten thousand dollars ($10,000), mandating a report to the Central Bank of Nigeria or the Securities and Exchange Commission when the mandated limit was exceeded.[61] These requirements were to ensure a move away from a cash-based to a cashless economy, whilst ensuring that regulatory agencies could formulate and implement practical futuristic policies. The Act achieved the aim of delisting Nigeria from the FATF's blacklist.

Importantly, two other notable laws, the Corrupt Practices and Other Offences Act 2000 which sets up the Independent Corrupt Practices and Other Related Offences Commission (ICPC) and the Economic and Financial Crimes Commission (EFCC) Act 2002, also facilitated the delisting of Nigeria.[62] The ICPC focuses squarely on fighting corruption through investigations, arrests, prosecutions, corrective, preventative and educational responsibilities. The EFCC has a broader agenda, focused on the investigation and prosecution of all financial crimes.[63] The EFCC is also authorised to freeze bank accounts, seize assets or arrest suspects.[64] The Nigerian Financial Intelligence Unit (NFIU) is now domiciled within the Central Bank of Nigeria and serves as the national centre for the collation and analysis of suspicious transaction reports and other rel-

---

reports/InterMedia%20FII%20Nigeria%20W3%20%2030%20April%202016.pdf> accessed July 2016.

60 Money Laundering Act 2004, S1(1).

61 Ibid. S 2(1); S2 (2).

62 The Corrupt Practices and other Related Offences Act 2000 No.5 Laws of the Federation of Nigeria; the Economic and Financial Crimes Commission (Establishment) Act 2002.

63 Nuhu Ribadu, *Show Me the Money – Leveraging Anti-Money Laundering Tools to Fight Corruption in Nigeria: An Insider Story* (Centre for Global Development 2010) 16.

64 Economic and Financial Crimes Commission (Establishment) Act 2004, Section 7(1) (a).

evant information to money laundering. The NFIU previously derived its power from the Money Laundering Prohibition Act 2011, as amended in 2012 and the EFCC Act. In 2018, the Financial Intelligence Unit (Establishment) Act (NFIU Act)[65] became its main source of power. It is also responsible for establishing and maintaining relationships with other Financial Intelligence Units (FIUs) within the Egmont Group.

Following these legislations, there is appreciable progress in the way ML/TF is combatted in Nigeria through financial institutions. For instance, banks now implement the CDD requirements which ensure the creation and maintenance of paper trails. Suspicious transactions are highlighted to regulators and the management is held responsible for the acts and omissions in facilitating ML/TF.

Consequently, it is arguable that Nigerian and, indeed, African laws may be capable of curbing illicit crimes. EENA2 states that 'it is not as dire as one might think in…African countries – in fact, the letter of the law is pretty good'.[66] However, recently, the Egmont Group suspended Nigeria for failing to enact legislations to autotomise the country's NFIU from the EFCC.[67] Nigeria is yet to take positive steps to avert an impending expulsion. Chukwuma Utazi, the Chairman of the Nigerian Senate Committee on Anti-Corruption has stated that 'they (Egmont) already said that if we did not comply, they would expel us, so there is no fresh news there…we are working towards it, nothing has been done'.[68] This response illustrates a nonchalant approach to addressing an issue pending for over five years. In June 2018, Nigeria finally took swift steps to avoid impending expulsion by enacting the NFIU Act, consequently granting the NFIU independent and operational autonomy.[69] Indeed, the government's slack demonstrates legislators' reactive approach to addressing pressing issues.

LEGISLATIVE CHANGES IN EMERGING ECONOMIES RESULTING FROM AML/CFT LAWS

Legislation-inspired changes are more profound in EEs, taking China as an example. China's history indicates the existence of ML/TF during the ancient period (2000 BC), when all properties were vested in the ruler.[70] Merchants had engaged in extortion, bribery and subsequent investment of these properties in

---

65 See NFIU Act, 2018.

66 EENA2, Senior Counsel, Financial Integrity Unit, IMF, Interview with EENA2, 'Telephone Call' (2017).

67 Damilola Oyedele, 'Egmont: Senate, House Disagree on NFIA as Threat of Nigeria's Expulsion Looms' (*Thisday*, 6 February 2018) <https://www.thisdaylive.com/index.php/2018/02/06/egmont-senate-house-disagree-on-nfia-as-threat-of-nigerias-expulsion-looms/> accessed 11 February 2018.

68 Ibid.

69 See, s. 2(2), NFIU Act 2018.

70 Sterling Seagrave, *Lord of the Rim* (Bantam Press, London 1997).

other jurisdictions, circumventing restrictions imposed by the government.[71] Measures devised to curb the appropriation of properties proved insufficient in the face of varied ways of laundering.

Like ACs, the first legislation came as a result of China's accession to the 1988 Vienna Convention.[72] These laws could only combat drug crime.[73] Subsequent legislation included other predicate offences – in line with evolving international standards.[74]

China's evolving laws were inspired by responses to external pressures, for instance, from the FATF. Two thematic areas standout – customer due diligence and reporting.

There is evidence that CDD legislation facilitated the active fight against illicit crimes.[75] Prior to the legislation, there was no evidence that Chinese banks, especially smaller banks, implemented CDD requirements.[76] Thus, it is unsurprising that the first regulation requiring customers to use genuine names to open bank accounts was in 2000.[77] Lack of CDD requirements cloaked launderers in anonymity, enabling them to operate without detection. China has now implemented CDD requirements to combat ML/TF following FATF's stipulations,[78] thus potentially reducing laundering opportunities through financial institutions.

Law has also changed the culture regarding 'reporting' of suspicious transactions by financial institutions. China's 2003 AML/CFT legislation introduced the country's pioneer suspicious transactions reporting requirement. However, due to legislative capacity challenges, it failed to capture FATF current

---

71 Nigel Morris-Cotterill, 'Money Laundering' [2001] 124 Foreign Policy 16–20.
72 The Chinese Government signed the convention on December 20, 1998 and handed over the instrument of accession on December 25, 1989. The convention came into effect in China on November 11, 1990. NB: In 1979, prior to the criminalization of money laundering internationally, Art. 312 Chinese Criminal Law criminalized activities receiving, and handling proceeds of crime.
73 Ibid.
74 In 2001, 'terrorist financing' was included and in 2006, other financial crimes/predicate offences were included. Previously, in 1997 only drug and organised crime, terrorism and smuggling were covered.
75 'Rules for Anti-Money Laundering by Financial Institutions' and the 'Administrative Rules for the Reporting of Large-Value and Suspicious Transaction by Financial Institutions'; Temenos, 'Identifying Anti Money Laundering Issues in Chinese Banks' (*Asian Banker Researcher*) <https://www.theasianbanker.com/assets/media/dl/whitepaper/Asian%20Banker%20White%20Paper%20-%20China%20Anti-Money%20Laundry%20(English).pdf> accessed 4 June 2016.
76 Prior to 2003.
77 Xue Bin Li, 'Money Laundering and its Regulation in China' (UMI Dissertation Publishing 2009) 256.
78 Rules for Anti-Money Laundering by Financial Institutions, Administrative Rules for the Reporting of Large-Value and Suspicious RMB Payment Transactions and the Administrative Rules for the Reporting by Financial institutions of Large-Value and Suspicious Foreign Exchange Transactions has been extended to cover all financial institutions.

recommendations 9–12 and 20–23 on reporting.[79] In the absence of appropriate prescriptive guidelines on detection and reporting of suspicious transactions, compliance officers honoured the laws in breach. The shortcomings of the AML regulations do not overshadow its advantages. It detailed the thresholds for identifying suspicious transactions[80] and imposed penalties for non-compliance with reporting requirements, which emphasised its drive to foster a robust corporate governance culture. Non-compliance by persons occasioned disciplinary sanctions, usually in the form of fines.[81] In serious cases, business licences could be revoked.[82]

Considering that transplantation of global standards was key to advancing its economic vision, China enacted stricter AML/CFT laws, sometimes graver than international standards. For instance, whilst international standards impose financial penalties or imprisonment for tax evasion as a predicate offence,[83] the Chinese government made it a capital offence.[84] This approach has gained scholarly support. Shuceng suggests that modifications of the punishment regimes have contributed to reduced criminal offences in China.[85] Subsequent cross-country empirical studies support Shuceng's suggestion, showing how tougher money laundering regulations, particularly those that criminalise feeding activities or improved disclosure are linked to lower levels of money laundering.[86]

Given the foregoing legislative alignment with global standards, it is fair to postulate that China's legislators have stronger capacity. Therefore, despite legislative omissions regarding the reporting of suspicious transactions, the law allowed for effective implementation. This warranted the 2016 International

---

79 *FATF* (n 7).
80 For instance, it required financial institutions to identify suspicious transactions on the basis of set thresholds for daily transfers from companies and/or individuals for which CDD is required. For minimum transaction, CDD is not required, for instance, where the property insurance contracts paid in cash is a single amount insurance premium less than RMB 10,000 or foreign currency of value US$1,000 or equivalent. This indicates that not all cases fall under this bracket; it is wide but not too wide.
81 Penalties include disciplinary sanction or revolving qualification to hold a post, a fine of RMB 500,000 to the individual and/or RMB 20,000 up to RMB5 million to the organization.
82 PricewaterhouseCoopers, Know Your Customer: Quick Reference Guide (PwC, January 2016) <https://www.pwc.com/gx/en/financial-services/publications/assets/pwc-anti-m oney-laundering-2016.pdf> accessed 17 May 2017.
83 *FATF* (n 20).
84 The death penalty was eventually ended in 2011, see Ian Jeffries, *Political Developments in Contemporary China: A Guide* (First published 2011, Routledge 2011) 128; Chris Higg, China Ends Death Penalty for 13 Economic Crimes (*BBC News Shanghai*, February 2011) <http://www.bbc.co.uk/news/world-asia-pacific-12580504> accessed 11 February 2016; NB: The effectiveness is however questionable as only a few people were actually executed.
85 Wang Shucheng, 'Predictions on the Development and Direction of Legislation', in Yuwen W. Li (ed.) *The China Legal Development Yearbook* (Volume 2, 2009).
86 Alberto Chong and Florencio Lopez-de Silanes, 'Money Laundering and Its Regulation' [2015] 27 Journal of Economics and Politics 1, 25.

Narcotics Control Strategy Report (INCSR) which recorded China's milestones in addressing the early challenges posed by lack of relevant laws.[87] This milestone demonstrates the legislators' awareness of China's economic and international relations agenda, including the need to maintain its global reputation.

Law as the Bedrock of Financial Regulation: A Rejoinder

The weakness or absence of AML/CFT laws in certain countries has revealed that tough laws may not necessarily be a precondition for effective regulation.[88] Davis and Trebilcock reinforce this with empirical reports, which indicate that there is limited correlation between enhanced legal systems and development.[89] Additionally, law and economics scholars have argued that statutory laws are either immaterial or ineffective.[90] Moreover, it can be argued, further to the principal-agent theory, that laws can be gamed as countries have the power to manipulate and direct behaviour given their interpretation of the law. Consequently, it is imperative to question the need for statutory law in AML/CFT regulation. Scholars have postulated five situations where laws may not be ideal for robust regulation.

First, it is argued that laws are misdirected, and the unintended consequences thereof are increased predicate offences. Chong and Lopez De Silanes argue that from legal and economic perspectives, the ineffectiveness of money laundering legislation is responsible for the misdirection of regulatory policies which focus mainly on laundering acts, as opposed to predicate offences.[91] They argue that regulatory focus on predicate offences will eventually lead to a reduction in ML/TF crimes, given that ML/TF is an outcome of predicate offences.[92] They also posit that AML/CFT statutes have not only been inactive in combating initial predicate offences of drug crimes, but have further perpetuated other crimes such as kidnapping and smuggling.[93] Resultantly, it is argued that AML/CFT regulation is immaterial and disadvantageous, as it increases demand for services by inventing new crimes, fostering the creation of a new criminal industry to evade

---

87 U.S. Department of State, '2016 International Narcotics Control Strategy Report: Countries/Jurisdictions of Primary Concern – China' (U.S. Department of State, 2016) <https://www.state.gov/j/inl/rls/nrcrpt/2016/vol2/253391.htm> accessed 11 February 2017; Tax Justice Network, 'Financial Secrecy Index' (Tax Justice Network, 30 January 2018) <http://www.financialsecrecyindex.com/database/China.xml#t129> accessed 11 February 2018.

88 *Chong, Lopez-De-Silanes* (n 86).

89 Kevin Davis and Michael Trebilock, 'What Role Do Legal Institutions Play in Development' (Draft for the IMF Conference of 2nd Generation Reform, October 1989).

90 R.H Coase, 'The Nature of the Firm' Economica [2007] 4 (16); *Chong, Lopez-De-Silanes* (n 86).

91 *Chong, Lopez-De-Silanes* (n 86).

92 Ibid.

93 Ibid.

new laws.[94] Though compelling, this argument does not present the true nature of AML/CFT laws which undoubtedly includes predicate offences. Additionally, certain predicate offences such as tax evasion or kidnapping have separate laws which can be read alongside AML/CFT laws.

The second perspective posits that the reputation of financial institutions alongside enforcement actions by courts are sufficient preconditions for effective regulation of ML/TF. This argument recognises that potentially damaging penalties on financial institutions can propel robust regulation. For instance, Organisation for Economic Co-operation and Development's (OECD's) blacklisting of tax havens restricts the activities of institutions within the sanctioned countries, causing reputational damage and leading to improved regulation and compliance.[95] Furthermore, it also acknowledges the role of courts in 'law-making'.[96] Lending credence to this position, La Porta et al. and North argue that irrespective of the content of the law, better enforcement could be associated with lower levels of criminal activity – including money laundering.[97] However, this perspective that court-driven enforcement is sufficient to tackle ML/TF and render AML/CFT regulation needless is limited given that in the absence of legislative structures, regulation may not have the force of law. It fails to recognise the difference between legislation (laws enacted by the legislature or the governing body of a country)[98] and regulation (the process of monitoring and enforcing legislation or a written instrument containing rules built on laws).[99] Thus, for instance, where the legislature enacts a law requiring telecommunication companies to register all Subscriber Identity Module (SIM) card users, the relevant regulatory body is duty-bound to guide implementation of the law. This underscores that law informs regulation and enforcement.

Thirdly, scholars have postulated that legislation that is not backed by tough regulatory measures would not serve as a precondition for effective regulation.[100]

---

94   Richard Rhan , 'The Case Against Federalising Airport Security' (CATO Institute, 2001) <http://www.cato.org/publications/commentary/case-against-federalizing-airport-se curity> accessed 16 August 2016.
95   Robert Kudrie, 'Did Blacklisting Hurt the Tax Havens?' [2009] 12 (1) Journal of Money Laundering Control 1,3; OECD, 'List of Uncooperative Tax Havens' <http://www.oecd .org/countries/monaco/listofunco-operativetaxhavens.htm> accessed 17 January 2017.
96   William Hornblower, 'A Century of "Judge-Made" Law' [1907] 7 (7) CLR.
97   Rafael La Porta, Florencio Lopez-de-Silanes, Andrei Shleifer and Robert Vishny 'The Quality of Government' [1999] 15 (1) The Journal of Law, Economics and Organisation 222, 235; North Douglass, *Growth and Structural Change* (W.W. Norton, New York, 1981).
98   Some authors have however defined both to mean the same thing, for instance, Christine Parker defines regulation to include 'laws, formal and informal orders, subordinate rules issued by all levels of government'. See OECD, 'Reducing the Risk of Policy Failure: Challenges for Regulatory Compliance' (*OECD*, 2000) <https://www.oecd.org/gov/regul atory-policy/1910833.pdf> accessed 20 July 2016.
99   Julia Black, 'Critical Reflections on Regulation' (2002) 27 Australian Journal of Legal Philosophy 1, 11.
100 Mark Roe, 'Corporate Law's Limits' [2002] 31 (2) Journal of Legal Studies 233–271, Columbia Law and Economics Working Paper No.186.

This can be illustrated by the weak regulation of beneficial ownership in Nigeria, Togo and China, notwithstanding their tough legislation which signals a gaming of the law.[101] Beneficial ownership which refers to the 'real ownership' of funds or stocks held in trust or corporate vehicles is an identified avenue for ML/TF.[102] 'Nominees' who hold assets on trust have no executive authority over their clients' business affairs but are merely charged for use of their details on official documents. In certain instances, the nominee is usually unaware of the owner's true identity. Weak regulatory measures on beneficial ownership mean that funds may be laundered through this structure by industries that have evolved to meet the demands of individuals and organisations seeking privacy for legitimate and illegitimate reasons.[103] These weak regulatory measures can however be supplanted by parliamentary committees, the ombudsman, competition commissions or judicial review.[104] The parliamentary committee's role was decisive in ensuring financial due process in the Nigerian Securities and Exchange Commission.[105]

Fourthly, there is a global challenge to evaluate the effectiveness of AML/ CFT legislations and resulting regulations. Academics have noted the difficulties in estimating the annual cost of laundering due to varying and evolving money laundering techniques, especially in underground banking methods.[106] There remains a concern that actions based on AML/CFT laws would be inaccurate and ineffective. Levi and Gilmore contend that it was never clear that measures such as confiscation and monitoring constituted a significant condition for success.[107]

101 TI, 'Were G20 Corruption Promises Nothing More than a Photo –Op?' (12 November 2015) (TI, 2015) <http://www.transparency.org/news/feature/were_g20_corruption _promises_nothing_more_than_a_photo_op> accessed 1 January 2016; Mimi Lau, 'Loophole for the Corrupt: China and US worst in G20 for Transparency over "Real Ownership" of Shares and Companies' (South China Morning Post: Policies and Politics 12 November 2015) <http://www.scmp.com/news/china/policies-politics/article/1878350/ loophole-corrupt-china-and-us-worst-g20-transparency?__hstc=52789303.810863f5634 170c81c80dbc356af6baa.1450137600060.1450137600061.1450137600062.1&__hssc =52789303.1.1450137600063&__hsfp=1119992871> accessed 21 May 2016.
102 FATF, 'FATF Guidance on Transparency and Beneficial Ownership' (*FATF*, 2014) <http: //www.fatf-gafi.org/media/fatf/documents/reports/Guidance-transparency-beneficial -ownership.pdf> accessed 1 April 2016; *Temenos* (n 75).
103 FATF GAFI, Financial Action Task Force, 'Summary of the First Mutual Evaluation Report Anti-Money Laundering and Combating the Financing of Terrorism – Peoples Republic of China' (*FATF*, 29 June 2007) <http://www.fatf-gafi.org/media/fatf/documents/reports /mer/MER%20China%20full.pdf> accessed 10 June 2016.
104 Georgina Lawrence, 'Who Regulates the Regulators' (Centre for Study of Regulated Industries, Occasional Paper 16, 2012) 27 <http://www.bath.ac.uk/management/cri/ pubpdf/Occasional_Papers/16_Lawrence.pdf> accessed 11 February 2017.
105 Idris Kasumu's Blog, 'Arunma Oteh Faces Query Over Hostilities in SEC' (*Idris Kamusu's Blog*, 10 May 2012) <http://idriskasumu.blogspot.co.uk/2012/05/> accessed 11 February 2017.
106 Michele Fletcher, 'China's Underground Bank' (Global Financial Integrity, 16 July, 2014) <http://www.gfintegrity.org/chinas-underground-bank/> accessed 21 January 2016.
107 M. Levi and William Gilmore, 'Terrorist Finance: Money Laundering and the Rise of Mutual Evaluation: A New Paradigm for Crime Control' [2002] 4 (2) European Journal of Law Reform 87.

This indictment can be backed by the 2015 INCSR which revealed that China's involvement in money laundering is still growing, as it currently leads the world in illicit capital flow.[108] Additionally, in 2016, the International Narcotics Control Board (INCB) raised concerns over increased drug trafficking and laundering in West African States.[109] This reveals the challenges in gathering empirical data for measuring the effectiveness of AML/CFT laws.[110] This scenario indicates that although contextually different, these jurisdictions suffer similar issues relating to mining data and combating illicit crimes.

Lastly, there is the argument on the cost involved in legislation and regulations. Studies have shown that, in certain jurisdictions, money laundering harms bank efficiency,[111] particularly given the cost-implication of compliance. However, compliance-related cost is not comparable to the risk money laundering could pose to the financial system, if it contributes to a financial crisis. Recent studies have however illustrated that tougher AML/CFT regulations are associated with reduced levels of ML/TF, particularly those that criminalise predicate offences and improve disclosure.[112]

Other arguments that critique the position of law as the bedrock of financial regulation include the role of market forces and customary norms. Posner[113] and Lessig[114] postulate that the assumption that legislation is the bedrock of regulatory effectiveness and compliance is erroneous and empirically unsubstantiated, as compliance is not a sequence of regulatory efforts. Posner attributes effective regulation to community customary norms rather than legislation,[115] whilst Lessig attributes it to market forces.[116] Taking such factors as primary influencers to compliance as opposed to law comes with consequences. Market forces can be manipulated, and customary norms do not necessarily take into consideration the interests of all parties – women for instance are usually prejudiced by customary norms in developing countries.[117]

---

108 See US Department of State, Diplomacy in Action, '2015 International Narcotics Control Strategy Report' (US Department of State, 2015) <http://www.state.gov/j/inl/rls/nrcr pt/2015/> accessed 30 April 2016.

109 Africanews, 'UN: Drug Trafficking on the rise in West Africa' (*Africanews*, 2 March 2016) <http://www.africanews.com/2016/03/02/un-drug-trafficking-on-the-rise-in-west-afr ica/> accessed 20 July 2017.

110 It is imperative to decipher if the AML/CFT structure evolved stronger in countries that have more developed laws and legal structures.

111 Donato Masciandaro and Alessandro Portolano, 'It Takes Two to Tango: International Financial Regulation and Off-shore Centers' (2003) Universita di Lecee Department of Economics Working Paper No.11/4 <https://papers.ssrn.com/sol3/papers.cfm?abstract _id=289541> accessed 1 May 2016.

112 *Chong, Lopez-De-Silanes* (n 86).

113 Richard Posner, 'Social Norms and the Law: An Economic Approach' [1997] 87 (2) The American Economic Review 365, 368.

114 Lawrence Lessig, 'The Zones of Cyberspace' [1996] 48 (5) Stanford Law Review 1403, 1406.

115 *Posner* (n 113).

116 *Lessig* (n 114).

117 *Posner* (n 113).

The above responses to the rejoinder illustrate that the role of law in financial regulation cannot be displaced. For this reason, the vagueness of the FATF soft laws have facilitated increased public-private partnerships in combating ML/TF.[118] Wlike argues that this explains the shift from rule-based to risk-based regulation, where banks engage in self-regulation unless indicators of risk are detected. The FATF has acknowledged these principles on the basis of pragmatism.[119] This pragmatism contributes to the argument that the development of law does not necessarily translate to robust AML/CFT regulations. Nevertheless, as shown above, in the absence of robust laws, proactive steps are usually not taken by ACs/EEs to combat illicit crimes. The effectiveness of legislations is however not solely dependent on transplantation, but on the design of the law.

Design of the Law

Where laws would serve as a precondition for effective regulation, the content and drafting technique employed is vital. Poorly drafted laws give room for subjective interpretation by regulators and financial institutions, which facilitates gaming of the law, thus resulting in breach. Bossu and Chew assert that the problems with banking laws are not inherent in local circumstances but attributable to challenges in drafting and designing laws globally.[120] However, given the positioning of developed countries in training ACs/EEs in legislative drafting through their agencies, it can be assumed that the robustness of laws are subject to jurisdictional circumstances.[121]

The question then is, to what extent have international network bodies like the FATF and Basel Committee on Banking Supervision (BCBS) provided sufficient legislative or regulatory guidance to ACs/EEs? This question is posed against the background of the FATF recommendations and exemplified with Recommendation 3 on criminalisation.

Recommendation 3 (Money Laundering Offence) states that 'Countries should criminalise money laundering on the basis of the Vienna Convention and the Palermo Convention. Countries should apply the crime of money laundering

118 Marie Wilke, 'Emerging Informal Network Structures in Global Governance: Inside the Anti-Money Laundering Regime' [2008] 77 (4) Nordic Journal of International Law 509, 511; See 'Wolfsberg Anti-Money Laundering Principles for Private' (The Wolfsberg Group, 2012) <http://www.wolfsberg-principles.com/pdf/standards/Wolfsberg-Private-Banking-Prinicples-May-2012.pdf> accessed 10 June 2016.
119 Jared Wessel, 'The Financial Action Task Force: A Study in Balancing Sovereignty with Equality in Global Administrative Law' [2007] 13 Widener Law Review 169, 193; Marie Wilke, 'Emerging Informal Network Structures in Global Governance: Inside the Anti-Money Laundering Regime' [2008] 77 (4) Nordic Journal of International Law 509, 518.
120 *Bossu and Chew* (n 31).
121 Victor Thuronyi, 'Drafting Tax Legislation' (Tax Law Design and Drafting: IMF, 1996) 2 <https://www.imf.org/external/pubs/nft/1998/tlaw/eng/ch3.pdf> accessed 11 February 2017.

to all serious offences, with a view to including the widest range of predicate offences'.[122]

'Should', the operational word in Recommendation 3, which also resonates in other recommendations, reflects the persuasive nature of the framework document. The soft law documents express more of a moral obligation than a mandatory requirement. The non-mandatory signpost to the Vienna and Palermo Conventions leaves room for over-inclusion or under-inclusion in legislative drafting. For this reason, legislative documents in various countries do not meet up with the expectations of the recommendations. Hinterseer argues that the leverage given to legislators places them in a quandary between controlling the abuse of financial services and penalising those who utilise these services legitimately.[123] The soft law adaptation system has however created a situation where financial institutions may be unduly penalised despite compliance with obligations mandated by criminal law.[124] This illustrates the limitation of the FATF as an inter-governmental body blindsided to law-making but focused on standard setting.

This shortcoming is further highlighted by the recommendations review (or selection process). Potential recommendations are proposed to the FATF plenary by the FATF's Policy Development Group.[125] The plenary then presents the proposal before its members and associate members to deliberate on its adoption. Noting the power asymmetry in the deliberation process, EENA5, a GIABA staff member stated that 'there are powers that their opinions supersede the others'.[126] Acknowledging this, Rose Cecily contended that recommendations are produced by the consensus reached by largely developed like-minded states.[127] However developed, precision is sometimes forfeited for compromise during the negotiation process. Thus, without conceding transparency and flexibility, the FATF should ensure that there is an element of certainty afforded to legislative drafters to carry out their duties effectively or risk the gaming of the law.[128]

Primary and secondary legislation should have well-defined rules governing supervision of financial institutions. For instance, they should encompass

122 *FATF* (n 8).
123 Kris Hinterseer, *Criminal Finance: The Political Economy of Money Laundering in a Comparative Legal Context* (Kluwer Law International 2002) 290.
124 Despite the dearth of detailed analyses, governments have instituted extensive ML/TF legislative controls that criminalises ML/TF and facilitates prosecution. Inevitably, criminalisation raises juridical and practical challenges on interpretation and enforcement, and its interface with civil law areas.
125 Nicholas Ryder, Magaret Griffiths and Lachmi Singh, *Commercial Law: Principles and Policy* (CUP, 2012).
126 EENA5, Researcher, GIABA Interview with EENA5, 'Telephone Call' (2017).
127 Cecily Rose, *International Anti-Corruption Norms: Their Creation and Influence on Domestic Legal Systems* (OUP 2015) 55.
128 This can be done thoroughly through its explanatory notes/plenary meetings.

independence, accountability, resourcing and legal protection for supervisors.[129] The inclusion of these would indicate the required absence of government or industry interference with the role of the supervisor to avoid regulatory capture.[130] The mandate of the supervisor and the ambits of his powers should be properly set out. It should be clearly stated whether the supervisors will be granted executive powers over banking laws, or limited powers which would be determined based on the implementation of regulations.[131] Both options have implications; whilst the former grants the supervisor broad regulatory powers in unforeseen instances and grants the opportunity to catch up with advances not captured by legislation, it however makes regulation susceptible to arguments that it was not established on sufficient legal grounds. Contrariwise, where subject to regulations, it restricts the ability of supervisors to react to issues not expressly stated by the legislation. Limiting the discretionary powers of the supervisor harms the market, as it may lead to frequent update of the law, which regulatory bodies and institutions may struggle to adjust to.

For the above reason, the IMF/World Bank provides technical assistance to enable legislative draftsmen to construct robust laws. However, does this legal guidance take into consideration the level of development of countries or their local circumstances? In collaboration with the United Nations Office on Drugs and Crime (UNODC), the IMF crafted model legislation on money laundering for countries to adopt.[132] Such model laws come across as a prototype that does not address the particular local circumstances of countries. EENA3 argues that the legal development of countries is not factored into discussions on law formulation, rather, the process of law-making smacks of quasi-imperialism.[133] He exemplifies this with the case of Sri Lanka which was pushed to adopt AML/CFT laws by the IMF, without factoring in its weak legal system or its attempt to settle a war with the Tamel Tigers, an insurgent group that would have viewed the adoption of the AML/CFT standards as bad faith.

EENA1 however argues that the IMF does not necessarily engage in a 'one-size-fits-all' approach, but spends time discussing with countries and customising standards.[134] He posits that such modifications take into consideration the legal development, framework and culture of countries. EENA1 exemplifies

129 BCBS, 'Consultative Document: Core Principles for Effective Banking Supervision' (BCBS, 20 March 2012) <http://www.bis.org/publ/bcbs213.pdf> accessed 1 February 2016.

130 Pierre C. Boyer and Jorge Ponce, 'Regulatory Capture and Banking Supervision Reform' [2012] 8 (3) Journal of Financial Stability 1, 10.

131 *BCBS* (n 129); Marc Quintyn and Michael W. Taylor, 'Regulatory and Supervisory Independence and Financial Stability' (2002) IMF Working Paper WP/02/46 <https://www.imf.org/external/pubs/ft/wp/2002/wp0246.pdf> accessed 19 November 2016.

132 UNODC, 'Model Legislation' (*UNODC*) <https://www.unodc.org/unodc/en/money-laundering/Model-Legislation.html> accessed 10 August 2017.

133 EENA3, Anti-Money Laundering Specialist (CAMS), Expert Witness and Former Banking Regulator (FDIC), Interview with EENA3, 'Telephone Call' (2017).

134 EENA1, Consulting Counsel, Financial Integrity Unit, IMF, Interview with EENA1, 'Telephone Call' (2017).

his stance by alluding to recommendation 4 on *Confiscation and Provisional Measures* which clearly states that 'Countries should consider adopting measures that allow...proceeds or instrumentalities to be confiscated without requiring a criminal conviction (non-conviction based confiscation)...to the extent that such a requirement is consistent with the principles of their domestic law'. Although precise, this standard allows for some manoeuvre to give precedence to domestic law when drafting legislation or regulations, a feature that model laws may be blindsided to. Conceding, EENA1 asserts that prior to the institutionalisation of discussions that served as a prelude to technical assistance, ACs were involved in 'copying, pasting and publishing laws' such as the penalty of 15 years for ML/TF, which were not often implemented.[135] EENA1 acknowledges that the involvement of ACs, coupled with the deference to their domestic legislation has led to the inclusion of pieces of legislation in the right place in the legal framework. Examples include the addition of standards relating to criminalisation in the country's criminal code and the reduction of sanctions from five to ten years imprisonment.[136] These were achievable mainly through partnership with Inter-Governmental Group Against Money Laundering in West Africa (GIABA). Although better design of the law has led to remarkable improvement in technical compliance, this does not translate to effective compliance.

EENA1's arguments, though practical, do not acknowledge that the transplantation of AML/CFT laws in ACs was simply to evade sanctions of the FATF. Hence whilst a penalty of 15 years might have been unsuitable, ACs adopted it to avoid sanctions and repercussions that flow thereof. Additionally, whilst recommendation 4 may have provided room for 'domestic requirements', alongside recommendations 37 and 39, other recommendations impose a blanket requirement. This would severely limit the IMF's ability to tailor-fit legislations to a country's domestic challenges or its ability to take into consideration the level of legal development, without breaching its collective principal arrangement with the FATF.

The literature on the design of the law is however incomplete without an appraisal of the current and potential lawmakers. EENA1 argues that prosecutors and legislators alike, inclusive of law schools and students, are wary of new topics on how to fight financial crime and hence kick against them. An example of such an area is civil confiscation, a FATF recommendation that permits the confiscation of proceeds of crime without a criminal conviction.[137] This is largely rejected in countries where laws require that a civil confiscation can only commence after a criminal conviction, because it is regarded as an affront on traditional legal structures. Such countries usually refuse to amend their laws to reflect the evolving requirement of standards. This is also the case with the FATF requirement on criminal liability of legal persons, that is, the conviction of a legal entity misused by criminals. Countries have however failed to amend their laws

---

135   Ibid.
136   Ibid.; Money Laundering (Prohibition) Act 2011 Explanatory Memorandum.
137   *EENA1* (n 134).

for non-conformity with national laws and norms. This indicates that although the design of laws is seemingly good, there is still room for improvement to eliminate existing bottlenecks.

The design of law reiterates the argument that law is insufficient as a sole precondition for robust regulation of AML/CFT as it can be gamed. Additionally, the strength of well-designed laws cannot be divorced from broader political and economic settings in which they function.[138] Therefore, law must be discussed in concert with confidence as preconditions for effective regulation.

Confidence as a Precondition for Effective Regulation

Absence of confidence in financial institutions destabilises an orderly market and increases market volatility. This warrants action from financial regulators to make and enforce regulations aimed at resolving a destabilised market. Governments across jurisdictions devote resources and manpower to guarantee against systemic and non-systemic risk to the market. Otherwise, the market may remain volatile, resulting in an unexpected crash, which would trigger loss of confidence.

Ruxiev and Dow assert that confidence is the backbone of financial institutions and systems and is thus necessary in a free enterprise system.[139] Presenting a graphical representation of this assertion, they liken the financial system to an inverted pyramid built on confidence in outside money held as reserves in the central bank by commercial banks.[140] If confidence in outside money falls, there is a danger that the entire inverted pyramid of the private financial sector may collapse.[141] This indicates that internal and external factors contribute significantly to the build-up of confidence.

To this end, this chapter argues that effective regulation requires confidence. Confidence in this context is further subdivided into four thematic areas; confidence in financial stability, political and governmental systems, institutional systems and regulation and enforcement. To explain these, it is imperative to understand the concept of confidence.

Defining Confidence

Black's Law Dictionary defines 'confidence' as 'trust, reliance (or) grounds of trust'.[142] The interchangeable nature of the words indicate that 'trust' and 'con-

---

138 Cheryl Gray, 'Reforming Legal Systems in Developing and Transitional Countries' [1997] Finance and Development 14, 14.

139 Kobil Ruziev & Sheila Dow, 'A Re-Evaluation of Banking Sector Reforms in Transition Economies: Intentions and Unintended Consequences' *in* Kobil Ruziev and Nicholas Perdikis (eds.) Development and Reforms in Financial Economies (Taylor & Francis 2016) 88.

140 Ibid.

141 Ibid.

142 The Black's Law Dictionary (*The Law Dictionary*) <http://thelawdictionary.org/confidence/> accessed 1 January 2016.

fidence' are not mutually exclusive. Confidence is derived from the legitimate expectations of specific actions from people or institutions due to the rules, conventions and morals which dictate their activities.[143] Kaufman and Ciesolka postulate that this expectation is built on trust in robust regulatory frameworks and actors loyalty to the framework and each other.[144] Where such trust is established, investors can entrust a financial institution with the management of their assets and depositors will be restrained from withdrawing banked funds at the slightest sign of market turbulence. Legitimate expectations can however be violated, resulting in financial crises and devastating effect on financial stability and integrity. Therefore, confidence is critical.

Murphy argues that financial regulations should be constructively designed to mitigate risks in stressed conditions and be seen as mitigating such risk to stimulate confidence.[145] The appearance of a crack in the system occasioned by information asymmetry can cause a mini crisis of confidence leading to investor withdrawal.[146] This denotes a twofold problem. Firstly, withdrawal – a catalyst for increased cash transaction[147] which facilitates ease of laundering across weak borders. Secondly, information asymmetry between financial institutions, regulators and stakeholders. In such instances, stakeholders' confidence and their rational expectations will not be dependent on the actual health of individual banks, but moulded on the chance of future bailouts, hence relying on information on government's financial constraints and bailout policy.[148]

Scholars have argued that drastic alterations in stakeholders' confidence are only affected by massive scandals[149] such as the Asian crisis.[150] While this is usually

---

143 Bernhard Schlink, 'Wirtschaft und ertrauen' *in Berhand Schlink Vergewisserungen u ber politik, schreiben und Glauben* (Zurich: Diogenes Verlag, 2005).

144 Christine Kaufmann & Mirja Ciesolka, 'Wann Baute Noah die Arche – Vermo gensverwaltung als Akteurin einer nachhltigen Marktenwicklung' *in* Peter R Isler and Romeo Cerutti (eds.), *Vermogensverwaltung III* (Zurich: Schriftenreihe Nr. 105 des Europainstututes an der Universitat Zurich 2010) 3.

145 David Murphy, *Maintaining Confidence* (LSE Financial Markets Group Research Centre, 2012).

146 Sophia Grene, 'European Banks Suffer a Mini Crisis of Confidence' (Financial Times March 6, 2016) <https://next.ft.com/content/daf9f04a-e07d-11e5-8d9b-e88a2a889797> accessed 2 January 2016.

147 *Ruziev, Dow* (n 139).

148 Se Jik Kim and Ashoka Mody, 'Managing Confidence in Emerging Market Bank Runs' (2004) IMF Working Paper WP/04/235, 26 <https://www.imf.org/en/Publications/WP/Issues/2016/12/31/Managing-Confidence-in-Emerging-Market-Bank-Runs-17847> accessed 18 June 2–16.

149 Lindsay A. Owens, 'The Polls – Trends, Confidence in Banks, Financial Institutions and Wall Street, 1971–2011' [2012] 76 (1) Public Opinion Quarterly 142, 147.

150 Augustine Pang and Yeo Su Lin, 'Crisis Aftermath: Image Reinvention in Restoring Corporate Reputation and Regaining Stakeholder Confidence' (Nanyang Technological University, 2014) <http://www.wkwsci.ntu.edu.sg/Research/Pages/Crisis-Aftermath-Image-Reinvention-in-Restoring-Corporate-Reputation-and-Regaining-Stakeholder-Confidence.aspx> accessed 13 May 2016; Patthanij Gonjanar and Supawadee Suttirak, 'The

the case, pockets of mini crises of confidence indicate that business cycles affect public opinion in this domain. Murphy stressed how important it is for investors to believe that banks can absorb losses in stressed conditions, observing that well-capitalised banks do fail, but confidence in them allows these banks survive long enough to correct problems that may arise.[151]

These arguments illustrate that 'confidence' vested in the ability of financial regulatory bodies to deliver cannot be underestimated. Confidence serves as a guide to financial regulators, keeping them abreast of public opinion in financial regulation and is a check against illicit activities in financial institutions.

CONFIDENCE IN FINANCIAL STABILITY

ML/TF weakens financial institutions and poses harm to the stability of the financial market as a whole. When stakeholders evaluate accessible information on financial markets, findings of illicit crimes can destroy their confidence. To retain their confidence in the system, there must be a clear framework for crisis management, resolution, discipline and prevention.

A crisis management structure sends a message to stakeholders that potential disruptions to financial stability would be properly managed.[152] A lender of last resort, which is usually a central bank and robust deposit insurance system, falls within the framework of crisis management.[153] Their roles are critical for systemic protection against financial instability. Central to their mandate is minimising the likelihood of a bank run whilst also protecting depositors and retaining their confidence in the financial system.[154] The presence and effectiveness of these institutions enhance stakeholder confidence in financial stability.

Crisis management institutions have their distinct functions, including the mandate to curtail illicit crimes. Central banks offer loans to financial institutions with liquidity problems,[155] particularly those that pose systemic risk.[156] This mandate is discretionary. Goodhart contends that central banks would usually

---

Effects from Asia's Financial Crisis: Factors Affecting on the Value Creation of Organisation' [2012] 3 (16) International Journal of Business and Social Science 78, 81.

151 *Murphy* (n 145).

152 Dalvinder Singh and John Raymond LaBrosse, 'Developing a Financial Crisis Management' [2012] 2 OCED Financial Market Trends 1, 8.

153 Arnoud W.A. Boot & Matej Marinc, 'Crisis Management and Lender of Last Resort in the European Banking Market' *in* Pietro Alessandrini, Michele Fratianno and Alberto Zazzaro (eds.) *The Changing Geography of Banking and Finance* (Springer, 2009) 234.

154 Nicholas J. Ketcha, 'Deposit Insurance System Design and Considerations' [1999] 7 Strengthening the Banking System in China: Issues and Experience, Policy Paper 221, 223; James Barth, Cindy Lee and Triphon Phumiwasana, 'Deposit Insurance Schemes' [2013] Encyclopedia of Finance 207, 208; *Singh, LaBrosse*, (n 152) 1, 3.

155 Charles Goodhart, 'Balancing Lender of Last Resort Assistance with Avoidance of Moral Hazard' *in* Frank Heinemann, Ulrich Kluh and Sebastian Watzk (eds.) *Monetary Policy, Financial Crises and the Macroeconomy: Festschrift for Gerhard IIIing* (Springer, 2017) 20.

156 Ibid.

not support the most egregiously badly-behaved banks,[157] indicating that where banks are heavily dependent on laundered funds for liquidity and suffer a solvency crisis, such banks are unlikely to receive support from the central banks. For example, the Bank of Credit and Commerce International (BCCI), which although had become 'too big to fail' could not be restructured with liquidity provision by the Bank of England (BoE) due to large-scale evidence of fraud, money laundering and terrorist financing.[158] Hence, the BoE let the bank fail. Whilst this may lead to a short-term crisis of confidence, long-term, stakeholders would support the government's decision.

The deposit insurance system protects depositors from losses caused by a bank's inability to pay its debts when due as a result of bank failure.[159] This is usually done by insuring customers' deposits up to a certain limit.[160] However, the deposit insurers are only required to pay eligible depositors and not launderers, demonstrating that endemic cases of financial crime can undermine the deposit insurers pay-out mandate. This indicates that some due diligence is mandatory to delineate clean money from illicit funds in the process of transfer of funds from a collapsed bank. The presence of a deposit insurer can lead to a moral hazard; a situation whereby financial institutions take on more risk than necessary given the desensitised approach of insured customers to the bank's risk appetite.[161] However, profit-maximising launderers would be deterred from depending on such bailouts and may seek alternative, non-regulated institutions to deposit their funds. This may no doubt protect the desensitised customers and elevate their confidence in financial stability.

In addition to crisis management structures, market discipline also provides confidence in financial stability and serves as a precondition for effective regulation. This form of discipline, which complements official supervision, is utilised where there is unavoidable information asymmetry between financial institutions and their supervisors or forbearance associated with political considerations.[162] These circumstances place an onus on market participants to monitor financial institutions and discipline excessive risk-taking behaviours.[163] Market discipline is however largely dependent on the dissemination

---

157 Ibid.
158 Senator John Kerry and Senator Hank Brown, *The BCCI Affair: A Report to the Committee on Foreign Relations* (102nd Congress 2nd Session Senate Print 1-2-140) 358.
159 Patricia A. McCoy, 'The Moral Hazard Implications of Deposit Insurance: Theory and Evidence' (Seminar on Current Developments in Monetary and Financial Law, October 2006) 8.
160 Ibid.
161 Ibid. 1; Gillian Garcia, 'Deposit Insurance and Crisis Management' (2000) IMF Working Paper WP/00/57/2000, 19 <https://www.imf.org/external/pubs/ft/wp/2000/wp0057.pdf> accessed 10 January 2017.
162 Constantinos Stephanou, 'Rethinking Market Discipline in Banking: Lessons from the Financial Crisis' *in* Panagiotis Delimatsis and Nils Herger, *Financial Regulation at the Crossroads: Implications for Supervision* (Wolters luwer, 2011) 212.
163 Ibid.

of information within the market, appropriate incentives to reward well-managed institutions and arrangements that ensure that investors are not insulated from the consequences of their decisions.[164] Where market discipline is robust, information such as governments' lending or guarantee of lending is disclosed. Furthermore, governments are not permitted to influence or override commercial decisions to achieve public policy objectives.[165] Given the complementary nature of this disciplinary approach to official supervision, it engineers improved compliance in financial stability.[166] For this reason, there is improved emphasis on market discipline as illustrated by Pillar 3 in the Basel II framework which is focused on obtaining empirical data on banks' capital, risk profile and risk assessment.[167]

Financial institutions saddled with ML/TF problems are prone to concentration, operational, legal and reputational risks.[168] The reflection of these risks to the market however undermine the confidence of stakeholders, especially depositors and investors, prompting withdrawal of funds from the affected bank or country.

In handling risks that undermine effective regulation, supervisors and relevant authorities are to identify high-risk sectors and ensure proper direction of resources. These risks differ in presentation and in manifestation and thus would require a tailored approach towards their resolution. This would improve internal and external confidence within the system.

CONFIDENCE IN THE POLITICAL AND GOVERNMENTAL SYSTEM

Confidence in the political system is vital for financial stability, serving as a precondition for effective regulation. Political systems that create an atmosphere where rule of law prevails and crime is punished deter ML/TF activities and, more importantly, create confidence in FIs. This can be attributed to the fact that FIs become increasingly adherent to prescribed regulations, knowing that breach would result in severe penalties and reputational damage. This indicates a top-down approach where the scene is set by the executives elected or appointed into power.

This top-down approach requires that governments do not compromise on sound macroeconomic policies for effective regulation. In the absence of sound policies, discrepancies such as astronomical spending by government, excessive

---

164 *BCBS* (n 2).
165 BIS, 'Working Paper on Pillar 3 – Market Discipline' (2001) *BCBS* <https://www.bis.org /publ/bcbs_wp7.pdf> accessed 10 November 2016.
166 *Stephanou* (n 162).
167 *BIS* (165).
168 Kern Alexander Kern, Rahul Dumale and John Eatwell, *Global Governance of Financial Systems: The International Regulation of Systemic Risk* (OUP, 2006); BCBS, 'Sound Management of Risks Related to Money Laundering and Financing of Terrorism' (*BCBS*, June 2017) <http://www.bis.org/bcbs/publ/d405.pdf> accessed August 2017.

shortage or supply of liquidity may affect financial stability.[169] Furthermore, certain government policies may specifically use banks and other financial intermediaries as instruments and this may inhibit effective supervision.[170] Where this is allowed to flourish, the state in question would not experience effective regulation.

Sequential patterns in ACs have indicated that government representatives may be actively involved in ML/TF,[171] exemplified in Sub-Saharan ACs where corruption is an integral part of the political fabric. In Sierra Leone, government officials were recently embroiled in the laundering of UKAid for 'peacekeeping' in excess of £1million.[172] In Uganda, education ministers embezzled £800,000 intended for schools.[173] Reports indicate that corrupt officials in Senegal, Equatorial Guinea and Nigeria have used their children to embezzle funds overseas.[174] These actions are antithetical to financial stability and the dictates of good governance, thereby undermining confidence in the governments. Former South Africa's president, Jacob Zuma, faced a no-confidence vote partly due to corruption allegations, which warranted his removal from office.[175] Similarly, there was an unsuccessful coup attempt on the current president of Equatorial Guinea due to prevalent corruption and inequality.[176] Where the government is successful in curtailing intelligence leakage, the resulting information asymmetry may create a false sense of confidence in the political and financial system.

Confidence in the political and governmental system also encompasses political will. This requires that governments must fight corruption and be publicly

169 Anand Sinha, 'Financial Sector Regulation and Implications for Growth' (CAFRAL-BIS International Conference on Financial Sector Regulation for Growth, Equity and Financial Stability in the Post-Crisis World, Mumbai, November, 2011).

170 Examples of such policies include accumulation of large quantities of government securities, reduced access to capital markets due to government controls or growing imbalances; degradation of asset quality after loose monetary policies; and government-directed lending or forbearance requirements as an economic policy response to deteriorating economic conditions.

171 David Thompson, 'Panama Papers: Putin Associates Linked to "Money Laundering"'(*BBC News*, 2 April 2016) <http://www.bbc.co.uk/news/world-europe-35918845> accessed 2 May 2016.

172 Robert Rayner and Steven Swinford, 'Wikileaks Cables: Millions in Overseas Aid to Africa was Embezzled' (*The Telegraph*, 5 February, 2011) <http://www.telegraph.co.uk/news/worldnews/wikileaks/8304640/WikiLeaks-cables-millions-in-overseas-aid-to-Africa-was-embezzled.html> accessed 10 July 2017.

173 Ibid.

174 Anne Look, 'Investigations Underway into Corruption and Embezzlement in West Africa' (*Voice of Africa*, 5 December 2012) <https://www.voanews.com/a/west-Africa-corruption-investigation/1558980.html> accessed 19 August 2016.

175 Alexander Winning, 'South Africa's Zuma Faces new No-confidence Vote this Month' (*Reuters*, 2 February 2018) <https://uk.reuters.com/article/uk-safrica-politics/south-africas-zuma-faces-new-no-confidence-vote-this-month-idUKKBN1FM1B9> accessed 10 February 2018.

176 Business Day, 'Clashes in Equatorial Guinea after Thwarted Coup' (Business Day, 4 January 2018) <https://www.businesslive.co.za/bd/world/africa/2018-01-04-clashes-in-equatorial-guinea-after-thwarted-coup/> accessed 10 February 2018.

perceived to be doing so. Resultantly, there would be effective regulation of regulators, publication of enforcement actions, timely judicial decisions and effective partnership for repatriation of laundered assets. Furthermore, independence of the legislative and law enforcement agencies would be guaranteed to ensure that they are not prey to corruption, under-resourced or demoralised. Without such circumstances backed by political will, the presence of sturdy legislation as a precondition for effective regulation would be invalidated. Political will and the resultant AML/CFT regime will encourage domestic coordination and exchange of information amongst the various domestic parties at policy and operational levels.[177]

CONFIDENCE IN THE INSTITUTIONAL SYSTEM

Confidence in the institutional system is largely dependent on agencies external to FIs. Government regulations, budgetary allocations and factors such as the global financial crisis play a vital role in ensuring trust in FIs in any economy.

Positive governmental regulations are crucial in building and sustaining confidence as a precondition for effective regulation. These regulations ensure a suitable political and economic climate for investment and business. Where, however, government policies create a hostile environment that facilitates corruption, high inflation and unemployment rates coupled with low social wellbeing, FIs would be unable to carry out their day-to-day business satisfactorily.[178] This indicates that the public's confidence in institutions may be pro-cyclical.[179] So, when countries experience a sharp rise in unemployment, there is a dramatic decline in public confidence in national governments and financial sectors.[180] This suggests that decline in confidence may sometimes be a standard response to a cyclical downturn.[181] Thus, governments must be challenged to ensure long-term domestic growth as opposed to short-term investment, to engineer confidence within FIs.

Additionally, there are concerns that budget constraints contribute to the loss of confidence in FIs. Insufficient funding provision to equip regulatory bodies with the technical skills to combat illicit crimes promotes an environment where criminals are permitted to thrive. Additionally, on a tight budget, regulators

---

177 The World Bank, 'Combating Money Laundering and the Financing of Terrorism: A Comprehensive Training Guide' (*The World Bank*, 2016) <http://siteresources.worldbank.org/FINANCIALSECTOR/Resources/CombattingMLandTF.pdf> accessed 12 April 2016 and 10 July 2017.

178 Montfort Mlachila, Dennis Dykes, Sabrina Zajc, Paul-Harry Aithnard, Thorsten Beck, Mthuli Ncube and Oskar Nelvin, 'Banking in Sub-Saharan Africa: Challenges and Opportunities' (European Investment Bank, January 2013) <http://www.eib.org/attachments/efs/economic_report_banking_africa_en.pdf> accessed 10 July 2017.

179 Betsey Stevenson and Justin Wolfers, 'Trust in Public Institutions over Business Cycle' (2011) Federal Reserve Bank of San Francisco Working Paper Series 11/2011, 4 <https://www.frbsf.org/economic-research/files/wp11-11bk.pdf> accessed 5 March 2016.

180 Ibid.

181 Ibid.

usually work with fewer staff or unmotivated staff in comparison with staff of FIs, otherwise known as under-regulation which may result in regulatory arbitrage. Recog nising the occurrence of this situation in ACs, interviewee EENA4 stated that, 'from all African countries, Nigeria has the most resources directed to curb ML/TF, but it is usually diverted'.[182] Such diversion leads to under-provision of necessary resources which has socio-economic consequences.

Budget constraints effects are evidenced by the limited regulation on inter-net and mobile use, which is wherecrime in ACs/EEs are directed.[183] Within the African continent, Nigeria records the highest overall value of fraud.[184] The 2015 Nigeria Deposit Insurance Corporation (NDIC) report disclosed a 15.71% increase in fraud cases.[185] It revealed that most fraudulent activities were particu-larly relating to internet banking and bank card fraud.[186] Undoubtedly, these activ-ities pose significant cost to the Nigerian economy and hinder financial inclusion. It illustrates the limited regulatory powers, capacity and resources in addressing these issues.[187] Globally, Brazil and India are ranked second and third, respec-tively in the list of countries with the highest fraud levels.[188] These include credit card and internet fraud which facilitate ML/TF. The false sense of security pro-jected by banks in Brazil has done little to salvage the situation.[189] For instance, a 2014 financial cyber threat report ranked Brazil second in online banking fraud and financial malware.[190] The situation seems to be worsening with research show-ing that cyber-attacks grew by 197% and online fraud by 20% in 2014.[191] The

182 EENA4, Interview with Anonymous, 'Telephone Call' (2017).

183 Jayshree Chavan, 'Internet Banking-Benefits and Challenges in an Emerging Economy' [2013]1 (1) International Journal of Research in Business 19, 23.

184 Sahara Reporters, 'Nigeria is the Most Fraudulent Country in Africa, KPMG Report Says' (Sahara Reporters, 23 November 2012) <http://saharareporters.com/2012/11/23/ni geria-most-fraudulent-country-africa-kpmg-report-says> accessed 10 July 2016.

185 NDIC, 'NDIC Releases 2015 Annual Report' (NDIC, 2015) <http://ndic.gov.ng/ndic-r eleases-2015-annual-report/> accessed 10 May 2017.

186 Ibid.

187 Abel Ezeoha, 'Internet Banking Strategy in a Highly Volatile Business Environment: The Nigerian Case' in *E-Banking and Emerging Multidisciplinary Processes: Social, Economical and Organizational Models* (Business Science Reference) 76.

188 Shirley Inscoe, 'Global Consumers: Losing Confidence in the Battle against Fraud' (*Aite*, June 2014) <http://www.aciworldwide.com/-/media/files/collateral/global-consu mers-losing-confidence-in-the-battle-against-fraud-report> accessed 21 March 2016. The United Arab Emirates (UAE) has the highest rate of fraud overall at 44%, followed by China at 42%, and India and the United States at 41% each (Figure 1).

189 Fernando Guerreiro De Lemos, President of Banrisul boasted, 'Our bank is a leader in banking technology' See, Forbes Custom 'Brazil: Confidence is the Keyword' (*Forbes Custom*), <http://www.forbescustom.com/EconomicDevelopmentPgs/BrazilP1.html> accessed 1 May 2016.

190 Kaspersky Lab Report, Financial Cyber Threats in 2014 (Kaspersky Lab Report, February 2015) <https://securelist.com/files/2015/02/KSN_Financial_Threats_Report_2014 _eng.pdf> accessed 2 May 2016.

191 Centre of Studies, 'Response and Treatment of Security Incidents in Brazil' (Centre of Studies, 28 July 2015) <http://diariodocomercio.com.br/noticia.php?tit=numero_de_ata ques_ciberneticos_cresceu_197&id=157314> accessed 2 May 2016.

effect is reduced stakeholder confidence as customers who have once experienced fraud are less likely to continue using the banking mode that exposed them to that risk.[192] It also indicates the need for customers to be properly informed of fraud levels and their responsibility to safeguard their bank details.[193]

The global financial crisis is also an external force that affects confidence. The crisis accentuated a shift in investment from developed countries to ACs/EEs who were not so severely hit by the financial crisis.[194] This shift offered stakeholders an opportunity to diversify their risks beyond developed countries. The 2014 OECD report stated that whilst confidence in FIs in general declined in OECD countries, it increased in other countries, including Russia[195] and Brazil.[196] These reports indicate the need for FIs in emerging economies to continually ensure compliance with regulatory authorities to retain confidence in their financial systems. It also requires that FIs accept their pivotal role in the fight against ML/TF.[197]

Scholars, however, believe that although highly resisted by practitioners, the obligations of banks and other FIs to curtail ML/TF is unlikely to diminish soon[198] because they are able to monitor the movement of funds. Professor Rider states:

> it is not surprising that increasingly those who handle other people's money have been placed in the forefront of attacks on money laundering...of course, it is a very unpleasant place to be, particularly if you are ill prepared, ill advised, unsupported and probably entirely sacrificial.[199]

From Rider's statement, two factors which are required for improved functionality and confidence in the institutional system can be deduced. First, efficiency of

192 *Inscoe* (n 188).
193 Ibid.
194 International Trade Forum Magazine, 'New World Order: Shifting Markets in Trade, Investment and Opportunity' [2010] 2 International Trade Forum; OECD, *Society at a Glance 2014: OECD Social Indicators* (OECD Publishing, 2014); Lindsay Owens, 'Confidence in Banks, Financial Institutions and Wall Street, 1971–2011' [2011] 76 (1) Public Opinion Quarterly 142, 147.
195 OECD, Society at a Glance 2014: OECD Social Indicators (OECD Publishing, 2014).
196 Forbes Custom 'Brazil: Confidence is the Keyword' (*Forbes Custom*), <http://www.forb escustom.com/EconomicDevelopmentPgs/BrazilP1.html> accessed 1 May 2016 – Brazil, land of the samba, Sugar Loaf Mountain and Copacabana beach, is also distinguishing itself in the midst of the worldwide financial crisis by the resilience of its economic performance.
197 Vern Mckinley, 'After the Crisis: Revisiting the "Banks Are Special" and "Safety Net" Doctrines' (Mercatus Research – George Mason University 2015) <https://www.mercatus .org/system/files/McKinley-Are-Banks-Special.pdf> accessed July 2017.
198 Steven Beattie, Donald Lamson and Marc Oliver Schmidt, 'Anti-Money Laundering Issues for Financial Institutions' (*Financier Worldwide*, December 2013) <http://www.financier worldwide.com/anti-money-laundering-issues-for-financial-institutions/#.Vw6nV7TF vkI> accessed 10 January 2016.
199 Barry Rider, 'The Limits of the Law: An Analysis of the Interrelationship of the Criminal and Civil Control in the Control of Money Laundering' [1999] 2 (3) Journal of Money Laundering Control 209, 210.

FIs in curtailing ML/TF backed by supervision and secondly, an institution supported by insurance in the event of a mishap. These two factors are not mutually exclusive but are contradictory. The paradox is that the presence of an insurance system would allow banks to engage in excessive risk-taking, with the knowledge that they would be bailed out.[200] The resolution of these goals requires effective and continuous supervision to set risk parameters whilst ensuring that regulatory capture is avoided.

In light of the above, regulatory agencies are to ensure that FIs have a framework to facilitate strict adherence to AML/CFT regulations as a precondition for entry and continued operation in the market. This would foster a culture of accountability where efficiency is also measured by the competence and reputation of board members in adhering to the AML/CFT regulatory requirements. Such an atmosphere would protect the reputation of FIs and the public interest in their integrity. Operationalising this framework comes with challenges. For instance, regarding financial secrecy laws, certain jurisdictions mandate FIs' staff like lawyers and other bank professionals to honour the confidentiality of their contract with their client(s).[201] However, their position as gatekeepers in curtailing illicit crimes places them in a legal quandary whereby the contract on confidentiality may be honoured in breach to uncover illegality. Scholars and practitioners have argued that bank secrecy may sometimes be for legitimate purposes[202] like tax avoidance. Whilst acknowledging that illegal use can occasion untold hardships, there are significant cost implications associated with appropriately distinguishing legitimate from illegitimate use.[203] Moreover, any less than universally applied bank secrecy policy can have stringent adverse consequences for institutions, triggering a race to the bottom. Conversely, strict adherence to FATF recommendations by institutions can unveil the rot in non-compliant institutions. In these instances, there are increased possibilities of customers wishing to safeguard their savings or interests by moving their business to more adherent institutions. Additionally, dissolving bank secrecy laws for AML/CFT risks can trigger competition within FIs and drive customers to underground banking, especially in ACs which are still largely unbanked and unregulated.

Thus, it is evident that resolving this dilemma requires the building, acceptance and integration of the culture of integrity within FIs in such a way that is not antithetical to the business of banking. Although countries vary in their adoption of laws, policies and standards aimed at combating AML/CFT as well as in the quality of their institutional framework and general level of development, an

---

200 Adhering to the laws may cause even the best regulatory system to err in their supervision.

201 For instance, in Brazil bank secrecy cannot occur without the judiciary's approval. See Jorge Nemr, 'Brazil' *in* Gwendoline Godfrey and Francis Neate, *Bank Confidentiality* (5th edn, IBA, 2011).

202 Hinterseer argues that financial secrecy laws are said to protect private assets from public authorities' wrongful expropriation *Hinterseer* (n 123) 286.

203 This should be executed in a manner that curtails compliance cost and comparative disadvantage on legal service providers.

optimal institutional framework should encompass certain key traits. Examples of these traits include an operative corporate governance where the tone is set at the top, as well as continuous staff training.[204] The challenge is however not usually one of intention but of complexity and execution.[205] To this end, Wheatley argues that 'it is not straightforward to govern individuals' behaviour in large, heavily stratified banking institutions. Invariably, it takes time'.[206]

This illustrates the difficulty for FIs to control the risk posed by their staff based on individual behavioural values and choices. In seeking measurable conclusions, value judgements are to be made and competitive peer evaluations may replace standard appraisals.[207]

The effect of curtailing these factors is financial stability and improved confidence of stakeholders in FIs.

CONFIDENCE IN REGULATION AND ENFORCEMENT

The robustness of regulation is dependent on the strength of the law and legal structures in place. Law is crucial in determining the framework of regulations and providing a safe and sound banking system. For this reason, Cheffins argues that in the absence of laws, and the legal protections that flow thereof, investors will be deterred from investing in an affected country, but would consider it risky and fear possible exploitation.[208] Recognising this, the BCBS highlights the role of the law as a precondition for effective regulation.[209] Hinterseer contends that legal measures such as regulations will remain subject to market discipline because information blind spots will permit money laundering to fester.[210] However, this view ignores the study by Masciandaro which highlights the inverse relationship between the degree of diffusion of ML activities and AML regulation in a given economy.[211] This indicates that tougher regulation can reduce ML and its feeder activities, controlling for other country characteristics, legal enforcement and potential endogeneity.[212] This is particularly so because, in reaction to regula-

---

204 On customer relationship, forgery detection etc. to build confidence from within whilst managing existing relationships.

205 Martin Wheatley, 'Debating Trust and Confidence in Banking' (*Financial Conduct Authority*, 28 May 2015) <https://www.fca.org.uk/news/debating-trust-and-confidence-in-banking-> accessed 3 December 2015 and 10 May 2016.

206 Ibid.

207 Ibid.

208 Brian Cheffins, 'Does Law Matter? The Separation of Ownership and Control in the United Kingdom' (2000) ESRC Centre for Business Research, University of Cambridge Working Paper No 172, 463 <https://www.cbr.cam.ac.uk/fileadmin/user_upload/centre-for-business-research/downloads/working-papers/wp172.pdf> accessed 8 May 2016.

209 *BCBS* (n 129).

210 *Hinterseer* (n 123) 414.

211 Donato Masciandaro, 'Money Laundering: The Economics of Regulation' [1999] 7 European Journal of Law and Economics 225, 239.

212 *Chong, Lopez-De-Silanes* (n 86).

tions, financial intermediaries mandatorily engage in CDD, ensure transparency in financial dealings and construct a culture that facilitates accountability.

Adopting a suitable enforcement mechanism is crucial in curtailing ML/ TF, allowing for the collection of information and the setting of rules that sanction misconduct. It also fosters a safe and sound banking system, expanding public disclosure, transparency, enhanced financial reporting and audit.[213] Two enforcement mechanisms can be adopted; the compliance-based approach (CBA) and/or the deterrence-based approach (DBA).[214] Adopting a mechanism is dependent on factors, such as the gravity of the approved person's offence, the perception of the regulatory agencies and the characteristics of the offender or institution.[215] During examination of FIs, regulatory bodies consider the identity, personal history and responsiveness of the regulated to sanctions or assistance.[216] They also consider whether the regulated is engaged in a business, the fall of which poses systemic risk. If the regulated's activities would not have disastrous consequences on the economy, the regulator can use the CBA. Where, however, the activity of the regulated carries grave consequences, e.g., when it relates to the liquidity of a bank, the regulator may use the DBA. These approaches are not mutually exclusive. The CBA focuses on creating an avenue for interaction between the regulator and the regulated,[217] to ensure that it complies with regulatory rules. The DBA is focused on imposing sanctions and retributions[218] to serve as deterrence. This exposes FIs to a variety of sanctions which may be punitive or non-punitive.[219] FIs may also be subjected to legal claims, with possible civil, administrative or criminal sanctions.[220]

Confidence in institutions is based on the potency and immediacy of prescribed actions, the regulatory institutions' ability to follow through, the frequency of interactions with regulatory institutions and possible publication of enforcement actions. The enforcement activities and design of adopted regulations are vital in determining and influencing compliance. Becker and Stigler argue that institutions comply with regulations when they believe that non-compliance will be harshly dealt with.[221]

213 Gary Becker, 'Crime and Punishment: An Economic Approach' *in* Nigel Fielding, Alan Clarke and Robert Witt (eds.), *The Economic Dimensions of Crime* (Macmillan Press Ltd) 15.
214 Dalvinder Singh, *Banking Regulation of UK and US Financial Markets* (Ashgate Publishing 2007) 113–115.
215 Ibid.
216 i.e., whether a political citizen, an amoral calculator or organizationally incompetent. Ibid 113–115.
217 Ibid. 113 -115.
218 Ibid.
219 Ibid. (n 232).
220 Ibid. (n 232).
221 Gary Becker, 'Crime and Punishment: An Economic Approach' *in* Nigel Fielding, Alan Clarke and Robert Witt (eds.), *The Economic Dimensions of Crime* (Macmillan Press Ltd)

The deterrent effect of criminal punishment, the harshest form of DBA is highly contested. Reviews on the impact of varying levels of punishment do not suggest that harsher sanctions deter illicit activities.[222] Moreover, Coglianese et al. emphasise that the organisationally incompetent may not be amenable to criminal sanctions.[223] Black further expressed fears that criminal sanctions would not impact behaviours long-term.[224] The practicalities of holding bank officials responsible for fiduciary duties or to a criminal prosecution are also problematic.[225] The practical and conceptual difficulties that occasion this method of enforcement have led to the advancement by Brummer of the compliance-based approach.[226] He asserts that effective monitoring systems can have important deterrent effects, having been designed to deter and prevent launderers from using FIs as conduits for illicit transfers.[227] However persuasive the compliance approach seems, it does not exist in a vacuum, as it occurs within the context of an application of legal rules.[228]

Enforcement mandates that in the absence of regulatory capture,[229] regulatory agencies must be willing to authorise FIs to comply with AML/CFT regulations in the form of negotiated non-compliance. Publicity of enforcement actions has

---

15; George Sigler, 'The Optimum Enforcement of Laws' *in* Gary Becker and William Landes (eds.) *Essays in the Economics of Crime and Punishment* (NBER 1974).

222 Anthony Doon and Cheryl Webster, 'Sentence Severity and Crime: Accepting the Null Hypothesis' [2003] 30 Crime and Justice 143, 146.

223 Cary Coglianese, Elizabeth K. Keating, Michael L. Micheal and Thomas J. Healey, 'The Role of Government in Corporate Governance' [2004] 1243 Faculty Scholarship 219, 234 cf with Lois M. Musikali, 'Why Criminal Sanctions Still Matter in Corporate Governance' [2009] International Company and Commercial Law Review 1.1.

224 Julia Black and David Kershaw, 'Sanctions for Bank Directors: Response from Professor Julia Black and Professor Kershaw, London School of Economics and Political Science' (LSE Collections 11 January 2013) <http://www.lse.ac.uk/collections/law/news/San ctions%20-%20submission%20from%20Black%20and%20Kershaw%2011%20Jan%202013 .pdf> accessed 16 July 2013.

225 William Cohan, 'How Wall Street's Bankers Stayed Out of Jail' (*The Atlantic*, September 2015) <http://www.theatlantic.com/magazine/archive/2015/09/how-wall-streets-b ankers-stayed-out-of-jail/399368/> accessed 1 January 2016; Jed Rakoff, 'The Financial Crisis: Why Have No High-Level Executives Been Prosecuted' (*The New York Review of Books*, 2014) <http://www.nybooks.com/articles/2014/01/09/financial-crisis-why-no -executive-prosecutions/> accessed 13 January 2016.

226 Chris Brummer, 'How International Financial Law Works and How It Doesn't' [2011] 99 Georgetown Law Journal 257, 290; John Braithwaite and Philip Petit, Not *Just Deserts. A Republican Theory of Criminal Justice* (Oxford: Clarendon Press 1990) 3.

227 *Brummer* (n 226); Levi Michael and Peter Reuter, 'Money Laundering' [2006] Crime and Justice 289, 296.

228 Compliance entails applying measures designed to attain the legal mandate, with the regulator being primarily concerned with improved outcomes rather than prosecution results; see Keith Hawkins, *Law as Last Resort: Prosecution Decision-Making in a Regulatory Agent* (OUP 2002) 253.

229 Emerging economies have better compliance; however, compliance levels are still substandard. For more information on negotiated non-compliance between the inspector and the enforcement officer, see Peter Grabosky and John Braithwaite, *Of Manners Gentle: Enforce-*

also been undertaken in various jurisdictions, to punish erring financial institutions and deter others from engaging in sharp practices or economic crimes. By so doing, governments define what is considered acceptable, hoping that policymakers ensure that unacceptable activities are less economically attractive. This is no doubt a way to eliminate the benefits of crime through a deterrent approach, including sanctions. It is however recognised that deterrence is not necessarily the best option for certain institutions, as already discussed.

In light of this, regulatory bodies' ability to ensure robust enforcement systems aimed at improving confidence in the financial system depends on the quality of their workforce and the levels of interaction between regulatory bodies. Their effectiveness in achieving these is dependent on their understanding of the nature of criminal expertise and the cultural aspect of criminal organisations. However, in the absence of sturdy capacity and collaboration, expertise would be stretched and unable to deliver. This is typified with Nigeria, alongside other developing countries where ill-equipped regulatory bodies are unable to combat regulatory deficiencies, including illicit crimes.[230] In Brazil, although regulators are equipped with trained quality supervisors, this is challenged by the limited numerical capacity of its workforce.[231] Consequently, their ability to effectively combat ML/TF is restricted.

This argument is also applicable to the judicial system. The strength of the judiciary serves as a vital precondition for effective regulation. It plays a pivotal role in building stakeholder confidence in a financial system that offers significant protection. Cheffins asserts that a reliable and corrupt-free court system is crucial for speedy dispensation of justice, serving as a catalyst for confidence building in investors.[232] This argument emphasises that a corrupt system delays and possibly denies justice. It also creates an atmosphere where illicit activities become acceptable. This results in increased utilisation of a country's 'weak points' by criminal syndicates, confident in their profit maximisation in the face of the inability of judicial structures to issue sound judgements. This was the situation in Brazil, as recorded in its 2010 FATF Mutual Evaluation Report. It noted that although sentences and convictions were recorded for ML/TF, these were insignificant compared to the size of the country and the sophistication of its financial

ment Strategies of Australian Business Regulatory Agencies (First published 1986, OUP in association with Australian Institute of Criminology) 230.

230 Peter Reuter, 'Illicit Financial Flows and Governance: The Importance of Disaggregation' (World Development Report, 2017) <http://pubdocs.worldbank.org/en/67701148 5539750208/WDR17-BP-Illicit-Financial-Flows.pdf> accessed 2 February 2018; OECD, 'Illicit Financial Flows from Developing Countries: Measuring OECD Responses' (*OECD*, 2014) <https://www.oecd.org/corruption/Illicit_Financial_Flows_from_Developing _Countries.pdf> accessed 12 February 2018.

231 Alba Kiihl, 'U.S. and Brazil AML Audit Comparative Analysis How a Review of AML Legislation and Practices Can give a Board of Directors the Confidence to Invest – or Not' (*ACAMS*, 2011) <http://www.acams.org/wp-content/uploads/2015/08/US-and-Brazil-AML-Audit-Comparative-Analysis-Alba-Kiihl.pdf> accessed 14 June 2017.

232 *Cheffins* (n 208).

system.[233] In response, Brazil introduced specialised trial courts in financial crimes and money laundering to ensure improvements in the quality of decisions and information exchange.[234] This novel approach ensures that quality judgements are not sacrificed on the altar of expediency, especially given the complexities of cases involving ML/TF. Consequently, Brazil has been making strides towards combating corruption in the judiciary, particularly by improving the interface between the regulators, police, judiciary and public prosecution.[235]

Improving the capacity of judges can contribute positively to the financial market. La Porta et al. support this assertion with empirical research indicating a strong correlation between the strength of a country's law and order and the size of its equity market.[236] This suggests that an independent and efficient judiciary may guide and determine investment from other countries[237] whilst ensuring that erring FIs are punished effectively. However, the expertise and ability of judges can be hindered by existing laws which may cause lawyers to exploit procedural irregularities to favour their claim; or simply stall the case. Courts may not have the necessary legal tools to ensure that the goals of criminal law are achieved.[238] In instances that concern substantive law, judges are sometimes forced to engage in judicial activism to bring the purpose of legislations to life. This would be necessary where the tools provided by the legislature are insufficient to ensure conviction. This is imperative as statistics have illustrated that lower levels of enforcement are invariably related with higher levels of ML activities.[239] This indicates that well-crafted laws in corporate bankruptcy, contract, private property, tax, consumer protection and financial regulation are consistently enforced through a well-structured public infrastructure. In the absence of these, there can be a weakening of financial systems, markets and confidence. Thus, countries are charged with improving their legal systems.[240]

In the presence of structured and robust laws, regulatory institutions and enforcement agencies must work closely to ensure access to information and swift action in curbing illicit crimes. The conflict of interest that hinders this cooperation becomes clearer when the issue of trust between enforcement agencies and FIs is broached. Whilst FIs presume that clients are innocent until guilty, the law enforcement agencies think otherwise because they realise that swift action

---

233 FATF, 'Brazil Mutual Evaluation Report 2010' (*FATF*) <http://www.fatf-gafi.org/media/fatf/documents/reports/mer/MER%20Brazil%20full.pdf> accessed 10 May 2016
234 2003 by Resolution No 314/2003 of the Federal Justice Council.
235 See the Judgement of Criminal Case no 470 (The Mansalao Case) by the Brazilian Supreme Federal Court.
236 Rafael La Porta, Florencio Lopez-de-Silanes, Andrei Shleifer and Robert Vishny, 'Legal Determinants of External Finance' [1997] 11 (3) The Journal of Finance 1131, 1132.
237 Ibid.
238 *Chong, Lopez-De-Silanes* (n 86).
239 Ibid. 78, 106.
240 See Demirguc-Kunt and Detragiache, 'The Determinants of Banking Crises in Developing and Developed Countries' [1998] 45 (1) IMF Staff Papers 82–109.

is needed to freeze or confiscate the assets of a suspect.[241] Notwithstanding their differences, the strategies of enforcement bodies in supplementing regulatory approaches in combating illicit crimes cannot however be undermined.

Differences in the Transplantation and Confidence Trajectory between African Countries and Brazil, Russia, India, China and South Africa (the BRICS)

From the foregoing discourse, it is evident that transplantation and confidence patterns differ in ACs/EEs. For instance, Nigeria's AML/CFT standards suffered from legislative and enforcement lapses that hindered implementation. Conversely, China opted for stricter legislative and enforcement standards to ensure implementation of standards. EENA1 asserts that these differences are attributable to variances in compliance levels and strength of institutions.[242] EENA1 acknowledges that all ACs are unique, however, corruption is a rife issue and stifles the growth of sturdy institutions.[243] He adds that whilst corruption is rife within the BRICS, these countries have been more proactive in combating these illicit crimes.[244] More so, the BRICS have an agenda to build reputable institutions to facilitate cross-border information exchanges, an agenda that is not firmly on the table of ACs.

Concurring with EENA1, EENA2 states that 'by having more at stake, having an AML/CFT framework that is consistent with the international standards is a bigger priority for EEs than for African states'.[245] This is attributable to EEs financial sector size and interlinkage of these financial sectors with other financial sectors within and outside the region. Thus, EEs are subject to scrutiny by other jurisdictions and groupings like the OECD and G7. Consequently, it becomes a political matter to adopt the AML/CFT laws and ensure a conducive environment for this to thrive. In contrast, ACs have a more contained and smaller financial sector. Thus, ACs have other pressing issues to focus on which is exclusive of an established AML/CFT framework.

Another explanation for the disparity in legal transplantation and confidence in ACs/EEs is their timeline of ascension to the FATF membership. EENA1 stated that 'BRICS became members of the FATF in the late 90s – now they are going through their third or fourth mutual evaluations...whereas African countries only became members of the FSRBs post-2001'.[246] Whilst membership is not necessarily a catalyst for improved transplantation and confidence, it can be deduced that early ascension allowed the BRICS understand the FATF standards better,

---

241 *Hinterseer* (n 123).
242 *EENA1* (n 134).
243 Ibid.
244 Ibid. (n 257).
245 *EENA2* (n 66).
246 *EENA1* (n 134).

and faster. The lapse of time before the ascension of ACs to associate membership positions undoubtedly hindered their ability to adapt to the standards, transplant them and improve their confidence levels.

Perspective on Compliance with Global Standards

Academics have increasingly scrutinised factors that precipitate government compliance with international instruments.[247] The economics perspective argues that compliance is determined by a comparative analysis between the supposed benefits of non-compliance with the probability of detection and punishment.[248] Therefore, an effective enforcement system with severe punishment will ensure that compliance is attractive to amoral calculators.[249] Political determinants of compliance are largely dependent on the direction of country leaders' political will and the reaction of pressure groups to non-compliance.[250] Bounded rationality and behavioural theory postulates that there are operational risks which undermine compliance – these risks are triggered by the limits of organisations in processing and acting on information.[251] Alternative explanations include social norms,[252] negative effect of formal sanctions, deterrent impact, legitimacy and trust.[253] In certain instances, compliance is determined by moral obligations and social influence.[254]

An appraisal of the varying compliance perspectives provides an understanding of the interplay between international agreements, domestic politics and financial

247 Beth Simmons, 'International Law and State Behavior: Commitment and Compliance in International Monetary Affairs' [2000] 94 (4) American Political Science Review 819–835; Harold Koh, 'Review: Why Do Nations Obey International Law?' [1997] 106 (8) The Yale Law Journal 2599–2642; Andrew Guzman, 'A Compliance Based Theory of International Law' [2002] 90 (6) California Law Review, 1823–1887; Benedict Kingsbury, 'The Concept of Compliance as a Function of Competing Conceptions of International law' [1998] 19 Mich. J. International Law 345–368; Oran Young, *Compliance With Public Authority* (Baltimore: JHUP, 1979); Ronald B. Mitchell, 'Regime Design Matters: International Oil Pollution and Treaty Compliance' [1994] 48 (3) International Organizations 425, 439.
248 *Becker* (n 221) 46.
249 Robert Kagan and John Scholz, 'The "Criminology of the Corporation" and Regulatory Enforcement Strategies' *in* K. Hawkins and J.M. Thomas (eds.) *Enforcing Regulation* (Boston, Mass: Kluwer-Nijhoff 1084) 323.
250 Emmanuel C. Areno, 'Beyond Lip Service: Using Social Contracts to Achieve Participatory and Accountable Governance in the Philippines' *in* Carmen Malena (eds.) *From Political Won't to Political Will: Building Support for Participatory Governance* (Kumarian Press, 2009) 246.
251 James March and Herbert Simon, *Organizations* (1st edn, 1958, 3rd edn, Blackwell Business 1993).
252 John Coffee, 'Do Norms Matter? A Cross-Country Evaluation' [2001] 149 (6) University of Pennsylvania Law Review 2151, 2175.
253 John Scholz and Mark Lubell, 'Trust and Taxpaying: Testing the Heuristic Approach to Collective Action' [1988] 42 (2) American Journal of Political Science 398–417.
254 Jon Sutinen and Keith Kuperan, 'A Socio-Economic Theory of Regulatory Compliance' [1999] 26 (1) International Journal of Social Economics 174, 178; Ian Ayres & John Braithwaite, *Responsive Regulation* (OUP 1992) 124.

institutions on ML and counter-terrorism.[255] Examining the perspectives reveals that the motivations for compliance are either calculated, normative or social[256] and operate as a legal or non-legal factor. As a result, policy responses for enhanced compliance have moved from a pure-command and control approach to one favouring a mix of enforcement strategies as listed in the regulatory pyramid.[257] These changes are predicated on the general agreement that the borderless nature of illicit crimes warrants an internationally coordinated response[258] managed by IFIs, tackled through cooperation amongst states and implemented by states.[259] This logic is premised on the fact that the AML/CFT regime is only as strong as the weakest link in the chain, because astute criminals would reroute their finances to countries with weaker regimes.[260]

Regarding AML/CFT regulation, the crucial question is whether the commitment of ACs/EEs to the FATF standards and compliance interests are aligned? What factors influence their regulatory and compliance responses? The next section will address this succinctly, given that the following chapters discuss this in more detail.

Compliance as a Function of Legal Factors

Scholars have argued that various legal factors affect the compliance of countries to domesticated international standards. Whilst Yepes refers to cultural, institutional, socio-economic and financial factors,[261] Simmons refers to reputational concerns as one of the most crucial factors that propel compliance.[262] Kal Raustiala and Anne-Marie Slaughter[263] refer to enforcement and legalisation as some factors that influence compliance. However, this book restricts these legal factors to democracy and rule of law, enforcement and the mirroring of law.

---

255 Beth E. Whitaker, 'Compliance Among Weak States: Africa and the Counter Terrorism Regime' [2010] 36 Review of International Studies 640, 644.

256 Winter Soren and Peter May, 'Motivation for Compliance with Environmental Regulations' [2001] 20 (4) Journal of Policy Analysis and Management 678, 680.

257 Ian Ayres & John Braithwaite, *Responsive Regulation* (OUP 1992).

258 Jason Sharman, 'Power and Discourse in Policy Diffusion: Anti-Money Laundering in Developing States' [2008] 52 (3) International Studies Quarterly 635, 640.

259 Peter Romaniuk, 'Institutions as Swords and Shields: Multilateral Counter-terrorism Since 9/11' [2010] 36 Review of International Studies 591, 594.

260 This is not always the case as criminals know that even if they move their finances to such states, the odds might not favor them. It is not a veritable land for investment as opposed to countries like England which promises higher investment returns.

261 Concepcion Yepes, 'Compliance with the AML/CFT International Standard: Lessons from a Cross-Country Analysis' (2006) IMF Working Paper 11/177, 17 <https://www.imf .org/external/pubs/ft/wp/2011/wp11177.pdf> accessed 10 July 2015.

262 *Simmons* (n 247).

263 Kal Raustiala & Anne-Marie Slaugher, 'International Law, International Relations and Compliance' *in* Walter Carlnaes, Thomas Risse and Beth Simmons (eds.) *The Handbook of International Relations* (Sage Publications, Ltd., 2002) 538, 539–542.

Compliance Engineered by Democracy and Rule of Law

Key amongst factors that influence government's compliance to international instruments is the presence of domestic political institutions driven by democracy.[264] Studies suggest that non-democratic governments are less likely to comply as opposed to liberal democratic governments.[265] Reasons for this include the democratic government's respect for legal processes through the judiciary or the presence of domestic interest groups.[266] Civil societies, court processes and democratic political constituencies may act as enforcement mechanisms pressuring governments to comply. Consequently, Simons argues that governments with respect for rule of law and stable democracy are unlikely to harm their reputation by breaching commitments to standards.[267] Conversely, the restriction on human rights in dictatorial regimes will prevent activists pushing the government for results.[268] These arguments suggest that democracies are reliable partners in ensuring compliance with AML/CFT regulations.[269]

However, it may be too simplistic to assume that non-democratic countries are not compliant with international standards, or that countries with entrenched rule of law comply. Other factors may come into play that propel countries to comply notwithstanding the rule of law status, such as the culture or imperative need of a country.

Enforcement-Driven Compliance

According to the enforcement model, compliance occurs 'in the shadow of the law', given that state behaviour can be shaped by concerns about the possibility of adjudication, rule enforcement and legal sanctions.[270] Within the context of AML/CFT regulation, the FATF does not have an adjudicatory framework or process to resolve conflicts and mandate compliance, thus foreclosing the possibility of international adjudication.[271] This shortcoming has however not limited

---

264 Helen Milner, *Interests, Institutions and Information: Domestic Politics and International Relations* (PUP, 1997) 110.
265 Beth Simmons, 'Compliance with International Agreements' [1998] Annual Rev. Polit. Sci.75, 83; Anne-Marie Slaughter, 'International law in a World of Liberal States' [1995] EJIL 503, 534.
266 Andrew Guznam, 'International Law: A Compliance Based Theory of International Law' [2002] California Law Review 1823–1887. This is not always the case, with the recent rise in social networking usage, sometimes the loudest voice is what counts and not necessarily the perception of pressure groups.
267 *Simmons* (n 265).
268 The dictatorial nature of Cameroonian and Chadian governments has curtailed compliance.
269 They may be anti-compliance advocates. Conversely, authoritarian governments may comply better with global AML/CFT standards.
270 Olu Fasan, 'Compliance with WTO Law in Developing Countries: A Study of South Africa and Nigeria' (PhD Thesis, London School of Economics 2006).
271 Norman Magurura, *The Global Anti-Money Laundering Regulatory Landscape in Less Developed Countries* (Routledge, Taylor & Francis Group, London and New York, 2012), which gives a suggestion for the FATF to legitimise itself.

its ability to drive compliance through sanctioning. This idea is central to the economics perspective which is focused on a comparative analysis between the cost and benefit of compliance.[272] The assumption is that states' motivation to comply with standards is influenced by their interests and only in manipulating benefits and costs defined in terms of those interests can compliance be achieved.[273] Therefore, where enforcement powers are used, severe punishment will ensure that compliance is attractive even to amoral calculators.[274]

Enforcement in this context refers to mechanisms such as sanctions. Within the framework of international law, the aim of enforcement is to put 'measures (in place) to ensure the observance of rules'.[275] As stated, the FATF executes enforcement through reputational damage of countries, further isolating them from the global financial market. This stimulates a strong deterrence for countries that want to remain strong players in the market.

However, counterarguments hold that compliance is better induced through active management instruments, such as verification, review and monitoring.[276] The FATF provides such enforcement tools through the Mutual Evaluation Reports (MER).[277] Mutual evaluations entail gathering information on countries to decipher their compliance levels. Information derived from this 'review and verification process' forms the basis for further interactions with countries and decisions on sanctions.

Active management and enforcement cannot however be totally divorced. Koh observes that the success of the management model is sometimes dependent on the 'shadow of sanctions, however rare or remote that possibility might be'.[278] This indicates that whilst dialogue established through monitoring and review may be ineffective on their own, when backed with sanctions – countries may be willing to comply. So also, countries may be unresponsive to sanctions or threat of the same in the absence of persuasiveness.

Additionally, the enforcement and management models derive their validity from laws and regulations. Laws and regulations are not constricted to serving as preconditions for effective regulation but work to ensure compliance within states. For laws and regulations to ensure compliance within states, national

---

272 Alan Skyes and Eric Posner, 'An Economic Analysis of State and Individual Responsibility under International Law' (2006) Coase-Sandor Working Paper Series in Law and Economics 279/2006 <https://chicagounbound.uchicago.edu/cgi/viewcontent.cgi?article=1042&context=law_and_economics> accessed 6 March 2016.
273 Ibid.
274 *Kagan and Scholz* (n 249).
275 Tam Christian, 'Enforcement' *in* G. Ulfstein, T.Marauhn and A. Zimmermann (eds.). *Making Treaties Work* (CUP, 2007) 319–407.
276 Abram Chayes and Antonio Handler Chayes, *The New Sovereignty: Compliance with International Regulatory Agreements* (HUP, 1995) 197.
277 FATF, 'Mutual Evaluations' (*FATF*) <http://www.fatf-gafi.org/publications/mutualevaluations/?hf=10&b=0&s=desc(fatf_releasedate)> accessed 5 January 2017.
278 Koh Harold, 'Why do Nations Obey International Law' [1997] 106 Yale Law Journal 2599, 2639.

legislation and implementation is necessary.[279] Laws are symbolic and catalyse practical changes because laws usually serve as the primary basis upon which courts can enforce judgement, or regulators issue penalties in cases of AML/ CFT.

However, as earlier discussed, enshrined laws may not always be a determinant factor for compliance, even when non-compliance results in reputational damages. Black argues that it is overly simplistic to assume that putting laws in place would result in predictions on improved compliance solely based on reputational concerns.[280] This indicates the likely repulsion towards laws and the need for laws and regulations to be translated to regulatory practice. This requires that regulatory bodies make clear their mandate. A clear mandate may however not result in formal adherence to regulations, especially when such a mandate is prescriptive or technologically outdated.

Law: A Mirroring of Society?

An age-old argument is that laws reflect how a society views itself. Friedman states that 'legal systems do not float in some cultural void, free of space and time and social context: necessarily, they reflect what is happening in their own societies'.[281] Vago also argues that law reflects the intellectual, social, economic and political climate of its time.[282] Wendel Holmes's statement that 'the law, wherein, as a magic mirror, we see reflected, not only our lives, but the lives of all men that have been', encapsulates the mirroring thesis of law.[283] This view is reflected by Teubner's autopoiesis which views law as a deeply integrated aspect of society, and that the external environment influences law only as it is filtered through legal discourse.[284] According to this author, autopoietic systems, such as laws construct their images of other systems only through the distorting lens of their perceptual view.[285] When domestic laws which are considered legitimate conflict with international laws, the latter may be internalised gradually or not at all.[286] These arguments illustrate that law provides a representation of a society's values and norms.

---

279 Daniel Ho, 'Compliance and International Soft law: Why Do Countries Implement the Basel Accord' [2002] Journal of International Economic Law.
280 Julia Black, Martyn Hopper and Christa Band, 'Making a Success of Principles-Based Regulation' [2007] 1 (3) Law and Financial Markets Review 191, 194.
281 Lawrence Friedman, 'Borders: On the Emerging Sociology of Transnational Law' [1996] 32 Stan.J.Int'l L 65, 72.
282 Steven Vago, *Law and Society* (Englewood Cliffs, N.J: Prentice-Hall, 1981).
283 Oliver Holmes, Jr., *The Speeches of Oliver Wendell Holmes* (Cambridge, MA, 1981).
284 Gunther Teubner, *Law as an Autopoietic System* (Oxford/Cambridge, Blackwell Publishers, 1993); Niklas Luhmann, 'The Autopoiesis of Social Systems' *in* Felix Geyer and Jonannes Van Zouwen (eds.) *Sociocybernetic Paradoxes: Observation, Control and Evaluation of Self Steering Systems* (SAGE Publications, India, 1986).
285 Ibid.
286 Ibid. (n 299).

This argument has faced a myriad of contestation, particularly from the notion of transplantation of international law.[287] Transplantation holds that the transfer of rules, principles and legal concepts from one legal system to another usually occasions some measure of legal transformation, either voluntarily or otherwise.[288] Roos et a.l argue that laws are crossing geographical and cultural boundaries[289] and this has an impact on the social ordering of law.

Nevertheless, it is recognised that the surrounding social circumstances determine how rules are interpreted or function.[290] To that effect, the design or construction of globally applicable standards for governance should entail some flexibility for universal adaptability. Consequently, IFIs and the FATF should take into consideration the peculiarities of countries in crafting standards. It must not only interact with a set of countries, but all countries involved should have a say in the adaptability and applicability of standards for suitability.

Legal factors cannot by themselves drive compliance, but they work in tandem with non-legal factors. Non-legal factors are variable and not developed on the basis of legal considerations. They are nevertheless instrumental in shaping compliance responses of states.

Compliance as a Function of Non-Legal Factors

An examination of the preconditions that allow for effective regulation has given pointers to certain factors that can influence compliance outside the law. Five main factors are discussed. These include (1) political will, domestic conditions and policy priorities; (2) compliance-based reputational concerns; (3) legitimacy; (4) globalisation and integration; and (6) technical capacity and resources.

Political Will, Domestic Conditions and Policy Priorities

The concept of political will is elusive and ambiguous with various scholars defining it contextually.[291] However, this book adopts the definition by Post et al., that political will is the 'extent of committed support amongst key decision makers for a particular policy solution to a particular problem'.[292] This perspective reveals that political will is usually the collective aspiration of a majority of citizens within a country represented by decision-makers. These aspirations are reflected in budgetary allocations,[293] drive of civil societies, pro-regulatory interest groups,

---

287 Alan Watson, *The Evolution of Law* (Baltimore: JHUP, 1985).

288 Ibid.; Brian Z. Tamanaha, *A General Jurisprudence of Law and Society* (OUP, 2001).

289 R. Jagtenberg, E. Orucu and A. de Roos, 'Introduction', *in* Jagtenberg et al. (eds.), Transfrontier Mobility of Law (Boston: Kluwer Law International, 1995).

290 *Watson* (n 287).

291 Lori Post, Amber N.W. Raile and Eric Raile, 'Defining Political Will' [2010] 38.4 Politics & Policy 653, 653.

292 Ibid. 653, 659.

293 Ibid. (n 306) 653, 668.

voice of the people and determination of the different arms of government. This reveals that domestic conditions and policy priorities are crucial in generating political will.

Domestic conditions are also indicated in the system of government operational within a state. Scholars have argued that the level of democracy of states determines their compliance records.[294] They argue that internal structures, including budgetary allocations, reflect the policy priorities and the domestic conditions of a state.[295] Also, domestic politics has long been understood to determine the state's decision to accept international obligations.[296]

Yet, in certain instances, political will is foisted on a country through its external agreements. The extent to which this can produce compliance is however debatable. For instance, there are expectations that involvement of ACs/EEs with the FATF would propel political will within these states and translate to improved compliance. In such instances, compliance is largely dependent on the perception by states that the FATF's recommendations reflect their national interests and priorities.[297] For instance, countries faced with high-level predicate offences, including high crime rates, terror attacks, capital flight, tax evasion and diminishing financial stability are more inclined to comply with these recommendations to combat these difficulties. States that are predominately financially inclusive also tend to be more compliant with AML/CFT regimes.[298]

However ideal this may seem, the degree of political will and institutional commitment in responding to AML/CFT regulations may produce varying demands of accountability.

Compliance Based on Reputational Concerns

Scholars have argued that reputation affects state behaviour.[299] Goldsmith and Posner believe that states refrain from violating treaties or non-legal agreements simply because they are motivated by the need to avoid reputational loss.[300] Reputation encourages states to comply with international law.[301] This reputa-

---

294 *Slaughter* (n 265); Helen Milner and Andrew Moravcsik (eds.), *Power, Interdependence and Non-State Actors in World Politics* (PUP, 2009).
295 *Post, Raile, Raile* (n 291).
296 Beth Simmons, *Mobilizing for Human Rights: International Law in Domestic Politics* 23–56 (CUP 2009) 130.
297 Tatiana Tropina, 'Do Digital Technologies Facilitate Illicit Financial Flows?' (World Development Report: Digital Dividends, 2016) <http://pubdocs.worldbank.org/en/396 751453906608518/WDR16-BP-Do-Digital-Technologies-Facilitate-Illicit-Financial-Fl ows-Tropina.pdf> accessed 10 February 2017.
298 Hennie Ester et al., 'Implementing FATF Standards in Developing Countries and Financial Inclusion – Findings and Guidelines' (First Initiative, 2008) <http://cenfri.org/documen ts/AML/AML_CFT%20and%20Financial%20Inclusion.pdf> accessed 4 June 2016.
299 Jack GoldSmith & Eric Posner, *The Limits of International Law* (2005) 159.
300 Ibid. (n 314) 98.
301 Andrew Guzman, 'Reputation and International Law' [2005] 34 Ga J. Int'l n & Comp. L 379, 381.

tional perspective can be applied to the AML/CFT regime derived from the desire for financial stability and integrity – factors that can affect the reputation or credibility of countries. It also forms the basis for understanding the FATF's sanction through listing of countries.

Reputational concerns are not necessarily always external to a country; sometimes they are internal. For instance, the pressure for compliance with AML/CFT standards can come from large localised institutions which are more predisposed to comply for reputational reasons.[302] Such banks recognise that a 'good reputation' would enable them to compete effectively in the market. These efforts sometimes serve as a catalyst for increased national regulatory supervision on banks and other FIs.

There are concerns about the role of reputation in ensuring compliance. Downs and Jones argue that states have multiple reputations, not a single reputation.[303] So, whilst a state has a good reputation for complying with environmental standards, it may have a negative record for complying with ML standards. This suggests that reputations vary according to commitments. Consequently, with increasing global integration, reputational concerns alone are insufficient to ensure improved compliance,[304] as states would comply with standards that are more likely to be beneficial, or agreements with high sanctions that have a detrimental effect on their economy.

Legitimacy and Its Effect on Compliance

Legitimacy is crucial in encouraging compliance with regulatory standards and in motivating behavioural responses.[305] Proactive compliance with international law would be improved when institutions are considered legitimate; permitting ownership, inclusiveness and procedural fairness.[306] This is ingrained in Shaffer's perspective that legitimacy must be able to stand the test of input, throughput and output.[307] According to Tyler, such compliance is a catalyst for voluntary observance of the law and is preferred due to its cost-effective

---

302 S.G. Ashby and S.R.Daikon, 'The Value of Corporate Risk Management: Empirical Evidence from Large UK Companies' [1996] 1 (2) Risk Decision and Policy, 203–215; *Simmons* (n 247).

303 George W. Downs and Michael Jones, 'Reputation, Compliance and International Law' [2002] 31 JLS 95, 97.

304 Ibid.

305 Julia Black, 'Constructing and Contesting Legitimacy and Accountability in Polycentric Regulatory Regimes' [2008] 2 Regulation & Governance 138, 148.

306 Gregory Shaffer, *Transnational Legal Ordering and State Change* (Cambridge Studies in Law and Society, 2014).

307 Ibid. 50; cf with Bodnasky who asserts that legitimacy can be viewed in terms of representativeness, procedures and effectiveness. See Daniel Bodansky, 'The Legitimacy of International Governance: A Coming Challenge for International Environmental Law?' [1999] 93 (3) American Journal of International Law 596.

nature.[308] This varies from formal or constructive compliance by countries, which necessitates higher enforcement cost and is usually achieved through coercion.[309]

Given that the G7 and certain OECD countries formulated the FATF's standards, the extent to which 'associate members' can perceive the FATF or its standards as legitimate is questionable. The membership asymmetry within the FATF has occasioned arguments that a global hegemony exists[310] which facilitates an agency slack. This explains why the FATF has yet to gain acceptability and its ability to engineer compliance by ACs/EEs has been stalled. For this reason, it is argued that the FATF's standards and processes should be re-engineered, particularly its sanction scheme.[311]

Scholars have however argued that any re-engineering in favour of legitimacy ignores that fundamentally, soft law bodies such as the FATF are epistemic authorities. Hulsee and Kerwer argue that the FATF standards are derived from expertise rather than membership politics.[312] Acceding to this, Vibert asserts that the IFIs/TGNs belong to the knowledge world where their decision-making skills are dependent on their epistemic authority.[313] They draw on the procedure of the natural and social sciences to identify complications and frame policy responses.[314] This illustrates the FATF's projection as legitimate on the basis of the expertise wielded by its secretariat and staff in its processes. A position blindsided to the politics of the agenda within the institution and its effect on the FATF's rude design and compliance. The politics is evident in the composition of the experts from the private and public sectors who are mainly representatives of developed countries, a configuration that does not encompass or represent the views of developing countries. It is thus capable of undermining developing countries effectiveness with the FATF standards. This suggests that any re-structuring should de-politicise the FATF and ensure an expertise-based process that is inclusive of the views of developing countries.

---

308 Tom R. Tyler, *Why People Obey the Law* (PUP, 2006).
309 Cf with Rainer Hulsee who argues that coercion may be more cost effective and simpler for institutions to disseminate an unpopular regime. Rainer Hulsee, 'Even Clubs Can't Do Without Legitimacy: Why the Anti-Money Laundering Blacklist Was Suspended' [2008] 2 Regulation and Governance 459, 460.
310 Mark Suchman, 'Managing Legitimacy: Strategic and Institutional Approaches' [1995] 20 (3) Academy of Management Review 571, 588; Eric Helleiner, 'State Power and the Regulation of Illicit Activity in Global Finance' *in* R.H. Friman and P. Andreas (eds.) *The Illicit Global Economy and State Power* (Rowman & Littlefield, Lanham, 1999) 76.
311 As there was an absence of 'voice-able' members in standards formulation, lack of representativeness and procedural unfairness in its processes, thus hindering effectiveness.
312 Dieter Kerwer and Rainer Hulsee, 'How International Organisations Rule the World: The Case of the Financial Action Task Force on Money Laundering' [2011] 2 Journal of Int'l Stud. 50, 55.
313 Frank Vibert, 'Reforming International Rule-Making' [2012] 3 (3) Global Policy 391, 392.
314 Ibid.

Globalisation and Integration

Several macroeconomic variables determine a country's level of integration to the global financial market. These include a country's level of financial exposure, openness, relevance, transparency or the interconnectedness of its banking and financial markets.[315] The IMF utilises these indices in determining the systematic importance of a country.[316] Such categories separate countries whose financial sectors potentially impact on systemic stability from those that do not and subjects the former to a heightened surveillance process.[317] These variables arguably affect the level of compliance to international standards.

Countries plugged into the international economy arguably have more incentives to comply for two reasons: the level of supervision by multilateral institutions and the potential effect of sanctions. Supervision, which usually entails monitoring, can reveal the shortcomings of countries, a catalyst for reputational damages that such countries would rather avoid. Furthermore, the FATF sanctions meted out and backed by the IFIs have the effect of limiting the involvement of these countries in global economic activities – a position countries are uncomfortable about. Conversely, it can be argued that countries not connected to the international global economy may defer compliance knowing the limited effect of sanctions on them.

Nevertheless, the ability of countries not classed as 'systemically important countries' to renege on AML/CFT compliance is largely limited by the involvement of IFIs. As a precondition for financial assistance, IFIs have incorporated law reforms and compliance requirements.[318] Additionally, multilateral institutions and FIs within highly integrated countries use compliance with accredited standards to determine potential finance opportunities or threats within developing countries.[319]

Consequently, although the impact of globalisation and integration in propelling compliance cannot be overlooked, it need not be overelaborated. This is because countries have internal reasons that can propel compliance irrespective of external pressure.[320] More difficult is the position whereby internal factors within the country prevent compliance.

---

315 IMF, 'Mandatory Financial Stability Assessment under the FSAP' (*IMF*, 24 September 2014) <https://www.imf.org/external/np/fsap/mandatoryfsap.htm> accessed 4 May 2016 – warranting South Africa's compliance levels.

316 Ibid.

317 IMF, 'Mandatory Financial Stability Assessments Under the FSAP: Update' (*IMF*, 15 September 2013) <https://www.imf.org/external/np/pp/eng/2013/111513.pdf> accessed 7 October 2017.

318 I. Fletcher, L. Mistelis and M. Cremona (eds.) *Foundations and Perspectives of International Trade Law* (London: Sweet & Maxwell, 2001).

319 Ibid.

320 G. Garrett, 'Global Markets and National Politics: Collusion Course or Virtuous Circle?' [1998] 52 (4) International Organization.

Technical Capacity and Resources

Technical capacity of countries is crucial in ensuring compliance to international standards. Within the private and regulatory sector, a new market has emerged for lawyers, accountants, auditors, economists, front desk officers and other professionals. These gatekeepers are responsible for ensuring that the FATF recommendations are adhered to, particularly as regards strict CDD. It requires that financial transactions are monitored, and prompt reports made to the FIU where suspicion arises. These responsibilities require staff training in requisite skills required to drive the new market.[321] Therefore, intensified training is necessary to ensure compliance.

Training is also required due to the increased use of technology in facilitating illicit transfers. Internet penetration and evolving payment methods have increased the vulnerability of financial systems to a new form of risk. Regulators and operators are to get acquainted with the new processes of transfers, such as cryptocurrencies, so as to ensure that their countries are not adversely affected by illicit autonomous transfers.

In recognition of the need for capacity building, IFIs provide technical assistance to countries. The aim is to ensure that countries can address the vulnerabilities within their system locally. This is largely dependent on the country's political will, which is reflected through its interactions with IFIs and the resources it approves for this purpose. In the absence of resources, the countries' ability to combat illicit crimes would be significantly limited, illustrating the interaction between varying non-legal factors.

An important point is that the source of funding may determine its influence on compliance. For instance, international funding may come with preconditions and specificity which is likely to ensure improved compliance resulting from the build-up of preconditions for effective regulation. However, when funding is from a government's budget, it usually comes without conditions and lacks the transparency associated with foreign funding.

It is imperative to state however that adequate training and funding may not always translate to improved compliance because the 'human factor' element cannot be overlooked. Training and resources are no guarantee that staff cannot be manipulated, or funds diverted.

Setting out Factors that Influence Compliance

The literature on compliance has been examined with the aim of explaining internal and external compliance drivers in ACs/EEs. In line with the core argument of this book, these factors are set out as legal and non-legal factors, both of which are not mutually exclusive (Table 3.1).

---

321 *Shaffer* (n 306) 76.

Table 3.1 Legal and Non-Legal Compliance Drivers

Legal Factors	Description
Compliance engineered by democracy and rule of law	This refers to factors such as 'democratic' or 'non-democratic' governments, judicial independence and respect for the rule of law
Enforcement- driven compliance	This refers to factors such as legal sanctions, 'instruments of active monitoring' such as monitoring or surveillance, effective contract law and sturdy judicial systems
Law mirroring society	Culture (e.g., remittances/financial inclusions)
Non-Legal Factors	*Description*
Political will, domestic conditions and policy priorities	Government stance, pressure groups/civil societies
Compliance based on reputational concerns	Reputation, sanctions
Legitimacy and its effect on compliance	Perception of legality of institution
Globalisation and integration	Position of countries within the global financial market
Technical capacity and resources	Human and financial resources, training, technological advancements

Benchmarking Compliance Ratings

Notwithstanding the above drivers of compliance that impact on a country's compliance levels, the IFIs/FATF benchmark all countries to the same standards using the same methodology. To appreciate the impact of this, it is crucial to understand the concept of benchmarking.

Benchmarks are indicators that measure the achievements of set goals and are widely used to track market developments. They serve as a guide to investors and determine the direction of investments.[322] This instrument has been used in diverse areas, including the health industry[323] and service productivity industry,[324] to achieve improved compliance. Originally coined to improve compliance with

---

322 European Parliament News, 'Benchmarks: Restoring Confidence in the Financial Market' (European Parliament News, 6 April 2016) <http://www.europarl.europa.eu/news/en /news-room/20160404STO21313/benchmarks-restoring-confidence-in-the-financial-m arkets> accessed 23 July 2016.

323 Susanne Wait and Ellen Noite, 'Benchmarking Health Systems: Trends, Conceptual Issues and Perspectives' [2005] 12 (5) Benchmarking: An International Journal 436, 437.

324 Stephan Klingner, Stepanie Pravemann and Michael Becker, 'Service Productivity in Different Industries' [2015] 22 (2) Benchmarking: An International Journal 238–253.

policy goals, international organisations have usurped it to circumvent their enforcement problems.[325]

Countries are adjudged to be compliant to AML/CFT regulations by the extent to which they conform to FATF indicators or other regulatory benchmarks.[326] The extent of compliance is determined by a measure of combination of technical compliance, and effectiveness in meeting defined outcomes.[327] In both estimates of compliance, there is a measure of benchmarking; whilst the technical compliance approach adopts a more rigid methodology, the effectiveness measure adopts an open but exploratory language.[328]

Technical compliance with FATF recommendations is categorised into four different levels: Compliant, Largely Compliant, Partially Compliant and Non-Compliant.[329] Compliance is measured using the FATF's 40 recommendations.[330] Effectiveness provides an appreciation of a country's AML/CFT framework, measuring how defined outcomes are achieved.[331]

The FATF methodology presents the illusion that its benchmarks are supposed to highlight the best practice attainable by countries, indicating a purpose focused on fostering creativity and encouraging improvements, allowing countries to learn from each other.[332] The implication, however, is that states are urged to emulate these standards, failing which they would face enforcement sanctions.

The benchmarking process which is a ground for sanctioning countries is fallible. Firstly, the FATF reports may be unreliable. For instance, monitoring and measurement of compliance are done through mutual evaluations, self-assessment surveys and progress reports[333] carried out by FATF staff in agreement with related FIs and criminal justice agencies. The ratings produced from this technical exercise are generalised. In India (as with other EEs), only about three FIs are assessed along with several regulatory bodies. In a country with over 93 commercial banks, an assessment of only three FIs cannot be reflective of actual compliance levels. It is immaterial that an examination of regulatory bodies, criminal justice agencies and relevant ministries are also carried out, as a 'clear picture' can only be obtained directly from FIs, which serve as first point of call, providing information to other bodies. Blacklisting a country based on an unrepresentative assessment of compliance levels is unsatisfactory. Lombardo asserts that the judgement of performance is strictly formal, assessing the legal

---

325 Andre Broome and Joel Quirk, 'The Politics of Numbers: The Normative Agendas of Global Benchmarking' [2015] 41 Review of International Studies 813, 817.
326 *FATF* (n 20).
327 Ibid.
328 Ibid (n 342).
329 Ibid.
330 Ibid.
331 Ibid.
332 John Williams, Cheryl Brown and Anita Springer, 'Overcoming Benchmarking Reluctance: A Literature Review' [2012] 19 (2) Benchmarking: An International Journal 255–276.
333 Kern Alexander, Rahul Dhumale and John Eatwell, *Global Governance and International Standard Setting* (OUP 2006) 71.

implementation of the standard does not adequately reflect the de facto attainment of the policy goals contained in the standard.[334]

Secondly, the subjective nature of data collection poses various problems. For instance, the FATF methodology has an open and closed perception-based index which asks specific questions linked to industry experience, instead of simply measuring the perception of money laundering in a particular country. However, the variance in such reports as the Basel AML Index 2015 and the FATF NCCT 2015 list demonstrates the difficulty associated with subjective criteria.[335] For instance, whilst the FATF lists Algeria, Ecuador and Myanmar as countries with strategic AML/CFT deficiencies and high risk, Basel AML Index only list Myanmar as one of the top ten highest risk countries.[336] Additionally, whilst the FATF MER-derived statistics of China list it as one of the most compliant countries, the Basel AML Index classifies China as a country with high risk.[337] The result is that key institutions in certain jurisdictions may stretch data to meet the most renowned standard setter's policy objectives.[338] Countries in the lower regions of the ranking would be the most likely to engage in these sharp practices in a bid to avoid associated financial stigma and reputational damage, indicating existent information asymmetry.

Flowing from this is the argument that countries may become immune to the ranking process. For instance, it may be easier to report notorious countries like Afghanistan, overlooking its growing ability to combat AML/CFT. In comparison, reporting countries such as China, which is assumed to be clean, would demand a higher threshold requiring substantial proof. This could demotivate those that come out at the top of the ranking.[339]

The backlash that has trailed the culture of benchmarking has classed this concept as a power-based instrument for two reasons. Firstly, it is negotiated by groups with conflicting interests. This is evident in the composition of FATF members with China, an EE, which has diverse socio-political interests from countries like the United Kingdom and the United States, although

---

334 Dean Lombardo, *Benchmarking: An Adviser's Guide to Client Engagement Model* (2013).

335 International Centre for Asset Recovery (ICAR), Basel AML Index 2015 Report, <https ://index.baselgovernance.org/sites/index/documents/Basel_AML_Index_Report_2015 .pdf> accessed 20 June 2016; Thomson Reuters, 'Country Risk Ranking' (Thomas Reuters) <https://risk.thomsonreuters.com/products/thomson-reuters-country-risk-ranki ng> accessed 20 July 2016.

336 ICAR, 'Basel AML Index 2015 Report' (*ICAR*, 2015) <https://index.baselgovernance. org/sites/index/documents/Basel_AML_Index_Report_2015.pdf> accessed 20 June 2016; FATF, 'FATF Public Statement – 27 February 2015' (*FATF*, 27 February 2015) <http://www.fatf-gafi.org/publications/high-riskandnon-cooperativejurisdictions/d ocuments/public-statement-february-2015.html> accessed 15 January 2017.

337 Ibid.

338 Wendy Espeland and Michael Sauder, 'Rankings and Reactivity: How Public Measures Recreate Social Worlds' [2007] 113 (1) American Journal of Sociology 1. 28.

339 Adam Oliver, 'The Folly of Cross-Country Ranking Exercise' [2012] 7 Health, Policy and Law 15, 15.

the interest of the latter set of countries trumps that of the EEs. Secondly, its resulting policies and sanctions are imposed on groups that are not privy to the negotiation process, particularly developing countries.[340] Expounding on this, EENA4 stated that 'the ICRG usually list developing countries. Whereas, the money flows from these countries are much less than that from developed countries...it [the ICRG list] does not represent a totality of the countries not complying'.[341] EENA4's statement illuminates the subjectivity of the benchmarking process which usually seeks to sanction non-member countries as reflected in the International Country Risk Guide's (ICRG's) black-2 and grey lists.[342] It is deplorable that irrespective of the grievous consequences of these listings, including the financial isolation of countries – the listing criteria is unclear and concealed.

Yet, FATF compliance remains mandatory despite the democratic deficit in negotiations and listing processes. Additionally, the lack of preconditions for robust AML/CFT regulations coupled with the variances in internal country circumstances are not considered in subjecting ACs to the same standards, yet these countries are benchmarked similarly. Countries may react by producing false compliance standards. This situation unearths a legitimacy crisis unparticular to the FATF. More damning financial scandals involving benchmarks such as libor and eurolibor have shown the benchmarking system's susceptibility to manipulations. These benchmarks were used to price European Union (EU) citizen's mortgages, loans and other forms of lending. However, the daily values of these were usually determined and manipulated by a few big players in the market. Therefore, it is critical for benchmarking administrators to be independent, registered and carefully selected to ensure a transparent process.

Independent benchmarking administrators are critical in addressing concerns on the formulation and classification of benchmarking indicators. The conceptual framework of benchmarking is important given the effect of the benchmarking process noted by the exercise of the determinants of compliance backed by statistical evidence. Furthermore, it is against this benchmark that determinants for compliance are deduced.

---

340 James Caporaso and Joerg Wittenbrinck, 'The New Modes of Governance and Political Authority in Europe' [2006] 13 (4) Journal of European Public Policy; Anna Van Der Vleuten and Mieke Verloo, 'Ranking and Benchmarking: The Political Logic of New Regulatory Instruments in the Field of Gender Equality and Anti-Corruption' [2012] 40 (1) Policy and Politics. 71, 85. The G7 countries who spearheaded the initiation of the FATF have a greater say in the negotiation of recommendations; Kern Alexander, Rahul Dhumale and John Eatwell, *Global Governance of Financial Systems* (OUP, 2006) 72.

341 EENA4 (n 182).

342 FATF, 'High-Risk and Non-Cooperative Jurisdictions' (*FATF*) <http://www.fatf-gafi .org/publications/high-riskandnon-cooperativejurisdictions/more/more-on-high-risk -and-non-cooperative-jurisdictions.html?hf=10&b=0&s=desc(fatf_releasedate)> accessed 10 June 2017.

Conclusion

'Law and confidence', factors which are crucial to ensuring a conducive environment for transplantation of laws in ACs/EEs are weak. Law matters, but most importantly, the design of law is crucial in propelling compliance and averting gaming of the law. Law however does not work in a vacuum but is largely dependent on confidence. Confidence in financial stability, institutions, governmental and political systems, and enforcement structures. Confidence would ensure that FIs are held accountable and regulations are effective and able to ensure financial stability. These factors are however lacking in ACs/EEs, an indication that ACs/EEs will be incapable of effectively transplanting or implementing FATF's standards. This is particularly so for ACs due to the enhanced effect of corruption and belated understanding of the FATF standards, coupled with their absence of integration within the global economy. Yet, due to the subjection of states to AML/CFT regulation, they are mandated to comply or face sanctions.

The preconditions for effective regulation and variances in the internal country structures feed into the compliance drivers that are determinants of compliance levels. Compliance drivers, categorised into legal and non-legal factors, are not always internal to a country and may in certain instances be external – not within the control of the country's authorities. The legal factors considered include democracy and rule of law, enforcement and mirroring of the law. Political will, domestic conditions and policy priorities, reputational concerns, legitimacy, globalisation and capacity are non-legal factors found to have an impact on the compliance level of countries with AML/CFT standards. It is however noteworthy that none of these factors can influence compliance solely, rather, they work in tandem and are interlinked.

Further Reading

1. Abel Ezeoha, 'Internet Banking Strategy in a Highly Volatile Business Environment: The Nigerian Case', *in E-Banking and Emerging Multidisciplinary Processes: Social, Economical and Organizational Models* (Business Science Reference) <https://www.irma-international.org/chapter/internet-banking-strategy-highly-volatile/46230/>.
2. Abram Chayes and Antonio Handler Chayes, *The New Sovereignty: Compliance with International Regulatory Agreements* (HUP 1995).
3. Adam Oliver, 'The Folly of Cross-Country Ranking Exercise' [2012] 7 Health, Policy and Law 15–17.
4. Adegboyega Ige, 'A Review of the Legislative and Institutional Frameworks for Combating Money Laundering in Nigeria' [2011] 1 NIALS.
5. Africanews, 'UN: Drug Trafficking on the Rise in West Africa' (*Africanews*, 2 March 2016) <http://www.africanews.com/2016/03/02/un-drug-trafficking-on-the-rise-in-west-africa/> accessed 20 July 2017.
6. Ajayi Adegboyega Isaac, 'Military Regimes and Nation Building in Nigeria, 1966–1999' [2013] 5 (7) African Journal of History and Culture 138–142.
7. Alan Skyes and Eric Posner, 'An Economic Analysis of State and Individual Responsibility under International Law' (2006) Coase-Sandor Working Paper

Series in Law and Economics 279/2006 <https://chicagounbound.uchicag o.edu/cgi/viewcontent.cgi?article=1042&context=law:and_economics> accessed 6 March 2016.

8. Alan Watson, *The Evolution of Law* (JHUP 1985).
9. Albert Venn Dicey, *Introduction to the Study of the Law of the Constitution* (Macmillian and CO, London, 1985).
10. Alberto Chong and Florencio López-de-Silanes. 'Money Laundering and Its Regulations' [2015] 27 (1) Economics & Politics 86.
11. Alexander Winning, 'South Africa's Zuma Faces New No-Confidence Vote this Month' (*Reuters*, 2 February 2018) <https://uk.reuters.com/article/uk-s africa-politics/south-africas-zuma-faces-new-no-confidence-vote-this-month-idUKKBN1FM1B9> accessed 10 February 2018.
12. Aljazeera News, 'UK Suspends Uganda Aid Over Corruption' (*Aljazeera News*, 12 November 2012) <http://www.aljazeera.com/news/africa/2012/11/20121117155051480786.html> accessed 15 June 2017.
13. Andre Broome and Joel Quirk, 'The Politics of Numbers: The Normative Agendas of Global Benchmarking' [2015] 41 Review of International Studies.
14. Andrew T. Guzman, 'A Compliance Based Theory of International Law' [2002] 90 (6) California Law Review.
15. Andrew T. Guzman, 'Reputation and International Law' [2005] 34 Georgia Journal of International and Comparative Law.
16. Anne-Marie Slaughter, 'International Law in a World of Liberal States' [1995] European Journal of International Law, 6 (3), 503–538.
17. Anne Look, 'Investigations Underway into Corruption and Embezzlement in West Africa' (*Voice of Africa*, 5 December 2012) <https://www.voanews.com/a/west-Africa-corruption-investigation/1558980.html> accessed 19 August 2016.
18. Anna Van Der Vleuten and Mieke Verloo, 'Ranking and Benchmarking: The Political Logic of New Regulatory Instruments in the Field of Gender Equality and Anti-Corruption' [2012] 40 (1) Policy and Politics.
19. Anthony Doon and Cheryl Webster, 'Sentence Severity and Crime: Accepting the Null Hypothesis' [2003] 30 Crime and Justice.
20. Arnoud W.A. Boot and Matej Marinc, 'Crisis Management and Lender of Last Resort in the European Banking Market', *in* Pietro Alessandrini, Michele Fratianno and Alberto Zazzaro (eds.), *The Changing Geography of Banking and Finance* (Springer, Boston, MA, 2009).
21. S.G. Ashby and S.R. Daikon, 'The Value of Corporate Risk Management: Empirical Evidence from Large UK Companies' [1996] 1 (2) Risk Decision and Policy.
22. Austine Ejovi, Mgbonyebi Charles and Akpokighe Okiemute Raymond, 'Corruption in Nigeria: A Historical Perspective' [2013] 3 (16) Research Humanities and Social Sciences Journal.
23. Barry Rider, 'The Limits of the Law: An Analysis of the Interrelationship of the Criminal and Civil Control in the Control of Money Laundering' [1999] 2 (3) Journal of Money Laundering Control.
24. BCBS, 'Consultative Document: Core Principles for Effective Banking Supervision' (*BCBS*, 20 March 2012) <http://www.bis.org/publ/bcbs213.pdf> accessed 1 February 2016.
25. BCBS, 'Sound Management of Risks Related to Money Laundering and Financing of Terrorism' (*Basel Committee on Banking Supervision*, June 2017) <http://www.bis.org/bcbs/publ/d405.pdf> accessed August 2017.

26. Bernhard Schlink, 'Wirtschaft und ertrauen', in *Berhand Schlink Vergewisserungen u ber politik, schreiben und Glauben* (Diogenes Verlag, Zurich, 2005) <https://www.amazon.co.uk/Vergewisserungen-Bernhard-Schlink/dp/3257064837>.

27. Beth Whitaker, 'Compliance among Weak States: Africa and the Counter Terrorism Regime' [2010] 36 Review of International Studies.

28. Beth Simmons, 'Compliance with International Agreements' [1998] Annual Review of Political Science 75, 83; Anne-Marie Slaughter, 'International Law in a World of Liberal States' [1995] 6 (3) EJIL 265.

29. Beth Simmons, 'International Law and State Behavior: Commitment and Compliance in International Monetary Affairs' [2000] 94 (4) American Political Science Review 247.

30. Beth Simmons, *Mobilizing for Human Rights: International Law in Domestic Politics* 23–56 (CUP 2009).

31. Betsey Stevenson and Justin Wolfers, 'Trust in Public Institutions over Business Cycle' (2011) Federal Reserve Bank of San Francisco Working Paper Series 11/2011, 4 <https://www.frbsf.org/economic-research/files/wp11-11bk.pdf> accessed 5 March 2016.

32. BIS, 'Working Paper on Pillar 3 – Market Discipline' (2001) Basel Committee on Banking Supervision <https://www.bis.org/publ/bcbs_wp7.pdf> accessed 10 November 2016.

33. Benedict Kingsbury, 'The Concept of Compliance as a Function of Competing Conceptions of International law' [1998] 19 Michigan Journal of International Law.

34. Brian Cheffins, 'Does Law Matter? The Separation of Ownership and Control in the United Kingdom' (2000) ESRC Centre for Business Research, University of Cambridge Working Paper No. 172, 468 <https://www.cbr.cam.ac.uk/file admin/user_upload/centre-for-business-research/downloads/working-paper s/wp172.pdf> accessed 8 May 2016.

35. Brian Tamanaha, *A General Jurisprudence of Law and Society* (OUP 2001).

36. Cary Coglianese, Elizabeth K. Keating, Michael L. Micheal and Thomas J. Healey, 'The Role of Government in Corporate Governance' [2004] 1243 Faculty Scholarship.

37. Cecily Rose, *International Anti-Corruption Norms: Their Creation and Influence on Domestic Legal Systems* (OUP 2015).

38. Centre of Studies, Response and Treatment of Security Incidents in Brazil (Centre of Studies, 28 July 2015) <http://diariodocomercio.com.br/noticia.p hp?tit=numero_de_ataques_ciberneticos_cresceu_197&id=157314> accessed 2 May 2016.

39. Cheryl Gray, 'Reforming Legal Systems in Developing and Transitional Countries' [1997] Finance and Development. <https://issat.dcaf.ch/ser/download/2312/20094/Reforming%20Legal%20Systems%20in%20Developing%20and%20Transitional%20Countries%20Gray%20(1997).pdf>.

40. Chibuike Uche, 'The Adoption of a Money Laundering Regime in Nigeria' [1988] 1 (3) JMLC.

41. Chinn Menzie and Ito Hiro, 'What Matters for Financial Development? Capital Controls, Institutions and Interactions' [2006] 81 (1) Journal of Development Economics.

42. Concepcion Verdugo Yepes, 'Compliance with the AML/CFT International Standard: Lessons from a Cross-Country Analysis' (2006) IMF Working Paper

11/177, 17 <https://www.imf.org/external/pubs/ft/wp/2011/wp11177.pdf> accessed 10 July 2015.

43. Constantinos Stephanou, 'Rethinking Market Discipline in Banking: Lessons from the Financial Crisis', *in* Panagiotis Delimatsis and Nils Herger (eds.), *Financial Regulation at the Crossroads: Implications for Supervision* (Wolters Kluwer, The Netherlands, 2011).

44. R. Cooter and H.B. Schafer, *Solomon's Knot: How Law Can End the Poverty of Nations* (First published 2012, PUP 2012).

45. Charles Goodhart, 'Balancing Lender of Last Resort Assistance with Avoidance of Moral Hazard' *in* Frank Heinemann, Ulrich Kluh and Sebastian Watzk (eds.), *Monetary Policy, Financial Crises and the Macroeconomy: Festschrift for Gerhard IIIing* (Springer, Dordrecht, 2017).

46. Chris Brummer, 'How International Financial Law Works and How It Doesn't' [2011] 99 Georgetown Law Journal 257, 290.

47. Chris Higg, 'China Ends Death Penalty for 13 Economic Crimes (*BBC News Shanghai*, February 2011) <http://www.bbc.co.uk/news/world-asia-pacific-12580504> accessed 11 February 2016.

48. Christine Kaufmann and Mirja Ciesolka, 'Wann Baute Noah die Arche – Vermo gensverwaltung als Akteurin einer nachhltigen Marktenwicklung', *in* Peter R. Isler and Romeo Cerutti (eds), *Vermogensverwaltung III* (Schriftenreihe Nr. 105 des Europainstututes an der Universitat Zurich, Zurich, 2010).

49. Dalvinder Singh, *Banking Regulation of UK and US Financial Markets* (Ashgate Publishing 2007).

50. Dalvinder Singh and John LaBrosse, 'Developing a Framework for Effective Financial Crisis Management' [2012] 2 OECD Journal: Financial Market Trends.

51. Dalvinder Singh and John LaBrosse, 'Developing a Financial Crisis Management' [2012] 2 OCED Financial Market Trends.

52. Daniel Ho, 'Compliance and International Soft Law: Why Do Countries Implement the Basel Accord' [2002] 5 (3) Journal of International Economic Law.

53. Daniel Bodansky, 'The Legitimacy of International Governance: A Coming Challenge for International Environmental Law?' [1999] 93 (3) American Journal of International Law.

54. Damien Gayle, 'Foreign Criminals Use London Housing Market to Launder Billions of Pounds' (*The Guardian*, 25 July 2015) <https://www.theguardian.com/uk-news/2015/jul/25/london-housing-market-launder-offshore-tax-havens> accessed 10 August 2017.

55. David Murphy, *Maintaining Confidence* (LSE Financial Markets Group Research Centre 2012).

56. David Thompson, 'Panama Papers: Putin Associates Linked to "Money Laundering"'(*BBC News*, 2 April 2016). <http://www.bbc.co.uk/news/world-europe-35918845> accessed 2 May 2016.

57. Dean Lombardo, *Benchmarking: An Adviser's Guide to Client Engagement Model* (Lulu.com 2013).

58. A. Demirguc-Kunt and E. Detragiache, 'The Determinants of Banking Crises in Developing and Developed Countries' [1998] 45 (1) IMF Staff Papers.

59. Dieter Kerwer and Rainer Hulsee, 'How International Organisations Rule the World: The Case of the Financial Action Task Force on Money Laundering' [2011] 2 Journal of the International Studies.

60. Donato Masciandaro, 'Money Laundering: The Economics of Regulation' [1999] 7 European Journal of Law and Economics.

61. Donato Masciandaro and Alessandro Portolano, 'It Takes Two to Tango: International Financial Regulation and Off-Shore Centers' (2003) Universita di Lecee Department of Economics Working Paper No.11/4 <https://papers. ssrn.com/sol3/papers.cfm?abstract_id=289541> accessed 1 May 2016.

62. B.J. Dudley, *Instability and Political Order: Politics and Crisis in Nigeria* (Ibadan University Press 1973).

63. Emmanuel C. Areno, 'Beyond Lip Service: Using Social Contracts to Achieve Participatory and Accountable Governance in the Philippines', *in* Carmen Malena (ed.), *From Political Won't to Political Will: Building Support for Participatory Governance* (Kumarian Press, Sterling, VA, 2009) 246.

64. Eric Helleiner, 'State Power and the Regulation of Illicit Activity in Global Finance', *in* R.H. Friman and P. Andreas (eds.), *The Illicit Global Economy and State Power* (Rowman & Littlefield, Lanham, MD, 1999) 76.

65. European Parliament News, 'Benchmarks: Restoring Confidence in the Financial Market' (*European Parliament News*, 6 April 2016) <http:// www.europarl.europa.eu/news/en/news-room/20160404STO21313/ benchmarks-restoring-confidence-in-the-financial-markets> accessed 23 July 2016.

66. FATF, 'Brazil Mutual Evaluation Report 2010' (*FATF* 2010) <http://www .fatf-gafi.org/media/fatf/documents/reports/mer/MER%20Brazil%20full .pdf> accessed 10 May 2016.

67. FATF, 'FATF Guidance on Transparency and Beneficial Ownership' (*FATF*, 2014) <http://www.fatf-gafi.org/media/fatf/documents/reports/Guidance -transparency-beneficial-ownership.pdf> accessed 1 April 2016.

68. FATF, 'FATF Public Statement –27 February 2015' (*FATF*, 27 February 2015) <http://www.fatf-gafi.org/publications/high-riskandnon-cooperative jurisdictions/documents/public-statement-february-2015.html> accessed 15 January 2017.

69. FATF, 'High-Risk and Non-Cooperative Jurisdictions' (*FATF*) <http://www .fatf-gafi.org/publications/high-riskandnon-cooperativejurisdictions/more /more-on-high-risk-and-non-cooperative-jurisdictions.html?hf=10&b=0&s =desc(fatf_releasedate)> accessed 10 June 2017.

70. FATF, 'Methodology: For Assessing Technical Compliance with the FATF Recommendations and the Effectiveness of AML/CFT System' (*FATF*, 2013) <http://www.fatf-gafi.org/media/fatf/documents/methodology/FATF%20 Methodology%2022%20Feb%202013.pdf> accessed 10 August 2017.

71. FATF, 'Mutual Evaluations' (*FATF*) <http://www.fatf-gafi.org/publications/ mutualevaluations/?hf=10&b=0&s=desc(fatf_releasedate)> accessed 5 January 2017.

72. FATF, 'The FATF Recommendations' (*FATF*, 2013) <http://www.fatf-gafi .org/media/fatf/documents/recommendations/pdfs/fatf_recommendations .pdf> accessed 12 May 2015.

73. FATF GAFI, Financial Action Task Force, 'Summary of the First Mutual Evaluation Report Anti-Money Laundering and Combating the Financing of Terrorism – Peoples Republic of China' (*FATF*, 29 June 2007) <http://www .fatf-gafi.org/media/fatf/documents/reports/mer/MER%20China%20full .pdf> accessed 10 June 2016.

74. Fernando Guerreiro De Lemos, President of Banrisul boasted, 'Our Bank is a Leader in Banking Technology' See Forbes Custom 'Brazil: Confidence is the Keyword' (*Forbes Custom*), <http://www.forbescustom.com/EconomicDevelopmentPgs/BrazilP1.html> accessed 1 May 2016.

75. Financial Inclusion Insights, 'Nigeria: Wave 3 Report, FII Tracker Survey Conducted August–September 2015' (*FinInclusion.org*, 2015) <http://finclusion.org/uploads/file/reports/InterMedia%20FII%20Nigeria%20W3%20%2030%20April%202016.pdf> accessed July 2016.

76. I. Fletcher, L. Mistelis and M. Cremona (eds.), *Foundations and Perspectives of International Trade Law* (Sweet & Maxwell 2001).

77. Forbes Custom, 'Brazil: Confidence is the Keyword' (*Forbes Custom*), <http://www.forbescustom.com/EconomicDevelopmentPgs/BrazilP1.html> accessed 1 May 2016.

78. Frank Vibert, 'Reforming International Rule-Making' [2012] 3 (3) Global Policy.

79. Gary Becker, 'Crime and Punishment: An Economic Approach' *in* Nigel Fielding, Alan Clarke and Robert Witt (eds.), *The Economic Dimensions of Crime* (Macmillan Press Ltd, UK, 2000).

80. G. Garrett, 'Global Markets and National Politics: Collusion Course or Virtuous Circle?' [1998] 52 (4) International Organization.

81. George Downs and Michael Jones, 'Reputation, Compliance and International Law' [2002] 31 JLS.

82. George Sigler, 'The Optimum Enforcement of Laws', in Gary Becker and William Landes (eds.), *Essays in the Economics of Crime and Punishment* (NBER 1974).

83. Georgina Lawrence, 'Who Regulates the Regulators' (Centre for Study of Regulated Industries, Occasional Paper 16, 2012) 27 <http://www.bath.ac.uk/management/cri/pubpdf/Occasional_Papers/16_Lawrence.pdf> accessed 11 February 2017.

84. Gerard Caprio, Jr, 'Financial Regulation after the Crisis: How Did We Get Here and How Do We Get Out?' [2013] Federal Reserve of San Francisco Proceedings.

85. Gillian Garcia, 'Deposit Insurance and Crisis Management' (2000) IMF Working Paper WP/00/57/2000, 19 <https://www.imf.org/external/pubs/ft/wp/2000/wp0057.pdf> accessed 10 January 2017.

86. Gregory Shaffer, *Transnational Legal Ordering and State Change* (Cambridge Studies in Law and Society 2014).

87. Harold Koh, 'Review: Why Do Nations Obey International Law?' [1997] 106 (8) The Yale Law Journal.

88. Helen Milner, *Interests, Institutions and Information: Domestic Politics and International Relations* (PUP 1997).

89. Helen Milner and Andrew Moravcsik (eds.), *Power, Interdependence and Non-State Actors in World Politics* (PUP 2009).

90. Hemeiri Shahar and Lee Jones, 'Regulatory Regionalism and Anti-Money Laundering Governance in Asia' [2015] 69 (2) Australian Journal of International Affairs.

91. Hennie Bester, Doubell Chamberlain, Louis De Koker, Christine Hougaard, Ryan Short, Anja Smith and Richard Walker, 'Implementing FATF Standards in Developing Countries and Financial Inclusion – Findings and Guidelines'

(*First Initiative*, 2008) < http://cenfri.org/documents/AML/AML_CFT%20and%20Financial%20Inclusion.pdf> accessed 4 June 2016.

92. Hilton McCann, *Offshore Finance* (CUP 2009).
93. Hyun Shin, 'Reflections on Northern Rock: The Bank Run that Heralded the Global Financial Crisis' [2009] 23 (1) Journal of Economic Perspectives.
94. IAIS, 'Guidance Paper on Anti-Money Laundering and Combating the Financing of Terrorism' (Insurance Fraud Sub-Committee 2004).
95. Ian Ayres and John Braithwaite, *Responsive Regulation* (OUP 1992).
96. Ian Jeffries, *Political Developments in Contemporary China: A Guide* (First published 2011, Routledge 2011).
97. Idris Kasumu's Blog, 'Arunma Oteh Faces Query Over Hostilities in SEC' (Idris Kamusu's Blog, 10 May 2012) <http://idriskasumu.blogspot.co.uk/2012/05/> accessed 11 February 2017.
98. IMF, 'Canada: Financial Sector Assessment Program: IOSCO Objectives and Principles of Securities Regulation – Detailed Assessment of Implementation 2014' (IMF Country Report No. 14/73, 2014).
99. IMF, 'Anti-Money Laundering/Combating the Financing of Terrorism Topics – The Fund's Involvement in AML/CFT' (*IMF*) (2014) <https://www.imf.org/external/np/leg/amlcft/eng/aml1.htm> accessed 20 June 2016.
100. IMF, 'Mandatory Financial Stability Assessment under the FSAP' (*IMF*, 24 September 2014) <https://www.imf.org/external/np/fsap/mandatoryfsap.htm> accessed 4 May 2016 – Warranting South Africa's compliance levels.
101. IMF, 'Mandatory Financial Stability Assessments under the FSAP' (International Monetary Fund, 15 September 2013) <https://www.imf.org/external/np/pp/eng/2013/111513.pdf> accessed 7 October 2017.
102. IOSCO, 'Methodology for Assessing Implementation of the IOSCO Objectives and Principles of Securities Regulation' (OICU-IOSCO, February 2008).
103. International Trade Forum Magazine, 'New World Order: Shifting Markets in Trade, Investment and Opportunity' [2010] 2 International Trade Forum; Organization for Economic Cooperation and Development, Society at a Glance 2014: OECD Social Indicators (OECD Publishing 2014).
104. Jack GoldSmith and Eric Posner, *The Limits of International Law* (OUP, New York, 2005).
105. Jackie Johnson, 'Blacklisting: Initial Reactions, Responses and Repercussion' [2001] 4 (2) Journal of Money Laundering Control.
106. R. Jagtenberg, E. Orucu and A. de Roos, 'Introduction', *in* A.J. De Roo, E. Örücü and Robert W. Jagtenberg (eds.), *Transfrontier Mobility of Law* (Kluwer Law International, Boston, MA, 1995).
107. James March and Herbert Alexander Simon, *Organizations* (1st edn, 1958, 3rd edn, Blackwell Business 1993).
108. James Barth, Cindy Lee and Triphon Phumiwasana, 'Deposit Insurance Schemes' [2013] Encyclopedia of Finance.
109. Jared Wessel, 'The Financial Action Task Force: A Study in Balancing Sovereignty with Equality in Global Administrative Law' [2007] 13 Widener Law Review.
110. James Caporaso and Joerg Wittenbrinck, 'The New Modes of Governance and Political Authority in Europe' [2006] 13 (4) Journal of European Public Policy.
111. Jason C. Sharman, 'Power and Discourse in Policy Diffusion: Anti-Money Laundering in Developing States' [2008] 52 (3) International Studies Quarterly.

112. Jayshree Chavan, 'Internet Banking-Benefits and Challenges in an Emerging Economy' [2013]1 (1) International Journal of Research in Business.

113. John Williams, Cheryl Brown and Anita Springer, 'Overcoming Benchmarking Reluctance: A Literature Review' [2012] 19 (2) Benchmarking: An International Journal.

114. John Coffee, 'Do Norms Matter? A Cross-Country Evaluation' [2001] 149 (6) University of Pennsylvania Law Review.

115. Jon G. Sutinen and Keith Kuperan, 'A Socio-Economic Theory of Regulatory Compliance' [1999] 26 (1) International Journal of Social Economics 174, 178; Ian Ayres and John Braithwaite, *Responsive Regulation* (OUP 1992).

116. Jorge Nemr, 'Brazil' *in* Gwendoline Godfrey, *Nate and Godfrey: Bank Confidentiality* (5th edn, IBA 2011).

117. Julia Black, 'Critical Reflections on Regulation' [2002] 27 Australian Journal of Legal Philosophy.

118. Julia Black, 'Constructing and Contesting Legitimacy and Accountability in Polycentric Regulatory Regimes' [2008] 2 Regulation & Governance.

119. Julia Black, Martyn Hopper and Christa Band, 'Making a Success of Principles-Based Regulation' [2007] 1 (3) Law and Financial Markets Review.

120. Julia Black and David Kershaw, 'Sanctions for Bank Directors: Response from Professor Julia Black and Professor Kershaw, London School of Economics and Political Science' (*LSE Collections*, 11 January 2013) <http://www.lse.ac.uk/collections/law/news/Sanctions%20-%20submission%20from%20Black%20and%20Kershaw%2011%20Jan%202013.pdf> accessed 16 July 2013.

121. Kal Raustiala and Anne-Marie Slaughter, 'International Law, International Relations and Compliance', *in* Walter Carlnaes, Thomas Risse and Beth Simmons (eds.), *The Handbook of International Relations* (SAGE Publications, Ltd., London, 2002).

122. Kaspersky Lab Report, 'Financial Cyber Threats in 2014' (*Kaspersky Lab Report*, February2015) <https://securelist.com/files/2015/02/KSN_Financial_Threats_Report_2014_eng.pdf> accessed 2 May 2016.

123. Ketcha Nicholas, 'Deposit Insurance System Design and Considerations' [1999] 7 Strengthening the Banking System in China: Issues and Experience, Policy Paper.

124. Keith Hawkins, *Law as Last Resort: Prosecution Decision-Making in a Regulatory Agent* (OUP 2002) 253.

125. Kevin Davis and Michael Trebilock, 'What Role Do Legal Institutions Play in Development' (Draft for the IMF Conference of 2nd Generation Reform, October 1989).

126. Kern Alexander, Rahul Dhumale and John Eatwell, *Global Governance of Financial Systems* (OUP 2006).

127. Kern Alexander, Rahul Dhumale and John Eatwell, *Global Governance and International Standard Setting* (OUP 2006).

128. Klaus J. Hopt, 'Corporate Governance of Banks after the Financial Crisis', *in* E. Wymeersch, K.J. Hopt and G. Ferrarini (eds.), *Financial Regulation and Supervision, A Post-Crisis Analysis* (OUP, 2012) 3.

129. Klaus Hopt, 'Better Governance of Financial Institutions' (2013) *European Corporate Governance Institute Working Paper* 207/2013, 23 <http://personal.lse.ac.uk/schustee/hopt%20governance.pdf> accessed 6 May 2016.

130. Kobil Ruziev and Sheila Dow, 'A Re-Evaluation of Banking Sector Reforms in Transition Economies: Intentions and Unintended Consequences', *in* Kobil Ruziev and Nicholas Perdikis (eds.), *Development and Reforms in Financial Economies* (Taylor & Francis, 2016).

131. Koh Harold, 'Why Do Nations Obey International Law' [1997] 106 Yale Law Journal.

132. Kris Hinterseer, *Criminal Finance: The Political Economy of Money Laundering in a Comparative Legal Context* (Kluwer Law International 2002).

133. Lawrence Friedman, 'Borders: On the Emerging Sociology of Transnational Law' [1996] 32 Stanford Journal of International Law.

134. Lawrence Lessig, 'The Zones of Cyberspace' [1996] 48 (5) Stanford Law Review.

135. M. Levi and Gilmore William, 'Terrorist Finance: Money Laundering and the Rise of Mutual Evaluation: A New Paradigm for Crime Control' [2002] 4 (2) European Journal of Law Reform.

136. Leonardo Borlini, 'The Financial Action Task Force: An Introduction' (*U4 Brief*, January 2015) <https://assets.publishing.service.gov.uk/media/57a 0898ee5274a27b2000137/U4Brief-2015-02WEB.pdf> accessed 18 March 2016.

137. Lindsay Owens, 'Confidence in Banks, Financial Institutions and Wall Street, 1971–2011' [2011] 76 (1) Public Opinion Quarterly.

138. Lindsay Owens, 'The Polls – Trends, Confidence in Banks, Financial Institutions and Wall Street, 1971 – 2011' [2012] 76 (1) Public Opinion Quarterly.

139. Lori Ann Post, Amber N.W. Raile and Eric D. Raile, 'Defining Political Will' [2010] 38 (4) Politics & Policy 653.

140. Lois M. Musikali, 'Why Criminal Sanctions Still Matter in Corporate Governance' [2009] 20 (4) International Company and Commercial Law Review.

141. Marie Wilke 'Emerging Informal Network Structures in Global Governance: Inside the Anti-Money Laundering Regime' [2008] 77 (4) Nordic Journal of International Law.

142. Marc Quintyn and Michael W. Taylor, 'Regulatory and Supervisory Independence and Financial Stability' (2002) IMF Working Paper WP/02/46 <https://www.imf.org/external/pubs/ft/wp/2002/wp0246.pdf> accessed 19 November 2016.

143. Mark Medish, 'Lesson from Economies in Transition During Global Financial Crisis', *in* Joseph R. Sisignano, Wiliam C. Hunter and George Kaufman (eds.), *Global Financial Crises: Lessons from Recent Events* (Bank for International Settlement Federal Reserve Bank of Chicago, 2000).

144. Mark Roe, 'Corporate Law's Limits' [2002] 31 (2) Journal of Legal Studies 233–271, Columbia Law and Economics Working Paper No.186.

145. Mark Suchman, 'Managing Legitimacy: Strategic and Institutional Approaches' [1995] 20 (3) Academy of Management Review.

146. Martin Wheatley, 'Debating Trust and Confidence in Banking' (Financial Conduct Authority, 28 May 2015) <https://www.fca.org.uk/news/debatin g-trust-and-confidence-in-banking-> accessed 3 December 2015 accessed 10 May 2016.

147. Michael Ogbedi, 'Political Leadership and Corruption in Nigeria Since 1960: A Socio-Economic Analysis' [2012] 1 (2) Journal of Nigeria Studies.

148. Michele Fletcher, 'China's Underground Bank' (Global Financial Integrity, 16 July, 2014) <http://www.gfintegrity.org/chinas-underground-bank/> accessed 21 January 2016.

149. Mimi Lau, 'Loophole for the Corrupt: China and US Worst in G20 for Transparency over 'Real Ownership of Shares and Companies' (*South China Morning Post: Policies and Politics*, 12 November 2015) <http://www.scmp .com/news/china/policies-politics/article/1878350/loophole-corrupt-chi na-and-us-worst-g20-transparency?__hstc=52789303.810863f5634170c8 1c80dbc356af6baa.1450137600060.1450137600061.1450137600062.1&_ _hssc=52789303.1.1450137600063&__hsfp=1119992871> accessed 21 May 2016.

150. Montfort Mlachila, Dennis Dykes, Sabrina Zajc, Paul-Harry Aithnard, Thorsten Beck, Mthuli Ncube and Oskar Nelvin, 'Banking in Sub-Saharan Africa: Challenges and Opportunities' (European Investment Bank, January 2013) <http://www.eib.org/attachments/efs/economic_report_banking_africa_en .pdf> accessed 10 July 2017.

151. NDIC, 'NDIC Releases 2015 Annual Report' (*NDIC*, 2015) <http://ndic .gov.ng/ndic-releases-2015-annual-report/> accessed 10 May 2017.

152. Nicholas Ryder, Magaret Griffiths and Lachmi Singh, *Commercial Law: Principles and Policy* (CUP 2012).

153. Nigel Morris-Cotterill, 'Money Laundering' [2001] 124 Foreign Policy.

154. Niklas Luhmann, 'The Autopoiesis of Social Systems', *in* Felix Geyer and Jonannes Van Der Zouwen (eds.), *Sociocybernetic Paradoxes: Observation, Control and Evaluation of Self Steering Systems* (SAGE Publications, India, 1986).

155. Nlerum Okogbule, 'Combating Money Laundering in Nigeria: An Appraisal of the Money Laundering Act 2004' [2007] 28 (2) Statute Law Review.

156. Norman Magurura, *The Global Anti-Money Laundering Regulatory Landscape in Less Developed Countries* (Routledge, Taylor & Francis Group 2012).

157. North Douglass, *Growth and Structural Change* (W.W. Norton 1981).

158. Nuhu Ribadu, *Show Me the Money – Leveraging Anti-Money Laundering Tools to Fight Corruption in Nigeria: An Insider Story* (Centre for Global Development 2010).

159. OECD, 'Illicit Financial Flows from Developing Countries: Measuring OECD Responses' (*OECD*, 2014) <https://www.oecd.org/corruption/Illicit_Finan cial_Flows_from_Developing_Countries.pdf> accessed 12 February 2018.

160. OECD, 'List of Uncooperative Tax Havens' <http://www.oecd.org/count ries/monaco/listofunco-operativetaxhavens.htm> accessed 17 January 2017.

161. OECD, 'Reducing the Risk of Policy Failure: Challenges for Regulatory Compliance' (OECD, 2000) <https://www.oecd.org/gov/regulatory-policy /1910833.pdf> accessed 20 July 2016.

162. OECD, 'Society at a Glance 2014: OECD Social Indicators' (OECD Publishing, 2014).

163. Ogbewere Bankole Ijewereme, 'Anatomy of Corruption in the Nigeria Public Sector: Theoretical Perspectives and Some Empirical Explanations' [2015] SAGE Open.

164. Oliver Wendell Holmes, Jr., *The Speeches of Oliver Wendell Holmes* (Harvard Univerisity Press 1981).

165. Olu Fasan, 'Compliance with WTO Law in Developing Countries: A Study of South Africa and Nigeria' (PhD Thesis, London School of Economics 2006).

166. Oran Young, *Compliance with Public Authority* (JHUP 1979).

167. Patricia A. McCoy, 'The Moral Hazard Implications of Deposit Insurance: Theory and Evidence' (Seminar on Current Developments in Monetary and Financial Law, October 2006).

168. Patthanij Gonjanar and Supawadee Suttirak, 'The Effects from Asia's Financial Crisis: Factors Affecting on the Value Creation of Organisation' [2012] 3 (16) International Journal of Business and Social Science.

169. Peter Grabosky and John Braithwaite, *Of Manners Gentle: Enforcement Strategies of Australian Business Regulatory Agencies* (First published 1986, OUP in association with Australian Institute of Criminology).

170. Peter Reuter, 'Illicit Financial Flows and Governance: The Importance of Disaggregation' (World Development Report, 2017) <http://pubdocs.world bank.org/en/677011485539750208/WDR17-BP-Illicit-Financial-Flows.p df> accessed 2 February 2018.

171. Peter Romaniuk, 'Institutions as Swords and Shields: Multilateral Counter-Terrorism Since 9/11' [2010] 36 Review of International Studies.

172. Pierre Boyer and Jorge Ponce, 'Regulatory Capture and Banking Supervision Reform' [2012] 8 (3) Journal of Financial Stability.

173. Pricewaterhouse Coopers, 'Know Your Customer: Quick Reference Guide' (*PwC*, January 2016) <https://www.pwc.com/gx/en/financial-services/ publications/assets/pwc-anti-money-laundering-2016.pdf> accessed 17 May 2017.

174. R.H. Coase, 'The Nature of the Firm' [2007] 4 (16) Economica.

175. Rafael La Porta, Florencio Lopez-de-Silanes, Andrei Shleifer and Robert Vishny, 'Legal Determinants of External Finance' [1997] 11 (3) The Journal of Finance.

176. Rafael La Porta, Florencio Lopez-de-Silanes, Andrei Shleifer and Robert Vishny 'The Quality of Government' [1999] 15 (1) The Journal of Law, Economics and Organisation.

177. Rahmat Mohamad, 'Access to International Justice: The Role of the International Criminal Court in Aiding National Prosecutions of International Crimes' [2012] 1 (2) AALCO Journal of International Law.

178. Rainer Hulsee, 'Even Clubs Can't Do Without Legitimacy: Why the Anti-Money Laundering Blacklist Was Suspended' [2008] 2 Regulation and Governance.

179. Richard W. Rhan, 'The Case against Federalising Airport Security' (CATO Institute, 2001) <http://www.cato.org/publications/commentary/case-a gainst-federalizing-airport-security> accessed 16 August 2016.

180. Robert Baldwin, Martin Cave and Martin Lodge, *Understanding Regulation: Theory, Strategy and Practice* (First published 2012, 2nd edn, OUP 2014).

181. Robert Booth, 'MPs Decry 'Failed' Effort to Stop UK Property Money Laundering' (*The Guardian*, 15 July 2016) <https://www.theguardian.com /money/2016/jul/15/mps-decry-inadequate-efforts-stop-money-laundering -uk-property> accessed 10 August 2017.

182. Robert Kagan and John T. Scholz, 'The "Criminology of the Corporation" and Regulatory Enforcement Strategies', in K. Hawkins and J.M. Thomas (eds.), *Enforcing Regulation* (Kluwer-Nijhoff, Boston, MA, 1984).

183. Robert Kudrie, 'Did Blacklisting Hurt the Tax Havens?' [2009] 12 (1) Journal of Money Laundering Control.
184. Robert Tignor, 'Political Corruption in Nigeria before Independence' [1993] 31 (2) Journal of Modern African Studies.
185. Robert Rayner and Steven Swinford, 'Wikileaks Cables: Millions in Overseas Aid to Africa Was Embezzled' (*The Telegraph*, 5 February 2011) <http://www.telegraph.co.uk/news/worldnews/wikileaks/8304640/WikiLeaks-cables-millions-in-overseas-aid-to-Africa-was-embezzled.html> accessed 10 July 2017.
186. Richard Posner, 'Social Norms and the Law: An Economic Approach' [1997] 87 (2) The American Economic Review.
187. Saby Ghoshray, 'Compliance Convergence in FATF Rulemaking: The Conflict between Agency Capture and Soft Law' [2014–2015] 59 New York Law School Law Review.
188. Sahara Reporters, 'Nigeria is the Most Fraudulent Country in Africa, KPMG Report Says' (*Sahara Reporters*, 23 November 2012) <http://saharareporters.com/2012/11/23/nigeria-most-fraudulent-country-africa-kpmg-report-says> accessed 10 July 2016.
189. Scholz John and Mark Lubell, 'Trust and Taxpaying: Testing the Heuristic Approach to Collective Action' [1988] 42 (2) American Journal of Political Science.
190. Scott Senccal, Murat Akuyev and Yulia Somomakhina, 'Offshores Restricted from Participation in Privatisation and Acquisition of Russian Strategic Companies' (*Cleary Gottlieb, Alert Memorandum*, 10 July 2017) <https://www.clearygottlieb.com/~/media/cgsh/files/2017/publications/alert-memos/offshores-restricted-from-participation-in-privatizations-and-acquisitions-of-russian-7-10-17.pdf> accessed 21 August 2017.
191. Senator John Kerry and Senator Hank Brown, *The BCCI Affair: A Report to the Committee on Foreign Relations* (102nd Congress 2nd Session Senate Print 102–140, 2011).
192. Se Kim and Ashoka Mody, 'Managing Confidence in Emerging Market Bank Runs' (2004) IMF Working Paper WP/04/235, 26 <https://www.imf.org/en/Publications/WP/Issues/2016/12/31/Managing-Confidence-in-Emerging-Market-Bank-Runs-17847> accessed 18 June 2016.
193. Shirley W. Inscoe, 'Global Consumers: Losing Confidence in the Battle against Fraud' (*Aite*, June 2014) <http://www.aciworldwide.com/-/media/files/collateral/global-consumers-losing-confidence-in-the-battle-against-fraud-report> accessed 21 March 2016.
194. Sophia Grene, 'European Banks Suffer a Mini Crisis of Confidence' (*Financial Times*, 6 March 2016) <https://next.ft.com/content/daf9f04a-e07d-11e5-8d9b-e88a2a889797> accessed 2 January 2016.
195. Sterling Seagrave, *Lord of the Rim* (Bantam Press 1997).
196. Stephan Klingner, Stepanie Pravemann and Michael Becker, 'Service Productivity in Different Industries' [2015] 22 (2) Benchmarking: An International Journal.
197. Steven Vago, *Law and Society* (Prentice-Hall 1981).
198. Steven Beattie, Donald Lamson and Marc Oliver Schmidt, 'Anti-Money Laundering Issues for Financial Institutions' (*Financier Worldwide*, December 2013) <http://www.financierworldwide.com/anti-money-laundering-issues-for-financial-institutions/#.Vw6nV7TFvkI> accessed 10 January 2016.

199. Stijin Classens, Daniela Klingebiel and Luc Laeven, 'Resolving Systemic Financial Crisis: Policies and Institutions' (2004) *3377 The World Bank*, 13 <http://documents.worldbank.org/curated/en/306631468780599186 /126526322_20041117165058/additional/wps3377.pdf> accessed 18 November 2015.

200. Tam Christian, 'Enforcement', in G. Ulfstein, T. Marauhn and A. Zimmermann (eds.), *Making Treaties Work* (CUP 2007).

201. Tatiana Tropina, 'Do Digital Technologies Facilitate Illicit Financial Flows?' (World Development Report: Digital Dividends, 2016) <http://pubdocs. worldbank.org/en/396751453906608518/WDR16-BP-Do-Digital-Tech nologies-Facilitate-Illicit-Financial-Flows-Tropina.pdf> accessed 10 February 2017.

202. Tax Justice Network, 'Financial Secrecy Index' (Tax Justice Network, 30 January 2018) <http://www.financialsecrecyindex.com/database/China.xml #t129> accessed 11 February 2018.

203. Tax Justice Network-Africa, *Why Africa Should Stand Up for Tax Justice* (Pambazuka Press 2011).

204. Temenos, 'Identifying Anti Money Laundering Issues in Chinese Banks' (Asian Banker Researcher) <https://www.theasianbanker.com/assets/media/dl/whi tepaper/Asian%20Banker%20White%20Paper%20-%20China%20Anti-Money %20Laundry%20(English).pdf> accessed 4 June 2016.

205. Gunther Teubner, *Law as an Autopoietic System* (Blackwell Publishers 1993).

206. The Associated Press, 'Late Nigerian Dictator Looted Nearly $500 Million, Swiss Say' (*New York Times*, 19 August 2004) <http://www.nytimes.com/20 04/08/19/world/late-nigerian-dictator-looted-nearly-500-million-swiss-say .html> accessed 29 September 2017.

207. The Joint Forum, 'Initiatives by the BCBS, IAIS and IOSCO to Combat Money Laundering and the Financing of Terrorism' (June 2003) <http:// www.bis.org/publ/joint05.pdf> accessed 1 May 2016.

208. The World Bank, 'Combating Money Laundering and the Financing of Terrorism: A Comprehensive Training Guide' (The World Bank, 2016) <http: //siteresources.worldbank.org/FINANCIALSECTOR/Resources/Comb attingMLandTF.pdf> accessed 10 July 2017.

209. Thomson Reuters, 'Country Risk Ranking' (Thomas Reuters) <https://risk.th omsonreuters.com/products/thomson-reuters-country-risk-ranking> accessed 20 July 2016.

210. TI, 'Were G20 Corruption Promises Nothing More than a Photo –Op?' (12 November 2015) (Transparency International, 2015) <http://www.transpare ncy.org/news/feature/were_g20_corruption_promises_nothing_more_than _a_photo_op> accessed 1 January 2016.

211. Tom Tyler, *Why People Obey the Law* (PUP 2006).

212. T. Ulen, 'The Uneasy Case for Competition Law and Regulation as Decisive Factors in Development: Some Lessons for China', *in* M. Faure and Z. Xang (eds.), *Competition Policy and Regulation. Recent Developments in China, the US and Europe* (Edward Elgar, Cheltenham, UK, 2011).

213. UNODC, 'Model Legislation' (*UNODC*) <https://www.unodc.org/unodc/ en/money-laundering/Model-Legislation.html> accessed 10 August 2017.

214. U.S. Department of State, '2016 International Narcotics Control Strategy Report: Countries/Jurisdictions of Primary Concern – China' (U.S.

Department of State, 2016) <https://www.state.gov/j/inl/rls/nrcrpt/2016/vol2/253391.htm> accessed 11 February 2017.

215. US Department of State, Diplomacy in Action, '2015 International Narcotics Control Strategy Report' (US Department of State, 2015) <http://www.state.gov/j/inl/rls/nrcrpt/2015/> accessed 30 April 2016.

216. Vern Mckinley, 'After the Crisis: Revisiting the "Banks Are Special" and "Safety Net" Doctrines' (Mercatus Research – George Mason University, 2015) <https://www.mercatus.org/system/files/McKinley-Are-Banks-Special.pdf> accessed July 2017.

217. Victor Thuronyi, 'Drafting Tax Legislation' (Tax Law Design and Drafting: IMF, 1996) 2 <https://www.imf.org/external/pubs/nft/1998/tlaw/eng/ch3.pdf> accessed 11 February 2017.

218. Walter Rodney, *How Europe Underdeveloped Africa* (Bogle L'Ouverture Publications Ltd 1988).

219. Wang Shucheng, 'Predictions on the Development and Direction of Legislation', *in* Yuwen W. Li (ed.), *The China Legal Development Yearbook* (Volume 2, 2009) Brill.

220. Wendy Nelson Espeland and Michael Sauder, 'Rankings and Reactivity: How Public Measures Recreate Social Worlds' [2007] 113 (1) American Journal of Sociology.

221. Soren C. Winter and Peter J. May, 'Motivation for Compliance with Environmental Regulations' [2001] 20 (4) Journal of Policy Analysis and Management.

222. Marie Wilke, 'Emerging Informal Network Structures in Global Governance: Inside the Anti-Money Laundering Regime' [2008] 77 (4) Nordic Journal of International Law.

223. William Cohan, 'How Wall Street's Bankers Stayed Out of Jail' (*The Atlantic*, September 2015) <http://www.theatlantic.com/magazine/archive/2015/09/how-wall-streets-bankers-stayed-out-of-jail/399368/> accessed 1 January 2016.

224. William Hornblower, 'A Century of "Judge-Made" Law' [1907] 7 (7) CLR.

225. 'Wolfsberg Anti-Money Laundering Principles for Private' (The Wolfsberg Group, 2012) <http://www.wolfsberg-principles.com/pdf/standards/Wolfsberg-Private-Banking-Prinicples-May-2012.pdf> accessed 10 June 2016.

226. Wouter Bossu and Dawn Chew, 'But We Are Different!' 12 Common Weaknesses in Banking Laws, and What to Do about Them (2015) IMF Working Paper WP/15/2000 <https://poseidon01.ssrn.com/delivery.php?ID=5761210200030200820971020190920780640000430770330240240750020020420740000250831080291040811020460100300040021170981161160880240920720710250710930710070951080770890100300860006021071&EXT=pdf> accessed 19 May 2016.

227. Xue Bin Li, *Money Laundering and Its Regulation in China* (UMI Dissertation Publishing 2009) 256.

4 The Agency Relationship between Collective Principals and Their Interaction with African Countries and Emerging Economies

Introduction

Information sharing is crucial in combating financial crimes. Hence, the collaboration between International Financial Institutions (IFIs) and the Financial Action Task Force (FATF) is aimed at presenting a synchronized global approach to counter illicit crimes, thereby facilitating information sharing with agents. The collective principals (IFIs/FATF) interact with agents (countries) to advance transparency of information and cure any underlining asymmetries. Findings however reveal that countries with the highest degree of integration and potential compliance levels have the strongest incentive to interact with IFIs/FATF. African countries (ACs) do not fall within this category and to evade sanctions, these countries interact strategically with the collective principals. Yet, financial crime remains a borderless crime and can flow from ACs to highly integrated countries. Acknowledging this, the interaction between these countries is examined to determine how compliance is generated in these instances.

The first section examines the relationship between the collective principals. The evolution of their relationship is examined in light of anti-money laundering and counter-terrorist financing (AML/CFT) rulemaking, implementation and compliance measures aimed at fostering standardization for application ease. The second section focuses on the relationship between the collective principals and agent-states. It analyses how the level of integration with the global financial system and perceived compliance levels play a role in resolving or escalating information asymmetry. It further considers how information asymmetry can hinder cross-border transactions between countries at various ends of the spectrum of global financial integration and compliance. Regarding cross-border banking, it contends that countries converge better when it serves their self-interest and they have capacity. The monitoring and sanctioning tools employed by the collective principals in evading the shortcomings associated with information asymmetry are considered. The third section concludes the analysis.

Rule Design, Implementation and Compliance

The reverse and continuing agency relationship postulate that all developed and developing countries are agents to the collective principals (IFIs/FATF). This means that African countries and emerging economies (ACs/EEs) fall within the purview of agents to the collective principals. As the proximate principal (PP) within this context, the FATF has the authority, as delegated from the agents, to issue rules which incorporate compliance measures. IFIs, as extended principals (EP) only have the authority to assess compliance levels, provide technical assistance (TA), organize high-level meetings and back up sanctions by the PP. However, in discharge of their assessment responsibilities, IFIs usually acquire practical knowledge of the workability or suitability of rules. This grants them the expertise to advise the PP on the amendment of or addition to certain existing rules/standards.

It is against this background that this chapter discusses the evolution of the relationship between the collective principals in rulemaking, implementation and compliance aimed at ensuring a unified approach to combating money laundering/terrorist financing (ML/TF). Whilst recognizing that 'ideally' all countries delegate authority to collective principals for this purpose, this is not inclusive of ACs that are uninvolved in the delegation process. Therefore, their interests are not reflected at any stage or are discounted as unparalleled to the global economy's direction. This has occasioned agency slack aimed at ensuring continued compliance in a bid to retain their corner within the global economy.

Rule Design: Relationship between the FATF and IFIs

The FATF, with assistance from IFIs, constructs global recommendations for transplantation to nation-states (agents). Agents, i.e., national legislators, ensure that transplanted recommendations transcribed to legislations reflect the principals' objectives. A deviation, which may be in favour of local factors, may necessitate sanctions in the form of financial isolation from the international financial market.

Recommendations/Standards for transplantation created by principal(s) are referred to as 'soft law', a nomenclature attributed to the creation of a global order through the stipulation of best practices applicable to autonomous countries and organisations.[1] These recommendations which set benchmarks that 'gives advice to many'[2] gain their peculiarity from capturing rulemaking through the use of voluntary standards injected with a measure of flexibility.[3] These standards form a category of rules that address public policy issues.[4] This form of recommendation design is employed to solve cross-border issues affecting various countries, adding to the world's predictability.[5] This is a major stabilising factor in a world where relative power is rapidly shifting.

---

1   Rainer Hulsse and Dieter Kerwer, 'Global Standards in Action: Insights from Anti-Money Laundering Regulations' [2007] 14 (5) Organization 625, 627.
2   Brunsson Nils, 'Standardization as Organization' *in* M. Egeberg and P. Laegried (eds.) *Organizing Political Institutions: Essays for Johan P. Olsen* (Oslo: Scandinavian University Press, 1999) 109 –128.
3   *Hulsse and Kerwer* (n 1).
4   Ibid.
5   Frank Vibert, 'Reforming International Rule Making' [2012] 2 (3) Global Policy 391, 391.

Arguably, there are profound differences between hard law and soft law instruments, and the spaces they regulate. For instance, though borne out of negotiations with actors that are seemingly bound by a unified objective, unlike hard law, 'soft laws' lack binding enactment power.[6] Organisations such as the Basel Committee on Banking Supervision (BCBS) that are involved in setting best practices on banking capital requirements typify this.[7] The BCBS's role requires it to undertake a large amount of rulemaking due to the uncertainty in its regulatory niche.[8] Consequently, these rules are sometimes classified as 'hard-law' due to their precision and requirements on countries to legislate on the guidelines. This extends the concept beyond treaties[9] which are employed to deal with areas of law that have some measure of certainty such as trade or monetary policy. Additionally, with hard law, there is reliance on military intervention, coercive diplomacy and economic means for binding powers.[10] Such enforcement approaches are unavailable with soft law. However, unlike soft law rules which can be easily reassessed,[11] hard law is rigid, with changes to treaty agreements possible only through costly and burdensome renegotiation.[12]

There is a dichotomy between hard and soft law rules in the context of international law. However, the hardening of soft law boundaries through separate legal instruments internationally or domestically denotes a continuum within which several instruments of coercion or persuasion exist.[13] Nevertheless, its source is usually not authoritative or binding. It is within this setting that the FATF, the foremost standard-setting body for AML/CFT sits.[14]

Ideally, international rules should permit regulatory space to ensure its adaptability. Vibert contends that in engineering compliance, international rulemaking does not in fact overregulate an area.[15] This can be attributable to the 'mirroring' of law which postulates that the design or construction of globally applica-

---

6   Dinah Shelton, 'Normative Hierarchy in International Law' [2006] 100 AM. J. Int'l/ 291, 319.

7   Kerwer Dieter, 'Rules that Many Use: Standards and Global Regulation' [2005] 12 (4) Governance 611, 619; Timothy Meyer, 'Soft Law as Delegation' [2008] 32 (3) Fordham International Law Journal 888, 892.

8   Ibid.

9   Raustiala Kal and Anne-Marie Slaughter, 'International Law, International Relations and Compliance' [2002] 02 (2) Princeton Law & Public Affairs Paper 538, 539.

10 Gallarotti Giulio, 'Soft Soft Power: What it Is, Why it's Important, and the Conditions for its Effective Use' [2011] 4 (1) Journal of Political Power 25, 29.

11 For instance, the FATF recommendations were reassessed in 2001, 2012.

12 Wilson, Ernest J., 'Hard Power, Soft Power, Smart Power' [2008] 616 (1) The Annals of the American Academy of Political and Social Science.

13 Brooke A. Smith-Windsor, 'Hard Power, Soft Power Reconsidered' [2000] 1 (3) Canadian Military Journal 51, 52. Soft law is hardened in application, but its source is usually not authoritative or binding, see *Meyer* (n 7).

14 Saby Ghoshray, 'Combating Threats to the International Financial System: The Financial Action Task Force: Compliance Convergence in FATF Rulemaking: The Conflict Between Agency Capture and Soft Law' [2014/2015] 59. N.Y.L School Review 521, 528.

15 *Vibert* (n 5).

ble rules for governance should reflect countries' socio-economic and political peculiarities. Hence, flexibility of international rules is required for universal adaptability. Put simply, laws reflect how societies see themselves.[16] Therefore, the creation of these rules/standards through networks requires that actors construct and convey them in a way that appreciates the uniqueness of countries.[17] The actors in this case are staff of international institutions, such as the FATF, the International Monetary Fund (IMF) and the World Bank. As principals, these actors must interact with representatives of member states' legislature to ensure that rules adopted are suitable to those states. This ensures that rules adopted result in the best outcomes for global regulation of ML/TF in the form of financial integrity and stability. More importantly, these actors must also interact with themselves to ensure synchronisation of rules which makes for easy adaptability.

INTERACTION BETWEEN PRINCIPALS IN RULEMAKING

The FATF manages global regulation in AML/CFT through a comprehensive array of recommendations related to prescribed conduct.[18] However, its lack of an internal constitution or constituent charter[19] and a non-direct supervisory enforcement ability renders its laws soft. This seeming deficiency is resolved by two means. Firstly, its issue of specific guidelines for prudent behaviour and publication of compliance levels of countries. These ensure that the FATF recommendations become a comprehensive governance framework for member and non-member jurisdictions.

Secondly, through collaboration with established supranational bodies such as the IMF, the United Nations Security Council (UNSC) and the World Bank who have observatory membership on the FATF.[20] Such engagements reveal that the FATF does not act in isolation when prescribing recommendations, since assessment reports from IFIs are fed back into the re-modelling of the FATF standards.[21] Recommendation 1 of the FATF which adopts a risk-based approach to

16 Gregory Shaffer, 'Transnational Legal Process and State Change' [2012] 37 (2) Law & Social Inquiry 229, 238.
17 Ibid. 229, 259. They are constructed or conveyed by actors, including government officials, members of international secretariats, professionals/business representatives and civil society representatives.
18 FATF, 'The FATF Recommendations' (*FATF*, 2012) <http://www.fatf-gafi.org/media/ fatf/documents/recommendations/pdfs/FATF_Recommendations.pdf> accessed 13 April 2017.
19 James T. Gathii, 'The Financial Action Task Force and Global Administrative Law' (2010) J Prof. Law 197, 198; Beth Simmons, 'International Efforts Against Money Laundering' *in* Dinah Shelton (ed.), *Commitment and Compliance: The Role of Non-Binding Norms in the International Legal System* (OUP, 2000, First Published 2000) 255.
20 FATF, 'FATF Members and Observers' (*FATF*) <http://www.fatf-gafi.org/about/memb ersandobservers/> accessed 13 April 2017.
21 FATF, 'Procedures for the FATF Fourth Round of AML/CFT Mutual Evaluations' (*FATF*, 2013) <http://www.fatf-gafi.org/media/fatf/documents/methodology/FATF-4th-Rou nd-Procedures.pdf> accessed 10 April 2017.

technical compliance illustrates this. It is argued to have been included to douse the FATF's legitimacy crisis as requested by the IFIs.[22]

Additionally, these relationships have compelled the FATF to exert authority as a legitimate supervisory body capable of setting international standards.[23] The FATF also gains its normative authority through its working relationship with the United Nations Counter-Terrorism Committee (UNCTC) and endorsement of its recommendations by the Sanctions Committee of the UNSC.[24] The global endorsement of various recommendations through specific UNSC resolutions has significantly contributed to enhancing the FATF status as a supervisory body, transforming its recommendations from mere prescriptions to legitimate legal norms.[25]

An examination of the relationship between the FATF and the IFIs reveals a collective principal framework, with the FATF as the PP and the IFIs as EPs to the agents in the context of rulemaking. This position is attributable to the actors' individual and collaborative roles in the realisation that so long as they are bound by principal responsibilities, no principal of nation-states is an island.[26] Rather, efficiency is derived when expertise and specializations are harnessed. Cooperation in this circumstance can be defined to include exchange of information, analysis, views and deliberations on best practices between IFIs and FATF officials.[27]

A scrutiny of the FATF and IFIs partnership illustrates how the FATF cultivated these relationships to advance its objectives. IFIs now provide technical assistance and carry out assessments on the soundness or vulnerabilities of economies to ML/TF. Previously, the IMF was solely responsible for providing short-term loans to stabilise members' balance of payments concerns,[28] whilst the Bank was responsible for providing long-term loans for development projects.[29] Such disparity in their specializations required no collaboration or consultation. However, these institutions began to overlap their mandates over

---

22 Sean Hagan, 'Revision to the Financial Action Task Force (FATF) Standard – Information Note to the Executive Board' (*IMF*, July 2012) <https://www.imf.org/external/np/pp/eng/2012/071712a.pdf> accessed 11 May 2017.

23 *Ghoshray* (n 14).

24 FATF, 'Briefing Briefing to the United Nations Security Council Committee, New York' (26,October 2009) <http://www.un.org/en/sc/ctc/docs/statements/2009_10_26_fatf_brief.pdf> accessed 19 April 2017.

25 Kenneth Blazejewski, 'The FATF and Its Institutional Partners: Improving the Effectiveness and Accountability of Trans-Governmental Networks' [2008] 22 Temp. Int'l & Comp LJ 1, 14; *Ghoshray* (n 14).

26 James Boughton, 'Tearing Down Wall' (IMF 1990–1999) 82.

27 Ibid.; *FATF* (n 21).

28 IMF 'Articles of Agreement' <https://www.imf.org/external/pubs/ft/aa/pdf/aa.pdf> accessed 26 April 2017.

29 IMF and IBRD, 'Articles of Agreement: International Bank for Reconstruction and Development' [1944] <http://siteresources.worldbank.org/EXTARCHIVES/Resources/IBRD_Articles_of_Agreement.pdf> accessed 10 April 2017.

time, requiring partnership and continuous discussions for effective division of labour.[30] In 1997, the Bank-Fund Financial Sector Liaison Committee was established to oversee collaboration between the two institutions, a process which culminated in the creation of the Financial Sector Assessment Program (FSAP) in 1999.

The integration of these institutions was not without hitch. The IMF's mission chiefs consistently complained of the World Bank's bureaucracy or indifferent response. Conversely, World Bank staff complained that the IMF staff were inflexible and too quick to draw conclusions.[31] Indicating that irrespective of similar structures and culture of staff cross-fertilisation, the ethos within these organizations varied, hindering effective collaboration. Through this period of IFIs collaboration, their relationship with the FATF was strained. Although the FATF considered a relationship expedient, the IFIs did not. Indeed, the IFIs' initial reception of the FATF's proposal for collaboration was lukewarm.[32] They expressed concern that AML/CFT lay outside their mandate.[33]

However, some elements of coordination between these institutions existed for two reasons. Firstly, IFIs and the FATF are created and largely funded by the same set of countries – a commonality that led to frequent networked meetings. Secondly, the role of the IFIs in assessing compliance level of countries in specific areas and providing technical expertise based on its FSAP reports – a niche which was crucial in expanding the FATF's reach. This meant that coordinated meetings were vital.[34] The latter reason propelled the FATF to seek partnership with the IFIs post the commencement of the FSAP, of which the Report of the Observance of Standards and Codes (ROSC) is a key component.[35] The ROSC is particularly relevant as it reports on the implementation of 12 benchmarks of good practice earmarked by the IMF as areas relevant to the financial and economic soundness of the state.[36] One of the benchmarks is the FATF AML/CFT

---

30 *Boughton* (n 26).

31 Ibid.

32 Pete Engardio, 'Commentary: Don't Use the IMF to Push U.S. Foreign Policy' (Bloomberg, 26 November 2001) <https://www.bloomberg.com/news/articles/2001-11-25/commentary-dont-use-the-imf-to-push-u-dot-s-dot-foreign-policy> accessed 10 April 2017.

33 IMF and the World Bank, 'Anti-Money Laundering and Combatting the Financing of Terrorism (AML/CFT): Materials Concerning Staff Progress Towards the Development of a Comprehensive AML/CFT Methodology and Assessment Process' (*IMF and World Bank*, 2002) <http://www.imf.org/External/np/mae/aml/2002/eng/061102.pdf > accessed 10 April 2017.

34 Given the role of the IFIs in monitoring and implementing the FATF's recommendations, which overlaps the FATF's standards formulation mandate, meetings ensure coordinated efforts that save resources without unnecessary overlaps. This is crucial in engineering changes to set recommendations.

35 *Blazejewski* (n 25) 1, 30.

36 IMF Factsheet, Standards and Codes: The Role of the IMF (*IMF Factsheet*, 2017) <http://www.imf.org/About/Factsheets/Sheets/2016/08/01/16/25/Standards-and-Codes?pdf=1> accessed 10 April 2017.

recommendations. Its inclusion signalled a recognition of the macroeconomic problems posed by ML/TF.[37] Hence, the ROSC has been identified as a means of assessing its recommendations amongst non-member states of the FATF. This move was partly based on the FATF's membership shortage which necessitated partnership to penetrate hard-to-reach states through the voluntary FSAP instruments.[38] More importantly, the 9/11 attack propelled the IFIs to engage collaboratively with the FATF and align with its participation schedule[39] as endorsed by their boards.[40]

Consequently, the IFIs engaged in a 12-month pilot programme to include FATF recommendations within the FSAP and Offshore Centre Program (OFC) assessment, whilst the FATF and its regional bodies continued their mutual evaluations.[41] This scheme, which facilitated an effective working relationship between the necessary actors,[42] was not without its difficulties. For instance, IFIs continually critiqued the FATF recommendations for not considering the peculiarities of countries. The FATF's subsequent adoption of a risk-based AML/CFT approach propelled the IFIs to re-endorse the recommendations and work hand in hand to ensure reflective standards.[43] This relationship has been cemented by information and staff cross-fertilisation. In particular, the IMF has employed FATF staff in its Financial Integrity Group (FIG), a unit of its legal department involved in FSAP preparations and provision of technical assistance to countries combating ML/TF.

As expected, the relationship between these actors created a division of labour in executing the FSAP. Whilst the IFIs jointly worked on building the AML/CFT framework for developing and EEs, the IMF was solely responsible for that of developed countries. As stated, they have minimal roles to play in rule design as their task is restricted to the assessment of and compliance with FATF

37 IMF, 'Financial System Abuse, Financial Crime and Money Laundering – Background Paper' (*IMF*, 2001) <http://www.imf.org/en/Publications/Policy-Papers/Issues/2016/12/31/Financial-System-Abuse-Financial-Crime-and-Money-Laundering-Background-Paper-PP128> accessed 10 February 2017.
38 IMF Press Release No.14/447, 'Press Release: IMF Executive Board Concludes Review of the FSAP' (2014) < http://www.imf.org/external/np/sec/pr/2014/pr14447.htm> accessed 12 April 2017. Both IFIs had 184 member countries and over 120 participated voluntarily in the FSAP. See IMF and the World Bank, 'Financial Sector Assessment Program – Review, Lessons and Issues Going Forward' (2005) <https://www.imf.org/External/np/fsap/2005/022205.htm> accessed 11 April 2017.
39 IMF and the World Bank, 'Financial Sector Assessment Program – Review, Lessons and Issues Going Forward' (2005) <https://www.imf.org/External/np/fsap/2005/022205.htm> accessed 11 April 2017.
40 IMF and the World Bank, Twelve Month Pilot Program of Anti-Money Laundering and Combatting the Financing of Terrorism (AML/CFT) Assessments 7 (2004) <https://www.imf.org/external/np/aml/eng/2004/031004.pdf> accessed 10 April 2017.
41 Ibid.
42 IMF, 'The IMF and the World Bank' (2016) <http://www.imf.org/en/About/Factsheets/Sheets/2016/07/27/15/31/IMF-World-Bank> accessed 10 February 2017.
43 *Hagan* (n 22).

recommendations. However, these are crucial in highlighting policy issues that can be imputed in the modification of the recommendations. This implies that IFIs continually deal with issues related to AML/CFT rule design through their interaction with the FATF. Thus, over time, staff of IFIs developed substantial expertise relevant to AML/CFT regulation.[44]

The interaction between these institutions is further heightened by the establishment of country and regional bodies. These are crucial for resolving information asymmetry and ensuring compliance with standards. Thus, whilst the FATF established FATF-Styled Regional Bodies (FSRBs),[45] the IMF/World Bank both have regional and country offices.[46] FSRB member countries inducted after 1990 were included to ensure improved representation, because the plenary meetings grant countries an opportunity to air their opinions only through regional bodies. FSRB member countries are classed as 'associate members' of the FATF.

The FSRB was praised as an ingenious means of globalising the FATF without losing its decision-making process. The extent to which the creation and collaboration are equitable is however questionable due to the FATF's composition, its decision-making process and the sanctioning mechanism.

The FATF cadre, which is responsible for framing decisions on AML/CFT, is composed of the plenary, president, steering group and secretariat.[47] Within this structure, the secretariat, through the instrumentality of the Policy Development Group (PDG) is responsible for developing global policies and best practices[48] which receive assent from the plenary – the body with the authority to adopt FATF standards, guidance and reports.[49] The secretariat assists the president in running daily activities alongside coordinating work groups.[50] The president convenes and chairs meetings of the plenary and steering group and oversees the secretariat.[51]

---

44 IMF, 'Intensified Work on Anti-Money Laundering and Combating Financing of Terrorism (AML/CFT): Joint Progress Report on the Work of the IMF and World Bank' (*IMF*, April 2002) <https://www.imf.org/External/np/mae/aml/2002/eng/041702.pdf > accessed 7 July 2017.

45 APG, 'FATF & FSRB' (*APG*) <http://www.apgml.org/fatf-and-fsrb/page.aspx?p=940 65425-e6aa-479f-8701-5ca5d07ccfe8> accessed 10 July 2017; U.S Department of State: Diplomacy in Action, 'The Financial Action Task Force and FATF-Style Regional Bodies' (US Department of State) <https://www.state.gov/j/inl/rls/nrcrpt/2015/vol2/239046.htm> accessed 10 July 2017.

46 Tine Hanrieder, *International Organization in Time: Fragmentation and Reform* (1st edn, OUP 2015) 119.

47 FATF, 'Financial Action Task Force Mandate (2012–2020)' (2012) <http://www.fatf -gafi.org/media/fatf/documents/FINAL%20FATF%20MANDATE%202012-2020.pdf> accessed 13 April 2017.

48 FATF, 'FATF Secretariat' (*FATF*, 2017) <http://www.fatf-gafi.org/about/fatfsecretaria t/> accessed 20 January 2017.

49 *FATF* (n 47).

50 Ibid.

51 Ibid.

The workings of the secretariat and plenary sessions show the lack of equity in the standards-making process. For instance, the secretariat's workings reveal the influence of Organisation for Economic Co-operation and Development (OECD) countries in the daily processes of the FATF. This influence is to the exclusion of 'associate members' whose input is only required at the plenary sessions – which are held three times a year.[52] During these sessions, all the votes of 'associate members' count as one as compared to core members that exercise one vote each. This restricts the extent to which the voices of associate members are considered in the design of standards. Furthermore, the FATF, which is housed by the OECD can only employ OECD citizen staff,[53] a provision which impliedly excludes ACs/EEs from participating in the daily workings of the secretariat. This highlights the minimal input of ACs in the formulation of policies or the daily workings of the FATF. Yet, the FATF would wield coercive powers against them.[54]

The disparity amongst countries in the FATF standard-setting process is also commonplace in the IFIs' decision-making process. For instance, in the IFIs' head offices, the Board's voting structure is ingrained in their decision-making process, which relies on the existing quota configuration. Thus, a country's vote is dependent on its funding contribution to the IFIs.[55] The United States has the largest quota with approximately 82.99 million Special Drawing Rights (SDRs)[56] which totals 831,406 billion dollars. The United States is followed by Japan, China, Germany, France and the United Kingdom, four of which are part of the G7. Collectively, all other countries of the world hold 23.2% voting rights,[57] with Africa holding only 5.6% of the overall votes.[58] This is similar to the World Bank system where voting rights are determined by each country's agreed annual contribution to the Bank[59] which reflects how much weight the country carries in the world economy.[60]

52   Their ability to frame recommendations/decisions at meetings are restricted due to their limited involvement in driving discourses or agendas.

53   OECD: Better Policies for Better Lives, 'OECD Careers' (*OECD*) <http://www.oecd.org/careers/whatwelookfor.htm> accessed 20 January 2016.

54   As members of the FATF, the Brazil, Russia, India, China, South Africa (BRICS) countries are however privy to the plenary discussions and can sit as president of the FATF; the extent of their influence in this role is however debatable.

55   Ngaire Woods, *The Globalizers: The IMF, the World Bank and their Borrower* (CUP, 2006) 22–24.

56   IMF, 'IMF Members' Quotas and Voting Power, and IMF Board of Governors' (*IMF*, 24 January 2017) <https://www.imf.org/external/np/sec/memdir/members.aspx#U> accessed 24 January 2017.

57   Ibid.; IMF, 'Illustration of Proposed Quota and Voting Shares' (*IMF*, 2010) <http://www.imf.org/external/np/sec/pr/2010/pdfs/pr10418_table.pdf> accessed 15 July 2016.

58   Ibid.

59   World Bank, 'IBRD Articles of Agreement' (*World Bank*, 1989) <http://siteresources.worldbank.org/EXTABOUTUS/Resources/ibrd-articlesofagreement.pdf> accessed 20 June 2017.

60   *Woods* (n 55).

The quota diversity is also enshrined in the executive directors (EDs) spread. The Bank has 26 EDs, the largest stakeholders of this decision-making organ – the United States, Japan, France, the United Kingdom, China, Russia and Saudi Arabia each have one ED appointed by their countries.[61] Other members are grouped into 16 constituencies, each electing one ED. This structure gives European countries the second-highest representation, whilst all ACs have three EDs.[62] Given that a bloc can only have one vote, developing countries and ACs have limited say in AML/CFT matters, notwithstanding that these are ML/FT-prone countries. Undoubtedly, this overarching decision-making process is unreflective of the diverse membership of these institutions, heightened by their undemocratic decision-making process.

Despite the shortcomings of these institutions, there is a trajectory of strengthened collaboration in standard-making as a step towards curbing illicit crimes. Legitimacy concerns plague the collective principal's agenda. Nonetheless, their interaction has presented a united front for countries combating ML/TF by instituting rules that provide for a coordinated compliance approach to illicit crimes.

Implementation and Compliance: Relationship between IFIs and the FATF

Legislations are inadequate without implementation and compliance. Implementation denotes the operationalisation of legislative requirements, whilst compliance warrants that such actions be done in strict adherence to laws and regulations. Hence, when a Financial Intelligence Unit (FIU) is established, the FATF recommendation 29 is deemed implemented; compliance is achieved when this is done in alignment with the law.

Compliance would however only be effective and accorded value where it converges with internal ethics. Therefore, compliance is effective when it considers the values of countries. The effectiveness of such compliance can be gleaned from an instance where strict customer due diligence (CDD) is mandated to operate within a cash-based society. Such rule would result in a regulatory paradox as it would defeat the overarching aim of financial integrity, whilst facilitating ML/TF outside the banking system. For example, country (A) may be adjudged to have 'low level of effectiveness' and may not evade the opprobrium of the law, whereas country (B) adopting the CDD/ know your customer (KYC) in a cashless society would be deemed to have a 'high level of effectiveness'. This is worsened for country (A) as compliance comes with its costs. Although the principals (FATF/IFIs) consider these costs as necessary to protect institutions within countries

---

61 World Bank, *A Guide to the World Bank* (Third Edition, The World Bank) 9.

62 Although some other ACs are merged with foreign countries in bloc 21 where Egypt and Libya are classed with middle eastern states, so also Ghana and Tunisia and Algeria are merged in bloc 16. See IBRD, 'Voting Power of Executive Directors' (*Corporate Secretariat*, 6 February 2017) <http://siteresources.worldbank.org/BODINT/Resources/278027-1215524804501/IBRDEDsVotingTable.pdf> accessed 21 February 2017.

from rule transgression and consequent regulatory sanction, the agents (financial and non-financial institutions) consider it unnecessary, cumbersome and a hindrance to profit.

The above scenario between the principals and country (A) agent depicts a conflict of interest thus warranting continuous monitoring by the principals and necessitating further collaboration between these actors to foster systematical information exchange. In theory, this may potentially guarantee the elimination of conflicts of interest and the integrity of the international financial system. It would also place an extra policing role on principals, requiring them to monitor and report on compliance activities within states. Furthermore, the principals would be privy to private information which may affect rule modifications to cure the defects faced by country (A). In practice, it may be more complex given the absence of preconditions for effective regulation.

Within the context of rule implementation and compliance, the IFIs are the principals and the agent states institutions are the agents. Hence, the agents include financial and non-financial institutions, regulatory bodies, enforcement bodies and the judicial and executive arm of government. As is the case in legislative interactions, the principals present a united front in their interactions with agents, to ensure a standardized approach devoid of quality disparities.

INTERACTIONS BETWEEN PRINCIPALS IN SETTING IMPLEMENTATION
AND COMPLIANCE FRAMEWORKS

Presently, an intimate collaboration exists between the IFIs and the FATF, aimed at ensuring implementation of and compliance with the FATF standards. This however was not always the case. Upon engagement in assessments of compliance levels by the FATF, the IFIs expressed that their mandate restricted them from engaging in assessments of law enforcement issues throughout the pilot programme.[63] This position was solidified by the IMF Board which stated that it would be 'inappropriate' for the IMF to become involved in law enforcement issues.[64] It therefore limited itself to assessing FATF criteria which it considered 'macro-economically relevant'.[65] However, the rigorousness of the IFIs' assessments of implementation to the exclusion of enforcement necessitated the FATF to call for a revision of the IMF's decision on the ground that it hindered the production of fully integrated assessments.

---

63 IMF and the World Bank, 'Anti-Money Laundering and Combatting the Financing of Terrorism: Review of the Quality and Consistency of Assessments Reports and the Effectiveness of Coordination' (2006) <https://www.imf.org/external/np/pp/eng/2006/041806r.pdf> accessed 11 April 2017.
64 IMF and World Bank, 'Anti-Money Laundering and Combatting the Financing of Terrorism (AML/CFT): Proposals to Assess a Global Standard and to Prepare ROSCs' (2002) <http://www.imf.org/external/np/mae/aml/2002/eng/071702.pdf> accessed 15 April 2017.
65 Ibid.

This limited framework which deterred effective collaboration between principals necessitated revision. Consequently, the FATF beckoned the IFIs to reassess this limitation and revise their evaluation approach, to become more comprehensive.[66] The IMF Board subsequently adopted the FATF recommendations as a regular component of its FSAP and OFC programmes, and the World Bank[67] followed suit.[68] This has improved communication between both institutions and created room for expert reliance on information exchange.

This partnership has facilitated AML/CFT implementation and compliance. Blazejewsji contends that collaboration between the principals contributes to AML/CFT implementation in five ways.[69] Firstly, through assessments conducted by the IFI programmes which evaluate AML/CFT measures within countries. He contends that the programmes contained within the FSAP and OFC are far-reaching and comprehensive. By June 2006, IFIs had assessed over 60 jurisdictions on compliance with the FATF recommendations.[70]

Secondly, the IFIs aligned their assessment methodology with that of the FATF to facilitate uniform benchmarking of recommendations.[71] This was concretised by the fact that these standards became the only ROSC standards for which the IFIs accepted assessments conducted by external partners.[72]

Thirdly, the IFIs maintain quality control, standardization and coordination of AML/CFT assessments.[73] These came in response to an IMF report which revealed a 'high degree of variability in the quality of reports' and between ongoing efforts to increase assessment quality.[74] Hence the IFIs have worked to ensure

---

66 *IMF & The World Bank* (n 40).

67 IMF, 'Public Information Notice No.04/33: IMF Executive Board Reviews and Enhances Efforts for Anti-Money Laundering and Combatting the Financing of Terrorism' (2 April 2004) <https://www.imf.org/en/News/Articles/2015/09/28/04/53/pn0433> accessed 6 April 2017; IMF, 'Press Release No. 04/70: IMF, World Bank Enhance Efforts at Combating Money Laundering, Terrorist Financing' (2 April 2004) <http://www.imf.org/external/np/sec/pr/2004/pr0470.htm> accessed 4 February 2017.

68 2003–2004 the FATF stated that its 'key priority' was to develop its relationship with IFIs to ensure global action in combatting ML/TF.

69 *Blazejewski* (n 25) 15, 31.

70 US Department of Treasury, 'Implementation of Legislative Provisions Relating to the International Monetary Fund: A Report to Congress 11' (United States Department of the Treasury, March 2006) <https://www.treasury.gov/resource-center/international/int-monetary-fund/Documents/2015%20IMF%20Legislative%20Mandates%20Report.pdf> accessed 10 May 2017.

71 The World Bank and the IMF, 'Financial Sector Assessment: A Handbook' (2005) <http://documents.worldbank.org/curated/en/306701468337879923/pdf/337970rev0Final0Assessment01PUBLIC1.pdf> accessed 10 June 2016.

72 IMF, 'Public Information Notice No.11/74: IMF Executive Board Reviews Efforts in Anti-Money Laundering and Combating the Financing of Terrorism' (27 June 2011) <http://www.imf.org/external/np/sec/pn/2011/pn1174.htm> accessed 6 April 2017.

73 IMF, 'Anti-Money Laundering/Combating the Financing of Terrorism (AML/CFT)' <https://www.imf.org/external/np/leg/amlcft/eng/aml2.htm> accessed 10 April 2017.

74 *IMF and World Bank* (n 63).

consistency and harmonisation across the ROSCs produced by various assessing bodies,[75] and across all methodologies for assessing compliance;[76] this avoids duplication of efforts.[77]

Fourthly, the IFIs top-down perspective on AML/CFT monitoring permits their staff to analyse global trends and common weaknesses in implementation of AML/CFT measures. Such reports include the IMF Progress Report on the OFC programme which provides an exhaustive profile of compliance with FATF recommendations within the offshore countries that participate in OFC programmes.[78] Its 2005 Financial Sector Assessment Handbook highlighted some common weaknesses amongst national AML/CFT regulatory systems; so did the FATF's Mutual Evaluation Reports (MERs) of countries.[79]

Lastly, the IFIs undertake technical capacity building to enable countries to achieve maximum implementation requirements. Technical assistance, which includes training of regional[80] and country-level supervisors, has focused on how to conduct mutual evaluations in compliance with the common methodology.[81] What becomes evident is that the IFIs serve as a bedrock of the FATF's efforts to advance implementation of recommendations amongst non-FATF member states, as their involvement has led to a more robust fight against ML/TF. Blazejewski reveals the principals' collaborative approach in ensuring implementation and compliance with set recommendations transcribed to national laws and regulations.

Having discussed how collective principals engage in formulating rules and in guiding implementation and compliance, it is imperative to understand how these principals engage with agent-states.

Agency Theory: Interactions between the Collective Principals and Agent-States in Rule Making, Implementation and Compliance

The application of the agency theory (discussed in chapter 2) provides the theoretical framework to understanding potential agency problems that can arise from the principal or agent's side. For instance, agent states may slack in transplanting or implementing rules. Conversely, the principals may retort by engaging

---

75 Ibid.

76 Mario Giovanoli, 'A New Architecture for the Global Financial Market: Legal Aspects of International Standards Setting' *in* Mario Giovanoli (ed.) *International Monetary Law, Issues for the New Millennium* (OUP, 2000) 3–59.

77 Ibid.

78 *IMF and the World Bank* (n 40).

79 Ibid.

80 IMF, 'IMF Policy Paper: Review of the Fund's Strategy on Anti-Money Laundering and Combating the Financing of Terrorism' (*IMF*, February 2014) <https://www.imf.org/external/np/pp/eng/2014/022014a.pdf> accessed 10 May 2016.

81 IMF Legal Department, 'Suppressing the Financing of Terrorism: A Handbook for Legislative Drafting' (*IMF*, 2003) <https://www.imf.org/external/pubs/nft/2003/SFTH/pdf/SFTH.pdf> accessed 1 June 2016.

observatory tools, such as sanctions, technical assistance or high-level meetings. A misunderstanding of the agency slack or the agent state may however occasion misapplication of observatory tools, further perpetuating agency problems. For instance, utilizing sanctions where technical assistance should be used can weaken agent states' incentive to comply with the AML/CFT standards.

A fitting resolution of agency problems requires that any existing information asymmetry between the principals and the agent is addressed. For this to occur, two crucial factors are taken into consideration. Firstly, the level of integration of a country within the global financial market; and secondly, their perceived compliance levels with the FATF standards.[82] The level of integration is largely dependent on quantitative factors that underscore membership of the FATF such as the gross domestic product (GDP) of a country, the size of its financial institutions market and its per capita income.[83] It also encompasses qualitative factors such as the financial sector's openness and the potential of that country's systemic risk on the global financial architecture.[84] Countries with these attributes are classed as 'systematically important' by the IMF, signifying the need for heightened supervision to avoid risk of contagion should a crash occur.

The second factor, the perceived compliance level of countries addresses the attainment by countries of the necessary preconditions for effective regulation and incorporates the legal development of countries according to the FATF recommendations.

The table below shows the extent to which these factors play a role in triggering or addressing agency problems:

The following three conclusive categories are drawn from examining Table 4.1:

a. High priority (HP) is associated with countries with high level of integration despite their compliance levels, indicating a need for sustained surveillance, assessment and reduced information asymmetry. However, information asymmetry may exist where a HP country has low compliance with the AML/CFT rules, as opposed to where such country has high compliance.

b. Low priority (LP) is associated with medium or low level of integration with high level of compliance. In those countries, the risk to financial stability and integrity is low; there is minimal need to hinder information sharing.

c. Mid priority (MP) is associated with countries with low level of integration and low compliance levels. The risk these countries pose to global financial stability and integrity is considered minimal. There is however a high incentive to hinder information sharing so as to avoid sanctions. Most ACs fall within this category.

---

82 This conclusion was reached by examining of the compliance pattern of countries assessed by the FATF.

83 FATF, 'FATF Membership Policy' (*FATF*) <http://www.fatf-gafi.org/about/membersan dobservers/fatfmembershippolicy.html > accessed 11 October 2017.

84 Ibid.

Table 4.1 Factors that Influence/Trigger Information Asymmetry between Principals and Agents in AML/CFT Regulation.

S/No	Priority Level	Level of Integration[a]	Compliance Level	Effect on Financial Stability and Integrity[b]
1.	High priority	High	Low	Elevated
2.	Low priority	Medium	High	Minimal
3.	Mid priority	Low	Low	Minimal
4.	Low priority	Low	High	Very minimal
5.	High priority	High	High	Very minimal

[a] Level of integration is dependent on factors such as country GDP, size of financial institutions, per-capita income and openness of the financial sector. High integrated countries are developed countries and/emerging economies such as India and China. Medium integrated countries are certain emerging economies. Low integrated countries are developing countries and underdeveloped countries.
[b] *Elevated* = situation where the effect or risk of ML/TF lapses would have heightened effect on financial stability and integrity. *Minimal* = situation where the risk of ML/TF materializing would have marginal impact on financial stability and integrity. *Very minimal* = where the risk of ML/TF would have very marginal impact on financial stability and integrity.

HP countries which are 'highly integrated' but with perceived low level of compliance to the AML/CFT standards would be a concern to the collective principals because low compliance can affect financial stability and integrity. Brazil, a member of the FATF falls within this category. Principals carry out mutual evaluations that determine the extent of each country's compliance. Knowing that sanctions follow weak compliance, HP countries may choose to engage strategically with the principals. Supporting this assertion, Crawford and Sobel argue that when governments anticipate correction strategies by the principals which threaten capital flow and access to market, they may decide to omit or manipulate statistics.[85] With the IMF, these countries may simply request non-publication of the FSAP report, hence destroying any potential harm the market may read into their low compliance level. In a bid to document compliance in context, the mutual evaluation methodology requires that countries inform IFIs of any significant problems that arise in compliance. Whilst this ensures that the shortcomings are understood, agents are aware that these are not necessarily taken into consideration by the market or the IFIs, hence their strategic communication.

Where, however, HP countries are classed as 'highly integrated' within the global financial system and have high compliance levels, they would still be classed as high priority although they pose minimal risk to the economy.[86] This

---

85   Crawford Vincent and Sobel Joel, 'Strategic Informational Transmission' [1982] Econometrica: Journal of the Econometric Society, 1431, 1451; Manne Henry, *Insider Trading and the Stock Market* (First Edition, Free Press, 1996).
86   India and China fall within this category.

decision is necessary given that supervision is continuous, hence their placement on the IMF's Article IV surveillance. The IMF understands that though the risk these countries pose is minimal, a crisis may escalate if a bubble exists. This may have a catastrophic effect on other countries. The US role in the global financial crisis exemplifies the situation, where vulnerability in the US financial market had a catastrophic global effect. Consequently, given the high compliance levels to formulation of legislative standards and implementation, these countries are less likely to have an incentive to omit or hinder information sharing, thereby limiting the chances of information asymmetry.

The limited asymmetry or agency slack in this circumstance can be attributed to the fact that however limited their roles are, these countries, particularly EEs, are part of the rulemaking. Additionally, their financial institutions (FIs) are strongly consulted in the re-modelling of standards due to the growing maturity of their finance industry. Most practices introduced as part of the FATF rules are not necessarily very foreign to them due to their economic growth rate that has mandated numerous changes. Therefore, compliance does not require extensive re-modelling or re-learning.

LP countries with medium or low degree integration with potentially high compliance levels pose minimal risk to global financial stability or integrity. Hence their classification as 'low priority'.[87] The IMF has not classed these countries as systematically important given their limited contribution to the global world product (GWP) and per capita income, coupled with their limited openness and transparency. In such countries where potential compliance is high, the possibility of information asymmetry is reduced except in instances where compliance is a charade.

MP countries with a low degree of integration with the global financial economy and low compliance levels have limited impact on financial stability and integrity.[88] Despite their low degree of integration, they are considered mid priority because money laundering is a borderless crime and can flow across all countries. Additionally, agency concerns are raised because these countries are willing to protect their fragile space within the financial market, attract businesses and provide career advancement opportunities for their politicians. Hence, these countries are likely to manipulate information during mutual evaluations, sometimes leading to regulatory capture. EENA2, a staff member at a global multilateral bank mentioned that he did not trust the report of certain FSRBs – a concern that was pervasive within these institutions, even with the quality assurance standards.[89]

---

87   South Africa falls within this category, although one of Africa's largest economies and a member of the FATF, the IMF has not classed South Africa as systemically important given its limited contribution to the global world product (GWP) and per capita income, coupled with its limited openness and transparency.
88   This category includes Nigeria, Ghana, Togo and other ACs with low compliance levels.
89   EENA2, Interview with EENA2, 'Telephone Call' (2017).

IFIs usually engage in technical assistance programmes in recognition that low compliance is sometimes attributable to lack of human and technical resources. In certain instances, low compliance may be attributable to the agent acting in his own interest instead of the principal's which is financial stability and integrity. Thus, are there any conflicting goals between governments of countries and IFIs/FATF? It would be expected that they share the same goals. Dijkstra finds that politicians do not necessarily follow the national interest but act opportunistically to maximise their economic benefits, such as salary, public reputation and power.[90] Therefore, there is usually no political will. Such countries can be likened to the amoral calculator, requiring sanctions and technical assistance.

Low compliance may be because countries that are not well integrated into the global financial system largely focus on home-grown issues, such as financial exclusion. Consequently, these countries may issue standards that fall below the FATF's CDD expectations. Thus, where compliance levels are deteriorating, countries are incentivised to delay information sharing or de-escalate the gravity of information, issues potentially solvable by observatory tools.

Clearly, a high degree of integration and high compliance is the only conclusive category where countries have a strong incentive to share information that allows the principal to make informed decisions. However, countries are not isolated and efforts by the FATF to reduce conflicts between MP/LP and HP have proved difficult.

Agency Theory: Integration between High Priority (A) and Mid Priority Countries (C) – the Domination of Self Interests?

Integration gives room for laundered money to flow between HP, MP and LP countries given their engagement in trade and financial transactions. This engagement is mutually beneficial as foreign investors from HP countries are keen on investing in MP countries to maximise profit. MP countries also want to attract, protect and retain foreign investments to enhance their integration into the global financial market. Thus, as the countries' interests converge, the need for collaboration and information sharing for continued trade increases. MP countries' interest causes them to comply and share information on AML/CFT to avoid de-risking. Conversely, HP countries comply and share information to ensure profit maximisation.

Yet, HP countries do not necessarily profit, even when the self-interest of countries converge. Rather, they engage in a balancing act between profit maximisation and ensuring compliance via information sharing, an exercise that does not necessarily make economic sense. This is because MP countries terrain makes it difficult for HP countries to apply the FATF measures strictly, else they lose profit. Therefore, HP countries usually de-risk. Where they decide not to,

---

90   Robert Dijkstra, 'Accountability of Financial Supervisory Agencies: An Incentive Approach' [2010] 11 (2) Journal of Banking Regulation 115, 122.

because of the importance of the business in question, an agency relationship may be established where, as principal, HP countries set conditions for compliance and information sharing with the FI in MP countries they wish to enter into a relationship with. Where the business is perceived as crucial to the country or institution in question, the MP country would align with the conditions. But, to what extent can MP countries comply?

Compliance by agents may largely be undermined by their capacity deficit. For instance, agents strive to accede to their principal's conditions, particularly where the countries have historical, economic and cultural ties. The United Kingdom (principal) and the Commonwealth states (agent) exemplifies this, given their colonial history. This history has engendered migration from the Commonwealth to the United Kingdom, catalysing increased remittances from the UK migrants to relatives in their home countries.[91] Such cash flow requires increased collaboration of both parties' interest, as these channels can be used to launder funds. Remittances are however more in the interest of agent-states. Without true reciprocal interest, the interest of developed countries takes precedence. Therefore, whilst their laws aim to ensure transparency through the licencing and regulation of remittances,[92] they also hinder remittances flowing out of the country. Conversely, given the lack of regulatory resources in manpower, skills and finances, unlicensed remittance operators thrive in the Commonwealth.[93] The regulatory approach of the United Kingdom may hinder information sharing and instead facilitate underground remittances across jurisdictions. This indicates that institutional capacity becomes an issue when states are integrated. Hence, identifying overlapping interests that would drive compliance and resolve agency issues is critical.

Arguably, reciprocal interest is present when there is a continuous business that is of systemic importance to both countries – such as in the case of correspondent banking (CB). CB

> is the provision of a current or other liability account, and related services, to another financial institution, including affiliates, used for the execution of third party payments and trade finance, as well as its own cash clearing,

---

91 Carlos Vargas-Silva, 'Migrant Remittances to and from the UK' (*The Migration Observatory at the University of Oxford*, 24 February 2016) <http://www.migrationobservatory .ox.ac.uk/resources/briefings/migrant-remittances-to-and-from-the-uk/ > accessed 10 March 2017; Catalina Amuedo-Dorantes, 'The Good and the Bad in Remittance Flows' (IZA World of Labor, November 2014) <https://wol.iza.org/uploads/articles/97/pdfs/ good-and-bad-in-remittance-flows.pdf> accessed 10 May 2017.

92 The Payment Services Regulations 2017.

93 CBN, 'Press Release: Activities of Illegal International Money Transfer Operators' (*Central Bank of Nigeria*, 2016) <https://www.cbn.gov.ng/out/2016/ccd/press%20release%20on %20illegal%20imtsos.pdf> accessed 10 July 2017; *The Economist*, 'Africa Money Transfers, Let them Remit' (*The Economist*, 20 July 2013) <https://www.economist.com/news/midd le-east-and-africa/21581995-western-worries-about-money-laundering-are-threatening-ec onomic-lifeline> accessed 10 November 2017.

Table 4.2 Determination of Self-Interest: Interaction between HP and MP countries

Agent (mid priority) Respondent bank	Principal (High Priority) Sustained correspondent banking Correspondent bank	Ad hoc correspondent banking
Sustained Correspondent Banking	(a) Potential for coordination	(b) Conflicts of interest and potential for coordination problems
Ad hoc Correspondent Banking	(c) Conflicts of interests and potential for coordination problems	(d) Lack of compliance incentive

liquidity management and short-term borrowing or investment needs in a particular currency.[94]

It ensures that 'respondent' banks extend their services using foreign 'correspondent' banks as a proxy in places where the 'respondent' bank has no physical presence, but the correspondent bank does.[95] CB however poses ML/TF risks, as the correspondent bank does not have direct contact with the customer, but relies on the respondent bank's CDD processes, which may be inadequate. The effect is that the correspondent bank may unintentionally allow other FIs with inadequate AML/CFT systems and their customers, direct access to the global banking landscape.

Usually, the business is crucial to both countries and in line with the FATF Guidance on 'Private Sector Information Sharing',[96] institutions would be incentivised to share information and illustrate compliance. This is particularly where the banking relationship is sustained and not 'ad hoc'. However, this is not always the case, particularly where legal or operational challenges hinder information sharing and compliance. This is illustrated by Table 4.2.

In category (a), both the principal and agent would share information and comply with the FATF recommendations, given their mutual best interest to do

---

94 The Wolfsberg Group, 'Wolfsberg Anti-Money Laundering Principles for Correspondent Banking' (*The Wolfsberg Group* 2014) <https://sic.gov.lb/intorg/Wolfsberg%20Correspondent%20Banking%20Principles%20(2014).pdf> accessed 10 March 2016.; BIS, 'Committee on Payments and Market Infrastructure: Correspondent Banking' (*BIS*, July 2016) <https://www.bis.org/cpmi/publ/d147.pdf> accessed October 2016; Michaela Erbenova, Yan Liu et al., 'The Withdrawal of Correspondent Banking Relationships: A Case for Policy Action' (IMF Staff Discussion Note, June 2016) <https://www.imf.org/external/pubs/ft/sdn/2016/sdn1606.pdf> accessed 10 October 2016.
95 This is done in exchange for a fee.
96 FATF, FATF Guidance: Private Sector Information Sharing (*FATF*, November 2017) <http://www.fatf-gafi.org/media/fatf/documents/recommendations/Private-Sector-Information-Sharing.pdf> accessed January 2018.

so. Compliance is unlikely to be fool-proof due to legal and operational challenges in the respondent bank's country. Some legal issues that currently undermine the respondent bank's ability to facilitate compliance include lack of clarity about the legal position on information sharing and differing regulatory requirements. These issues coupled with issues such as when the policy objectives are at variance with the FATFs can undermine compliance. This may also include the preference for data protection over national security by the respondent bank, at variance with the principal's preference. Operational challenges include inadequate IT tools, varying data formats and the cultural disposition towards the value of information. Herring noted that the asymmetries of human and natural resources, coupled with weak legal infrastructure and corrupt processes may hinder the respondent bank's ability to align with the correspondent's standards.[97] Instead, this entrenches conflict of interest.

In category (b), the CB relationship is ad hoc for the principal but sustained for the agent. The agent has a stronger compliance incentive. The principal may not have an incentive to investigate the agent's books to ensure compliance, and this may undermine the agent. Given the principal's HP position, even an ad hoc arrangement may be caught by their home country regulators or the FI institution's culture, thereby facilitating information sharing and compliance.

In category (c), the principal has a higher incentive to comply, but the agent has relatively low incentive to comply and may slack to the dissatisfaction of the principal, who may then be forced to de-risk. Agency slack by the respondent bank may be due to the supervisory body's or financial institution's staff capacity challenges.

In category (d), the principal and agent lack compliance incentive given the ad hoc nature of their business. However, where the principal is not an amoral calculator or is subject to strict 'in-country' regulation, it would be in its interest to comply. This may indeed propel the compliance of the agent.

In the four different scenarios, the correspondent banks, as principal, are willing to enable their FIs to be used by the respondent for a fee. The principal is however subject to more rigorous regulation given their location within 'high priority' countries. Therefore, it is more in their interest to comply to standards. Therefore, institutions in these countries usually exercise some form of control over the agent countries by setting down conditions necessary to establish and maintain business relationships, particularly where the respondent country has significant reputational risk factors, such as corruption.

Regulatory institutions such as FIUs or Central Banks in MP and HP countries also collaborate on information sharing due to the traffic of transactions between their countries. Resultantly, institutions usually converge on information sharing when it is in their interest and diverge when it is not. For instance,

97 Richard Herring, 'Conflicts between Home and Host Country Prudential Supervisors' <http://citeseerx.ist.psu.edu/viewdoc/download?doi=10.1.1.543.1482&rep=rep1&type =pdf> accessed 19 March 2018.

in line with the Consolidated FATF Standards on Information Sharing,[98] the United Kingdom and Nigeria have entered into a memorandum of understanding to facilitate the return of stolen assets from Nigeria.[99] This process has been frustrated by the conditions the United Kingdom has put in place before any such return can be made. EENA6 argues that the mandatory requirement for Nigeria to make a formal request, and the numerous legal requirements that follow, have stifled the process for repatriation of funds.[100] Whilst some scholars have attributed this to the need to ensure that returned stolen wealth is utilized judiciously by Nigeria,[101] various experts have argued that the United Kingdom has stifled this process because it is not in its interest to return stolen wealth.[102] This shows how, as principal, the HP countries' strategic interest continues to colour compliance and implementation, illustrating how economic interest can shape the political interest of powerful countries.

The convergence pattern of FIs and regulatory bodies indicate that these institutions converge better when they have the same objective of financial stability, legal powers and processes, similar supervisory tools and capacity.[103] Divergence on any of these factors would occasion a gap in information sharing, even when the MP country is desirous of converging. Therefore, players need to be able to facilitate compliance by all parties, including other countries and the IFIs/FATF. For instance, the United States gave Pakistan some funding to incentivise the country to stop terror on Afghanistan.

To circumvent agency issues, the principals (IFIs/FATF) engage agent-states (MP/HP/LP) in various ways. These ways include high-level meetings, assessments, technical assistance and sanctions. These supervisory or monitoring engagements to cure agency issues would be discussed in the context of rule formulation and compliance/implementation.

98　FATF 'The Consolidated FATF Standards on Information Sharing: Relevant Excerpts from the FATF Recommendations and Interpretative Notes' (*FATF*, November 2017) <http://www.fatf-gafi.org/media/fatf/documents/recommendations/pdfs/Consolidated-FATF-Standards-information-sharing.pdf> accessed 10 February 2017.

99　Channels Television, 'Nigeria, UK Sign Agreement on Stolen Assets' (Channels Television, 30 August 2016) <https://www.channelstv.com/2016/08/30/nigeria-uk-sign-agreement-stolen-assets/> accessed 10 February 2017; Vanguard, 'Nigeria, UK Sign MOU on Return of Stolen Assets' (*Vanguard*, 30 August 2016) <https://www.vanguardngr.com/2016/08/nigeria-uk-sign-mou-return-stolen-assets/> accessed 10 February 2017.

100　EENA6, GIABA, Interview with EENA6, 'Telephone Call' (2017).

101　UN and the World Bank, 'Stolen Asset Recovery (StAR) Initiative: Challenges, Opportunities, and Action Plan' (United Nations and World Bank, June 2007) <https://siteresources.worldbank.org/NEWS/Resources/Star-rep-full.pdf> accessed 10 June 2016.

102　For instance, due to the cost involved in the process. See Natanel Abramov, 'Why States Struggle to Repatriate looted assets' (*Financial Times*, 11 May 2016) <https://www.ft.com/content/322c1854-dcb9-3e31-a191-6651afd5776b> accessed 10 October 2016; Adamu Abuh, 'British Envoy Gives Conditions for Repatriating Stolen Funds to Nigeria' (*The Guardian*, 21 January, 2016) <https://guardian.ng/news/british-envoy-gives-condition-for-repatriating-stolen-funds-to-nigeria/#comment-section> accessed 10 July 2016.

103　Kal Raustiala 'The Architecture of International Cooperation: Trans-governmental Networks and the Future of International Law' [2002] 43 (1) Va. J. Int'l L 1, 61.

Interaction between Principal(s) and Agents (Country Legislators)[104]

As discussed in the previous chapter, local laws usually mirror society. Therefore, legislatures are to ensure that laws are contextualised whilst checking on the executive arm of government.[105] In combating ML/TF, legislators have to imbibe international rules which may compromise the law's contextualization. Legislators may have to serve two masters – their local constituencies and global financial integrity and stability. Whilst the latter is projected to serve the global good, the former may be protectionist and competitive. Hence, in transplanting AML/CFT rules, legislators have the arduous task of striking a balance, ensuring that recommendations are carefully crafted into law, to ensure effective implementation.

Transplantation is necessary because rules are not always home-grown to certain states. For instance, the FATF recommendations were derived from the combination of national strategies from Switzerland, the United Kingdom and the United States, in collaboration with the international recommendations of the Basel Committee from 1988 which was drafted by the United States.[106] Although ACs/EEs did not partake in moulding these laws, the FATF, backed by the IFIs, mandates implementation. This requirement places an onus on the countries' legislatures to give such recommendations the force of law by embedding them in their national systems.[107]

The principals' collaborative efforts give the agent states little leeway to contest or amend rules produced by the FATF and its cohorts. This is despite the fact that recommended rules affect domestic affairs, inter alia, banking policies and ML/TF regulation of recipient countries. Therefore, the interaction between principals and agents is not aimed at formulation of global rules. Most recommendations promulgated in 1990 have not been scrapped; they have only undergone some modifications, most profoundly – following the 9/11 attack, and later on, the global financial crisis.[108] This illustrates that there is room for ex-post

---

104   Andrew Cornford, 'Basel II and Developing Countries' [2008] 2 (31–32) Finance & Bien Commun, Cairn Info 69–78; *Hulsee and Kerwer* (n 1); Independent Evaluation Office of the IMF, 'The IMF's Interactions with Its Member Countries: Issues Paper for an Evaluation by the Independent Evaluation Office (IEO)' (*IMF*, 2008) <http://www.ieo-imf.org/ieo/files/issuespapers/051508.pdf> accessed 10 May 2017; Independent Evaluation Office of the IMF, 'Evaluation Report: IMF Interactions with Member Countries' (*IMF*, 2009) <http://www.ieo-imf.org/ieo/files/completedevaluations/A.%20%20Full%20Text%20of%20Main%20Report.pdf> accessed 20 May 2017.
105   The Parliamentary Network, 'Parliamentary Workshop at the Annual Meetings 2016' (World Bank Group, IMF 2016) <http://www.parlnet.org/sites/default/files/Agenda-MP-workshop-annual-meetings2016.pdf > accessed 21 January 2017.
106   Mark Pieth and Gemma Aiolfi, 'The Private Sector Becomes Active: The Wolfsberg Process' [2003] 10 (4) Journal of Financial Crime 359, 359–360; John Braithwaite and Peter Drahos, *Global Business Regulation* (1st edn, CUP, 2000).
107   Ibid.
108   Ben Hayes, 'Counter-Terrorism, "Policy Laundering" and the FATF: Legalizing Surveillance, Regulating Civil Society' <http://www.statewatch.org/analyses/no-171-fafp-report.pdf> accessed 10 January 2017.

rulemaking which entails the modification of international standards for efficiency and effective transplantation.

The ex-post rule modification process necessitates interaction between the FATF/IFIs (principals) and country legislators (agents). The purpose is to facilitate information exchange geared towards contextual global standards and efficient in-country structures. The interaction process, which employs the use of observatory tools and incentives, is usually facilitated by the principal. This process occurs through different methods:

1. High-level meetings.
2. Technical assistance.
3. Sanctions.

While there is no precise sequence, the principals do not usually commence interactions with the imposition of sanctions.

High-level meetings (HLMs), as an observatory tool, provide an avenue for information exchange between actors to facilitate rule modification processes. These take into consideration the underlying factors that precipitate legislative compliance differentials amongst countries. For instance, a country may have financial secrecy laws that prohibit the extraterritorial application of laws of other states. This situation actively hinders efforts to combat global ML/TF.[109] Thus, the principals would seek to understand the underlying reason. Where non-compliance stems from lack of structures uncontemplated by the FATF at its drafting stage, such as the cash-based economy or the solid minerals ML/TF trade risk, the principals will seek to amend its recommendations or guide documents to take these into considerations. Thus, HLMs are a two-way process, usually organised by the principals, agents or third parties (civil societies).

As the PP, the FATF engages in HLMs with its members, FSRB members and country legislators in order to resolve legislative deficiencies. Sometimes, such meetings are held through intermediaries. With the FATF's review of Nigeria's proposed legislation, an intermediary was employed to engage in HLMs with the FATF officials who appraised the draft and found it suitable for the purpose intended.[110] The decision to appoint an intermediary was because he was best-positioned to get information the other party would not necessarily give out.

A more intense relationship exists between the IFIs and country legislators. Their engagement occurs at multiple levels, sometimes through the IMF's Article IV surveillance and allows IFIs familiarise legislators with the FATF

---

109   James O'Kane, *The Crooked Ladder: Gangsters, Ethnicity and the American Dream* (New Brunswick: Transaction Publishers, 1992).

110   Scoop Independent News WikiLeaks, 'Cablegate: Nigeria: Economic and Financial Crimes Act Passed' (Scoop Independent News WikiLeaks, 24 February 2004) <http://www.scoop.co.nz/stories/WL0402/S00051/cablegate-nigeria-economic-and-financial-crimes-act-passed.htm> accessed 1 April 2017.

recommendations whilst listening to their concerns.[111] The IFIs would deal with in-country legislative committees focused on economic issues and/or interactions with parliamentary networks.[112] Whilst the former occurs through seminars, briefings, mission visits or visiting delegations at the IMF/Bank, the latter occurs through organised conferences and workshops in partnership with parliamentary umbrella groups.[113] Both processes are targeted at ensuring compliance with the FATF standards on sturdy legislations.

In a 2004 report, the Executive Working Group stressed that the IMF should 'expand its outreach and listen to legislators to improve the understanding of the political and social context in which economic decisions are taken...(and) help build understanding of the IMF'.[114] Consequently, there has been improved interactions between the IFIs and states, as illustrated by the yearly parliamentary network workshop meetings,[115] the July 2015 Vienna workshop for MP countries across Central Asia and the Caucasus. In 2014, programmes for parliamentarians were held in Mozambique and Tanzania. These meetings give the IFIs an improved understanding of the socio-economic and political context in which transplantation occurs.[116]

Additionally, the African Union's *High Panel on Illicit Financial Flows from Africa*,[117] designd by experts drawn from continental and IFIs recommended actions to combat Africa's illicit crimes. A key recommendation was that 'clear and concise laws' should be passed to regulate trade mispricing (TM). TM is the deliberate over-invoicing of imports or under-invoicing of exports by local entities, usually to avoid tax or levies.[118] Although TM is a predominant means

111 IMF, 'Guide for IMF Staff Outreach to Legislators' (*IMF*, 4 January 2006) <https://www.imf.org/external/np/exr/leg/eng/guide.htm> accessed 1 April 2017.
112 The Parliamentary Network on the World Bank & IMF <http://www.parlnet.org/node> accessed 10 April 2017; The Global Organisation of Parliamentarians Against Corruption (GOPAC) <http://gopacnetwork.org> accessed 10 April 2017; The NATO Parliamentary Assembly and the Commonwealth Parliamentary Association (CPA) <http://www.nato-pa.int> accessed 1 April 2017.
113 IMF, 'Guide for IMF Staff Outreach to Legislators' (*IMF*, 4 January 2006) <http://www.imf.org/external/np/exr/leg/eng/guide.htm> accessed 10 May 2018
114 IMF, 'Factsheet: The IMF and Legislators' (*IMF*, 9 January 2017) <http://www.imf.org/external/np/exr/facts/leg.htm> accessed 1 May 2017.
115 World Bank Group and the IMF, 'Parliamentary Workshop at the Annual Meetings 2016' (The Parliamentary Network on the World Bank & IMF) <http://www.parlnet.org/sites/default/files/Agenda-MP-workshop-annual-meetings2016.pdf> accessed 10 April 2017.
116 *IMF* (n 116); *Daily Post*, 'Full Test of Saraki's Speech as Lagarde Visits Senate' (*Daily Post*, 6 January 2016) <http://dailypost.ng/2016/01/06/full-text-of-sarakis-speech-as-lagarde-visits-senate/> accessed 11 March 2017.
117 Commissioned by the AU/ECA Conference of Ministers of Finance, Planning and Economic Development, 'Report of the High Level Panel on Illicit Financial Flows from Africa' <http://www.uneca.org/sites/default/files/PublicationFiles/iff_main_report_26feb_en.pdf> accessed 10 April 2017.
118 Ann Hollingshead, 'The Implied Tax Revenue Loss from Trade Mispricing' [2010] Global Financial Integrity 1, 13.

of laundering in ACs, it is only highlighted by the FATF Best Practices Paper for combating Trade-Based Money Laundering (TBML)[119] and not given the focus required through the FATF recommendations. Delston and Walls contend that the Best Practices Paper for TBML and FATF recommendations should be harmonised, as the recommendations should demand that traders adopt CDD, KYC and Suspicious Transaction Reports (STR) reporting protocols. Otherwise, companies may ignore the risk TBML poses.[120] This proposal contradicts the FATF's Best Practice Paper which cautions against undue regulatory burdens on legitimate businesses. The FATF viewpoint is supported by McSkimming who asserts that there is minimal evidence of the ill-effect of TBML and little consideration as to whether systematic monitoring of trade systems would be cost-effective.[121] Nevertheless, the findings of this HLM cannot be discarded, given their impact on Africa's financial integrity.

The extent to which these interactions promote strategic AML/CFT standards and effective transplantation is however debatable. Although highly promoted, it assumes that its agents (legislative members) are well versed in political and socio-economic situations within countries and have the expertise required to draft. This is not necessarily the case, as elected legislators usually have minimal knowledge of social circumstances surrounding drafted/sponsored bills.[122] They are more concerned with the procedure for assent, a shortcoming attributable to nepotistic election process. This is usually remedied by working with experts from different agencies or third sectors who do not usually accompany legislators to such HLMs. In the process of briefing and debriefing, information may get lost in transmission.

Furthermore, political will is usually absent, because of fear of getting trapped by enacted legislations on AML/CFT. EENA4 noted this, stating that Angola is yet to institute checks against politically exposed persons (PEPs).[123] This shortcoming is remediable by HLMs, which provide a platform for networks between legislators and their interactions with IFIs/FATF. This may engineer some competitive pressure amongst agents to comply; however, this may elicit varying responses based on resources, expertise and political will.

---

119   FATF, 'FATF Guidance Document: Best Practices Paper, Best Practices on Trade Based Money Laundering' (*FATF*, 2008) <http://www.fatf-gafi.org/media/fatf/documents/recommendations/BPP%20Trade%20Based%20Money%20Laundering%202012%20COVER.pdf> accessed 10 July 2017.
120   Ross Delston and Stephen C. Walls, 'Reaching Beyond Banks: How to Target Trade-Based Money Laundering and Terrorist Financing outside the Financial Sector' [2009] 41 The Case Western Reserve Journal of International Law 85, 103.
121   McSkimming Samuel, 'Trade Based Money Laundering: Responding to an Emerging Threat' [2010] 2 Deakin LR. 37.
122   Robert Rotberg, 'Africa Legislative Effectiveness' (Africa and Asia: The Key Issues) <https://robertrotberg.wordpress.com/2013/10/16/african-legislative-effectiveness/> accessed 5 July 2017.
123   EENA4, Counsel, Financial Integrity Unit, IMF Interview with EENA4, 'Telephone Call' (2017).

Additionally, HLMs have revealed a top-down approach where developing and emerging countries meet the principals to seek solutions for their home-grown questions, rather than quizzing them on the suitability of recommendations or laws.[124] However, this is an inconclusive statement given that HLMs are not only sparsely held but are rarely publicised. There is therefore insufficient evidence on interactions between principals and agents. Nonetheless, the practice has continued because it is capable of generating political will from low-income countries' legislatures. It also empowers them with requisite information[125] to push for increased resources in combating ML/TF, challenge the executive arm of government and facilitate national coordination amongst agencies.[126]

Secondly, technical assistance (TA) bridges information asymmetry between the principal and the agent in the re-modification and transplantation of standards. TA, which is carried out at national and regional levels, can be defined as 'non-financial assistance provided by local and international specialists which take the form of information sharing, expertise dissemination, transmission of working knowledge and consulting services'.[127] The IMF refers to this as 'building human and institutional capacity within a country to help government implement more effective policies, leading to better economic outcomes.'[128] This description unveils a two-way stream; while it provides an opportunity for the agent to learn from principals and improve their drafting compliance levels, it also allows the principals to build their knowledge base on the agent to tailor their assistance programmes.

TA is mainly employed because IFIs/FATF recognize that low capacity countries struggle to translate standards to legislation.[129] For instance, in Nigeria, concerns were raised that 'lawmakers and stakeholders in the financial sector are

---

124 As noticed in the IMF/World Bank (WB) Spring Meetings 2017 – a representative from the Central Bank of Ghana sought recommendations on how current financial issues in Ghana could be resolved.

125 Such as predicate offence in other countries so as to ensure that legislations cover predicate offences in originating countries. In addition, legislators would review reports of assessment of their country, identify their own shortcomings and make amendments.

126 FATF, 'Guidance on Capacity Building for Mutual Evaluations and Implementation of the FATF Standards within Low Capacity Countries' (29 February 2008) <http://www.fatf -gafi.org/media/fatf/documents/reports/Capacity%20building%20LCC.pdf> accessed 10 June 2017; *GOPAC* (n 114).

127 UNESCO, 'Technical Assistance in Cultural Governance' (*UNESCO*) <http://www.unes co.org/new/en/culture/themes/cultural-diversity/cultural-expressions/programmes/ technical-assistance/what-is-technical-assistance/> accessed 10 April 2017.

128 IMF, 'Factsheet: IMF Capacity Development' (IMF, 19 April 2017) <http://www.imf. org/en/About/Factsheets/Capacity-Development-Technical-Assistance-and-Training> accessed 1 April 2017.

129 FATF, 'Guidance on Capacity Building For Mutual Evaluations and Implementation of the FATF Standards Within Low Capacity Countries' (29 February 2008) <http:// www.fatf-gafi.org/media/fatf/documents/reports/Capacity%20building%20LCC.pdf> accessed 4 February 2018; it however carries this out in conjunction with or prior to a mutual evaluation.

generally unfamiliar with AML/CFT issues.'[130] Consequently, the FATF advocated for, and implemented robust interactions through a national coordination committee that included legislators and justice ministries/agencies involved in legal policy, legislative drafting and mutual legal assistance. This robust national level TA recognizes that although legislators are at the forefront of enacting laws, they are supported by other institutions that play a vital role in drafting and formulating legislation in accordance with international standards.

At the regional level, the FSRB are also involved in training justice ministry/agencies staff. For instance, inbuilt in the Eastern and Southern Africa Anti-Money Laundering Group (ESAMMG) strategic plan for 2012–2015 was the need to consolidate regional AML/CFT capacity building, training and awareness-raising programmes.[131] This position resonates with GIABA. However, training is usually provided on request from the FSRB. Thus, although GIABA noted that countries like Benin, Mali and Cote d'Ivoire needed support to strengthen their AML/CFT framework, it did not provide direct assistance because there was no formal request.[132] To forestall information asymmetry through TA, the FATF Training and Research Institute (TRIEN) was established to grant government officials in FATF member countries access to comprehensive training and research programmes.[133]

The specialised TA provided by the IMF is a sequel to surveillance which identifies areas where TA can have the greatest impact. Thus, in certain countries, TA is focused on building institutional and human capacity for effective policy drafting. Although granted voluntarily, countries must pass the IMF guidelines which are in the form of prioritisation filters to engage in TA.[134] IMF staff do not proceed on a one-way training stream but provide tailor-made assistance through engagement with countries over a period of time, thus, potentially resolving asymmetries.[135]

---

130   The Inter-Governmental Action Group Against Money Laundering in West Africa (GIABA).
131   Eastern and Southern African Anti-Money Laundering Group (ESAAMLG), 'Strategic Plan April 2012–March 2015' <http://www.esaamlg.org/documents_storage/2013-1-4-16-4-51_strategic_plan_2012-2015.pdf> accessed 9 April 2017.
132   GIABA, 'Member States: Republic of Benin' (GIABA) <http://www.giaba.org/member-states/benin.html> accessed 7 April 2017; GIABA, 'Member States: Republic of Mali' (*GIABA*) <http://www.giaba.org/member-states/mali.html> accessed 10 June 2016; GIABA, 'Member States: Republic of Cote d'Ivoire' <http://www.giaba.org/member-states/cote_divoire.html> accessed 10 March 2017.
133   FATF, 'FATF Training and Research Institute (TREIN)' (*FATF*, 20 September 2016) <http://www.fatf-gafi.org/fr/publications/recommandationsgafi/documents/trein-institute.html?hf=10&b=0&s=desc(fatf_releasedate)> accessed 1 March 2017.
134   Requests are prioritized based upon filters such as program areas, policy initiatives, impact and commitment, availability of external financing and regional diversity.
135   Bretton Woods Project, 'IMF Technical Assistance' (*Bretton Woods Project*, 13 March 2014) <http://www.brettonwoodsproject.org/2014/03/inside-institutions-imf-technical-assistance/> accessed 10 March 2017.

The IMF has also included regional and country approaches in technical assistance through the establishment of nine regional centres and various country offices.[136] Thus, TA can be tailored to legislative guidance, such as enabling countries legislate effectively on pertinent issues such as laws guiding the formation of the FIUs or restricting ML/TF through PEPs. The World Bank has done this through its sponsorship of the Joint Initiative by the Bank of Sierra Leone and Transnational Organised Crime Unit (TOCU) in drafting a National Procedure on Anti-Terrorism and Proliferation Financing.[137] This was facilitated during a three-day workshop attended by relevant stakeholders such as the UN and other key bodies, where steps were agreed to curb illicit crimes. The interaction between IFIs/FATF and countries illustrates continuous engagement with agents.

There are however difficulties in the effectiveness of TA projects in promoting successful AML/CFT strategies. For instance, TA is mostly led by regional and international bodies, usually in blocs of two-day workshops. Such sessions are facilitated using a top-down approach where experts from developed countries provide technical-knowhow without being conversant with the full socio-economic and political issues in the host country. This prevents national stakeholders from contributing to the global standards or transplanting effectively and thus hinders the 'global' nature of the FATF recommendations. For example, the FATF's TRIEN pulls government officials from member countries to engage in comprehensive training and research – which is then disseminated to low-capacity countries with less mature AML/CFT regimes.[138]

TA for each country usually occurs once within a five-year time frame, the last in Africa being in 2012. This is ineffective given the fast changes in ML. For instance, cryptocurrencies are a new and evolving way for ML, a subject scarcely considered in 2012. As already noted, training is usually offered to legislators who delegate drafting responsibilities to expert bodies or staff. This creates another agency relationship where information asymmetry thrives. However, follow-up MERs and ROSCs usually reveal an improvement in legislative drafts post TA, illustrating that despite the limitations of this observatory and information

---

136 Since 1993, the IMF included a regional approach towards technical assistance, establishing nine regional centers globally, allowing for quicker dissemination and specific tailoring of assistance to meet the needs of the regions. The pioneer regional center was established in the Pacific region in 1993, then the Caribbean regional center. Since 2002, five centers have been established in the Sub-Saharan Africa region as part of the IMF's Africa Capacity Building Initiative, to improve the coordination of capacity-building technical assistance in the Poverty Reduction Strategy Paper (PRSP) process. Two further regional centers were established in the Middle East in 2004 and in Central America and the Dominican Republic in 2009.

137 GIABA, (*GIABA*) <http://www.giaba.org/member-states/sierra_leone.html> accessed 10 March 2017.

138 Attendance is also extended to the judicial ministries and agencies involved in rulemaking and the legal drafters within the regulatory bodies inter alia, the Central Bank and the Securities and Exchange Commission – as input is necessary from both the legislative and regulatory fronts.

exchange tool, it has provided a platform for improved law-making, which is vital in combating ML/TF.

Thirdly, principals also interact with agents through sanctions, incentives or conditionalities. The distinction between incentives and sanctions are not always clear. Wagner states that, 'incentives are often considered to be weak sanctions.'[139] However, some differences exist between them. Incentives involve granting of political and economic benefit to a country in exchange for specific policy adjustments.[140] They are used to foster and maintain cooperative goodwill amongst states as it usually involves interactions and agreements aimed at encouraging legislators to enact the requisite laws to avoid the FATF's listing. Conversely, sanctions are hard, hostile instruments or penalties which mandate a country to carry out a specific activity when there is a breach of international standards. Sanctions entail minimal interaction and take away rather than grant specific advantages to countries. Consequently, Wagner contends that sanctions are more effective than incentives because states value the marginal unit of a good taken away through sanctions more than the benefit of the same amount added through incentives.[141] Although closely related, conditionalities are neither sanctions or loans. Rather, they are conditions attached to the provision of benefits such as loans, debt relief or bilateral trade.[142]

The instrument used by the principal to enhance the agent's compliance to the FATF standards depends on the level of compliance and intensity of interactions. Conditionalities may be used to build interactions with agents and forestall or rectify a breach. Sanctions are restricted to post-breach occurrence. This can be typified with the case of a developing country failing to comply with the FATF recommendations 3 and 5, which mandate the criminalisation of ML/TF based on the Vienna and Palermo Conventions. In such case, the principals would most likely issue a sanction or mandate compliance through conditionalities.[143] Such a hard stance may unearth the low level of interaction prior to and during assessments which occasioned a low compliance level. Hence, sanctions in the form of listing would merit public censure through the placement of such countries on the FATF's 'high risk and non-cooperative jurisdictions lists'. Countries placed on this list would have to engage with FATF officials to facilitate de-risking as public censure may threaten financial flow and hinder market access.

139   Harrision Wagner, 'Economic Inter-Dependence, Bargaining Power and Political Influence' [1988] 42 (3) International Organisation 461–483.

140   Ibid.; Han Dorussen, 'Mixing Carrots with Sticks: Evaluating the Effectiveness of Positive Incentives' [2001] 38 (2) Journal of Peace Research 251, 260.

141   *Wagner* (n 141).

142   Carlos Santiso, 'Good Governance and Aid Effectiveness: The World Bank and Conditionality' [2001] 7 (1) The Georgetown Public Policy Review 1, 12; Alexander Kentikelenis, Thomas Stubbs and Lawrence King, 'IMF Conditionality and Development Policy Space 1985–2014' [2016] 23 (4) Review of International Political Economy 544, 548.

143   FATF, 'High-Risk and Non-Cooperative Jurisdictions' (*FATF*) <http://www.fatf-gafi.org/countries/#high-risk> accessed 10 February 2017.

The level of engagement is however dependent on the specific list on which a jurisdiction is placed. First, 'jurisdiction with serious strategic deficiencies for which the FATF has called its members to apply counter-measures based on substantial risk to the international financial system'. This means that the country must show FATF officials that significant measures are being taken to remedy deficiencies.[144] Secondly, 'jurisdictions with strategic deficiencies that have developed an action plan'. This means the FATF would only seek to ensure that the country implements its action plans whilst calling on its members to apply enhanced due diligence proportionate to the risk posed. Although it seems likely that countries with legislative deficiencies would be placed on the first list only, in the absence of legislative guidance, implementation would be problematic.

To avoid being listed, several countries have improved their interactions prior to assessments and ensured that their laws are properly transplanted. This was the case in Nigeria, where last-minute efforts were initiated to avert sanctions over money laundering.[145] After being blacklisted, Ghana strengthened its interactions and was de-listed the next year.[146] The effectivity of this interaction in ensuring transplantation and contributing to improved FATF standards is however questionable, because of conflict of interest and information asymmetry. For instance, in rushing to evade blacklisting, countries may engage in sham compliance by drafting legislation deemed suitable on paper. However, legislators may not follow up on other legislative roles, such as ensuring checks on the regulators and executive. Furthermore, legislators who work hand in hand with the government may also draft legislation to combat supposed enemies of the government or target opponents, safe in the knowledge that the 'immunity cloak' prevents certain government officials from facing the wrath of the law.[147] This information may be fed to the principal as improved compliance, whereas it is simply the roadmap to implementing ML/TF.

Interaction between Principals and Agents in Implementation and Compliance

The interaction between principals on the implementation of, and compliance with, AML/CFT standards foster a unified approach towards agent-states. Within the agency model adopted by this chapter, the principal delegates standards

144   FATF, 'Improving Global AML/CFT Compliance: On-going Process – 24 February 2017' (*FATF*, 24 February 2017) <http://www.fatf-gafi.org/publications/high-riskand non-cooperativejurisdictions/documents/fatf-compliance-february-2017.html> accessed 12 March 2017.

145   Martins Oloja, 'Nigeria Rushes to Avert Sanction over Money Laundering Law' (*The Guardian*, 27 September 2012) <http://odili.net/news/source/2012/sep/27/16.h tml> accessed 10 March 2017.

146   Modern Ghana, 'Ghana Exits Blacklist; Nigeria Enacts Terrorism (Prevention) (Amendment) Act 2013' (*Modern Ghana*, 22 February 2013) < https://www.modernghana.com/news/44 7311/1/ghana-exits-fatf-blacklist-nigeria-enacts-terroris.html > accessed 20 June 2016.

147   Norman Mugarura, *The Global Anti-Money Laundering Regulatory Landscape in Less Developed Countries* (1st edn, Routledge 2016).

according to which regulatory and enforcement bodies ensure implementation and compliance. Such delegation grants authority to agents to carry out tailored projects following the principal's objective post legislation. This illustrates the continuous need for interaction between actors to forestall agency slack post legislation. The delegated and uninterrupted interaction further illustrates the 'disaggregation of the state'. Although the state is preserved as sovereign, the primary body responsible for implementation and compliance, the agents derive authority from the principal's mandate which has been concretised via national legislation. This legitimises the interaction and network between principals and agents.

As stated, agents within states include regulatory bodies, such as the Securities and Exchange Commission, Central Banks, FIUs etc. These institutions, each answerable to their own global principals who are concerned about ML/TF issues, have dual roles in ensuring compliance with AML/CFT regulations. Firstly, they ensure the construction and synchronisation of regulatory rules for robust supervision of financial institutions that pose ML/TF risk. Secondly, they interact with financial institutions through supervisory and enforcement powers, utilised to checkmate non-compliance and protect the integrity of the international financial system. These institutions have enforcement divisions within their offices to enable swift response to cases of ML/TF alert, and collaborate with other agents, such as the state's enforcement officers and the judiciary.

The issue then is how the collective principals interact with the agents to ensure the resolution of conflict of interests for effective compliance with AML/CFT rules.

As earlier stated, the interaction between the principal(s) and the agent is mainly through

1. High-level meetings.
2. Assessments.
3. Technical assistance.
4. Enforcement actions.

HLM inform effective transplantations and input into the FATF rules update. Such high-level meetings occur through conferences, seminars, workshops or in-country meetings. Conferences may be organised by the principal, agent or a third party. For instance, the Cambridge International Economic Crime Symposium, which is usually attended by regulatory/enforcement officers and Principal representatives, is organized by academics to foster high-level interaction to curb financial crime.[148]

The IFIs spring meetings also gather private sector executives, regulators, lawyers and third parties to discuss regulatory and compliance issues.[149] The

---

148 CIDDEC, 'The Cambridge International Symposium on Economic Crime' (*CIDDEC*) <http://www.crimesymposium.org > accessed 01 May 2017.

149 IMF Blog, 'IMF Spring Meetings 2017: Keeping Growth on Track' (*IMF Blog*, 28 April 2017) <https://blogs.imf.org/2017/04/28/imf-spring-meetings-2017-keeping-growth -on-track/ > accessed 2 May 2017.

2017 spring meetings saw intense focus on Fintech and digital financial inclusion, with discussions on tackling regulatory issues that these raise.[150] In-country meetings are also held as a prelude to technical assistance, with staff and members of various ministries and institutions – financial and non-financial. These meetings provide networked interaction between connected parties, a step towards strengthening the relationship of regulators and institutions with the enforcement agencies – such as the police who are considered extraneous to institutions profit ratio.[151]

The interaction between various actors is premised on the fact that combating ML/TF requires a co-dependent relationship between these institutions. In certain instances, the IFIs hold inter-ministerial meetings with country representatives, especially where it perceives that political will is the main issue at hand. The translation of these meetings to improved compliance and input into the FATF rules is plausible but remains contentious. This is because although networked interactions may ensure that regulators and enforcement officers have a better relationship, a financial institution may remain unwilling to work effectively with enforcement officers at the expense of prosecutions or profit expected from ML transactions.[152] Moreover, as would be seen, home-grown compliance/enforcement solutions may sometimes be best suited to resolve compliance difficulties. In such situations, the FATF may seek to ensure that its rules reflect other means of compliance.

IFIs/FATF assess implementation or compliance to monitor adherence to set FATF standards.[153] However, their modes of operation differ. The difference is predicated on the intrusiveness of their projects. For instance, the FATF carries out mandatory assessments through its mutual evaluation of a country's compliance level to its standards.[154] This exercise is usually carried out by secretariat staff and member country assessors[155] or in particular cases, a composition approved by the FATF President.[156] These may include pre-trained FSRB members or in cases of joint evaluations, staff of IFIs. These officials spend ten days within countries, assessing their private and public sector offices for technical compliance, and recently, the effectiveness of their AML/CFT regime.[157] These in-country assessments do not occur in a vacuum but are based on prior research at the secretariat.

---

150 Ibid.
151 Jack Harvey and Simon Ashon, 'Regulatory Capture: Anti-Money Laundering Policy: A Response to the Activity of Criminals or of Agencies?' *in* Petrus van Duyne, Almir Maljevic, Georgios Antonopoulos, Jack Harvey and Klaus von Lampe (eds.) *The Relativity of Wrongdoing: Corruption, Organized Crime, Fraud and Money Laundering in Perspective* (The Authors, Wolf Legal Publishers, 2015) 300.
152 *EENA6* (n 102).
153 *Blazejewski* (n 25) 1, 23.
154 Ibid. 1, 16.
155 *FATF* (n 21).
156 Ibid.
157 Ibid; FATF, 'Mutual Evaluations' (*FATF*) <http://www.fatf-gafi.org/publications/mutualevaluations/more/more-about-mutual evaluations.html?hf=10&b=0&s=desc(fatf_releasedate)> accessed 01 April 2017.

This includes reviews of reports from countries via the 'technical compliance update questionnaire' which, combined with the previous MERs, follow-ups and 'information on effectiveness' of countries AML/CFT regime is utilised to pre-assess a country's compliance level.[158] The country, sometimes in collaboration with the assessment team, makes a risk-based decision on focus areas during the onsite visits.[159] Findings from these time-bound evaluations are however, rarely discussed with countries to understand reasons for non-compliance. Instead, discussions are based on the need to justify findings. The short period allotted to a country's representative during the plenary session reflects this;[160] although countries engage in discussions on the initial two drafts of the MERs and are permitted to respond, evaluation reports published post-adoption by the plenary session rarely reflect changes to the MERs.[161] Thereafter, the MERs are published, a process designed to publicly shame the agents within a country into compliance. This step signals agency slack, with resultant interaction between the principal and agent to remedy defects. Although the FATF assessment process facilitates interaction with countries, it is intrusive, usually reporting on technical compliance and effectiveness from a perspective of non-ownership. This position may actually shroud the true compliance level of a country.

Conversely, the IFIs interact with agents through FSAP programmes.[162] The FSAP identifies risks and vulnerabilities that hinder compliance to FATF standards.[163] BRICs, along with 25 other countries with systemically important financial sectors are required to undertake mandatory financial assessments under FSAP. This decision warranted the inclusion of the FSAP under the IMF Article IV surveillance. It acknowledges that ML/TF may cause macroeconomic and financial instability which can be facilitated by these countries that are largely connected and pose contagion risk.[164] In such cases, the IMF enters discussions with the central bank governor or financial ministers of such countries in order to generate political support to combat ML/TF. This suggests that the IMF

---

158 *FATF* (n 157).

159 Ibid.

160 Ibid. (n 161).

161 Ibid.

162 IMF, 'Review of the Financial Sector Assessment Program: Further Adaptation to the Post Crisis Era' (*IMF*, September 2014) <https://www.imf.org/en/Publications/Policy-Papers/Issues/2016/12/31/Review-of-the-Financial-Sector-Assessment-Program-Further-Adaptation-to-the-Post-Crisis-Era-PP4893> accessed 10 December 2017.

163 Ibid.

164 IMF, 'Financial Sector Assessment Program (FSAP)' (*IMF*, 03 April 2017) <http://www.imf.org/external/NP/fsap/fssa.aspx> accessed 10 April 2017; IMF, 'Integrating Stability Assessments Under the Financial Sector Assessment Program into Article IV Surveillance' (*IMF*, 27 August 2010) <http://www.imf.org/external/np/pp/eng/2010/08/2710.pdf> accessed 27 March 2017; IMF, 'Press Release No14/0: IMF Executive Board Reviews Mandatory Financial Stability Assessments Under the Financial Sector Assessment Program' (13 January 2014) <https://www.imf.org/external/np/sec/pr/2014/pr1408.htm> accessed 10 May 2016.

has greater interaction with these countries. Conversely, the Evaluation Report of the Independent Evaluation Office of the IMF illustrates that IMF interactions are least effective with advanced and large EEs.[165] They were most effective with developing countries.[166] This may be attributable to the fact that instead of discussions, the IFIs impose conditionalities on certain developing countries to mandate legislation and subsequent compliance with FATF standards. These conditionalities are usually beneficial in ensuring actual compliance but have the disadvantage of altering the democratic ideal and accountability model of governance.[167]

Nevertheless, the FSAP has remained largely voluntary in developing countries. Through its creation of the ROSC, the FSAP reports on member states implementation of AML/CFT recommendations.[168] Reports produced from the assessment exercises are also reviewed in partnership with countries. As publication of such reports is at the discretion of the country in question,[169] a country may withhold publications that might have disastrous consequences for it. This illustrates how IFIs uphold and respect sovereignty.

Furthermore, interaction between countries and IFIs is largely dependent on the stage of assessment. At the pre-assessment stage, IFIs are usually involved in extensive research on countries; thus, interaction is usually limited to exchange of information which arms the IFIs with additional material data on the country in question.[170] The provision of this information entails a process of self-reflection, which gives the regulatory/enforcement bodies and FIs sufficient time to plan the assessment procedures. Interaction between principals and agents is more intense during the assessment, as the IFIs usually engage with regulatory bodies, FIs and other market participants (e.g., insurance agencies, pension funds, mutual funds) to gain a robust understanding of market developments, structure, outlook and risk management practices.[171] This requires a two-way communication for robust understanding of the purpose of the FSAP and the importance of

165　IEO of the IMF, 'IMF Interactions with Member Countries' (*Independent Evaluation Office of the IMF*, 2009) <http://www.ieo-imf.org/ieo/files/completedevaluations/A.%20%20Full%20Text%20of%20Main%20Report.pdf> accessed 2 April 2017.

166　Ibid.

167　Ngaire Woods, 'Unelected Government: Making the IMF and the World Bank More Accountable' (Brookings, March 1 2003) <https://www.brookings.edu/articles/unelected-government-making-the-imf-and-the-world-bank-more-accountable/ > accessed 1 July 2017; John Hilary, 'Africa: Dead Aid and the Return of Neoliberalism' [2010] 52 (2) Race & Class 81, 83.

168　IMF, 'List of Standards, Codes and Principles Useful for Bank and Fund Operational Work and for which Reports on the Observance of Standards and Codes are Produced' (*IMF*, November 2002) <http://www.imf.org/external/standards/scnew.htm> accessed 10 May 2016.

169　Ibid.

170　IMF, 'FSAP: Frequently Asked Questions' (*IMF*, 01 August 2016) <https://www.imf.org/external/np/fsap/faq/#q20> accessed 9 January 2017.

171　Ibid.

participation for propelling international financial stability. This project is usually carried out in collaboration with the country representative of IFIs, thus making for a more responsive assessment. Additionally, although assessment occurs within a two-week time frame, the presence of a country representative of the IFIs resident in host countries significantly bridges existent information asymmetry, as these actors can furnish assessors with adequate context and information.

The results of assessments are crucial in determining the direction of the principal's relationship with the agent state. Thus, where the agent is considered an 'amoral calculator'[172] in the sense that the regulatory body and institutions are driven by profit or the probability of being caught, the principal may categorise the agent state under 'high-risk and non-cooperative jurisdictions'. This 'list' sanction requires FATF core members and other jurisdictions to apply countermeasures to protect the international financial system from the ongoing and substantial ML/TF risk emanating from that country.[173] Conversely, an agent-state may be considered to be either a 'political citizen' who will adhere to regulations considered of public interest, even in the absence of political will. Or 'organisationally incompetent', where it has ineffective internal governance to propel compliance. In these cases, the principal will interact with these agent-states through continuous monitoring and TA. Sometimes, there is no clear-cut solution, and the deficiency of a country falls within grey areas. The IFIs may then decide that a country needs both sanctions and TA.

When an agent-state is intimated of the need for TA, it may or may not request for this service. Any request must be approved by the principals (IFIs). Trainings are offered on how to scrutinise financial and non-financial institutions under their purview without falling prey to 'regulatory capture', and on confidence maintenance in the financial system.[174] Such training ensures that these regulatory bodies are knowledgeable on how to identify credible data from institutions and respond effectively to ML/TF risk, by drafting or updating regulations to fill any regulatory vacuum.

Training is also offered on how to synchronise efforts with enforcement agencies such as FIUs, the police and courts to ensure swift and effective measures to combat ML/TF. The IFIs also train judges and judicial agencies to handle ML/TF evidence, so as to bring every case to an even-handed end. Such training is

172   Robert Kagan and John Scholz, 'The Criminology of the Corporation and Regulatory Enforcement Strategies' *in* J.T in Hawkins K and Thomas J. (eds.) *Enforcing Regulation* (Boston, Kluwer-Nijhoff Publishing 1984).

173   FATF, 'Public Statement 24' (*FATF*, 24 February 2017) <http://www.fatf-gafi.org/publications/high-riskandnon-cooperativejurisdictions/documents/public-statement-february-2017.html> accessed 4 March 2017.

174   *Harvey and Ashon* (n 153). Regulatory capture is where the regulated system is operated in the interests of regulatory firms rather than the general public, see Martin Ricketts, 'Economic Regulation: Principles, History and Methods' *in* Michael Crew and David Parker (eds.) *International Handbook on Economic Regulation* (Edward Elgar Publishing, 2016) 34–62.

however not country-bound given the borderless nature of illicit crimes. The IFIs also encourage cross-border interactions via FIUs for real-time exchange of information in cases of cross-border crimes. The FATF wields sanctions with the IFIs' backing when an agent is in breach of its recommendations. In such cases, the principal publicly 'lists' non-compliance. It also requires the submission of a progress report from the country and requests that FIs in other member countries give special attention to any transaction involving the 'listed' country. Where the country is a member, the membership is suspended. Osborne notes that the allied influence of observer members of the FATF would ensure that recalcitrant states bear the consequences of their actions.[175]

Despite the harsh stance taken against non-compliant countries, the problem-solving capacity of principals has been thrown into question as a result of cases of alleged agent-state failure. For instance, despite sanctions and training offered to the appropriate agents, money is still moved without any report being flagged for follow-up. In Nigeria, the Central Bank, the Nigerian Financial Intelligence Unit (NFIU) and the Economic and Financial Crimes Commission received training from the principals to fortify their staff with skills against ML/TF risk. These engineered the indigenous political will to come up with home-grown solutions to combat financial crimes. The Bank Verification Number (BVN) exercise, one of such schemes, interlinks all financial accounts held by one individual.[176] The aim is to promote transparency within the financial system and combat illicit crimes.[177] Also, a single treasury account was introduced by the Federal Government of Nigeria to ensure that all funds belonging to government parastatals are kept with the Central Bank.[178] The aim is to prevent diversion of state funds and enable the Central Bank to keep track of disbursements. These solutions received support from civic organizations such as BudgIT which applies technology to track financial disbursement and expenditure.[179]

Nevertheless, there remained a gap in implementation and compliance. A news report uncovered through financial whistleblowing revealed that with approval from the presidency, government parastatals had received sums in excess of $50 million in cash, which were stored in apartments.[180] This indicates

175   Duncan Osborne, 'The Financial Action Task Force and the Legal Profession' [2014–2015] 59 NYL Sch. LR 421.

176   Ehi Esoimeme, 'A Critical Analysis of the Bank Verification Number Project Introduced by the Central Bank of Nigeria' [2015].

177   Ibid.

178   Okechukwu Innocent, Chukwurah Daniel and Iheanacho Emmanuel, 'An Analysis of Pros and Cons: Treasury Single Account Policy in Nigeria' [2015] 5 (4) Arabian Journal of Business and Management Review (OMAN Chapter) 20, 23.

179   BudgIT, 'budgiT' (*BudgiT*, 2017) <http://yourbudgit.com/about-us/> accessed 10 July 2017.

180   Sani Tukur, 'How Nigerians Can Make Money, be Protected in New Whistle Blowing Policy – Finance Minister' (*Premium Times*, September 21 2016) <http://www.premiumtimesng.com/news/headlines/218643-nigerians-can-make-money-protected-new-whistle-blowing-policy-finance-minister.html> accessed 16 July 2017.

that such solutions just encouraged cash circulation amongst PEPs. This shows the limit of the FATF recommendations in combating ML/TF. Whilst GIABA focused solely on financial/non-financial institutions as a conduit of funds for PEPs, there is limited focus on the origin of these funds – the government coffers itself.

Furthermore, institutions responsible for overseeing governmental laundering have repeatedly failed to work hand in hand with the NFIU or the Economic and Financial Crimes Commission (EFCC) to see cases to conclusion. Indigenous actions taken on the back of political will further illustrate the positive agency slack within the actors. It reveals that TA programmes do not necessarily facilitate information exchange that inculcates the peculiarities of states which principals are sometimes unaware of. Rather, it cultivates a top-down approach where principals delegate to agents without fully contracting on unknown issues.

Additionally, the interaction between principal and agent-states fails to capture the complex dual role of regulatory compliance officers who are charged with combating ML/TF whilst maintaining confidence in the financial market. These roles are however conflicted in states where the regulator decriminalises, choosing instead to ridicule a company publicly by exposing the financial crime. The general public may lose confidence in the integrity of such a market. This implies treading a line between enforcing adherence to the FATF recommendations whilst evading release of information that would possibly damage the institution's repute. Contrary to the tenets on which the FATF was built, regulatory bodies may be slacking from their delegation when protecting FIs from a 'run' and ensuring financial stability. Such slack may be corrected by finding a balance through TA and high-level meetings, as sanctions would prove unsuitable. This shows the interaction between instruments the principal uses to monitor the agent and improved technical compliance and effectiveness.

Conclusion

This chapter commences by examining the relationship between the collective principals, (IFIs and the FATF). Their relationship's evolution is examined in light of AML/CFT rulemaking, coupled with the implementation and compliance measures. It argues that the synergy between the Collective Principals (CPs) was crucial in expanding the FATF's reach. This was a catalyst for the division of labour and specialization in the assessment of AML/CFT standards, whilst also allowing the CPs present a united front devoid of quality disparities. This synergy, driven by the FATF, was undermined by the exclusion of ACs from contributing to the standards-making process despite being subjected to enforcement measures.

The interaction between agent-states and CPs is then examined. It argued that two factors are crucial for understanding information asymmetry between these actors on ML/TF issues: the level of a country's integration with the global financial system and its perceived compliance levels. It finds that the incentive for information sharing is highest when a country is 'highly integrated' with perceived high compliance levels. In opposite situations, the countries would usually engage strategically with the principal in order to evade observatory tools or sanctions. However, whilst robust, this perspective is limited in its inability to consider the borderless nature of crime given that laundering can originate from 'low integrated' countries to other countries. Acknowledging this flow of money between countries, this chapter examines the interaction between 'highly integrated' and 'mid-integrated' countries. A pictorial representation illustrates that these countries examined share information only when it is in their self-interest to, particularly when there is a continuous financial business that is of systemic importance to both parties. It however argues that even when countries are willing to exchange viable information, they may be limited by capacity challenges.

It also argues that where information asymmetry continually thrives, the CPs are privy to tools to rein in the agent-states. The tools utilized are dependent on the circumstances in question. The application of the inappropriate tool may indeed lead to an under-regulation, as the tool would be inadequate.

Further Reading

1. Adamu Abuh, 'British Envoy Gives Conditions for Repatriating Stolen Funds to Nigeria' (*The Guardian*, 21 January, 2016) <https://guardian.ng/news/british-envoy-gives-condition-for-repatriating-stolen-funds-to-nigeria/#comment-section> accessed 10 July 2016.
2. Andrew Cornford, 'Basel II and Developing Countries' [2008] 2 *Finance & Bien Commun, Cairn Info* 31–32.
3. Alexander Kentikelenis, Thomas Stubbs and Lawrence King, 'IMF Conditionality and Development Policy Space 1985–2014' [2016] 23 (4) *Review of International Political Economy.*
4. Ann Hollingshead, 'The Implied Tax Revenue Loss from Trade Mispricing' [2010] *Global Financial Integrity.*
5. APG on Money Laundering, 'FATF & FATF Style Regional Bodies' (*APG*) <http://www.apgml.org/fatf-and-fsrb/page.aspx?p=94065425-e6aa-479f-8701-5ca5d07ccfe8> accessed 10 July 2017.
6. BIS, 'Committee on Payments and Market Infrastructure: Correspondent Banking' (Bank for International Settlement, July 2016) <https://www.bis.org/cpmi/publ/d147.pdf> accessed October 2016.
7. Ben Hayes, 'Counter-Terrorism, "Policy Laundering" and the FATF: Legalizing Surveillance, Regulating Civil Society' <http://www.statewatch.org/analyses/no-171-fafp-report.pdf> accessed 10 January 2017.
8. Beth Simmons, 'International Efforts Against Money Laundering' *in* Dinah Shelton (ed.) *Commitment and Compliance: The Role of Non-Binding Norms in the International Legal System* (Oxford University Press, Oxford, 2000, First Published 2000).
9. Bretton Woods Project, 'IMF Technical Assistance' (*Bretton Woods Project*, 13 March 2014) <http://www.brettonwoodsproject.org/2014/03/inside-institutions-imf-technical-assistance/> accessed 10 March 2017.
10. John Braithwaite and Peter Drahos, *Global Business Regulation* (1st edn, Cambridge University Press, 2000).

11. Brooke A. Smith-Windsor, 'Hard Power, Soft Power Reconsidered' [2000] 1 (3) Canadian Military Journal.

12. Brunsson Nils, 'Standardization as Organization' *in* M. Egeberg and P. Laegried (eds.) *Organizing Political Institutions: Essays for Johan P. Olsen* (Scandinavian University Press, Oslo, 1999).

13. BudgiT, 'budgiT' (*BudgiT*, 2017) <http://yourbudgit.com/about-us/> accessed 10 July 2017.

14. Catalina Amuedo-Dorantes, 'The Good and the Bad in Remittance Flows' (IZA World of Labor, November 2014) <https://wol.iza.org/uploads/article s/97/pdfs/good-and-bad-in-remittance-flows.pdf> accessed 10 May 2017.

15. Carlos Santiso, 'Good Governance and Aid Effectiveness: The World Bank and Conditionality' [2001] 7 (1) *The Georgetown Public Policy Review*.

16. Carlos Vargas-Silva, 'Migrant Remittances to and from the UK' (*The Migration Observatory at the University of Oxford*, 24 February 2016) <http://www.migr ationobservatory.ox.ac.uk/resources/briefings/migrant-remittances-to-and-fr om-the-uk/> accessed 10 March 2017.

17. CBN, 'Press Release: Activities of Illegal International Money Transfer Operators' (*Central Bank of Nigeria*, 2016) <https://www.cbn.gov.ng/out/2016/ccd/ press%20release%20on%20illegal%20imtsos.pdf> accessed 10 July 2017.

18. Channels Television, 'Nigeria, UK Sign Agreement on Stolen Assets' (*Channels Television*, 30 August 2016) <https://www.channelstv.com/2016/08/30/ni geria-uk-sign-agreement-stolen-assets/> accessed 10 February 2017.

19. CIDDEC, 'The Cambridge International Symposium on Economic Crime' (*CIDDEC*) <http://www.crimesymposium.org> accessed 01 May 2017.

20. Commissioned by the AU/ECA Conference of Ministers of Finance, Planning and Economic Development, 'Report of the High Level Panel on Illicit Financial Flows from Africa' <http://www.uneca.org/sites/default/files/ PublicationFiles/iff_main_report_26feb_en.pdf> accessed 10 April 2017.

21. Vincent Crawford and Joel Sobel, 'Strategic Informational Transmission' [1982] Econometrica: Journal of the Econometric Society.

22. Dinah Shelton, 'Normative Hierarchy in International Law' [2006] 100 American Journal of International Law.

23. Duncan E. Osborne, 'The Financial Action Task Force and the Legal Profession' [2014–2015] 59 *New York Law School Law Review*.

24. Eastern and Southern African Anti-Money Laundering Group (ESAAMLG), 'Strategic Plan April 2012–March 2015' <http://www.esaamlg.org/documen ts_storage/2013-1-4-16-4-51_strategic_plan_2012-2015.pdf> accessed 9 April 2017.

25. Ehi Eric Esoimeme, 'A Critical Analysis of the Bank Verification Number Project Introduced by the Central Bank of Nigeria' [2015].

26. FATF, 'Briefing Briefing to the United Nations Security Council Committee, New York' (26 October 2009) <http://www.un.org/en/sc/ctc/docs/st atements/2009_10_26_fatf_brief.pdf> accessed 19 April 2017.

27. FATF, 'FATF Guidance Document: Best Practices Paper, Best Practices on Trade Based Money Laundering' (*FATF*, 2008) <http://www.fatfgafi.org/m edia/fatf/documents/recommendations/BPP%20Trade%20Based%20Money %20Laundering%202012%20COVER.pdf> accessed 10 July 2017.

28. FATF, 'FATF Guidance: Private Sector Information Sharing' (*FATF*, November 2017) <http://www.fatf-gafi.org/media/fatf/documents/recommendations /Private-Sector-Information-Sharing.pdf> accessed January 2018.

29. FATF, 'FATF Members and Observers' (*FATF*) <http://www.fatf-gafi.org/about/membersandobservers/> accessed 13 April 2017.

30. FATF, 'FATF Membership Policy' (*FATF*) <http://www.fatf-gafi.org/about/membersandobservers/fatfmembershippolicy.html> accessed 11 October 2017.

31. FATF, 'FATF Secretariat' (*FATF*, 2017) <http://www.fatf-gafi.org/about/fatfsecretariat/> accessed 20 January 2017.

32. FATF, 'FATF Training and Research Institute (TREIN)' (*FATF*, 20 September 2016) <http://www.fatf-gafi.org/fr/publications/recommandationsgafi/documents/trein-institute.html?hf=10&b=0&s=desc(fatf_releasedate)> accessed 1 March 2017.

33. FATF, 'Financial Action Task Force Mandate (2012–2020)' (2012) <http://www.fatf-gafi.org/media/fatf/documents/FINAL%20FATF%20MANDATE%202012-2020.pdf> accessed 13 April 2017.

34. FATF, 'Guidance on Capacity Building for Mutual Evaluations and Implementation of the FATF Standards within Low Capacity Countries' (29 February 2008) <http://www.fatf-gafi.org/media/fatf/documents/reports/Capacity%20building%20LCC.pdf> accessed 10 June 2017.

35. FATF, 'High-Risk and Non-Cooperative Jurisdictions' (*FATF*) <http://www.fatf-gafi.org/countries/#high-risk> accessed 10 February 2017.

36. FATF, 'Improving Global AML/CFT Compliance: On-going Process – 24 February 2017' (*FATF*, 24 February 2017) <http://www.fatf-gafi.org/publications/high-riskandnon-cooperativejurisdictions/documents/fatf-compliance-february-2017.html> accessed 12 March 2017.

37. FATF, 'The FATF Recommendations' (*FATF*, 2012) <http://www.fatf-gafi.org/media/fatf/documents/recommendations/pdfs/FATF_Recommendations.pdf> accessed 13 April 2017.

38. FATF, 'Mutual Evaluations' (*FATF*) <http://www.fatf-gafi.org/publications/mutualevaluations/more/more-about-mutual evaluations.html?hf=10&b=0&s=desc(fatf_releasedate)> accessed 01 April 2017.

39. FATF, 'Procedures for the FATF Fourth Round of AML/CFT Mutual Evaluations' (*FATF*, 2013) <http://www.fatf-gafi.org/media/fatf/documents/methodology/FATF-4th-Round-Procedures.pdf> accessed 10 April 2017.

40. FATF, 'The Consolidated FATF Standards on Information Sharing: Relevant Excerpts from the FATF Recommendations and Interpretative Notes' (*FATF*, November 2017) <http://www.fatf-gafi.org/media/fatf/documents/recommendations/pdfs/Consolidated-FATF-Standards-information-sharing.pdf> accessed 10 February 2017.

41. FATF, 'Public Statement 24' (*FATF*, 24 February 2017) <http://www.fatf-gafi.org/publications/high-riskandnon-cooperativejurisdictions/documents/public-statement-february-2017.html> accessed 4 March 2017.

42. FATF, 'Guidance on Capacity Building for Mutual Evaluations and Implementation of the FATF Standards Within Low Capacity Countries' (29 February 2008) <http://www.fatf-gafi.org/media/fatf/documents/reports/Capacity%20building%20LCC.pdf> accessed 4 February 2018.

43. Frank Vibert, 'Reforming International Rule Making' [2012] 2 (3) *Global Policy*.

44. Gallarotti Giulio, 'Soft Soft Power: What it Is, Why it's Important, and the Conditions for its Effective Use' [2011] 4 (1) Journal of Political Power.

45. GIABA, (GIABA) <http://www.giaba.org/member-states/sierra_leone.ht ml> accessed 10 March 2017.

46. Gregory Shaffer, 'Transnational Legal Process and State Change' [2012] 37 (2) *Law & Social Inquiry.*

47. Han Dorussen, 'Mixing Carrots with Sticks: Evaluating the Effectiveness of Positive Incentives' [2001] 38 (2) Journal of Peace Research.

48. Harrision Wagner, 'Economic Inter-Dependence, Bargaining Power and Political Influence' [1988] 42 (3) *International Organisation.*

49. IMF and IBRD, 'Articles of Agreement: International Bank for Reconstruction and Development' [1944] <http://siteresources.worldbank.org/EXTAR CHIVES/Resources/IBRD_Articles_of_Agreement.pdf> accessed 10 April 2017.

50. IMF 'Articles of Agreement' <https://www.imf.org/external/pubs/ft/aa/ pdf/aa.pdf> accessed 26 April 2017.

51. IMF and the World Bank, 'Anti-Money Laundering and Combatting the Financing of Terrorism (AML/CFT): Materials Concerning Staff Progress Towards the Development of a Comprehensive AML/CFT Methodology and Assessment Process' (IMF and World Bank, 2002) <http://www.imf.org/E xternal/np/mae/aml/2002/eng/061102.pdf> accessed 10 April 2017.

52. IMF and World Bank, 'Anti-Money Laundering and Combatting the Financing of Terrorism (AML/CFT): Proposals to Assess a Global Standard and to Prepare ROSCs' (2002) <http://www.imf.org/external/np/mae/aml/2002 /eng/071702.pdf> accessed 15 April 2017.

53. IMF and the World Bank, 'Anti-Money Laundering and Combatting the Financing of Terrorism: Review of the Quality and Consistency of Assessments Reports and the Effectiveness of Coordination' (2006) <https://www.imf .org/external/np/pp/eng/2006/041806r.pdf> accessed 11 April 2017.

54. IMF and the World Bank, 'Financial Sector Assessment Program – Review, Lessons and Issues Going Forward' (2005) <https://www.imf.org/External/ np/fsap/2005/022205.htm> accessed 11 April 2017.

55. IMF and the World Bank, 'Twelve-Month Pilot Program of Anti-Money Laundering and Combating the Financing of Terrorism (AML/CFT) Assessments: Joint Report on the Review of the Pilot Program' (IMF and World Bank, 2004) <http://www.imf.org/external/np/aml/eng/2004/0 31004.pdf> accessed 12 March 2017.

56. IMF and the World Bank, 'Twelve Month Pilot Program of Anti-Money Laundering and Combatting the Financing of Terrorism (AML/CFT) Assessments 7' (2004) <https://www.imf.org/external/np/aml/eng/2004/ 031004.pdf> accessed 10 April 2017.

57. IMF, 'Anti-Money Laundering/Combating the Financing of Terrorism (AML/CFT)' <https://www.imf.org/external/np/leg/amlcft/eng/aml2 .htm> accessed 10 April 2017.

58. IMF Blog, 'IMF Spring Meetings 2017: Keeping Growth on Track' (*IMF Blog*, 28 April 2017) <https://blogs.imf.org/2017/04/28/imf-spring-meetings -2017-keeping-growth-on-track/> accessed 2 May 2017.

59. IMF, 'Factsheet: IMF Capacity Development' (*IMF*, 19 April 2017) <http:// www.imf.org/en/About/Factsheets/Capacity-Development-Technical-Assis tance-and-Training> accessed 1 April 2017.

60. IMF, 'Factsheet: The IMF and Legislators' (*IMF*, 9 January 2017) <http://www.imf.org/external/np/exr/facts/leg.htm> accessed 1 May 2017.

61. IMF, 'Financial Sector Assessment Program: Frequently Asked Questions' (*IMF*, 01 August 2016). <https://www.imf.org/external/np/fsap/faq/#q20> accessed 9 January 2017.

62. IMF, 'Financial System Abuse, Financial Crime and Money Laundering – Background Paper' (*IMF*, 2001) <http://www.imf.org/en/Publications/Policy-Papers/Issues/2016/12/31/Financial-System-Abuse-Financial-Crime-and-Money-Laundering-Background-Paper-PP128> accessed 10 February 2017.

63. IMF, 'Guide for IMF Staff Outreach to Legislators' (*IMF*, 4 January 2006) <http://www.imf.org/external/np/exr/leg/eng/guide.htm> accessed 10 May 2018.

64. IMF, 'Illustration of Proposed Quota and Voting Shares' (*IMF*, 2010) <http://www.imf.org/external/np/sec/pr/2010/pdfs/pr10418_table.pdf> accessed 15 July 2016.

65. IMF, 'Intensified Work on Anti-Money Laundering and Combating Financing of Terrorism (AML/CFT): Joint Progress Report on the Work of the IMF and World Bank' (*IMF*, April 2002) <https://www.imf.org/External/np/mae/aml/2002/eng/041702.pdf> accessed 7 July 2017.

66. IMF, 'IMF Members' Quotas and Voting Power, and IMF Board of Governors' (*IMF*, 24 January 2017) <https://www.imf.org/external/np/sec/memdir/members.aspx#U> accessed 24 January 2017.

67. IMF, 'IMF Policy Paper: Review of the Fund's Strategy on Anti-Money Laundering and Combating the Financing of Terrorism' (*IMF*, February 2014) <https://www.imf.org/external/np/pp/eng/2014/022014a.pdf> accessed 10 May 2016.

68. IMF Legal Department, 'Suppressing the Financing of Terrorism: A Handbook for Legislative Drafting' (*IMF*, 2003) <https://www.imf.org/external/pubs/nft/2003/SFTH/pdf/SFTH.pdf> accessed 1 June 2016.

69. IMF, 'Press Release No. 04/70: IMF, World Bank Enhance Efforts at Combating Money Laundering, Terrorist Financing' (2 April 2004) http://www.imf.org/external/np/sec/pr/2004/pr0470.htm.

70. IMF, 'Press Release No14/0: IMF Executive Board Reviews Mandatory Financial Stability Assessments Under the Financial Sector Assessment Program' (13 January 2014) <https://www.imf.org/external/np/sec/pr/2014/pr1408.htm> accessed 10 May 2016.

71. IMF, 'Public Information Notice No.11/74: IMF Executive Board Reviews Efforts in Anti-Money Laundering and Combating the Financing of Terrorism' (27 June 2011) <http://www.imf.org/external/np/sec/pn/2011/pn1174.htm> accessed 6 April 2017.

72. IMF, 'Review of the Financial Sector Assessment Program: Further Adaptation to the Post Crisis Era' (*IMF*, September 2014) <https://www.imf.org/en/Publications/Policy-Papers/Issues/2016/12/31/Review-of-the-Financial-Sector-Assessment-Program-Further-Adaptation-to-the-Post-Crisis-Era-PP4893> accessed 10 December 2017.

73. Independent Evaluation Office of the IMF, 'Evaluation Report: IMF Interactions with Member Countries' (IMF, 2009) <http://www.ieo-imf.o

rg/ieo/files/completedevaluations/A.%20%20Full%20Text%20of%20Main %20Report.pdf> accessed 20 May 2017.

74. IMF, 'The IMF and the World Bank' (2016) <http://www.imf.org/en/Abo ut/Factsheets/Sheets/2016/07/27/15/31/IMF-World-Bank> accessed 10 February 2017.

75. GIABA, 'Member States: Republic of Benin' (*GIABA*) <http://www.giaba .org/member-states/benin.html> accessed 7 April 2017.

76. GIABA, 'Member States: Republic of Cote d'Ivoire' <http://www.giaba.org/ member-states/cote_divoire.html> accessed 10 March 2017.

77. GIABA, 'Member States: Republic of Mali' (*GIABA*) <http://www.giaba.org /member-states/mali.html> accessed 10 June 2016.

78. IBRD, 'Voting Power of Executive Directors' (Corporate Secretariat, 6 February 2017) <http://siteresources.worldbank.org/BODINT/Resources/278027-1 215524804501/IBRDEDsVotingTable.pdf> accessed 21 February 2017.

79. IMF Factsheet, 'Standards and Codes: The Role of the IMF' (*IMF Factsheet*, 2017) <http://www.imf.org/About/Factsheets/Sheets/2016/08/01/16 /25/Standards-and-Codes?pdf=1> accessed 10 April 2017.

80. James M. Boughton, 'Tearing Down Wall' (IMF, 1990–1999).

81. James M, O'Kane, *The Crooked Ladder: Gangsters, Ethnicity and the American Dream* (Transaction Publishers, New Brunswick, 1992).

82. James T. Gathii, 'The Financial Action Task Force and Global Administrative Law' [2010] Journal of Professional Law.

83. John Hilary, 'Africa: Dead Aid and the Return of Neoliberalism' [2010] 52 (2) *Race & Class*.

84. Kal Raustiala 'The Architecture of International Cooperation: Trans- governmental Networks and the Future of International Law' [2002] 43 (1) Virginia Journal of International Law 1.

85. Kenneth S. Blazejewski, 'The FATF and Its Institutional Partners: Improving the Effectiveness and Accountability of Trans-Governmental Networks' [2008] 22 Temple International and Comparative Law Journal.

86. Dieter Kerwer, 'Rules That Many Use: Standards and Global Regulation' [2005] 12 (4) *Governance* 611, 619.

87. Henry Manne, *Insider Trading and the Stock Market* (1st edn, Free Press, 1996).

88. Mario Giovanoli, 'A New Architecture for the Global Financial Market: Legal Aspects of International Standards Setting' *in* Mario Giovanoli (eds.) *International Monetary Law, Issues for the New Millennium* (Oxford University Press, Oxford, 2000).

89. Mark Pieth and Gemma Aiolfi, 'The Private Sector Becomes Active: The Wolfsberg Process' [2003] 10 (4) Journal of Financial Crime.

90. Oloja Martins , 'Nigeria Rushes to Avert Sanction over Money Laundering Law' (*The Guardian*, 27 September 2012) <http://odili.net/news/source/2 012/sep/27/16.html> accessed 10 March 2017.

91. Martin Ricketts, 'Economic Regulation: Principles, History and Methods' *in* Michael Crew and David Parker (eds.) *International Handbook on Economic Regulation* (Edward Elgar Publishing, 2016).

92. Samuel McSkimming, 'Trade Based Money Laundering: Responding to an Emerging Threat' [2010] 2 *Deakin Law Review*. 37.

93. Michaela Erbenova, Yan Liu et al., 'The Withdrawal of Correspondent Banking Relationships: A Case for Policy Action' (IMF Staff Discussion Note, June

2016) <https://www.imf.org/external/pubs/ft/sdn/2016/sdn1606.pdf> accessed 10 October 2016.

94. Modern Ghana, 'Ghana Exits Blacklist; Nigeria Enacts Terrorism (Prevention) (Amendment) Act 2013' (*Modern Ghana*, 22 February 2013) <https://ww w.modernghana.com/news/447311/1/ghana-exits-fatf-blacklist-nigeria-ena cts-terroris.html> accessed 20 June 2016.

95. Natanel Abramov, 'Why States Struggle to Repatriate Looted Assets' (*Financial Times*, 11 May 2016) <https://www.ft.com/content/322c1854-dcb9-3e31 -a191-6651afd5776b> accessed 10 October 2016.

96. Ngaire Woods, *The Globalizers: The IMF, the World Bank and Their Borrower* (Cambridge University Press, 2006).

97. Norman Mugarura, *The Global Anti-Money Laundering Regulatory Landscape in Less Developed Countries* (1st edn, Routledge, 2016).

98. Okechukwu Innocent, Chukwurah Daniel and Iheanacho Emmanuel, 'An Analysis of Pros and Cons: Treasury Single Account Policy in Nigeria' [2015] 5 (4) Arabian Journal of Business and Management Review (OMAN Chapter) 20, 23.

99. Organization for Economic Co-operation and Development: Better Policies for Better Lives, 'OECD Careers' (OECD) <http://www.oecd.org/careers/wh atwelookfor.htm> accessed 20 January 2016.

100. Pete Engardio, 'Commentary: Don't Use the IMF to Push U.S. Foreign Policy' (*Bloomberg*, 26 November 2001) <https://www.bloomberg.com/news/arti cles/2001-11-25/commentary-dont-use-the-imf-to-push-u-dot-s-dot-foreign -policy> accessed 10 April 2017.

101. Rainer Hulsse and Dieter Kerwer, 'Global Standards in Action: Insights from Anti-Money Laundering Regulations' [2007] 14 (5) *Organization*.

102. Raustiala Kal and Anne-Marie Slaughter, 'International Law, International Relations and Compliance' [2002] 2 (2) *Princeton Law & Public Affairs Paper*.

103. Richard Herring, 'Conflicts Between Home and Host Country Prudential Supervisors' <http://citeseerx.ist.psu.edu/viewdoc/download?doi=10.1.1 .543.1482&rep=rep1&type=pdf> accessed 19 March 2018.

104. Robert A. Kagan and John T. Scholz, 'The Criminology of the Corporation and Regulatory Enforcement Strategies' *in* J.T. Hawkins and K. and J. Thomas (eds.) *Enforcing Regulation* (Kluwer-Nijhoff Publishing, Boston, 1984).

105. Robert Dijkstra, 'Accountability of Financial Supervisory Agencies: An Incentive Approach' [2010] 11 (2) Journal of Banking Regulation.

106. Robert Rotberg, 'Africa Legislative Effectiveness' (Africa and Asia: The Key Issues) <https://robertrotberg.wordpress.com/2013/10/16/african-legis lative-effectiveness/> accessed 5 July 2017.

107. Ross Delston and Stephen C. Walls, 'Reaching Beyond Banks: How to Target Trade-Based Money Laundering and Terrorist Financing Outside the Financial Sector' [2009] 41 The Case Western Reserve Journal of International Law 85, 103.

108. Saby Ghoshray, 'Combating Threats to the International Financial System: The Financial Action Task Force: Compliance Convergence in FATF Rulemaking: The Conflict Between Agency Capture and Soft Law' [2014/2015] 59. *New York Law School Review*.

109. Sani Tukur, 'How Nigerians Can Make Money, be Protected in New Whistle Blowing Policy – Finance Minister' (*Premium Times*, 21 September 2016)

<http://www.premiumtimesng.com/news/headlines/218643-nigerians-can
-make-money-protected-new-whistle-blowing-policy-finance-minister.html>
accessed 16 July 2017.

110. Scoop Independent News WikiLeaks, 'Cablegate: Nigeria: Economic and
Financial Crimes Act Passed' (*Scoop Independent News WikiLeaks*, 24 February
2004) <http://www.scoop.co.nz/stories/WL0402/S00051/cablegate-niger
ia-economic-and-financial-crimes-act-passed.htm> accessed 1 April 2017.

111. Sean Hagan, 'Revision to the Financial Action Task Force (FATF) Standard –
Information Note to the Executive Board' (*IMF*, July 2012) <https://www
.imf.org/external/np/pp/eng/2012/071712a.pdf> accessed 11 May 2017.

112. *The Economist*, 'Africa Money Transfers, Let Them Remit' (*The Economist*, 20
July 2013) <https://www.economist.com/news/middle-east-and-africa/2
1581995-western-worries-about-money-laundering-are-threatening-economic
-lifeline> accessed 10 November 2017.

113. The NATO Parliamentary Assembly and the Commonwealth Parliamentary
Association (CPA) <http://www.nato-pa.int> accessed 1 April 2017.

114. The Parliamentary Network on the World Bank & IMF <http://www.parlnet
.org/node> accessed 10 April 2017.

115. The Parliamentary Network, 'Parliamentary Workshop at the Annual Meetings
2016' (World Bank Group, IMF, 2016) <http://www.parlnet.org/sites/d
efault/files/Agenda-MP-workshop-annual-meetings2016.pdf> accessed 21
January 2017.

116. The Wolfsberg Group, 'Wolfsberg Anti-Money Laundering Principles for
Correspondent Banking' (The Wolfsberg Group, 2014) <https://sic.gov.lb
/intorg/Wolfsberg%20Correspondent%20Banking%20Principles%20(2014).
pdf> accessed 10 March 2016.

117. The World Bank and the IMF, 'Financial Sector Assessment: A Handbook'
(2005) <http://documents.worldbank.org/curated/en/3067014683378
79923/pdf/337970rev0Final0Assessment01PUBLIC1.pdf> accessed 10
June 2016.

118. Timothy Meyer, 'Soft Law as Delegation' [2008] 32 (3) Fordham International
Law Journal.

119. Tine Hanrieder, *International Organization in Time: Fragmentation and
Reform* (1st edn, Oxford University Press, 2015).

120. UNESCO, 'Technical Assistance in Cultural Governance' (UNESCO) <http:
//www.unesco.org/new/en/culture/themes/cultural-diversity/cultural-exp
ressions/programmes/technical-assistance/what-is-technical-assistance/>
accessed 10 April 2017.

121. UN and the World Bank, 'Stolen Asset Recovery (StAR) Initiative: Challenges,
Opportunities, and Action Plan' (United Nations and World Bank, June 2007)
<https://siteresources.worldbank.org/NEWS/Resources/Star-rep-full.pdf>
accessed 10 June 2016.

122. US Department of State: Diplomacy in Action, 'The Financial Action Task
Force and FATF-Style Regional Bodies' (US Department of State) <https:/
/www.state.gov/j/inl/rls/nrcrpt/2015/vol2/239046.htm> accessed 10 July
2017.

123. US Department of Treasury, 'Implementation of Legislative Provisions Relating
to the International Monetary Fund: A Report to Congress 11' (United States
Department of the Treasury, March 2006) <https://www.treasury.gov/resou

rce-center/international/int-monetary-fund/Documents/2015%20IMF%2 0Legislative%20Mandates%20Report.pdf> accessed 10 May 2017.

124. *Vanguard*, 'Nigeria, UK Sign MOU on Return of Stolen Assets' (*Vanguard*, 30 August 2016) <https://www.vanguardngr.com/2016/08/nigeria-uk-sign -mou-return-stolen-assets/> accessed 10 February 2017.

125. Ernest J. Wilson, 'Hard Power, Soft Power, Smart Power' [2008] 616 (1) The Annals of the American Academy of Political and Social Science.

126. World Bank, *A Guide to the World Bank* (3rd edn, The World Bank, 2011).

127. World Bank Group and the IMF, 'Parliamentary Workshop at the Annual Meetings 2016' (The Parliamentary Network on the World Bank & IMF) <http://www.parlnet.org/sites/default/files/Agenda-MP-workshop-annual -meetings2016.pdf> accessed 10 April 2017.

5 Determinants of Africa's Compliance Levels to the Global Anti-Money Laundering Regime

Introduction

The efficiency of the global anti-money laundering and counter-terrorist financing (AML/CFT) regime is largely dependent on the capability of countries to adopt and implement it. The majority of African countries (ACs) are however beset with socio-economic, legal and political challenges which impede their ability to transplant and comply, notwithstanding the Financial Action Task Force's (FATF's) introduction of the risk-based approach. Consequently, the question is whether the commitment of ACs to the AML/CFT regime can be aligned with their compliance interests and capacity. Whilst the FATF argues that socio-economic, political and legal challenges should have no impact on compliance outcomes, these factors cannot be divorced because, empirically, the absence thereof hinders the compliance trajectory of states.

The first section examines ACs, acknowledging the historical and socio-economic dissimilarities between them. These considerations are not unconnected to the challenges faced by ACs in meeting the AML/CFT standards. Rather, they reinforce the need for a framework that would facilitate compliance, given that Africa serves as a fertile ground for money laundering/terrorist financing (ML/TF). The second section examines the seemingly indigenous attempt to combat illicit crimes through the framework of the African Union (AU) and the FATF-styled regional bodies (FSRBs). The third section explores the regulatory environment across ACs, illustrating that most ACs are inundated by an interaction of legal and non-legal factors which affect or determine their compliance levels and regulatory responses. The fourth section presents the compliance levels of countries to the FATF recommendations and empirically evaluates the factors that influence the attainment of such compliance levels. It illustrates that premature regulatory environments coupled with socio-economic challenges may indeed affect compliance. The fifth section knits the other sections together and concludes.

African States: Context

Examining Africa's socio-economic history reveals a chronology of setbacks, arguably from the pre-colonial era. Although commodities trade was buoyant between ACs and the industrialised world during the early 19th century, there were structural inadequacies which hindered the continent's economic growth.[1] This argument, advanced by Davidson, is restricted by its perception of Africa's setbacks as internal and distinct from colonialism.[2] Davidson does not acknowledge that before formal colonialism, external institutions affected Africa's interrelationship with developed countries.[3] Trading activities that preceded colonisation occasioned the political subjugation of parts of Africa to Europe.[4] Pre-colonial relations led to the conquest of Africa by Europe.[5] Therefore, whilst internal structural shortcomings might have affected Africa's economy, the role of external forces cannot be discounted.

Perhaps, the socio-economic issues were exacerbated during the colonial era, where all ACs, barring Ethiopia and Liberia, were subjected to colonial rule.[6] Refuting the effect of colonialism, scholars have argued that Asian countries suffered a similar colonial fate, but their economies improved within a generation after independence.[7] Whilst credible, this argument discounts the history of economic exploitation and psychological damage which ravaged Africa.[8] The later part of the 19th century evidenced this; it was marked by capital and labour shortage, a catalyst of slave trade.[9] Slave trade involved the trade of persons for goods and the settlement of the colonisers within Africa. Africans were used as labourers to harvest export items such as minerals and commodities.[10] Empirical findings indicate that slave trade hindered the economic performance of countries.[11] Colonial banks

1 Basil Davidson, *The African Genius: An Introduction to African Social History* (Little, Brown and Company, 1969). West African countries traded in salt, gold, cola nut and slaves, whilst Southern Africa developed trade with China and India in iron, ivory and gold. In return, they received porcelain, heads and Persian/Arab Pots. As a result of Islamic influence, Northern Africa traded with Arab countries. See Randall L. Pouwels, *The African and Middle Eastern World, 600–1500* (OUP, 2005).

2 *Davidson* (n 1).

3 Edward Alpers, 'Rethinking African Economic History: A Contribution to the Discussion of the Roots of Under-Development' [1973] 3 (3) Ufahamu A Journal of African Studies 97, 100; A.G. Hopkins, 'The New Economic History of Africa' [2009] 50 (2) Journal of African History 155, 166.

4 K. Dike, *Trade and Politics in the Niger Delta* (OUP, 1956); James Fenske, 'The Causal History of Africa: A Response to Hopkins' [2010] 25 (2) Economic History of Developing Regions 1, 17.

5 Walter Rodney, *How Europe Underdeveloped Africa* (Bogle-L'Ouverture Publications, 1972).

6 Leigh Gardner, 'Was Independence Really Better than Colonial Rule? A Comparative Study of Liberia and Sierra Leone' [2013] 1, 3.

7 The Economist, 'The Heart of the Matter' (*The Economist*, 11 May 2000) <http://www.economist.com/node/333437> accessed 20 October 2017.

8 Ibid.

9 Biodun Olamosu and Andy Wynne, 'Africa Rising? The Economic History of Sub-Saharan Africa' (*International Socialism*, 2015) <http://isj.org.uk/africa-rising/#footnote-263-14> accessed 18 October 2017.

10 Pius Okigbo, 'Problem, Crisis or Catastrophe: Any Exit for African Economies in the 1990s?' [1993] 3 Nigerian National Merit Award Lectures (Fountain Publications).

11 Nathan Nunn, 'The Long-term Effects of Africa's Slave Trades' [2008] 123 (1) The Quarterly Journal of Economics 139, 144.

within ACs were also complicit in preserving the monopolistic position of colonies in the export-import trade, through the provision of less favourable bank credit to Africans, than to Europeans.[12] Such limited credit, including the export trend which still subsists, has made ACs more susceptible to vagaries of changing global prices and external shocks than most diversified economies.[13]

The subsequent introduction of neoliberal policies, such as privatisation, increased integration and deregulation in the 1980s worsened Africa's position within the global financial system. ACs became more susceptible to external shocks.[14] This occasioned inequality within the continent.[15] For instance, economically, the continent is dominated by Nigeria with 405.1 billion dollars of nominal gross domestic product (GDP).[16] Nigeria is followed by Egypt, Algeria, Morocco and Angola with a cumulative GDP of 679.6 billion dollars,[17] whilst Sao Tome and Principe, Comoros, The Gambia and Guinea-Bissau rank the least with a cumulative GDP of 2.98 billion dollars.[18] Regionally, North Africa is the least poor region, closely followed by Southern Africa.[19] Indeed, 90% of the poorest people in Africa live in East, Central and West Africa,[20] a situation that illustrates the inequalities triggered by a combination of external and internal factors.

More disturbing is the economic inequality that liberalisation has created between Africa and the industrialised world. Africa holds only 4.4% of the world's GDP based on purchasing-power-parity (PPP) share of world total.[21] This is neg-

12 Chibuike Uche, 'Foreign Banks, Africans, and Credit in Colonial Nigeria, c. 1890–1912' [1999] 4 Economic History Review, LII 699, 699; Chibuike Uche, 'Indigenous Banks in Colonial Nigeria' [2010] 43 (3) The International Journal of African Historical Studies 467, 472.

13 Thankdika Mkandawire and Charles C. Soludo (eds.) *Our Continent, Our Future: African Perspectives on Structural Adjustment* (Codesria, 1999) 42.

14 Cull Robert, Lemma Senbet and Macro Sorge, 'Deposit Insurance and Financial Development' (2005) World Bank Policy Research Working Paper 2682, 16 <http://document s.worldbank.org/curated/en/813041468739789102/pdf/multi0page.pdf> accessed 18 November 2017.

15 *Olamosu and Wynne* (n 9).

16 AfDB, 'African Economic Outlook 2017' (*AfDB*, 2017) <https://www.afdb.org/fileadmin /uploads/afdb/Documents/Publications/AEO_2017_Report_Full_English.pdf> accessed 18 October 2017.

17 IMF, 'World Economic Outlook: Subdued Demand, Symptoms and Remedies' (*IMF*, October 2016) <http://www.imf.org/external/pubs/ft/weo/2016/02/#front> accessed 18 October 2017; The World Bank, 'The World Bank in Africa' (*The World Bank*, 2017) <http: //www.worldbank.org/en/region/afr/overview> accessed 18 October 2017.

18 IMF, 'World Economic Outlook: Subdued Demand, Symptoms and Remedies' (*IMF*, October 2016) <http://www.imf.org/external/pubs/ft/weo/2016/02/#front> accessed 18 October 2017.

19 Sabrina Alkire, Christoph Jindra, Gisela Robles and Ana Vaz, 'Multidimensional Poverty in Africa' (*OPHI Briefing 40*, 2016) <http://www.ophi.org.uk/wp-content/uploads/Global -MPI-2016-8-pager.pdf> accessed 18 October 2017.

20 Ibid.

21 IMF, 'IMF DataMapper: GDP Based on PPP, Share of World' (*IMF World Economic Outlook Database*, April 2017) <http://www.imf.org/external/datamapper/PPPSH@WEO/ OEMDC/WEOWORLD/ADVEC/MAE> accessed 10 October 2017.

ligible when compared to the BRICS's cumulative 32.02% share, with China alone holding 18.26%.[22] These statistics provide a prism through which to examine the degree of integration with the global economy. Contrary to emerging economies (EEs), ACs have a lower degree of financial integration with the global economy.[23] This demonstrates Africa's challenges to creating an inclusive financial system, a factor crucial for financial sector development and improved economic performance.[24] The effect is that ACs are more likely to suffer from poverty and stunted financial growth.[25]

The resulting shortcomings from integration deficit is further revealed by examining Africa's banking system. It is characterised by a high interest margin[26] usually triggered by low competition in domestic banking, weak property rights and lack of financial infrastructure.[27] Additionally, African financial systems only deliver on a limited range of products at high costs. The financial sector reforms in the 1980s were however not all bad news. Stirred by improvements in global conditions and the advent of technology, these reforms connected Africa to the rest of the world and led to improved performance in the real and financial sectors.[28] Consequently, until recently, Africa's finance and stock markets experienced slow but uninterrupted growth, irrespective of low capitalisation and liquidity.[29] Surprisingly, the continent proved resilient during the global financial crisis. ACs, particularly the East Africa Community (EAC), have taken to regional financial integration, with blocks of countries establishing a common market, custom union and common currency.[30]

Notwithstanding the laudable performance in terms of regional financial integration, Africa's financial markets are significantly less developed than other

22 Ibid.
23 Benedicte Christensen, 'Financial Integration in Africa: Implications for Monetary Policy and Financial Stability' [2014] 76 BIS Paper 11, 11; AfDB, 'Financial Sector Integration in Three Regions of Africa' (*AfDB*, 2010) <https://www.afdb.org/fileadmin/uploads/afdb /Documents/Project-and-Operations/AfDB%20Regional%20Financial%20Integration%2 0REPORT_EN.pdf> accessed 19 October 2017.
24 Lemma Senbet and Isaac Otchere, African Stock Markets (*IMF*, 2008) <https://www.imf .org/external/np/seminars/eng/2008/afrfin/pdf/senbet.pdf> accessed 20 October 2017.
25 *Christensen* (n 23); AfDB, 'Financial Sector Integration in Three Regions of Africa' (*AfDB*, 2010) <https://www.afdb.org/fileadmin/uploads/afdb/Documents/Project-and-Oper ations/AfDB%20Regional%20Financial%20Integration%20REPORT_EN.pdf> accessed 19 October 2017; Cyn-Young Park and Rogelio Mercado, 'Financial Inclusion, Poverty and Income Inequality in Developing Asia' (2015) ADB Economics Working Paper Series 426, 7 < https://www.adb.org/sites/default/files/publication/153143/ewp-426.pdf> accessed 19 November 2017; Ross Levine, 'Finance and Growth: Theory and Evidence' (2004) NBER Working Paper Series 10766, 84 <http://www.nber.org/papers/w10766 .pdf> accessed 19 November 2017.
26 *Christensen* (n 23).
27 Ibid.
28 *Senbet and Otchere* (n 24).
29 Ibid.; Allen Franklin et al., 'The African Financial Development and Financial Inclusion Gaps' [2014] 23 (5) Journal of African Economies 614, 621.
30 *Christensen* (n 23).

markets on all indicators of financial development.[31] Hence, regulators have sought to achieve financial broadening and inclusion through adherence to the Basel III requirements whilst facilitating improved access to financial products or services.[32] However, it is indeed questionable if the level attained by Nigeria or Egypt in terms of financial growth can be replicated in other countries given the diversity of countries within Africa.[33] Other financial markets within Africa are relatively underdeveloped and fragmented, further hindering effective replication.

Notwithstanding the low degree of integration of ACs to the global economy, certain countries pose a risk to the global financial system given the high rate of corruption and financial crimes. Sub-Saharan Africa countries were recently ranked with an average score of 31,[34] with 0 meaning highly corrupt and 100 meaning clean.[35] Country-by-country differences also exist; whilst Botswana and Cape Verde rank as the least corrupt ACs, Somalia, Sudan, South Sudan and Guinea-Bissau rank highest on corrupt standard globally.[36] Consequently, there is increased poverty, injustice and stunted development of food security, health facilities, educational services and infrastructure in these countries, and Africa as a whole.[37]

For the above reason, *The Economist* once referred to Africa as a 'hopeless continent' that would continually suffer series of crises until it was able to develop a consciousness to resolving corruption.[38] More unflattering is the United Nations Economic Commission for Africa (UNECA) estimates that the continent loses about US$50 billion annually to illicit dealings, most of which is looted by government officials and business leaders to developed countries.[39] This demon-

---

31 Christopher Green, Colin Kirkpatrick and Victor Murinde, 'Finance for Small Enterprise Growth and Poverty Reduction in Developing Countries' [2006] 18 (7) Journal of International Development 1017, 1027.

32 Beck Thorsten and Samuel Munzele Maimbo, (eds.) *Financial Sector Development in Africa: Opportunities and Challenges* (World Bank Publications, 2012) 4.

33 *Green, Kirkpatrick and Murinde* (n 31).

34 This falls below 43, the global average score. See, TI, 'Corruption Perceptions Index 2016' (*Transparency International*, 25 January 2017) <https://www.transparency.org/whatwedo /publication/corruption_perceptions_index_2016> accessed 19 October 2017.

35 Ibid.

36 Ibid. (n 34).

37 Mohamed Sultan, 'How Illicit Financial Flows Drain African Economies' (*Open Society Foundations*, 21 April 2014) < https://www.opensocietyfoundations.org/voices/how-illic it-financial-flows-drain-african-economies > accessed 20 October 2017; Theophilous Chiviru, 'Panama Papers Reveal Africa Losing Billions to Corruption and Bribery' (*One.org*, 16 August 2016) <https://www.one.org/international/blog/panama-paper-reveals-africa-los ing-billions-to-corruption-and-bribery/> accessed 19 October 2017.

38 The Economist, 'Hopeless Africa' (*The Economist*, 11 May 2000) <http://www.economist .com/node/333429> accessed 20 October 2017.

39 *The Guardian*, 'Africa Losing Billions from Fraud and Tax Avoidance' (*The Guardian*, 2 February 2015) <https://www.theguardian.com/global-development/2015/feb/02/a frica-tax-avoidance-money-laundering-illicit-financial-flows> accessed 20 October 2017. Commissioned by the AU/ECA Conference of Ministers of Finance, Planning and Eco-

strates the lax structures and culture in Africa that permit and foster laundering. More interestingly, it also illustrates that developed countries provide gateways for illicit transfers in the shape of anonymous offshore companies and investment entities which enable the facilitation of stolen funds overseas.[40] Such gateways however have catastrophic effects on developed economies, contributing directly or indirectly to the financing of crime or terror.[41]

Undoubtedly, a correlation exists between Africa's historical context and its current socio-economic structures. Africa's colonial history has catalysed lack of robust financial institutions (FIs), redundant political will, corruption, financial inequality and lack of education. Although the IFIs/FATF view these as factors that hinder countries attaining full compliance with the FATF recommendations, these factors are somewhat peculiar to ACs. Therefore, ACs need a suitable framework that allows them combat illicit crimes. Not one that has arguably set them up to fail.

Importantly, given the threat that illicit crimes pose to the global economy and the sustainability of Africa's economic growth, Africa has developed a framework to combat ML/TF.

Africa's Response to AML/CFT

Responding to international pressures and certain homegrown factors, some ACs have taken reactive steps by formulating, signing and domesticating conventions[42] via national legislations. Consequently, in 2002, action plans were developed to ensure compliance to ML/TF in Africa.[43]

The African Peer Review Mechanism (APRM), an initiative of the New Partnership for Africa's Development (NEPAD),[44] was launched to reinvigor-

---

nomic Development, 'Illicit Financial Flows: Report of the High Level Panel on Illicit Financial Flows from Africa' (*Track it! Stop It! Get It!*, 2014) <https://www.uneca.org/sites/default/files/PublicationFiles/iff_main_report_26feb_en.pdf> accessed 20 October 2017.

40 Aljazeera, 'How to Rob Africa' (*Aljazeera*, 8 November 2012) <http://www.aljazeera.com/programmes/peopleandpower/2012/11/201211714649852604.html> accessed 19 October 2017; Roberto Saviano, 'The Real Threat to Britain's Borders is the Flow of Dirty Money' (*The Guardian*, 23 June 2016) <https://www.theguardian.com/commentisfree/2016/jun/23/real-threat-britain-borders-flow-dirty-money-eu> accessed 20 October 2017.

41 Peter Reuter (eds.), *Draining Development? Controlling Flows of Illicit Funds from Developing Countries* (The World Bank, 2012).

42 In 1999, the Organization of African Unity (OAU, now AU) adopted a Convention on the Prevention and Combating of Terrorism (the Algiers Convention).

43 See Charles Goredema and Anneli Botha, 'Africa's Commitment to Combating Crime and Terrorism: A Review of Eight NEPAD Countries' [2004] 3 African Human Security Initiative 1, 3. In 2004, the AU adopted a protocol to the Algiers Convention, which addressed commitments to criminalise the financing of terrorism.

44 Similar to the Organisation for Economic Cooperation and Development (OECD) reviews, the APRM entails periodic reviews of policies and practices of participating states to measure progress on mutually agreed goals and compliance with adopted economic goals.

ate the African voice in decisions concerning Africa. The APRM recognised the relationship between ML and corruption (ML/C) and put in place a corruption control mechanism aimed at fostering the implementation of banking and financial standards under its thematic area of economic governance.[45] A brainchild of Africa's experience, the APRM illustrates that poor governance in one country can have far-reaching negative implications on a region or continent.[46]

The ML/C objective is assessed against the standards and codes of the United Nations and African Union on ML/C, the FATF recommendations and the International Standards on Auditing.[47] Participating countries are subject to a five-stage review process.[48] The risk-based approach[49] benchmarks backed by indicators come in the form of open questions requiring documentary evidence in certain instances.[50] Examining the APRM processes shows that it synchronised international and regional standards with the aim of propelling implementation of standards, thus revealing external influence.[51]

Nonetheless, the language of the APRM, which lacked precision, and its assessment processes warranted subjective and conflicting interpretations, thus lacking measurability. Also, staff of universities and research institutions are responsible for filling out assessment questionnaires.[52] Thus, contrary to the objectivity portrayed by the APRM process,[53] the resulting Country Review Reports (CRR) are

---

45 Anthony Afful-Dadzie et al., 'Tracking Progress of African Peer Review Mechanism (APRM) Using Fuzzy Comprehensive Evaluation Method' [2014] 43 (8) Kybermetes 1193, 1194.

46 *Goredema and Botha* (n 43) 1, 1.

47 NEPAD Secretariat, 'NEPAD/ HSGIC/03-2003/APRM/Guideline/OSCI, 6th Summit of the NEPAD Heads of State and Government Implementation Committee; Nigeria Objectives, Standards, Criteria and Indicators for the African Peer Review Mechanism' (*NEPAD Secretariat,* 2003) <http://www.chr.up.ac.za/chr_old/hr_docs/arpm/docs/book5.pdf> accessed 20 July 2015.

48 AU and NEPAD, 'Guidelines for Countries to Prepare for and Participate in the African Peer Review Mechanism (APRM)' (*AU and NEPAD,* 2003) <http://www1.uneca.org/Portals/ nepad/Documents/Guidelines-for-Countries-to-APRM.pdf> accessed 10 March 2015; G.M. Ukertor and A.G. Gabriel., 'African Peer Review Mechanism: Nigeria's Democracy and Good Governance' [2009] 7 (1) Journal of Research National Development; Ross Herbert and Steven Gruzd, 'Taking Stock of the African Peer Review Mechanism' [2007] 14 (1) South Africa Journal of International Affairs 5, 5; Kanbur Ravi, 'The African Peer Review Mechanism (APRM): An Assessment of Concept and Design' [2004] 31 (4) Politikno 1, 3.

49 It recognizes that participating countries have varied developmental levels and each country's assessment and the assistance granted is tailored to its developmental level. APRM Base Document, Paragraph 17 in Guidelines for Countries to Prepare for and to Participate in the African Peer Review Mechanism (APRM).

50 *Ravi* (n 48) 1, 3.

51 AU and APRM, 'Revised Country Self-Assessment Questionnaire for the African Peer Review Mechanism' (AU and APRM) <http://aprm-au.org/admin/pdfFiles/aprm_questi onnaire.pdf> accessed 10 July 2017.

52 The APRM requires that its questionnaires be filled by a cross-section of the society, thus involving government bodies, civil societies etc.; *Anthony Afful-Dadzie et al.* (n 45).

53 The requirement that questionnaires be filled by a cross-section of the society.

prejudiced. For instance, the cases of Burkina Faso[54] and Nigeria[55] illustrate characteristic differences. Whilst both countries had evident ML/TF threats given their porous borders and cash-based economy, the 2008 CRRs, assuming that ML/TF were alien to ACs, reported that ML did not seem to be a concern for both countries; TF was also unmentioned in the reports.[56] Nigeria however interpreted the standards differently and took action to combat ML/C by legislating and putting legal structures in place to ensure enforcement.[57] Consequently, Nigeria introduced laws on TF and fortified its regulatory policies. Subsequently, Burkina Faso also promulgated laws on ML.[58] Whether the legislative progress was due to the APRM cannot be ascertained, particularly given the initial flippant attitude by Burkina Faso and Nigeria's desire to leave the FATF's blacklist.[59]

Furthermore, it is indeed disputed whether the independent panel or heads of states were able to call Burkina Faso to order during its non-compliance period resulting from the misrepresented CRR. The APRM was a voluntary consensus-oriented mechanism.[60] Unlike the FATF or the International Monetary Fund/World Bank (IMF/WB), the APRM does not issue sanctions or impose conditionalities through aid. It does not blacklist or threaten suspension[61] when countries fail to meet the required benchmark on AML/CFT. The APRM mechanism presumes that voluntary participation entrenches sovereignty and indicates political will and would thus facilitate good governance, peace and security.[62] In practice, lack of compulsion may occasion difficulties in accession and compliance.[63] This demonstrates why 18 ACs have refused to subject themselves to the APRM

54 APRM, 'Country Review Report of Burkina Faso: Country Review Report No 9' (*African Peer Review Mechanism*, May 2008) <http://www1.uneca.org/Portals/aprm/Documents/CountryReports/BurkinaFaso.pdf> accessed 10 July 2016.

55 APRM, 'Country Review Report of Nigeria: Country Review Report No 8' (*African Peer Review Mechanism*, June 2008) <http://www1.uneca.org/Portals/aprm/Documents/CountryReports/Nigeria.pdf> accessed 10 July 2016.

56 *APRM* (n 54); *APRM* (n 55).

57 Agu Onyebuchi, Simon Nwankwo and Onwuka Onuka, 'Combating Money Laundering and Terrorist Financing – The Nigerian Experience' [2016] 4 (1) International Journal of Business and Law Research 29, 35.

58 Law No. 026 – 2006/ AN of 28 November 2006 (AML Act).

59 Patrick Bond, 'Removing Neo-colonialism's APRM Mask: A Critique of the African Peer Review Mechanism' [2009] 36 (122) Review of African Political Economy 595, 602.

60 Rachel Mukamunana and J.O. Kuye, 'Revisiting the African Peer Review Mechanism: The Case for Leadership and Good Governance in Africa' [2005] 3 (40) Journal of Public Administration 590, 596.

61 *Herbert and Gruzd* (n 48) 1, 8.

62 Hanafi Hammed and Sarinus Kabo, 'African Peer Review Mechanism and Crisis of Good Governance in Africa' [2013] 19 Journal of Law, Policy and Globalization 1, 25.

63 Jackkie Cilliers, 'Peace and Security through Good Governance? A Guide to the NEPAD African Peer Review Mechanism' [2003] 70 Pretoria: Institute for Security Studies 1, 14; Ross Herbert, 'Becoming my Brother's Keeper' [2003] 1. E-Africa: Electronic Journal of Governance and Innovation 7, 9.

evaluations[64] and, more fundamentally, erring countries have the opportunity to withdraw.[65] Contrary to expectations, the non-enforcement approach of the APRM is likely to reinforce non-compliance and thus fail to incentivise political will. This informs why Hammed and Kobo advocate for sanctions,[66] emphasising the imperative need for an indigenous mechanism to ensure compliance.[67] Without an appropriate monitoring and evaluation structure to ensure data analysis, the APRM will remain a cosmetic exercise without effect in the real world of policy and decision-making.[68]

The APRM is further critiqued on the ground that its review process is a measure to assure international creditors of Africa's determination to repudiate intolerable practices.[69] It therefore appears as a donor-imposed plan, repackaged under an alleged African ownership.[70] This argument indicates the non-preservation of sovereignty as supposed 'African' decisions are externally influenced. For instance, the engineering of NEPAD by ACs was supported by the Group of Eight (G8).[71] It is however realised that Africa cannot combat ML/TF in isolation. Thus in 2002, the APRM's steering committee proposed an action plan to adopt and strengthen AML/CFT laws and promote compliance with international AML/CFT standards.[72] Further to this, the APRM forum approved the African Development Bank (AfDB) as one of the partners to support the peer review process.[73] The AfDB comes with a form of compulsion given that its

---

64 Adejoke Babington-Ashaye, 'The African Peer Review Mechanism at Ten: From Lofty Goals to Practical Implementation' (AfricLaw, 19 March 2013) <http://africlaw.com/2013/03/19/the-african-peer-review-mechanism-at-ten-from-lofty-goals-to-practical-implementation/> accessed 10 May 2016.

65 *Mukamunana and Kuye* (n 60) 590, 596.

66 *Hammed, Kabo* (n 62).

67 *Ravi* (n 48) 1, 2.

68 Karen Odhiambo, 'Evaluation Capacity Development in Kenya' (Paper Presented at the Workshop Organized by the Development Bank of Southern Africa, the African Development Bank and the World Bank, Johannesburg 2000); Appiah Koranteng, 'Evaluation Capacity in Ghana' (Workshop by the Development Bank of Southern Africa, the African Development Bank and the World Bank, Johannesburg 2000).

69 Sommet Kananaskis Summit Canada, 'G8 Africa Action Plan' (Sommet Kananskis Summit, 2002) <http://www.owen.org/wp-content/uploads/G8-AAA.pdf> accessed 11 April 2015; G8 countries, through the Africa Action Plan (AAP), have promised *enhanced partnerships* if ACs can hold themselves to the principles of democratic and economic reform and social investment, through the self-monitoring instrument of the APRM. Paragraph 7 of the AAP is very informative: "The peer review process will inform our considerations of eligibility for enhanced partnerships".

70 *Bond* (n 59); *Babington-Ashaye* (n 64).

71 *Sommet Kananaskis Summit Canada* (n 69).

72 *Goredema and Botha* (n 43) 1, 9.

73 NEPAD Secretariat, 'African Peer Review Mechanism Organization and Process' (*NEPAD Secretariat*, 2003) <http://www1.uneca.org/Portals/aprm/Documents/book4.pdf> accessed 10 May 2016. Also approved were the Organs/Units of the AU, the United Nations Economic Commission for Africa (UNECA) and the UN Development Program Regional Bureau for Africa.

Articles of Association entrust it with fiduciary responsibility to ensure that the proceeds of any loan it makes or guarantees are used only for the loan's purpose.[74] The aim is to prevent fraudulent transactions that may disguise the origins of proceeds of crimes/profits from corruption and use of the banks.[75] Additionally, the AfDB has assisted in ensuring that laws and strategies comply with international standards and norms.[76] It has also intervened to guarantee that Financial Intelligence Units (FIUs) work together, thus promoting a unified approach to combating AML/CFT.[77]

Notwithstanding its shortcomings, the APRM has been lauded for appreciating the historical contexts and developmental stages of ACs. Upon this premise, it has stated that all countries are not expected to reach their highest level of performance simultaneously. This has however not encouraged countries to ratify and implement its processes. For instance, although the African Union (AU) AML convention was adopted in 2003, at the same time as the UN convention,[78] the AU convention has been ratified by fewer states, illustrating no respect for the AU's likely reactions.[79]

Hence, FSRBs, headed and run by African nationals (with international organisations as observers), have been perceived as more promising for curbing regional and continental ML. It is assumed that the African nationals are well versed in local issues, thus giving regions leeway in deciding their risk-based approach (RBA) in line with their peculiarities. For instance, the Central Bank of Nigeria and Kenyan regulators supervise the niche created by mobile banking within the context of a more relaxed customer due diligence (CDD).[80] So far other regions in Africa have set up their regional bodies. These regional efforts signify Africa's willingness to comply, but compliance levels have been far from impressive.

---

74 AfDB/African Development Fund, 'Bank Group Strategy for the Prevention of Money Laundering and Terrorist Financing in Africa' (AfDBAfrican Development Fund, May 2007) <https://www.afdb.org/fileadmin/uploads/afdb/Documents/Policy-Documents/10000012-EN-STRATEGY-FOR-THE-PREVENTION-OF-MONEY-LAUNDERING_01.pdf> accessed 10 May 2015.
75 Ibid.
76 Ibid. (n 74).
77 Ibid.
78 Humphrey Moshi, 'Fighting Money Laundering: The Challenges in Africa' [2007] 152 Institute for Security Studies Papers 1, 10–12.
79 In 2005, pioneering Pan-African meeting of national anti-corrupt bodies recommended that assistance with identifying areas of convergence/divergence between multilateral anti-corruption instruments be given to AU members to facilitate national implementation.
80 CBN, 'Regulatory Framework for Mobile Payments Services in Nigeria' (*CBN*) <http://www.cenbank.org/OUT/CIRCULARS/BOD/2009/REGULATORY%20FRAMEWORK%20%20FOR%20MOBILE%20PAYMENTS%20SERVICES%20IN%20NIGERIA.PDF> accessed 21 December 2014; CGPA, 'Update on Regulation of Branchless Banking in Kenya' (*CGAP*, January 2010) <https://www.cgap.org/sites/default/files/CGAP-Regulation-of-Branchless-Banking-in-Kenya-Jan-2010.pdf> accessed 21 December 2014.

Compliance by African States

IFIs have argued that despite the internal factors that propel compliance to international standards, ACs are subject to the same standards as other countries. The logic is that the AML/CFT regime is only as strong as the weakest link in the chain. Given the borderless nature of ML/TF crimes, astute criminals would reroute their finances to countries with weaker regimes.[81] Consequently, failure to meet the compliance levels required in acceding to those standards would warrant financial isolation and reputational damage. This hard stance does not take into consideration the historical or socio-economic peculiarities of ACs that hinder compliance. By using the same benchmarking structure for every country, it can be argued that ACs are simply set up to fail, a catalyst for unmerited sanctions.

Scholars have increasingly sought to understand the reason for varying compliance levels across ACs.[82] Flowing from the pre-conditions for effective regulations and the compliance drivers discussed in this book, this chapter argues that ACs are inundated by legal and non-legal factors which affect compliance with international instruments. These factors may be subject to a balancing act between internal and external drivers which determine the degree of compliance.[83] However, whilst external drivers may propel formal or creative compliance due to the implementation resistance, internal drivers may propel proactive compliance if properly guided. EENA1 argues that this is not always correct, given that 'change from within is often impossible, sometimes because of vested interest and – often times – it's because of habit...[and] it is difficult to change habit'.[84] This indicates the need for a balancing act between internal and external

---

81 In certain instances, criminals are aware that such states have low-returns investments as opposed to countries like England with higher investment returns. Jason Sharman, 'Power and Discourse in Policy Diffusion: Anti-Money Laundering in Developing States' [2008] 52.3 International Studies Quarterly 635, 641; Peter Romaniuk, 'Institutions as Swords and Shields: Multilateral Counter-terrorism Since 9/11' [2010] 36 Review of International Studies 591, 596; *Moshi* (n 78). Due to institutionalized corruption, ACs failed to acknowledge the damaging economic effect of laundering – Abayomi Mumuni, *Global Terrorism and Its Effects on Humanity* (Wsgf Pty Limited, 2016); Amado Philip de Andre, 'Organized Crime, Drug Trafficking, Terrorism: The New Achilles' Heel of West Africa' (*Fride*, 2008) <http://fride.org/descarga/COM_Achilles_heel_eng_may08.pdf> accessed 10 July 2016.

82 Beth Simmons, 'International Law and State Behavior: Commitment and Compliance in International Monetary Affairs' [2000] 94 (4) American Political Science Review 819, 819; Harold Koh, 'Review: Why Do Nations Obey International Law?' [1997] 106 (8) The Yale Law Journal 2598, 2645–2659; Andrew Guzman, 'A Compliance Based Theory of International Law' [2002] 90 (6) California Law Review 1823–1887; Benedict Kingsbury, 'The Concept of Compliance as a Function of Competing Conceptions of International Law' [1998] 19 Mich. J. International Law 345, 346; Oran Young, *Compliance with Public Authority* (Baltimore: JHUP 1979); Ronald Mitchell, 'Regime Design Matters: International Oil Pollution and Treaty Compliance' [1994] 48 (3) IO 425–458.

83 Beth Whitaker, 'Compliance among Weak States: Africa and the Counter Terrorism Regime' [2010] 36 Review of International Studies 639, 644.

84 EENA1, Consulting Counsel, Financial Integrity Unit, IMF, Interview with EENA1, 'Telephone Call' (2017).

drivers for compliance, given that where external drivers push for compliance in a manner that does not encapsulate the peculiarities of ACs, it may occasion a regulatory paradox – where standards adopted are counterproductive.

Compliance as a Function of Legal Factors

As a function of legal factors, however debatable, compliance is chiefly influenced by three factors:

1. Law reflecting society.
2. Enforcement-driven compliance.
3. Compliance engineered by democracy and rule of law.

Evaluating these factors in turn illustrates how a robust regulatory environment backed by sturdy legal factors are crucial determinants for effective compliance. Where these factors are not effectively ingrained within a country, they hinder countries' compliance with AML/CFT recommendations irrespective of the external factors.

LAW: MIRRORING SOCIETY TO COMBAT ML/TF

As discussed, the indigenous attempt by ACs to curtail ML/TF proved unsuitable and recorded limited success. It was modelled on the existing international standards alongside the perception that illicit crimes, particularly terror funding, were alien to the ACs. Hence, ACs did not proactively legislate or implement frameworks to combat these crimes.[85] This lackadaisical attitude, which reflects law as 'mirroring society', was further aided by the voluntary consensus decision-making process which lacked sanctions to call countries to order.

Yet, there remained an urgency to curtail these illicit crimes, which worsened with the liberalisation of markets. Consequently, ACs paid more attention to the vast range of general and specialised international institutions established to ensure that every country transplanted and implemented the FATF recommendations via legislation.[86] This shift in attention focused on the 'transplantation of laws' was not voluntary or through rational responses to material incentives. Rather, it can be attributable to external pressure to fulfil obligations under international agreements.[87] Sharman attributes the willingness of states to transplant

85 GIABA, 'Overview of GIABA Operations from 2004 to 2013' (*Giaba*, 2014) <https://www.giaba.org/media/f/693_599_GIABA-Overview-2004-2013-English.pdf> accessed 10 July 2016.
86 William F. Wechsler., 'Follow the Money' (*Foreign Affairs*, 2001) <https://www.foreignaffairs.com/articles/2001-07-01/follow-money> accessed 10 May 2015.
87 Only a few ACs legislated on AML/CFT prior to the FATF recommendations. See the Ethiopian Anti-Terrorism Law of 1954; The Penal Code No 85 of the Arab Republic of Egypt 1937 which contains AML/CFT provisions in Article 86–102.

laws to the diffusion of policies.[88] He argues that the AML/CFT regime's diffusion amongst 'weak states' is driven by discursive power-based mechanisms, a combination of direct coercion, mimicry and competition.[89] Whilst direct coercion works to ensure legislation and implementation through sanctions, mimicry is focused on the transplantation of standards to law within states. The fact that mimicry backed by coercion can elicit compliance in ACs gives credence to how powerful states may influence compliance through international institutions, not the growing indices of ML/TF in the African terrain.

The extent to which this external influence catalysed for proactive compliance is questionable. Although the international regulatory standards proved largely workable in developed jurisdictions, they have proved unsuitable and ineffective in stimulating proactive compliance in various ACs. This compliance deficiency is further perpetuated by the weak legal and institutional structures, embedded in a culture of pervasive corruption. These challenges beg the question, to what extent can laws be transplanted in a way that stimulates compliance?

Legal comparativists have engaged in a discourse on the practicality of transplantation. Watson contends that the idea that law mirrors society is a fallacy, as change in the law is divorced from the workings of any historical, socio-economic or cultural substratum – but is rather a function of rules imported from another legal system.[90] Consequently, he argues that legal transplantation is practical and easy. Differences within jurisdictions do not limit the transferability of laws.[91] It is against this backdrop that Sharman postulates that developing or perceived 'weak countries' mimic developed countries' laws and implementation strategies. This perspective sees laws or rules as culture neutral and assume that they can be transported across countries. Consequently, Sharman argues that developing countries adopt laws and implementation strategies for two distinct but interrelated reasons: to replicate pioneering countries' recorded successes and as a mere symbolic exercise to avoid a penalty or receive associated benefits.[92] The results of these are seen in marginally improved compliance ratings granted to countries that have replicated laws which were not modified to fit into a country's local context by a comprehensive risk assessment.[93]

Legrand however disputes Watson's perspective. He argues that rules are more than a series of inscribed words, but rather, are contextual.[94] Hence, words can-

---

88 *Sharman* (n 81) 635, 636.

89 Ibid.; Daniel W. Drezner's, *All Politics is Global: Explaining International Regulatory Regime* (Princeton: PUP, 2007) 5, 75.

90 Alan Watson, *Legal Transplants: An Approach to Comparative Law* (Scottish Academic Press, 1974).

91 Ibid.

92 *Sharman* (n 81) 635, 647; Anne-Marrie Slaughter, *A New World Order* (PUP 2004) 6.

93 See the FATF Country reports; countries that have adopted legislations have better compliance ratings than countries that have not.

94 Pierre Legrand, 'The Impossibility of "Legal Transplants"' [1997] 4 Masstricht J. Eur. & Comp.L. 111, 115.

not be divorced from their historical, socio-economic, cultural or ideological underpinnings. Therefore, when rules are technically integrated into a different legal order, the host jurisdiction will understand it differently because of cultural differences and distance between the originator and host jurisdiction. Thus, the interpretation of a rule within a different context would be subjective, given the insensitivity of the originator to the cultural dissimilarities of the host jurisdiction.[95] Consequently, the crucial element of the rule's meaning does not survive the journey from one legal system to another. Therefore, as the understanding of the rule changes, so does the meaning.[96] Against this background, Legrand argues that legal transplantation does not take place.[97]

The AfDB supports this position, arguing that locally researched policies are better suited to ensure sustainable development for Africa than the transplantation of international laws or standards.[98] Spataru-Neguru further contends that there is evidential proof that transplanted laws usually cannot achieve the same results or fulfil the same aims.[99] This argument assumes that results caused by laws are limited to a specific time and place. Sharman buttresses this with evidence that AML policy effectiveness in developing countries have remained marginal, whether categorised as successful in disrupting criminal finance and illegal activities, or in terms of greater benefit for the society which overrides the cost of regulation itself.[100] Thus, although transplantation leads to improved compliance ratings, the proactive compliance levels are neither unusually high nor low, illustrating that states are merely concerned with achieving minimum acceptable standards.[101]

However, other scholars have argued that treaties and conventions can be easily transplanted, since they are rooted in negotiations amongst countries

---

95 Ibid. (n 94) 111, 117.
96 Ibid. 111, 114.
97 Ibid. 111, 118.
98 AfDB, 'Africa Must Develop Relevant Knowledge for Its Problems' 2014 < http://www .afdb.org/en/news-and-events/article/africa-must-develop-relevant-knowledge-for-its-p roblems-13692/ >accessed 16 April 2015. Contrary to assumptions, transplantation is a healthy sign that a country is actively looking for solutions and options, rather than waiting for the host country to impose conditions, which do not fit their needs – María Gaitán, 'The Challenges of Legal Transplants in a Globalized Context: A Case Study on "Working" Examples' (2014) Dissertation, University of Warwick.
99 Apart from the United States, the AML/CFT regime has not proved cost effective in other developing countries that participated in building the regime.
100 A majority of OECD countries routinely carry out or even legally mandate the use of Regulatory Impact Assessments or Regulatory Impact Statements (OECD) 2007. The OECD has advanced the latter approach as the most revered international practice in assessing regulation.
101 Mariano-Florentino Cueller, 'The Tenuous Relationship Between the Fight Against Money Laundering and the Disruption of Criminal Finance' [2003] 93.2 Journal of Criminal Law and Criminology 311, 465; Jake Kendall and Jan Sonnenschein, 'Many Transactions in Sub-Saharan Africa Still in Cash' (*Gallup*, June 11 2012) <http://www.gallup.com/poll /155126/transactions-sub-saharan-africa-cash.aspx> accessed 28 April 2015.

reflecting general interests. They argue that given the convergence of countries to address AML/CFT, such laws cannot be designed in isolation. Barak-Erez contends that AML legislations are not necessarily 'mimicked' as it is expected that the international model or conventions can lead to similar laws in host countries.[102] These arguments ignore the composition of international AML/CFT standard-setting bodies, which excludes ACs and thus suffers from democratic deficit. According to Legrand, this restricts host states (which in this case are ACs) from realising the originators' vision of their world.[103] This deficit hinders the originator's ability to decipher how its circumstances differ from the host states. Instead of organising diversity of discourse around varying cultural forms, what is noticed is a crowding towards uniformisation.[104] It can be argued that a more democratic standard-setting body would ensure an inclusive strategy that considers the perspective of less developed states, making ACs more inclined to comply proactively.

Berliner asserts that transplantations along regional lines are more effective.[105] Whilst this might be true, it constitutes a facilitating condition rather than a causal mechanism. The AU model illustrated a lack of indigenous enthusiasm in combating ML/TF. Nonetheless, the establishment of the FSRBs has, even if in a limited way, created the context to ensure that transplanted laws work effectively.

ENFORCEMENT-DRIVEN COMPLIANCE

In the absence of an adjudicatory structure, the FATF 'list' non-compliant/high-risk countries publicly. This sanctioning strategy is aimed at ensuring observance to set standards.[106] Resolving or circumventing this 'stick' warrants some measure of compliance.[107] Nigeria made history as the first West African country

---

102 Daphne Barak-Erez, 'The International Aspects of Comparative Law' [2008] 13 Colum. J.Eur.L. 477, 484.

103 *Legrand* (n 94) 111, 114.

104 Ibid. 111, 118.

105 Berliner Daniel, 'Follow Your Neighbor? Regional Emulation and the Design of Transparency Policies' (2013) KFG Working Paper 55, 17 < http://userpage.fu-berlin.de/kfgeu/kfgwp/wpseries/WorkingPaperKFG_55.pdf > accessed 10 May 2016; Daniel Berowitz, Katharina Pistor and Jean-Francois Richard, 'Economic Development, Legality and the Transplant Effect' [2003] 41(1) European Economic Review 165, 167; Beth A. Simmons and Zachary Elkins, 'The Globalisation of Liberalisation: Policy Diffusion in the International Political Economy' [2004] 98 (1) American Political Science Review 171, 187.

106 Tam Christian, 'Enforcement' *in* Ulfsein G., Marauhn T. and Zimmermann (eds.) *Making Treaties Work* (CUP, 2007) 391–410.

107 Chr. Michelsen Institute, 'Profiting from Corruption: The Role and Responsibility of Financial Institutions' [2009] 31 U4 Brief; Jason C. Sharman, 'The Bark Is the Bite: International Organizations and Blacklisting' [2009] Review of International Political Economy 1, 15; Dieter Kerwer and Rainer Hulsse, 'Explaining International Organizations: How International Organizations Rule the World: The Case of the Financial Action Task Force on Money Laundering' [2011] UN Studies Association, Berlin 61; Rainer Hulsse, 'Even Clubs Can't Do Without Legitimacy: Why the Anti-Money Laundering Blacklist Was Sus-

to fall into the category of non-compliant countries.[108] Nigeria was blacklisted following the FATF's realisation that it was unwilling to legislate on, or implement the AML/CFT legislation.[109] Furthermore, at the national level, the FATF noticed that prosecutions against persons or sanctions against banks for failing to carry out their duties were rare.[110] The lackadaisical nature and willingness to hide information were also demonstrated by the reluctance of Nigerian officials to cooperate with the FATF evaluation team during their fact-finding mission. Egypt was blacklisted on similar grounds.[111]

To avoid the harsh repercussions of this sanction, these countries aligned with the AML/CFT regime's request by legislating on and subsequently institutionalising structures to combat illicit crimes.[112] Training was also provided to improve the capability of judges to bring cases to an equitable end. Subsequently, these countries were delisted. Although blacklisting has been able to secure formal compliance, its ability to secure proactive compliance has been questioned.[113] This indicates that although countries may comply with the 'black letter' laws, they might remain deficient in reality. This is the case with most ACs that remain largely deficient despite their expected compliance. (See Figure 5.1.) Put simply, external pressure on a country with weak enforcement institutions does not translate to robust AML/CFT regulation, implementation and compliance.

Moreover, countries unconcerned with the adverse effect of blacklisting may remain uncooperative and thus non-compliant. For instance, some ACs have remained on the Non-Cooperative Countries and Territories (NCCTs) list without taking the requisite steps to correct the situation.[114] Conversely, there is evidence that the sanction system itself is fallible, as international institutions do not

---

pended' [2008] 2 (4) Regulation and Governance 459, 465. 'Blacklisting' is now known as the 'call on members to apply counter-measures list' or the 'call for enhanced due diligence risk proportionate to the risk arising from defaulting countries'. However, the implication remains the same.

108 Rainer Hulsse, 'Even Clubs Can't Do Without Legitimacy: Why the Anti-Money Laundering Blacklist Was Suspended' [2008] 2 (4) Regulation and Governance 459.

109 Jubril Olabode Aka, *Blacks Greatest Homeland* (IUniverse, 2006) 210; Jubril Olabode Aka, *Great Presidents of Nigeria 4th Republic* (Trafford Publishing 2012) 276.

110 GIABA, 'Mutual Evaluation Report: AML/CFT: Nigeria' (*GIABA*, 2008) 95 < https:/ /www.giaba.org/media/f/299_Mutual%20Evaluation%20Report%20of%20Nigeria.pdf > accessed 9 April 2015.

111 Jeanne Giraldo and Harold Trinkunas, *Terrorist Financing and State Responses: A Comparative Perspective* (SUP, 2007).

112 Mail & Guardian, Africa's Best Read, 'Nigeria A Risky Prospect for South African Banks' (*Mail & Guardian*, 31 August 2005) <http://mg.co.za/article/2005-08-31-nigeria-a-risky-prospect-for-sa-banks> accessed 12 March 2015. This aligns with the functionalist argument that states comply with out of reputational concerns, see Robert O. Keohane, *After Hegemony: Cooperation and Discord in the World Political Economy* (PUP 1984); *Sharman* (n 107) 1, 3.

113 *Hulsse* (n 107) 459, 467.

114 This may however be more structural than deliberate given that internal institutions may be unable to support their activities.

discontinue aid transfers to failing countries.[115] Neither do FIs cease transactions with erring countries.[116] For these reasons, arguments have been advanced in favour of non-coercive means of compliance.

Non-coercive compliance measures are usually induced through instruments of active management, such as monitoring or review.[117] These oversight measures are instituted through the FATF's Mutual Evaluation Reports (MER) which entails the gathering and review of information on the compliance levels of all countries.[118] Information so derived form the basis for further interactions with countries and inform decisions on sanctions. This indicates that active management and enforcement sanctions are interrelated. For instance, prior to the blacklisting of Nigeria – the FATF pushed for active management to facilitate compliance. However, this was hindered by bureaucracy in Nigeria and lack of political will, which culminated in the FATF sanctioning Nigeria. This sanction propelled Nigeria to become subservient to the instruments of active management. This works vice versa: countries that may be unresponsive sanction threat in the absence of some measure of persuasiveness.

Collectively, the enforcement and management models are sometimes largely dependent on the degree to which rule of law is entrenched in a country, and the operationalisation of democracy. A country without these factors may undermine the effectiveness of the AML/CFT compliance regime.

COMPLIANCE ENGINEERED BY DEMOCRACY AND RULE OF LAW

The rule of law is the notion that powers of state and government can only be exercised legitimately when following applicable laws and laid down procedures.[119] This connotes that government officials and citizens are bound to act consistently with the law.[120] The rule of law is a prerequisite for democracy and democratic practice, and it also protects democracy.[121] Against this backdrop, Simons argues that governments with respect for the rule of law and stable

115 This applies to Pakistan which, although by 14 February 2018 was regarded as a country with serious deficiencies in formulating an AML/CFT action plan, has remained a perpetual recipient of foreign aids; as has Ghana.

116 See Ralph Orlowski, 'Commerzbank Fined $1.5bn for Doing Business With Sanctioned Iran and Sudan' (*RT*, 13 March 2015) < http://rt.com/business/240353-commerzbank -billion-fine-sanctions/> accessed 14 May 2015.

117 Abram Chayes and Antonia Chayes, *The New Sovereignty: Compliance with International Regulatory Agreements* (HUP, 1995).

118 FATF, 'Mutual Evaluations' (FATF) < http://www.fatf-gafi.org/publications/mutuale valuations/?hf=10&b=0&s=desc(fatf_releasedate) > accessed 5 January 2017.

119 Peter Shivute, 'The Rule of Law in Sub-Saharan Africa – An Overview' [2009] Human Rights and the Rule of Law in Namibia 213, 213.

120 Francis Fukuyama, 'Why is Democracy Performing So Poorly' [2015] 26 (1) Journal of Democracy 11, 18; Brian Tamanaha, *On the Rule of Law: History, Politics Theory* (CUP, 2004).

121 *Fukuyama* (n 120).

democracy are unlikely to harm their reputation by breaching commitments to standards.[122] These arguments strongly link the rule of law and democracy. These factors are crucial in determining the degree of compliance with the AML/CFT recommendations through the enhancement of institutional and government staff capacity.

Hence, it is unsurprising that the presence of domestic and democratic political institutions are identified as critical internal factors that influence government's compliance with international instruments.[123] This is backed by studies which suggest that undemocratic governments are less likely to comply than liberal democratic governments.[124] The reasons for this include the democratic government's respect for the legal process, human rights, electoral processes or domestic interest groups.[125] Domestic interest groups, including civil societies and democratic political constituencies, are usually constrained within undemocratic governments and can pressurise democratic governments to comply. The limitations of governmental institutions and civil groups in ensuring compliance by ACs can be gleaned from the 2016 Democracy Index which demonstrates that no AC has attained full democracy.[126] Rather, most ACs fall within the purview of hybrid or authoritarian democracy.[127] Whilst the former refers to countries with weak rule of law, civil society and judiciary, the latter refers to states where political pluralism is absent or highly circumscribed, with no free or fair elections, and government-controlled media.[128]

For example, Nigeria, as a hybrid democracy, disregarded its growing corruption index and resulting capital flight between 2010 and 2015.[129] The growing incidences of terrorism, kidnaps and economic inequality resulting from corruption compelled civil societies to champion the 'Bring Back our Girls' campaign. The Goodluck Jonathan-led administration, fearing it would not be re-elected during the next election, took more active steps to arrest the situation in Nigeria; sadly, the efforts could not salvage their defeat at the polls.[130]

---

122 Beth Simmons, 'Compliance with International Agreements' [1998] Annual Rev. Polit. Sci. 1, 13; Anne-Marie Slaughter, 'International Law in a World of Liberal States' [1995] EJIL 503, 511.

123 Helen Milner, *Interest, Institutions and Information: Domestic Politics and International Relations* (PUP, 1997).

124 *Simmons* (n 122); *Slaughter* (n 122).

125 *Guzman* (n 82). With the recent rise in use of social network, sometimes the loudest voice counts and not necessarily the perception of pressure groups.

126 *The Economist*, 'Democracy Index 2016: Revenge of the "Deplorables"' (A Report by The Economist Intelligence Unit, 2016) < http://felipesahagun.es/wp-content/uploads/20 17/01/Democracy-Index-2016.pdf > accessed 11 November 2017.

127 Ibid.

128 Ibid. (n 126).

129 Ibid.

130 Arit John, 'What's Wrong with Our Well Intentioned Boko Haram Coverage' (*The Wire*, 9 May 2014) < http://www.thewire.com/politics/2014/05/whats-wrong-with-our-well -intentioned-boko-haram-coverage/361993/ > accessed 2 June 2015; Monica Mark,

The recent backlash against the Kenyan election process which occasioned threats of internet shutdown is also another example.[131] The Kenyan judiciary salvaged the election irregularities by annulling the election and declaring a re-run.[132] This illustrates the rule of law drives certain institutions within hybrid-democracy countries. Conversely, in authoritarian governments, the restriction on human rights may prevent interest groups from pushing the government for results.[133] However, other political factors may propel their compliance. These arguments suggest that proper democracies are more reliable partners in ensuring compliance with AML/CFT, a shortcoming in ACs.[134]

ACs' inability to embrace full democracy is further buttressed by their low rating on the Rule of Law Index, particularly in relation to the Regulatory Enforcement factor.[135] Botswana, Senegal, Ghana and Morocco are the only ACs ranked amongst the top 50 countries globally.[136] Others are ranked in the bottom 100, with Ethiopia, Egypt and Zimbabwe ranking the lowest.[137] There is evidence that the rule of law has declined for 70% of ACs over the past decade.[138] This shortfall indicates that the mere existence of formal laws does not translate to unbiased implementation or enforcement. The law may in certain

---

'Obiageli Ezekwesili: When They Took The Girls, Our Government Went Under' (*The Guardian*, 28 December 2014) <http://www.theguardian.com/world/2014/dec/28/obiageli-ezekwesili-bring-back-our-girls-boko-haram-school-kidnapping > accessed 12 May 2015; Faith Karimi, '24 Killed in Post-Election Violence in Kenya, Rights Group Says' (CNN, 13 August 2017)< http://edition.cnn.com/2017/08/12/africa/kenya-elections-protests/index.html > accessed 21 October 2017.

131 Njeri Wangari, 'Kenyans Fear a Possible Internet Shutdown During 2017 Presidential Election' (*Mail & Guardian Africa*, 16 January 2017) < http://mgafrica.com/article/2017-01-16-kenyans-fear-a-possible-internet-shutdown-during-2017-presidential-election > accessed 10 May 2017.

132 Jason Burke, 'Kenyan Election Annulled after Result Called Before Votes Counted, Says Court' (*The Guardian*, 20 September 2017) < https://www.theguardian.com/world/2017/sep/20/kenyan-election-rerun-not-transparent-supreme-court > accessed 1 November 2017.

133 Cameroon and Chad have been ineffective in ensuring compliance due to the dictatorial nature of their governments.

134 *The Economist* (n 126). Interestingly, an authoritarian government may be best suited to comply with international agreements on ML/TF, for instance, China's case.

135 World Justice Project, 'Rule of Law Index' (*World Justice Project*, 2016) < https://worldjusticeproject.org/sites/default/files/documents/RoLI_Final-Digital_0.pdf > accessed 9 November 2017.

136 Ibid.

137 Ibid.

138 Karen McVeigh and Kate Hodal, 'Rule of Law Declines for 70% of Africans over Past Decade, Warns Ibrahim Index' (*The Guardian*, 3 October 2016) < https://www.theguardian.com/global-development/2016/oct/03/rule-of-law-declines-70-per-cent-africans-over-past-decade-ibrahim-index-governance > accessed 9 November 2017; Mo Ibrahim Foundation, 'A Decade of African Governance 2006–2015' (*Ibrahim Index of African Governance Index Report*, 2016) < http://s.mo.ibrahim.foundation/u/2016/10/0118 4917/2016-Index-Report.pdf?_ga=2.32642366.1457805273.1510188763-132223 7499.1510188763 > accessed 9 November 2017.

instances be used to perpetuate inequality. For example, in non-liberal regimes, like Zimbabwe, political leaders can legitimise undemocratic rules, such as tenure elongation amendments to the constitution.[139] In more liberal democracies, like Ghana, the law can be used to ensure that political leaders have prolonged immunity to enable them evade prosecution for illicit transactions, at the expense of the country's economic development. Consequently, it may be overgeneralising to assume that only undemocratic countries would be antagonistic to compliance pressures, or that countries with entrenched rule of law would comply. Other factors, like culture, the country's imperative need or sanctions, affect compliance.

Whilst external sanctions may potentially be crucial in remedying the shortcomings of democracy and rule of law – a step which can alter countries' incentive to comply, impact-related challenges must be considered. Sanctions are largely expensive for ACs. The law and economics approach that the rule of law will be adhered to if the cost of non-compliance is higher than benefits illustrates the position of ACs. For example, certain ACs may comply with the FATF recommendations in the belief that 'associate membership' through the FSRBs may outweigh the alternative of financial exclusion. Some considerations include enhanced financial integration, improved FIs and regulatory space or the attraction of foreign investments to strengthen their economies. Forced 'benefits' through sanctions may however trigger sham compliance which may be formal or creative, as opposed to proactive compliance.

Given the shortcomings of external sanctions, IFIs more readily utilise the management models. Notwithstanding, the effectiveness of monitoring and evaluation is dependent on the validity of laws, regulations and institutions. The rule of law is not necessarily just symbolic; it catalyses practical changes. As a 'precondition for effective regulation', law is one of the critical primary bases upon which institutions can ensure compliance with the AML/CFT regulations.

Non-Legal Factors that Affect Compliance

It would be overly simplistic to assume that putting laws in place will result in improved compliance, solely based on reputational concerns.[140] Therefore, this section argues that there are non-legal factors which support the legal factors that ensure compliance. These are:

1. Compliance based on reputational concerns.
2. Political will, domestic conditions and policy priorities.

---

139 Aljazeera, 'Zimbabwe's Mugabe Signs New Constitution' (Aljazeera, 22 May 2013) < http://www.aljazeera.com/news/africa/2013/05/2013522105015147596.html > accessed 10 May 2016.
140 Julia Black, Martyn Hopper and Christa Band, 'Making a Success of Principles-Based Regulation' [2007] 1 (3) Law and Financial Markets Review 191–204.

3. Technical capacity and resources.
4. Legitimacy and its effect on compliance.
5. Globalisation and integration.

COMPLIANCE BASED ON REPUTATIONAL CONCERNS

Despite their reputational damage, some ACs usually undertake speedy trans-plantation or unreasoned copying of unsuitable rules to avert sanctions. As earlier mentioned, Nigeria's suspension from the Egmont Group was met with legislative indifference for over five years – even with the reputational implications. Conversely, Nigerian FIs pushed for the adoption of legislations to evade sanctions recognising its implications for their continued service and expansion plans. This shows a stark misalignment of the objectives of FIs, regulators and legislators, which must converge for reputation concerns to have the desired effect.

The reputational damage of being blacklisted includes limiting foreign investments, increased cost of remittances or hindering correspondent banking relationships (CBR), given the high regulatory checks required to conduct business with 'listed countries'.[141] The AfDB stated that 'the existence of money laundering would reflect poorly on (a) country's governance reputation and would be taken into account in decisions about future lending in the country'.[142] This would impact the private sector, affecting risk views and investment ratings. Nash states that '[w]estern investors and banks are currently reducing the number of correspondent banks they interact with that are based in Africa...due to their (in)ability to demonstrate that they have the right AML procedures and systems in place'.[143] This severance of CBR or other transactional engagements, known as 'de-risking', recently occasioned the termination of CBR between Deutsche Bank (High Priority – HP countries) and Africa (Mid Priority – MP countries).[144]

---

141 Clay Lowery, 'Unintended Consequences of Anti-Money Laundering Policies in Poor Countries – A CGD Working Group Report' (*Centre for Global Development*, 2015) <https ://www.cgdev.org/sites/default/files/CGD-WG-Report-Unintended-Consequences-A ML-Policies-2015.pdf > accessed 7 November 2017; William Lawrence, 'Money Laundering Compliance for Africa?' (*bbrief*, 9 June 2017) <https://www.bbrief.co.za/2017/06 /09/money-laundering-compliance-africa/ > accessed 10 July 2017.

142 World Bank and IMF Global Dialogue Series, 'Anti-Money Laundering and Combating the Financing of Terrorism – Regional Videoconference: Anglophone West Africa Region – The Gambia, Ghana, Nigeria and Sierra Leone' (World Bank and IMF Global Dialogue Series) <http://documents.worldbank.org/curated/en/620291468751786123/pdf/ 271830Anti1money0laundering00West0Africa.pdf> accessed 15 May 2017.

143 Imogen Nash, 'Why Financial Institutions based in Africa Should Have Robust Compliance Systems in Place' (*Accuity*, 10 August 2016) < https://accuity.com/accuity-insight s-blog/why-financial-institutions-based-in-africa-should-have-robust-compliance-systems -in-place/ > accessed 7 November 2017.

144 *The Economist*, 'A Crackdown on Financial Crime Means Global Banks Are De-risking' (*The Economist*, 8 July 2017) < https://www.economist.com/news/international/21724 803-charities-and-poor-migrants-are-among-hardest-hit-crackdown-financial-crime-means > accessed 10 August 2017.

This was done chiefly to avoid reputational risks to the bank.[145] The SWIFT report indicates a more dire picture, showing that de-risking in Africa is on the rise with Angola losing 37% of foreign counterparties and Mauritius losing at least 18% between 2013 and 2015.[146] Nigeria has however managed to maintain limited international de-risking, although there is evidence that local banks have severed relationships with other African banks or services deemed risky – such as bureau de change and money transmission companies.[147] The de-risking exercise negatively affects the African economy, as such relationships strengthen financial integration.[148]

The adverse effect of de-risking includes the challenge of accessing products and services, such as international wire transfers – a predicament which can result in consumers engaging in alternative, less regulated channels. To avoid this, ACs are pressured into compliance with AML/CFT to retain their clients.[149] This pressure may facilitate increased compliance or may in fact occasion a paradox, thus worsening compliance in certain countries. Where the latter occurs, it usually indicates challenges within a country's regulatory environment that warrants internal changes. These may include improvements in regulatory processes in order to build reputation within the global financial market. This would counteract the paradox of de-risking as a catalyst for financial exclusion or the ousting of customers.

Management of FIs may also project the need to protect banking activities, as a means of levelling the playing field. These institutions may then force regulatory bodies to adopt uniform regulations so as to avoid a race to the bottom as competitors' price each other out on the international markets. Thus, banks with domestic and international competitive advantages pressure regulators to implement the law in order to attract international business, whereas banks with high compliance that acknowledge the irrevocable harm which ML/TF can do to reputation and integrity will advertise their compliance levels to attract investors

---

145 Michaela Erbenova, Yan Liu et al., 'The Withdrawal of Correspondent Banking Relationships: A Case for Policy Action' (*IMF Staff Discussion Note*, 2016) < https://www.imf.org/external/pubs/ft/sdn/2016/sdn1606.pdf > accessed 10 January 2017.

146 Swift, 'De-risking in Africa on the Rise, according to Latest SWIFT Data' (*Swift*, 24 August 2016) < https://www.swift.com/insights/press-releases/de-risking-in-africa-on-the-rise_according-to-latest-swift-data > accessed 10 March 2017.

147 Ibid.; Note that this can also be attributed to the CBN's stipulated guidelines on investments that banks can hold.

148 SWIFT, 'Addressing the Unintended Consequences of De-Risking – Focus on Africa' (*Swift*, Information Paper, August 2016) < https://www.swift.com/node/35121 > accessed 10 March 2017; Otaviano Canuto and Veronica Ramcharan, 'De-Risking is De-Linking Small States from Global Finance' (*HuffPost*) <https://www.huffingtonpost.com/otaviano-canuto/de-risking-is-de-linking_b_8357342.html > accessed 11 March 2017.

149 The Commonwealth, 'Disconnecting from Global Finance: The Impact of AML/CFT Regulations on Commonwealth Developing Countries' (*The Commonwealth*, 2016). <http://thecommonwealth.org/sites/default/files/inline/DisconnectingfromGlobalFinance2016.pdf> accessed 10 March 2017.

and depositors. However, banks or countries with compliance challenges, which nevertheless still attract financial investment, may remain immune to reputational concerns. In the long run, lapses in such countries by FIs are noticed by the markets and regulators. This will inevitably attract sanctions or in some cases – withdrawal of licences. These external pressure points expose the reputational concerns that occasion non-compliance,[150] which adversely affects the banking industry.

POLITICAL WILL, DOMESTIC CONDITIONS AND POLICY PRIORITIES

It is expected that appreciation of the adverse effect of ML/TF on an economy would cultivate political will, which would effectively facilitate compliance and thereby build a nation's economy. This suggests that when government leaders appreciate, by empirical evidence, that ML/TF occasions capital flight[151] and hinders the effectiveness of monetary policies, they would actively curtail such crimes.[152] Such assumptions are premised on the rational perspective that countries want to curtail macroeconomic issues that hinder economic development.[153]

Evidently, this is not always the case. For instance, indices in Nigeria show capital flight in billions of dollars to Dubai and Washington by chief executive officers of banks.[154] According to a former governor of the Central Bank of Nigeria, such 'bank officials had economic power...(and) had bought political protection... they had financed elections of officers...every time I said it was time for us to take action, people said to me, you can't touch these people, you'll be sacked... they will kill you'.[155] This revelation shows the interrelationship between heads of FIs and government officials, a situation which creates regulatory arbitrage, and undermines the regulator's ability to generate political will. This position of arbitrage is however not constant, particularly in countries where there is perceived threat of terror by the government in power,[156] significant loss of government

---

150 Michael Imeson and Alastair Sim, 'Regulation and Your Reputation' White Paper < http://www.sas.com/resources/whitepaper/wp_24359.pdf > accessed 1 June 2015.

151 Liliana Rojas-Suarez, 'Risk and Capital Flight in Developing Countries' (1990) International Monetary Fund, IMF Working Paper 0440, 15 < https://www.cgdev.org/doc/experts/Risk_Cap_Flight_Dev_Countries.pdf > accessed 19 November 2016.

152 Hippolyte Fofack and Leonce Ndikumana, 'Capital Flight and Monetary Policy in African Countries' (2014) Political Economy Research Institute, Working Paper Series 362, 2 < https://www.africaportal.org/publications/capital-flight-and-monetary-policy-in-african-countries/ > accessed 17 November 2016.

153 S. Ajayi, 'Capital Flight and Economic Development in Africa' [2014] 55 Capital flight from Africa: Causes, Effects and Policy Issues 1, 20.

154 *Premium Times*, 'Sanusi Lamido Explodes: How Vested Interests are Killing Nigeria' (*Premium Times*, 13 January 2014) < https://www.premiumtimesng.com/news/153212-sanusi-lamido-explodes-how-vested-interests-are-killing-nigeria.html > accessed 10 March 2016.

155 Ibid.

156 African leaders in counties that have experienced previous terror attacks will be more willing unlike states that have not experienced same – *Whitaker* (n 83) 639, 646.

revenue or proactive civil societies. In such cases, there is political will to combat ML/TF and meet international standards.[157] For example, the national assembly of Kenya recently enacted the Proceeds of Crime and Anti-Money Laundering (Amendment) Act 2017, imposing stiff penalties for economic crime. This law, coming shortly before a pivotal Kenyan election, may indicate strong political will accelerated by civil societies and threats by the electorates.

Political will is however not always internally generated at the domestic level; it may also be externally engendered through a hub that facilitates cross-country regulatory interactions. Such a hub, usually created by soft law bodies like the FATF, produces a competitive atmosphere where national authorities start to perceive international banking regulation as a technique for guarding against systemic risk or threat of ML/TF. Hence, national authorities in ACs may start to impose additional pressure on governments to implement laws, knowing that FIs with reduced fraud are less likely to experience collapse which may trigger systemic risk. This provides security but also works to facilitate the reparation of capital laundered back to the country of origin. In certain instances, political will may be foisted on a country through its external agreements, such as the United Nations Convention Against Illicit Traffic in Narcotic Drugs and Psychotropic Substances.[158]

The extent to which a combination of soft and hard law can propel political will within states with weak institutional structures is debatable. Notwithstanding how political will is generated, it may be hindered by domestic conditions, such as thriving corruption, cultural and socio-political contestation. In ACs, for instance, there is a thriving culture of 'man-know-man' within and between FIs, regulatory bodies and customers, which facilitates illicit transactions. Unsurprisingly, corruption indexes reveal that 92% of all ACs score below 50% of 100% – averaging 33%, considerably lower than the global average.[159] Africa cannot achieve improved compliance with this level of corruption, which cripples the continent's ability to effectively adhere to the AML/CFT regime. It compromises the efficiency of various institutions, including the judiciary, the executive. It also affects the ability of private institutions to hold erring customers to account.[160]

---

157 Sojin Lim, 'Compliance with International Norms: Implementing the OECD DAC Principles in South Korea' [2014] 11 (6) Globalisation 859–874; Anna Markovska and Nya Adams 'Political Corruption and Money Laundering: Lessons from Nigeria' [2015] 18 (2) JMLC 169, 169.

158 United Nations Convention against Illicit Traffic in Narcotic Drugs and Psychotropic Substances (1988) < https://www.unodc.org/pdf/convention_1988_en.pdf > accessed 10 July 2016.

159 TI, 'Corruption Perception Index 2014' (*Transparency International*) <https://www.transparency.org/cpi2014/results > accessed 10 July 2016.

160 David Chaikin and Jason Sharman, *Corruption and Money Laundering: A Symbiotic Relationship.*(Palgrave Macmillan, 2009); see also World Bank, 'World Development Report 2011: Conflict, Security and Development' 264 (*The World Bank*, 2011) < https://siteresources.worldbank.org/INTWDRS/Resources/WDR2011_Full_Text.pdf > accessed 10 July 2016.

By way of illustration, the banking sector's effectiveness as gatekeepers requires identification and prevention of the influx of illicit funds into the economy. This is largely dependent on the tone or culture set by senior management of banks. But, in certain ACs, senior management has fallen short of this responsibility. A 2012 KPMG survey revealed that 34% of boards of directors do not take active interest in AML issues,[161] the weakest region being West Africa. In Nigeria, bank managers have aided and promoted corrupt practices by permitting secrecy, authorising the doctoring of or refusing to disclose statements of suspicious account holders who are subject to investigation by regulatory bodies.[162] The endorsement of these acts is enshrined in the 'big man culture', which entices bank officials to aid politically exposed persons (PEPs) transfer illicit funds without reporting a breach of AML/CFT requirements.[163] These acts furnished some directors lavish lifestyles until the perpetrators were charged for corruption.[164] It is startling to note that no FI has been sanctioned for lapses in its ML practices,[165] though the Financial Conduct Authority (FCA) has fined a Nigerian subsidiary bank for failures in its AML controls.[166] Sanctions on a bank would not only cause reputational damage in a competitive market,[167] it would also alter the tolerant culture of bank officials to ML/TF cases.

Africa's judiciary also suffers from corruption. In Nigeria, serious cases of ML have not reached their expected conclusion.[168] This is usually the case with PEPs who bribe their way to freedom.[169] Certain landmark cases have revealed the corruption in the judiciary as regards ML in Nigeria; for instance, the case of former Governor James Ibori of Delta State. Despite overwhelming evidence, a Nigerian

---

161 KPMG, Africa AML Survey 2012 (KPMG) <https://www.kpmg.com/ZA/en/IssuesAn dInsights/ArticlesPublications/Financial-Services/Documents/KPMG%202012%20A frica%20Anti-Money%20Laundering%20Survey.pdf > accessed 1 June 2015.

162 Sani Turkur, 'Nigerian Banks Aid Corruption – EFCC' (*Premium Times*, 10 September 2012). <http://www.premiumtimesng.com/business/99682-nigerian-banks-aid-corrup tion-efcc.html > accessed 3 June 2015.

163 Alexandra Evans, 'The Utility of Informal Networks to Policy Makers' *in* David Martin Jones, Ann Lane and Paul Schulte (eds.) *Terrorism, Security and the Power of Informal Networks* (Edward Elgar, 2010) 18.

164 Marwan Haruna Abdulkarim, 'The Nigerian Banking Revolution' < http://www.gamji .com/article8000/NEWS8790.htm > accessed 10 March 2017.

165 Benson Esomojumi, NFIU to Sanction Banks over Money Laundering (*Nigeria Commu- nications Week*, 30 August 2013) <http://nigeriacommunicationsweek.com.ng/e-financia l/nfiu-to-sanction-banks-over-money-laundering> accessed 14 April 2015.

166 FCA, 'FCA Fines Guaranty Trust Bank (UK) Ltd £525,000 for Failures in its Anti-Money Laundering Controls' (*Financial Conduct Authority*, 17 September 2013) < http://www .fca.org.uk/news/fca-fines-guaranty-trust-bank-uk-ltd > accessed 21 March 2015.

167 Antoinette Verhage, 'Between the Hammer and the Anvil? The Anti-Money Laundering – Complex and its Interactions with the Compliance Industry' [2009] 52 Crime Law Soc. Change 1, 12.

168 Abdullahi Shehu, *Strategies and Techniques of Prosecuting Economic and Financial Crimes* (GIABA Secretariat, 2012) 61–76.

169 Ibid.

judge dismissed the case 'for lack of merit'.[170] Other instances in Nigeria have illustrated that cases concerning PEPs who are cronies of the government are usually not seen to a conclusive end[171] or ex-convicts are subsequently pardoned.[172] Other ACs have similar instances, albeit to a smaller extent. Angola has had no record of enforcement or prosecution of ML-related offences to date. Botswana, Niger, Sierra Leone, Kenya and Uganda are reported to have poor prosecutions or conviction levels despite the numerous investigations carried out.[173]

Also, cases of TF have not received the right attention from the courts. Prominent cases against businessmen on the allegation of laundering funds aimed at financing a terrorist organisation – Hezbollah.[174] These cases were however struck out on the application of the prosecutor.[175] Subsequently, the United States Government stated that it had frozen all assets owned by the accused persons and banned them from dealing with US persons. Similarly, a former Nigerian senator was charged with assisting and funding Boko Haram. The judge dismissed the case on the grounds of insufficient evidence, disregarding evidence that may have warranted a finding of guilt beyond reasonable doubt.[176]

Notably, the judiciary's attitude is not solely reflective of corruption; it also illustrates the absence of judicial independence. Judges may be pressured into dispensing unmerited decisions through coercion or bribery, a practice rife in ACs. These constraints are however not unusual as legal scholars posit that domestic regimes uncharacterised by rule of law and the independence of the judiciary

170 Bolaji Akinola, *Authority Stealing: How Greedy Politicians and Corporate Executives Loot the World's Most Populous Black Nation* (AuthorHouse, 2012) 122.
171 GIABA, 'Annex to Nigeria 2nd Follow Up Report, Money Laundering Convictions' (*GIABA*) < https://www.giaba.org/media/f/305_Annexe > accessed 12 March 2015.
172 Nnenna Ibeh, 'US Threatens Sanctions Against Nigeria over Pardon for Ex-Convict Alamieyeseigha, Bulama' (*Premium Times*, 16 March 2013) <http://www.premiumti mesng.com/news/125112-u-s-threatens-sanctions-against-nigeria-over-pardon-for-ex -convict-alamieyeseigha-bulama.html > accessed 21st May 2015.
173 Tanzania recently reported 14 instituted cases following the 2016 AML legislation. Whilst ahead of neighboring states, it must address its failure to prosecute. Conversely, it can be argued that corruption level is not a determinant factor to the level of compliance. Botswana is the least corrupt AC, yet remains deficient in AML/CFT regulations.
174 Hezbollah Financer in Nigeria Exposed (*Money Jihad*, March 3, 2015) < https://moneyji had.wordpress.com/2015/03/03/hezbollah-financier-in-nigeria-exposed/ > accessed May 1 2015.
175 Nnenna Ibeh, 'America Bans Owners of Amigo Supermarket, Wonderland Amusement Park over Alleged Terrorist Activities' (*Premium Times*, June 15 2015) <http://www.prem iumtimesng.com/news/top-news/177962-america-bans-owners-of-amigo-supermarke t-wonderland-amusement-park-over-alleged-terrorist-activities.html > accessed March 7 2015.
176 *Premium Times*, 'Senator Ndume Contacted Boko Haram Leader 73 Times In One Month Says SSS' (*Sahara Reporters*, 12 December 2012) <http://saharareporters.com/2012 /12/12/senator-ndume-contacted-boko-haram-leader-73-times-one-month-says-sss-pr emium-times;> accessed 12 April 2015.

are less likely to comply with international obligations.[177] Conversely, empirical evidence has also confirmed that countries with sturdier legal and regulatory systems have better developed financial intermediaries[178] – indicating that law does matter.[179]

Private and public sectors' actions on ML/TF reflect the mind of the executive body of the country. Some past corrupt PEPs accused of ML/TF were later granted state pardon,[180] with the right to run for public office. The government rejected efforts to demolish alleged terror-funders businesses.[181] The constitutional cloak of immunity, which insulates some PEPs from judicial proceeding whilst in office, also presents difficulties for developing countries.[182] These instances reveal the absence of political will to curb ML/TF in Africa, which aids and perpetuates non-compliance.

Treatises on corruption in FIs, the judiciary and executive arms of government may suggest that internal domestic factors drive and affect compliance to international AML/CFT standards. Scholars accede to the effect of discursive mechanism in pressurising countries to adopt AML/CFT regime, but have argued that this in itself does not equate to straightforward success.[183] They argue instead that countries themselves, through regulatory regionalism, dictate the process of implementation and enforcement, which is shaped by their wider socio-political contestations.[184] This argument recognises that trans-governmental regulatory networks like the FATF do not operate by establishing and empowering supra-

177 Concepcion Yepes, 'Compliance with the AML/CFT International Standard: Lessons from a Cross-Country Analysis' (2011) International Monetary Fund Working Paper WP/11/177, 9 < https://papers.ssrn.com/sol3/papers.cfm?abstract_id=1899578 > accessed 19 April 2015.

178 Ross Levine, 'Law, Finance and Economic Growth' [1999] 8 (1) Journal of Financial Intermediation 1, 10.

179 Brian Cheffins, 'Does Law Matter? The Separation of Ownership and Control in the United Kingdom' (2000) ERSC Centre for Business Research, University of Cambridge Working Paper 172 < https://www.cbr.cam.ac.uk/fileadmin/user_upload/centre-for-business-research/downloads/working-papers/wp172.pdf > accessed 19 April 2015.

180 Emmanuel Edukugho, 'Alamieyeseigha: Unpardonable Pardon' (Vanguard, 23 March 2013) < https://www.vanguardngr.com/2013/03/alamieyeseigha-unpardonable-pardon / > accessed 10 April 2015.

181 Nnenna Ibeh, 'America Bans Owners of Amigo Supermarket, Wonderland Amusement Park over Alleged Terrorist Activities' (*Premium Times*, 5 March 2015) < https://www.vanguardngr.com/2013/03/alamieyeseigha-unpardonable-pardon/ > accessed 10 April 2015.

182 Ngozi Okonjo-Iweala, *Reforming the Unreformable: Lessons from Nigeria* (The MIT Press, Cambridge Massachusetts, London 2012) 82.

183 Navin Beekarry, 'The International Anti-Money Laundering and Combatting the Financing of Terrorism Regulatory Strategy: A Critical Analysis of Compliance Determinants in International Law' [2010] 31 Nw. J. Int'l L. & Bus 137, 190.

184 By the FATF standards, compliance and enforcement is measured by the number of confiscations and convictions – Shahar Hameiri and Lee Jones, 'Regulatory Regionalism and Anti-Money Laundering Governance in Asia' [2014] Australian Institute of International Affairs 1, 4.

national authorities to oversee issues directly, but rather by transforming regulatory apparatuses and processes that states must adopt. They posit that regulatory regional governance occurs by transforming rather than supplanting statehood so that states enact regional governance initiatives domestically.[185] Thus, the FATF only dictates but does not implement or enforce these recommendations, rather enforcement is reserved to FSRBs to coordinate mutual peer reviews aimed at eliciting compliance.[186]

Myanmar, which shares similarities with certain ACs,[187] typifies the cultural and socio-political contestations which determine a country's compliance. Myanmar legislated on AML/CFT and was subsequently de-blacklisted. However, it remained on the FATF's list of countries with AML/CFT strategic deficiencies. Myanmar was not especially known as a country complacent with the culture of laundering through banks.[188] The adopted legislations were instruments to undermine groups considered disloyal to the ruling regime as opposed to tackling predicate crimes, indicating deliberate flouting of the FATF recommendations.[189] Certain ACs, like Myanmar, use their structures of AML/CFT regimes to witch-hunt opposition parties or past military dictators. This demonstrates why though ACs have been removed from the watch list, they are still largely deficient. Funds are lost through the low level of compliance and the rates of corruption and terrorist activities leave much to be desired.

States that are predominantly financially inclusive tend to be more compliant to AML/CFT regimes.[190] ACs however operate cash-based economies,[191] which

185 Shahar Hameiri and Lee Jones, 'Regulatory Regionalism and Anti-Money Laundering Governance in Asia' [2014] Australian Institute of International Affairs 1, 7; Hameiri Shahar and Kanishka Jayasuriya, 'Regulatory Regionalism and the Dynamics of Territorial Politics: The Case of the Asia- Pacific Region' [2011] 59 Political Studies, 1, 21.

186 Cf with Drezner Daniel, 'The New World Order' [2007] 86.2 Foreign Affairs 34–46 who argues that it reflects the capacity of the great powers – mainly the US and European Union – to use sanctions to coerce weaker states to adopt their preferred rules, via regional organizations like the APG, of which the US is a member. Hameiri and Jones disagree, arguing that FATF and FSRBs are not supranational institutions overriding natural sovereignty as assumed, rather the hubs of a regional network, coordinating domestic agencies to manage transnational problems. See Shahar Hameiri and Lee Jones, 'Regulatory Regionalism and Anti-Money Laundering Governance in Asia' [2014] Australian Institute of International Affairs.

187 In terms of unsophisticated legal systems, corruption, unemployment, basic and undeveloped infrastructures etc.

188 Shahar Hameiri and Lee Jones, 'Regulatory Regionalism and Anti-Money Laundering Governance in Asia' [2014] Australian Institute of International Affairs 1, 4.

189 Ibid. 1, 5.

190 Hennie Bester, Doubell Chamberlain, Louis de Koker, Christine Hougaard, Rayn Short, Anja Smith and Richard Walker, 'Implementing FATF Standards in Developing Countries and Financial Inclusion: Findings and Guidelines' (*First Initiative*, 2008) <http://cenfri .org/documents/AML/AML_CFT%20and%20Financial%20Inclusion.pdf > accessed 10 May 2015.

191 States where more than 50% of their economic transactions are conducted in cash and the majority of the populations are unbanked.

leave room for uncontrolled and unregulated cash movement, thus perpetuating laundering and the financing of terror.[192] Verdugo-Yepes illustrates that developing countries most likely to be cash-based economies comply to a lesser degree with the AML/CFT standard.[193] Hence, the limitations in compliance do not rest so much in imperfect laws as in the lack of capability to monitor and counter ML through the informal sector.[194] The informal sector's poor enforcement levels described as 'lackluster or non-existent' are attributable to the absence of information to prompt prosecution.[195] Paradoxically, the AML/CFT regime itself prompts financial exclusion by barring the financially vulnerable and marginalised citizens from the financial system.[196] This is because persons in the lower economic strata may not possess banks' requirements for requisite IDs, address or proof of address.[197] Thus, the prospects of ML are increasingly rife, with criminals able to move dirty money within and across borders. Many ACs, rich in either oil or precious stones, frequently launder funds around the continent using these commodities,[198] thereby hindering Africa's economic development.

Corruption, financial exclusion and other socio-political contestations illustrate the arguments put forward by scholars who recognise that domestic factors determine the likelihood of actual or proactive compliance.[199] This underscores the inability of ACs to effectively converge. Furthermore, the discourse on political will and domestic conditions and their relationship with compliance illustrates that the narrative behind policies and political change is set within the broader culture of a country which determines what is most deserving of focus, from a scale of varying socio-political and economic interests.[200] The policy priorities

192 Ronald Mynhardt and Johan Marx, 'Anti-Money Laundering Recommendations for Cash Based Economies in West Africa' [2013] 11 (1) Corporate Ownership and Control 24, 25.

193 *Verdugo-Yepes* (n 177). Humphrey P.B. Moshi, 'Fighting Money Laundering: The Challenges in Africa' [2007] 152 Institute for Security Studies Papers 1, 10–12.

194 *Mynhardt and Marx* (n 192) 24, 29.

195 Norton Rose Fulbright, 'Prominence of Money Laundering in Africa, 10 things to know' (*Norton Rose Fulbright*, February 2014) <http://www.nortonrosefulbright.com/knowl edge/publications/113161/prominence-of-money-laundering-in-africa-br-ten-things-to -know > accessed 1 June 2015.

196 *Bester, Chamberlain, Koker, Hougaard, Rayn Short, Smith and Walker* (n 190).

197 Verdugo-Yepes agrees that compliance is correlated with a country's economic development, see *Verdugo-Yepes* (n 177).

198 *Norton Rose Fulbright* (n 195); GIABA Report, 'The Nexus Between Small Arms and Light Weapons and Money Laundering and Terrorist Financing in Africa' (*GIABA*, 2013) < https ://www.giaba.org/media/f/613_519_GIABA%20SALW%20Nexus-final.pdf > accessed 10 May 2015.

199 Andrea Lenschow, Duncan Liefferink, and Sietske Veenman., 'When the Birds Sing. A Framework for Analyzing Domestic Factors behind Policy Convergence' [2005] 12 (5) Journal of European Public Policy 797, 800; John Mearsheimer, 'The False Promise of International Institutions' [1994–95] 19 (3) International Security 5–49.

200 Andrea Lenschow, Duncan Liefferink, and Sietske Veenman, 'When the Birds Sing. A Framework for Analyzing Domestic Factors behind Policy Convergence' [2005] 12 (5) Journal of European Public Policy 797, 801.

of a country or region can be evaluated by its budgetary focus.[201] Countries like Kenya and Nigeria apportion their highest budgetary allocation to security to ensure stability and economic growth. This focus is however undermined by corruption solidified through 'immunity' granted to PEPs and issues concerning financial inclusion – a key determinant of AML/CFT compliance.[202] Thus, whilst the FATF recommendations focus on FIs – the real damage is done outside these institutions. Hence, the current FATF recommendations and other international standards do not appear to advance practical and realistic methods of preventing and detecting ML/TF in a predominantly cash-based economy, or in countries reliant on a parallel banking system and informal value transfer. These issues are prominent in Africa and deserve tailored solutions.

TECHNICAL CAPACITY AND RESOURCES

The capacity of regulatory and institutional officers to carry out their duties efficiently determines the degree of compliance. The AML/CFT regime has progressively expanded from banks to encompass other businesses that criminals might explore to launder or transfer illicit funds. Thus, insurance companies, lawyers, accountants, bureau de change and casinos are mandated to be actively involved in ensuring compliance with the FATF recommendations.[203] This requirement particularly encompasses suspicious transaction reporting (STR) and CDD.[204] However, carrying out these tasks in Africa requires technical skills to deal with complicated software,[205] which staff of financial and non-financial institutions may not be well acquainted with.

The dearth of technical capacity can be illustrated with the inability to use or objectively translate reports of software-generated STRs.[206] For example, reports forwarded to the FIUs by officials are those that raise suspicion of ML/TF activ-

---

201 Ibid. 797, 807.
202 TI, 'When Immunity Becomes a License to Break the Law' (*Transparency International*, 29 April 2013) < https://www.transparency.org/news/feature/when_immunity_becomes_a_licence_to_break_the_law > accessed 10 July 2017.
203 FATF, 'FATF Recommendation (FATF, 2012) < http://www.fatf-gafi.org/media/fatf/documents/recommendations/pdfs/FATF%20Recommendations%202012.pdf > accessed 10 February 2017.
204 *FATF* (n 203) recommendation 10.
205 For instance, SAS, Norkom, World Check, etc., see Antoinette Verhage, 'Between the Hammer and the Anvil? The Anti-Money Laundering-Complex and Its Interactions with the Compliance Industry' [2009] 52 Crime Law Soc. Change 1, 18; Gandy Oscar Jr, 'Data Mining, Surveillance and Discrimination in the Post 9/11 Environment' *in* Haggerty Kevin and Ericson Richard (eds.) *The New Politics of Surveillance and Visibility* (Toronto: UTP 2006) 381.
206 Antoinette Verhage, 'Between the Hammer and the Anvil? The Anti-Money Laundering-Complex and Its Interactions with the Compliance Industry' [2009] 52 Crime Law Soc. Change 1, 18; Margaret Rouse, 'Anti-Money Laundering Software (AML)' (*Tech Target*) <http://searchfinancialsecurity.techtarget.com/definition/anti-money-laundering-software-AML > accessed 15 April 2015; Gilles Favarel-Garrigues, Thierry Godefroy, Pierre Las-

ity. However, this is not always the case due to the officials' subjectivity in filtering STR which can lead to erroneous judgements, thus permitting some ML/TF cases to go unnoticed. This shortcoming was highlighted by the FATF MER report on Nigeria, which underscored instances of inappropriate filing of Cash Transaction Reports (CTRs) and worse still, instances where CTRs were filed in place of STRs.[207] Evidently, the pressure to provide reports to regulators are attributed to reputational benefits instead of the main aim of combating illicit crimes.[208] The FATF evaluation team echoed their fears that FIs did not have a clear understanding of how to determine suspicious activity or the significance of incorrect CTRs reporting on the effectiveness of AML/CFT regulation.[209]

Furthermore, illicit transactions still go unnoticed as departments within banks operate in silos, meaning the compliance department may be oblivious of the business of the retail or business banking divisions.[210] This creates a risk where links between a customer and an account used for illicit crimes are missed, particularly with the exclusion of the compliance department from the business of banking. This has been exacerbated by the risk assessment criterion, which diminishes the standard requirements for opening or maintaining a bank account in cash-based economies,[211] where a large segment of the population may not have proper verification documents.[212] The ability of FIs to effectively ascertain the extent of documentation that suffices determines to a large extent the level of compliance of ACs to AML/CFT requirements.

The compliance of the regulated may be undermined by ineffective regulatory supervision.[213] The regulator's ability to enhance compliance may be hindered by

coumes, 'Reluctant Partners? Banks in the Fight against Money Laundering and Terrorism Financing in France' [2011] 42 (2) Security Dialogue 179, 183.

207 GIABA, 'Mutual Evaluation Report: Anti-Money Laundering and Combating the Financing of Terrorism: Nigeria' (*GIABA*, 2008) 95 < https://www.giaba.org/media/f/299_M utual%20Evaluation%20Report%20of%20Nigeria.pdf > accessed 9 April 2015.

208 Ericson, Richard, 'Ten Uncertainties of Risk Management Approaches to Security' [2006] 48 (3) Canadian Journal of Criminology and Criminal Justice 345, 352.

209 Banks' response will determine the area of the FIU's risk matrix in order to identify the areas within the financial sector that would require increased supervision.

210 *Lawrence* (n 141).

211 See the Central Bank of Nigeria's know your customer (KYC) requirement for mobile banking – Central Bank of Nigeria, 'Regulatory Framework for Mobile Payments Services in Nigeria' (Central Bank of Nigeria) <http://www.cbn.gov.ng/out/circulars/bod/ 2009/regulatory%20framework%20%20for%20mobile%20payments%20services%20in%20 nigeria.pdF> accessed 11 April 2015.

212 KPMG, 'Global Anti-Money Laundering Survey 2011, How Banks Are Facing up to the Challenge (*KPMG*, 2011) <https://www.kpmg.com/UK/en/IssuesAndInsights/Artic lesPublications/Documents/PDF/Advisory/global-aml-survey-2011-main-report.p df> accessed 2 June 2015; *Bester, Chamberlain, Koker, Hougaard, Rayn Short, Smith and Walker* (n 190).

213 Jun Tang and Lishan Ai, 'Combating Money Laundering in Transition Countries: The Inherent Limitations and Practical Issues' [2010] 13 (3) Journal of Money Laundering Control 215–225.

limited knowledge, technical capacity, resources and evaluation mechanisms.[214] For instance, the FATF report on Nigeria noted that regulatory authorities were unaware of the FATF standard of $1000 for off-wire transactions and were unable to cite a reference illustrating that a lower threshold for occasional wire transfers existed.[215] This knowledge gap illustrates difficulties in enforcing proper sanctions. Additionally, regulators' evaluation is usually preceded by formal information to the regulated on the proposed period of evaluation. This gives the regulated institutions time to prepare their books to meet the regulator's requirements, making it more difficult to identify pitfalls and issue sanctions. Currently, none of the related regulatory bodies in Nigeria has issued sanctions for AML/ CFT, a situation which prompted the US to threaten action.[216] These shortcomings evidence that resources are to be directed at training and re-training to ensure compliance – short of this, the ability of ACs to meet the regime's requirements will be challenged.

Capacity deficit is also evident in the various arms of government. Across ACs, legislators fail to grasp the fundamentals of the law, prosecutors fail to ensure admissible evidence is retrieved and preserved and the judiciary has insufficient training to effectively address cases of ML/TF. In the absence of properly crafted laws, criminals will use the existing lacunae to their advantage, thus weakening compliance. This is also the case with the judiciary and law enforcement agencies. Consequently, the IMF, World Bank, International Bar Association and various other global organisations have embarked on training in various ACs, to improve the capacity of staff to deal with AML/CFT cases.

Capacity deficit is also dependent on inadequate infrastructure to effectively monitor information received by the various agencies responsible for analysing and reporting instances of AML/CFT. The FIUs across countries have repeatedly decried lack of necessary infrastructures to effectively carry out their duties.[217] The primary reason is lack of requisite funding to boost institutional capacity and promote interagency coordination and international cooperation.[218] It is therefore unsurprising that given the relatively low GDP and weak framework for financial

---

214 Ibid.
215 GIABA, 'Mutual Evaluation Report: Anti-Money Laundering and Combating the Financing of Terrorism: Nigeria' (*GIABA*, 2008) 95 < https://www.giaba.org/media/f/299_M utual%20Evaluation%20Report%20of%20Nigeria.pdf > accessed 9 April 2015.
216 *The Guardian,* 'U.S May Probe Nigerian Banks over Terror Funding' (*The Guardian,* 2014) < http://theguardianmobile.com/readNewsItem1.php?nid=29350 > accessed 12 April 2015.
217 George Kieh and Kelechi Kalu, *West Africa and the U.S. War on Terror* (Routledge, Taylor & Francis Group, London and New York, 2013); Musonda Simwayi and Muhammed Haseed, 'The Role of Financial Intelligence Units in Combating Money Laundering: A Comparative Analysis of Zambia, Zimbabwe and Malawi' [2011] 15 (1) Journal of Money Laundering Control 112–134.
218 IMF, 'Anti-Money Laundering and Combating the Financing of Terrorism (AML/CFT) Report on the Review of the Effectiveness of the Program' (*IMF*, 11 May 2011) < http:// www.imf.org/external/np/pp/eng/2011/051111.pdf > accessed 11 May 2015.

regulation, ACs have low compliance levels. Moreover, externally sourced funds may influence operations. To this extent, Uganda and Tanzania's dependence on foreign aid marginally improved their compliance levels, as these funds have the conditionality to be fulfilled prior to the release of tranches.[219] Lack of funding or sudden reduction in funds can adversely affect compliance levels.[220]

GLOBALISATION AND INTEGRATION

Globalisation and strengthening financial integration occasioned a degree of financial exposure and openness that ACs were unprepared for. The resulting neoliberal policies worsened Africa's position within the global financial market, making countries more susceptible to shocks. With low GDP economies, coupled with laxity towards resolving AML/CFT deficiencies, ACs have not been classed as 'strategically or systemically important'. They are thereby excluded from the core FATF membership status. Consequently, their agency relationship with the IFIs permits agency slack which manifests in formal or creative compliance aimed at avoiding sanctions that further isolate them from the market. This slack is particularly through their communication strategy with IFIs which may be geared at projecting sham compliance to avert sanctions.

Yet, ACs already have a limited degree of integration and may only comply given their trade or capital interests. Coupled with the lack of political will and other domestic factors that hinder compliance, this facilitates illicit crimes.[221] Moreover, it can be argued that these class of countries with limited connection to the global financial market may indeed defer compliance, knowing that sanctions would have a limited effect on them.

Debunking this argument, scholars have argued that globalisation and integration drive competition amongst countries and this may catalyse proactive compliance with the AML/CFT regime.[222] This aligns with the position that countries that have implemented the AML/CFT regime are more attractive to foreign investors than countries which have not. This may however not always be the case, as countries with lax regulations may attract investments, a situation that can lead to a race to the bottom. Given the global minimum standards to which all countries are mandated to adhere to, there is a mechanism of competition which creates policy interdependence, as countries implement AML/CFT laws to avoid the adverse effects of non-compliance.[223] This is however not peculiar to AML/CFT regulations, it exists in other policy areas like tax and expatriate laws as well.

219 *Whitaker* (n 83) 639, 654.
220 Ibid. 647.
221 Garrett Geoffrey, 'Global Markets and National Politics: Collusion Course or Virtuous Circle?' [1998] 52 (4) *International Organization* 787, 823.
222 *Sharman* (n 81) 635, 649.
223 Ibid.

Nevertheless, the ability of ACs who are not classed as 'systemically important' to renege on AML/CFT compliance is somewhat curtailed by the involvement of IFIs. For instance, as a prerequisite for financial assistance, IFIs have incorporated law reforms and compliance requirements.[224] Additionally, multilateral institutions and FIs use compliance with accredited standards to determine potential finance opportunities or threats.[225] Whilst this may suggest that the scope for slack is addressed, this is not necessarily correct. For instance, if a FI within a HP country is entering into a business with another FI in an MP country, the domination of self-interests may resurface, particularly if the transaction is ad hoc for the principal and agent. In such situations, the incentive to comply is low for both institutions, although it is higher for the HP country FI due to its mandated adherence to international standards and subjection to high regulatory standards. Where however, it is a continuous transactional relationship for both FIs, both countries are incentivised to comply to maximise profit. However, differing legal framework, policies and capacity means that the MP FI is less able to comply, thereby forcing the HP FI to de-risk so as to avert any possible home or international sanction. This serves as another explanation for the de-risking of African banks by Deutsche Bank.[226]

This difficulty is further exacerbated by the delegation of gatekeeper responsibilities to private institutions. Sharman notes that similar to the Basel 2 requirement where the task of determining capital requirements was assigned to banks, assigning and guarding against AML/CFT risk has been increasingly delegated to private firms.[227] These firms are required to flag up high-risk countries and ensure extra scrutiny to guarantee safe transaction with such countries. However, due to their subjectivity, firms may fall back on casual impressions and shared stereotypes in making conclusions as to which countries are high and low risk.[228] On this basis, FIs in regulated states are assumed to be more risk-averse than in unregulated states. Sharman argues that the effect is ousting a country from an 'in group' thus warranting reputational damage.[229] This is based on the argument that AML standards are not in themselves effective in lowering risk but serve as an indicator of membership of an 'in group'. Such position suggests that compliance response to competition is an involuntary measure and without competition, and occasioning loss, some countries would not implement AML/CFT laws. It is however not independent from coercion, which in itself forms the 'in group' membership.

---

224 Ian Fletcher, Loukas Mistelis, and Marise Cremona, (eds.) *Foundations and Perspectives of International Trade Law* (London: Sweet & Maxwell, 2001).
225 Ibid.
226 *The Economist* (n 144).
227 Zoe Lester, 'Risk Management and the Risk Attached to Money Laundering and Terrorist Financing' (Money Laundering Risk Conference, Sydney, Australia, July 2006); *KPMG* (n 212).
228 Firms are usually unconcerned with the result of sanctions caused by their wrongful assessments.
229 *Sharman* (n 81) 635, 649.

Despite indications that ACs are keen to integrate with the global financial market, this aspiration is hindered by their culture and capacity. For instance, FIs in developed or EEs are owned by shareholders with dispersed ownership. Conversely, African FIs are usually family-owned and run.[230] Hence, customers do not have the same political recourse to demand regulatory reform as opposed to countries. The absence of recourse for stakeholders largely undermines compliance. More so, these countries do not have the needed technological or expert capacity to ensure compliance.

The literature on globalisation and integration has indicated that supranational influences can only determine compliance level of ACs to a limited extent. Homegrown factors are paramount to ensuring effective compliance to AML/CFT. Given this fact, the FATF, the IMF/WB have intensified efforts to ensure compliance, by providing the assistance required to ensure effective capacity building and training in Africa. The extent to which this has ensured compliance would require a cross-country analysis based on country review.

LEGITIMISATION

Legitimacy of institutions and standards is considered crucial for stimulating pro-active compliance with regulatory standards.[231] This is predicated on the perception of its ownership, inclusiveness and procedural fairness ingrained in its processes and standards.[232] Given the establishment and formulation of FATF standards by a non-inclusive club of Group of Seven (G7) countries to the exclusion of ACs, ACs postulated that a global hegemony exists.[233] The subsequent attempt at resolving this 'legitimacy crisis' through the FSRBs has been deemed inadequate.

Buttressing the absence of legitimacy in Inter-Governmental Group against Money Laundering in West Africa (GIABA), EENA5 mentioned that GIABA did not evolve from rational incentives, but rather, external pressure from Nigeria's blacklisting.[234] EENA5 stated that 'one of the conditions to be removed from that

---

230 Gomiluk Otokwala, 'Wither Family Shareholding in Developing Countries' (2010) available at SSRN 1714526.

231 Julia Black, 'Constructing and Contesting Legitimacy and Accountability in Polycentric Regulatory Regimes' (2008) LSE Law, Society and Economy Working Papers < http://www.lse.ac.uk/law/people/academic-staff/julia-black/Documents/black2.pdf > accessed 10 March 2015.

232 Gregory Shaffer, *Transnational Legal Ordering and State Change* (Cambridge Studies in Law and Society, 2014); cf with Bodnasky who asserts that legitimacy can be viewed in terms of representativeness, procedures and effectiveness. Bodansky, 'The Legitimacy of International Governance: A Coming Challenge for International Environmental Law?' [1999] 93 (3) American Journal of International Law 596, 604.

233 Mark Suchman, 'Managing Legitimacy: Strategic and Institutional Approaches' [1995] 20 (3) Academy of Management Review 571, 588; Eric Helleiner, 'State Power and the Regulation of Illicit Activity in Global Finance'. *in* R.H. Friman and P. Andreas (eds.) *The Illicit Global Economy and State Power* (Rowman & Littlefield, Lanham, 1999).

234 EENA5, Researcher, GIABA, Interview with EENA5 'Telephone Call' (2017).

list was (for Nigeria) to become a strong pillar in dealing with the problem of ML/ TF in West Africa'.[235] Such expectation was bestowed on Nigeria given its economic influence in Africa and the involvement of its citizens in illicit crimes across West Africa. But given the lack of ownership or inclusion in the FATF standards making process at the time, GIABA remained dormant for a period of four years, due to limited understanding of the FATF's standards. Consequently, compliance, which required adherence to 'dead letter standards' was met with scarce observance.

The absence of legitimacy is further evidenced by the processes involved in the re-evaluation of standards. EENA5 asserts that the recommendations review process is based on a participatory process where all countries, divided into groups, discuss and contribute to proposals by the Policy Development Group (PDG) during the plenary sessions. However, when making final decisions 'there are powers and opinions that supersede the others', with opinions from developed countries dwarfing those of ACs.[236]

Furthermore, FIs from ACs are rarely ever consulted given their perceived premature status.[237] This perspective illustrates the semi-exclusive nature of the FATF's decision-making process regarding its standards and how that challenges countries' sovereignty. Accordingly, EENA5 asserts that any review process is belated as 'no review will take the interest of African states into consideration'.[238] His perspective is predicated on the fallibility of the FATF in encapsulating African states' input in its standards. Acceding to this, Singer argues that in heterogeneous societies, for substantive legitimacy, the law must strike a balance between recognising differences in worldviews and enabling society to function as a cohesive entity.[239] The FATF does not currently have this provision.

What becomes evident is that from ACs' perspective, the FATF's recommendations and processes lack legitimacy. This shortcoming is heightened by FATF sanctions which single out countries for financial isolation and reputational damage. This perspective aligns with Shaffer's stance that countries would be hindered from voluntary proactive compliance to international law in the absence of input, output and throughput legitimacy.[240] Instead, they would engage in formal or creative compliance to evade sanctions. This would necessitate higher enforcement costs to ensure compliance through coercion, but the result would be limited progress on effectiveness.[241]

Vibert scrutinises the perception that proactive compliance is subject to the institution of legitimacy, asserting that bodies such as the FATF have epistemic authority,

---

235 Ibid.
236 Ibid. (n 235).
237 Ibid.
238 Ibid.
239 Michael Singer, 'Legitimacy Criteria for Legal Systems' [2006] 17 (2) Kings Law Journal 229–253.
240 *Shaffer* (n 232).
241 Cf with Rainer Hulsee who argues that coercion may be more cost effective and simpler for institutions to disseminate an unpopular regime. *Hulse* (n 107) 459, 466.

which is based on expertise that confers legitimacy.[242] This position is blindsided to the institution's internal politics and its effect on the FATF's rule design and compliance. The politics is evident in the composition of experts from the private and public sectors who are mainly representatives of developed countries, a configuration that does not encompass or represent the views of developing countries. It is thus capable of stifling the effectiveness of these countries to the FATF standards. This indicates that any re-structuring should de-politicise the FATF and ensure a truly 'expertise' process that include the views of developing countries.

Cross-Country Analysis of Compliance to AML/CFT Regime: Financial Sector Assessment Programme (FSAP) and FATF.

Assessing the Financial Sector Assessment Programme : The Procedure

The FSAP assesses a country's financial stability by measuring its compliance with international standards. The aim is to evaluate the attainment of minimum standards on rules and a country's ability to absorb stress. The result of the FSAP is the Financial System Stability Assessment (FSSA), a vital document in the IMF's Surveillance process and Financial Sector Assessment (FSA) for the World Bank. The FSAP report signals the respect the IMF/World Bank have for sovereign boundaries given that countries are not mandated to partake in the FSAP process. Even upon participation, countries have a say in whether the FSAP is published and what part can be excluded from publication.[243] This is aimed at promoting country ownership of financial stability reform and encouraging voluntary rather than pressured participation.[244] It would also encourage compliance from countries wishing to be assessed in order to attract foreign capital. This rationale propels countries to prepare adequately to ensure they are fit for assessments that will illustrate their conformity with the IMF/World Bank designs.[245]

Assessment of FSAP Country Review

AML/CFT regulation is an aspect of the FSAP review programme; however, its concentration is wider as it encompasses prudential supervision and management. Thus, its focus on AML/CFT in this context is usually sparse; hardly concentrating on all areas and has neither depth nor any particular approach. This is evident

---

242 Frank Vibert, 'Reforming International Rule Making' [2012] 3 (3) Global Policy 391, 392.
243 Paul Kupiec, 'The IMF-World Bank Financial Sector Assessment Program: A View from the Inside' *in* Douglas D. Evanoff and George G. Kaufman (eds.), *Systematic Financial Crisis, Resolving Large Bank Insolvencies* (World Scientific, 2005) 71.
244 Leonard Seabrooke and Eleni Tsiongou, 'Revolving Doors and Linked Ecologies in the World Economy: Policy Locations and the Practice of International Financial Reform' (2009) CSRG Working Paper 260/09, 15 < https://warwick.ac.uk/fac/soc/pais/research /researchcentres/csgr/papers/workingpapers/2009/26009.pdf > accessed 10 July 2015.
245 Ibid.

in country reports. For instance, Nigeria's AML/CFT focus was on pensions and insurance.[246] In contrast, Algeria focused on AML/CFT as a means of facilitating financial deepening across all sectors.[247] Country assessment reports vary based on content, quality and institutional findings, which complicate the ability to make effective cross-country analysis and comparisons.[248]

By February 2015, only 18 of the 54 ACs had undergone the FSAP procedure and had their FSSA published.[249] Amongst them, only 11 had AML/CFT discussed in their reports,[250] indicating the apathetic attitude of ACs towards AML/CFT regulations. Conversely, it may indicate the incapability of ACs to adequately adopt or implement the AML/CFT recommendations or the FSAPs focus on other areas. This is paradoxical as the FSAP was assumed to have a wider reach, able to ensure uniform widespread application of recommendations.[251]

Despite the lack of participation, the FSAP reports illustrate resonating themes cutting across countries. These include strategic deficiencies in the AML/CFT legal framework, weak regulatory supervision, absence of a robust enforcement and implementation apparatus, absence of the technical ability to combat ML/TF especially in banks where the CDD and STR were defective, the presence of new laws which could not be assessed and the absence of FIU links across countries. It is difficult to comprehensively evaluate the merits, shortcomings and impact of the AML/CFT programme and implementation, or draw founded conclusions due to the summary nature of the assessment reports.

Assessment of the Financial Action Task Force Country Reports

The FATF monitors a country's implementation and compliance with its recommendations in two main ways: a self-assessment and a mutual evaluation.[252] The self-assessment exercise is carried out by the countries themselves. This exer-

---

246 IMF, 'Nigeria: Financial Sector Stability Assessment' (IMF, 2013) < https://www.imf .org/external/pubs/ft/scr/2013/cr13140.pdf > accessed 10 July 2015.

247 IMF, 'Algeria: Financial System Stability Assessment' (IMF, June 2014) < https://www .imf.org/external/pubs/ft/scr/2014/cr14161.pdf > accessed 10 July 2015.

248 Marco Arnone and Pier Carlo Padone, 'Anti-Money Laundering by International Institutions: A Preliminary Assessment' [2008] 26 (3) European Journal of Law and Economics 361, 369.

249 Algeria, Cameroon, Central Africa Republic, Chad, Comoros, Congo, Gabon, Ghana, Morocco, Mozambique, Namibia, Nigeria, Rwanda, Senegal, South Africa, Tanzania, Tunisia and Uganda.

250 Algeria, Central African Republic, Congo, Ghana, Morocco, Mozambique, Namibia, Nigeria, Rwanda, South Africa and Tunisia.

251 This can be attributed to the voluntary nature of the FSAP.

252 FATF, 'Methodology for Assessing Technical Compliance with the FATF Recommendations and the Effectiveness of the AML/CFT Systems' (*FATF*, February 2013) <http://www.fatf-gafi.org/media/fatf/documents/methodology/fatf%20methodology%2022%20feb%202013.pdf > accessed 21 May 2015; AML/CFT Evaluations and Assessments, Handbook for Countries and Assessors, (April 2009) < http://www.fatf-gafi.org/media/fatf/documents/reports/Handbook%20for%20assessors.pdf > accessed 1 June 2015.

cise, which requires completing questionnaires, enables them to evaluate their progress in the implementation of specialist standards.[253] Officials of the FATF who undertake the on-site mutual evaluation task in countries depend on the self-assessment reports for preliminary information.[254] An analysis of the information garnered forms the bedrock of the discussions at plenary meetings, where the country's compliance level is decided.

Unlike the FSAP, the only point where countries can influence the MER's content is during the self-assessment stage and to a limited extent during the country dialogue concerning the MER. The FATF does not require consent from a country to publish its extensive findings. To that extent, it can be argued that it encroaches on the sovereignty of countries.

EMPIRICAL ASSESSMENT OF FATF COUNTRY REPORTS

An assessment of countries' MER is carried out to determine the level of compliance to AML/CFT. Each qualitative assessment is recoded into a number to permit a quantitative analysis. Officially each recommendation (rec.) can be scored based on one of five possible assessments methodology as follows:

- NA (0) = Not Applicable   (A requirement or part of it does not apply due to the country's the structural, legal or institutional features.)
- NC (1) = Non-Compliant   (There are shortcomings, with a large majority of the essential criteria not being met.)
- PC (2) = Partially Compliant   (The country has taken some substantive action and complies with some of the essential criteria.)
- LC (3) = Largely Compliant   (There are minor shortcomings, with a large majority of essential criteria being fully met.)
- C (4) = Compliant   (Recommendation is fully observed with respect to all essential criteria.)

The assessment of each recommendation is mapped out into a 5-valued measure where 0 is the minimum and 5 is the maximum.

ANALYSIS OF AML/CFT BY COUNTRIES AND GEOGRAPHICAL DISTRIBUTION

Figure 5.1 represents a plot indicating the percentage score of compliance of 38 ACs with the 40 FATF recommendations. Data is derived from each country's mutual evaluation reports spanning 2007 to 2015. Consequently, changes in updated MERs have been reflected in the compliance levels to the exclusion of post-2015 MERs. Of the countries examined, 30 of them are deemed to be <50%

253 Ibid.
254 FATF, 'Mutual Evaluations' (FATF) < http://www.fatf-gafi.org/topics/mutualevaluat ions/ > accessed 1 June 2015.

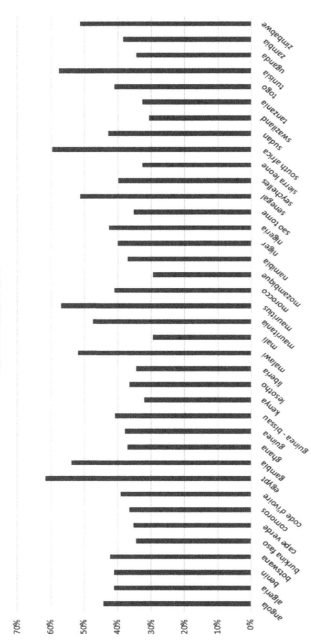

Figure 5.1 Technical Compliance Levels of African Countries to the FATF Recommendations (Derived from the MERs of Countries' FATFs.

compliant with the FATF recommendations. Only seven are deemed to be >50% compliant. The statistics indicate low level of compliance by ACs. Figure 5.1 shows that Egypt is the most compliant AC, followed by Tunisia, Mauritius, the Gambia, Malawi, Senegal and Zimbabwe. The weakest frameworks are those of Burkina Faso, Liberia, Tanzania, Sierra Leone, Kenya, Swaziland, Mozambique and Mali.

The weakest frameworks were mainly in the area of TF regulation, and sanctions related thereto.[255] Thus, since TF was added to the FATF recommendations, ACs are yet to comprehend and implement these requirements for compliance purposes. Weakness is also noted in recommendation 10 (CDD), thus bolstering the argument about absence of capacity to effectively address the requirements of this recommendation.[256] Countries also contend with recommendations relating to the additional measures for specific customer control,[257] indicating the pervasive nature of corruption and ineptitude in African financial regulatory institutions. Regarding recommendation 14 ('money or value transfer services'), it is doubtful that the vast efforts required to identify, register and monitor these services are likely to be an immediate priority.

Figure 5.2 presents a plot of the average score based on detailed assessments. Countries are grouped according to the following geographical category: North Africa (Region 9), South Africa (Region 8), West Africa (Region 6) and East Africa (Region 7). On a 100% scale, it emerges that no region achieves a compliance level of 50%. East Africa with a compliance level of 34% is the least compliant region in Africa,[258] followed by Western Africa[259] with 39% compliance. Southern Africa is 43% compliant,[260] whilst North Africa is the most compliant region in Africa with 49%.[261] It is however imperative to note that an estimated assessment is not reflective of the regions' actual compliance levels. Certain regions have more countries than others and some countries in particular regions were not assessed. It is therefore inappropriate to conclude that East Africa is the least compliant region in Africa.

ANALYSIS BY FATF RECOMMENDATIONS

Figure 5.3 highlights the compliance levels with the FATF recommendations. The clearest deficiencies noted regarding country compliance levels are mainly in

---

255 *FATF* (n 203) Recommendation 5, 6, 7 and 8.
256 *KPMG* (n 212); *Bester, Chamberlain, Koker, Hougaard, Rayn Short, Smith and Walker* (n 190).
257 *FATF* (n 203) Recommendation 12, 13, 14, 15 and 16.
258 Comoros, Uganda, Tanzania and Kenya.
259 Gambia, Senegal, Nigeria, Benin, Guinea Bissau, Togo, Niger, Cote d'Ivoire, Guinea, Ghana, Cape Verde, Liberia, Sao Tome and Principe, Burkina Faso, Sierra Leone and Mali.
260 Mauritius, Malawi, Zimbabwe, Angola, Botswana, Seychelles, Zambia, Lesotho, Namibia, Swaziland and Mozambique.
261 Egypt, Tunisia, Mauritania, Sudan, Algeria and Morocco.

Recommendation

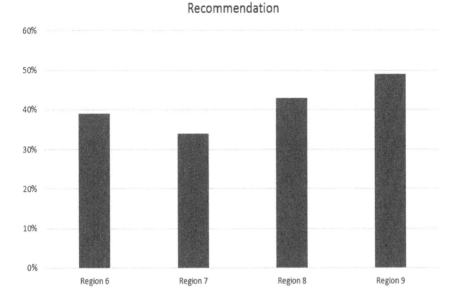

Figure 5.2 Africa's Compliance to the FATF Recommendations by Regions.

'Designated Non-Financial Businesses and Professions'.[262] These recommendations mandate effective regulation by casinos, real estate agents, dealers in precious
metals and stones, lawyers, and trust and company service providers, to ensure
that their businesses do not aid ML/TF. This recognises that money launderers
and terror funders exploit other lucrative and less regulated or licensed avenues
to transfer illicit funds.[263] For activities like casinos, there are differences in regulatory climates in each AC. Whilst countries like South Africa suffer from discrepancies in its supposed casino regulation,[264] in Nigeria casino regulation is relatively

262 See FATF Recommendation 22, 23, 28 – FATF, 'International Standards on Combating
Money Laundering and the Financing of Terrorism & Proliferation' (*The FATF Recommendations*, February 2012) <http://www.fatf-gafi.org/media/fatf/documents/recommend
ations/pdfs/fatf_recommendations.pdf> accessed 20 April 2015, with the score of 1.05,
1.12 and 1.1, respectively, lower than the average of 1.66.
263 Jan Mcmillen, 'Online Gambling: Challenges to National Sovereignty and Regulation'
[2000] 18 (4) Prometheus 391–410. Casinos are lucrative in Africa and have continued
to grow at healthy rates – see PwC page 9, Raising the stakes in Africa Gambling Outlook:
2014–2018 South Africa • Nigeria • Kenya 3rd Annual Edition November 2014 <http:/
/www.pwc.co.za/en_ZA/za/assets/pdf/gambling-outlook-2014.pdf > accessed 10 May.
264 Professor Sphiwe Nzimande, Dr. Stephen Louw, Mr Clement Mannya, Ms Adheera Bodasing, Ms Astrid Ludin, 'Review of the South African Gambling Industry and its Regulation,
a report prepared by the Gambling Review Commission – Final Report submitted to the
Minister of Trade and Industry, September 2010.

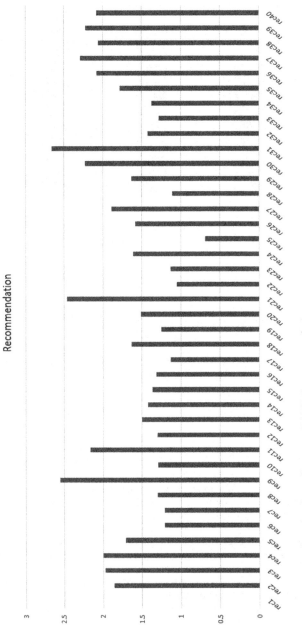

Figure 5.3 Analysis by Compliance to FATF Recommendations.

recent, accounting for the huge number of unlicensed casinos. Contrariwise, in Kenya and Zimbabwe, gambling is encouraged; however, its regulation is growing due to internal conflicts.[265]

This is particularly worrisome because they relate to actions and procedures which require the identification of customers domestically and across borders. This illustrates the need for more determined action on the side of non-financial sector regulators and supervisors. This also applies to recommendation 25, which requires countries to put in place measures to curb unlawful use of persons and legal arrangement by launderers. It states that 'countries should ensure that there is adequate, accurate and timely information on the beneficial ownership and control of legal persons that can be obtained or accessed in a timely fashion by competent authorities', indicating that specific actions are required to be taken by the government to support both regulatory bodies and FIs. That this is the lowest scoring recommendation shows the lackadaisical attitude of the authorities.

Surprisingly, the statistics reveal that the recommendation with the highest level of compliance in Africa is recommendation 31 on the power of law enforcement and investigative bodies, with a score of 2.7, well above the average of 1.66. This is followed by recommendation 9 on financial institution secrecy laws, with a score of 2.6. If this is correct, it can be interpreted to mean that financial secrecy laws are not inhibiting implementation. It is therefore paradoxical that the score on recommendation 25 on 'transparency and beneficial ownership' is low, given that beneficial ownership can only really thrive where there is financial secrecy. Compliance literature reveals that Africa's investigative and enforcement structures are weakly developed.[266] It is therefore worrisome when weakly developed areas are considered the most complied to by ACs.

CAVEATS

There are limitations associated with the general applicability of this study. Firstly, the FATF data quality is questionable, given that the data sources are usually gathered from national regulatory institutions subjected to limited regulation. Thus, recommendations are often interpreted in a manner that makes them appear compliant. Secondly, due to resource constraints, as regards finances and human capacity, intelligence and data supplied by these regulatory bodies may not reflect the accurate compliance level with the regulatory standards. Thirdly, only 37 countries have undertaken an MER, as opposed to 54 ACs. This indicates limited representativeness, illustrating the difficulties with undertaking a meaningful cross-country comparison using the limited sample of countries with published detailed assessments. Thus, the FATF's recommended course of action

---

265 Tonderayi Mukeredzi, 'Young Zimbabweans Warming up to Gambling' (*AfricaRenewal Online*) <http://www.un.org/africarenewal/web-features/young-zimbabweans-warming -gamblingaa > accessed 17 May 2015.

266 *Shehu* (n 168). *Whitaker* (n 83) 639, 655.

may not always be consistent with the trajectory of domestic law and any measurement for compliance is deficient.

Conclusion

Africa's socio-economic history reveals the effect of liberalisation on the African economy and the resulting diversity amongst countries. For ACs, liberalisation was premature and placed considerable pressure on their trade and finance. This worsened Africa's position within the global financial system as countries became more susceptible to external shock. Consequently, this led to inequality amongst countries in Africa, with certain banking and financial markets performing better than others. The rein of the colonial exploits, which had ingrained corruption, lack of political will and financial inequality in countries across Africa, further restricted the growth of markets, whilst facilitating illicit crimes.

Yet, Africa's response to combating illicit crimes was tailored to meeting international standards that did not recognise their challenges. This necessitated a home-grown approach that would preserve the sovereignty of ACs whilst remedying the democratic deficit at the international level. However, the APRM created by the AU was unable to meet with demands. This was due to its lack of enforcement powers, dependence on international bodies, procedural difficulties and the absence of a truly indigenous approach to curtailing illicit crimes.

Therefore, ACs have remained subject to international standards despite their compliance challenges. The FSAP and the FATF evaluation reports buttress this, as only seven countries achieved over 50% compliance rate, with only Egypt achieving over 60% but less than 70%. An examination of the compliance drivers within ACs as a function of legal and non-legal factors however illustrates that despite the drive to comply to evade sanctions, internal factors challenge compliance in ACs.

Albeit restricted in scope, it is hopeful that the recent AU partnership with the AfDB will improve compliance levels of ACs. However, the proper functioning of the AML/CFT regime in Africa would require a more active involvement of properly coordinated national regulatory bodies.

Further Reading

1. A.G. Hopkins, 'The New Economic History of Africa' [2009] 50 (2) *Journal of African History.*
2. Abayomi Mumuni, *Global Terrorism and Its Effects on Humanity* (Wsgf Pty Limited, 2016).
3. Abdullahi Shehu, *Strategies and Techniques of Prosecuting Economic and Financial Crimes* (GIABA Secretariat, 2012).
4. Abram Chayes and Antonia Handler Chayes, *The New Sovereignty: Compliance with International Regulatory Agreements* (Harvard University Press, 1995).
5. Adejoke Babington-Ashaye, 'The African Peer Review Mechanism at Ten: From Lofty Goals to Practical Implementation' (AfricLaw, 19 March 2013)

<http://africlaw.com/2013/03/19/the-african-peer-review-mechanism-at -ten-from-lofty-goals-to-practical-implementation/> accessed 10 May 2016.

6. AfDB, 'African Economic Outlook 2017' (AfDB, 2017) <https://www.afd b.org/fileadmin/uploads/afdb/Documents/Publications/AEO_2017_Repo rt_Full_English.pdf> accessed 18 October 2017.

7. AfDB, 'Africa Must Develop Relevant Knowledge for Its Problems' (AfDB, 2014) <http://www.afdb.org/en/news-and-events/article/africa-must-d evelop-relevant-knowledge-for-its-problems-13692/> accessed 16 April 2015.

8. AfDB, 'Financial Sector Integration in Three Regions of Africa' (AfDB, 2010) <https://www.afdb.org/fileadmin/uploads/afdb/Documents/Project-and -Operations/AfDB%20Regional%20Financial%20Integration%20REPORT _EN.pdf> accessed 19 October.

9. Agu Bertram Onyebuchi, Simon Nwankwo and Onwuka Ifeanyi Onuka, 'Combating Money Laundering and Terrorist Financing – The Nigerian Experience' [2016] 4 (1) *International Journal of Business and Law Research* 29, 35.

10. Alan Watson, *Legal Transplants: An Approach to Comparative Law* (Scottish Academic Press, 1974).

11. Alexandra Evans, 'The Utility of Informal Networks to Policy Makers' *in* David Martin Jones, Ann Lane and Paul Schulte (eds.) *Terrorism, Security and the Power of Informal Networks* (Edward Elgar, Cheltenham, 2010).

12. Aljazeera, 'Zimbabwe's Mugabe Signs New Constitution' (Aljazeera, 22 May 2013) <http://www.aljazeera.com/news/africa/2013/05/201352210501 5147596.html> accessed 10 May 2016.

13. Allen Franklin et al., 'The African Financial Development and Financial Inclusion Gaps' [2014] 23 (5) *Journal of African Economies.*

14. Amado Philip de Andre, 'Organized Crime, Drug Trafficking, Terrorism: The New Achilles' Heel of West Africa' (Fride, 2008) <http://fride.org/descarga/ COM_Achilles_heel_eng_may08.pdf> accessed 10 July 2016.

15. AML/CFT Evaluations and Assessments, 'Handbook for Countries and Assessors' (April 2009) <http://www.fatf-gafi.org/media/fatf/documents/ reports/Handbook%20for%20assessors.pdf> accessed 1 June 2015.

16. Andrea Lenschow, Duncan Liefferink and Sietske Veenman, 'When the Birds Sing. A Framework for Analyzing Domestic Factors behind Policy Convergence' [2005] 12 (5) *Journal of European Public Policy.*

17. Andrew Guzman, 'International Law: A Compliance Based Theory of International Law' [2002] 90 (6) *California Law Review.*

18. Anna Markovska and Nya Adams 'Political Corruption and Money Laundering: Lessons from Nigeria' [2015] 18 (2) *JMLC.*

19. Anne-Marie Slaughter, *A New World Order* (Princeton University Press, 2004).

20. Anne-Marie Slaughter, 'International Law in a World of Liberal States' [1995] 6 (3) *EJIL.*

21. Anthony Afful-Dadzie et al., 'Tracking Progress of African Peer Review Mechanism (APRM) Using Fuzzy Comprehensive Evaluation Method' [2014] 43 (8) *Kybermetes* 1193, 1169.

22. Antoinette Verhage, 'Between the Hammer and the Anvil? The Anti-Money Laundering-Complex and Its Interactions with the Compliance Industry' [2009] 52 *Crime Law Social Change.*

23. Appiah Koranteng, 'Evaluation Capacity in Ghana' (Workshop by the Development Bank of Southern Africa, the African Development Bank and the World Bank, Johannesburg, 2000).

24. APRM, 'Country Review Report of Nigeria: Country Review Report No 8' (African Peer Review Mechanism, June 2008) <http://www1.uneca.org/Por tals/aprm/Documents/CountryReports/Nigeria.pdf> accessed 10 July 2016.

25. AU and APRM, 'Revised Country Self-Assessment Questionnaire for the African Peer Review Mechanism' (AU and APRM) <http://aprm-au.org/a dmin/pdfFiles/aprm_questionnaire.pdf> accessed 10 July 2017.

26. AU and NEPAD, 'Guidelines for Countries to Prepare for and Participate in the African Peer Review Mechanism (APRM)' (AU and NEPAD, 2003) <http://www1.uneca.org/Portals/nepad/Documents/Guidelines-for-Countries -to-APRM.pdf > accessed 10 March 2015.

27. Basil Davidson, *The African Genius: An Introduction to African Social History* (Little, Brown and Company, 1969).

28. Beck Thorsten and Samuel Munzele Maimbo (eds.) *Financial Sector Development in Africa: Opportunities and Challenges* (World Bank Publications, 2012).

29. Benedict Kingsbury, 'The Concept of Compliance as a Function of Competing Conceptions of International Law' [1998] 19 *Michigan Journal of International Law*.

30. Benedicte Vibe Christensen, 'Financial Integration in Africa: Implications for Monetary Policy and Financial Stability' [2014] 76 *BIS Paper*.

31. Berliner Daniel, 'Follow Your Neighbor? Regional Emulation and the Design of Transparency Policies' (2013) KFG Working Paper 55, 17 <http://userpage .fu-berlin.de/kfgeu/kfgwp/wpseries/WorkingPaperKFG_55.pdf> accessed 10 May 2016.

32. Beth A. Simmons, 'Compliance with International Agreements' [1998] *Annual Review of Political Science*.

33. Beth A. Simmons and Zachary Elkins, 'The Globalisation of Liberalisation: Policy Diffusion in the International Political Economy' [2004] 98 (1) *American Political Science Review*.

34. Beth Elise Whitaker, 'Compliance among Weak States: Africa and the Counter Terrorism Regime' [2010] 36 *Review of International Studies*.

35. Biodun Olamosu and Andy Wynne, 'Africa Rising? The Economic History of Sub-Saharan Africa' (International Socialism, 2015) <http://isj.org.uk/africa-rising/#footnote-263-14> accessed 18 October 2017.

36. Bodansky, 'The Legitimacy of International Governance: A Coming Challenge for International Environmental Law?' [1999] 93 (3) *American Journal of International Law*.

37. Bolaji Akinola, *Authority Stealing: How Greedy Politicians and Corporate Executives Loot the World's Most Populous Black Nation* (AuthorHouse, 2012).

38. Boldwin Anugwara, 'Curbing Corruption in Banking Sector' (*Newswatch Times*, 22 March 2014) <http://www.mynewswatchtimesng.com/curbing -corruption-banking-sector/> accessed 5 May 2015.

39. Brian Cheffins, 'Does Law Matter? The Separation of Ownership and Control in the United Kingdom' (2000) *ERSC Centre for Business Research, University of Cambridge Working Paper 172* <https://www.cbr.cam.ac.uk/fileadmin/

user_upload/centre-for-business-research/downloads/working-papers/wp1 72.pdf> accessed 19 April 2015.

40. Brian Tamanaha, *On the Rule of Law: History, Politics Theory* (Cambridge University Press, 2004).

41. Clay Lowery, 'Unintended Consequences of Anti-Money Laundering Policies in Poor Countries – A CGD Working Group Report' (Centre for Global Development, 2015) <https://www.cgdev.org/sites/default/files/CGD -WG-Report-Unintended-Consequences-AML-Policies-2015.pdf> accessed 7 November 2017.

42. Charles Goredema and Anneli Botha, 'African Commitments to Combating Terrorism: A Review of Eight NEPAD Countries' (2004) *AHSI Paper 3.* African Human Initiative, Pretoria.

43. Chibuike Uche, 'Indigenous Banks in Colonial Nigeria' [2010] 43 (3) *The International Journal of African Historical Studies.*

44. Chibuike Ugochukwu Uche, 'Foreign Banks, Africans, and Credit in Colonial Nigeria, c. 1890–1912' [1999] 4 *Economic History Review, LII.*

45. Christopher J. Green, Colin Kirkpatrick and Victor Murinde, 'Finance for Small Enterprise Growth and Poverty Reduction in Developing Countries' [2016] 18 (7) *Journal of International Development.*

46. Chr. Michelsen Institute, 'Profiting from Corruption: The Role and Responsibility of Financial Institutions' [2009] 31 *U4 Brief.*

47. Concepcion Verdugo-Yepes, 'Compliance with the AML/CFT International Standard: Lessons from a Cross-Country Analysis' (2011) International Monetary Fund Working Paper WP/11/177, 6 <https://papers.ssrn.com/s ol3/papers.cfm?abstract_id=1899578> accessed 19 April 2015.

48. Cull Robert, Lemma Senbet and Macro Sorge, 'Deposit Insurance and Financial Development' (2005) World Bank Policy Research Working Paper 2682, 16 <http://documents.worldbank.org/curated/en/813041468739789102/ pdf/multi0page.pdf> accessed 18 November 2017.

49. Cyn-Young Park and Rogelio V. Mercado, 'Financial Inclusion, Poverty and Income Inequality in Developing Asia' (2015) *ADB Economics Working Paper Series 426,* 7 <https://www.adb.org/sites/default/files/publication/153143 /ewp-426.pdf> accessed 19 November 2017.

50. Damilola Oyedele, 'Egmont: Senate, House Disagree on NFIA as Threat of Nigeria's Expulsion Looms' (Thisday, 6 February 2018) <https://www.thi sdaylive.com/index.php/2018/02/06/egmont-senate-house-disagree-on -nfia-as-threat-of-nigerias-expulsion-looms/> accessed 11 February 2018.

51. Daniel Berowitz, Katharina Pistor and Jean-Francois Richard, 'Economic Development, Legality and the Transplant Effect' [2003] 41(1) *European Economic Review.*

52. Daniel W. Drezner, *All Politics is Global: Explaining International Regulatory Regime* (Princeton University Press, 2007).

53. Daphne Barak-Erez, 'The International Aspects of Comparative Law' [2008] 13 *Columbia Journal of East European Law.*

54. David Chaikin and Jason C. Sharman, *Corruption and Money Laundering: A Symbiotic Relationship* (Palgrave Macmillan, USA, 2009).

55. Dieter Kerwer and Rainer Hulsse, 'Explaining International Organizations: How International Organizations Rule the World: The Case of the Financial

Action Task Force on Money Laundering' [2011] 61 *UN Studies Association, Berlin.*

56. Doubell Chamberlain, Louis de Koker, Christine Hougaard, Rayn Short, Anja Smith and Richard Walker, 'Implementing FATF Standards in Developing Countries and Financial Inclusion: Findings and Guidelines' (First Initiative, 2008) <http://cenfri.org/documents/AML/AML_CFT%20and%20Financi al%20Inclusion.pdf> accessed 10 May 2015.

57. Edward Alpers, 'Rethinking African Economic History: A Contribution to the Discussion of the Roots of Under-Development' [1973] 3 (3) *Ufahamu A Journal of African Studies.*

58. Emmanuel Edukugho, 'Alamieyeseigha: Unpardonable Pardon' (*Vanguard*, 23 March 2013) <https://www.vanguardngr.com/2013/03/alamieyeseigha -unpardonable-pardon/> accessed 10 April 2015.

59. Eric Helleiner, 'State Power and the Regulation of Illicit Activity in Global Finance' *in* R.H. Friman and P. Andreas (eds.) *The Illicit Global Economy and State Power* (Rowman & Littlefield, Lanham, 1999).

60. Ericson Richard, 'Ten Uncertainties of Risk Management Approaches to Security' [2006] 48 (3) *Canadian Journal of Criminology and Criminal Justice.*

61. Faith Karimi, '24 Killed in Post-Election Violence in Kenya, Rights Group Says' (CNN, 13 August 2017)<http://edition.cnn.com/2017/08/12/africa/keny a-elections-protests/index.html> accessed 21 October 2017.

62. FATF, 'FATF Recommendation 10' (FATF, 2012) <http://www.fatf-gafi .org/media/fatf/documents/recommendations/pdfs/FATF%20Recommend ations%202012.pdf> accessed 10 February 2017.

63. FATF, 'FATF Recommendation 12, 13, 14, 15 and 16' (FATF, 2012) <http: //www.fatf-gafi.org/media/fatf/documents/recommendations/pdfs/FATF %20Recommendations%202012.pdf> accessed 10 February 2017.

64. FATF, 'FATF Recommendation 20 and 21' (FATF, 2012) <http://www .fatf-gafi.org/media/fatf/documents/recommendations/pdfs/FATF%20R ecommendations%202012.pdf> accessed 10 February 2017.

65. FATF, 'Mutual Evaluations' (FATF) <http://www.fatf-gafi.org/publications/ mutualevaluations/?hf=10&b=0&s=desc(fatf_releasedate) > accessed 5 January 2017.

66. FATF, 'Methodology for Assessing Technical Compliance with the FATF Recommendations and the Effectiveness of the AML/CFT Systems' (FATF, February 2013) <http://www.fatf-gafi.org/media/fatf/documents/meth odology/fatf%20methodology%2022%20feb%202013.pdf> accessed 21 May 2015.

67. FATF, 'Mutual Evaluations' (FATF) <http://www.fatf-gafi.org/topics/mut ualevaluations/ > accessed 1 June 2015.

68. FCA, 'FCA Fines Guaranty Trust Bank (UK) Ltd £525,000 for Failures in its Anti-Money Laundering Controls' (Financial Conduct Authority, 17 September 2013) <http://www.fca.org.uk/news/fca-fines-guaranty-trust-ban k-uk-ltd> accessed 21 March 2015.

69. Francis Fukuyama, 'Why is Democracy Performing So Poorly' [2015] 26 (1) *Journal of Democracy.*

70. Frank Vibert, 'Reforming International Rule Making' [2012] 3 (3) *Global Policy.*

71. Gandy Oscar Jr, 'Data Mining, Surveillance and Discrimination in the Post 9/11 Environment' *in* Kevin Haggerty and Richard Ericson (eds.) *The New Politics of Surveillance and Visibility* (UTP, Toronto, 2006) 381.
72. Garrett Geoffrey, 'Global Markets and National Politics: Collusion Course or Virtuous Circle?' [1998] 52 (4) *International Organization*.
73. George Klay Kieh and Kelechi Kalu, *West Africa and the U.S. War on Terror* (Routledge, Taylor & Francis Group, London, 2013).
74. GIABA, 'Annex to Nigeria 2nd Follow Up Report, Money Laundering Convictions' (GIABA) <https://www.giaba.org/media/f/305_Annexe> accessed 12 March 2015.
75. GIABA, 'Mutual Evaluation Report: Anti-Money Laundering and Combating the Financing of Terrorism: Nigeria (Inter-Governmental Action Group Against Money Laundering in West Africa, 2008) 95 <https://www.giaba .org/media/f/299_Mutual%20Evaluation%20Report%20of%20Nigeria.pdf> accessed 9 April 2015.
76. GIABA, 'Overview of GIABA Operations from 2004 to 2013' (GIABA, 2014) <https://www.giaba.org/media/f/693_599_GIABA-Overview-2004-2013 -English.pdf> accessed 10 July 2016.
77. GIABA Report, 'The Nexus Between Small Arms and Light Weapons and Money Laundering and Terrorist Financing in Africa' (GIABA, 2013) <https:/ /www.giaba.org/media/f/613_519_GIABA%20SALW%20Nexus-final.pdf> accessed 10 May 2015.
78. Gilles Favarel-Garrigues, Thierry Godefroy and Pierre Lascoumes, 'Reluctant Partners? Banks in the Fight against Money Laundering and Terrorism Financing in France' [2011] 42 (2) *Security Dialogue*.
79. Gomiluk Otokwala, 'Wither Family Shareholding in Developing Countries' (2010) available at SSRN 1714526.
80. Gregory Shaffer, *Transnational Legal Ordering and State Change* (Cambridge Studies in Law and Society, 2014).
81. Hameiri Shahar and Kanishka Jayasuriya, 'Regulatory Regionalism and the Dynamics of Territorial Politics: The Case of the Asia- Pacific Region' [2011] 59 Political Studies.
82. Hanafi A. Hammed and Sarinus E. Kabo, 'African Peer Review Mechanism and Crisis of Good Governance in Africa' [2013] 19 *Journal of Law, Policy and Globalization*.
83. Harold Hongju Koh, 'Review: Why Do Nations Obey International Law?' [1997] 106 (8) *The Yale Law Journal*.
84. Helen Milner, *Interest, Institutions and Information: Domestic Politics and International Relations* (Princeton University Press, 1997).
85. Hippolyte Fofack and Leonce Ndikumana, 'Capital Flight and Monetary Policy in African Countries' (2014) *Political Economy Research Institute, Working Paper Series 362*, 2 <https://www.africaportal.org/publications/capital-fligh t-and-monetary-policy-in-african-countries/> accessed 17 November 2016.
86. Humphrey P.B. Moshi, 'Fighting Money Laundering: The Challenges in Africa' [2007] 152 *Institute for Security Studies Papers*.
87. Ian Fletcher, Loukas Mistelis and Marise Cremona, (eds.) *Foundations and Perspectives of International Trade Law* (Sweet & Maxwell, London, 2001).
88. Illicit Financial Flows, 'Report of the High-Level Panel on Illicit Financial Flows from Africa' (Track it! Stop It! Get It!, 2014) <https://www.uneca.org/sites

/default/files/PublicationFiles/iff_main_report_26feb_en.pdf > accessed 20 October 2017.

89. IMF, 'Algeria: Financial System Stability Assessment' (IMF, June 2014) <https://www.imf.org/external/pubs/ft/scr/2014/cr14161.pdf.

90. IMF, 'IMF DataMapper: GDP Based on PPP, Share of World' (IMF World Economic Outlook Database, April 2017) <http://www.imf.org/external /datamapper/PPPSH@WEO/OEMDC/WEOWORLD/ADVEC/MAE> accessed 10 October 2017.

91. IMF, 'International Standards on Combating Money Laundering and the Financing of Terrorism & Proliferation' (The FATF Recommendations, February 2012) <http://www.fatf-gafi.org/media/fatf/documents/reco mmendations/pdfs/fatf_recommendations.pdf> accessed 20 April 2015.

92. IMF, 'World Economic Outlook: Subdued Demand, Symptoms and Remedies' (IMF, October 2016) <http://www.imf.org/external/pubs/ft/weo/2016/ 02/#front> accessed 18 October 2017.

93. Imogen Nash, 'Why Financial Institutions Based in Africa Should Have Robust Compliance Systems in Place' (Accuity, 10 August 2016) <https://accuity .com/accuity-insights-blog/why-financial-institutions-based-in-africa-should -have-robust-compliance-systems-in-place/> accessed 7 November 2017.

94. GIABA, 'Mutual Evaluation Report: Anti-Money Laundering and Combating the Financing of Terrorism: Nigeria (Inter-Governmental Action Group Against Money Laundering in West Africa, 2008) 95 <https://www.giaba .org/media/f/299_Mutual%20Evaluation%20Report%20of%20Nigeria.pdf> accessed 9 April 2015.

95. IMF, 'Anti-Money Laundering and Combating the Financing of Terrorism (AML/CFT) Report on the Review of the Effectiveness of the Program' (IMF, 11 May 2011) <http://www.imf.org/external/np/pp/eng/2011/051111. pdf> accessed 11 May 2015.

96. Jackkie Cilliers, 'Peace and Security Through Good Governance? A Guide to the NEPAD African Peer Review Mechanism' [2003] 70 *Pretoria: Institute for Security Studies.*

97. James Fenske, 'The Causal History of Africa: A Response to Hopkins' [2010] 25 (2) Economic History of Developing Regions.

98. Jan Mcmillen, 'Online Gambling: Challenges to National Sovereignty and Regulation' [2000] 18 (4) Prometheus 391–410.

99. Jason C. Sharman, 'Power and Policy Diffusion: Anti-Money Laundering in Developing States' [2008] 52 (3) International Studies Quarterly.

100. Jason C. Sharman, 'The Bark is the Bite: International Organizations and Blacklisting' [2009] 16 (4) Review of International Political Economy.

101. Jeanne Giraldo and Harold Trinkunas, *Terrorist Financing and State Responses: A Comparative Perspective* (SUP, 2007).

102. John Mearsheimer, 'The False Promise of International Institutions' [1994– 1995] 19 (3) International Security.

103. Jubril Olabode Aka, *Blacks Greatest Homeland (IUniverse, 2006) 210; Jubril Olabode Aka, Great Presidents of Nigeria 4th Republic* (Trafford Publishing, 2012).

104. Julia Black, 'Constructing and Contesting Legitimacy and Accountability in Polycentric Regulatory Regimes' (2008) *LSE Law, Society and Economy Working Papers* <http://www.lse.ac.uk/law/people/academic-staff/julia-bl ack/Documents/black2.pdf> accessed 10 March 2015.

105. Julia Black, Martyn Hopper and Christa Band, 'Making a Success of Principles-Based Regulation' [2007] 1 (3) Law and Financial Markets Review 191–204.

106. Jun Tang and Lishan Ai, 'Combating Money Laundering in Transition Countries: The Inherent Limitations and Practical Issues' [2010] 13 (3) Journal of Money Laundering Control 215–225.

107. Kanbur Ravi, 'The African Peer Review Mechanism (APRM): An Assessment of Concept and Design' [2004] 31 (2) Politikon.

108. Karen McVeigh and Kate Hodal, 'Rule of Law Declines for 70% of Africans over Past Decade, Warns Ibrahim Index' (*The Guardian*, 3 October 2016) <https://www.theguardian.com/global-development/2016/oct/03/rule-o f-law-declines-70-per-cent-africans-over-past-decade-ibrahim-index-governan ce> accessed 9 November 2017.

109. Karen Odhiambo, 'Evaluation Capacity Development in Kenya' (Paper Presented at the Workshop Organized by the Development Bank of Southern Africa, the African Development Bank and the World Bank, Johannesburg. 2000).

110. K.O. Dike, *Trade and Politics in the Niger Delta* (Oxford University Press, 1956).

111. KPMG, 'Africa AML Survey 2012' (*KPMG*) <https://www.kpmg.com/ZA /en/IssuesAndInsights/ArticlesPublications/Financial-Services/Documents/ KPMG%202012%20Africa%20Anti-Money%20Laundering%20Survey.pdf> accessed 1 June 2015.

112. KPMG, 'Global Anti-Money Laundering Survey 2011, How Banks Are Facing up to the Challenge' (*KPMG*, 2011) <https://www.kpmg.com/UK/en/ IssuesAndInsights/ArticlesPublications/Documents/PDF/Advisory/global -aml-survey-2011-main-report.pdf> accessed 2 June 2015.

113. Leigh Gardner, 'Was Independence Really Better Than Colonial Rule? A Comparative Study of Liberia and Sierra Leone' [2013].

114. Leonard Seabrooke and Eleni Tsiongou, 'Revolving Doors and Linked Ecologies in the World Economy: Policy Locations and the Practice of International Financial Reform' (2009) *CSRG Working Paper 260/09*, 15 <https://warwick.ac.uk/fac/soc/pais/research/researchcentres/csgr/papers /workingpapers/2009/26009.pdf> accessed 10 July 2015.

115. Lemma W. Senbet and Isaac Otchere, *African Stock Markets* (*IMF*, 2008) <https://www.imf.org/external/np/seminars/eng/2008/afrfin/pdf/senbet .pdf> accessed 20 October 2017.

116. Liliana Rojas-Suarez, 'Risk and Capital Flight in Developing Countries' (1990) IMF Working Paper 0440, 15 <https://www.cgdev.org/doc/experts/Risk_C ap_Flight_Dev_Countries.pdf> accessed 19 November 2016.

117. *Mail & Guardian*, Africa's Best Read, 'Nigeria A Risky Prospect for South African Banks' (*Mail & Guardian*, 31 August 2005) <http://mg.co.za/article /2005-08-31-nigeria-a-risky-prospect-for-sa-banks> accessed 12 March 2015.

118. Marco Arnone and Pier Carlo Padone, 'Anti-Money Laundering by International Institutions: A Preliminary Assessment' [2008] 26 (3) European Journal of Law and Economics.

119. Margaret Rouse, 'Anti-Money Laundering Software (AML)' (Tech Target) <http://searchfinancialsecurity.techtarget.com/definition/anti-money-la undering-software-AML> accessed 15 April 2015.

120. María Paula Reyes Gaitán, The Challenges of Legal Transplants in a Globalized Context: A Case Study on "Working" Examples' (2014) Dissertation, University of Warwick.

121. Mariano-Florentino Cueller, 'The Tenuous Relationship Between the Fight Against Money Laundering and the Disruption of Criminal Finance' [2003] 93 (2) *Journal of Criminal Law and Criminology*.

122. Mark C. Suchman, 'Managing Legitimacy: Strategic and Institutional Approaches' [1995] 20 (3) *Academy of Management Review*.

123. Marwan Haruna Abdulkarim, 'The Nigerian Banking Revolution' <http://www.gamji.com/article8000/NEWS8790.htm> accessed 10 March 2017.

124. Michaela Erbenova, Yan Liu et al., 'The Withdrawal of Correspondent Banking Relationships: A Case for Policy Action' (IMF Staff Discussion Note, 2016) <https://www.imf.org/external/pubs/ft/sdn/2016/sdn1606.pdf> accessed 10 January 2017.

125. Michael Imeson and Alastair Sim, 'Regulation and Your Reputation' *White Paper* <http://www.sas.com/resources/whitepaper/wp_24359.pdf> accessed 1 June 2015.

126. Mohamed Sultan, 'How Illicit Financial Flows Drain African Economies' (*Open Society Foundations*, 21 April 2014) <https://www.opensocietyfoundat ions.org/voices/how-illicit-financial-flows-drain-african-economies> accessed 20 October 2017.

127. Monica Mark, 'Obiageli Ezekwesili: When They Took The Girls, Our Government Went Under' (*The Guardian*, 28 December 2014) <http://www .theguardian.com/world/2014/dec/28/obiageli-ezekwesili-bring-back-our-girls-boko-haram-school-kidnapping> accessed 12 May 2015.

128. Musonda Simwayi and Muhammed Haseed, 'The Role of Financial Intelligence Units in Combating Money Laundering: A Comparative Analysis of Zambia, Zimbabwe and Malawi' [2011] 15 (1) Journal of Money Laundering Control.

129. Nathan Nunn, 'The Long-term Effects of Africa's Slave Trades' [2008] 123 (1) The Quarterly Journal of Economics.

130. Navin Beekarry, 'The International Anti-Money Laundering and Combatting the Financing of Terrorism Regulatory Strategy: A Critical Analysis of Compliance Determinants in International Law' [2010] 31 Northwestern Journal of International Law & Business.

131. NEPAD Secretariat, 'African Peer Review Mechanism Organization and Process' (NEPAD Secretariat, 2003) <http://www1.uneca.org/Portals/ aprm/Documents/book4.pdf> accessed 10 May 2016.

132. NEPAD Secretariat, 'NEPAD/ HSGIC/03-2003/APRM/Guideline/OSCI, 6th Summit of the NEPAD Heads of State and Government Implementation Committee; Nigeria Objectives, Standards, Criteria and Indicators for the African Peer Review Mechanism' (NEPAD Secretariat, 2003) <http://www.chr.up.ac .za/chr_old/hr_docs/arpm/docs/book5.pdf> accessed 20 July 2015.

133. Ngozi Okonjo Iweala, *Reforming the Unreformable: Lessons from Nigeria* (The MIT Press, Cambridge, MA, 2012).

134. Nnenna Ibeh, 'America Bans Owners of Amigo Supermarket, Wonderland Amusement Park over Alleged Terrorist Activities' (*Premium Times*, 15 June 2015) <http://www.premiumtimesng.com/news/top-news/177962-amer ica-bans-owners-of-amigo-supermarket-wonderland-amusement-park-over-all eged-terrorist-activities.html> accessed March 7 2015.

135. Njeri Wangari, 'Kenyans Fear a Possible Internet Shutdown During 2017 Presidential Election' (*Mail & Guardian Africa*, 16 January 2017) <http://

mgafrica.com/article/2017-01-16-kenyans-fear-a-possible-internet-shutdown -during-2017-presidential-election> accessed 10 May 2017.

136. Norton Rose Fulbright, 'Prominence of Money Laundering in Africa, 10 Things to KNOW' (*Norton Rose Fulbright*, February 2014) <http://www.nort onrosefulbright.com/knowledge/publications/113161/prominence-of-m oney-laundering-in-africa-br-ten-things-to-know> accessed 1 June 2015.

137. Oran R. Young, *Compliance with Public Authority* (JHUP, Baltimore, 1979).

138. Otaviano Canuto and Veronica Ramcharan, 'De-Risking is De-Linking Small States from Global Finance' (*HuffPost*) <https://www.huffingtonpost.com /otaviano-canuto/de-risking-is-de-linking_b_8357342.html> accessed 11 March 2017.

139. Patrick Bond, 'Removing Neo-colonialism's APRM Mask: A Critique of the African Peer Review Mechanism' [2009] 36 (122) Review of African Political Economy.

140. Paul Kupiec, 'The IMF-World Bank Financial Sector Assessment Program: A View from the Inside' *in* Douglas D. Evanoff and George G. Kaufman (eds.) *Systematic Financial Crisis, Resolving Large Bank Insolvencies* (World Scientific, Canada, 2005).

141. Peter Reuter (ed.), *Draining Development? Controlling Flows of Illicit Funds from Developing Countries* (The World Bank, 2012).

142. Peter Romaniuk, 'Institutions as Swords and Shields: Multilateral Counter-Terrorism Since 9/11' [2010] 36 Review of International Studies.

143. Peter Shivute, 'The Rule of Law in Sub-Saharan Africa – An Overview' [2009] Human Rights and the Rule of Law in Namibia 213, 213.

144. Pierre Legrand, 'The Impossibility of "Legal Transplants"' [1997] 4 Masstricht Journal of European and Comparative Law.

145. Pius Okigbo, 'Problem, Crisis or Catastrophe: Any Exit for African Economies in the 1990s?' [1993] 3 *Nigerian National Merit Award Lectures* (Fountain Publications).

146. *Premium Times*, 'Sanusi Lamido Explodes: How Vested Interests are Killing Nigeria' (*Premium Times*, 13 January 2014) <https://www.premiumtimesn g.com/news/153212-sanusi-lamido-explodes-how-vested-interests-are-killing -nigeria.html> accessed 10 March 2016.

147. Sphiwe Nzimande, Stephen Louw, Clement Mannya, Adheera Bodasing and Astrid Ludin, *Review of the South African Gambling Industry and its Regulation, a Report Prepared by the Gambling Review Commission – Final Report Submitted to the Minister of Trade and Industry* (September 2010).

148. Rachel Mukamunana and J.O. Kuye, 'Revisiting the African Peer Review Mechanism: The Case for Leadership and Good Governance in Africa' [2005] 3 (40) JPA.

149. Rainer Hulsse, 'Even Clubs Can't Do Without Legitimacy: Why the Anti-Money Laundering Blacklist Was Suspended' [2008] 2 (4) Regulation and Governance.

150. Ralph Orlowski, 'Commerzbank Fined $1.5bn for Doing Business With Sanctioned Iran and Sudan' (*RT*, 13 March 2015) <http://rt.com/business /240353-commerzbank-billion-fine-sanctions/> accessed 14 May 2015.

151. Randall L. Pouwels, *The African and Middle Eastern World, 600–1500* (Oxford University Press, 2005).

152. Robert O. Keohnane, *After Hegemony: Cooperation and Discord in the World Political Economy* (Princeton University Press, 1984).

153. Roberto Saviano, 'The Real Threat to Britain's Borders is the Flow of Dirty Money' (*The Guardian*, 23 June 2016) <https://www.theguardian.com/commentisfree/2016/jun/23/real-threat-britain-borders-flow-dirty-money-eu> accessed 20 October 2017.

154. Ronald B. Mitchell, 'Regime Design Matters: International Oil Pollution and Treaty Compliance' [1994] 48 (3) International Organizations.

155. Ronald H. Mynhardt and Johan Marx, 'Anti-Money Laundering Recommendations for Cash Based Economies in West Africa' [2013] 11 (1) Corporate Ownership and Control.

156. Ross Herbert and Steven Gruzd, 'Taking Stock of the African Peer Review Mechanism' [2007] 41 (1) *SAJIA*.

157. Ross Herbert, 'Becoming my Brother's Keeper' [2003] 1. *E-Africa: EJGI.*

158. Ross Levine, 'Finance and Growth: Theory and Evidence' (2004) *NBER Working Paper Series 10766*, 84 <http://www.nber.org/papers/w10766.pdf> accessed 19 November 2017.

159. Sabrina Alkire, Christoph Jindra, Gisela Robles and Ana Vaz, 'Multidimensional Poverty in Africa' (OPHI Briefing 40, 2016) <http://www.ophi.org.uk/wp-content/uploads/Global-MPI-2016-8-pager.pdf> accessed 18 October 2017.

160. Sani Turkur, 'Nigerian Banks Aid Corruption – EFCC' (*Premium Times*, 10 September 2012) <http://www.premiumtimesng.com/business/99682-nigerian-banks-aid-corruption-efcc.html> accessed 3 June.

161. 'Senator Ndume Contacted Boko Haram Leader 73 Times In One Month Says SSS' – *Premium Times* (Sahara Reporters, 12 December 2012) <http://saharareporters.com/2012/12/12/senator-ndume-contacted-boko-haram-leader-73-times-one-month-says-sss-premium-times> accessed 12 April 2015.

162. Shahar Hameiri and Lee Jones, 'Regulatory Regionalism and Anti-Money Laundering Governance in Asia' [2014] 69 (2) *Australian Institute of International Affairs.*

163. S. Ibi Ajayi, 'Capital Flight and Economic Development in Africa' [2014] 55 *Capital Flight from Africa: Causes, Effects and Policy Issues.*

164. Sojin Lim, 'Compliance with International Norms: Implementing the OECD DAC Principles in South Korea' [2014] 11 (6) *Globalization.*

165. Sommet Kananaskis Summit Canada, 'G8 Africa Action Plan' (Sommet Kananskis Summit, 2002) <http://www.owen.org/wp-content/uploads/G8-AAA.pdf> accessed 11 April 2015.

166. Swift, 'Addressing the Unintended Consequences of De-Risking – Focus on Africa' (Swift, Information Paper, August 2016) <https://www.swift.com/node/35121> accessed 10 March 2017.

167. Swift, 'De-risking in Africa on the Rise, according to Latest SWIFT Data' (*Swift*, 24 August 2016) <https://www.swift.com/insights/press-releases/de-risking-in-africa-on-the-rise_according-to-latest-swift-data> accessed 10 March 2017.

168. Tam Christian, 'Enforcement' *in* G. Ulfsein, T. Marauhn and A. Zimmermann (eds.) *Making Treaties Work* (Cambridge University Press, Cambridge, 2007).

169. Thankdika Mkandawire and Charles C. Soludo (eds.) *Our Continent, Our Future: African Perspectives on Structural Adjustment* (Codesria, 1999).

170. The Commonwealth, 'Disconnecting from Global Finance: The Impact of AML/CFT Regulations on Commonwealth Developing Countries' (*The*

Commonwealth, 2016) <http://thecommonwealth.org/sites/default/files/inline/DisconnectingfromGlobalFinance2016.pdf> accessed 10 March 2017.

171. *The Economist*, 'A Crackdown on Financial Crime Means Global Bank Are De-risking' (*The Economist*, 8 July 2017) <https://www.economist.com/news/international/21724803-charities-and-poor-migrants-are-among-hardest-hit-crackdown-financial-crime-means> accessed 10 August 2017.

172. *The Economist*, 'Democracy Index 2016: Revenge of the "Deplorables"' (A Report by The Economist Intelligence Unit, 2016) <http://felipesahagun.es/wp-content/uploads/2017/01/Democracy-Index-2016.pdf> accessed 11 November 2017.

173. *The Economist*, 'Hopeless Africa' (*The Economist*, 11 May 2000) <http://www.economist.com/node/333429> accessed 20 October 2017.

174. *The Economist*, 'The Heart of the Matter' (*The Economist*, 11 May 2000) <http://www.economist.com/node/333437> accessed 20 October 2017.

175. *The Guardian*, 'Africa Losing Billions from Fraud and Tax Avoidance' (*The Guardian*, 2 February 2015) <https://www.theguardian.com/global-development/2015/feb/02/africa-tax-avoidance-money-laundering-illicit-financial-flows> accessed 20 October 2017.

176. *The Guardian*, 'U.S. May Probe Nigerian Banks over Terror Funding' (*The Guardian*, 2014) <http://theguardianmobile.com/readNewsItem1.php?nid=29350> accessed 12 April 2015.

177. Theophilous Chiviru, 'Panama Papers Reveal Africa Losing Billions to Corruption and Bribery' (One.org, 16 August 2016) <https://www.one.org/international/blog/panama-paper-reveals-africa-losing-billions-to-corruption-and-bribery/> accessed 19 October 2017.

178. The United Nations Convention against Illicit Traffic in Narcotic Drugs and Psychotropic Substances (1988) <https://www.unodc.org/pdf/convention_1988_en.pdf> accessed 10 July 2016.

179. The World Bank, 'The World Bank in Africa' (*The World Bank*, 2017) <http://www.worldbank.org/en/region/afr/overview> accessed 18 October 2017.

180. TI, 'Corruption Perception Index 2014' (TI) <https://www.transparency.org/cpi2014/results> accessed 10 July 2016.

181. TI, 'Corruption Perceptions Index 2016' (TI, 25 January 2017) <https://www.transparency.org/whatwedo/publication/corruption_perceptions_index_2016> accessed 19 October 2017.

182. TI, 'When Immunity Becomes a License to Break the Law' (Transparency International, 29 April 2013) <https://www.transparency.org/news/feature/when_immunity_becomes_a_licence_to_break_the_law> accessed 10 July 2017.

183. Tonderayi Mukeredzi, 'Young Zimbabweans Warming up to Gambling' (*AfricaRenewal Online*) <http://www.un.org/africarenewal/web-features/young-zimbabweans-warming-gambling> accessed 17 May 2015.

184. G.M. Ukertor and A.G. Gabriel, 'African Peer Review Mechanism: Nigeria's Democracy and Good Governance' [2009] 7 (1) *Journal of Research National Development*.

185. Walter Rodney *How Europe Underdeveloped Africa* (Bogle-L'Ouverture Publications, 1972).

186. William F. Wechsler, 'Follow the Money' (*Foreign Affairs*, 2001) <https://www.foreignaffairs.com/articles/2001-07-01/follow-money> accessed 10 May 2015.

187. William Lawrence, 'Money Laundering Compliance for Africa?' (*bbrief*, 9 June 2017) <https://www.bbrief.co.za/2017/06/09/money-laundering-complia nce-africa/> accessed 10 July 2017.

188. World Bank and IMF Global Dialogue Series, *Anti-Money Laundering and Combating the Financing of Terrorism – Regional Videoconference: Anglophone West Africa Region – The Gambia, Ghana, Nigeria and Sierra Leone* (World Bank and IMF Global Dialogue Series) <http://documents.worldbank.org /curated/en/620291468751786123/pdf/271830Anti1money0launderi ng00West0Africa.pdf> accessed 15 May 2017.

189. World Bank, 'World Development Report 2011: Conflict, Security and Development' (The World Bank, 2011) 264 <https://siteresources.worldban k.org/INTWDRS/Resources/WDR2011_Full_Text.pdf> accessed 10 July 2016.

190. World Justice Project, 'Rule of Law Index' (World Justice Project, 2016). <https://worldjusticeproject.org/sites/default/files/documents/RoLI_Final -Digital_0.pdf> accessed 9 November 2017.

191. Zoe Lester, 'Risk Management and the Risk Attached to Money Laundering and Terrorist Financing' (Money Laundering Risk Conference, Sydney, July 2006).

6 Anti-Money Laundering and Counter-Terrorist Financing (AML/CFT) Regime

Compliance within Emerging Economies (EE)

Introduction

The BRICS economies (Brazil, Russia, India, China and South Africa) have created newer inequalities of power and influence regionally and globally. Although inherently diverse in terms of socio-economic and political structures, the BRICS's agreement is perceived as a threat to the existing international financial institutions (IFIs). This is particularly due to the BRICS's accelerating economic progression. Resultantly, the BRICS were conferred the Financial Action Task Force (FATF) membership to drive compliance regionally, whilst facilitating financial stability. However, compliance drivers within the BRICS indicate a possible misalignment between the expectations of the FATF and the reality of the BRICS to deliver on compliance. Consequently, the extent to which the BRICS membership translates to improved compliance and perception of legitimacy is debatable.

The first section provides a brief background to the BRICS and their emergence as an economic bloc. It highlights the BRICS's interrelationship with reference to their socio-economic and political position with the United States. The second section focuses on the inclusion of the BRICS as FATF members, examining whether such inclusion, however belated, propelled improved compliance with the FATF recommendations. The third section examines determinants of BRICS's compliance with the FATF's standards, through the lens of legal and non-legal factors, that may be internal or external to emerging economies (EEs). The fifth section draws the strands together.

Background to BRICS Countries

Although recognised as developing countries by Kenny Chiu and Dominic Wilson et al.,[1] Lord Jim O'Neil accorded the BRICS the status of 'emerging

---

1 Kenny Chiu, 'Analysis of the Economic Development Prospects of BRICS Countries' (*ENSafrica*, 28 July 2014) <http://www.mondaq.com/southafrica/x/330536/international+trade+investment/Analysis+Of+The+Economic+Development+Prospects+Of+BRICS+Count

economies' given their economic growth.[2] The global power and influence that EEs wield justifies such status. EEs house a large percentage of the world's publicly owned banks and account for about 40% of the world's population.[3] China is recognised as the world factory, Brazil as the raw material base, Russia as a hub of petrol, India as the white-collar centre and South Africa as a resource reservoir.[4] Collectively, the BRICS account for 30% of global GDP[5] and control 43% of global foreign exchange reserves.[6] Admittedly, these features distinguish the BRICS from developing countries that have low GDP, underdeveloped industries and low standard of living levels.[7]

Given the characteristics and stage of development of BRICS,[8] the implications are that they are already creating newer inequalities of power and influence in relation to smaller or developing African and Asian states.[9] Additionally, the BRICS are attempting to checkmate Western supremacy through their augmented position in the global economy. The financial crisis catalysed this agenda, stimulating investors looking for alternative investment destinations to diversify their portfolio into the BRICS,[10] thereby amplifying their position within the global economy and IFIs/Trans-governmental Networks (TGNs).

ries> accessed 23 February 2016; Dominic Wilson and Roopa Purushothaman, 'Dreaming with BRICs: the Path to 2050' [2003] 99 Global Economic Paper 1, 3.

2 Jim O'Neil, 'Building Better Global Economic BRICs' [2001] 66 Global Economics Paper S.04; Ellen Brown, 'Just who is Responsible for Deregulation?' (*Illusion2Reality at* www.moreyroots.co.uk, 5 September 2015) <http://www.moneyroots.co.uk/#!the-banksters/c1ny7> accessed 23 February 2016; Gillian Tett, 'The Story of the BRICs' (*Financial Times,* 15 January 2010) <https://next.ft.com/content/112ca932-00ab-11df-ae8d-00144fea bdc0 > accessed 15 May 2016; Leslie Armijo, 'The BRICs Countries (Brazil, Russia, India and China) as Analytical Category: Mirage or Insight?' [2007] 31 (4) Asian Perspective 1, 2; *Wilson and Purushothaman* (n 1)1, 3.

3 Leszek Niewdana, *Money and Justice: A Critique of Modern Money and Banking System from the Perspective of Aristotelian and Scholastic Thoughts* (1st Published, Routledge Taylor & Francis Group 2015) 140.

4 Pavnesh Kuman, 'BRICS: The Rise of Sleeping Giant' [2013] 2 (1) Voice of Research 66, 66.

5 BRICS Russia UFA 2015, 'BRICS Reach 30 Percent of Global GDP' (*BRICS RUSSIA UFA,* 7 July 2015) <http://en.brics2015.ru/news/20150707/277026.html> accessed 23 February 2016.

6 Van Agtmael 'Think Again: The BRICS' (*Foreign Policy,* 8 October 2012) <http://foreignp olicy.com/2012/10/08/think-again-the-brics/> accessed 21 May 2016.

7 The World Bank, 'Data: World Bank Country and Lending Groups', (*The World Bank,* 2018) <https://datahelpdesk.worldbank.org/knowledgebase/articles/906519-world-bank-coun try-and-lending-groups> accessed 2 February 2018.

8 Mohsin Habib & Leon Zurawwicki, 'Corruption in Large Developing Economies: The Brazil, Russia, India and China' *in* Subhash Jain (eds.) *Emerging Economies and the Transformation of International Business – Brazil, Russia, India and China* (BRICs) (Edward Elgar, Cheltenham, UK, 2006) 452.

9 Robert Holton, *Global Inequalities* (1st Published, Macmillan Palgrave, 2014) 20; European Parliament, Directorate-General for External Policies, *The Role of BRICS in the Developing World* (European Parliament, 2012) 34.

10 *Tett* (n 2).

However, the BRICS's political disconnect has raised concerns that their clustering as EEs was an awkward fusion.[11] The BRICS have individual and divergent political ambitions[12] somewhat linked to the United States (US). The strategic triangular relationship between India, China and the United States epitomises the US link, which, although tense, is necessary to combat terrorism occasioned by financial liberalisation.[13] The strains in the relationship are evident in differences between China and the US on issues such as human rights, product pirating and unfair trading practices.[14] The US-India relationship is equally strained, given India's opposition to the US movement against communism and the US's subsequent uncertainties about India's nuclear programme.[15] Despite their differences, India and China are mending fences to develop stronger ties, but the US remains uncomfortable with these developments.[16]

As protagonists of the cold war, the historical disagreements between Russia and the US were deepened by the US-led North Atlantic Treaty Organisation (NATO) alliance to combat the Soviet Union,[17] a recognised nuclear superpower.[18] More recently, the US alliance against Russia facilitated its suspension from the Group of Eight (G8), given Russia's annexation of Crimea.[19] Consequently,

---

11 Vidya Nadkarni, 'Introduction' *in* Vidya Nadkarni and Norma C. Noonan, *Emerging Powers in a Comparative Perspective: The Political and Economic Rise of the BRIC* (First published 2012, Bloomsbury 2013) 3.; Colin Sparks, 'How Coherent is the BRICS Grouping' *in* Kaarle Nordenstreng and Daya Kishan Thussu (eds.) *Mapping BRICS Media* (Routeledge 2015). This fusion was faulted for excluding South Africa, given its economic prominence in Africa. South Africa was later added in 2010, a move opposing scholars perceived as a mismatch. Even with South Africa's sophisticated financial service base, its GDP of $351 billion has undermined its global economic growth drive – see Frank William, 'International Business Challenge: Does Adding South Africa Finally Make the BRIC Countries Relevant' [2013] 12 (1) Journal of International Business Research 1, 5; Economic Development & Growth in Ethekwini, 'Building Better BRICS: South Africa's Inclusion into the Bloc' (*Ethekwini Municipality*, 2012) <http://www.durban.gov.za/Resource_Centre/edge/Documents/Building%20Better%20BRICS%20-%20South%20Africa%27s%20Inclusion%20into%20the%20Bl.pdf> accessed 10 May 2016.

12 *Nadkarni* (n 11) 3.

13 Ananya Chatterjee, 'India-China-United States: The Post-Cold War Evolution of a Strategic Triangle' [2011] 5 (3) Political Perspectives 74, 75.

14 Ibid.

15 Ibid.

16 Tridivesh Maini, 'What the US Gets Wrong about India's Relationship with China' (*The Diplomat*, March 13 2016) <http://thediplomat.com/2016/03/what-the-us-gets-wrong-about-indias-relationship-with-china/> accessed 13 May 2016.

17 Pravdu Ru, 'NATO: Built Against USSR, doomed to Lose Battle Against Russia' (*Pradu Ru*, 2016) <http://www.pravdareport.com/news/world/europe/05-04-2016/134065-nato_bloc-0/> accessed 21 May 2016.

18 Jim Nichol, 'Russian Political, Economic and Security Issues and U.S Interests' (Congressional Research Service, 31 March 2014) <https://fas.org/sgp/crs/row/RL33407.pdf> accessed 21 May 2016.

19 Oleg Remizov, 'Discourses and Emotions in Narration of the Annexation of Crimean Peninsula by the Russian Federation' (Master's Thesis, University of Tartu 2015); Braun Aurel,

Russia has intensified its political and trade agreement with China.[20] However, Russia has shown little evidence that it intends to backtrack on its human rights stance, which the United States disagrees with.[21] However, the United States and Russia work together to counter global terrorism.[22]

Brazil and South Africa have dissimilar relationships with the United States. Although historically perceived to be pro-American given its role in the Second World War, Brazil has had a relatively distant relationship with the United States and is currently seeking equality with the United States.[23] However, South Africa (SA) has a unique relationship with the United States given its influence in combating apartheid.[24] The United States and SA have also maintained bilateral trade agreements,[25] despite their diplomatic minefield on issues such as SA's oil trade with Iran[26] and the recently resolved poultry import duties.[27] Additionally, SA depends on the United States for aid.[28] Conversely, Brazil has minimal aid

---

'Tougher Sanctions Now: Putin's Delusional Quest for Empire' [2014] 177 (2) World Affairs 34, 40.

20 Mark Katz, 'The Big Winner form Ukraine Crisis? China' (*Fareed Zakaria GPS, Special to CNN*, 6 June 2014) <http://globalpublicsquare.blogs.cnn.com/2014/06/06/the-big-w inner-from-ukraine-crisis-china/>accessed 21 April 2016.

21 For instance, banning of gay marriages.

22 US DoS, 'Country Reports on Terrorism 2012' (*US DoS Publication*, May 2013) <https ://www.state.gov/documents/organization/210204.pdf> accessed 30 May 2016; Brazil and China have become partners in commodity trading, allowing Brazil to triangulate U.S. interest in the region with China. It also reduced U.S. leverage in the region, given china's willingness to finance projects and engage with leaders therefore acting outside the previous hemispheric consensus. See Eric Farnsworth, 'America Must Take Brazil Seriously' (*The National Interest*, June 15, 2015) <http://nationalinterest.org/feature/america-must-take -brazil-seriously-13111?page=2> accessed 1 January 2016.

23 Giselle Datz and Joel Peters, 'Brazil and the Israeli-Palestinian Conflict in the New Century: Between Ambition, Idealism and Pragmatism' [2013] 2 (2) Journal of Foreign Affairs 1, 12; Luiz Bandeira, 'Brazil and the United States: From Dependency to Equality' (*Open Democracy*, 20 November 2003) <https://www.opendemocracy.net/democracy-americanpower/ article_1599.jsp> accessed 10 January 2017.

24 Christopher McCoy, 'America's Role in the End of South African Apartheid' [2011] Journal of International Affairs at UCSD <https://prospectjournal.org/2011/10/21/americas-ro le-in-the-end-of-south-african-apartheid/> accessed 13 January 2017.

25 Such as the Trade and Investment Framework Agreement (TIFA) and other agreements backed by the Africa Growth and Opportunity Act (AGOA).

26 Scott Firsing, 'A New "Rough Patch" in U.S.-South Africa Relations' (*International Policy Digest*, 4 May 2012) <https://intpolicydigest.org/2012/05/04/a-new-rough-patch-in-u -s-south-africa-relations/> accessed 13 January 2017.

27 William Watson, 'Antidumping Fowls Out: U.S.-South Africa Chicken Dispute Highlights the Need for Global Reform' (*Free Trade Bulletin No. 62 Cato Institute*, 19 October 2015) <https://www.cato.org/publications/free-trade-bulletin/antidumping-fowls-out-us-s outh-africa-chicken-dispute-highlights> accessed 10 January 2017.

28 Peter Pedroncelli, '12 Biggest African Recipients of Foreign Aid from the United States' (AFK Insider, 12 May 2017) <https://afkinsider.com/139167/12-biggest-african-recipi ents-of-foreign-aid-from-the-united-states/4/> accessed 10 February 2018; U.S. DOS, 'U.S. Relations with South Africa' (U.S. Department of State, 12 January 2018) <https:// www.state.gov/r/pa/ei/bgn/2898.htm > accessed 10 February 2018.

dependence but its relationship with the United States is defined along the lines of trade/investment.[29]

The BRICS's political and economic systems vary. China and Russia are authoritarian regimes, as opposed to Brazil, India and SA which are democratic.[30] It is therefore problematic for BRICS to unite on shared political values. Their economic ambitions and systems also differ. History reveals that SA's capitalism, which was racially driven, is now dipped in socialist interventions.[31] Russia and China share a special economic relationship in their investment as capitalist economies.[32] Larry Ong and Lee Edwards, however, disagree, arguing that China and Russia run communist economies.[33] Recent developments and evidence contradict this stance.[34] Moreover, undisputedly, Brazil and India are capitalist economies.[35] The underlining economic structures in the BRICS have revealed varying levels of economic development, with China leading the other countries in the league.[36]

Liberalisation and the resulting heightened integration of the BRICS in the global economy have precipitated discussions on whether economic development can be solely attributed to a phase of radical reregulation.[37] Holton contends that

29 Bronti DeRoche, 'The Ways the US Benefits from Foreign Aid to Brazil' (The Borgen Project, 26 January 2018) <https://borgenproject.org/u-s-benefits-from-foreign-aid-to-brazil /> accessed 10 February 2018.

30 Laetitia Mottet, 'Cooperation and Competition among the BRICS Countries and other Emerging Powers', (French Centre for Research on Contemporary China, March 2013) <http://www.cefc.com.hk/uf/file/researchpapers/BRICS%20report/BRICS%20report .pdf> accessed 10 January 2017.

31 Marian Tupy, 'The Myth of Social African Capitalism' (*Cato Institute*, 12 May 2004) <https ://www.cato.org/publications/commentary/myth-south-african-capitalism> accessed 13 January 2017; Richard Sklar, 'Beyond Capitalism and Socialism in Africa' [1988] 26.1 The Journal of Modern African Studies 1, 20.

32 Young Kim, 'Economic Transition in China and Russia' [2015] 1 European Scientific Journal 355, 364.

33 Larry Ong, 'Is China Still Communist?' (*Epoch Times*, 11 January 2017) <http://www.thee pochtimes.com/n3/2208716-is-china-still-communist/> accessed 13 January 2017; Lee Edwards, 'Yes Communism is Still with us' (The *Heritage Foundation*, 23 June 2015) <http: //www.heritage.org/research/commentary/2015/6/yes-communism-is-still-with-us> accessed 13 January 2017.

34 Colin Clark, 'Economic Development in Communist China' [1976] 84 (2) Journal of Political Economy 239, 239; Pranab Bardhan, 'The Contradictions of China's Communist Capitalism' (*Project Syndicate*, 16 July 2015) <https://www.project-syndicate.org/commen tary/china-stock-market-crash-communism-capitalism-by-pranab-bardhan-2015-07?bar rier=accessreg> accessed 13 January 2017.

35 Sibal Rajeev, 'Varieties of Capitalism and Firm Performance in Emerging Markets: An Examination of the Typological Trajectories of India and Brazil' (PhD Dissertation, The London School of Economics and Political Science, 2014).

36 Cynthia Roberts, 'Building the New World Order BRIC by BRIC' [2011] 6 The European Financial Review 4.

37 N.K. Singh, 'New Money Laundering Threats for Emerging Economies' (Global Programme Against Money Laundering, United Nations, Office for Drug Control and Crime Prevention – Attacking the Profits of Crime: Drugs, Money and Laundering).

it can partly be attributed to state-managed basis of selection and partial regulation.[38] Partial deregulation has heightened the importance of these markets, especially regarding the risk of money laundering (ML) and consequent risks to financial stability. These partial deregulations, in the form of relaxed exchange control[39] and a move away from current account convertibility, pose risks to the financial system, especially through the erosion of the foreign exchange reserves and increase volatility. These risks are also present in the move towards the privatization of public monopolies. The deregulation of the financial system has been accompanied by a simultaneous reform in the capital market, leading to increasing integration and rapid technological changes, which amalgamates markets and increases capital flows within the global arena. This illustrates how ML/terrorist financing (TF) risks within EEs are multifaceted and not peculiar to one financial sector.

Given their historically entrenched differences in economic and political interests,[40] coupled with global integration, scholars have argued that the credibility and longevity of a sturdy BRICS union is uncertain.[41] The doubt is mainly in the ability of the BRICS to bring about lasting change in the global economic and political order.[42] This perspective highlights the inherent heterogeneity of BRICS and casts doubt on their ability to champion change in the global economy and political order. Despite these divergences, the BRICS have exhibited a remarkable degree of cohesion, providing a peaceful and stable international environment, conducive to economic modernisation and growth.[43] They also share a common aspiration for greater representation in international organisations, heightened by their traditional conceptions of state sovereignty.[44] This has led to improved positioning and voting slots within international organisations and network bodies.[45]

38 *Holton* (n 9) 20.
39 Morris Goldstein and Nicholas Lardy, 'China's Exchange Rate Policy: An Overview of Some Key Issues' (China Exchange Rate Policy Peterson Institute for International Economics, October 2007).
40 *Mottet* (n 30).
41 Ramesh Thakur, 'How Representative are BRICS' [2014] 35.10 Third World Quarterly 1791, 1792.
42 Marko Juutinen and Jyrki Kakonen 'Battle for Globalization? BRICS and US Mega-Regional Trade Agreements in a Changing World Order' (New Delhi: Observer Research Foundation, 2016) <http://www.orfonline.org/wp-content/uploads/2016/03/Book_Battle-For-Globalisation.pdf> accessed 10 May 2017.
43 Michael Glosny, 'China and the BRICs: A Real (but Limited) Partnership in a Unipolar World' [2010] 42 (1) Polity 100, 126; Roberts Cynthia, 'Challengers or Stakeholders? BRICs and the Liberal World Order' [2010] 42 (1) Polity 1, 5.
44 Luke Glanville, 'The Antecedents of "Sovereignty as Responsibility"' [2011] 17 (2) European Journal of International Relations 233–255; Christian Brutsch and Mihaela Papa, 'Deconstructing the BRICS: Bargaining Coalition, Imagined Community or Geopolitical Fad?' [2013] 6 (3) Chinese Journal of International Politics 299, 308.
45 Martin Muller, *How Brazil, Russia, India and China view BRIC in Yvette Sanchez, Claudia Franziska Bruhwiler, Transculturalism and Business in the BRIC States: A Handbook* (Rout-

The BRICS Membership of the FATF

Brazil was the first EE to become a FATF member in 2000, 11 years after the FATF's formation. Other countries became members between 2003 and 2007.[46] The BRICS belated membership of the FATF has raised questions about whether such positioning can foster improved compliance with the AML/CFT recommendations.[47] The membership pattern reveals the coercive inclusion of EEs in exchange for the perceived gains of reputational advancements. Membership places countries on a pedestal that improves their compliance drive given the competition that arises between the networked staff. For this reason, the BRICS were granted membership based on their economic growth, efforts in combatting illicit crimes and regional influence.[48]

Conversely, it can be argued that membership can only facilitate compliance when it is voluntary and legitimate. Inherent in this viewpoint is the interrogation of the FATF's membership strategies which are deemed coercive. This is based on the acknowledgement that the EEs' agenda of financial growth largely conflicts with the IFIs/TGNs agenda for financial integrity. Hence membership through sanctions is considered necessary. Yet, this has proved unworkable as it is only when such strategies are perceived as legitimate that they can promote the acceptance of transnational norms and convey state change. Such voluntary membership would promote belief in the FATF as a legitimate rule-maker to be complied with based on appropriateness and not consequence.[49]

These competing perspectives help in providing explanations regarding the emergence of the BRICS as FATF member countries. To further explore this, the section will investigate the trigger for membership, whether it was voluntary or coercive and the impact of the inclusion strategies on compliance.

A historical review of the FATF's membership pattern reveals power-play between Western countries – the rule-makers, and the BRICS as rule-takers. Countries classified as rule-takers were often coerced into compliance with the hope of accelerated FATF membership. For instance, Russia's membership accession was due to pressure from its placement on the Non-Cooperative Countries

ledge 2014). UN General Assembly voting patterns have improved as BRICS countries have higher input.

46 FATF Membership Timeline for EEs: South Africa (2003), Russia (2003), China (2007) and India (2006).

47 Maira Rocha Machado, 'Financial Regulation and International Criminal Policy: the Anti-Money Laundering System in Brazil and Argentina' (2007) Law & Society Association Annual Conference 7/2007, 50 <https://bibliotecadigital.fgv.br/dspace/bitstream/handl e/10438/2777/WP7.pdf> accessed 19 October 2015.

48 FATF, 'Process and Criteria for Becoming a FATF Member' (*FATF*) <http://www.fatf-gafi .org/about/membersandobservers/membershipprocessandcriteria.html> accessed 1 May 2016.

49 Kerwer Dieter and Rainer Hulsse, 'How International Organizations Rule the World: The Case of the Financial Action Task Force on Money Laundering' [2011] 2 J Int. Organ Stud 50, 59.

and Territories (NCCT) list.[50] Also, the public hearing on SA's Financial Intelligence Centre bill indicated that the country's compliance and subsequent membership was due to fear of being blacklisted.[51] Moreover, authors of the 1998 Brazilian Law 9613, drafted in response to the FATF's requirements, noted that its creation was dependent on their contacts with a U.S. representative on drugs, a relationship which placed a more onerous burden on them than the influence of the FATF.[52] This provides insights into the continued hegemony of the United States over other countries. Thus, the overall membership process reveals that the FATF's initial members did indeed wield authoritarian powers over non-members, indicating an encroachment on their sovereignty.

The coercive inclusion of the EEs further exposed the two-way bargain between rule-makers and rule-takers – financial integrity for accountability and reputational benefits. Series of financial crises and terror activities, particularly the 9/11 propelled the Western desire for financial integrity. To achieve this, Western states utilised the backing of IFIs/TGNs to penalise non-compliant states, an act that tarnished their accountability image. Consequently, states aspired to reach the FATF's requirement for membership to evade sanctions. Yang, however, debunks claims that China was coerced into FATF membership, arguing instead that the accession to membership was beneficial to the Chinese government and its private sector.[53] This suggests that China's inclusion served as a momentum to actively combat illicit crimes. Peter Knaack advances a stronger argument, that China's over-compliance and membership were based on the need to remain a major player in the global economy, by protecting its reputation.[54] This indicates a subliminal form of coercion.

Arguments that the FATF's inclusion of the BRICS has resolved democratic deficiency and existing legitimacy crises have been challenged. Kerwer and Hulsee argue that the inclusion of the BRICS enhances the FATF's geographical balance and remedies agitations that the organisation lacks accountability and legitimacy.[55] Accordingly, the Organisation for Economic Cooperation and

50 Peter Lilley, 'Dirty Dealing: the FATF "Blacklist"' (www.DirtyDealing.net, 2006) <http://www.dirtydealing.org/IMAGES/fatfblacklist/The%20FATF%20Blacklist.pdf> accessed 15 January 2016; NewEurope, 'FATF Decides to Cross Russia off Blacklist' (*NewEurope*, 20 July 2002) <https://www.neweurope.eu/article/fatf-decides-cross-russia-blacklist/> accessed 21 January 2016.

51 Parliamentary Monitoring Group, 'Financial Intelligence Centre Bill: Hearings' (*PMG*, 22 March 2001) <https://pmg.org.za/committee-meeting/418/> accessed 10 January 2016.

52 Heinrich-Boll-Stiftung and Regine Schonenberg (eds.), *Transnational Organized Crime: Analyses of a Global Challenge to Democracy* (Transcript Verlag Bielefeld, 2013).

53 Cedric Lam and Liu Yang, 'China Joins the FATF' (*The Anti-Fraud Network*, September 2007) <http://antifraudnetwork.com/2007/09/china-joins-the-fatf/> accessed 14 January 2016.

54 Peter Knaack, 'An Unlikely Champion of Global Finance: Why is China Exceeding International Banking Standards?' [2017] 46 (2) Journal of Current Chinese Affairs 41, 65.

55 *Kerwer and Hulsse* (n 49) 50, 60; Anne-Marie Slaughter, 'Disaggregated Sovereignty: Towards the Public Accountability of Global Government Networks' [2004] 39 (2) Government and Opposition 159, 165.

Development (OECD)-dominated FATF membership[56] has grown to accommodate 'strategically important countries'[57] including the BRICS. Accommodating the BRICS seemingly grants them the privileges of original members – the power to participate in devising global standards on AML/CFT.[58] Such steps revealed the FATF's perception of legitimacy, where democratic inclusion triumphs technical expertise.[59] Consequently, the FATF sought to enhance its input legitimacy, promoting the belief that its rules are decided openly and fairly.[60] Nevertheless, the extent to which the BRICS participate in the standard-setting of established recommendations is questionable, given their belated inclusion and the backing of IFIs.

The Position of the BRICS Prior to and after Their FATF Membership

Prior to their inclusion as core FATF members, the BRICS were part of the FATF-style regional bodies (FSRBs), which are classed as 'associate members'.[61] FSRBs are each regarded as one organisation representing the interest of all its member countries; hence, the BRICS could not individually exert membership of the FATF, without their respective FSRB platforms. Interestingly, the relevant FSRBs (covering the BRICS) were created between 1997 and 2004. Thus, before they attained full FATF membership, the BRICS could also be regarded as 'non-members'.

A gaping disparity existed in voting patterns and treatment between the FATF members and its associates/non-members. Resultantly, whilst the initial FATF members were entitled to one vote each, each FSRB was collectively entitled to one vote.[62] This pragmatically restrictive voting structure was designed to avoid an unwieldy consensus-driven process. Therefore, membership was restricted to countries with advanced and sophisticated financial activities. These countries

---

56 The G7 members, the European Commission, Australia, Austria, Belgium, Luxembourg, Netherlands, Spain, Sweden and Switzerland – on establishment in 1989.

57 FATF – IX, 'Financial Action Task Force on Money Laundering, Annual Report, 1997–1998' (FATF – IX) <http://www.fatf-gafi.org/media/fatf/documents/reports/1997%201998%20ENG.pdf?TSPD_101_R0=be9bbd19c394a0f96d9bc7e799853062eD90000000000000000d501cd89ffff0000000000000000000000000000005a8d916b00d7bfb32c> accessed 10 January 2017.

58 Kern Alexander, Rahul Dhumale and John Eatwell, *Global Governance of Financial Systems: the International Regulation of Systemic Risk* (OUP 2006).

59 *Kerwer and Hulsse* (n 49) 50, 58.

60 Ibid. 50, 56.

61 U.S. DoS, 'The Financial Action Task force and FATF-Style Regional Bodies' (U.S Department of State, 2015) <https://www.state.gov/j/inl/rls/nrcrpt/2015/vol2/239046.htm> accessed 4 February 2018.

62 Maria Machado, 'Similar in their Differences: Transnational Legal Processes Addressing Money Laundering in Brazil and Argentina' in Gregory Shaffer (eds.) *Transnational Legal Ordering and State Change* (CUP, New York, 2013) 61; Domitilla Sagramoso, *Russia's Western Orientation after 11th September: Russia's Enhanced Cooperation with NATO and the European Union* (Rubbettino Editore 2004).

are perceived to have expert knowledge on AML/CFT, given their interactions with diverse advanced forms of illicit crimes over time. The voting consensus from this pool of states is then translated into laws and applied globally. Sidelined from the voting process, the BRICS had to contend with applying decided recommendations despite their seeming unsuitability to its local concerns.

Additionally, before the revision of the FATF's provisions in 2003, reputational damage through coercion was achieved through country placement on the NCCT list.[63] Russia was on this list till 2002,[64] resulting in reduced investment, cross-border trade and banking.[65] Conversely, members were only subject to a form of peer pressure.[66] However, upon the creation of most FSRBs by 2004, the coercive procedure imposed on non-members was made applicable to members also – one of self-assessment and peer pressure.[67] This somewhat bridged the gap between FATF members and non-members. However, the practical effect has not changed, as non-compliant member states (not part of the core member countries) are subject to more intensive peer pressure as a result of their global standing.[68]

With the BRICS membership of the FATF, it remains to be seen whether there has been any substantial change in their treatment by the initial members. Evident changes are expected, particularly since the BRICS now have equal voting powers as the initial members. Mochado however contends that although the distribution of voting powers is relevant in attributing legitimacy to the process, the FATF conceals information about the quality of the decision process.[69] The technical capacity and number of experts play a crucial role in the political discussions of Mutual Evaluation Reports (MERs) and adoptions of decisions at FATF plenary meetings.[70] Evidence however shows that most experts sent for

---

63 The NCCT process started in 2000; Alldridge Peter, 'Money Laundering and Globalization' [2008] 35 (4) Journal of Law and Society 437–463; Kenneth Blazejewski, 'The FATF and Its Institutional Partners: Improving the Effectiveness and Accountability of Trans-governmental Networks' [2008] 22 Temple International and Comparative Law Journal 1, 45; Norman Mugarura, 'The Global Anti-Money Laundering Court as a Judicial and Institutional Imperative' [2011] 14 (1) Journal of Money Laundering Control 60.

64 Victoria Lavrentieva, 'Russia Taken off Financial Blacklist' (*The Moscow Times*, 2002) <http://www.themoscowtimes.com/sitemap/free/2002/10/article/russia-taken-off-financial-blacklist/242953.html> accessed 1 December 2015.

65 Ibid.

66 Cecily Rose, *International Anti-Corruption Norms: their Creation and Influence on Domestic Legal Systems* (1st edn, OUP 2015) 199.

67 In 2006, all non-members were de-listed. Some IFIs like the IMF and the World Bank started to play an active role in conducting evaluations of non-member countries based on the FATF Methodology for assessing compliance.

68 *Cecily Rose* (n 66) 199.

69 *Machado* (n 47); Chris Bummer, *Soft Law and the Global Financial System: Rule Making in the 21st Century* (CUP, 2011) 307.

70 The technical experts play a crucial role in the preparation of the national reports and in the negotiation with the assessment team.

in-country evaluations are drawn from the US.[71] Besides, there are limits on the number of experts sent from different countries. Thus, the reports on countries may indeed be distorted by biases, regarding the actual participation of countries. Machado emphasises that appreciating the procedural fairness regarding actual participation is difficult, being largely dependent on the ability to scrutinise documents which detail participation processes, direct observation and in-depth interviews.[72] Accordingly, it is questionable whether legitimacy should rely on representation in IFIs (given differences in actual participation), the structuring of global agendas and development of global recommendations.

Responding to concerns about lack of legitimacy, the FATF democratised its presidency, making it rotational amongst members.[73] Barring India, other BRICS have served their presidency tenure.[74] The presidency role is undermined by the absence of guidelines for the decision-making processes.[75] The FATF has no strict rules regarding who could overrule its decisions, although no two members can hold out the group on a particular decision.[76] Additionally, the FATF's hierarchy reveals that the president's role is subject to the FATF plenary decisions.[77] Furthermore, ascendency to presidency is allegedly voluntary, countering arguments that it was a reward for Brazil's Financial Intelligence Unit (FIU) senior officers' proactivity.[78] The voluntary nature of the presidency reveals the limits in influencing decisions or discussions at plenary meetings. Thus, the sitting president can only bring his own style in setting the agenda.[79]

The marginalisation of the BRICS is further emphasised by their representation in the International Monetary Fund (IMF) and the World Bank, IFIs which form the backbone for the FATF's enforcement process. Being late entrants to these institutions, the BRICS are sidelined in decision-making given their limited

---

71 This was obvious from reading over 40 assessment reports.

72 *Machado* (n 47).

73 FATF, 'FATF Presidency' (*FATF*) <http://www.fatf-gafi.org/about/fatfpresidency/> accessed 1 May 2016.

74 Presidency of the FATF: China 2001–2002 (Clarie Lo); South Africa 2005–2006 (Prof. Kader Asmal); Brazil 2008–2009 (Antonio Gustavo Rodrigues); Russia 2013–2014 (Vladirmir Nechaev); FATF, '25 Years and Beyond: the Financial Action Task Force' (*FATF*, 2014) <http://www.fatf-gafi.org/media/fatf/documents/brochuresannualreports/FATF%2025%20years.pdf?TSPD_101_R0=1495c41e79bcbd390bbe7629e106108ajF50000000000000000d501cd89ffff00000000000000000000000000005a8d95e80048c055d7> accessed 14 January 2017.

75 House of Lords, European Union Committee, 'Money Laundering and the Financing of Terrorism: Evidence' (19th Report of Session 2008–09 Volume II: Evidence, 22 July 2009) 169.

76 Ibid.

77 The Financial Action Task Force Mandate (2012–2013).

78 Maira Machado, 'Transnational Legal Processes Addressing Money Laundering in Brazil and Argentina' in Gregory Shaffer (eds.) *Transnational Legal Ordering and State Change* (CUP, 2013).

79 Ibid.

quota and voting rights.[80] The BRIC'S voting powers at the IMF are not reflective of their tremendous economic growth.[81] This is because these institutions
align with the US's desire for financial stability. The marginalisation of the BRICS
within IFIs is backed by a long history of G7 supremacy, individually and within
the FATF or connected bodies. For instance, the Treaty of Nanking ratified by
China in 1843, on the free sale of opium between the US and China placed onerous obligations on China, with none on the US.[82] Consequently, the US waged
war against Chinese ports to compel them to trade on the agreed merchandise.[83]
Similarly, the G7 excluded India from discussions on counter-terrorism, although
India had experience dealing with related issues.[84] Resentment by the BRICS can
catalyse some level of non-compliance.[85]

The BRICS desired to form their agenda outside Western control,[86] thus altering the international order. They seek to undo biased treatments enshrined in
international bodies or treaties established when they were seemingly toothless.
One way to cure this is by reviewing the treaties and procedures that have historically existed within international organisations.[87] An alternative is to establish a similar organisation, for instance, the BRICS development bank. These
options indicate the BRICS's aspiration, stemming from a history of political
marginalisation of the South due to colonialism and its legacies, for a multipolar,
equitable and democratic world order.[88] Brazil has called for an end to American
dominance,[89] whilst China has pushed for reform of IMF global currencies.[90]

80 Alonso Soto, 'BRICS Bank to Defy Western Clout in Global Finances' (*Reuters*, 11 July
   2014)   <http://uk.reuters.com/article/uk-brics-summit-idUKKBN0FG1SG20140711>
   accessed 14 March 2016.
81 Ibid.
82 Bruce Jones, *Still Ours to Lead: America, Rising Power and the Tension Between Rivalry and
   Restraint* (The Brookings Institution, 2014) 58.
83 Ibid.
84 Peter Romaniuk, *Multilateral Counterterrorism: The Global Politics of Cooperation and Contestation* (First Published 2010, Routledge) 57.
85 Peter Andreas and Ethan Nadelmann, *Policing the Globe: Criminalization and Crime Control Control in International Relations* (1st edn, OUP, 2006); Karin Helgesson and Ulrika
   Morth, *Securitization, Accountability and Risk Management – Transforming the Public Security Domain* (Routledge, 2012).
86 *Brutsch and Papa* (n 44) 299, 304; Miller Tyler, 'Addressing the Economic and Political
   Rise of the BRICS Countries through Neoliberal International Relations Theory' (Master's
   Thesis, Towson University, 2013).
87 Eduardo Viola, 'The BRICS in the International System: Very Relevant Countries, but a Group
   of Limited Importance' in Gustavo Lins Riberio, Tom Dwyer, Antonadia Borges, Eduardo
   Viola (eds.), *Social, Political and Cultural Challenges of the BRICS* (Langaa RPCIG, 2015).
88 Laurence Piper, 'The BRICS Phenomenon: From Regional Economic Leaders to Global
   Political Players' (2015) BICAS Working Paper 3/2015, 3 <https://www.tni.org/files/
   download/bicas_working_paper_3_piper.pdf> accessed 15 January 2017.
89 Andres Cala, 'Brazil's Challenge to US Dominance' (*Consortiumnews.com*, 2 October 2013)
   <https://consortiumnews.com/2013/10/02/brazils-challenge-to-us-dominance/>
   accessed 2 January 2016.
90 Domenico Lombardi and Hongying Wang, (eds.) *Enter the Dragon: China in the International Financial System* (Centre for International Governance Innovation, 2015).

Western countries' advancement has placed them in the forefront of global governance, thus culminating in the perspective that their actions are laced with good intentions. However, other states perceive these actions as a threat to their sovereignty. The marginalisation perception may cause countries to resist or induce sham compliance in a bid to find favour with countries that caused the marginalisation.

Furthermore, at the national level, membership does not guarantee immunity from ML/TF. The BRICS suffer from corruption, which is inextricably linked to ML.[91] The absence of sturdy political will obstructs enforcement measures to combat these ills. For instance, India's emerging status as a regional financial centre, its access to drugs and the prevalence of underground banking has made it an attractive ML hub.[92] Distinguishing between internal and international ML, Vijay argues that India's strict foreign exchange laws restrict cross-border ML.[93] This distinction however fails to consider how internal ML fosters cross-border ML. For instance, the exploitation of the informal remittance system to launder funds abroad,[94] or the case of politically exposed persons (PEPs) who launder funds internally but engage in cross-border investments through proxies.

In certain instances, the problem is not the absence of, but rather misguided, political will aligned with corrupt practices. Across various countries, the incumbent government dismantles opposition by alleging corruption,[95] whilst overlooking corrupt practices within its ranks. The recent Deutsche Bank laundering

91 OECD, 'CleanGovBiz Integrity in Practice: Money Laundering' (OECD) <http://www.oecd.org/cleangovbiz/toolkit/moneylaundering.htm>accessed 21 February 2016; Money Laundering Bulletin, 'Building FATF Evaluations BRIC by BRIC' (*Money Laundering Bulletin*) <http://www.moneylaunderingbulletin.com/legalandregulatory/governmentan dinternationalbodies/building-fatf-evaluations-bric-by-bric--1.htm> accessed 21 February 2016.

92 US DoS: Bureau for International Narcotics and Law Enforcement Affairs, 'International Narcotics Control Strategy Report: Volume II Money Laundering and Financial Crimes' (United States Department of State, March 2017) <https://www.state.gov/document s/organization/268024.pdf> accessed 16 August 2017; Ramanand Garge, 'Combating Financing of Terror: an Indian Perspective' (Vivekandanda International Foundation, Occasional Paper, October 2015) <http://www.vifindia.org/sites/default/files/combating-f inancing-of-terror-an-indian-perspective.pdf> accessed 10 March 2017.

93 Vijay Singh, 'Controlling Money Laundering in India – Problems and Perspectives', (Annual Conference on Money and Finance in the Indian Economy, India, January 2009).

94 Elod Takats, 'International Enforcement Issues', in Donato Masciandaro, Elod Takats and Brigitte Unger, *Black Finance: The Economies of Money Laundering* (Edward Elgar, 2007); FATF Report, Money Laundering through Money Remittance and Currency Exchange Providers (*FATF Report*, 2010) <http://www.fatf-gafi.org/media/fatf/ML%20through %20Remittance%20and%20Currency%20Exchange%20Providers.pdf> accessed 23 January 2017.

95 *Asian Tribune*, 'Arrest of Yoshita a Political Witch Hunting: Police Denied Allegation' (*Asian Tribune* 1 February 2016) <http://www.asiantribune.com/node/88502> accessed 21 January 2017; *The Financial Express*, 'BJP Describes Robert Vadra's "Witch-Hunt" Claim As "Farcical"' (*The Financial Express*, 22 November 2015) <http://www.financial express.com/article/india-news/bjp-describes-robert-vadras-witch-hunt-claim-as-farcical /169116/> accessed 1 February 2016.

probe implicated close personal and political associates of Vladimir Putin,[96] revealing the public-private sector tolerant perception of laundering and corruption within Russia.

Remittances also pose compliance problems for the BRICS, especially India and China, both of which receive the largest amounts.[97] Anonymity and expediency usually make remittances the preferred choice for launderers. ML is prevalent in Brazil's various financial sectors[98] and has now come to encompass its sporting sector, particularly football.[99] Brazil's location and natural resources also make it vulnerable to drug-related laundering.[100]

Increased liberalisation, coupled with partial deregulation and misguided political will, ensures that the involvement of EEs in formulation of AML/CFT standards does not translate to improved AML/CFT regulation within each sovereign state. This is partly why international prudential regulation is postulated as an antidote for AML/CFT in EEs.

The concern however is that the BRICS union is a marriage of convenience, given their conflicting interests, and may not have the capacity to shape the dynamic of the international system.[101] More recently, the slowdown of the BRICS economies has raised questions as to whether they deserve to sit at 'the table'.[102] Notwithstanding these concerns, a new economic order is emerging,[103] which has caused the IMF to alter its structure.[104] China now has the third-largest

---

96 *The Moscow Times*, 'Putin Associates Implicated in Deutsche Bank Moscow Laundering Probe' (*Moscow Times*, October 16 2015) <http://www.themoscowtimes.com/business/article/putin-associates-implicated-in-deutsche-bank-moscow-laundering-probe/539451.html > accessed 15 June 2016; Martin Arnold, Deutsche Bank Eyes Russian Pullback Amid Money Laundering Probe (*Financial Times*, 11 September 2015) <http://www.ft.com/cms/s/0/8533caca-58ae-11e5-9846-de406ccb37f2.html#axzz3z2fVDQkE> accessed 10 May 2016

97 The World Bank, International Migration at All-Time High (*The World Bank*, 18 December 2015 <http://www.worldbank.org/en/news/press-release/2015/12/18/international-migrants-and-remittances-continue-to-grow-as-people-search-for-better-opportunities-new-report-finds> accessed 1 February 2016.

98 Colin Watterson, 'More Flies with Honey: Encouraging Formal Channel Remittances to Combat Money Laundering' [2013] 91 Texas Law Review 711, 712–717; Roberto Delmanto Junior, 'The World Cup in Brazil: Fighting Against Money Laundering and Corruption' South-Western Journal of International Law [2014] 21 SW. J. Int'l L. 143.

99 Kenneth Korosi, Kristen Brown, Christina Marquez, Mauricio Salazar and Sophia Segura, 'Sporting Events as Sites of International Law, Society and Governance: the 2014 Brazilian World Cup: Forward' [2010] 21 Southwestern Journal of International Law, Sw. J. Int'l L. 1.

100 Oaula Miraglia, 'Drugs and Drug Trafficking in Brazil: Trends and Policies' [2016] Foreign Policy at Brookings.

101 *Eduardo Viola* (n 87); *Agtmael* (n 6).

102 *Piper* (n 88).

103 The potential growth of the BRICS beyond China and India has been questioned. However, with the United States and Europe headed for economic stagnation and recession – it called for deeper international cooperation. See *Agtmael* (n 6); Tereza De Castro, 'Trade Among BRICS Countries: Changes Towards Closer Cooperation?' [2013] 16 (3) Central European Review of Economic Issues 131, 133.

104 IMF, 'IMF Members' Quotas and Voting Power, and IMF Board of Governors' (*IMF*, 4, June 2016) <https://www.imf.org/external/np/sec/memdir/members.aspx> accessed

IMF quota (its currency was resolved); also, the BRIC economies were placed amongst the ten largest members of the IMF.[105] Unfortunately, the US Congress only passed the bill amending the IMF quota allocation in 2016, six years after an agreement was negotiated with the US Congress to make the change.[106] The extent to which this would occasion improved compliance is yet to be seen.

The Determinants of Compliance to AML/CFT in Emerging Economies

Chapter 3 highlights certain legal factors that are crucial in understanding the compliance trajectory of countries. These are supported by non-legal factors such as political will, domestic conditions and globalisation which are crucial drivers of compliance. The extent to which these factors catalyse improved compliance within EEs is dependent on their effect on EE and how this aligns with the FATF's compliance methodologies.

Legal factors

Chapter 3 shows that law matters.[107] Julio Faundez argues that law is the main source of the formal rules and provides enforcement mechanisms that strengthen the credibility of commitments made by economic and political actors.[108] The position of law in setting the foundation for EEs to comply is contestable. Consequently, this section examines how law is decisive in determining the AML/CFT compliance levels of countries. This is examined in the context of three legal factors: law reflecting society, enforcement-driven compliance, democracy and rule of law.

LAW MIRRORING SOCIETY

Scholars have claimed that the dissemination of the AML/CFT regime to EEs was 'illegitimate' given that it involved coercive and persuasive schemes by the

June 4 2016); IMF, 'Acceptances of the Proposed Amendment of the Articles of Agreement on Reform of the Executive Board and Consents to 2010 Quota Increase' (*IMF*, 31 May 2016) <http://www.imf.org/external/np/sec/misc/consents.htm#a2> accessed 10 May 2017.

105 IMF, 'Press Release: IMF Managing Director Christine Lagarde Welcomes U.S. Congressional Approval of the 2010 Quota and Governance Reforms' (*IMF*, 18 December 2015) <https://www.imf.org/en/News/Articles/2015/09/14/01/49/pr15573>   4   June 2016.

106 Bretton Woods Agreement Act, Section 5 [22 U.S.C. 286c] 1962, amended and effected in 2016; John Ross, 'China's New Position in Global Economic Governance' (*China.org .cn*, 10 February 2016) <http://china.org.cn/opinion/2016-02/10/content_37752043 .htm> accessed 10 May 2016.

107 See Julio Faundez, 'Douglass North's Theory of Institutions: Lessons for Law and Development' [2016] 8 (2) Hague Journal on the Rule of Law 373, 404.

108 Ibid.

G7 countries that established the FATF.[109] Additionally, although the BRICS were excluded from decision-making processes, there was an expectation that they would translate the FATF recommendations to law via national legislation under the FATF's scrutiny. This expectation occasioned the adoption of laws which did not necessarily 'mirror' society and hence its application and effectiveness has raised questions.

What would 'law mirroring society' look like within the BRICS? It is difficult to predict. However, one can imagine that China might have focused on laws tailored to addressing remittances and secrecy in its informal banking sector. This assumption is predicated on China's formal banking system's slow development, which only became operative in the 20th century.[110] To illustrate, although China's plague with extortion and bribery can be traced back to 2000 BC, it was combatted with limited measures.[111] In the 19th century, the *Piaohao*, China's first traditional banking structures which operated as remittances, further escalated the avenues for illicit transfers.[112] These channels, although properly structured, ran largely unregulated despite the currency exchange and ML risk posed. Rather, the informal banking structures operated successfully on the culture of trust which promoted secrecy of transactional exchanges. Law mirroring the society would have indicated heightened focus on the informal sector which might have included lax regulation on remittances and laws to promote financial secrecy.[113] Such regulations might simply have been a reflection of the information asymmetry between the regulator and the regulated, coupled with the culture of trust.

SA presents a different perspective. Organised crime escalated in the country given its historical transition from apartheid to democracy.[114] The apartheid regime thrived on proceeds of illicit crimes, and the democratic government was no exception.[115] This informed the lackadaisical attitude towards combatting illicit crimes. Additionally, the weak legal framework at the time would have

109 BCBS, 'Consultative Document: Customer Due Diligence for Banks' (*Bank for International Settlements*, January 2001) <https://www.bis.org/publ/bcbs77.pdf> accessed 19 May 2016.
110 Robert L. Worden, Andrea Matles Savada and Roland E. Dolan (eds.) *China: A Country Study* (Washington: GPO for the Library of Congress, 1987).
111 Sterling Seagrave, *Lord of the Rim* (Bantam Press, London 1997).
112 *Worden, Savada and Dolan* (n 110).
113 This explains China's weak bank secrecy regulation – see Wang Wei, 'Bank Secrecy in China' (Bank Secrecy Symposium, Singapore, March 2016) and why Chinese banks failed to engage in Customer Due Diligence (CDD) till post-2003 upon the FATF recommending incorporation.
114 Jenny Irish and Kevin Qhobosheane, 'South Africa' in Peter Gastrow (ed.) *Penetrating State and Business: Organised Crime in Southern Africa, Volume 2* (Pretoria, ISS, Monograph 89, 2003).
115 Hennie van Vuuren, 'Apartheid Grand Corruption: Assessing the Scale of Crimes of Profit in South Africa from 1976 to 1994' (*Institute for Security Studies*, May 2006) <https://www.files.ethz.ch/isn/123917/2006_05_29.pdf> accessed 10 July 2017.

frustrated attempts to combat such crimes.[116] SA subsequently introduced criminal laws to combat organised groups that profited from crimes.[117] Whilst this may allow for launderers to be imprisoned, it would hinder the ability to recover the proceeds of crime through civil confiscation. Thus, law mirroring society would at best strangulate efforts at combatting illicit crimes.

Russia painted a dire picture of absence of specific laws to ensure that illicit crimes were effectively combatted, signposting a society where absence or inadequacy of laws was symptomatic of 'law mirroring' acceptable societal values of corruption and organised crime.[118]

Recognising that if law is allowed to 'mirror society' in the BRICS – there would be a risk to the international financial market, particularly given the growing degree of integration of the BRICS into the global economy, the discursive power-based mechanism came into play.[119] Consequently, China adopted the Vienna and Palermo Conventions.[120] China has put laws in place to ensure convergence with the FATF standards[121] to maintain foreign policy relationships with the US for trade and development, particularly after 9/11.[122] China's convergence was also triggered by the need to remain a competitive player in the global financial market through compliance to avoid the risk of reputational damage.[123] Whilst China displayed some willingness to comply for intrinsic reasons, this is not necessarily the case with other countries.

116 See O'Malley, '08 August 1998: Hofmeyr, Willie' (O'Malley, 1998) <https://www.nel sonmandela.org/omalley/index.php/site/q/03lv00017/04lv00344/05lv01183/06lv0 1224.htm> accessed 10 July 2017.

117 Ibid.; South African Law Commission, 'Issue Paper 1, Project 104, Money Laundering and Related Matters' (South African Law Commission, 24 May 1996).

118 Delphine Defossez, 'The Current Challenges of Money Laundering Law in Russia' [2017] 20 (4) Journal of Money Laundering Control 367–385.

119 Jason Sharman, 'Power and Policy Diffusion: Anti-Money Laundering in Developing States' [2008] 52 (3) International Studies Quarterly 635, 652. This accords with Daniel W. Drezner's, *All Politics is Global: Explaining International Regulatory Regime* (Princeton: PUP 2007) 5, 75.

120 The Chinese Government signed the convention on 20 December 1998 and handed over the instrument of accession on 25 December 1989. The convention became effective on 11 November 1990. Note that in 1979, before the criminalization of ML internationally, Art. 312 of Chinese Criminal Law criminalised activities of receiving and handling proceeds of crime.

121 In 2001, China included 'terrorist financing' and in 2006 included other financial crimes/ predicate offences; it was expanded to cover only drug and organised crime, terrorism and smuggling in 1997. The Rules for Anti-Money Laundering by Financial Institutions, Administrative Rules for the Reporting of Large-Value and Suspicious RMB Payment Transactions and the Administrative Rules for the Reporting by Financial institutions of Large-Value and Suspicious Foreign Exchange Transactions have been extended to cover all financial institutions.

122 Xue Bin Li, 'Money Laundering and Its Regulation in China' (PhD Thesis, Cardiff University, 2009).

123 *Knaack* (n 54) 41, 65.

Scholars have argued that SA's convergence was predicated on external coercion and mimicry, in addition to intrinsic domestic factors.[124] Arguably, the central need to combat illicit crimes driven by the transition from apartheid to democracy led SA to enact new democratically motivated laws. However, Zakhele argues that external mimicry was proactively brought to bear, which inspired convergence to the FATF's AML/CFT standards by SA authorities.[125] Thus, whilst domestic factors created incentives to mimic, actual actions were driven externally, given the threat of the FATF's enforcement processes. It was not until 1992 that SA adopted its first AML legislation which showed sturdy awareness of the Vienna Convention.[126] D'Oliveira agrees that the timing of the Drugs and Drug Trafficking Act 1992 and the subsequent Proceeds of Crime Act 1996 indicated a desire to accede to the Vienna Convention post-apartheid.[127] The statement of a representative at the public hearing of the Financial Intelligence Centre Bill in 2002 exemplified external pressures on SA, thus: '[w]e have the sword of the FATF hanging over our heads and the patience of the international community is reaching its end'.[128] Undoubtedly, the external pressures may have coerced compliance with the standards, but the extent of compliance this has stimulated is debatable.

Russia's experience, although largely different from China's, was slightly similar to SA's. Given its unprecedented ML rate, capital flight and corruption, Russia was blacklisted by the FATF.[129] Failure to enact laws to curb these illicit crimes, largely exacerbated by privatisation policies in 1992, exposed Russia's acquiescence to such illicit crimes at every government level.[130] The reports of the possible laundering of IMF credits through the Bank of New York in 1999 mounted pressure to blacklist Russia.[131] The FATF blacklisted Russia as a direct external coercion to compel it to observe the FATF recommendations by legislating on AML/CFT. Russia then enacted the Combatting the Laundering of Income Obtained by Criminal Means law in 2001.[132] This law not only compelled FIs to report suspicious transactions above $20,000, it also established an FIU to act on such reports. The law also compelled law enforcement agencies to prosecute cases.[133] Additionally, after 9/11, Vladimir Putin tightened the illicit crime rules

---

124 Hlophe Zakhele, 'Regulating Money Laundering in Developing Countries: A Critical Analysis of South Africa's Incorporation and Implementation of the Global FATF Standards' (PhD Thesis, Kings College London, 2013).
125 Ibid.
126 Drugs and Drug Trafficking Act 1992.
127 See also Jan d'Oliviera, 'International Co-operation in Criminal Matters: The South African Contribution' [2003] 16 (3) *South African Journal of Criminal Justice* 323, 333.
128 *Parliamentary Monitoring Group* (n 51).
129 Elena Chinyaeva, 'Russia and the FATF Blacklist' [2002] 1.3 Russia and Eurasia Review (*The Jamestown Foundation*, 2 July 2002) <https://jamestown.org/program/russia-and -the-fatf-blacklist/> accessed 10 November 2017.
130 Ibid.
131 Ibid. (n 129).
132 Ibid.
133 Ibid.

with a decree establishing criminal penalties for bank officials who did not report suspicious transactions. In 2002, Russia was delisted and following its economic growth and seeming adherence to the FATF's recommendations, it gained the prestigious FATF membership in 2003.

Examining the 'law mirroring international standards' across countries illustrates that the FATF regime led to tailored laws and, in certain instances, harsher sanctions. It can be argued that this may have led to reduced illicit crimes. Shuceng concurs and submits that the modification of punishment regimes has contributed to reduced criminal offences in China.[134] For instance, the death penalty for citizens who embezzle funds has been largely effective.[135] This supports external pressures to facilitate compliance, given harsher applicable sanctions.

Given the systemic risk of the BRICS to the global economy, they were invited to membership of the FATF and, barring SA, have been classed as 'systemically important' by the IMF. Being so categorised comes with mandatory Financial Stability Assessments (FSA) under the Financial Sector Assessment Programme (FSAP), given the importance of their financial sectors and the impending risk of contagion they pose. It also signifies a growing relationship between IFIs and EEs, which can ensure that EEs comply with the IFIs' requirements and avoid agency slack.

Yet, 'law mirroring international standards' is not always ideal, as the FATF requirements backed by the IFIs do not usually indicate concrete understanding of the country's culture within which it operates. Indeed, this may facilitate, rather than curb illicit crimes. For example, recommendation 14 of the FATF requirements mandates registration and licensing of remittances;[136] it is usually read with the customer due dilligence (CDD) and reporting requirements. Likewise, given the inter-linkages established between remittances and terror funding, regulatory bodies have been empowered to report, freeze or confiscate terror funding when suspicion is raised or ascertained.[137] Although aimed at ensuring transparency, examining the FATF's language and purpose reveals the superimposition of existing formal financial sector regulatory and supervisory practices onto the informal transfer systems.[138] In countries like China or India, remittances are built

---

134 Wang Shucheng, 'Predictions on the Development and Direction of Legislation' *in* Yuwen W. Li (ed.) *The China Legal Development Yearbook*, (Volume 2, 2009).

135 Ian Jeffries, *Political Developments in Contemporary China: A Guide* (First published 2011, Routledge 2011) 386. The death penalty was eventually ended in 2011, see also Chris Higg, 'China Ends Death Penalty for 13 Economic Crimes' (*BBC News Shanghai*, February 2011) <http://www.bbc.co.uk/news/world-asia-pacific-12580504> accessed 11 February 2016. The limited execution undermines its effectiveness.

136 FATF, 'The FATF Recommendations' (*FATF*, 2012) <http://www.fatf-gafi.org/media/fatf/documents/recommendations/pdfs/FATF_Recommendations.pdf> accessed 7 August 2012.

137 Ibid.

138 Samuel Maimbo, 'The Regulation and Supervision of Informal Remittance Systems: Emerging Oversight Strategies' (Current Developments in Monetary and Financial Law, November 2004).

on a culture of trust and operate through a complex web of transactions[139] which are deemed the safest means of transmitting funds. Therefore, such regulations might only succeed in pushing their services underground,[140] as evidenced by the growing rate of unregistered remittance intermediaries in both countries.[141] This medium is considered the largest source of financial flows to developing countries, exceeding the foreign direct investment in some countries.[142]

This feeds into Legrand's argument that transplantation must be contextual, considering the cultural, historical and socio-economic sensibilities of the recipient country.[143] Otherwise, it may be rejected by the recipient state.[144] Local conditions generate acceptance or resistance to crucial policies or practices; therefore, lessons should be learned in a manner that reinforces, rather than transforms local practices.[145] This can be achieved by empowering local policy makers to investigate and proffer solutions to suit their domestic contexts rather than applying incompatible international standards to local realities.[146] These analyses indicate that transplantation effected in developed-emerging economies is not necessarily suitable, but rather policy responses should be designed with recipient countries for proactive compliance. Whilst this has arguably been addressed by BRICS membership of the FATF, it does not solve the pending problem, as these countries only have minimal say in the re-formulation of standards.

Given their need for tailored solutions to addressing ML/TF, the BRICS have established a BRICS Council on AML/CFT.[147] This council serves as a platform for participating countries to consolidate BRICS actions on Counter terrorist financing (CTF) and the intensification of training programmes, especially through the Network AML/CFT.[148] These actions indicate increased ownership

---

139 Ibid.

140 Ibid.; Walter Perkel, 'Money Laundering and Terrorism: Informal Value Transfer System' [2004] 41 (1) AM Crim. L Rev. 183, 198.

141 Nikos Passas, 'Financial Intermediaries – Anti-Money Laundering Allies in Cash-Based Societies?' [2015] 10. U4 Brief 1,7; Michelle V. Remo, 'Stop Illegal Remittance Agents, BSP Urged' (*Inquirer.net*, 14 November 2012) <http://business.inquirer.net/93066/stop-illegal-remittance-agents-bsp-urged> accessed 15 March 2016.

142 Dietmar Meyer and Adela Shera, 'The Impact of Remittances on Economic Growth: an Econometric Model' [2017] 18 (2) Economia 147, 147.

143 Pierre Legrand 'The Impossibility of "Legal Transplants"' [1997] 4 Masstricht J. Eur. & Comp.L 111, 118–119.

144 Manuhuia Barcham, 'South-South Policy Transfer: The Case of the Vanuatu Ombudsman's Office' [2003] 18 (2) Pacific Economic Bulletin 108–116.

145 Eduardo Gonzales, 'Policy Transfer in the Philippines: Can it Pass the Localization Test?' [2007] 2.1 JOAAG.

146 Ibid.

147 Daniel Berliner, 'Follow Your Neighbor? Regional Emulation and the Design of Transparency Policies' (2013) KFG Working Paper 55, 17 <http://userpage.fu-berlin.de/kfgeu/kfgwp/wpseries/WorkingPaperKFG_55.pdf> accessed 10 May 2016; Simmons Beth and Zachary Elkins, 'The Globalisation of Liberalisation: Policy Diffusion in the International Political Economy' [2004] 98 (1) American Political Science Review 171, 187.

148 BRICS, 'The BRICS Handover Report: 2015–2016', (*BRICS*, 2016) 65/66 <en.brics2015.ru/load/885248> accessed 10 December 2017.

and accountability by these countries. However, the extent to which this can translate to long-term change is to be seen.

ENFORCEMENT-DRIVEN COMPLIANCE

Concerns about the possibility of enforcement actions shape behaviour.[149] At the national level, compliance by key actors are sometimes focused on evading enforcement actions. This is because breach of certain FATF recommendations which are enshrined in national legislations are backed by sanctions ranging from fine to imprisonment. When meted on an individual or institution by enforcement agencies or the court, it can lead to reputational damage. For this reason, it serves as a key driver of compliance with AML/CFT regulation, particularly in countries where legal structures are robust to sanction-erring criminals.

At the international level, the FATF enforces its rules through measures aimed at facilitating compliance.[150] Blacklisting of erring countries is one of such measures – which comes with reputational damage and financial isolation. All EEs, but Russia, were able to circumvent this enforcement action.[151] Whilst the other EEs transplanted the FATF recommendations to ensure a conducive environment for compliance, Russia did not. Consequently, Russia's high rate of capital flight, corruption and ML went unchecked. The sanction however propelled compliance by Russia. As earlier discussed, there is evidence that EEs simply transplanted rules and seemingly complied with same to evade sanctions.

Strengthened laws and improved implementation measures sometimes signal an increasing attempt at compliance by the BRICS. For instance, the 2015 FATF compliance statistics indicate that whilst Russia averaged 68% compliance to the FATF recommendations, Brazil averaged 63%.[152] It can be argued that these results, following their attainment of a core FATF membership position, are because of the attendant compliance responsibilities. Examining the criteria for membership reveals a different perspective. A criterion requires that a country should not have eight or more non-compliant (NC) or partially compliant (PC) ratings for technical compliance.[153] Additionally, countries must not be rated NC/PC on recommendations 2, 5, 10, 11 and 20.[154] Moreover, low effectiveness on seven or more of the 11 effectiveness outcomes would disqualify a country

---

149 David G. Victor, Kal Raustaila and Eugene B. Skolnikoff (eds.), *The Implementation and Effectiveness of International Environmental Commitments: Theory and Practice* (International Institute for Applied System Analysis, 1998).

150 Tam Christian, 'Enforcement' *in* G. Ulfsein, T. Marauhn and A. Zimmermann (eds.). *Making Treaties Work* (CUP, 2007) 391–410.

151 Daniel Ho, 'Compliance and International Soft law: Why Do Countries Implement the Basel Accord' [2002] 5 (3) Journal of International Economic Law 647–688.

152 See Figure 6.1.

153 *FATF* (n 46).

154 Ibid.

from meeting the membership standards.[155] Attaining these standards without membership status will definitely ensure improved compliance levels of any country. It can therefore be argued that compliance can be attributable to the internal financial regulatory dynamics of EEs coupled with external coercion or persuasion. Acceding to this, Yepes argues that a strong correlation exists between countries' economic development and their compliance levels, notwithstanding the risk-based approach currently adopted.[156]

That compliance levels are improving may also be suggestive of the success of the FATF's enforcement strategies. However, although countries are complying with 'black letter' requirements, they may indeed remain deficient on the effectiveness levels. Additionally, there is limited evidence that there is significantly improved 'actual or proactive' compliance.[157] For instance, Brazil's technical compliance does not parallel its effectiveness.[158] This shortfall can be attributed to the absence of ownership in the process of standard making, coupled with the coercive strategies employed to facilitate compliance. This counters the argument that the involvement of the BRICS in combatting illicit crime was dependent on increased financial liberalisation and the need to curtail infiltration of illicit funds.[159] It rather illustrates that in the absence of voluntary compliance backed by ownership, formal or creative compliance will thrive, even with sturdy enforcement infrastructure to facilitate compliance.

The above argument does not however invalidate the impact of 'listing' on a country. Given the BRICS membership of the FATF, there is some political impetus to ensure continued compliance. Nevertheless, membership provides some shield from the consequences of non-compliance which may only be circumvented through de-risking. Hence, the member countries may be de-incentivised, given their 'sacred' position. To curtail this moral hazard, the FATF listed Turkey, a member country, for deficiencies in its compliance.[160] This rare and singular act has not provided a paradigm shift for EEs and developed countries who are resolute in their membership protection from financial isolation or reputational damage. Recognising this shortcoming, the IMF recently identified

---

155 Ibid. (n 153).
156 Concepcion Verdugo-Yepes, 'Compliance with the AML/CFT International Standard: Lessons from a Cross-Country Analysis' (2006) IMF Working Paper 11/177, 17 <https://www.imf.org/external/pubs/ft/wp/2011/wp11177.pdf> accessed 10 July 2015.
157 Rainer Hulsse, 'Even Clubs Can't Do Without Legitimacy: Why the Anti-Money Laundering Blacklist Was Suspended' [2008] 2 (4) Regulation and Governance 459, 465.
158 FATF, 'Outcomes of the Plenary Meeting of the FATF, Valencia, 21–23 June 2017' (*FATF*, June 2017)<http://www.dt.tesoro.it/export/sites/sitodt/modules/document i_it/prevenzione_reati_finanziari/prevenzione_reati_finanziari/FATF_Outcomes_of_the _Plenary_meeting_of_the_June_2017_FATF.pdf> accessed September 2017.
159 *Piper* (n 88); Charalampos Efstahopoulos, 'India and Global Governance: the Politics of Ambivalent Reform' [2016] 53 International Politics 239–259; *Jones* (n 82).
160 *Financial Times*, 'Turkey's Banking Blacklist Risk' (*Financial Times*, 16 October 2012) <https://www.ft.com/content/bbfe16f0-01c8-357e-84d4-4cce12d1e6b4> accessed 1 January 2016.

the BRICs as countries which need a higher level of surveillance through FSAP. The reason was to heighten IMF's interactions with BRICS's representatives to identify and work towards curtailing any likely agency slack, such as the materialisation of risks in a manner that can occasion systemic risk. This usually occurs through an intense monitoring and review of information on compliance levels of the BRICS institutions.[161] This process of monitoring through evaluations and any resulting compliance variable explains the BRICS behaviour. Information derived from such exercises usually forms the basis for further interactions with countries and informs decisions on sanctions. Thus, active management and enforcement sanctions are interrelated.

COMPLIANCE ENGINEERED BY DEMOCRACY AND RULE OF LAW

The argument that rule of law and stable democracy are pre-requisites for improved compliance is challengeable when examined through the BRICS's perspective.[162] This challenge can be attributed to the differences amongst the BRICS and their perception of the Western values. For instance, whilst Brazil,[163] India[164] and SA follow the Western notion of democracy, China and Russia do not.[165] Also, China has an authoritarian governmental system and[166] Russia has a managed democracy.[167] Surprisingly, China and Russia's governance approach has not undermined their compliance to AML/CFT standards.[168]

China's compliance position undermines Simmons's argument which suggests that non-liberal democratic governments are less likely to ensure compliance than liberal democracies.[169] Simmons argues that this is due to their lack of respect for

161 Abram Chayes and Antonia Chayes, *The New Sovereignty: Compliance with International Regulatory Agreements* (HUP, 1995).

162 Beth Simmons, 'Compliance with International Agreements' [1998] Annual Rev. Polit. Sci.; Anne-Marie Slaughter, 'International Law in a World of Liberal States' [1995] EJIL 503, 511.

163 Brazil, a civil law country, commenced re-democratization in 1985 after several decades of military rule.

164 India is a pluralistic, common law country.

165 Ernest Bower, 'Economic Imperative in Southeast Asia' in Craig Cohen and Josiane Gabel (eds.) 2015 Global Forecast: Crisis and Opportunity (Centre for Strategic & International Studies) 68 <https://cryptome.org/2014/11/csis-global-2015.pdf> accessed 30 November 2016.

166 China, a civil law country became a market-oriented mixed economy under one-party rule in the 1980s, with a political system more decentralised, but with limited democratic processes internal to the party.

167 Helmut Reisen, '"Democracy" and "Corruption" in the BRICS' (*Shifting Wealth*, 5 August 2016) <http://shiftingwealth.blogspot.co.uk/2016/08/democracy-and-corruption-in-brics.html> accessed 16 November 2017; Russia, a civil law country, began democratisation in the early 1990s post-Soviet Union. Russia's transition from command economy to market economy is still ongoing.

168 *Knaack* (n 54) 41, 65.

169 *Simmons* (n 162) 1, 12.

human rights, legal processes and democratic political constituencies, coupled with acquiescence to high level of illicit activities occurring in the economic bloc.[170] Undoubtedly, China has these deficiencies as by the 2016 democracy index, China is classed as authoritarian and rated 136 of 160 countries.[171] This ranking means that existing formal institutions have limited substance, non-transparent elections and disregard for civil liberties. The 2016 rule of law index ranks China as 80th of 113 countries, an indication of entrenched corruption, a weak criminal justice system and fragile regulatory enforcement structures.[172] Surprisingly, these shortcomings have not hindered China's compliance with AML/CFT standards.[173]

Brazil and South Africa's position further weaken Simmons's argument on democracy as a pre-requisite for compliance with international standards. These historical democratic countries have failed to attain China's compliance levels with AML/CFT standards. For instance, Brazil's successful historical protests for democracy over four years (1984–1988)[174] instilled a spirit of resilience in its people who demanded for rule of law and democratic values. Hence, civil societies unreservedly and strongly combat political corruption, particularly as regards wasteful spending.[175] Recently, angered by corruption allegations against President Dilma Rousseff, over one million Brazilians protested for her removal, a move strengthened by the Brazilian Congress.[176] Nelson Mandela empowered South Africans to fight injustice, occasioned by weak political structures. Most protests have targeted service delivery for socially disadvantaged indigent citi-

---

170 Ibid, 13; *Slaughter* (n 162) 503, 511; Andrew Guznam, 'International Law: A Compliance-Based Theory of International Law' [2002] 90 (6) California Law Review 1826, 1888.

171 *The Economist*, 'Democracy Index 2016: Revenge of the "Deplorable"' (A report by The Economist Intelligence Unit) <http://felipesahagun.es/wp-content/uploads/2017/01/Democracy-Index-2016.pdf> accessed 16 December 2016.

172 World Justice Project, 'Rule of Law Index 2016' (*World Justice Project*, 2016) <https://worldjusticeproject.org/sites/default/files/documents/RoLI_Final-Digital_0.pdf> accessed 10 May 2017.

173 Roda Mushkat, 'China's Compliance with International Law: What Has been Learned and the Gaps Remaining' [2011] 20 (1) Pacific Rim Law & Policy Journal Association 41, 68; Josh Kimbrell, 'Why BRICS Are Bad for America: Inside the Effort to Undermine U.S. Predominance' (*RedState*, 12 April 2017) <https://www.redstate.com/joshkimbrell/2017/04/12/brics-bad-america-inside-effort-undermine-u.s.-predominance/> accessed 10 July 2017.

174 Astrid Prange, 'Brazil Remembers its Struggle for Democracy' (*DW*, 10 April 2014) <http://www.dw.com/en/brazil-remembers-its-struggle-for-democracy/a-17554707> accessed 16 November 2017.

175 Patrick Heller, 'BRICS from Below: Counter-Power Movements in Brazil, India and South Africa' (*Open Democracy*, 30 April 2015) <https://www.opendemocracy.net/patrick-heller/brics-from-below-counterpower-movements-in-brazil-india-and-south-africa> accessed 16 November 2017.

176 Jill Langlois, 'Soggy Protesters Demand Impeachment of Brazil's President: "We have to Fight for Better"' (*LA Times*, 21 May 2017) <http://www.latimes.com/world/mexico-americas/la-fg-brazil-protests-20170521-story.html> accessed 10 July 2017.

zens.[177] Remarkably, these aesthetically high levels of democracy and rule of law in Brazil and SA have not necessarily translated to high levels of AML/CFT compliance levels in excess of China's ratings.

It is however arguable that, unlike China, Brazil and SA provide some form of protection that allows their citizens involvement in the democratic processes. Consequently, China's compliance with international standards does not necessarily equate to national translation of global norms that combat illicit crimes whilst promoting the peoples' agenda. This entrenchment of democratic values in other EEs cannot be overlooked, particularly in light of their political and historical underpinnings which allow them to thrive and engineer compliance from within.

Compared with the other BRICS countries, India is a model country where compliance to AML/CFT reflects democracy and rule of law. India ranks 32nd out of 160 countries on the democracy index; has a robust electoral system and an independent civil liberties presence which is arguably propelled by the Gandhi movement. From the Gandhi era, Indians, disillusioned by the political class that saw themselves as law, would campaign against the government to ensure accountability.[178] This intensified in 2011, when members of a civil society established a political party which won 67 of the 70 seats in Delhi State Assembly in 2015.[179] Consequently, most protests have been focused on ensuring service delivery for its socially disadvantaged indigent citizens. Its high democracy ratings and the improving global ranking on the rule of law index,[180] has resulted in a steady rise in India's AML/CFT compliance levels.

Examining the BRICS indicates that China is indeed an exception. An environment with consolidated democracies usually underpins movement towards improved compliance.[181] This perception holds that sturdy civil societies are essential for a flourishing democracy and an environment where human rights, electoral processes and accountability are paramount. Hence, they propel compliance.[182] This explains Russia's struggle with compliance, given its weak political and economic institutions steeped in corruption and non-transparency or accountability at all governmental levels.[183] These shortcomings, bolstered by Russia's weak rule

---

177 Peter Alexander, 'Rebellion of the Poor: South Africa's Service Delivery Protests – A Preliminary Analysis' [2010] 37 Review of African Political Economy 25, 25.

178 Sarbeswar Sahoo, *Civil Society and Democratization in India: Institutions, Ideologies and Interests* (Routledge, 2013).

179 Parkes Riley and Ravi Roy, 'Corruption and Anti-Corruption: The Case of India' [2016] 32 (1) Journal of Developing Societies 73, 74.

180 World Justice Project, 'Rule of Law Index 2016' (*World Justice Project*, 2016) <https://worldjusticeproject.org/sites/default/files/documents/RoLI_Final-Digital_0.pdf> accessed 10 May 2017.

181 *Heller* (n 175).

182 This is not always the case; with heightened social networking usage, sometimes the loudest voice is what counts and not necessarily the perception of pressure groups.

183 Nandini Ramaujam et al., 'Rule of Law and Economic Development: a Comparative Analysis of Approaches to Economic Development across the BRIC Countries' (The Rule of

of law, have undermined its attempt to realise its economic potential,[184] trade liberalisation[185] and compliance to international standards despite its transition into a market economy. Commenting on this, Rivkin stated that 'Russia still has considerable work to do when it comes to establishing the rule of law… (and) in the creation of a genuinely independent and technocratic judiciary…for the enforcement of judgments..[186] The compliance limitations marked by external requirements and internal tensions challenge the need to monitor the dimensions of rule of law and democracy in relation to compliance.[187]

Recognising the shortcomings in compliance and the inadequacy of sanctions, particularly in Russia, IFIs started using management models, including membership. Other models include the review of countries' compliance shortcomings through assessments to evaluate compliance. This governance approach is supported by studies which emphasise the weak link between democracy and economic prosperity; after all, China's authoritarianist government has created more wealth.[188] However, no findings have buttressed that BRICS became democratic after making economic progress. Russia's ranking even presents evidence to the contrary.[189] The effectiveness of this governance alternative is still largely dependent on respect for rule of law and the efficacy of democracy within countries.

Non-Legal factors

Legal factors are not independent components, rather they are adjunct to political and resources issues. These adjunct issues, which are also compliance drivers in EEs, are examined to see how they affect compliance with AML/CFT standards. An overview of internal factors and external pressures, that occasioned FATF membership through coercion or subtle pressure, shows that the degree to which some of these factors are present, determines to a large extent the compliance levels of countries.

POLITICAL WILL, DOMESTIC CONDITIONS AND POLICY PRIORITIES

The degree of political will and institutional commitments in responding to AML/CFT regulations will determine, to a large extent, the varying degrees of compliance and accountability.

Law and Economic Development, December 2012) <https://www.mcgill.ca/roled/files/roled/mcgill_roled_report_2012.pdf > accessed 16 November 2017.

184 Ibid.
185 Elvis Ngatat, 'Trade Liberalisation within Intra-BRICS and the Rule of Law' [2016] 8 (2) Asian Journal of Law and Economics.
186 IBA, 'BRICS: Rule of law "Critically Important" to BRICS Success' (*IBA*, 11 June 2015) <https://www.ibanet.org/Article/NewDetail.aspx?ArticleUid=702cb343-8fdd-4b4a-962d-2f5fe40a0827> accessed 16 November 2017.
187 *Ramaujam et al.* (n 183).
188 *Reisen* (n 167).
189 Ibid.

It was expected that FATF membership would translate to improved political will for EEs to comply with FATF standards, thus ensuring improved compliance levels. These expectations assumed that strong economies must have had strong structures that promoted transparency within the government and private sector. Therefore, FATF membership would provide the needed impetus for political will within EEs to pursue refined legislative and regulatory reforms. Brazil, however, presents a different picture. The country was steeped in corruption, which hindered its compliance efforts. This was however short-lived.

In 2007, Brazil enacted the National Strategy to Combat Corruption and Money Laundering (ENCCLA), thereby indicating how political will drives accountability.[190] Adopting the ENCCLA demonstrated greater national commitment to combatting ML in light of internal corruption concerns. This was different from the US-driven transnational legal focus on TF; given that the ENCCLA demonstrated Brazil's response and accountability to national interests and concerns that were not necessarily part of transnational priorities. Brazil realised that whilst external demands are relevant, they are not the only considerations. The subsequent introduction of TF measures indicates that the ENCCLA alongside latter measures mediates between internal and external demands for accountability.[191] Consequently, the creation of an FIU[192] and a central authority,[193] combined with the shift of international cooperation responsibilities from the judiciary to the executive, and the introduction of specialised groups on financial crimes in Brazil's judiciary and Central Bank marked the move towards improved accountability.

The Panama papers incidence highlighted the differences in countries' reaction in addressing allegations of illicit crimes and facilitating accountability. Brazil passed a vote of no confidence on its president; China and Russia were silent. Nevertheless, collectively, the BRICS have displayed enormous political will through the introduction of the BRICS Council on AML/CFT. The BRICS agreed that their collective action on counter-terrorism financing should be consolidated. There was also a need to intensify training programmes, especially using the Network AML/CFT.[194] The BRICS also approved a proposal to permanently establish a secretariat for the BRICS Council on AML/CFT in Moscow. It remains to be seen the extent to which this can be translated to long-term change.

---

190 The National Strategy against Corruption and Money Laundering (Estrategia Nacional de Combate a Corrupcao e a Lavagem de Dinheiro) established in 2013, see OECD Public Governance Reviews, 'OECD Integrity Review of Brazil: Managing Risk for a Cleaner Public Service' (OECD, 2012). 72.
191 Ana Belotto and Marcelo Ribeiro, 'Compliance and Regulatory Developments in Brazil: Money Laundering and Corruption' (*Financier Worldwide*, June 2014) <http://www.fina ncierworldwide.com/compliance-and-regulatory-developments-in-brazil-money-launde ring-and-corruption/#.Vz4ht2NlmXR> accessed 13 June 2016.
192 *The National Strategy against Corruption and Money Laundering* (n 190)
193 Ibid.
194 *BRICS* (n 148).

National authorities which perceive compliance with AML/CFT standards as a means of combatting un-systemic risk and ensuring security can also propel the political will for tackling ML/TF. Although ML/TF may not be the immediate catalyst for bringing sectors down, they could be the participatory reason for institutional collapse. Sectors that are AML/CFT compliant are better able to withstand risks by eliminating or reducing the un-systemic risks that accompany financial integration. A country's compliance level may however be largely dependent on that of its neighbours. For example, to prevent a 'race to the bottom', countries with bank secrecy rules can compete more favourably internationally based on the recent Panama tax scandal example. Therefore, the activity of neighbouring nations can trigger a country's compliance or negate it.

Hence, although a country may have the political will, other domestic conditions may still hinder compliance. For instance, the ingrained culture of alternative remittances, such as Hawala, in various EEs, including China, Russia and India[195] largely due to their cash-based economies. Remittances are cheap, largely unregulated and kill paper trails. Transfer processes are dependent on the trust existent between community members and the remittance operator aided by a long history of use.[196] Consequently, remittance processes have escalated the agency slack between the BRICS and the IFIs largely because it lacks a formal registration process, which makes it attractive to users who prefer privacy or lack the requisite documentation. Regulation of Hawala is however significant given its volume[197] and vulnerability to ML/TF.[198] Any commodity can be subject of Hawala. This illustrates the porousness of the system.[199] Various Hawala forms have evolved, including internet- and mobile-based systems.[200]

Regulating Hawala, for instance, presents an effective way of addressing societal issues and ensuring compliance to FATF recommendations. However, regulatory responses must consider competing reactions. A weak response can embolden launderers to exploit any lapses in the Hawala systems, whilst a robust response may lead to proliferation contrary to reduction of underground services.[201] One of the impediments to regulation and compliance is the difficulty in detecting operators, who often camouflage their activities with legitimate busi-

195 Collins Watterson, 'Money Flies with Honey: Encouraging Formal Channel Remittances to Combat Money Laundering' [2013] 91 Texas Law Review 711, 712, 720; Adil Daudi, 'Note: The Invisible Bank: Regulating the Hawala System in India, Pakistan and the UAE' [2005] 15 Ind. Int'l & Comp. L. Rev 619, 654; *Singh* (n 93).
196 Ibid.
197 World Bank Group, Migration and Remittances Factbook 2016 (3rd edn, KNOMAD, 2016).
198 David Faith, 'The Hawala System' [2011] 2 (1) Global Studies, 23, 23.
199 Gold remains the most popular.
200 Manuel Orozco, Elisabeth Burgess and Netta Ascoli, 'Is there a Match Among Migration, Remittances and Technology' (*Inter-American Dialogue*, 30 September 2010) <http://archive.thedialogue.org/page.cfm?pageID=32&pubID=2501> accessed 14 November 2016.
201 Ibid.

nesses.[202] This makes detection, investigation and sanctioning of illicit crimes difficult, expensive and time-consuming. The ineffective regulatory efforts to register Hawala users demonstrate this difficulty. Of the projected 160,000 to 200,000 existing Hawala users in the US, only 38,859 got registered by January 2013.[203] This suggests that threats of sanctions or fines may in fact be unsuitable to compel compliance.

This situation suggests that Hawala banking systems are beyond the reach of regulation and raises questions about aligning or reconciling culture with existing regulation. Scholars have proposed the introduction of trust within the banking system using instruments for financial inclusion such as microfinance banking, mobile money[204] or internet transfers.[205] The extent to which these semi-regulated banking variations would be accepted by culture is however debatable. Acceptability would however provide investigative leads for law enforcement agencies, because transactions done through these means would generate an electronic record, while internet transfers generate IP addresses.[206]

Policy priorities of the BRICS are crucial in determining compliance with FATF recommendations. Compliance is largely dependent on states' perception that FATF recommendations reflect their national interests and priorities.[207] For instance, countries which sponsor state terrorism are unlikely to comply with FATF recommendations against their policy priorities and domestic conditions.

202 Charles B. Bowen, 'Hawala, Money Laundering and Terrorist Financing: Microfinance Lending as an End to Illicit Remittance' [2009] 37 Denv. J. Int'll and Policy 379, 393.

203 The Financial Crimes Enforcement Network (FinCEN) estimates that between 160,000 and 200,000 Monitory services operators (MSBs) are currently operating around the United States, see Bank Secrecy Act: FinCEN and IRS Need to Improve and Better Coordinate Compliance and Data Management Efforts (GAO-07-212, 15 December 2016) <https://www.gpo.gov/fdsys/pkg/GAOREPORTS-GAO-07-212/html/GAOREPOR TS-GAO-07-212.htm> accessed 10 March 2015.

204 Mobile Money Association of India and GSMA, 'Mobile Money: The Opportunity for India' (*MMAI/GSMA*, 13 November 2013) <https://www.gsma.com/mobilefordevel opment/wp-content/uploads/2013/12/MMAI-GSMA-on-Mobile-Money-in-India-for -RBI-Financial-Inclusion-Committee_Dec13.pdf> accessed 10 November 2017; Martha Reeves and Neha Sabharwal, 'Microfinance and Mobile Banking for the Bottom of the Pyramid' [2013] 7.2 Journal of Enterprising Communities: People and Places in the Global Economy 155, 155.

205 Alice Etim, 'Mobile Banking and Mobile Money Adoption for Financial Inclusion' [2014] 9 Research in Business and Economics Journal 1, 2.

206 FATF Report, 'Money Laundering Using New Payment Methods' (*FATF Report*, October 2010) <http://www.fatf-gafi.org/media/fatf/documents/reports/ML%20using%20New %20Payment%20Methods.pdf?TSPD_101_R0=9cb41d963f2572d210dd433c92353b15w I80000000000000000baeecd89ffff0000000000000000000000000005a8f20d10083 f1a37e> accessed 10 July 2017.

207 Tatiana Tropina, 'Do Digital Technologies Facilitate Illicit Financial Flows?' (2016) World Development Report: Digital Dividends 102953 <http://documents.worldbank.org/cura ted/en/896341468190180202/pdf/102953-WP-Box394845B-PUBLIC-WDR16-BP -Do-Digital-Technologies-Facilitate-Illicit-Financial-Flows-Tropina.pdf> accessed 10 July 2017.

However, countries faced with high-level predicate offences, including high crime rates, terror attacks, capital flight, tax evasion and diminishing financial stability are more inclined to comply with FATF recommendations to combat these difficulties. For instance, Brazil has extraordinary criminal rates;[208] as the largest exporter of goods, China tackles trade-based ML. Their emergence as new market-oriented economies worsens these issues, as criminals can operate on a world-wide scale.[209] The large volume of legitimate capital moving into the global financial economy, coupled with high remittances and insufficient regulatory controls have made it possible for funds to move around unregulated. Countries that value bank secrecy as a determinant of compliance are faced with stiff competition by countries which do not.

The domestic conditions are also indicated in the operative system of state governments. Scholars have argued that the level of democracy of states determines their compliance records.[210] They argue that internal structures, including budgetary allocations, reflect the policy priorities and the domestic conditions of a state.[211] Although debatable, domestic politics has long been understood to determine a state's decision to accept international obligations.[212]

COMPLIANCE BASED ON REPUTATIONAL CONCERNS

Unlike FIs in ACs, EEs have more to lose in terms of trade and financial integration if they are not compliant with the AML/CFT regulations. This is because a tainted reputation can adversely affect their businesses. The pressure for compliance may come from large banks which are more predisposed to comply for reputational reasons.[213] Large banks are also keen to display their compliance with international standards to compete globally and establish sturdy banks in developed economies. Thus, benchmarking for performance is valuable, as large banks usually have domestic and international competitive advantages. This may occasion positive regulatory capture whereby regulators are pressured to ensure

---

208   Paula Miraglia, 'Drugs and Drug Trafficking in Brazil: Trends and Policies' (*Foreign Policy at Brookings*, 2016) <https://www.brookings.edu/wp-content/uploads/2016/07/Miraglia-Brazil-final.pdf> accessed 10 December 2016.

209   Moamil, 'Drug Trafficking Among One of the Major Criminal Source of Money Laundering' [2015] 2 (1) International Journal of Multidisciplinary Research and Development 33, 35.

210   *Slaughter* (n 162) 503–538; Helen Milner and Andrew Moravcsik (eds.), *Power, Interdependence and Non-State Actors in World Politics* (PUP, 2009).

211   Lori Post, Amber Raile and Eric Raile, 'Defining Political Will' [2010] 38 (4) Politics & Policy 653, 653.

212   See also Beth Simmons, *Mobilizing for Human Rights: International Law in Domestic Politics* 23–56 (CUP 2009).

213   Deloitte, 'Meeting New Expectations: Foundational Considerations When Upgrading Know Your Customer Programs' (*Deloitte Centre for Financial Services*, 2015) <https://www2.deloitte.com/tr/en/pages/financial-services/articles/dcfs-know-your-customer.html> accessed 10 August 2017.

compliance with FATF recommendations across sectors to attract and ensure continued international investments and business.

The interaction between regulators and the regulated industry can occasion increased engagement in CDD requirements and other FATF recommendations, especially as these actively contribute to combatting fraud.[214] Conversely, non-compliance to CDD requirements contributes to fraud and operational risk. Given regulatory capture by large banks, CDD has increasingly become a concern for boards of directors and senior management, who are usually proactive in combatting ML/TF. These steps are taken in recognition that non-compliance to even soft law instruments can have reputational damage.[215] It indicates the FATF's standard of increased transparency and market pressure, as FATF recommendations now cover more domestic banks. Large banks' efforts to propel increased regulatory supervision indicate that proficient regulatory bodies are crucial in ensuring compliance.

These active steps towards improved compliance within EEs demonstrate limited reliance on their FATF membership to salvage them from the effect of non-compliance. This was particularly due to the knowledge that de-listing can be triggered in the event of dire shortcomings in compliance – a process which has an almost similar effect as blacklisting.

LEGITIMACY AND ITS EFFECT ON COMPLIANCE

The treatment faced by the BRICS as associate members and non-members has not been relegated to history. For this reason, the BRICS do not necessarily view the FATF as wholly legitimate irrespective of their positioning as strategically important countries. However, the BRICS persistently comply with the FATF standards. Their underlying agenda is to ensure their continued integration with the global financial market. For this reason, their compliance levels are usually above 50%.[216] However, given the internal issues faced by the BRICS, such as corruption, it is indeed questionable if their compliance levels are a true indication of their efforts to combat ML/TF. Indeed, compliance levels can be 'window dressed' and BRICS can strategically engage with its principals (the IFIs) to ensure continued integration.

To heighten their accountability, the BRICS developed a BRICS Council for AML/CFT, a move aimed to facilitate improved AML/CFT structures particularly centred on corruption.[217] Additionally, the BRICS sought a collaborative platform, free from bias which allowed for secure AML/CFT information

---

214 Ibid.
215 Andrew Guzman, 'A Compliance-Based Theory of International Law' [2002] 90 (6) California Law Journal 1826, 1888; *Simmons* (n 162) 1, 8.
216 See Figure 6.1.
217 Clarence Joseph, 'Establishing Comprehensive, Economic and Legal Approach to Risks and Threats in Anti-Money Laundering Regime' [2016] 13 Financial Security 1, 24.

exchange and the development of international mechanisms for confiscation and recovery of criminal assets within the BRICS.[218] The BRICS have taken on this additional responsibility because they recognise that effective AML/CFT and anti-corruption measures attract foreign direct investment and aid their global expansion plans. However, the BRICS Council for AML/CFT was established in 2015, and its effect is yet to be known.

GLOBALISATION AND INTEGRATION

Globalisation and integration come with attendant issues such as political strife between countries with varying values or increasing inter-bank relationship between countries. To the extent that certain banks establish their physical presence in other countries. This section will illustrate how these can affect a country's compliance with AML/CFT standards.

As demonstrated in chapter 3, political interrelationship is a determinant for compliance with AML/CFT regulations in the BRICS. Political strife between countries is likely to weaken external ties and internal institutions that drive regional or global compliance. For instance, the political strife between Russia and the West was arguably designed by Western states to weaken Russia geopolitically and reduce its threat to Western Europe and the NATO Alliance.[219] In pursuance of this objective, Russia was recently expelled from the G8 countries. The reason was the inability of Russia to enter into memoranda of understanding with Western countries to uncover cross-border ML/TF. Interestingly, Russia's political and economic stability is beneficial to the West as it could be a vital factor in international relations, particularly trade and the economy of the United States. Russia's expulsion from the G8 indicates a lack of diplomacy by the US and other Western countries in dealing with perceived allies and working together for a common good. The alternative argument however is that there is a balance between condoning Russia's infringement on Ukraine's sovereignty and protecting trade/finance agreements.

China has similar issues with the West, including territorial issues in its attempt to redefine its place amongst the West and the South. Furthermore, China is not content with Western interpretation of policies, such as the Western stance on human rights which may undermine China's attempts to curb illicit crimes through criminal sanctions.

Yet, global integration has seen BRICS enter into banking relationships with developed countries, and even establish subsidiary financial institutions in those countries. Stretching the agency theory enumerated in chapter 4 would indicate that High Priority (HP) countries classified as highly integrated (such as China) would be willing to sustain a high compliance level to ensure continued integration into the global economy. Hence, one may conclude that the propensity for

218 Ibid.
219 In relation to territorial issues with Western allies like Ukraine and Georgia.

China or India to comply to AML/CFT standards is higher. Particularly because, on paper, their procedures follow the host country's AML/CFT policies.[220]

Cases however illustrate the use of Chinese subsidiary banks abroad to facilitate money laundering or capital flight.[221] The UK regulator (the Financial Conduct Authority – FCA) has responded to these cases against the largest branches of the Industrial and Commercial Bank of China (ICBC) and the China Construction Bank Corp (CBB) by strengthening its inspection of them.[222] The United Kingdom's step indicates that the compliance by Chinese overseas banks is questionable. Henry Rui, an Ernst and Young partner for China stated that 'when they do funds transfer, they don't check the source of funds, which is very important in KYC...they just do the transactions'.[223] This is an indication that compliance may actually be lip service to regulation and these institutions would bypass compliance to win businesses. Rui attributes this to the recent history of AML in China which requires time for the country to be comfortable in meeting the international standards. Statistics however indicate that China's admirable compliance levels show evidence of the country's attempt to avert de-risking whilst maintaining its space within the global economy.[224]

TECHNICAL CAPACITY AND RESOURCES

Technical capacity is crucial in determining a country's compliance with the AML/CFT standards. Most BRICS countries have the technical capacity required to combat illicit crimes due to resources at their disposal and their interrelationship with IFIs/FATF. Their resource devotion and availability can be attributed to their need to protect their position in the international market. These give the EEs access to external technical assistance given the risk they pose to the global economy.

However, the BRICS do not always have all the expertise necessary to combat illicit crime. Evidence from various EEs reveal that there is no unified regulatory approach for combatting ML/TF, largely due to lack of capacity. In Brazil, for instance, the responsible agencies are the Central Bank, CVM (Securities Commission), SUSEP (Superintendencia de Seguros Privados; Agency of Private Insurances), and SPC (Secretaria de Previdencia Complementar; Secretary of Complementary Social Security). The FIU (COAF) is responsible for further investigation of suspicious transactions received from financial institutions and

220 Nick Kochan, 'Global Concern at AML Standards of Chinese Banks Abroad' (*WoltersKluwer*, 20 May 2016) <http://www.wolterskluwerfs.com/article/global-concern-at-aml-standards-of-chinese-banks-abroad.aspx> accessed 10 May 2017.
221 Ibid. For instance, the CBB had enforcement actions taken against it for non-compliance to CDD requirements. The Bank of China also allegedly smuggled more than 5 billion dollars out of Italy to China.
222 Ibid.
223 Ibid.
224 See Figure 6.1.

enforcement against same. There is however weak communication amongst these institutions.[225]

The Brazil 2010 MER stressed the disjointed system of communication in its criminal justice system.[226] It revealed the lack of a centralised database between the police, public prosecutors, FIs and the judiciary.[227] This resulted in a cumbersome process; where the judiciary had to apply to the central bank which received classified information. The request was then forwarded to the FIs for notification and documentation prior to submission to the judicial authority. This time-consuming process allowed for laundering prior to enforcement. This process has since been replaced by the BacenJud, an internet information request system that eliminates the middleman (the central bank), whilst permitting information exchange between the FIs and the judiciary.[228] The advantage of this system is that judges now have easy, fast and direct access to banking information. It also recognises orders for the lifting of financial secrecy as well as enforcement orders for the freezing of bank accounts. Partnerships are increasingly formed between regulatory institutions and regulators in a bid to ensure improved compliance.

Technical capacity can sometimes be undermined by corruption. Evidence from the private sector, particularly in light of the recent Panama and Paradise Papers incidences, illustrates a complacent approach to combatting illicit crimes.[229] In the private sector, a new market for lawyers, accountants, auditors, economists, front desk officers and other professionals has emerged, bestowing on them a gate-keeper responsibility of ensuring that FATF recommendations are adhered to. This responsibility specifically recognises that these professionals should carry out strict CDD. It requires that financial transactions are monitored, and prompt reports made to the FIU where suspicion arises. This responsibility requires that the staff be trained to acquire relevant skills to drive the new market.[230] This has been translated in the BRICS intensifying training programmes for relevant professionals. Despite this, Panama still happened[231] and involved all

---

225 FATF and GAFI, 'Mutual Evaluation Report: Anti-Money Laundering and Combating the Financing of Terrorism – Federative Republic of Brazil' (*FATF and GAFI*, 25 June 2010) <http://www.fatf-gafi.org/media/fatf/documents/reports/mer/MER%20Brazil%20full .pdf?TSPD_101_R0=af6a4c41a65469dddeef4499ce3e9c7cx270000000000000000baeec d89ffff00000000000000000000000000005a8f1dc900004dea87> accessed 17 July 2016.

226 Ibid.

227 Ibid. (n 227).

228 Banco Central Do Brasil, 'BACEN JUD 2.0: Manual Basico' (*Banco central Do Brasil*) <https://www.bcb.gov.br/fis/pedjud/ftp/manualbasico.pdf> accessed 7 February 2018.

229 Paul May, 'The Paradise Papers: Panama's Labyrinth' (Arachnys) <http://blog.arachnys .com/panamas-labyrinth> accessed 7 February 2018.

230 Gregory Shaffer, 'The Dimension and Determinants of State Change' *in* Gregory Shaffer (eds.) *Transnational Legal Ordering and State Change* (CUP, 2013).

231 For instance, in Brazil, corruption and crimes against national financial institutions including fraud, smuggling, embezzlement, drug trafficking and capital flight are considered as main crime sources. Terrorism and terrorist financing were excluded – see *FATF and GAFI* (n 225).

BRICS countries. The responses were surprising; Russia and China reacted by censoring all news items filtering into their countries. It became evident that bank officials were part of the process of securing the Panama deals. Clearly, technical capacity is hindered by corruption as it precipitates operational risk within institutions. Corruption is disastrous; it undermines staff professionalism and threatens effective judicial decisions. It appears that the Brazilian judiciary has taken a lax attitude to ML/TF cases before. For instance, only 11 cases have culminated in final convictions.[232]

This also extends to the ineffective regulation of increased technological use. To a large extent, this is a determinant for compliance in EEs,[233] given the wealth of the countries[234] and internet penetration. Within EEs, payment methods are continually evolving. The FATF has recognised that their vulnerability to ML/TF is predicated on the absence of specific regulations[235] and the sluggish adaptation of the regulators to ensure compliance.[236] Turner rejects the position that cyber payment and internet banking systems are extensions of the traditional banking system, arguing instead that they are game changers.[237] His position indicates the challenges that regulators are faced with in ensuring swift responses to combatting AML/CFT.

The pervasive nature of cybercrime further intensifies this challenge. Like ML via wire transfers, it is not subject to any regulator's jurisdiction. It is however faster and possible without paper trails, since programming entities sometimes provide services to the exclusion of banks. As the market for cyber criminals is expanding, with experts and social engineers leading the pack, so is the level of damage and consequential losses that can accrue. For example, a Brazilian group, 'Anonymous Brasil', unleashed cyber terror on Brazilian FIs' websites, including that of Citigroup in 2012.[238] India is plagued with similar issues; statistics reveal that 48% of Indians were cybercrime victims in 2015.[239] The damage in

232 Ibid.
233 Jonathan E. Turner, *Money Laundering Prevention: Deterring, Detecting, and Resolving Financial Fraud* (John Wiley & Sons, Inc. 2011).
234 Rosalba O'Brien, 'Latam Cyber Attacks Rise as Peru, Brazil Hackers Link up with Russians' (*Reuters*, 28 August 2015) <http://www.reuters.com/article/latam-cyberattack-idUSL5 N1134W520150828> accessed 14 January 2016.
235 Specific virtual currency regulations exist in Russia, although citizens are warned off payment sites as persons can unknowingly become vehicles for laundering.
236 Prepaid cards, internet payment services, mobile payment systems and virtual currencies, see *FATF Report* (n 206).
237 *Turner* (n 233) 194; Olivia Solon, 'Cybercriminals Launder Money Using in Game Currencies' (*Wired.Co.Uk*, 2013).
238 Intel Security, 'Net Losses: Estimating the Global Cost of CyberCrime' Economic Impact of Cybercrime II – Center for Strategic and International Studies (Intel Security, 2014) <https://csis-prod.s3.amazonaws.com/s3fs-public/legacy_files/files/attachments/140609_rp _economic_impact_cybercrime_report.pdf> accessed 15 July 2016; *O'Brien* (n 234).
239 Team PG, '48 Percent Indians Online Were Cyber Crime Victims Last Year: Norton' (*PGu-rus.com*, 20 November 2015) <https://www.pgurus.com/48-percent-indians-online-were -cyber-crime-victims-last-year-norton/> accessed 10 July 2016.

Russia is unprecedented, with hijackers doubling their income from USD 3.7 billion between 2011 and 2013.[240] Although Russian enforcement agencies have increasingly detected more cases, the effectiveness cannot be measured. These cyber attacks have occasioned stock market manipulations.[241]

Recognising the challenges posed by technology, Nobel Laureate Michael Spence recently stated that the BRICS slowdown is attributable to 'the disruptive impacts of digital technology, which are set to erode developing economies'.[242] This statement illustrates that technology, although a positive change, comes with challenges which hinder compliance to AML/CFT, puts customers at risk and challenges economic growth. Regrettably, Spence states that these countries 'have little or no control' over these obstacles that hinder their ability to achieve sustained high growth.

Cross-Country Analysis of Compliance to AML/CFT Regime: FATF

An assessment of the MER of countries is carried out to determine the level of country compliance to AML/CFT. The scoring of assessments is discussed in the previous chapter.[243]

Analysis of AML/CFT by Countries

Figure 6.1 represents a plot of the percentage score based on the FATF MER. The BRICS countries are individually represented on the basis of their MER results. Figure 6.1 displays India as the most compliant EE with 66.67%, closely followed by China with 66.03%. South Africa then follows these countries with 58.55%, Russia with 57.6% and Brazil with 54.49% compliance level. Brazil's troubling compliance level at 54% is however above that of 35 African countries, as 30 countries score below 50%.

This may be indicative that the membership within a club may promote increased compliance with its objectives. However, this chapter asserts that economic and legal development, not membership, occasions improved compliance. This is because countries like Mexico, Indonesia, Nigeria and Turkey (MINT) that are classified as EEs,[244] have achieved almost comparable compliance levels. Consequently, these results reflect that blacklisting and other implicit coercive

240 Willain Bynes and Robert Munro, *Money Laundering, Asset Forfeiture and Recovery and Compliance – A Global Guide* (Lexis Nexis, 2016).

241 Maarten Gehem, Artur Usanov, Erik Frinking and Michel Rademaker, *Assessing Cyber Security, A Meta-Analysis of Threats, Trends, and Responses to Cyber Attacks* (Hague International Centre for Strategic Studies, 2015).

242 *Reisen* (n 167).

243 See chapter 5.

244 BBC News, 'The Mint Countries: Next Economic Giants?' (*BBC News*, 6 January 2014) <http://www.bbc.co.uk/news/magazine-25548060> accessed 10 January 2017; Christine Easterfield, 'BRIC vs MINT – Comparing Emerging Markets Using Cambashi's

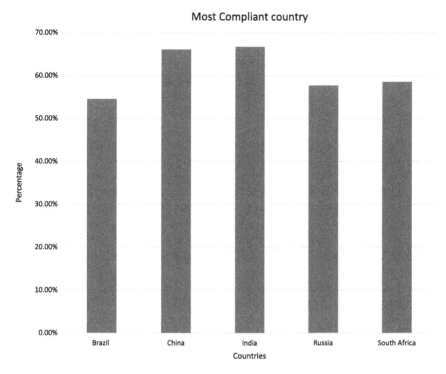

Figure 6.1 Technical Compliance Levels of the BRICS to the FATF Recommendations (Derived from the FATF MERs of countries).

measures of compliance induce potential members of the FATF to introduce high levels of supervision and enforcement structures which coincidentally is supported by their domestic structures. This can be deduced from the FATF membership policy which emphatically states that it considers, amongst other factors: 'the level of AML/CFT risks faced and the efforts to combat such risks…level of commitment to AML/CFT efforts'.[245]

The FATF considers these on a qualitative basis which is subjective and based on unquantifiable evidence. Although the method employed is questionable, what is evident is that the membership requirement is set at a high bar and countries are pushed to meet that bar by increased regulatory supervision and enforcement – actions which guarantee membership and warrant continuous compliance. This supports the argument that domestic factors and embedded coercion ensure compliance, not membership.

Updated Country Observation' (*Cambashi*) <http://www.cambashi.com/contentmgr/showdetails.php/id/2513/page/3> accessed 3 January 2016.
245 FATF, 'FATF Membership Policy' (*FATF*) <http://www.fatf-gafi.org/about/membersandobservers/fatfmembershippolicy.html> accessed 13 January 2016.

The question then is why the BRICS, why are these same measures not foisted on ACs? The response can be gleaned from the FATF membership requirement, which considers:

> the impact (of the country's financial system) on the global financial system...the degree of openness of the financial sector and its interaction with international markets...the level of adherence to financial sector standards and participation in international organizations.[246]

This demonstrates that developed countries are more likely to have sophisticated financial systems and impact on the global market, thus warranting their inclusion. Furthermore, they are also more likely to have advanced infrastructure and expertise to foster compliance to AML/CFT standards. Thus, it can be argued that the criterion for membership in itself fosters improved compliance within countries that aspire to get a seat at the FATF table. This explains why mandatory compliance to certain FATF recommendations, like recommendations 3, 5, 10, 11 and 20,[247] are easily achieved by the BRICS given their robust legal, economic and supervisory structure. IMF statistics buttress the increased supervisory quality in the BRICS countries. These requirements indeed make the BRICS regulation more robust and prepared to ensure compliance. Thus, when membership is aspired to and supported by domestic circumstances, compliance is less likely to be problematic.

Analysis by Recommendation and Topics

The clearest deficiency noted regarding country compliance levels is mainly as regards recommendation 17 on 'Reliance on Third Parties'. Third parties are classified as financial institutions or Designated Non-Financial Businesses and Professions (DNFBPs). The FATF believes that when permitted to rely on third parties, the financial institution granted that permission has the ultimate responsibility of ensuring that the third party is registered and carries out adequate due diligence (CDD)/record keeping. This deficiency can be attributed to the high level of unregulated money transfer business given the BRICS's high remittances. Additionally, businesses like casinos, real estate agents and dealers in precious stones face minimal regulation implementation and lack the expertise to supply adequate CDD/record keeping to the permitted institution. Lawyers, trust and service providers are also strictly regulated and owe confidentiality obligations to their clients. This explains the low level of compliance to recommendation 22 which requires DNFBPs to adhere to the FATF recommendations on CDD/record keeping.

Conversely, the statistics reveal that the recommendation with the highest level of compliance is recommendation 9 on financial secrecy, with a 95% score,

---

246 Ibid.
247 *FATF* (n 245).

well above the average 60.77%. This is followed by recommendation 31 on the powers of enforcement and investigative officers. If this is correct, then financial secrecy laws do not inhibit the implementation of the FATF recommendations. It is however paradoxical that recommendation 17 is low as recommendation 31 charges countries to empower their enforcement and investigative authorities to carry out their tasks effectively. It could however mean that these authorities have narrow focus, which is not inclusive of DNFBPs. This aligns with compliance literature on EEs which revealed that EEs' investigative and enforcement structures are sturdy but lacking in capacity. The absence of capacity has consequently occasioned a risk-based approach which, unfortunately, is not holistic.

An evaluation of Figure 6.2 illustrates improving compliance levels to CFT requirements by the BRICS and sturdy compliance to CDD requirements. This is different for ACs that although they do combat heavy terrorism, they have displayed weak compliance to the recommendations. This, again, can be attributed to lack of, or weak, expertise in ACs.

Conclusion

The BRICS have created newer inequalities of power and influence regionally and globally. Although inherently diverse in terms of culture, socio-political structures and economic policies, the agreement between these countries is a perceived threat to existing IFIs due to their accelerating economic progression. Based on their intrinsic powers and unprecedented economic growth, the BRICS

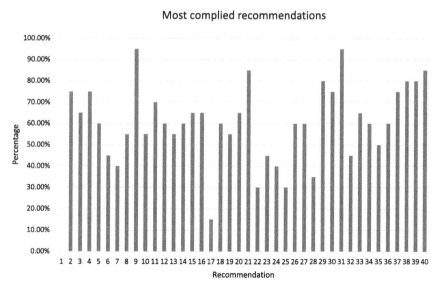

Figure 6.2 Analysis by Compliance to FATF Recommendations.

were selected as members to the FATF in a bid to drive improved compliance to AML/CFT recommendations, especially amongst regions.

Extending FATF membership to the BRICS was centred on varying jurisdictional reasons. Whilst the BRICS and the developing world viewed this membership as a means to gain increased representation within the FATF, the West's agenda was to ensure that the Global South's financial movement is not replete with illicit transactions. The power-play involved in negotiations between these 'North-South strategically important countries' was predicated on the assumption that representation would catalyse improved compliance to AML/CFT recommendations. This assumption however did not consider pertinent issues peculiar to the BRICS economies, such as diverse socio-economic, political and legal developmental levels. Furthermore, the FATF continues to exercise some restraint in including EEs as true core members and thus shapers of its standards. It had merely treated them as regulation-takers. The BRICS's coerced and belated membership has created a very unbalanced membership between EEs and the developed countries.

Against this background, this chapter argues that membership does not necessarily guarantee comparable representation or legitimacy; neither does it guarantee the overtly improved compliance of BRICS countries. It presents a contrary argument that 'representation' taints the socio-economic complexities inherent in these countries and their ability to comply. Worse still, it conceals the asymmetries occasioned by variances in the strength of legal structures reinforced by political and economic differences between FATF members. For membership to equate to legitimacy, there must be existent changes along existing political and economic global structures, arguing that this would ensure improved adherence to FATF recommendations.

It then considers the determinants of compliance to AML/CFT in EEs. It finds that compliance is based on varying factors which may be external or internal to individual jurisdictions. More so, external factors influence internal determinants of compliance. This is further buttressed by the FATF compliance standards which reveal that the standards of compliance are marginally higher in EEs than in African countries. This can be attributed to improved supervision in the select countries and stronger legal and financial systems which were grounds for membership and not an offshoot of membership.

Further Reading

1. Abram Chayes and Antonia Handler Chayes, *The New Sovereignty: Compliance with International Regulatory Agreements* (Harvard University Press, 1995).
2. Adil Anwar Daudi, 'Note: The Invisible Bank: Regulating the Hawala System in India, Pakistan and the UAE' [2005] 15 *Indiana International & Comparative Law Review*.
3. Alice S. Etim, 'Mobile Banking and Mobile Money Adoption for Financial Inclusion' [2014] 9 Research in Business and Economics Journal.
4. Alldridge Peter, 'Money Laundering and Globalization' [2008] 35 (4) Journal of Law and Society.

5. Alonso Soto, 'BRICS Bank to Defy Western Clout in Global Finances' (*Reuters*, 11 July 2014) <http://uk.reuters.com/article/uk-brics-summit-idUKKBN0F G1SG20140711> accessed 14 March 2016.
6. Ananya Chatterjee, 'India-China-United States: The Post-Cold War Evolution of a Strategic Triangle' [2011] 5 (3) *Political Perspectives.*
7. Andres Cala, 'Brazil's Challenge to US Dominance' (*Consortiumnews.com*, 2 October 2013) <https://consortiumnews.com/2013/10/02/brazils-chal lenge-to-us-dominance/> accessed 2 January 2016.
8. Andrew Guzman, 'A Compliance-Based Theory of International Law' [2002] 90 (6) California Law Journal.
9. *Asian Tribune*, 'Arrest of Yoshita a Political Witch Hunting: Police Denied Allegation' (*Asian Tribune*, 1 February 2016) <http://www.asiantribune.com /node/88502> accessed 21 January 2017.
10. Astrid Prange, 'Brazil Remembers its Struggle for Democracy' (*DW*, 10 April 2014) <http://www.dw.com/en/brazil-remembers-its-struggle-for-democ racy/a-17554707> accessed 16 November 2017.
11. Banco Central Do Brasil, 'BACEN JUD 2.0: Manual Basico' (*Banco Central Do Brasil*) <https://www.bcb.gov.br/fis/pedjud/ftp/manualbasico.pdf> accessed 7 February 2018.
12. BCBS, 'Consultative Document: Customer Due Diligence for Banks' (*Bank for International Settlements*, January 2001) <https://www.bis.org/publ/bcbs77 .pdf> accessed 19 May 2016.
13. BBC News, 'The Mint Countries: Next Economic Giants?' (*BBC News*, 6 January 2014) <http://www.bbc.co.uk/news/magazine-25548060> accessed 10 January 2017.
14. Beth Simmons, 'Compliance with International Agreements' [1998] 1 (1) Annual Review of Political Science.
15. Beth Simmons, *Mobilizing for Human Rights: International Law in Domestic Politics* (Cambridge University Press, 2009).
16. Kenneth Blazejewski, 'The FATF and Its Institutional Partners: Improving the Effectiveness and Accountability of Trans-governmental Networks' [2008] 22 Temple International and Comparative Law Journal.
17. Braun Aurel, 'Tougher Sanctions Now: Putin's Delusional Quest for Empire' [2014] 177 (2) World Affairs.
18. Bretton Woods, *Agreement Act*, Section 5 [22 U.S.C. 286c] 1962, amended and effected in 2016.
19. BRICS, 'The BRICS Handover Report: 2015–2016' (*BRICS*, 2016) 65/66 <en.brics2015.ru/load/885248> accessed 10 December 2017.
20. BRICS Russia UFA 2015, 'BRICS Reach 30 Percent of Global GDP' (*BRICS Russia UFA*, 7 July 2015) <http://en.brics2015.ru/news/20150707/277 026.html> accessed 23 February 2016.
21. Bronti DeRoche, 'The Ways the US Benefits from Foreign Aid to Brazil' (*The Borgen Project*, 26 January 2018) <https://borgenproject.org/u-s-benefits-f rom-foreign-aid-to-brazil/> accessed 10 February 2018.
22. Bruce Jones, *Still Ours to Lead: America, Rising Power and the Tension Between Rivalry and Restraint* (The Brookings Institution, 2014).
23. Cecily Rose, *International Anti-Corruption Norms: Their Creation and Influence on Domestic Legal Systems* (1st edn, Oxford University Press, 2015).

24. Cedric Lam and Liu Yang, 'China Joins the FATF' (*The Anti-Fraud Network*, September 2007) <http://antifraudnetwork.com/2007/09/china-joins-the -fatf/> accessed 14 January 2016.

25. Charalampos Efstahopoulos, 'India and Global Governance: the Politics of Ambivalent Reform' [2016] 53 International Politics 239–259.

26. Charles B. Bowen, 'Hawala, Money Laundering and Terrorist Financing: Microfinance Lending as an End to Illicit Remittance' [2009] 37 Denver Journal of International Law & Policy.

27. Chris Higg, 'China Ends Death Penalty for 13 Economic Crimes' (*BBC News Shanghai*, February 2011) <http://www.bbc.co.uk/news/world-asia-pacific-12580504> accessed 11 February 2016.

28. Christian Brutsch and Mihaela Papa, 'Deconstructing the BRICS: Bargaining Coalition, Imagined Community or Geopolitical Fad?' [2013] 6 (3) Chinese Journal of International Politics.

29. Christine Easterfield, 'BRIC vs MINT – Comparing Emerging Markets Using Cambashi's Updated Country Observation' (*Cambashi*) <http://www .cambashi.com/contentmgr/showdetails.php/id/2513/page/3> accessed 3 January 2016.

30. Christopher J. McCoy, 'America's Role in the End of South African Apartheid' [2011] Journal of International Affairs at UCSD <https://prospectjournal .org/2011/10/21/americas-role-in-the-end-of-south-african-apartheid/> accessed 13 January 2017.

31. Clarence Samuel Joseph, 'Establishing Comprehensive, Economic and Legal Approach to Risks and Threats in Anti-Money Laundering Regime' [2016] 13 Financial Security.

32. Colin Clark, 'Economic Development in Communist China' [1976] 84 (2) Journal of Political Economy.

33. Colin Sparks, 'How Coherent is the BRICS Grouping' *in* Kaarle Nordenstreng and Daya Kishan Thussu (eds.) *Mapping BRICS Media* (Routledge, 2015).

34. Collins Watterson, 'Money Flies with Honey: Encouraging Formal Channel Remittances to Combat Money Laundering' [2013] 91 Texas Law Review 711, 712, 720.

35. Concepcion Verdugo Yepes, 'Compliance with the AML/CFT International Standard: Lessons from a Cross-Country Analysis' (2006) IMF Working Paper 11/177, 17 <https://www.imf.org/external/pubs/ft/wp/2011/wp11177 .pdf> accessed 10 July 2015.

36. Cynthia Roberts, 'Building the New World Order BRIC by BRIC' [2011] 6 The European Financial Review 4.

37. Daniel E. Ho, 'Compliance and International Soft law: Why Do Countries Implement the Basel Accord' [2002] 5 (3) Journal of International Economic Law.

38. W. Daniel, Drezner, *All Politics is Global: Explaining International Regulatory Regime* (Princeton University Press, Princeton, 2007).

39. David Faith, 'The Hawala System' [2011] 2 (1) Global Studies.

40. Tereza De Castro, 'Trade Among BRICS Countries: Changes Towards Closer Cooperation?' [2013] 16 (3) Central European Review of Economic Issues.

41. Deloitte, 'Meeting New Expectations: Foundational Considerations When Upgrading Know Your Customer Programs' (*Deloitte Centre for Financial*

Services, 2015) <https://www2.deloitte.com/tr/en/pages/financial-services/articles/dcfs-know-your-customer.html> accessed 10 August 2017.

42. Delphine Defossez, 'The Current Challenges of Money Laundering Law in Russia' [2017] 20 (4) Journal of Money Laundering Control.

43. Dieter Kerwer and Rainer Hulsse, 'How International Organizations Rule the World: The Case of the Financial Action Task Force on Money Laundering' [2011] 1 (2) Journal of International Organization Studies.

44. Dietmar Meyer and Adela Shera, 'The Impact of Remittances on Economic Growth: An Econometric Model' [2017] 18 (2) Economia.

45. Domenico Lombardi and Hongying Wang (eds.), *Enter the Dragon: China in the International Financial System* (Centre for International Governance Innovation, 2015).

46. Dominic Wilson and Roopa Purushothaman, 'Dreaming with BRICs: The Path to 2050' [2003] 99 Global Economic Paper.

47. Domitilla Sagramoso, *Russia's Western Orientation after 11th September: Russia's Enhanced Cooperation with NATO and the European Union* (Rubbettino Editore, 2004).

48. Economic Development & Growth in Ethekwini, 'Building Better BRICS: South Africa's Inclusion into the Bloc' (Ethekwini Municipality, 2012) <http://www.durban.gov.za/Resource_Centre/edge/Documents/Building%20Better%20BRICS%20-%20South%20Africa%27s%20Inclusion%20into%20the%20Bl.pdf> accessed 10 May 2016.

49. Eduardo T. Gonzales, 'Policy Transfer in the Philippines: Can it Pass the Localization Test?' [2007] 2 (1) JOAAG.

50. Elena Chinyaeva, 'Russia and the FATF Blacklist' [2002] 1 (3) Russia and Eurasia Review (*The Jamestown Foundation*, 2 July 2002) <https://jamestown.org/program/russia-and-the-fatf-blacklist/> accessed 10 November 2017.

51. Ellen Brown, 'Just who is Responsible for Deregulation?' (Illusion2Reliality at www.moreyroots.co.uk, 5 September 2015) <http://www.moneyroots.co.uk/#!the-banksters/c1ny7> accessed 23 February 2016.

52. Elod Takats, 'International Enforcement Issues' *in* Donato Masciandaro, Elod Takats and Brigitte Unger (eds.) *Black Finance: The Economies of Money Laundering* (Edward Elgar, Cheltenham, UK/Northampton, MA, 2007).

53. Elvis Tankwa Ngatat, 'Trade Liberalisation Within Intra-BRICS and the Rule of Law' [2016] 8 (2) Asian Journal of Law and Economics.

54. Eric Farnsworth, 'America Must Take Brazil Seriously' (*The National Interest*, June 15, 2015) <http://nationalinterest.org/feature/america-must-take-brazil-seriously-13111?page=2> accessed 1 January 2016.

55. European Parliament, Directorate-General for External Policies, *The Role of BRICS in the Developing World* (European Parliament, 2012).

56. FATF and GAFI, 'Mutual Evaluation Report: Anti-Money Laundering and Combating the Financing of Terrorism – Federative Republic of Brazil' (*FATF and GAFI*, 25 June 2010) <http://www.fatf-gafi.org/media/fatf/documents/reports/mer/MER%20Brazil%20full.pdf?TSPD_101_R0=af6a4c41a65469dddeef4499ce3e9c7cx270000000000000000baeecd89ffff00000000000000000000000000005a8f1dc900004dea87> accessed 17 July 2016.

57. FATF, 'Process and Criteria for Becoming a FATF Member' (*FATF*) <http://www.fatf-gafi.org/about/membersandobservers/membershipprocessandcriteria.html> accessed 1 May 2016.
58. FATF – IX, 'Financial Action Task Force on Money Laundering, Annual Report, 1997–1998' (*FATF* – IX) <http://www.fatf-gafi.org/media/fatf/documents/reports/1997%201998%20ENG.pdf?TSPD_101_R0=be9bbd19c394a0f96d9bc7e799853062eD900000000000000000d501cd89ffff00000000000000000000000005a8d916b00d7bfb32c> accessed 10 January 2017.
59. FATF Report, 'Money Laundering Through Money Remittance and Currency Exchange Providers' (*FATF Report*, 2010) <http://www.fatf-gafi.org/media/fatf/ML%20through%20Remittance%20and%20Currency%20Exchange%20Providers.pdf> accessed 23 January 2017.
60. FATF, '25 Years and Beyond: the Financial Action Task Force' (*FATF*, 2014) <http://www.fatf-gafi.org/media/fatf/documents/brochuresannualreports/FATF%2025%20years.pdf?TSPD_101_R0=1495c41e79bcbd390bbe7629e106108ajF500000000000000000d501cd89ffff0000000000000000000000000000005a8d95e80048c055d7> accessed 14 January 2017.
61. FATF, 'FATF Membership Policy' (*FATF*) <http://www.fatf-gafi.org/about/membersandobservers/fatfmembershippolicy.html> accessed 11 October 2017.
62. FATF, 'FATF Presidency' (*FATF*) <http://www.fatf-gafi.org/about/fatfpresidency/> accessed 1 May 2016.
63. FATF, 'International Standards on Combating Money Laundering and the Financing of Terrorism & Proliferation: The FATF Recommendations' (*FATF*, 2012) <http://www.fatf-gafi.org/media/fatf/documents/recommendations/pdfs/FATF_Recommendations.pdf> accessed 7 August 2012.
64. FATF, 'Outcomes of the Plenary Meeting of the FATF, Valencia, 21–23 June 2017' (*FATF*, June 2017) <http://www.dt.tesoro.it/export/sites/sitodt/modules/documenti_it/prevenzione_reati_finanziari/prevenzione_reati_finanziari/FATF_Outcomes_of_the_Plenary_meeting_of_the_June_2017_FATF.pdf> accessed September 2017.
65. *Financial Times*, 'Turkey's Banking Blacklist Risk' (*Financial Times*, 16 October 2012) <https://www.ft.com/content/bbfe16f0-01c8-357e-84d4-4cce12d1e6b4> accessed 1 January 2016.
66. Frank William, 'International Business Challenge: Does Adding South Africa Finally Make the BRIC Countries Relevant' [2013] 12 (1) Journal of International Business Research.
67. Gregory Shaffer, 'The Dimension and Determinants of State Change' *in* Gregory Shaffer (ed.) *Transnational Legal Ordering and State Change* (Cambridge University Press, Cambridge, 2013).
68. Gillian Tett, 'The Story of the BRICs' (*Financial Times*, 15 January 2010) <https://next.ft.com/content/112ca932-00ab-11df-ae8d-00144feabdc0> accessed 15 May 2016.
69. Giselle Datz and Joel Peters, 'Brazil and the Israeli-Palestinian Conflict in the New Century: Between Ambition, Idealism and Pragmatism' [2013] 2 (2) Journal of Foreign Affairs.
70. Luke Glanville, 'The Antecedents of "Sovereignty as Responsibility"' [2011] 17 (2) European Journal of International Relations.

71. Michael Glosny, 'China and the BRICs: A Real (but Limited) Partnership in a Unipolar World' [2010] 42 (1) *Polity*.
72. Heinrich Boll-Stiftung and Regine Schonenberg (eds.), *Transnational Organized Crime: Analyses of a Global Challenge to Democracy* (Transcript Verlag Bielefeld, 2013).
73. Helmut Reisen, '"Democracy" and "Corruption" in the BRICS' (*ShiftingWealth*) <http://shiftingwealth.blogspot.co.uk/2016/08/democ racy-and-corruption-in-brics.html> accessed 10 July 2016.
74. Hlophe Zakhele, *Regulating Money Laundering in Developing Countries: A Critical Analysis of South Africa's Incorporation and Implementation of the Global FATF Standards* (PhD Thesis, Kings College London, 2013).
75. House of Lords, European Union Committee, *Money Laundering and the Financing of Terrorism: Evidence* (19th Report of Session 2008–09 Volume II: Evidence, 22 July 2009) 169.
76. Ian Jeffries, *Political Developments in Contemporary China: A Guide* (First published 2011, Routledge, 2011).
77. IMF, 'Acceptances of the Proposed Amendment of the Articles of Agreement on Reform of the Executive Board and Consents to 2010 Quota Increase' (*IMF*, 31 May 2016) <http://www.imf.org/external/np/sec/misc/consents .htm#a2> accessed 10 May 2017.
78. IMF, 'IMF Members' Quotas and Voting Power, and IMF Board of Governors' (*IMF*, 4 June 2016) <https://www.imf.org/external/np/sec/memdir/me mbers.aspx> accessed June 4 2016).
79. IBA, 'BRICS: Rule of law "Critically Important" to BRICS Success' (*IBA*, 11 June 2015) <https://www.ibanet.org/Article/NewDetail.aspx?ArticleUid =702cb343-8fdd-4b4a-962d-2f5fe40a0827> accessed 16 November 2017.
80. IMF, 'Press Release: IMF Managing Director Christine Lagarde Welcomes U.S. Congressional Approval of the 2010 Quota and Governance Reforms' (*IMF*, 18 December 2015) <https://www.imf.org/en/News/Articles/2015 /09/14/01/49/pr15573> 4 June 2016.
81. Jan d'Oliviera, 'International Co-operation in Criminal Matters: The South African Contribution' [2003] 16 (3) South African Journal of Criminal Justice.
82. Jason C. Sharman, 'Power and Policy Diffusion: Anti-Money Laundering in Developing States' [2008] 52 (3) International Studies Quarterly.
83. Jenny Irish and Kevin Qhobosheane, 'South Africa' in Peter Gastrow (ed.) *Penetrating State and Business: Organised Crime in Southern Africa*, Volume 2 (ISS, Monograph 89, Pretoria, 2003).
84. Jill Langlois, 'Soggy Protesters Demand Impeachment of Brazil's President: "We Have to Fight for Better"' (*LA Times*, 21 May 2017) <http://www.lati mes.com/world/mexico-americas/la-fg-brazil-protests-20170521-story.htm l> accessed 10 July 2017.
85. Jim Nichol, 'Russian Political, Economic and Security Issues and U.S Interests' (Congressional Research Service, 31 March 2014) <https://fas.org/sgp/crs/ row/RL33407.pdf> accessed 21 May 2016.
86. Jim O'Neil, 'Building Better Global Economic BRICs' [2001] 66 *Global Economics Paper S.04*.
87. John Ross, 'China's New Position in Global Economic Governance' (*China .org.cn*, 10 February 2016) <http://china.org.cn/opinion/2016-02/10/c ontent_37752043.htm> accessed 10 May 2016.

88. Jonathan E. Turner, *Money Launderings Prevention: Deterring, Detecting and Resolving Financial Fraud* (John Wiley & Sons, 2011).
89. Josh Kimbrell, 'Why BRICS Are Bad for America: Inside the Effort to Undermine U.S. Predominance' (*RedState*, 12 April 2017) <https://www.red state.com/joshkimbrell/2017/04/12/brics-bad-america-inside-effort-unde rmine-u.s.-predominance/> accessed 10 July 2017.
90. Julio Faundez, 'Douglass North's Theory of Institutions: Lessons for Law and Development' [2016] 8 (2) Hague Journal on the Rule of Law.
91. Karin Svedberg Helgesson and Ulrika Morth, *Securitization, Accountability and Risk Management – Transforming the Public Security Domain* (Routledge, 2012).
92. Kenneth Korosi, Kristen Brown, Christina Marquez, Mauricio Salazar and Sophia Segura, 'Sporting Events as Sites of International Law, Society and Governance: The 2014 Brazilian World Cup: Forward' [2010] 21 Southwestern Journal of International Law.
93. Kenny Chiu, 'Analysis of the Economic Development Prospects of BRICS Countries' (*ENSafrica*, 28 July 2014) <http://www.mondaq.com/southafr ica/x/330536/international+trade+investment/Analysis+Of+The+Economic +Development+Prospects+Of+BRICS+Countries> accessed 23 February 2016.
94. Kern Alexander, Rahul Dhumale and John Eatwell, *Global Governance of Financial Systems: The International Regulation of Systemic Risk* (Oxford University Press, 2006).
95. Kerwer Dieter and R. Hulsse, 'How International Organizations Rule the World: The Case of the Financial Action Task Force on Money Laundering' [2011] 2 Journal of International Organizations Studies.
96. Laetitia Mottet, 'Cooperation and Competition among the BRICS Countries and other Emerging Powers' (*French Centre for Research on Contemporary China*, March 2013) <http://www.cefc.com.hk/uf/file/researchpapers/ BRICS%20report/BRICS%20report.pdf> accessed 10 January 2017.
97. Larry Ong, 'Is China Still Communist? (*Epoch Times*, 11 January 2017) <http:/ /www.theepochtimes.com/n3/2208716-is-china-still-communist/> accessed 13 January 2017.
98. Laurence Piper, 'The BRICS Phenomenon: From Regional Economic Leaders to Global Political Players' (2015) BICAS Working Paper 3/2015, 3 <https:// www.tni.org/files/download/bicas_working_paper_3_piper.pdf> accessed 15 January 2017.
99. Lee Edwards, 'Yes Communism is Still with us' (*The Heritage Foundation*, 23 June 2015) <http://www.heritage.org/research/commentary/2015/6/yes-communism-is-still-with-us> accessed 13 January 2017.
100. Leslie Armijo, 'The BRICs Countries (Brazil, Russia, India and China) as Analytical Category: Mirage or Insight?' [2007] 31 (4) Asian Perspective.
101. Leszek Niewdana, *Money and Justice: A Critique of Modern Money and Banking System from the Perspective of Aristotelian and Scholastic Thoughts* (1st Published, Routledge Taylor & Francis Group, 2015).
102. Lori Ann Post, Amber N.W. Raile and Eric D. Raile, 'Defining Political Will' [2010] 38 (4) Politics & Policy.
103. Luiz Bandeira, 'Brazil and the United States: From Dependency to Equality' (*Open Democracy*, 20 November 2003) <https://www.opendemocracy.net/ democracy-americanpower/article_1599.jsp> accessed 10 January 2017.

104. Maira Machado, 'Financial Regulation and International Criminal Policy: the Anti-Money Laundering System in Brazil and Argentina' (2007) *Law & Society Association Annual Conference 7/2007, 50* <https://bibliotecadigital.fgv.br/ds pace/bitstream/handle/10438/2777/WP7.pdf> accessed 19 October 2015.
105. Manuel Orozco, Elisabeth Burgess and Netta Ascoli, 'Is There a Match Among Migration, Remittances and Technology' (*Inter-American Dialogue*, 30 September 2010) <http://archive.thedialogue.org/page.cfm?pageID=32 &pubID=2501> accessed 14 November 2016.
106. Manuhuia Barcham, 'South-South Policy Transfer: The Case of the Vanuatu Ombudsman's Office' [2003] 18 (2) Pacific Economic Bulletin 108–116.
107. Marian L. Tupy, 'The Myth of Social African Capitalism' (*Cato Institute*, 12 May 2004) <https://www.cato.org/publications/commentary/myth-south -african-capitalism> accessed 13 January 2017.
108. Mark N. Katz, 'The Big Winner form Ukraine Crisis? China' (*Fareed Zakaria GPS, Special to CNN*, 6 June 2014) <http://globalpublicsquare.blogs.cnn .com/2014/06/06/the-big-winner-from-ukraine-crisis-china/> accessed 21 April 2016.
109. Marko Juutinen and Jyrki Kakonen *Battle for Globalization? BRICS and US Mega-Regional Trade Agreements in a Changing World Order* (*Observer Research Foundation*, New Delhi, 2016) <http://www.orfonline.org/wp-co ntent/uploads/2016/03/Book_Battle-For-Globalisation.pdf> accessed 10 May 2017.
110. Martha Reeves and Neha Sabharwal, 'Microfinance and Mobile Banking for the Bottom of the Pyramid' [2013] 7 (2) Journal of Enterprising Communities: People and Places in the Global Economy.
111. Martin Arnold, 'Deutsche Bank Eyes Russian Pullback Amid Money Laundering Probe' (*Financial Times*, 11 September 2015) <http://www.ft.com/cms/s/0 /8533caca-58ae-11e5-9846-de406ccb37f2.html#axzz3z2fVDQkE> accessed 10 May 2016.
112. Martin Muller, *How Brazil, Russia, India and China View BRIC in Yvette Sanchez, Claudia Franziska Bruhwiler, Transculturalism and Business in the BRIC States: A Hand Book* (Routledge, 2014).
113. Michelle V. Remo, 'Stop Illegal Remittance Agents, BSP Urged' (*Inquirer.net* , 14 November 2012) <http://business.inquirer.net/93066/stop-illegal-re mittance-agents-bsp-urged> accessed 15 March 2016.
114. Miller Tyler, 'Addressing the Economic and Political Rise of the BRICS Countries Through Neoliberal International Relations Theory' (Master's Thesis, Towson University, 2013).
115. Moamil, 'Drug Trafficking Among One of the Major Criminal Source of Money Laundering' [2015] 2 (1) International Journal of Multidisciplinary Research and Development.
116. Mobile Money Association of India and GSMA, 'Mobile Money: The Opportunity for India' (*MMAI/GSMA*, 13 November 2013) <https://www .gsma.com/mobilefordevelopment/wp-content/uploads/2013/12/MMAI -GSMA-on-Mobile-Money-in-India-for-RBI-Financial-Inclusion-Committee _Dec13.pdf> accessed 10 November 2017.
117. Money Laundering Bulletin, 'Building FATF Evaluations BRIC by BRIC' (*Money Laundering Bulletin*) <http://www.moneylaunderingbulletin.com/

legalandregulatory/governmentandinternationalbodies/building-fatf-evalu
ations-bric-by-bric--1.htm> accessed 21 February 2016.

118. Morris Goldstein and Nicholas R. Lardy, 'China's Exchange Rate Policy: An Overview of Some Key Issues' (China Exchange Rate Policy Peterson Institute for International Economics, October 2007).

119. Norman Mugarura, 'The Global Anti-Money Laundering Court as a Judicial and Institutional Imperative' [2011] 14 (1) Journal of Money Laundering Control.

120. Nandini Ramaujam et al., 'Rule of Law and Economic Development: A Comparative Analysis of Approaches to Economic Development Across the BRIC Countries' (*The Rule of Law and Economic Development*, December 2012) <http://www.mcgill.ca/roled/files/roled/mcgill_roled_report_2012.pdf> accessed 16 November 2017.

121. NewEurope, 'FATF Decides to Cross Russia off Blacklist' (*NewEurope*, 20 July 2002) <https://www.neweurope.eu/article/fatf-decides-cross-russia-blacklist/> accessed 21 January 2016.

122. Nick Kochan, 'Global Concern at AML Standards of Chinese Banks Abroad' (*WoltersKluwer*, 20 May 2016) <http://www.wolterskluwerfs.com/article/global-concern-at-aml-standards-of-chinese-banks-abroad.aspx> accessed 10 May 2017.

123. Nikos Passas, 'Financial Intermediaries – Anti-Money Laundering Allies in Cash-Based Societies?' [2015] 10 U4 Brief.

124. N.K. Singh, 'New Money Laundering Threats for Emerging Economies' (Global Programme Against Money Laundering, United Nations, Office for Drug Control and Crime Prevention – Attacking the Profits of Crime: Drugs, Money and Laundering).

125. Oaula Miraglia, 'Drugs and Drug Trafficking in Brazil: Trends and Policies' [2016] *Foreign Policy at Brookings*.

126. OECD, 'CleanGovBiz Integrity in Practice: Money Laundering' (*OECD*) <http://www.oecd.org/cleangovbiz/toolkit/moneylaundering.htm>accessed 21 February 2016.

127. OECD Public Governance Reviews, *OECD Integrity Review of Brazil: Managing Risk for a Cleaner Public Service* (OECD, 2012) 72.

128. Oleg Remizov, 'Discourses and Emotions in Narration of the Annexation of Crimean Peninsula by the Russian Federation' (Master's Thesis, University of Tartu, 2015).

129. Olivia Solon, 'Cybercriminals Launder Money Using in Game Currencies' (*Wired.Co.Uk*, 2013).

130. O'Malley, '08 August 1998: Hofmeyr, Willie' (O'Malley, 1998) <https://www.nelsonmandela.org/omalley/index.php/site/q/03lv00017/04lv00344/05lv01183/06lv01224.htm> accessed 10 July 2017.

131. Parkes Riley and Ravi Roy, 'Corruption and Anti-Corruption: The Case of India' [2016] 32 (1) *Journal of Developing Societies* 73, 74.

132. Parliamentary Monitoring Group, 'Financial Intelligence Centre Bill: Hearings' (*PMG*, 22 March 2001) <https://pmg.org.za/committee-meeting/418/> accessed 10 January 2016.

133. Patrick Heller, 'BRICS from Below: Counter-Power Movements in Brazil, India and South Africa' (*Open Democracy*, 30 April 2015) <https://www.ope

ndemocracy.net/patrick-heller/brics-from-below-counterpower-movements-in-brazil-india-and-south-africa> accessed 16 November 2017.

134. Paula Miraglia, 'Drugs and Drug Trafficking in Brazil: Trends and Policies' (*Foreign Policy at Brookings*, 2016) <https://www.brookings.edu/wp-content/uploads/2016/07/Miraglia-Brazil-final.pdf> accessed 10 December 2016.

135. Paul May, 'The Paradise Papers: Panama's Labyrinth' (*Arachnys*) <http://blog.arachnys.com/panamas-labyrinth> accessed 7 February 2018.

136. Pavnesh Kuman, 'BRICS: The Rise of Sleeping Giant' [2013] 2 (1) Voice of Research 66, 66.

137. Peter Andreas and Ethan Nadelmann, *Policing the Globe: Criminalization and Crime Control in International Relations* (1st edn, Oxford University Press, 2006).

138. Peter Alexander, 'Rebellion of the Poor: South Africa's Service Delivery Protests – A Preliminary Analysis' [2010] 37 Review of African Political Economy 25, 25.

139. Peter Knaack, 'An Unlikely Champion of Global Finance: Why is China Exceeding International Banking Standards? [2017] 46 (2) Journal of Current Chinese Affairs 41, 65.

140. Peter Lilley, 'Dirty Dealing: the FATF "Blacklist" (*www.DirtyDealing.net*, 2006) <http://www.dirtydealing.org/IMAGES/fatfblacklist/The%20FATF%20Blacklist.pdf> accessed 15 January 2016.

141. Peter Pedroncelli, '12 Biggest African Recipients of Foreign Aid from the United States' (*AFK Insider*, 12 May 2017) <https://afkinsider.com/139167/12-biggest-african-recipients-of-foreign-aid-from-the-united-states/4/> accessed 10 February 2018.

142. Peter Romaniuk, *Multilateral Counterterrorism: the Global Politics of Cooperation and Contestation* (First Published, Routledge, 2010) 57.

143. Pierre Legrand, 'The Impossibility of "Legal Transplants"' [1997] 4 *Maastricht Journal of European and Comparative Law* 111, 118–119.

144. Pranab Bardhan, 'The Contradictions of China's Communist Capitalism' (*Project Syndicate*, 16 July 2015) <https://www.project-syndicate.org/commentary/china-stock-market-crash-communism-capitalism-by-pranab-bardhan-2015-07?barrier=accessreg> accessed 13 January 2017.

145. Pravdu Ru, 'NATO: Built Against USSR, doomed to Lose Battle Against Russia' (*Pradu Ru*, 2016) <http://www.pravdareport.com/news/world/europe/05-04-2016/134065-nato_bloc-0/> accessed 21 May 2016.

146. Rainer Hulsse, 'Even Clubs Can't Do Without Legitimacy: Why the Anti-Money Laundering Blacklist Was Suspended' [2008] 2 (4) Regulation and Governance 459, 465.

147. Ramanand Garge, 'Combating Financing of Terror: an Indian Perspective' (*Vivekandanda International Foundation*, Occasional Paper, October 2015) <http://www.vifindia.org/sites/default/files/combating-financing-of-terror-an-indian-perspective.pdf> accessed 10 March 2017.

148. Ramesh Thakur, 'How Representative are BRICS' [2014] 35 (10) *Third World Quarterly*.

149. Richard Sklar, 'Beyond Capitalism and Socialism in Africa' [1988] 26 (1) *The Journal of Modern African Studies* 1, 20.

150. Robert J. Holton, *Global Inequalities* (1st Published, Macmillan Palgrave, 2014) 20.

151. Robert L. Worden, Andrea Matles Savada and Roland E. Dolan (eds.) *China: A Country Study* (GPO for the Library of Congress, Washington, 1987).

152. Roberto Delmanto Junior, 'The World Cup in Brazil: Fighting Against Money Laundering and Corruption' [2014] 21 South-Western Journal of International Law 143.

153. Cynthia Roberts, 'Challengers or Stakeholders? BRICs and the Liberal World Order' [2010] 42 (1) Polity.

154. Roda Mushkat, 'China's Compliance with International Law: What Has been Learned and the Gaps Remaining' [2011] 20 (1) Pacific Rim Law & Policy Journal Association 41, 68.

155. Rosalba O'Brien, 'Latam Cyber Attacks Rise as Peru, Brazil Hackers Link up with Russians' (*Reuters*, 28 August 2015) <http://www.reuters.com/article/latam-cyberattack-idUSL5N1134W520150828> accessed 15 July 2016.

156. Samuel Munzele Maimbo, 'The Regulation and Supervision of Informal Remittance Systems: Emerging Oversight Strategies' (*Current Developments in Monetary and Financial Law*, November 2004).

157. Sarbeswar Sahoo, *Civil Society and Democratization in India: Institutions, Ideologies and Interests* (Routledge, 2013).

158. Scott Firsing, 'A New "Rough Patch" in U.S.-South Africa Relations' (*International Policy Digest*, 4 May 2012) <https://intpolicydigest.org/2012/05/04/a-new-rough-patch-in-u-s-south-africa-relations/> accessed 13 January 2017.

159. Sibal Rajeev, 'Varieties of Capitalism and Firm Performance in Emerging Markets: An Examination of the Typological Trajectories of India and Brazil' (PhD Dissertation, The London School of Economics and Political Science, 2014).

160. Beth Simmons and Zachary Elkins, 'The Globalisation of Liberalisation: Policy Diffusion in the International Political Economy' [2004] 98 (1) American Political Science Review.

161. Anne-Marie Slaughter, 'Disaggregated Sovereignty: Towards the Public Accountability of Global Government Networks' [2004] 39 (2) Government and Opposition.

162. Anne- Marie Slaughter, 'International Law in a World of Liberal States' [1995] 6 (3) European Journal of International Law.

163. South African Law Commission, 'Issue Paper 1, Project 104, Money Laundering and Related Matters' (South African Law Commission, 24 May 1996).

164. Sterling Seagrave, *Lord of the Rim* (Bantam Press, London, 1997).

165. Tam Christian, 'Enforcement' *in* G. Ulfsein, T. Marauhn and A. Zimmermann (eds.). *Making Treaties Work* (Cambridge University Press, Cambridge, 2007).

166. Tatiana Tropina, 'Do Digital Technologies Facilitate Illicit Financial Flows? (2016) *World Development Report: Digital Dividends* 102953 <http://documents.worldbank.org/curated/en/896341468190180202/pdf/102953-WP-Box394845B-PUBLIC-WDR16-BP-Do-Digital-Technologies-Facilitate-Illicit-Financial-Flows-Tropina.pdf> accessed 10 July 2017.

167. Team PG, '48 Percent Indians Online Were Cyber Crime Victims Last Year: Norton' (*PGurus.com*, 20 November 2015) <https://www.pgurus.com/48-percent-indians-online-were-cyber-crime-victims-last-year-norton/> accessed 10 July 2016.

168. *The Economist*, 'Democracy Index 2016: Revenge of the "Deplorable"' (A Report by The Economist Intelligence Unit) <http://felipesahagun.es/w p-content/uploads/2017/01/Democracy-Index-2016.pdf> accessed 16 December 2016.

169. *The Financial Express*, 'BJP Describes Robert Vadra's "Witch-Hunt" Claim As "Farcical"' (*The Financial Express*, 22 November 2015) <http://www.fina ncialexpress.com/article/india-news/bjp-describes-robert-vadras-witch-hunt-claim-as-farcical/169116/> accessed 1 February 2016.

170. *The Moscow Times*, 'Putin Associates Implicated in Deutsche Bank Moscow Laundering Probe' (*Moscow Times*, 16 October 2015) <http://www.them oscowtimes.com/business/article/putin-associates-implicated-in-deutsche -bank-moscow-laundering-probe/539451.html> accessed 15 June 2016.

171. The National Strategy Against Corruption and Money Laundering (Estrategia Nacional de Combate a Corrupcao e a Lavagem de Dinheiro) Established in 2013.

172. The World Bank, 'Data: World Bank Country and Lending Groups' (*The World Bank*, 2018) <https://datahelpdesk.worldbank.org/knowledgebase/a rticles/906519-world-bank-country-and-lending-groups> accessed 2 February 2018.

173. The World Bank, 'International Migration at All-Time High' (*The World Bank*, 18 December 2015) <http://www.worldbank.org/en/news/press-release /2015/12/18/international-migrants-and-remittances-continue-to-grow-as -people-search-for-better-opportunities-new-report-finds> accessed 1 February 2016.

174. Tridivesh Maini, 'What the US Gets Wrong about India's Relationship with China' (*The Diplomat*, 13 March 2016) <http://thediplomat.com/2016/03 /what-the-us-gets-wrong-about-indias-relationship-with-china/> accessed 13 May 2016.

175. United States Department of State, 'Country Reports on Terrorism 2012' (*United States Department of State* Publication, May 2013) <https://www.sta te.gov/documents/organization/210204.pdf> accessed 30 May 2016.

176. United States Department of State, 'Bureau for International Narcotics and Law Enforcement Affairs, International Narcotics Control Strategy Report: Volume II Money Laundering and Financial Crimes' (*United States Department of State*, March 2017) <https://www.state.gov/documents/organization/268024.pdf > accessed 16 August 2017.

177. U.S. Department of State, 'The Financial Action Task Force and FATF-Style Regional Bodies' (*U.S Department of State*, 2015) <https://www.state.gov/j/ inl/rls/nrcrpt/2015/vol2/239046.htm> accessed 4 February 2018.

178. U.S. Department of State, 'U.S. Relations with South Africa' (*U.S. Department of State*, 12 January 2018) <https://www.state.gov/r/pa/ei/bgn/2898.h tm> accessed 10 February 2018.

179. Antoine Van Agtmael, 'Think Again: The BRICS' (*Foreign Policy*, 8 October 2012) <http://foreignpolicy.com/2012/10/08/think-again-the-brics/> accessed 21 May 2016.

180. Victoria Lavrentieva, 'Russia Taken off Financial Blacklist' (*The Moscow Times*, 2002) <http://www.themoscowtimes.com/sitemap/free/2002/10/article/r ussia-taken-off-financial-blacklist/242953.html> accessed 1 December 2015.

181. Vidya Nadkarni, 'Introduction' *in* Vidya Nadkarni and Norma C. Noonan (eds.), *Emerging Powers in a Comparative Perspective: The Political and Economic Rise of the BRIC* (First published 2012, Bloomsbury, 2013).
182. Vijay Kumar Singh, 'Controlling Money Laundering in India – Problems and Perspectives', (Annual Conference on Money and Finance in the Indian Economy, India, January 2009).
183. Walter Perkel, 'Money Laundering and Terrorism: Informal Value Transfer System' [2004] 41 (1) *American Criminal Law Review.*
184. Wang Shucheng, 'Predictions on the Development and Direction of Legislation' *in* Yuwen W. Li (ed.) *The China Legal Development Yearbook* (Volume 2, 2009).
185. Wang Wei, 'Bank Secrecy in China' (Bank Secrecy Symposium, Singapore, March 2016).
186. Colin Watterson, 'More Flies with Honey: Encouraging Formal Channel Remittances to Combat Money Laundering' [2013] 91 Texas Law Review.
187. Willain H. Bynes and Robert J. Munro, *Money Laundering, Asset Forfeiture and Recovery and Compliance – A Global Guide* (Lexis Nexis, 2016).
188. William Watson, 'Antidumping Fowls Out: U.S.-South Africa Chicken Dispute Highlights the Need for Global Reform' (Free Trade Bulletin No. 62 *Cato Institute*, 19 October 2015) <https://www.cato.org/publications/free-trade-bulletin/antidumping-fowls-out-us-south-africa-chicken-dispute-highlights> accessed 10 January 2017.
189. World Bank Group, *Migration and Remittances Factbook 2016* (3rd edn, KNOMAD, 2016).
190. World Justice Project, 'Rule of Law Index 2016' (*World Justice Project*, 2016) <https://worldjusticeproject.org/sites/default/files/documents/RoLI_Final-Digital_0.pdf> accessed 10 May 2017.
191. Xue Bin Li, 'Money Laundering and Its Regulation in China' (PhD Thesis, Cardiff University, 2009).
192. Young Choul Kim, 'Economic Transition in China and Russia' [2015] 1 European Scientific Journal 355, 364.

7 Legitimacy – A Means of Levelling the Playing Field?

Introduction

Diffusing the Financial Action Task Force (FATF) standards to countries was achieved through a process of coercion and persuasion. Yet, African countries and emerging economies (ACs/EEs) implement the FATF standards, partly to avert any compromise to their funding from international financial institutions (IFIs). One reason why IFIs can wield such powers on anti-money laundering/counter-terrorist financing (AML/CFT) standards is because these standards are embedded in their conditionalities. Nevertheless, paradoxes still result from ACs/EEs implementation. The introduction of the risk-based approach (RBA) by the FATF to incorporate the peculiarities of countries in compliance ratings, with a view to resolving some legitimacy issues and agency slack, did not completely resolve the issue. Rather, continued implementation has only occasioned formal or creative compliance. For countries to attain proactive or actual compliance to the AML/CFT standards, the legitimacy of IFIs/FATF and the resulting standards are crucial. Additionally, a shift from RBA to the uncertainty-based approach (UBA) which is judgement-based and forward-looking may indeed be advisable.

The first section restates the concept and importance of legitimacy in AML/CFT regulation. The second section examines the FATF's strategies in rule design, implementation and compliance and the extent to which the legitimacy crisis is addressed. Additionally, it scrutinises the RBA and the extent to which it closes compliance differentials in ACs/EEs, thereby reducing agency slack and resolving the legitimacy crisis. It also appraises the UBA as an alternative to the RBA to ensure effective AML/CFT regulation. The third section scrutinises the attempts aimed at resolving legitimacy crisis and their possible feasibility. The fourth section questions why ACs/EEs still comply with AML/CFT standards, despite the legitimacy crisis and the regulatory paradoxes. The fifth section draws the strands together and concludes.

The Agency Quandary: Restating the Concept and Importance of Legitimacy

The exclusivity of FATF membership, which is biased against belated and associate members, reveals complexities in the institution's processes, which has worsened the legitimacy crisis. This crisis, which is evidenced by a lack of representation or input in global regulatory standards from these countries, was facilitated by the inherent overlap in the FATF's position as both principal and agent to developed countries. As discussed earlier, the FATF is the Group of Seven's (G7's) agent. The G7, whose member states are core FATF members, played an important role in formulating FATF standards. Conversely, the G7 countries remain bound by the FATF standards, which allows the FATF to evaluate their compliance and possibly issue sanctions. This places the FATF in a principal position to the G7.

Contrariwise, Brazil, Russia, India, China and South Africa (the BRICS) only have some measure of involvement in the FATF's standards re-formulation process, which demonstrates their role as 'rule-takers' because of their belated membership. ACs suffer a worse off fate with minimal input in standards re-formulation, which restricts them from contributing to the FATF standards and adding their peculiarities, yet ACs are still subject to the FATF rules. This connotes that the FATF relationship with its members is dependent on a hierarchy (core members, belated members and associate members). The resulting global asymmetry and the influence of G7 national/regulatory laws on international standards have raised questions about the FATF's legitimacy.

Whilst these shortcomings also exist in treaty bodies such as the IFIs, countries have continued to comply with conditionalities listed by them. This continued compliance can be attributable to arguments that treaty bodies derive their legitimacy from state consent[1] and thus have the power to mandate compliance. Without consent, clear legal structures to ensure accountability and democratic participation, trans-governmental institutions have continued to foster compliance to their standard. Legitimacy does not equate to 'legal', but rather, it is the 'perception of actors on the acceptability of an institution'.[2] That is, a process by which actors come to believe in the normative legitimacy of an object.[3] This perception grants decentralised bodies a basis for legitimacy and acceptance. The basis for an institution's legitimacy is rooted in how countries perceive their input, throughput and output.

---

1 Jan Klabbers, Anne Peters and Geir Ulfstein, *The Constitutionalization of International Law* (OUP, 2009) 39; Daniel M. Bodansky, 'The Legitimacy of International Governance: A Coming Challenge for International Environmental Law?' [1999] 93 (3) American Journal of International Law 596, 604; cf Nienke Grossman, 'The Normative Legitimacy of International Courts' [2012] 86 Temple Law Review 61,78 which argues that state consent and procedural fairness are insufficient to ground the legitimacy of institutions.

2 Ian Hurd, 'Legitimacy and Authority in International Politics' [1999] 53 (2) International Organization 379, 381; Chris Thomas, 'The Concept of Legitimacy and International Law' (2013) LSE Law, Society and Economy Working Papers 12/2013, 14< http://eprints.lse .ac.uk/51746/1/__libfile_repository_Content_Law%2C%20society%20and%20economic s%20working%20papers_2013_WPS2013-12_Thomas.pdf> accessed 10 November 2017; Julia Black, 'Constructing and Contesting Legitimacy and Accountability in Polycentric Regulatory Regimes' (2008) LSE Law, Society and Economy Working Papers 2/2008, 16 <http://eprints.lse.ac.uk/23040/1/WPS2008-02_Black.pdf>16 November 2017.

3 *Thomas* (n 2).

Without legitimacy, the FATF may be unable to inspire acceptance and compliance to its regulatory standards.[4] A body acknowledged as legitimate forms a reservoir of loyalty from which it can govern effectively.[5] So, where the FATF is considered legitimate by receiving actors, such actors are more likely to ensure actual or proactive compliance to set standards, than formal or constructive compliance.[6] Formal or constructive ('sham') compliance usually results from a regulator's quagmire to engage in ensuring adherence to laws that do not necessarily mirror society so as to avoid the compulsion of penalties.

ACs are examples of where the inability of law to reflect society can be problematic. For example, a country may be sanctioned if its economy is cash-based and it fails to achieve financial inclusion necessary for meeting the FATF's standards on curbing terror funding. Penalties may include restrictions on its credit lines or limitations on its involvement in the global financial market. These penalties would further exacerbate financial exclusion, worsening the country's capability to curb terrorist funding in-country and across borders. Black refers to this situation as a regulatory paradox, whereby regulation fails to change behaviour, manage risk or achieve any stated goals, but occasions unintended consequences.[7] To avoid this dilemma, legal authorities usually prefer that legitimacy is established to facilitate voluntary compliance. Furthermore, voluntary compliance is cost-effective because it is non-compulsive.[8]

Propelling Legitimacy and Ensuring Compliance: the FATF's Strategies

It is crucial to understand the legitimacy crisis's impact on the existing hierarchy of members within the context of the FATF's rulemaking and implementation processes. Countries' involvement in the FATF's processes shows a disparity – which is largely dependent on their membership hierarchy. This hierarchy determines the degree to which a particular country may engage in agency slack given the inability of standards and implementation processes to take cognisance of their historical and socio-economic peculiarities. It can be argued that this disparity not only encourages a regulatory paradox but sets up a set of countries to fail.

Legitimacy in FATF Rule/Standards Design

Legitimacy in designing rules goes to the root of the FATF's drafting process. This is demonstrable by the exclusive decision-making process which guides the

---

4 *Black* (n 2).
5 Tom Tyler, *Why People Obey the Law* (PUP, 2006) 281.
6 Rainer Hulsse, 'Even Clubs Can't Do Without Legitimacy: Why the Anti-Money Laundering Blacklist Was Suspended' [2008] 2 Regulation and Governance 459, 460.
7 Julia Black, 'Paradoxes and Failures: "New Governance" Techniques and the Financial Crisis' [2012] 75 (6) The Modern Law Review 1037, 1040.
8 *Tyler* (n 5) 4.

design of the rules. The restricted membership band which holds developed countries within the inner caucus, coupled with the FATF's location within the Organisation for Economic Co-operation and Development (OECD), exacerbates the process's exclusivity.[9] These are causes for concern when dealing with issues that require global convergence, as only a select group of countries are privy to the decision-making process for the FATF standards.[10]

Decisions about the content of recommendations are usually made by the secretariat and debated on during the plenary sessions.[11] These highlight difficulties in the FATF's secretariat location, given that the OECD's mandate only permits the employment of OECD nationals within the secretariat. This implies that ACs/EEs are foreclosed from partaking in the development of recommendations and may only offer consultative input.[12] This restricts active contribution of non-OECD countries to plenary sessions which are held three times a year. As discussions in these sessions mainly centre on ex-post rule design issues, the input of 'continuing agents' are effectively unheard.

The 'continuing agent's' limitations within the FATF can be contrasted with the position of ACs/EEs within the International Association of Deposit Insurers (IADI), a soft law forum for enhancing deposit insurance expertise worldwide.[13] This forum, which boasts over 100 members, has 85 countries involved in voting a representative council responsible for its rulemaking processes.[14] The IADI's platform allows for global convergence on deposit insurance issues, which has never been the case with the FATF, either at the rules development or guidance formulation stage. Without a IADI type umbrella body, the FATF gravitates towards a minority imposition of a global agenda. The resulting democratic deficit in rulemaking is manifested in the lack of participation by the majority of countries.[15] This can lead to standards that are not fairly applicable to ACs/EEs and may occasion unintended consequences. Vibert contends that such undemocratic rulemaking may undermine the rulemaking body's authority,[16] an effect that may curtail the efficiency of the FATF rules.

The absence of democracy in the drafting process is evidenced by the participation of private experts from developed states who dominate the content

---

9 James Jackson, 'The Financial Action Task Force: An Overview' (*Congressional Research Service*, 9 May 2012) <http://fas.org/sgp/crs/terror/RS21904.pdf> accessed 11 November 2017.
10 Kevin Shepherd, 'Guardians at the Gate: The Gatekeeper Initiative and the Risk-Based Approach for Transactional Lawyers' [2009] 43 (3) Real Prop. Tr. & Est. LJ 1.
11 FATF, 'FATF Secretariat' (*FATF*, 2017) < http://www.fatf-gafi.org/about/fatfsecretariat/> accessed 20 January 2017.
12 OECD: Better Policies for Better Lives, 'OECD Careers' (*OECD*) <http://www.oecd.org/careers/whatwelookfor.htm> accessed 20 January 2016.
13 IADI, 'Message from the Chairman' (*IADI*, 2016) <http://www.iadi.org/en/about-iadi/message-from-the-chairman/> accessed 10 November 2017.
14 . Ibid.
15 Ibid. (n 15).
16 Frank Vibert, 'Reforming International Rule-Making' [2012] 3 (3) Global Policy 391, 391.

of the FATF recommendations.[17] Such experts are involved in the consultation processes which serve as a prelude to the FATF standards' redrafting. They are usually drawn from institutions in developed countries given concerns about FIs/supervisory body experts' capacity from ACs/EEs.[18] Whilst this also affected the drafting process of the Basel II requirements, it was an unfounded fear.[19] Cornford argues that whereas developed countries focused on risk management due to the new financial products and services churned out periodically, developing countries usually have a narrower focus on traditional retail, private banking or investment banking.[20] This specialisation in developing countries means the technical capacity of their expertise cannot be underestimated.[21] Despite this criticism, the status quo remained. On this basis, Gathii characterises the rulemaking process by soft law bodies as a form of 'regulatory imperialism', where powerful nations dictate the pace, process and content of rulemaking.[22]

The absence of an avenue for democratic consensus on the content of the rules is further demonstrated by the private interests and landmark activities that prompted the inclusion of certain FATF recommendations. For instance, by 1970, the US banks, through laws instituted by the Bank Secrecy Act, were already adherent to regulations on cash reporting. In 1988 they beckoned on the G7 to impede the illegal drug market[23] through global application of these regulations so as to restrict countries from taking advantage of regulatory loopholes. Additionally, FIs in countries such as Switzerland and the United Kingdom already had customer due diligence/know your customer (CDD/KYC)

---

17 FATF, 'Consultation on Proposed Changes to the FATF Standards: Compilation of Responses from Designated Non-Financial Business and Professions (DNFBPs)' (*FATF*, 2011) <http://www.fatf-gafi.org/media/fatf/documents/publicconsultation/First%20pu blic%20consultation%20document%20responses%20dnfbp.pdf?TSPD_101_R0=692e4d2f 674f3e448a6e814befd6d8e6l4W0000000000000007501cd89ffff000000000000000 00000000000005a922327006825de3e> accessed 12 November 2017; FATF, 'Consultation on Proposed Changes to the FATF Standards: Compilation of Responses from the Financial Sector (PART ONE)' (*FATF*, 2012) <http://www.fatf-gafi.org/media/fatf/docu ments/publicconsultation/First%20public%20consultation%20document%20responses%20 financial%20sector%20part%201.pdf?TSPD_101_R0=e3d2a5c3ce8d0c7be6e842e3c9072 cfcl110000000000000007501cd89ffff00000000000000000000000000005a922384 00b9c8d0d1> accessed 12 November 2017.
18 Ibid.
19 Andrew Cornford, 'Basel II and Developing Countries' [2008] 2 Finance & Bien Commun 69, 69.
20 Ibid. 69, 70.
21 Ibid. (n 19) 69, 69.
22 James Gathii, The Financial Action Task Force and Global Administrative Law [2010] J. Prof. Law 1, 9; Jose Alvarez, Hegemonic International Law Revisited [2003] 97 AM.J.Int.L 873–887.
23 Mark Pieth and Gemma Aiolfi, 'The Private Sector Becomes Active: The Wolfsberg Process' [2003]10.4 Journal of Financial Crime 359, 359. NB: A portion of the FATF standards were also borrowed from binding international law, particularly the United Nation's Vienna Convention of 1988, an inclusion which has occasioned the hardening of the FATF soft law.

requirements ingrained in their legislations and their regulatory bodies enforced compliance.[24] France also mandated the inclusion of tax offences in the FATF's remit as a predicate offence as a requirement for its membership in 1989 – a position which although combatted by Switzerland, Luxemburg and Austria,[25] culminated in a compromise on its inclusion in 1996.[26] With the role played by private institutions within member countries in deciding on the foremost rules of the FATF, it would appear that it was a springboard for private institutions in developed countries to tackle global issues relating to tax, drugs and inefficient AML/CFT rules.[27]

Reacting to landmark activities such as 9/11 on the United States, the FATF expanded its regulatory rules to include recommendations on terrorist financing. Whereas evidence indicates that ACs had suffered spates of terror activities before 9/11, ACs' experiences were not considered severe enough to warrant alterations to the FATF recommendations. Similarly, in broadening its regulatory powers to inoculate the global financial system from exposures, the FATF reacted to the global financial crisis and not the Asian financial crisis.[28] This indicates a projection of the FATF founding members' priorities and interests founding members, with negligible focus on that of developing countries. This fails to recognise the varying nuances of developing countries but holds unrealistic expectations from these states to improve their laws to suit the requirements set by the developed countries.[29] This predicament may obstruct the distinctive progression of developing countries. This can be typified with the snail-like response of developing countries, especially ACs in legislating on issues that are perceived to hinder economic progression or go against the demands of their people. These include financial secrecy or countries not adhering to market economies.[30] Without representation, the resulting disproportionate rules applicable to all countries indicate an imposition of asymmetrically generated 'global standards', which is potentially damaging to ACs/EEs.[31] Gahtii contends that covenants of agency capture may

---

24 Ibid. 359, 359.
25 Mark Pieth and Gemma Aiolfi, 'Anti-Money Laundering: Levelling the Playing Field' (2003) Governance, Basel Institute on Governance 1, 9 <https://www.baselgovernance.or g/sites/collective.localhost/files/publications/biog_working_paper_01.pdf> accessed 10 November 2017.
26 FATF-VII, 'Financial Action Task Force on Money Laundering Annual Report 1995–1996' (*FATF*, 28 June 1996) <http://www.fatf-gafi.org/media/fatf/documents/reports/1995 %201996%20ENG.pdf> accessed 3 May 2017.
27 *Pieth and Aiolfi* (n 25).
28 *Jackson* (n 9).
29 *Gathii* (n 22) 873–887.
30 An interconnected market that requires open flow of capital may not be ideal for developing countries. The FATF imposes these obligations on these countries by the FATF through mandated compliance. Compliance by these countries sees a mirroring of the domestic laws of ACs/EEs to that of their Western counterparts. Consequently, ACs/EEs are usually faced with difficulties in the functioning of their economies.
31 *Alvarez* (n 22) 873–887.

have overtaken the FATF's intended policymaking agenda.[32] This recognises that although the FATF was commissioned to be a global AML/CFT rule setter, which warranted the later inclusion and endorsement of an RBA that takes into account the unique differences of countries into the FATF's rules, this is not necessarily the case.[33]

Without an option, ACs/EEs have conceded to transplanting the FATF standards through model legislations that do not necessarily fit their national terrain. This has come with a struggle given that these rules stifle any form of self-interest that propels proactive compliance. They also potentially set up ACs to fail on compliance levels, subjecting them to financial exclusion from the global market. Scholars have attributed this to the lack of moral, pragmatic or cognitively justifiable standards, making countries unwilling to accept them as legitimate.[34] Furthermore, the arguments on democratic deficit and legitimacy in rule design reveal that the asymmetric negotiation power between developed and developing countries continually shape FATF rules and guidance formulation.[35] This results in a recommended course of action that may not always be consistent with the domestic law's explicit guidance. This asymmetry has a continued effect on the implementation and compliance stage of FATF rules. Ghroshay states that the quandary between the two conflicting regimes can provide a window through which to view a jurisdiction's compliance deficit.[36]

Legitimacy in Rule Implementation and Compliance

For implementation and compliance to be effective, principals must resolve information asymmetries to understand the 'personality' of the agent-state, respond accordingly and avoid agency slack. As earlier stated, when a country is organisationally incompetent, sanctions may prove ineffective, and training would be more suited to ensuring compliance. The information needed to classify the agent-states to ensure that an effective response is given can only be garnered during the FATF's evaluation of its member states, its mutual evaluations in partnership with FATF-style regional bodies (FSRB) or the IFI's Financial Sector Assessment Programme (FSAP)/Art. IV surveillance. Whilst these means of fact-finding on implementation and compliance levels are seemingly legitimate, experts have argued that in reality they are not.

The FATF mutual evaluation process has been opined to be lacking legitimacy. Firstly, the process of selection of evaluators lacks transparency. The FATF, and the relevant FSRB, are responsible for choosing assessors with support and

---

32 *Gathii* (n 22).
33 Saby Ghoshray, 'Compliance Convergence in FATF Rulemaking: The Conflict Between Agency Capture and Soft Law' [2014/2015] 59 NYL. Sch.L. Rev. 521, 544.
34 *Black* (n 2).
35 *Ghoshray,* (n 33).
36 Ibid.

confirmation from the secretariat.[37] This is usually done in exclusion of inputs from the agent-state and results in a composition of external experts who although familiar with similar cross-border issues, are not necessarily conversant with pertinent issues in a particular country. The resulting asymmetry in composition was evident in the Nigerian mutual evaluation team which included assessors from the United Kingdom and the United States financial regulatory bodies together with a staff from the Inter-Governmental Group against Money Laundering in West Africa (GIABA).[38] Although seemingly balanced to produce an objective report, the involvement of external experts from hegemonic states may tilt the discussions of all representatives in their favour.[39] This was also the case with Mali's mutual evaluation which, when carried out by the World Bank, consisted mainly of representatives from the IFIs.[40] Whilst evaluating institutions may attribute the composition of evaluators to the need to guarantee neutrality of the assessment process, the absence of in-country input may colour the understanding of external experts who may not have a complete grasp of the home-grown situations of the country. The composition may thus result in biased reports that may hinder implementation and proactive compliance.

Secondly, the process and timing of fact-finding allows room for data manipulation. The pre-onsite evaluation visits mandate an export of information to the principal by the agent, based on responses to set questions.[41] This is usually done within a short time frame. As a result of the process and timing of information harvest, EENA2, a staff member of the International Monetary Fund (IMF), who had previous experience with the FATF, observed that to a large extent, reports by the FSRBs are untrustworthy. [42]A country's real situation is either concealed or exaggerated – somewhat to the detriment of international financial integrity. This illustrates the existing information asymmetry that hinders the IFIs'/FATFs' ability to understand the agent-states' 'personality'.

Thirdly, the manner of evaluation is disconcerting. EENA3 noted that FATF officials on mission to developing countries are 'like policemen who have no

---

37 FATF, 'Procedures for the FATF Fourth Round of AML/CFT Mutual Evaluations' (*FATF,* October 2013) <http://www.fatf-gafi.org/media/fatf/documents/methodology/FATF -4th-Round-Procedures.pdf> accessed 12 December 2017.

38 GIABA, 'Mutual Evaluation Report: Nigeria' (*GIABA,* 2008) <http://www.giaba.org/ media/f/299_Mutual%20Evaluation%20Report%20of%20Nigeria.pdf> accessed 10 June 2017.

39 Mushtaq Khan, 'The Political Economy of Inclusive Growth' *in* Luiz de Mello and Mark A Dutz (eds.) *OECD Promoting Inclusive Growth: Challenges and Policies (OECD, The World Bank,* 2012) 37; Diane Stone, 'Knowledge Networks and Global Policy' *in* Simon Maxwell and Diane Stone (eds) *Global Knowledge Networks and International Development;* Norman Girvan, 'Power Imbalances and Development Knowledge' (*Southern Perspectives on the Reform of the International Development Architecture,* 2007).

40 GIABA, 'Mutual Evaluation Report: Mali' (*GIABA,* 2008) <http://www.giaba.org/media /f/252_MALI_word_MER_english[1].pdf> accessed 10 June 2017.

41 Principal in this case are the IFIs/FATF and FSRB.

42 EENA2, Senior Counsel, Financial Integrity Unit, International Monetary Fund, Interview with EENA2, 'Telephone Call' (2017).

respect for state sovereignty',[43] given the manner they barge into countries to seek and publish information with varied input from the countries listed. The IFIs however adopt a more collaborative relationship with countries during their fact-finding mission, a process simplified by the presence of their in-country offices. They also publish their findings with permission from the concerned countries. This ensures that the IFIs are better placed than FATF to evaluate a country, understand its personality and issue sanction or incentives with minimal breach to state sovereignty.

It may however be impossible to categorise a country as having or projecting a single personality, given that whilst certain institutions in a particular country may be organisationally incompetent – not all are. This difficulty is heightened by the limited scope of each country's evaluation process, which only focuses on a set number of FIs and regulatory bodies. This further limits the ability to effectively categorise and deal with a country effectively. Thus, a wholesale sanction or incentive aimed at improving implementation or ensuring compliance may adversely affect certain institutions within a country whilst advancing others.

The trajectory of information asymmetry between countries and the IFIs/FATF reveals that the IFIs/FATF are not necessarily 'personality' seeking. Rather, they are driven by the faulty assumptions held by the hegemony bloc, that all countries have market economies with open flow dynamics. This supposition is based on the FATF's standards and sanctions – benchmarks which may sometimes harm the socio-economic and political fabric of less developed countries. Despite the aggregated personality attributable to a country, no sanction or incentive would prove effective in ensuring that countries are able to imbibe standards. This is especially so where developing countries are not particularly interconnected with the global economy, neither do they pose any substantial risk of contagion. Thus, they do not feel the impact of sanctions or incentives, which would at best further impose an onerous burden on such countries.

Sanctions, usually in the form of threats and public listing of non-compliant countries, may be imposed on countries alongside conditionalities, with the aim of coercing efficient implementation of rules.[44] Gahtii asserts that these are incompatible with the goal of achieving compliance across all countries.[45] This criticism flows from the shortcomings of the economic sanctions process, rooted in biased Mutual Evaluation Reports (MER) which highlight compliance variations across countries, thereby pressuring less compliant countries (LCCs) to offer implementation concessions even in the absence of a complete domestic ratification process.[46] LCCs are usually developing countries that are

---

43 EENA3, Anti-Money Laundering Specialist (CAMS), Expert Witness and Former Banking Regulator (FDIC), Interview with EENA3, 'Telephone Call' (2017).
44 Tim Wu, 'Agency Threats' [2010] 60 Duke LJ 1841, 1845.
45 *Gathii* (n 22).
46 Ben Hayes, 'Counter-terrorism, "Policy Laundering" and the FATF: Legalizing Surveillance, Regulating Civil Society' 11 (*Transnational Institute/Statewatch*, Mar. 2012) <http://www.statewatch.org/analyses/no-171-fafpreport.pdf> accessed 15 November 2017.

then subject to rules and sanctions manufactured by a select few wielding the FATF as a weapon to impose same on developing countries. These sanctions are blindsided because the absence of meaningful participation by LCCs in the consultation process forecloses their ability to benefit from wider coop-eration and information exchange. This makes it harder to ensure effective implementation and compliance. Conversely, participation would ensure that each country's peculiarities are considered in measuring implementation and compliance.

This hegemonic imposition proves counter-productive to targeted countries and undermines their sovereignty.[47] Todd condemns economic sanctions, stat-ing that historically, they have proved incapable of achieving the desired behav-ioural change which they seek within punished countries; instead, they negatively impact the general populace.[48] Todd also notes that the FATF's violation of inter-national law in imposing economic sanctions threatens the legitimacy and integ-rity of international efforts in combating money laundering/ terrorist financing (ML/TF), amounting to extraterritorial bullying.[49] This is because the FATF's 34 member countries make decisions on which countries to sanction and how, whereas the member countries, despite their non-compliance, are usually excused from sanctions. Developing countries have fiercely contested this phenomenon, arguing that guidelines and sanctions manufactured by a select few are imposed on a larger majority, without their freewill, thus curtailing the long-term stability and sustainability of the global system.[50]

Risk-Based Approach

To address these legitimacy concerns, Ghroshay asserts that the FATF adopted a RBA system to ensure that countries' developmental level and peculiarities are considered in the compliance assessment process.[51] The focus of the RBA, which is aimed at aiding countries understand and prioritise their ML/TF risks,[52] is two-fold: to strengthen global safeguards to ML/TF and to protect the integrity of the financial system by equipping governments with adequate tools against illicit crime.[53] To achieve these, the RBA requires countries, competent authorities and FIs to identify, assess and understand the ML/TF risks they are exposed to and

---

47 Todd Doyle, 'Cleaning Up Anti-Money Laundering Strategies: Current FATF Tactics Need-lessly Violate International Law' [2001] 24 Hous. J. Int'l Law 279, 289.
48 Ibid. 279, 281.
49 Ibid.
50 *Ghoshray*, (n 33) 521, 543.
51 Ibid. 521, 544. RBA was originally introduced in 2003 and 2007 but was restricted to certain recommendations. It became recognised as increasingly important and a basis for all standards in 2012.
52 FATF, 'FATF Guidance: National Money Laundering and Terrorist Financing Risk Assess-ment' (*FATF*, 2013) <http://www.fatf-gafi.org/media/fatf/content/images/National_ML_TF_Risk_Assessment.pdf> accessed 10 June 2017.
53 Ibid.

take commensurate measures to mitigate them effectively.[54] Additionally, countries are expected to understand the impact of the risk materialisation on their national economy, financial and non-financial sectors.[55]

Explaining the RBA, EENA1 states that

> if a country believes that 35% of its economy is informal and a substantial sum of money is laundered in cash, real estate or precious stones, regulators are to allocate resources to those areas and supervise effectively...less resources should be allocated to financial institutions and insurance bodies.[56]

This portrays an individualistic country-by-country approach that injects a measure of flexibility into the system, allowing the FATF standards adapt to multiple jurisdictional circumstances.[57] Acknowledging this, EENA1 states that institutions are also mandated to assess their risk, noting that 'if customs believe that cash couriers are utilised through the capital city airport, then there should be about ten people monitoring the airport capital and one person monitoring the land entry'.[58] This ensures the operationalisation of the RBA at the micro level. Ghroshay argues that under the RBA system, soft law evolves into tangible standards that mandate robust compliance because assessors consider and contain structural problems that hinder compliance in the MER, thus giving all countries a level playing ground.

Ghroshay's position is however not entirely correct and may pass off as somewhat idealistic in ensuring that each country's compliance reflects its peculiarities and risk projection. This is based on two factors: first, the ambiguity in the definition of risk and the conceptualisation of the RBA. Secondly, the literal interpretation of the FATF's statement on risk and compliance in its methodology for assessing technical compliance.

THE AMBIGUITY IN THE DEFINITION OF RISK AND THE CONCEPTUALISATION OF THE RBA

Firstly, whilst the FATF's denotation of a 'risk-based approach' described above seemed comprehensible, examining other FATF documents shows that there is ambiguity regarding the definition of 'risk'. For instance, the FATF's National Money Laundering and Terrorist Financing Risk Assessment omits the definition

---

54 Ibid.; Abdullahi Bello and Jackie Harvey, 'From a Risk-based Approach to an Uncertainty Based Approach to Anti-Money Laundering' [2017] 30 (1) Security Journal 1, 5.

55 *FATF* (n 52).

56 EENA1, Consulting Counsel, Financial Integrity Unit, International Monetary Fund, Interview with EENA1, 'Telephone Call' (2017).

57 FATF, FATF Guidance: Anti-Money Laundering and Terrorist Financing Measures and Financial Inclusion (*FATF*, February 2013) <http://www.fatf-gafi.org/media/fatf/documents/reports/AML_CFT_Measures_and_Financial_Inclusion_2013.pdf> accessed 10 June 2017.

58 *EENA1* (n 56).

of 'risk' but states that: 'Risk…(is) a function of three factors: threat, vulnerability and consequence'.[59]

The evasion of a precise definition of risk is an acknowledgement that the concept is multidimensional and nuanced.[60] Additionally, the absence of a definition within the concept of ML/TF may underpin poor implementation of the RBA.[61] Hence, Bello and Harvey define risk within the context of AML/CFT as 'a situation where the probability of an occurrence of an event is known and the resulting consequences are measurable'.[62] By this definition, the usage of the term 'risk', in application, will raise issues. This can be exemplified with the RBA expectations of the FATF which is evident in its Methodology for Assessing Technical Compliance. The document states that 'assessors should make clear in the mutual evaluation report…factors they have taken into account, why and how they have done so',[63] indicating that, at the country level, the FATF assumes that in-country regulators comprehend the likelihood that a particular 'conduit of transfer' is likely to be used to launder money and the outcome of such a decision. However, there are uncertainties to this. Firstly, it is difficult to ascertain the extent to which launderers utilise one conduit in comparison to other porous conduits. Secondly, it is difficult to justify the factors that are taken into account to label a sector more risk-prone to illicit transfers. Thirdly, if a conduit is categorised as being open to ML/TF risk, the regulators' likelihood of risk classification (high risk or low risk) and their resource allocation is unclear. Fourthly, how legitimate customers may react to being hindered from performing their businesses is unknown.[64]

However, despite the uncertainties surrounding the RBA, where in-country regulators fail to attain accurate risk valuation, it can adversely affect the country's overall compliance levels and the external assessors would be required to

59 *FATF* (n 52). Examining these factors reveals the porosity of the FATF's description of risk and the potential difficulties that may follow. Threat focuses on people, objects and activities which may cause harm to state, society or the economy. It includes criminals, terrorist groups, their facilitators and their ML/TF activities. This limits the law's reach, as persons who do not necessarily fall into this category may inadvertently be involved in laundering processes. See Hannah Kuchler, 'Cyber Criminals Eye Financial Markets for a Better Return on Investment' (*Financial Times*, 2014) <https://www.ft.com/content/2a11ee92-3cbc-11e4-871d-00144feabdc0> accessed 10 June 2017.

60 Yacov Y. Haimes, 'On the Complex Definition of Risk: A Systems-Based Approach' [2009] 29 (12) Risk Analyst 1647, 1648.

61 Killick Marcus and David Parody, 'Implementing AML/CFT Measures that Address the Risks and not Tick Boxes' [2007] 15.2 Journal of Financial Regulation and Compliance 210–216.

62 *Bello and Harvey* (n 54).

63 FATF, 'Methodology: For Assessing Technical Compliance with the FATF Recommendations and the Effectiveness of AML/CFT System' (*FATF*, 2013) <http://www.fatf-gafi.org/media/fatf/documents/methodology/FATF%20Methodology%2022%20Feb%202013.pdf> accessed 10 August 2017.

64 *Bello and Harvey* (n 54).

make estimations on a country's behalf,[65] therefore, further exacerbating agency slack and a legitimacy crisis. This outcome-focused approach is predicated on the assumption that an AML/CFT regulator can foretell the outcome of his decision and hence, should bear the responsibilities resulting therefrom. This is not necessarily true given that the 'probability of an outcome' may not be an accurate profiling technique to streamline conduits of transfers.

Critics have also argued that the RBA is not easily comprehended or honestly applied. EENA3 states 'I [went] to a country known for marijuana sale on every corner. Marijuana fields are within view of the capital city and the authorities never mentioned that they grow marijuana in their country'.[66] EENA3 attributed this to the fact that the RBA is not widely understood, the risk is not identified correctly, properly or honestly by countries.[67] Moreover, he argues that this is also a problem with assessors as there is a tendency for them to demand the same thing from every country. EENA4 attributes this deficiency to a shift in operation and culture as previously 'regulators were used to assessing institutions with a checklist...now they have to do a risk-based supervision – it's not familiar with a lot of people'.[68] This indicates the complexity in the application of this approach and the struggle countries have to encounter to meet the requirements. Noting this, EENA5 stated that 'conducting a national risk assessment is technical and resource intensive...[coupled] with risk profiling and profiling at every level...it takes about a year to get the risk status for a small country – not even a country like Nigeria'.[69] This complexity can indeed put countries under pressure to deliver, thereby occasioning agency slack. For this reason, there has been limited impact of the RBA on risk allocation or improved strategies.

The deficiency of the RBA can be attributable to various internal factors. These include inefficient collection of tax by countries and the reluctance to engage in forfeiture and confiscation of the proceeds of crime.[70] Related to those are the lack of political will, resources and political interference.[71] For instance, Angola has some corruption issues, but it will not want to talk about it. Also, the Nigerian President was criticised for admitting to the UK government that Nigeria is 'fantastically corrupt'.[72] Fearing likely listing by the FATF, countries are usually worried about revealing the true risk they face. Practitioners have coun-

---

65 FATF, 'Risk Based Approach for the Banking Sector' (*FATF*, October 2014) <http://www
.fatf-gafi.org/media/fatf/documents/reports/Risk-Based-Approach-Banking-Sector.pdf>
accessed 19 March 2018.
66 *EENA3* (n 43).
67 Ibid.
68 EENA4, Interview with EENA4 'Telephone Call' (2017).
69 EENA5, Researcher, GIABA, Interview with EENA5 'Telephone Call' (2017).
70 *EENA1* (n 56)
71 *EENA2* (n 42).
72 Bayo Oluwasanmi, 'Yes! Nigeria is "Fantastically Corrupt"' (*Sahara Reporters*, 16 May
2016) <http://saharareporters.com/2016/05/16/yes-nigeria-fantastically-corrupt-bayo
-oluwasanmi>accessed 10 May 2018.

tered the arguments on the deficiency of the RBA, arguing instead that when designed and used efficiently, the RBA can indeed lead to improved, targeted compliance of countries.[73] EENA1 and EENA4 acknowledge this but argue that the issues to implementation further hinder the effectiveness of the RBA.[74] For this reason, RBA is not leading to reforms yet.

These limitations of the RBA are also demonstrated at the institutional level. The regulator's risk profiling mechanism, which is dependent on the risk assessment of FIs, presumes that the higher the suspicion of FIs in AML/CFT, the higher the perceived risk. Hence, FIs' legal departments monitor contracts, whilst the compliance departments monitor the products/agreements of FIs, to ensure that any suspicion is addressed in accordance with the law. Differentiating suspicious from non-suspicious activity is an uphill task, which faults regulatory assumptions, as launderers are not easily identified apart from legal activities.[75] On this basis, Pellegrina and Masciandaro concede that the 'risk' terminology might have simply reflected the general movement to such approach within the broader regulation of financial markets.[76] Bello and Harvey however suggest that the 'uncertainty based approach'(UBA) which focuses not on the 'outcome of the decision' but on the process leading to the decision is a more suitable means of addressing ML/TF.[77]

To understand why the UBA is crucial for AML/CFT regulation, as opposed to the RBA, it is critical to distinguish these approaches. The UBA and the RBA are not mutually exclusive as they can both be incorporated within the meaning of uncertainty.[78] Thus, risk is considered as a subcategory of uncertainty, which is defined, measurable and predictable. Knight acknowledges this, stating that, whilst risk is also uncertainty, risk is a determinate uncertainty, whilst uncertainty is indeterminate.[79] Therefore, this means that whilst risk is somewhat known and measurable, uncertainty is unknown and unknowable.[80] Risk is, therefore, the

---

73 *EENA2* (n 42).

74 *EENA1* (n 56); *EENA4* (n 68).

75 Valsamis Mitsilegas, *Money Laundering Counter-Measures in the European Union: A Paradigm of Security Governance versus Fundamental Legal Principles* (Kluwer Law International, 2003).

76 Dalla Pellegrina and Donato Masciandaro, 'The Risk-Based Approach in the New European Anti-Money Laundering Legislations: a Law and Economics View' [2009] 5 (2) Review of Law and Economics 1, 3.

77 *Bello and Harvey* (n 54).; John S. Hammond, Ralph Keeney and Howard Raiffa, *Smart Choices: A Practical Guide to Making Better Decisions* (HUP, 2015) 112; Boris Holzer and Yuval Millo, 'From Risks to Second Order Danger in Financial Markets: Unintended Consequences of Risk Management Systems' [2005] 10 (2) New Political Economy.

78 Peter Miller, Liisa Kurunmäki and Ted O'Leary, 'Accounting, Hybrids and the Management of Risk' [2007] 33 (7–8) Accounting, Organizations and Society 942, 944.

79 Frank Knight, *Risk, Uncertainty and Profit* (First Published 1921, Dover Publications, Inc. New York).

80 Dionysious Demetis and Ian Angell, 'The Risk-Based Approach to AML: Representation, Paradox, and the 3rd Directive' [2007] 10 (4) Journal of Money Laundering Control 412, 413.

residual outcome of making uncertainty manageable by setting appropriate risk limits with defined parameters to control exposure. Conversely, with uncertainty, the probability may be known but the consequences remain unknown.

Unlike the RBA, decision-making within a UBA would provide a more accurate reflection of the uncertainties surrounding rationalisation of a conduit being more susceptible to the risk of ML/TF. This is because, given the nature of illicit transfers, regulators usually lack information about the possible consequences of their decision-making. In such situations where either the probability of the exposure to illicit crime is unclear and the precise consequence of the exposure to such crime is unknown, the UBA would be fit for purpose.[81] No doubt, this varies from the decision-making process within the RBA where it is expected that the consequence of decisions are known with certainty as to the outcome of such decisions.[82] Additionally, the RBA may misalign benefits and incentives between country regulators and the IFIs/FATF. This is particularly when the countries are aware that unveiling certain risk would warrant sanctions or reputational damage. For instance, countries would not be too quick to admit that they suffer from CDD deficiencies. Acknowledging this, as EENA4 stated, 'it is difficult to get officials to agree to the risk they face'.[83] This quagmire can be attributed to the variances in interest, as whilst IFIs/FATF are focused on combatting ML/TF, regulators are more inclined to focus on protecting the safety and soundness of banks with limited attention to ML/TF risk. For this reason, an agency slack arises where countries misinform the international community.

The inability of countries to understand or even measure risk and its likely outcome can be attributed to the nature of illicit crimes. For instance, to date, studies have been unable to quantify the amount of money laundered annually. Barone and Masciandaro argue that figures are usually 'pure speculation…or just invented'.[84] This poses a serious challenge to the RBA and largely renders its model unsuitable. For this reason, the implementation of the RBA has been criticised.[85]

The shortcomings of the RBA highlight the strengths of the UBA which is a viable alternative. With the UBA, countries would not necessarily be sanctioned for not properly identifying their risk, but rather, there is an implicit understanding

81 Carole Gibbs, Meredith Gore, Edmund McGarrell and Louie Rivers, 'Introducing Conservation Criminology: Towards Interdisciplinary Scholarship on Environmental Crimes and Risks' [2010] 1 (1) British Journal of Criminology 124, 135.

82 Paul Glimcher and Ernst Fehr, *Neuroeconomics: Decision Making and the Brain* (2nd edn, Amsterdam, Elsevier, 2014).

83 *EENA4* (n 68).

84 Raffaella Barone and Donato Masciandaro, 'Organised Crime, Money Laundering and legal Economy: Theory and Simulations' [2011] 32 (1) European Journal of Law and Economics 115, 116.

85 Stuart Ross and Michelle Hannan, 'Money Laundering Regulation and Risk-Based Decision Making' [2007] 10 (1) Journal of Money Laundering Control 106–115; *Demetis and Angell* (n 80) 412, 413.

that the nature of ML/TF, which makes it difficult to quantify risk, would be taken into consideration. In such situations, there is the recognition that regulators cannot be certain of the impact of ML via a particular conduct if the risk materialises.[86] Moreover, FIs are also uncertain about the nature of transactions given that transactions can be potentially financed with laundered funds or for terrorism purposes. Demetis and Angell state that although categories of risk are itemised for FIs, in practice, uncertainty is transferred to these categories.[87] As such, any attempts to fit a square peg in a round hole would be futile.

Interestingly, the UBA can be utilised by adopting Hammond et al.'s risk profile steps,[88] wherein concluding regarding areas that pose AML/CFT issues to countries, regulators can ask:

1. What are the uncertainties?
2. What are the possible outcomes of these uncertainties?
3. What are the chances of occurrences of each possible outcome?
4. What are the consequences of each outcome?

The crucial starting point is to identify each decision's objective, which in this case is to prevent illicit transfers.

The first step to this risk profiling approach for regulators is to decide on the available alternatives. For regulators, the decision is how to categorise a conduit as replete with ML/TF. Identifying an alternative requires the regulator to identify the uncertainties related with their decision. For the regulator, there are two significant uncertainties – a conduit is either frequently utilised for illicit transfers or it is not frequently used. Determining this is difficult, but regulators are to be guided by available statistics – which are scarce in ACs/EEs. Upon identification, the likely outcome of each uncertainty is outlined. As envisaged, specificity is not feasible in defining the outcome of each uncertainty.[89] Consequently, what is required is a broad but unique categorisation that would capture the likely outcomes. This leaves room for decision-making by the regulator but may also breed mistakes as the regulator can decide that a conduit poses ML/TF challenges, whereas it does not. The margin for error can however be minimised by dependence on accurate statistics and expert consultation, which involves the judgement-based approach (JBA).[90] JBA entails regulators looking forward to take account of a wide range of possible risks to the AML/CFT objectives.[91]

86 Elod Takats, 'A Theory of "Crying Wolf": The Economics of Money Laundering Enforcement' [2011] 27 (1) Journal of Law, Economics and Organization 32, 34.
87 *Demetis and Angell* (n 80) 412, 413.
88 *Hammond, Keeney and Raiffa* (n 77).
89 *Bello and Harvey* (n 54).
90 *Hammond, Keeney and Raiffa* (n 77).
91 Ellis Ferran, 'Where in the World is the EU Going' *in* Eilis Ferran, Niamh Moloney, Jennifer G. Hill and John Coffee (eds.) *The Regulatory Aftermath of the Global Financial Crisis* (CUP, 2012)

The information garnered can be used to decide the quantitative probability, expressed in percentages – that a conduit is largely or limitedly used to launder money. This is a very subjective approach which differs from the objective approach utilised by the RBA.[92] Unlike the UBA, the RBA does not focus on quantitative and qualitative analysis as it refers to such analysis as 'mere collection of…information'. RBA is largely dependent on the categorisation of risk through benchmarking as either medium-high, medium-low, etc.

An incentive-based system incorporated in the UBA may also ensure improved technical and effectiveness compliance to AML/CFT standards.[93] Therefore, where a conduit mainly used for regular transactions is classed as suspect, that conduit may experience withdrawal of use caused by regulators mishap. To prevent this, the regulator has a variety of choices, to consider the conduit as suspicious and report it or consider it as non-suspicious and document his position. Where it is suspicious, two uncertainties arise – the IFIs/FATF assessors may reward the regulators for curtailing the conduit's use. Conversely, the conduit may face decline in use due to reputational damage. Where classed as non-suspicious, the conduit will not lose customers and may even gain laundering customers who believe that they will now be subject to less intense supervision. However, this latter classification may indeed be erroneous as the conduit may actually be a hub for ML/TF. In such situations, whilst the RBA, in its focus on outcome, would mark the country as non-compliant in recommendation 1, which affects its effectiveness levels, the UBA would focus on the decision-making process. This indicates that a country must structure a format that would allow it to detect illicit transfers via various conduits, thereby curbing ML/TF.

Furthermore, an application of the RBA to countries also shows its inadequacies, particularly in securing accurate AML/CFT compliance levels. Whilst the RBA allows countries to designate resources in accordance with risk, it still categorises countries in the form of a Black2 or a grey list. This raises questions as to the arbitrary basis upon which countries are so classified.[94] Although most countries are sanctioned on the basis of the weakness of their financial and regulatory structure or the absence of political will, the FATF's mandate aims to ensure financial integrity and stability, a position which should aim at sanctioning countries with the most ML/TF activity. Although no concrete statistics exist, studies have indicated that the United States has the highest level of ML globally,[95] along

---

92 *Knight* (n 79).
93 Dalla Pellegrina and Donato Masciandaro, 'The Risk-Based Approach in the New European Anti-Money Laundering Legislations: A Law and Economics View' [2009] 5 (2) Review of Law and Economics 1, 3; *Takats* (n 86) 32, 34.
94 Countries classification may be arbitrary.
95 Burak Dolar and Shughart William, 'Enforcement of the USA Patriot Act's Anti-Money Laundering Provisions: Have Regulators Followed a Risk Based Approach?' [2011] 22 (1) Global Finance Journal 19, 20.

with the United Kingdom, particularly given its porous real estate market.[96] Yet, these countries are considered low risk and countries which are remotely connected to the global financial market, with lower levels of financial crime are continually classed as high risk due to structural issues. Bello and Harvey argue that this arbitrary designation contradicts a truly risk-based approach, typifying this with the case of Habib Bank, fined for not listing Pakistan and Kenya as high-risk countries.[97] Furthermore, although California has been classed as high risk within the United States,[98] suspicious transactions may not be flagged up as ones from Kenya would, given the FATF's asymmetrical risk basis.

THE LITERAL INTERPRETATION OF THE FATF'S STATEMENT ON RISK
AND COMPLIANCE IN ITS METHODOLOGY FOR ASSESSING TECHNICAL
COMPLIANCE

The FATF methodology for assessing compliance states clearly that: 'however, risks, materiality and structural or other contextual factors *should not be an excuse* for poor or uneven implementation of the FATF standards'.[99]

Whilst the FATF expects that structural reasons for non-compliance are highlighted in the MER document, the above statement illustrates that it does not expect such reasons to be a justification for, or a reason to condone non-compliance. EENA4 supports this line of argument, stating that

> you need to have your framework in place…a country cannot say "we have no capacity" or "we are slow in legislating" …[or] "we have corruption issues – so it is okay that we have not criminalised politically exposed persons" …we can understand why they haven't done so…but certain things cannot be excused.[100]

This is however a narrow perception of the factors that hinder compliance. For instance, should a country be rated lowly for not adequately complying with the CDD requirements where it was working to ensure financial inclusion? Such punishment would indicate the facilitation of continuously low compliance levels

---

96 Zlata Rodionova, 'London Property Market Turned into Money Laundering Safe Haven by Inadequate Supervision, MPs say' (*Independent*, 15 July 2016) <http://www.independent.co.uk/news/business/news/london-property-market-real-estate-money-laundering-overseas-foreign-buyers-mps-a7138176.html> accessed 10 July 2017.
97 *Bello and Harvey* (n 54).
98 *Hammond, Keeney and Raiffa* (n 77).; Boris Holzer and Yuval Millo, 'From Risks to Second Order Danger in Financial Markets: Unintended Consequences of Risk Management System' [2005] 10 (2) New Political Economy 223, 225.
99 FATF, 'Guidance for a Risk-Based Approach: The Banking Sector' (*FATF*, 2014) <http://www.fatf-gafi.org/media/fatf/documents/reports/Risk-Based-Approach-Banking-Sector.pdf> accessed 10 June 2017.
100 *EENA4* (n 68).

of developing countries despite the factors taken into account. Acknowledging this, EENA4 stated that

> The recommendations are very focused on the banks and it contravenes and goes against the cash-based economy. There is a huge chunk of money that is outside the bank that you cannot really assess. The recommendations hinder those countries that are less cash-based. You can say that you need to strengthen the banking sector and ensure that wire transfers are completely regulated – but does that really capture cash-based transfers. In some countries – people will buy houses with cash – it's only in more developed countries that you have bank transfers, cheques.... It's easier on the banking side to do CDD but maybe it's not easy on the cash that you follow. It's something that is a little bit more difficult.[101]

This further illustrates the continuous issue of asymmetrical compliance benchmarks which have an effect on the compliance level of countries, causing their placement on the grey or black2 list.

Furthermore, the methodology states that 'assessors should make clear in the MER...factors they have taken into account, why and how they have done so'.[102]

This indicates that even when structural reasons for non-compliance are highlighted in the MER, without an impact on the overall compliance level, assessors are mandated to comply and explain. This illustrates the onerous burden of ensuring that compliance reflects appropriate levels and not 'excused levels'.

Examining the conception of risk and the FATF's approach to it reveals that the current RBA may not necessarily lead to improved legitimacy or indeed the compliance of developing countries. EENA1 argues that, whilst theoretically, the RBA can ensure improved compliance, practically it is a struggle for countries. Furthermore, the impact cannot yet be ascertained because only a few countries conduct this risk-based exercise correctly.[103] Currently, it is not yet leading to reform, particularly in Africa.[104]

Through the Lens of Legitimacy

As noted, the FATF's rule design, implementation and compliance processes have unearthed a pervasive legitimacy crisis. This has occasioned the argument that amending power relationships through membership and inclusiveness would

---

101 Ibid.
102 FATF, 'Methodology: For Assessing Technical Compliance with the FATF Recommendations and the Effectiveness of AML/CFT System' (*FATF*, 2013) <http://www.fatf-gafi .org/media/fatf/documents/methodology/FATF%20Methodology%2022%20Feb%20 2013.pdf> accessed 10 August 2017.
103 *EENA1* (n 56).
104 Ibid.

resolve legitimacy concerns.[105] This perspective assumes that currently excluded countries can obtain membership which grants participation in deliberation processes by meeting the set FATF membership criteria. This argument is however blindsided to the realities of the FATF membership configuration, which is restricted to 'strategically important' countries.[106] This has seen only OECD countries, EEs and a few others become members on the basis of an elusive subjective selection process.[107]

Shortly after the accession of select countries, the FATF considered it expedient to close its membership doors in 1992 so as to 'preserve the efficiency of the task force'.[108] This action foreclosed the participation of all countries in the decision-making procedures – processes which although would have permitted dissenting viewpoints, it was alleged that it would result in bureaucracy and expensive decision-making.[109] Thus, at this point, there was the projection of ownership and legitimacy as secondary to efficiency. This raises concerns about whether the FATF acknowledges that its rules are unfavourable and may become subject to intense scrutiny, prompting refutation or delayed transplantation by developing countries. To achieve expediency, the FATF hastens its decision-making processes, which is even more detrimental to developing countries who are unable to input their perspective.

This closed membership structure poses two risks: firstly, countries excluded from 'core' membership positions may only render formal or creative compliance.[110] Secondly, it exposes the financial system to risk from countries not considered 'important'. Although these countries are subject to intense scrutiny, inappropriately crafted tools are applied to mandate compliance. This can be attributable to the absence of a degree of involvement in rule design which permits agency slack, correctable only in the presence of perfect information.

Whilst the FATF has refrained from expanding its membership, the IFIs have responded by altering their membership quota, granting EEs more weight in recognition of their rising economic powers.[111] The G20 has also taken up some

---

105 *Vibert* (n 16) 391, 391.
106 Why are the restrictions to strategically important countries? If the FATF does not think other countries pose serious risk, why does it add them as associate members in the first instance?
107 Wesley Kirton, 'Guyana Has Now Become a Strategically Important Country' (*Kaieteur News*, 15 May 2017) <http://www.kaieteurnewsonline.com/2017/05/15/guyana-has-now-become-a-strategically-important-country/> accessed 21 May 2017.
108 FATF, 'Financial Action Task Force on Money Laundering Report 1990–1991' (*FATF*, 13 May 1991) <http://www.fatf-gafi.org/media/fatf/documents/reports/1990%201991%20ENG.pdf> accessed 10 May 2017.
109 See FATF, Annual Report FATF 1990–1991 Paris, 13 May 1991 p. 19.
110 Doreen McBarnet, *Enforcing Ethics: New Strategies for Tackling Creative Compliance* [2007] Australian National University, Canberra.
111 BrettonWoods Project 'IMF & World Bank Decision-Making and Governance' (*Bretton-Woods Project*, 31 March 2016) <http://www.brettonwoodsproject.org/2016/03/imf-world-bank-decision-making-and-governance-existing-structures-and-reform-processes/> accessed 10 July 2017.

coordinating functions of the G7.[112] Although seemingly more inclusive, Vibert argues that these membership changes do not address two primary weaknesses in rule design, the failing abilities of the IFIs/ Trans-governmental Networks (TGNs) in problem solving and the undemocratic nature of rulemaking.[113]

Vibert argues that problem-solving abilities of IFIs/FATF lie not in membership but in informed knowledge and expertise.[114] He argues further that IFIs/ TGNs belong to the knowledge world where their decision-making skills depend on their epistemic authority.[115] They draw on the procedure of the natural and social sciences to identify complications and frame policy responses. This is supported by Kerwer and Hulsse who argue that trans-governmental organisations such as the FATF are objectively technocratic.[116] Thus, Vibert asserts that changes to membership arrangements may confound the problems of input legitimacy, confusing epistemic failure and democratic deficit.[117] The limitation to this argument is that it fails to recognise that improved membership representation may be crucial for a more robust knowledge bank at the IFIs/TGNs.

Discounting the possibility of a robust knowledge bank, Vibert advances the argument that there is no true democracy in international rulemaking.[118] He postulates that changing quotas in IFIs reflect the government and not the people. This defeats the argument on inclusivity from the start, for if they are democratic, IFIs/TGNs should reflect the people's preferences.[119] This recognises the complex high-level interactions that precede transplantations, whereby decisions applicable to the entire government are usually made to the exclusion of persons at the grassroots level. This illustrates how influences of international law usually barrage state and local governments. Furthermore, many citizens of countries unaware of FATF standards are subjected to the FATF's disclosure mandate laid out by its CDD/KYC requirements.

Nevertheless, it is acknowledged that the absence of democracy in IFIs/ TGNs may trigger hesitation in transplantation of standards by democratic and undemocratic countries alike. This is why these institutions continually declare their neutrality and legitimacy by projecting the tenets of democracy through their undertakings. These undertakings include ensuring equitable labour or

---

112 Gordon S. Smith, 'G7 to G8 to G20: Evolution in Global Governance' (CIGI G20 Papers, 6 May 2011) <https://www.cigionline.org/sites/default/files/g20no6-2.pdf> accessed 14 July 2017.
113 *Vibert* (n 16).
114 Ibid.
115 Ibid.
116 Dieter Kerwer and Rainer Hulsee, 'How International Organisations Rule the World: The Case of the Financial Action Task Force' [2011] 2 (1) Journal of International Organisation Studies.
117 *Vibert* (n 16) 391, 392.
118 Ibid.
119 To make the case that international decisions reflect the people's preferences, a huge number of assumptions have to be made about the way in which preferences are aggregated by government from the bottom up. *Vibert* (n 16).

intellectual property rights. However, the declaration of legitimacy is not a sufficient 'ingredient' for democracy, as without a dissenting opinion in governments or IFI/TGNs decision-making processes, democracy cannot exist. Contrariwise, in undemocratic regimes, opposing voices are subdued.

What becomes evident is that hegemonic subservience and agency capture shapes FATF policy making – resulting in democratic deficit. Democratic deficit in agency rulemaking is born out of the fundamentals of the underlining participatory conflict and is manifested in the data regarding the lack of meaningful participation by the majority of jurisdictions.[120] This in turn impacts countries' ability to close the compliance differential as they are not part of the process – whilst also foreclosing their ability to benefit from the wider cooperation and information exchange of a regulatory framework. The result is that affected jurisdictions may be compelled to comply with rules with no participatory linkage.[121] Conversely, when a country is part of the process, its compliance differential is less. This can be typified with the BRICS; although their level of participation in the FATF is questionable – their compliance differential is less.

To ensure that standards and laws by international bodies are respected, every aspect of decision-making must be democratic, in the sense that an option is provided to allow a contestation of the rule design or compliance process. What becomes evident is the need for a global platform that permits democracy. Whilst Vibert envisions this to be a global platform with a parliament, Mugarura envisages an adjudicatory framework.[122] Vibert concedes that Mugarura's approach may be a preferred option as an international juridical body would safeguard some form of legal pluralism allowing for delegation and fairness. The practicalities are however uncertain. Political elements may hinder the ability to rely on judicial structures, for example, when a court in one jurisdiction defers to another. Additionally, efforts to combine both political and juridical elements may result in 'cosmopolitan democracy'[123] which satisfies neither side.

Hence Vibert projects the alternative of an 'international agreement on international administrative procedure'. The idea is that international administrative procedures will apply to international rulemakers, where each institution would be bound to adhere to evidence-based procedures that underpin their epistemic authority. Additionally, each institution would be subject to external judicial review for recommendations and decisions. Finally, any such agreement would be subject to executive agreement of ministers or senior officials and the approval of national legislators – the bodies with the greatest claim to democratic legitimacy.

---

120 *Gathii* (n 22).
121 Todd Doyle, 'Cleaning Up Anti-Money Laundering Strategies: Current FATF Tactics Needlessly Violate International Law' [2002] 24 Hous. J. Int'l L. 279, 307.
122 Norman Mugarura, *The Global Anti-Money Laundering Regulatory Landscape in Less Developed Countries* (1st edn Routledge 2016) 209.
123 Daria Jarczewska, 'Critical Assessment of Cosmopolitan Democracy' (International Relations Students , 22 January 2013) <http://www.e-ir.info/2013/01/22/critical-assessment-of-cosmopolitan-democracy/> accessed 10 June 2017.

Vibert argues that this would mark the process of bringing constitutional order into the international level of decision-making. Apparently, this approach would ensure that all voices are brought to the table and expertise is no longer the most crucial factor in decision-making. However, in practice, the need to ensure the perspectives of various governments are taken into account during the review process would slow things down. Additionally, the belated involvement of countries may simply be a replication of the hegemonic agenda within these institutions.

This indicates the need to correct ownership, legitimacy and expertise simultaneously. A more inclusive platform, such as that of the International Association of Deposit Insurers[124] would ensure effective combative strategies, rather than an undemocratic platform with coercive powers. This would aid in reversing the debilitating financial consequences on non-compliant countries that were simply set up to fail, whilst enabling them to achieve true financial stability and integrity.

Regulatory Paradox: A Motive for Halting Continued Implementation of the FATF Standards by ACs/EEs?

The RBA will not permit non-compliance with any of the recommendations. ACs have to remain compliant with the FATF's technical and effectiveness recommendations to the same degree, only with narrowed focus on issues considered to pose higher AML/CFT risk. The problem with this is that the FATF standards, particularly on CDD/KYC, can propel socio-economic exclusion which has serious consequences for socio-economic development. This effect is averse to the FATF's financial inclusion objective. For the FATF, this is an unintended consequence, as driving an economy 'underground' can affect the regulators' ability to effectively monitor the abuse of financial systems and hinder their capability to detect crime. Furthermore, this regime which is external to ACs/EEs, can widen the gap between social classes whilst degenerating socio-economic exclusion in these countries. This is particularly so within ACs given the excesses of colonisation in the form of social and economic ills which the continent still grapples with.

These arguments portray the regulatory paradox that occurs in the absence of legitimacy of standards, a situation that weakens the effectiveness of standards and the compliance ratings of ACs/EEs. Consequently, it is imperative to ask, why ACs/EEs continue to implement the FATF standards. As discussed, ACs/EEs face a case of 'double illegitimacy'[125] that hinders their ability to 'opt out' of compliance given the inclusion of the FATF's recommendations within the IFIs' funding conditionalities. IFIs use standard setting bodies, including the FATF, to

---

124 IADI, 'Sharing Deposit Insurance Expertise with the World' (*IADI*, 2016) <http://www .iadi.org/en/> accessed 10 July 2017.

125 This is given that developed countries have a lesser quota, and hence, a lesser voice in the decision-making processes. Thus, it can be argued that some measure of 'double-illegitimacy' exists, particularly towards ACs.

determine and set conditionalities that countries have to adhere to.[126] The implication of this is that compliance with the IFIs' conditionalities are benchmarks against which decisions can be made about a country's credit worthiness.[127] This invariably means that when countries receive unfavourable ratings from credit rating agencies, which is highly likely with ACs, their ability to raise or issue debts at affordable rates may be compromised. The effect of this is worse for ACs and their private sector institutions, which rely largely on foreign investments and IFIs for capital. Going by the ratings which offer the international financial markets an estimate of the probability that borrowers will meet their debt obligations, it can be argued that ACs will be unable to access funding or even when they do, they will be subject to higher interest rates.[128] The IFIs' involvement necessitates a form of mandatory compliance, with the possibility of sanctions, severer than the FATF's blacklisting process.

Nevertheless, the pros of FATF implementation and compliance cannot be undermined. It aids good governance within financial and regulatory institutions, which will ensure that with adequate practices, sturdy institutions and resources, these institutions can promote financial integrity. Additionally, compliance can address corruption whilst improving global financial market integrity. Whilst seemingly logical, this position can be contested. For instance, whilst Zimbabwe has an AML/CFT compliance level of over 50%, it remains one of the most corrupt countries in Africa and globally.[129] This further indicates that compliance may be creative as opposed to actual. At present, even developed countries are yet to accurately ascertain how much is laundered yearly; therefore, it would be difficult to determine whether compliance to AML/CFT standards aids in fighting financial crime.

The shortcomings identified in the pros may indicate that countries may not find tangible reasons or output to combat AML/CFT but will continue to comply to ensure that their borrowing capabilities are not restrained. Hence, the FATF standards integration into the FSAP has no doubt aimed to utilise its root in state consent to enhance their legitimacy.[130] Consequently, the FATF standards have increasingly become perceived as legitimate by ACs/EEs. Whilst this would ensure that ACs strive to preserve their credit lines, ingraining the FATF standards within the IFIs conditionalities may have consequences. Such pessi-

---

126 K Alexander., R. Dhumale and J. Eatwell, *Global Governance of Financial Systems: The International Regulation of Systemic Risk* (OUP, New York, 2006).

127 Nadeem Haque, Donald Mathieson and Nelson Mark, 'Rating the Raters of Creditworthiness' (Finance & Development, March 1997)

128 G. Ferri, L-G Lui and J.E. Stiglitz, 'The Procyclical Role of Rating Agencies: Evidence from the East Asia Crisis' [1999] 28 (3) Economic Notes: Review of Banking, Finance and Monetary Economics 335, 335.

129 Transparency International, 'Corruption Perceptions Index 2016' (*Transparency International,* 2017) <https://www.transparency.org/news/feature/corruption_perceptions_index_2016> accessed 19 December 2017.

130 *Ghoshray* (n 33) 521, 544.

mism is due to the failings of the IFI's structural reforms, largely due to their unsuitability to the terrain – facilitated underdevelopment whilst hardly addressing the key issue it aimed to resolve – poverty.[131] This begs the rhetorical question, would the FATF recommendations achieve their intended output given the lack of legitimacy?

Against the backdrop of arguments which illustrate the coercive drive that engineers compliance in the presence of 'illegitimacy', this book argues that any further restructuring to include legitimacy must ensure that all actors (states), notwithstanding their hierarchy, are ingrained in the process of standard making and implementation. Including such fairness in procedures that are devoid of coercion would ensure that countries, particularly ACs, are voluntarily proactive towards convergence and meeting set goals.[132]

Conclusion

Although ACs/EEs adopted the FATF's standards, they have continued to implement them particularly due to the instrumentality of the IFIs. Their continued implementation has however only resulted in formal or creative compliance. The FATF's attempts to resolve this through the introduction of the RBA which was hoped to address the legitimacy crisis and resolve agency slack has proved futile. Scholars have promoted other options to resolving this. However, the UBA does hold some promise in resolving legitimacy issues and ingrained changes within institutions.

This chapter starts by re-emphasising the existence of a legitimacy crisis in AML/CFT regulation processes, as evidenced by the operations and strategy of IFIs/FATF in combatting these illicit crimes. It argues that the absence of legitimacy is most notable when applying standards to 'belated members' and associate members, which are 'rule-takers', with limited room to contribute to rulemaking. Hence, resulting laws do not necessarily mirror society. This occasions a regulatory paradox, for in certain cases, the standards, when translated to laws, achieve unintended consequences.

The legitimacy crisis is then examined in the context of rulemaking and implementation. It argues that belated attempts to include later members in rulemaking is a façade, a situation which leaves associate members in a worse off position given their limited ability to contribute to final decisions. The legitimacy crisis is further exacerbated by the implementation process, which mainly sees ACs penalised for compliance shortcomings. This is despite evidence that indicates that most compliance issues are within developed countries.

Whilst the RBA recently adopted by the FATF was aimed at resolving AML/CFT compliance differentials by taking into consideration the peculiarities of countries, its flawed conceptualisation has hindered its ability to achieve this

131 Ibid.
132 Ibid.

aim. Rather, this has aggravated the agency slack between IFIs/FATF and ACs/EEs particularly due to the difficulty in implementing the RBA which is outcome focused. Consequently, the argument advanced is that a UBA would be more suited to addressing the current agency slack as it shifts the focus to the process of decision-making as opposed to the outcome. Moreover, it can better incorporate the priorities of ACs/EEs. This would aid in resolving the legitimacy crisis which also requires a remodelling at the FATF level to mirror the IADI.

Further Reading

1. Abdullahi Usman Bello and Jackie Harvey, 'From a Risk-Based Approach to an Uncertainty Based Approach to Anti-Money Laundering' [2017] 30 (1) *Security Journal.*
2. K. Alexander, R. Dhumale and J. Eatwell, *Global Governance of Financial Systems: The International Regulation of Systemic Risk* (Oxford University Press, New York, 2006).
3. Andrew Cornford, 'Basel II and Developing Countries' [2008] 2 Finance & Bien Commun.
4. Bayo Oluwasanmi, 'Yes! Nigeria is 'Fantastically Corrupt' (*Sahara Reporters*, 16 May 2016) <http://saharareporters.com/2016/05/16/yes-nigeria-fanta stically-corrupt-bayo-oluwasanmi>accessed 10 May 2018.
5. Ben Hayes, 'Counter-terrorism, "Policy Laundering" and the FATF: Legalizing Surveillance, Regulating Civil Society 11' (*Transnational Institute/Statewatch*, March 2012) <http://www.statewatch.org/analyses/no-171-fafpreport.pdf> accessed 15 November2017.
6. Boris Holzer and Yuval Millo, 'From Risks to Second Order Danger in Financial Markets: Unintended Consequences of Risk Management Systems' [2005] 10 (2) *New Political Economy.*
7. BrettonWoods Project, 'IMF & World Bank Decision-Making and Governance' (*BrettonWoods Project*, 31 March 2016) <http://www.brettonwoodsproject .org/2016/03/imf-world-bank-decision-making-and-governance-existing-st ructures-and-reform-processes/> accessed 10 July 2017.
8. Burak Dolar and Shughart William, 'Enforcement of the USA Patriot Act's Anti-Money Laundering Provisions: Have Regulators Followed a Risk Based Approach?' [2011] 22 (1) Global Finance Journal.
9. Carole Gibbs, Meredith Gore, Edmund McGarrell and Louie Rivers, 'Introducing Conservation Criminology: Towards Interdisciplinary Scholarship on Environmental Crimes and Risks' [2010] 1 (1) British Journal of Criminology.
10. Chris A. Thomas, 'The Concept of Legitimacy and International Law' (2013) LSE Law, Society and Economy Working Papers 12/2013, 14 <http://epr ints.lse.ac.uk/51746/1/__libfile_repository_Content_Law%2C%20society%2 0and%20economics%20working%20papers_2013_WPS2013-12_Thomas.pdf> accessed 10 November 2017.
11. Dalla Pellegrina and Donato Masciandaro, 'The Risk-Based Approach in the New European Anti-Money Laundering Legislations: A Law and Economics View' [2009] 5 (2) Review of Law and Economics.

12. Daniel M. Bodansky, 'The Legitimacy of International Governance: A Coming Challenge for International Environmental Law?' [1999] 93 (3) American Journal of International Law.

13. Daria Jarczewska, 'Critical Assessment of Cosmopolitan Democracy' (International Relations Students, 22 January 2013) <http://www.e-ir.info /2013/01/22/critical-assessment-of-cosmopolitan-democracy/> accessed 10 June 2017.

14. Dionysious Demetis and Ian Angell, 'The Risk-Based Approach to AML: Representation, Paradox, and the 3rd Directive' [2007] 10 (4) Journal of Money Laundering Control.

15. Doreen McBarnet, *Enforcing Ethics: New Strategies for Tackling Creative Compliance* (Australian National University, Canberra, 2007).

16. Todd Doyle, 'Cleaning Up Anti-Money Laundering Strategies: Current FATF Tactics Needlessly Violate International Law' [2001] 24 Houston Journal of International Law.

17. Ellis Ferran, 'Where in the World is the EU Going' in Eilis Ferran, Niamh Moloney, Jennifer G. Hill and John Coffee (eds.) *The Regulatory Aftermath of the Global Financial Crisis* (Cambridge University Press, Cambridge, 2012).

18. Elod Takats, 'A Theory of "Crying Wolf": The Economics of Money Laundering Enforcement' [2011] 27 (1) Journal of Law, Economics and Organization.

19. FATF-VII, 'Financial Action Task Force on Money Laundering Annual Report 1995–1996' (*FATF*, 28 June 1996) <http://www.fatf-gafi.org/media/fatf/ documents/reports/1995%201996%20ENG.pdf> accessed 3 May 2017.

20. FATF, 'Consultation on Proposed Changes to the FATF Standards: Compilation of Responses from Designated Non-Financial Business and Professions (DNFBPs)' (*FATF*, 2011) <http://www.fatf-gafi.org/media/ fatf/documents/publicconsultation/First%20public%20consultation%20doc ument%20responses%20dnfbp.pdf?TSPD_101_R0=692e4d2f674f3e448a 6e814befd6d8e6l4W000000000000000007501cd89ffff000000000000000 00000000000005a922327006825de3e> accessed 12 November 2017.

21. FATF, 'Consultation on Proposed Changes to the FATF Standards: Compilation of Responses from the Financial Sector Part 1 and 2' (*FATF*, 2011) <http:/ /www.fatf-gafi.org/media/fatf/documents/publicconsultation/First%20pu blic%20consultation%20document%20responses%20financial%20sector%2 0part%202.pdf> accessed 4 June 2017.

22. FATF, 'FATF Guidance: Anti-Money Laundering and Terrorist Financing Measures and Financial Inclusion' (*FATF*, February 2013) <http://www.fatf -gafi.org/media/fatf/documents/reports/AML_CFT_Measures_and_Finan cial_Inclusion_2013.pdf> accessed 10 June 2017.

23. FATF, 'FATF Guidance: National Money Laundering and Terrorist Financing Risk Assessment' (*FATF*, 2013) <http://www.fatf-gafi.org/media/fatf/cont ent/images/National_ML_TF_Risk_Assessment.pdf> accessed 10 June 2017.

24. FATF, 'FATF Secretariat' (*FATF*, 2017) <http://www.fatf-gafi.org/about/ fatfsecretariat/> accessed 20 January 2017.

25. FATF, 'Financial Action Task Force on Money Laundering Report 1990–1991' (*FATF*, 13 May 1991) <http://www.fatf-gafi.org/media/fatf/documents/ reports/1990%201991%20ENG.pdf> accessed 10 May 2017.

26. FATF, 'Methodology: For Assessing Technical Compliance with the FATF Recommendations and the Effectiveness of AML/CFT System' (*FATF*, 2013)

<http://www.fatf-gafi.org/media/fatf/documents/methodology/FATF%20 Methodology%2022%20Feb%202013.pdf> accessed 10 August 2017.
27. FATF, 'Procedures for the FATF Fourth Round of AML/CFT Mutual Evaluations' (*FATF*, October 2013) <http://www.fatf-gafi.org/media/fatf /documents/methodology/FATF-4th-Round-Procedures.pdf>   accessed 12 December 2017.
28. FATF, 'Risk Based Approach for the Banking Sector' (*FATF*, October 2014) <http://www.fatf-gafi.org/media/fatf/documents/reports/Risk-Based-Approach-Banking-Sector.pdf> accessed 19 March 2018.
29. G. Ferri, L.-G. Lui and J.E. Stiglitz, 'The Procyclical Role of Rating Agencies: Evidence from the East Asia Crisis' [1999] 28 (3) *Economic Notes: Review of Banking, Finance and Monetary Economics.*
30. FATF, 'Guidance for a Risk-Based Approach: The Banking Sector' (*FATF*, 2014)   <http://www.fatf-gafi.org/media/fatf/documents/reports/Risk-B ased-Approach-Banking-Sector.pdf> accessed 10 June 2017.
31. Frank Knight, *Risk, Uncertainty and Profit* (First Published 1921, Dover Publications, Inc., New York, 2006).
32. Frank Vibert, 'Reforming International Rule-Making' [2012] 3 (3) *Global Policy* 391, 391.
33. GIABA, 'Mutual Evaluation Report: Mali' (*GIABA*, 2008) <http://www.giab a.org/media/f/252_MALI_word_MER_english[1].pdf> accessed 10 June 2017.
34. GIABA, 'Mutual Evaluation Report: Nigeria' (*GIABA*, 2008) <http://www .giaba.org/media/f/299_Mutual%20Evaluation%20Report%20of%20Nigeria .pdf> accessed 10 June 2017.
35. Gordon S. Smith, 'G7 to G8 to G20: Evolution in Global Governance (*CIGI G20 Papers*, 6 May 2011) <https://www.cigionline.org/sites/default/files/ g20no6-2.pdf> accessed 14 July 2017.
36. Hannah Kuchler, 'Cyber Criminals Eye Financial Markets for a Better Return on Investment' (*Financial Times*, 2014) <https://www.ft.com/content/2a1 1ee92-3cbc-11e4-871d-00144feabdc0> accessed 10 June 2017.
37. Ian Hurd, 'Legitimacy and Authority in International Politics' [1999] 53 (2) International Organization.
38. IADI, 'Message from the Chairman' (*IADI*, 2016) <http://www.iadi.org/en /about-iadi/message-from-the-chairman/> accessed 10 November 2017.
39. IADI, 'Sharing Deposit Insurance Expertise with the World' (*IADI*, 2016) <http://www.iadi.org/en/> accessed 10 July 2017.
40. James T. Gathii, 'The Financial Action Task Force and Global Administrative Law' [2010] *Journal of Professional Law.*
41. James K. Jackson, 'The Financial Action Task Force: An Overview' (*Congressional Research Service*, 9 May 2012) <http://fas.org/sgp/crs/terror/RS21904.pd f> accessed 11 November 2017.
42. Jan Klabbers, Anne Peters and Geir Ulfstein, *The Constitutionalization of International Law* (Oxford University Press, 2009).
43. John S. Hammond, Ralph Keeney and Howard Raiffa, *Smart Choices: A Practical Guide to Making Better Decisions* (Harvard University Press, 2015) 112.
44. Jose Alvarez, 'Hegemonic International Law Revisited' [2003] 97 The American Journal of International Law.

45. Julia Black, 'Constructing and Contesting Legitimacy and Accountability in Polycentric Regulatory Regimes' (2008) LSE Law, Society and Economy Working Papers 2/2008, 16 <http://eprints.lse.ac.uk/23040/1/WPS2008 -02_Black.pdf> accessed 16 November 2017.

46. Julia Black, 'Paradoxes and Failures: "New Governance" Techniques and the Financial Crisis' [2012] 75 (6) The Modern Law Review.

47. Kevin L. Shepherd, 'Guardians at the Gate: The Gatekeeper Initiative and the Risk-Based Approach for Transactional Lawyers' [2009] 43 (3) Real Property, Trust and Estate Law Journal 1.

48. Marcus Killickand David Parody, 'Implementing AML/CFT Measures That Address the Risks and not Tick Boxes' [2007] 15 (2) Journal of Financial Regulation and Compliance.

49. Mark Pieth and Gemma Aiolfi, 'Anti-Money Laundering: Levelling the Playing Field' (*Governance, Basel Institute on Governance*, 2003) 1, 9 <https://ww w.baselgovernance.org/sites/collective.localhost/files/publications/biog_wo rking_paper_01.pdf> accessed 10 November 2017.

50. Mushtaq Khan, 'The Political Economy of Inclusive Growth' *in* Luiz de Mello and Mark A. Dutz (eds.) *OECD Promoting Inclusive Growth: Challenges and Policies* (OECD, The World Bank, Paris, 2012).

51. Nadeem Haque, Donald Mathieson and Nelson Mark, 'Rating the Raters of Creditworthiness' (Finance & Development, March 1997).

52. Nienke Grossman, 'The Normative Legitimacy of International Courts' [2012] 86 Temple Law Review.

53. Norman Girvan, 'Power Imbalances and Development Knowledge' (Southern Perspectives on the Reform of the International Development Architecture, 2007).

54. Norman Mugarura, *The Global Anti-Money Laundering Regulatory Landscape in Less Developed Countries* (1st edn, Routledge, 2016).

55. OECD: Better Policies for Better Lives, 'OECD Careers' (*OECD*) <http:// www.oecd.org/careers/whatwelookfor.htm> accessed 20 January 2016.

56. Paul W. Glimcher and Ernst Fehr, *Neuroeconomics: Decision Making and the Brain* (2nd edn, Elsevier, Amsterdam, 2014).

57. Peter Miller, Liisa Kurunmäki and Ted O'Leary, 'Accounting, Hybrids and the Management of Risk' [2007] 33 (7–8) Accounting, Organizations and Society.

58. Raffaella Barone and Donato Masciandaro, 'Organised Crime, Money Laundering and Legal Economy: Theory and Simulations' [2011] 32 (1) European Journal of Law and Economics.

59. Rainer Hulsse, 'Even Clubs Can't Do Without Legitimacy: Why the Anti-Money Laundering Blacklist Was Suspended' [2008] 2 Regulation and Governance.

60. Saby Ghoshray, 'Compliance Convergence in FATF Rulemaking: The Conflict Between Agency Capture and Soft Law' [2014/15] 59 New York Law School Law Review.

61. Stuart Ross and Michelle Hannan, 'Money Laundering Regulation and Risk-Based Decision Making' [2007] 10 (1) Journal of Money Laundering Control.

62. Tim Wu, 'Agency Threats' [2010] 60 Duke Law Journal.

63. Todd Doyle, 'Cleaning Up Anti-Money Laundering Strategies: Current FATF Tactics Needlessly Violate International Law' [2002] 24 Houston Journal of International Law.

64. Tom R. Tyler, *Why People Obey the Law* (Princeton University Press, 2006).
65. Transparency International, 'Corruption Perceptions Index 2016' (*Transparency International*, 2017) <https://www.transparency.org/news/feature/corrupti on_perceptions_index_2016> accessed 19 December 2017.
66. Valsamis Mitsilegas, *Money Laundering Countermeasures in the European Union: A Paradigm of Security Governance Versus Fundamental Legal Principles* (Kluwer Law International, 2003).
67. Wesley Kirton, 'Guyana Has Now Become a Strategically Important Country' (*Kaieteur News*, 15 May 2017) <http://www.kaieteurnewsonline.com/2 017/05/15/guyana-has-now-become-a-strategically-important-country/> accessed 21 May 2017.
68. Yacov Y. Haimes, 'On the Complex Definition of Risk: A Systems-Based Approach' [2009] 29 (12) Risk Analyst.
69. Zlata Rodionova, 'London Property Market Turned into Money Laundering Sage Haven by Inadequate Supervision, MPs say' (*Independent*, 15 July 2016) <http://www.independent.co.uk/news/business/news/london-property-m arket-real-estate-money-laundering-overseas-foreign-buyers-mps-a7138176 .html> accessed 10 July 2017.

8 Explanations and Conclusion

Introduction

This book questions empirically, how the anti-money laundering and counter-terrorist financing (AML/CFT) framework's evolution has occasioned an agency slack which has an impact on attained Financial Action Task Force (FATF) compliance levels of countries. This chapter pulls together the main insights and conclusions from the previous chapters. It sets out to explain what compliance drivers African countries and emerging economies (ACs/EEs) respond to, how the agency relationship explains their behaviour and how the Regional Bureau Africa (RBA) may indeed not resolve the existing legitimacy crises.

The conclusion drawn from findings is that the FATF has a significant impact on AML/CFT governance in EEs even though their compliance level is still not at the optimum level, whilst its impact is negligible in ACs. These findings confirm the book's theoretical argument that the hierarchy of countries determines their compliance levels and communication strategy with international financial institutions (IFIs)/FATF. One possible explanation for this is that the AML/CFT policies are less reflective of the socio-economic and political terrain of ACs which are below the hierarchy and therefore, are less suitable in projecting proactive compliance within these countries.

Explanations and Conclusions by Research Questions

At the heart of this book are four research questions:

1. Has the evolution of IFIs/FATF facilitated an agency slack between these international institutions and ACs/EEs with resulting legitimacy crises?
2. Do the compliance drivers and level of compliance attained in ACs/EEs indicate a misalignment of incentives between these countries and IFIs/FATF?
3. What factors exacerbate information asymmetry between IFIs/FATF and ACs/EEs? Can the agency slack that arises from countries acting in their self-interest to hinder information sharing with other countries be resolved?

4. Does the risk-based approach sufficiently take into consideration the peculiarities of countries and facilitate increased legitimacy of the FATF?

The first question on the evolution of the IFIs/FATF, its resulting AML/CFT standards and the likely impact of this in creating an agency slack between these institutions and ACs/EEs was explored extensively through literature in chapter 2. This chapter examined the evolution of AML/CFT standards, the institutions central to its administration and the influences of these on state compliance. It argued strongly that these standards were crucial to facilitating financial integrity in cross-border relations. However, it found that the AML/CFT standards only inculcated the perspectives of a select group of developed countries (the Group of Seven. – G7), and hence, was better suited at combatting illicit crimes within these countries. Given the lack of transparency, accountability and legitimacy in the standards creation processes, this chapter asserts that ACs/EEs are more inclined to suffer a compliance deficit. This quandary is understood through the lens of the agency theory which unearths an agency slack in the relationship between IFIs/FATF and ACs/EEs, backed by a legitimacy crisis, showing that although ACs/EEs are disproportionately involved, there is a mandate for their compliance – an indication of hegemonic subjugation.

The second question on whether compliance drivers and the level of compliance attained in ACs/EEs indicate a misalignment of incentives between these countries and the IFIs/FATF was addressed in Chapters 3, 5 and 6. The statistics on compliance levels in ACs shows far from impressive attainments. Of the 37 ACs that are examined, only seven are deemed to be more than 50% compliant, and 30 are less than 50% compliant. A slightly improved image is seen with EEs with compliance levels ranging from 54% to 66.67%. Literature, however, indicates that these compliance levels may suggest that whilst ACs primarily strive for financial inclusion and EEs struggle for improved global integration – the FATF's focus is on integrity which may sometimes be tangential to the primary objectives of the bloc of countries. Consequently, the FATF's striving may come at the expense of the socio-economic and political peculiarities of these countries (cash-based, remittances, etc.) which hinders their unique development and may result in a regulatory paradox.

Moreover, the compliance drives which are expected to be effective in all countries, are seen to have different outcomes across ACs/EEs. More precisely, chapter 3 argues that law is crucial when designed properly, and most importantly, when backed with confidence. Confidence in financial stability, institutions, governmental and political systems, and enforcement structures. The extent to which these factors are instituted within ACs/EEs to ensure implementation and compliance is however questionable. This serves as an indication that ACs/EEs would be incapable of effectively transplanting or complying with the FATF standards. These pre-conditions feed into the compliance drivers categorised as legal and non-legal factors which can be internal or external to a country. It is against these 'drivers' that the compliance probability of ACs/EEs is examined.

In chapter 5, the compliance drivers enumerated in chapter 3 are examined within the context of Africa's socio-economic and political history. The current positioning of ACs in the global economy is also considered in determining how the compliance drivers actually define ACs' compliance with the FATF's standards. In examining compliance as a function of legal factors, the impact of democracy and rule of law, enforcement and law mirroring society are considered. Irrespective of the shortcomings ACs face in these areas, they still receive harsh sanctions for non-compliance. Most ACs sanctioned have reacted by projecting formal compliance in their engagements with IFIs/FATF so as to evade future sanctions. Such formal or sham compliance have seen laws in ACs mirror the FATF standards, some of which are antithetical to the ACs agenda on financial inclusion.

Legal compliance drivers are backed by non-legal drivers, such as reputation, political will, domestic conditions, resources and capacity deficits. Reputation's ability to drive compliance is restricted as most ACs shamed for non-compliance resorted to formal compliance. Political will, either internally or externally generated can be hindered by factors like corruption. Indeed, this limits the resources available to combat illicit crime.

Also crucial are the external compliance drivers of ownership and legitimacy. The belated associate membership of the ACs within FATF-style regional bodies (FSRBs) has tinted their perception of the FATF's legitimacy. This is particularly due to the perceived absence of input and ownership in the FATF standards and processes, especially on issues that concern them, a situation that leads to coerced or formal compliance, which is nevertheless apathetically low. Their low compliance is indicative of two things. Firstly, that although ACs are keen on integration and integrity within the global economy, their aspirations are hindered by culture and capacity. Secondly, the shortcomings of ACs indicate that subjecting these countries to the same standards, methodology and sanctions as other developed countries would be to ignore their heritage and socio-economic challenges whilst facilitating legitimacy issues. It would be setting these countries up to fail or permitting them to engage strategically with IFIs/FATF given their low integration with the global economy.

Chapter Six examines the impact of the compliance drivers enumerated in chapter 3 within Brazil, Russia, India, China, South Africa's. (BRICS's) socio-economic and political positioning. It starts by appraising the impact of legal factors as compliance drivers. On the rule of law and democracy, it finds that, contrary to the situation in ACs where these are key drivers, it is not the case with all the BRICS. Whilst these factors may indeed have some impact on compliance, the actual compliance levels would be shrouded in secrecy. This can be attributed to the law mirroring international standards – a situation which has led to the wholesale application of non-contextualised policies. For instance, the FATF's attempts at curtailing money laundering (ML) through remittances mirrors the requirements for curtailing ML through FIs, a process which is at best fallible. However, these situations can be remedied by enforcement actions that impact EEs, as these countries, keen on retaining their position within the international economy – respond positively to enforcement actions.

Flowing from enforcement is the non-legal driver – reputation. Evidence shows that EEs are keen to protect their reputation to ensure continued business with the West. This is strengthened by the resources at their disposal, coupled with their fortified technical capacity. Whilst this signal ingrained political will which can propel compliance, like ACs, such 'will' may be undermined by corruption. However, as opposed to ACs, globalisation and integration drives compliance in EEs, especially those like China that have established physical businesses in developed countries. There is, however, the concern that their procedures may only follow the host countries' AML/CFT policies on paper.

Crucially important are the external drives of ownership and legitimacy. Unlike ACs who are associate members of the FATF, the BRICS have gained membership, hence possibly augmenting their perception of the FATF as legitimate. Whilst the BRICS and developing world viewed this as a means to gain increased representation within the FATF, the Western agenda was to ensure that the financial movement to the Global South is not replete with illicit transactions. The power-play involved in negotiations between these 'North-South strategically important countries' was predicated on the assumption that representation would be a catalyst for improved compliance with AML/CFT recommendations. Conversely, the BRICS's coerced, and belated membership has created a very unbalanced membership between EEs and the developed countries. Against this background, this chapter argues that membership does not necessarily guarantee comparable representation or legitimacy; neither does it guarantee the overtly improved compliance of BRICS countries. It presents a contrary argument that 'representation' taints the socio-economic complexities inherent in these countries and their ability to comply. Worse still, it conceals the asymmetries occasioned by variances in the strength of legal structures reinforced by political and economic differences between FATF members. For membership to equate to legitimacy, there must be existent changes along existing political and economic global structures, arguing that this would ensure improved adherence to FATF recommendations.

The third set of questions are focused on the factors that exacerbate information asymmetry between IFIs/FATF and ACs/EEs. Additionally, it examines whether agency slack arises from countries acting in their self-interests to hinder information sharing. These questions are addressed in chapter 4 which uncovers the relationship between the collective principals and countries. This synergy examined through the agency theory unveils the power dynamics between developed countries, the institutions they create and lead and ACs/EEs. It reveals that the AML/CFT standards reflect the Global North's priorities and interests and is sublimated with covenants of agency capture which can hinder the unique development of ACs. Analysing the interaction between agent-states and the corrupt practices (CPs), it argues that two factors are crucial for understanding information asymmetry between these actors on ML/terrorist financing (TF) issues; the level of a country's integration with the global financial system and its perceived compliance levels. It finds that the incentive for information sharing is highest when a country is 'highly integrated' with perceived high compliance levels. In an opposite situation, the countries would usually engage strategically with the principal to evade observatory tools or sanctions.

Furthermore, acknowledging the flow of money within countries, the interaction between 'highly integrated' and 'mid-integrated' countries are examined. The chapter illustrates that these sets of countries share information only when it is in their self-interest, particularly when there is a continuous financial business that is of systematic importance to both parties. It, however, argues that even when low-integrated countries are willing to exchange viable information, they may be limited by capacity challenges. Where, however, information asymmetry continually thrives, the CPs are privy to tools to rein in the agent-states. The tools utilised are dependent on the circumstances in question and the application of the inappropriate tool may indeed lead to under-regulation, as the tool would at best be inadequate.

The fourth question is on whether the risk-based approach sufficiently considers the peculiarities of countries and facilitates increased legitimacy of the FATF? Chapter Seven addresses this. It argues that whilst the RBA recently adopted by the FATF was aimed at resolving AML/CFT compliance differentials by considering the peculiarities of countries, its flawed conceptualisation has hindered its ability to achieve this aim. Rather, this has aggravated the agency slack between IFIs/FATF and ACs/EEs particularly due to the difficulty in implementing the RBA which is outcome focused. Consequently, the argument advanced is that an uncertainty-based approach (UBA) would be more suited to addressing the current agency slack as it shifts the focus to the process of decision-making as opposed to the outcome. Moreover, it can better incorporate the priorities of ACs/EEs. This would help resolve the legitimacy crisis which also requires remodelling at the FATF level to mirror the International Association of Deposit Insurers (IADI).

Index

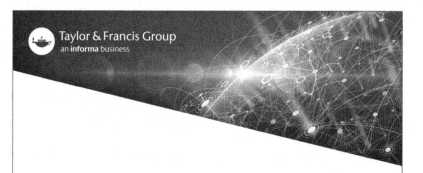

Printed in the United States
By Bookmasters